W9-BLI-432

MACROMEDIA®
Flash™ MX
2004

Hands-On Training

lynda.com/books

Rosanna Yeung | with Lynda Weinman

Macromedia Flash MX 2004 | H·O·T
Hands-On Training

By Rosanna Yeung
Developed with Lynda Weinman

lynda.com/books | Peachpit Press
1249 Eighth Street • Berkeley, CA • 94710
800.283.9444 • 510.524.2178
510.524.2221 (fax)
http://www.lynda.com/books
http://www.peachpit.com

lynda.com/books is published
in association with Peachpit Press,
a division of Pearson Education
Copyright ©2004 by lynda.com

ISBN: 0-321-20298-8

0 9 8 7 6 5 4

Printed and bound in the
United States of America

H•O•T | Credits

Original Design: Ali Karp, Alink Newmedia (*alink@earthlink.net*)

lynda.com Director, Publications: Garo Green (*garo@lynda.com*)

Project Manager: Jennifer Eberhardt

Copyeditor: Darren Meiss

Compositors: Rick Gordon and Debbie Roberti

Beta Testers: Robert Hoekman, Jr. and Crystal Waters

Cover Illustration: Bruce Heavin (*bruce@stink.com*)

Exercise Graphics: Domenique Sillett (*www.littleigloo.com*)

Indexer: Lisa Stumpf

Proofreaders: Kristy Hart and Beth Trudell

H•O•T | Colophon

The preliminary design for the H•O•T series was sketched on paper by Ali Karp | Alink Newmedia. The layout was heavily influenced by online communication—merging a traditional book format with a modern Web aesthetic.

The text in *Macromedia Flash MX 2004 H•O•T* was set in Akzidenz Grotesk from Adobe, and Triplex from Emigré. The cover illustration was painted in Adobe Photoshop and Adobe Illustrator.

This book was created using QuarkXPress 4, Adobe Photoshop 7, Macromedia Fireworks MX 2004, Microsoft Office XP, and Flash MX 2004 using Windows XP. It was printed on 50# Utopia at Phoenix Color.

Dedication

To all my students.
It's truly amazing to watch your creativity grow,
and I'm honored to play a small part in
making your dreams become a reality.
Thank you for inspiring me and
teaching me to stay young.

–Rosanna

Macromedia Flash MX 2004 | H•O•T _____ **Table of Contents**

Introduction

H·O·T
_____
Macromedia Flash MX 2004

A Note from Lynda Weinman

In my opinion, most people buy computer books in order to learn, yet it is amazing how few of these books are actually written by teachers. I take pride in the fact that this book was written by an experienced teacher who is familiar with training students in this subject matter. In this book, you will find carefully developed lessons to help you learn Macromedia Flash MX 2004—one of the most powerful animation and interactivity tools for the Web.

This book is targeted towards beginning-level Web developers who need a tool to create creative, powerful, and interactive Web sites. The premise of the hands-on exercise approach is to get you up to speed quickly in Flash MX 2004, while actively working through the book's lessons. It's one thing to read about a product, and an entirely other experience to try the product and get measurable results. Our motto is, "read the book, follow the exercises, and you will know the product." We've received countless testimonials to this fact, and it is our goal to make sure it remains true for all of our hands-on training books.

Many exercise-based books take a paint-by-numbers approach to teaching. While this approach works, it's often difficult to figure out how to apply those lessons to a real-world situation, or understand why or when you would use the technique again. What sets this book apart is that the lessons contain lots of background information and insights into each given subject, and they are designed to help you understand the process as well as the exercise.

At times, pictures are worth a lot more than words. When necessary, we have also included short QuickTime movies to show any process that's difficult to explain in text. These files are located on the **H•O•T CD-ROM** inside a folder called **movies**. It's our style to approach teaching from many different angles, because we know that some people are visual learners while others like to read, and still others like to get out there and try things. This book combines a lot of teaching approaches so you can learn Flash MX 2004 as thoroughly as you want to.

This book didn't set out to cover every single aspect of Flash MX 2004. The manual and many other reference books are great for that! What we saw missing from the bookshelves was a process-oriented tutorial that taught readers core principles, techniques, and tips in a hands-on training format.

We welcome your comments at **fl04hot@lynda.com**. Please visit our Web site as well, at **http://www.lynda.com**.

The support URL for this book is **http://www.lynda.com/products/books/fl04hot/**.

It's my hope that this book will give you a strong foundation in Flash MX 2004 and give you the necessary skills to begin developing animations and interactive Web sites. If it does, then we've accomplished the job we set out to do!

–Lynda Weinman

About the Author

Rosanna Yeung

Whoever told Rosanna that teaching was "work" sure hasn't witnessed her professorial multimedia magic at the Art Institute of California, where she teaches Web Design and Development classes. She's got this innate love for the creative freedom of the Web, and you can see the transference of her passion in the eyes of her students.

Rosanna's creative energy doesn't only exist in the classroom or on the Web. Don't be surprised if you see her donning Rasta braids with a flock of friends on boards, surfing the sea or the snow. She's done her time in the business world as well—starting her creative adventures behind the camera and microphone in radio, TV, and film and then transitioning to multimedia and Web design in the corporate sector before heading off to the teaching world. Her work at Ingram Micro is actually where her love for teaching began—by no one's fault but her own, Rosanna found herself working with other departments and their Web content almost daily. Her knowledge of the Web and patience and passion for teaching made her the integral link from a print medium to a dynamic Web resource.

When she's not writing on the chalkboard or surfing the Web, sea, or snow, you'll find her with her trusty companions—her husband, Alan, and her black Labrador, Forever—as they restore their new Eichler home in California.

Snapshots

Rosanna training Forever, her Labrador Retriever, for the Great Outdoor Animal Games. :-)

When Rosanna isn't stuck behind the computer, lately you can find her polishing up her fixer-upper Eichler home...

Rosanna as painter...

Rosanna as plumber...

Acknowledgments from Rosanna

A very special thanks to all of the wonderful and loving people who have helped me, directly and indirectly with this book. Each contribution was unique, subtle, and important. Your support of me and my work is not taken for granted.

My deepest thanks and appreciation go out to:

Garo Green, my mentor and friend. You were my most influential Web instructor, and it all started that day. Thank you for inspiring me in so many ways I can't even count. This book is by far one of the most challenging projects I've ever worked on. Thank you for taking each step with me, your guidance has been immeasurable and invaluable. Am I still your grasshopper?

Lynda Weinman, my coach. Thank you for this amazing opportunity. Not only have I taught many students with your books, but I have also learned so much writing this book with you! Thank you for your faith and confidence in me. I am truly honored to work with you and your team.

Shane Rebenschied, Robert Hoekman, Jr. and **Chad Corbin**, my contributing authors and my intermediate and advanced Flash gurus who I admire for your knowledge and guidance. Your work truly made this a better book. I'll miss our crazy conference calls and instant messages. Can't wait for your books to come out!

Robert Hoekman, Jr. and **Crystal Waters**, my beta testers. Thank you for all your hard work and for finding all the little (okay, sometimes big) oversights!

The **Peachpit** team, especially **Jennifer Eberhardt** and **Stephanie Wall**. Thank you for all your effort and professionalism.

Darren Meiss, my editor. Thank you so much for catching every single undotted i, uncrossed t, and extra space, and for keeping the continuity of the book consistent from chapter to chapter. Your attention to detail is amazing!

Rick Gordon and **Debbie Roberti**, my compositors. Your skills have made this book come together beautifully!

The creatives who made this book come to life. **Domenique Sillett** for the original artwork and designs, and **Patrick Miko** for providing the music.

My friends at **Crisp Digital**. **Ryan Regalado** and **Patrick Chang** for helping me develop exercises for the book; **Sasha Strauss** for always making me sound interesting; and **Tony Crisp** for allowing me to use your photo throughout the book.

Lynda Bui, my little grasshopper. Thank you for being another pair of eyes and helping me with the finishing touches.

The **Art Institute**. **Brad Janis** for your support and **Jonathon DeAscentis** for your enthusiasm and hard work to accommodate my tight schedule.

My **family** and **close friends**, especially my **Mom**, who's love never ends, **Ryan**, **Christian**, **Chuck**, the **Emnaces**, my family at **Saddleback Church**, and my **Hula Sistas** for being my cheerleaders. I know I've been MIA for months, I hope you guys still remember and recognize me. (I may have aged a bit through this process.) I promise to be at the next birthday party, baby shower, wedding, graduation, luau…and all the other celebrations we share together—I promise, promise, promise!!!

Alan Yeung, for your love, patience, and understanding. Thank you for putting up with all the long hours I spent cozying up to the computer instead of you. I am uncommonly blessed by your love and support, which have helped me climb many mountains. I love you.

Special thanks to **Patrick Miko** (`miko@ultrashock.com`) of `www.ultrashock.com` for allowing us to use his amazing collection of audio files.

And finally, my **God** who constantly provides me a quiet strength I could never have imagined.

How to Use This Book

Please read this section—it contains important information that's going to help you as you use this book. The following list outlines the information that is covered:

• The Formatting in This Book

• Interface Screen Captures

• Mac and Windows System Differences

• Opening Windows Files on a Mac

• A Note to Windows Users

• Making Exercise Files Editable on Windows Systems

• Making File Extensions Visible on Windows Systems

• Flash System Requirements—Authoring and Playback

• H·O·T CD-ROM Contents

The Formatting in This Book

This book has several components, including step-by-step exercises, commentary, notes, tips, warnings, and movies. Step-by-step exercises are numbered, and file names and command keys are bolded so they pop out more easily.

Captions and commentary are in italicized text: *This is a commentary*. File names/folders, command keys, menu commands, and URLs are bolded: **images** folder, **Ctrl+click**, **File > Open**, and **http://www.ultrashock.com**.

Interface Screen Captures

Most of the screen captures in the book were taken on a Windows machine using the XP operating system. The only time Macintosh shots were taken was when the interface differed from the Windows interface. I also own and use a Macintosh system, so I noted important differences when they occurred, and took screen captures accordingly.

Mac and Windows System Differences

Macromedia did a great job of ensuring that Flash MX 2004 looks and works the same between the Macintosh and Windows operating systems. However, some differences do exist. If you are using this book with one of the Windows operating systems, please be sure to read the section titled "A Note to Windows Users," carefully.

Opening Windows Files on a Mac

As you work with Flash MX 2004, you might need to open a PC-created file on a Macintosh. Because of this, I wanted to make sure you were aware of a little glitch that could cause you some confusion. The Macintosh has difficulty recognizing FLA files that were created on a PC. This means when using a Mac, you may not be able to simply double-click the FLA file that was created on a PC to open it. Instead, you will need to open Flash and then choose **File > Open**. At this point, you still may not see some of the FLA files when you use the Browse dialog box. You can get around this by changing the **Show** option to **All Files**. This will display all files in the folder. You can then save the file on your Mac, and it should then open normally when double-clicked.

A Note to Windows Users

This section contains essential information about making your exercise folders editable and making file extensions visible.

Making Exercise Files Editable on Windows Systems

By default, when you copy files from a CD-ROM to your Windows 98/2000/XP hard drive, they are set to read-only (write protected). This causes a problem with the exercise files, because you need to write over some of them. To remove this setting and make the files editable, use the following procedures:

1. Copy the chapter folder from the **H•O•T CD-ROM** to your hard drive.

---

2. Right-click the chapter folder and choose **Properties**.

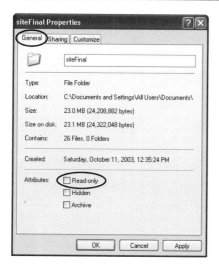

3. In the **General** tab, uncheck the **Read-only** check box. This will change the setting for all of the files that were selected. If **Archive** is selected, you can remove that check as well.

---

4. Click **OK**.

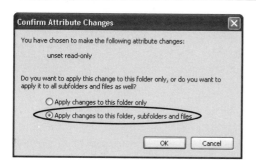

*Note: If there are other folders inside the chapter folder, change the attributes of those folders as well by selecting **Apply changes to this folder, subfolders and files** when the dialog box shown here appears.*

Making File Extensions Visible on Windows Systems

In this section, you'll see different examples of how to turn on file extensions for Windows 98, Windows 2000, and Windows XP. By default, Windows 98/2000 users will not be able to see file extension names such as .fla or .swf. Fortunately, you can change this setting!

Windows 98 Users:

1. Double-click the **My Computer** icon on your Desktop. **Note:** If you (or someone else) changed the name, it will not say **My Computer**.

2. Select **View > Folder Options**. This will open the **Folder Options** dialog box.

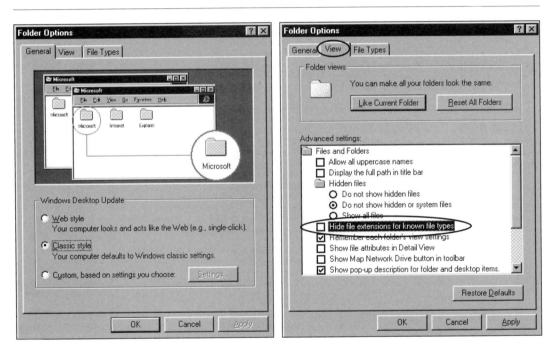

3. Click the **View** tab. This will open the **View** options screen so you can change the view settings of Windows 98.

4. Uncheck the **Hide file extensions for known file types** check box. This will make all of the file extensions visible.

Windows 2000 Users:

1. Double-click the **My Computer** icon on your Desktop. **Note:** If you (or someone else) changed the name, it will not say **My Computer**.

2. Select **Tools > Folder Options**. This will open the **Folder Options** dialog box.

3. Click the **View** tab. This will open the **View** options screen so you can change the view settings of Windows 2000.

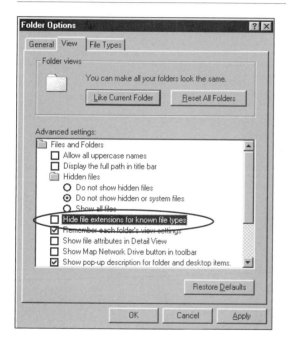

4. Make sure there is no checkmark next to the **Hide file extensions for known file types** option. This will make all of the file extensions visible.

Windows XP Users:

1. From the **Start** menu, choose **Control Panel**.

2. Click the **Folder Options** icon. This will open the **Folder Options** dialog box.

3. Click the **View** tab. This will open the **View** options screen so you can change the view settings of Windows XP.

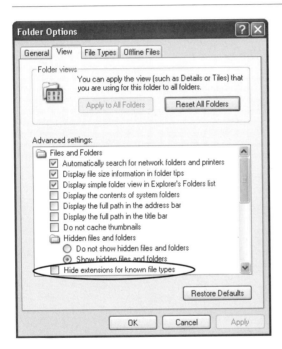

4. Make sure there is no checkmark next to the **Hide extensions for known file types** option. This will make all of the file extensions visible.

Flash MX 2004 System Requirements

This book requires that you use either a Macintosh operating system (Power Macintosh G3 running System 10.2.6 or later) or Windows 98, Windows 2000, or Windows NT 4.0, Windows ME, or Windows XP. You also will need a color monitor capable of 800 x 600 resolutions and a CD-ROM drive. I suggest that you have at least 256 MB of RAM in your system, because that way you can open Flash MX 2004 and a Web browser at the same time, more RAM than that is even better. The following chart cites Macromedia's system requirements.

Flash MX 2004 System Requirements	
AUTHORING	
Windows	**Macintosh**
600 MHz Intel Pentium III processor or equivalent	500 MHz PowerPC G3 processor
Windows 98 SE, Windows 2000, or Windows XP	Mac OS X 10.2.6 or higher
128 MB RAM (256 MB recommended)	128 MB RAM (256 MB recommended)
275 MB available disk space	215 MB available disk space
1024 x 768, 16-bit (thousands of colors) color display or better	1024 x 768, 16-bit (thousands of colors) color display or better
CD-ROM drive	CD-ROM drive
PLAYBACK	
Platform	**Browser**
Windows 98	Microsoft Internet Explorer 5.x, Netscape 4.7, Netscape 7.x, Mozilla 1.x, AOL 8, and Opera 7.11
Windows Me	Microsoft Internet Explorer 5.5, Netscape 4.7, Netscape 7.x, Mozilla 1.x, AOL 8, and Opera 7.11
Windows 2000	Microsoft Internet Explorer 5.x, Netscape 4.7, Netscape 7.x, Mozilla 1.x, CompuServe 7, AOL 8, and Opera 7.11
Windows XP	Microsoft Internet Explorer 6.0, Netscape 7.x, Mozilla 1.x, CompuServe 7, AOL 8, and Opera 7.11
Mac OS 9.x	Microsoft Internet Explorer 5.1, Netscape 4.8, Netscape 7.x, Mozilla 1.x, and Opera 6
Mac OS X 10.1.x or Mac OS X 10.2.x	Microsoft Internet Explorer 5.2, Netscape 7.x, Mozilla 1.x, AOL 7, Opera 6, and Safari 1.0 (Mac OS X 10.2.x only)

What's on the CD-ROM?

Exercise Files and the H·O·T CD-ROM

Your exercise files are located inside a folder called **exercise files** on the **H·O·T CD-ROM**. These files are divided into chapter folders, and you will be instructed to copy the chapter folders to your hard drive during many of the exercises. Unfortunately, when files originate from a CD-ROM, the Windows operating system defaults to making them write-protected, meaning that you cannot alter them. You will need to alter them to follow the exercises, so please read the section titled "A Note to Windows Users" for instructions on how to convert them to read-and-write formatting.

QuickTime Files on the H·O·T CD-ROM

There is a folder on the **H·O·T CD-ROM** called **movies** that contains several QuickTime tutorial movies for some of the exercises in this book. It's my hope that these movies will help you understand some of the more difficult exercises in this book by watching me perform them myself. If you like these movies, you should definitely check out the *Learning Macromedia Flash MX 2004 CD-ROM* at **http://www.lynda.com**, which contains several hours' worth of QuickTime movies on Flash MX 2004.

Demo Files on the CD-ROM

In addition to the exercise files, the **H·O·T CD-ROM** also contains a free 30-day trial version of Flash MX 2004 for Mac or Windows. All software is located inside the **software** folder on the **H·O·T CD-ROM**. I have included trial versions of the following:

• Macromedia Flash MX 2004

• Macromedia Dreamweaver MX 2004

• Macromedia Fireworks MX 2004

I also have included several players on the **H•O•T CD-ROM**. If you don't have these players installed already, you should install them before working with any exercise in this book that calls for one of them. All of the players are located inside the **software** folder. I have included the following:

• Flash Player 7

• Shockwave Player 8

In addition, **Patrick Miko** of **www.session12.com** was generous enough to donate a collection of audio files for you to use with the exercises in this book and your own projects. These files are located inside the **chap_13** folder. There is a folder for Macintosh users, which contains audio files in the AIFF format and another folder for Windows users, which contains audio files in the WAV format.

Also, the media files for this book including the bitmap graphics (found throughout the exercise folders) and all the video footage (located in the **chap_15** folder) were graciously donated for you to use with the exercises in this book and with your own projects. Additional thanks to **Charles Hollins**, for the photographs that were donated from Mountain High Ski Resort (Wrightwood, CA), and the video footage from **Tim Sigafoos**.

I.

Background Information

| Introducing the New Flash MX 2004 Product Line |
| Why Flash MX 2004? | What's New in Flash MX 2004? |
| Flash MX Professional 2004 | Project, Player, or Projector? |
| File Types Associated with Flash MX 2004 |
| Flash MX 2004 and Shockwave Players | Beyond Flash MX 2004 |

no exercise files

Macromedia Flash MX 2004 H•O•T

Most likely, if you've purchased a copy of Macromedia Flash MX 2004, you already know why you want to use the program. You might have experience building Web pages or using other graphics programs and want to increase your software skills for today's job market. However, some of you might not know the benefits of using Flash MX 2004 versus HTML for authoring a Web site. This chapter outlines the new Flash MX 2004 product line, what the differences are between Flash MX 2004 and Macromedia Flash MX Professional 2004, and answers the question, "Why use Flash MX 2004?" It also contains a summary of the notable new features and outlines some of the ways you can extend Flash MX 2004 content using other technologies such as CGI, XML, and JavaScript. I am sure that you are eager to dive into the hands-on exercises, so feel free to skim over this chapter. If you do decide to skim, be sure to take a look at the "What's New in Flash MX 2004?" section so you can see what's in store for you!

Introducing the New Flash MX 2004 Product Line

With this release of Flash, Macromedia has developed the program into two distinct solutions: **Flash MX 2004**, which you will be learning more about in this book, and **Flash MX Professional 2004**. **Flash MX 2004** is the solution for creating visually responsive Web content and interactive interfaces across platforms and devices; **Flash MX Professional 2004** is the development environment for teams building visually responsive and data-aware rich Internet applications, which require understanding advanced features beyond the scope of this book. In general, Flash MX Professional 2004 offers a more in-depth programming environment that allows teams to build data-rich Internet applications, as well as the integration of professional video editing tools to deliver high-quality immersive video experiences. You may be asking yourself, "Which program is right for me?" If you are new to creating media-rich content for the Web or are looking to familiarize yourself with the new features of Flash MX, then Flash MX 2004 is the way to go. If you are unsure whether you want to learn Flash MX 2004 or Flash MX Professional 2004, this chapter will go over a quick summary of features found only in the Flash MX Professional 2004 solution.

Why Use Flash MX 2004?

Flash MX 2004 has several key benefits, such as small file size, fast downloading speed, precise visual control, advanced interactivity, the capability to combine bitmap and vector graphics and include video and/or animation, and scalable and streaming content.

Download Speed

If you want to design a Web site that contains an abundance of visual content, download speed can be a major problem. As most of you know, nothing can be more frustrating than a slow-loading site. Even limited use of the compressed bitmap graphic file formats that are used for the Web (GIF and JPEG) can result in slow Web sites that frustrate visitors. Because of this, Web developers are often forced to alter their designs to be less visual.

Flash MX 2004 content is often smaller than HTML content because it uses its own compression scheme, which optimizes vector and bitmap content differently from GIFs or JPEGs. For this reason, Flash MX 2004 has become the delivery medium of preference for graphic-intensive Web sites.

Visual Control

Another great benefit of Flash MX 2004 is that it frees Web designers from many of the restraints of traditional HTML (HyperText Markup Language). Flash MX 2004 gives you complete and accurate control over position, color, fonts, and other aspects of the screen regardless of the delivery platform (Mac or Windows) or browser (Explorer or Netscape and others). This is a radical and important departure from traditional HTML authoring, which requires precise planning to ensure that graphics and content appear relatively similar and consistent on different computer platforms and with various Web browsers. Flash MX 2004 allows designers to focus on design instead of HTML workarounds.

Enhanced Interactivity

Although Flash MX 2004 is often known as an animation program, it also provides powerful interactivity tools that allow you to create buttons or free-form interfaces for site navigation that include sound and animation. With the release of Flash MX 2004, powerful improved scripting makes it possible to create presentations that are far more complex than standard HTML or JavaScript can achieve. This book covers interactivity in a number of later chapters.

Combine Vectors and Bitmaps

Most graphics on the Internet are **bitmap** graphics such as GIFs and JPEGs. The size of a bitmap file depends on the number of pixels it contains. Because of this, as the image dimensions increase, so does the file size and download time. In addition to file-size disadvantages, bitmap images that are enlarged to a size other than the original size of the image often appear distorted, out of focus, and pixelated.

Graphics created within Flash MX 2004 are composed of vectors. **Vector** graphics use mathematical formulas to describe the images, unlike bitmaps, which record information pixel by pixel and color by color. Vector graphics can offer much smaller file sizes and increased flexibility for certain types of images, such as those with solid color fills and typographic content. Some images will have a smaller file size as bitmaps, and some will be smaller as vectors. The neat thing about Flash MX 2004 is that you can use either type of image.

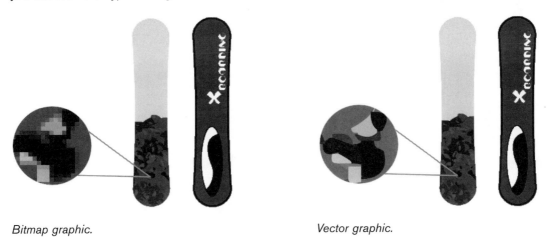

Bitmap graphic.   Vector graphic.

---

*A **bitmap** graphic is built pixel by pixel and color by color; a **vector** graphic is built from mathematical formulas. This means that a vector graphic will be the same file size regardless of its physical dimensions, but a bitmap graphic will grow and shrink in file size depending on how large or small it is. This makes it possible for Flash MX 2004 to create and display large vector images and animations without increasing file size.*

Video

The capability to embed video inside SWF files is a huge plus for creating media-rich Web sites, and the new video wizard inside of Flash MX 2004 makes it even easier. Being able to incorporate video opens the floodgates even further for the types of projects you can create using Flash MX 2004. You will have the chance to learn about the ins and outs of video in Chapter 15, "*Video.*"

Scalability

Because Flash MX 2004 movies can use vectors, they can be resized in any Web browser window and still retain their original scale and relative position. Most importantly, the file size of vector graphics is independent of their display size. This means it is possible to create full-screen vector animations that display at any resolution and that are only a fraction of the file size of a comparable bitmap graphic.

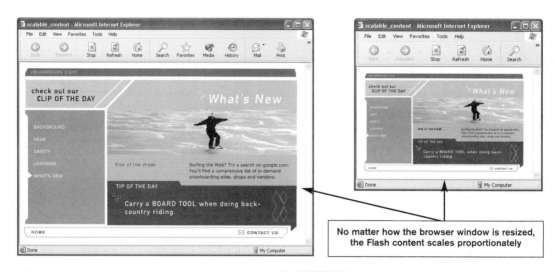

No matter how the browser window is resized, the Flash content scales proportionately

Flash MX 2004 content can be set to scale dynamically within the browser window, as shown here.

Does all of this mean you should use only vectors in your Flash MX 2004 movies? Absolutely not. Although Flash MX 2004 is known for its vector capabilities, its support of bitmap images is superb and far exceeds the support offered by HTML. Specifically, if you scale a bitmap image larger than its original size in HTML, the graphic will become distorted and unattractive. Flash MX 2004 allows bitmaps to scale, animate, and transform (skew, distort, and so on) without much image degradation. This means that you can, and often will, combine bitmap and vector images in your movies. The ability to deliver both bitmap and vector graphics together lets you create movies that look good at different resolutions and still deliver a bandwidth-friendly file size. Flash MX 2004 can even be used to convert bitmap images into vectors, which you will learn to do in Chapter 8, "*Bitmaps*."

Streaming Content

Vectors are not the only way Flash MX 2004 makes itself more bandwidth-friendly. Flash MX 2004 files download to Web browsers in small units. This allows the files to display some content while the rest is still downloading in the background. Ideally, the content will play more slowly than it downloads, so that the viewing experience is not interrupted. This method of playing one part of an entire Web site while the rest is still downloading is called **streaming**. It differs significantly from the way HTML files are downloaded and displayed in a browser, which takes place a page at a time.

With HTML, all content is organized into pages (HTML files). When you load a page, all the parts of its content are downloaded to the browser and then displayed. Flash MX 2004 movies, on the other hand, can be organized in a very different way.

Imagine a Web site with four or five pages. If it were a pure HTML site, each time you traveled from one page to another you would have to wait for the new page to download to the browser before being displayed. With a site built in Flash MX 2004, however, all of the "pages" could be contained in a single movie. When you visit the site, the first page would download and be displayed. While you were reading the first page, the other pages would be downloading in the background. When you clicked on a link to go to another page, it would be displayed instantly, with no download wait! This is the real beauty of streaming. When used correctly, it can allow you to build a site that eliminates a lot of unwanted waiting that plagues much of the Internet. You'll learn more about how to optimize your Flash MX 2004 content for streaming in Chapter 16, "*Publishing and Exporting.*"

What's New in Flash MX 2004?

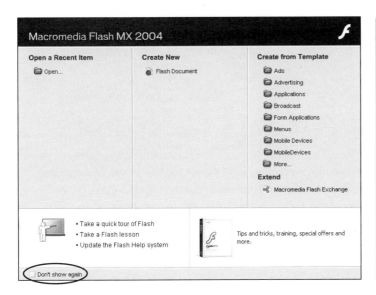
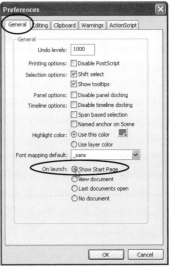

When you open the program, you will be prompted with the **Start Page**, which allows you to select from three start options. You can choose to open a recent file, create a new document, or create a new document from a template. At the bottom of the Start Page are helpful resources to get you started with the program. If you prefer not to see the Start Page each time you launch Flash MX 2004, you can click the **Don't show again** checkbox. To see the Start Page again, choose **Edit > Preferences** (Windows) or **Macromedia Flash MX 2004 > Preferences** (Mac) and in the **Preferences** dialog box under the **General** tab select **Show Start Page**.

Flash MX 2004 offers many upgraded and new features that enhance the program and make it even easier to work with. The following chart outlines the new features of the Flash MX 2004 product line. All features listed in the Flash MX 2004 solution are also included in the Flash MX Professional 2004 solution.

Flash MX 2004 Product Line New and Enhanced Features	
Feature	**Description**
Accessibility	Components and improved support for third-party plug-ins allows you to offer improved solutions for screen reading and closed captioning.
Adobe Illustrator support	Allows you to import Adobe Illustrator 10 files directly into Flash MX 2004 without losing vector representation of your source files. You will learn how to integrate Adobe Illustrator files in Chapter 18, "*Integration.*"
Adobe PDF support	Allows you to import Adobe PDFs for improved workflow.
Alias Text	Allows you to create crisp and legible text optimized for small display size. You will get a chance to work with Alias Text in Chapter 12, "*Working with Text.*"
Behaviors	Simplifies the creation of ActionScript so you can easily add inter-activity to your Flash MX 2004 movie without the need for explicit coding in the Actions panel. You will learn all about behaviors in Chapter 11, "*ActionScript Basics and Behaviors.*"
Cascading Style Sheets (CSS)	Allows you to create consistent design for HTML and Flash content. You can load XML or HTML files into your Flash MX 2004 movie with style-sheet specifications. You will get a chance to work with Cascading Style Sheets in Chapter 12, "*Working with Text.*"
Deployment Kit	Allows you to present appropriate content to end users more easily through the automatic player version detection kit. You will learn how to publish your Flash MX 2004 movies in Chapter 16, "*Publishing and Exporting.*"
Extensibility	Allows you to use third-party plug-ins, which can add functionality, text effects, high-resolution bitmap integration, and raster effects to your Flash MX 2004 movie.
FLV support	Allows you to play Flash MX 2004 video files back from disk directly from an FLV (Flash video) without the need to pack video into a SWF. You will learn more about Flash video in Chapter 15, "*Video.*"

continues on next page

Flash MX 2004 Product Line
New and Enhanced Features *continued*

Feature	Description
Help panel	The new Help panel allows you to access all Help information within the application and provides in-context reference and tutorials. You will learn more about the Help panel in Chapter 2, "*Interface.*"
History panel	Allows you to track the steps you've performed in your Flash MX 2004 document and convert those steps into reusable commands to automate repetitive tasks. You will learn more about the History panel in Chapter 2, "*Interface.*"
Search and Replace	Allows you to find and replace various elements within your Flash MX 2004 movie to increase your efficiency in the Flash MX 2004 authoring environment. You can create a search and replace for text, fonts, colors, symbols, sounds, video, and bitmaps within your Flash MX 2004 movie.
Spell check	Allows you to check the spelling in your Flash MX 2004 movie for improved workflow. You will learn how to spell check in Chapter 12, "*Working with Text.*"
Templates	Simplifies creating a new movie by giving you several new templates to choose from.
Timeline effects	Allows you to animate an object without using the timeline and keyframes to create animation. You will learn how to create Timeline effects in Chapter 7, "*Motion Tweening and Timeline Effects.*"
Unicode	Support for Unicode allows multilanguage authoring using any character set. This is an advanced feature and will not be covered in this book.
String panel	Facilitates deploying content into multiple languages by tracking strings for localization. This is an advanced feature and will not be covered in this book.
Video Import Wizard	Allows you to import and edit video clips with ease and provides additional control over frame ranges to be imported, reusable encoding settings, and new capabilities for cropping and color correction. You will work with the Video Import Wizard in Chapter 15, "*Video.*"

Flash MX Professional 2004

Flash MX Professional 2004 offers additional features that are not included in Flash MX 2004. The following chart outlines the features found only in the Flash MX Professional 2004 solution. These are features that are outside the scope of this book, and will not be covered because they are not included in the Flash MX 2004 solution.

Flash MX Professional 2004	
Feature	**Description**
Advanced components	More advanced components allow you to speed up the application development process.
Data binding	Data binding components easily display and respond to dynamic data
Data integration	Allows you to connect to data sources, including Web services, XML, SQL Server, and Macromedia Flash Remoting to make data-driven pages easy to author with minimal scripting.
Enhanced video quality and screen recording	Using the QuickTime FLV (Flash video) exporter, a new encoder is available with greater control and superior image quality for encoding video at larger frame sizes and higher frame rates.
Forms	The Forms programming environment allows you to easily develop interactive applications.
Pro video app integration	The QuickTime FLV (Flash video) Export plug-in enables third-party products that support QuickTime to export video files directly to the FLV format.
Project panel	The Project panel allows you to organize multiple files associated with your project and to work with a source control system.
Slides	The Slides authoring environment allows you to create highly interactive presentations.
Source code control	Integration with leading source control systems allows for improved team coordination.
Streaming media components	Allows for rapid development of FLV (Flash video) and MP3 files into video projects.

Project, Player, or Projector?

"Flash" as a term can be confusing. Macromedia uses the word interchangeably to include Macromedia Flash as an authoring tool, Macromedia Flash as a player, and Macromedia Flash as a stand-alone projector. The following chart should help set the groundwork for understanding the differences among the authoring tool, the player, and the stand-alone projector.

Macromedia Flash Applications	
Application	**Description**
Macromedia Flash authoring tool	The software application Flash MX 2004 is where you work to create and edit artwork, animation, add sound, and interactivity. The projects you create using the Flash MX 2004 authoring tool are stored in the FLA file format. Any changes to the Flash movie need to be edited in the production FLA file. Therefore, it's always wise to keep a copy of your FLA file. You cannot publish the FLA file to the Web, since it's a file that you use internally to edit and create Flash MX 2004 content. From the FLA file, you can export the SWF file format, which is inserted into an HTML document and published to the Web.
Macromedia Flash Player	The Macromedia Flash Player must be installed in the Web browser for end users to see Flash MX 2004 content in the SWF file. This player comes preinstalled in current Web browsers. If, for some reason, you do not have the Flash Player, you can download it from the Macromedia Web site for free.
Macromedia Flash Projector	Flash MX 2004 content can also be stored in stand-alone projectors that do not require the Web browser in order to play. These files can be distributed via email, on CD-ROMs, or on disk but are not typically distributed over the Web. The file extension for a Flash MX 2004 projector is .exe (Windows) or .hqx (Mac).

File Types Associated with Flash MX 2004

Flash MX 2004 media can be saved and output in many formats. The most common types of Flash MX 2004 files are project files, movie files, and projector files. The file types can become very confusing, because all of these are commonly referred to as "movies." The following list explains the three most prominent Flash MX 2004 formats. You will learn about all the file types that Flash MX 2004 can produce in detail in Chapter 16, "*Publishing and Exporting*."

Macromedia Flash File Types	
File Type	**Description**
Project file (.fla) Untitled.fla	The master project file format sometimes referred to as the "project file" and/or the "production file," stores all the settings and resources for your Flash MX 2004 project. You can reopen and reedit the FLA file at any time using the Flash MX 2004 Authoring Tool. (.fla stands for **FLA**sh.)
Movie file (.swf) Untitled.swf	The movie format sometimes referred to as the "published file" and/or the "optimized file" can be embedded in Web pages for Web-based Flash MX 2004 presentations. These files are generally not editable. (.swf stands for **S**mall **W**eb **F**ile.)
Windows Projector file (.exe) Untitled.exe **Mac Projector file (.hqx)** Untitled Projector	A stand-alone projector file can play on any computer without the need for the Macromedia Flash Player. Flash MX 2004 writes both Windows and Mac format projector files.

Caution: Player Required!

Flash MX 2004 content is not visible in a Web browser unless either the Macromedia Flash Player or the Shockwave Player has been installed in that browser. In the past, this has been seen as a serious limitation of the format, although over the past few years the number of Internet users who have the player has increased exponentially because current Web browsers now come with the Flash Player preinstalled.

Macromedia has hired an independent consulting firm to maintain an estimate of the number of Macromedia Flash Players that are in use. At the time of this writing, over 530 million Web users worldwide have a version of one of these players installed. The Macromedia Flash Player 7 comes preinstalled on all new browsers shipped by AOL, CompuServe, Microsoft, and Netscape. Additionally, all versions of Microsoft Windows 98 and newer and Apple OS 8 and newer operating systems include the plug-in.

Macromedia Players	
Macromedia Flash Player	The Macromedia Flash Player is used for viewing Macromedia Flash content on the Web. You can download the latest version of the Macromedia Flash Player at **http://www.macromedia.com/downloads/**. This player installs inside the player folder for your Web browser of choice.
Macromedia Shockwave Player	The Shockwave Player is used for viewing Macromedia Director content on the Web. You can download the latest version of the Shockwave Player at **http://www.macromedia.com/downloads/**.

Beyond Flash MX 2004

Flash MX 2004 is an incredibly powerful tool by itself. However, there are a few functions it can't perform. Here are some of the Web technologies you should know about if you want to extend Flash MX 2004 beyond its basic capabilities.

What's CGI?

A CGI (**C**ommon **G**ateway **I**nterface) script is a program that defines a standard way of exchanging information between a Web browser and a Web server. CGI scripts can be written in any number of languages (Perl, C, ASP, and others). If you plan on creating a complex Web application that requires the use of something like CGI, I recommend you work with a Web engineer who has experience creating these kinds of scripts. Flash MX 2004 can communicate with CGI scripts, although that topic is beyond the scope of this book.

For further information on using CGI, please check out the following links:

`http://www.cgidir.com/`

`http://www.cgi101.com/`

`http://www.icthus.net/CGI-City/`

What's XML?

XML (**EX**tensible **M**arkup **L**anguage) is a standard that has been developed to handle the description and exchange of data. XML enables developers to define markup languages that define the structure and meaning of information. Therefore, an XML document is much like a database presented in a text file. XML content can be transformed into a variety of different formats, including HTML, WML, and VoiceXML.

XML differs from HTML in that it is not predefined—you can create the tags and attributes. You can also use XML to create your own data structure and modify it for the data you want it to carry. In Flash MX 2004, you can use the XML object to create, manipulate, and pass that data. Using ActionScripting, a Flash MX 2004 movie can load and process XML data. As a result, an XML-savvy Flash MX 2004 developer can develop a movie that dynamically retrieves data from the external XML document instead of creating static text fields within a project file.

Just as HTML provided an open, platform-independent format for distributing Web documents, XML promises to be the open, platform-independent format for exchanging any type of electronic information. Like CGI, XML is also a topic beyond the scope of this book.

For further information on XML, take a look at the following links:

`http://www.ait-usa.com/xmlintro/xmlproject/article.htm`

`http://www.xml.com/`

`http://www.xml101.com/`

JavaScript and Flash MX 2004

Flash MX 2004's scripting language is referred to as **ActionScript**. ActionScript is based on another scripting language you may have heard of called **JavaScript**. Although they share a similar syntax and structure, they are two different languages. One way to tell them apart is that ActionScript uses scripts that are processed entirely within the Macromedia Flash Player, independently of the browser that is used to view the file. JavaScript, on the other hand, uses external interpreters that vary according to the browser used.

ActionScript and JavaScript can be used together because Flash MX 2004 gives you the ability to call JavaScript commands to perform tasks or to send and receive data. For many Flash MX 2004 developers, a basic knowledge of JavaScript makes learning ActionScript easier, because the basic syntax of the scripts and the handling of objects is the same in both languages. However, this is not a requirement for learning ActionScript.

You will be introduced to ActionScript in Chapter 11, "*ActionScript Basics and Behaviors.*" That chapter will give you hands-on experience in applying Flash MX 2004's powerful scripting language. For further information and tutorials about JavaScript and how to use it in conjunction with Flash MX 2004, check out the following links:

`http://www.javascript.com/`

`http://javascript.internet.com/`

`http://www.flashkit.com/links/Javascripts/`

That's a wrap for this chapter. You've familiarized yourself with the Flash MX 2004 product line, the new features of Flash MX 2004, and how to extend Flash content using various technologies. Now it's time to move on to the next chapter!

2.

Interface

Document Window	Timeline
Layer Controls	Edit Bar	Toolbar	Panels
Panel Keyboard Shortcuts	Custom Keyboard Shortcuts

no exercise files

Macromedia Flash MX 2004 H•O•T

If you are new to Flash MX 2004 you should not skip this chapter. Although you might be tempted to jump right in and begin with the hands-on exercises, take the time to read through this chapter first so you have a grasp of the Flash MX 2004 interface.

This chapter begins with an overview of the main components: the Timeline, stage, work area, and Toolbar, as well as the various panels in Flash MX 2004. This will be relatively short so you can get to the actual exercises as quickly as possible. After all, that's the best way to learn how these tools work. The overview in this chapter will make it easier for you to work with the various elements throughout the rest of the book.

If you are a veteran to the previous version, Flash MX, feel free to skim this chapter but be sure to check out the new panels in Flash MX 2004 such as the Behaviors panel, Help panel, History panel, and the Strings panel.

The Document Window

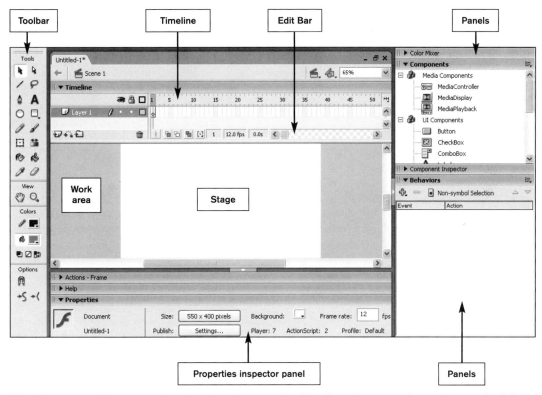

The document window contains six main elements: the Timeline, the stage, the work area, the Edit Bar, the Toolbar, and panels, including the Properties inspector shown here.

Each time you create a new document in Flash MX 2004, you are presented with a new blank **document window**. This window is divided into six main components:

Timeline: The Timeline is where you control the static and moving elements in the project file, using layers, frames, the playhead, and the status bar. All are described in detail in the next few pages.

Stage: The stage is where your animation, images, and content appear. It represents the visible area of your project. You will learn how to modify the properties of the stage, such as size, color, and frame rate, in Chapter 4, "*Animation Basics.*"

Work area: The light gray area around the stage is referred to as the work area. Nothing in the work area will be visible to the end user after you publish your movie. You can place objects here until you want them to appear on the stage. For example, if you want to animate a bird flying in from offstage, you can place the bird artwork offscreen in the work area so it appears to fly in from outside the stage area.

Edit Bar: The edit bar displays your current location inside the project file such as the name of the current scene, a number of buttons that let you edit scenes and symbols, and the Zoom box. This bar may change location based on whether your Timeline is docked or not. Docking and undocking the Timeline is discussed later in this chapter.

Toolbar: The Toolbar contains tools that are necessary when creating and editing artwork. This long vertical bar gives you access to just about every tool you will need to create and modify the objects in your Flash MX 2004 projects.

Panels: Panels are windows that contain tools and information to help you work in your project file more efficiently. Each of the panels can be used to view and modify elements within your project file. For example, the contents of the Properties inspector change depending on what is selected, and it allows you to make changes to the current selection quickly, right inside the panel. You will learn more about panels later in this chapter.

The Timeline

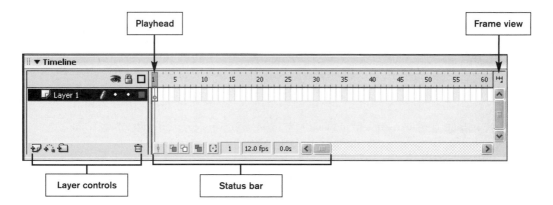

Timeline: The Timeline controls and displays all of the static and moving elements of your project over time, using frames and layers. In this section, you'll learn about the main elements of the Timeline. You will get hands-on experience later as you go through the exercises.

Playhead: The playhead indicates which frame in the Timeline is currently displayed on the stage. Once you have artwork on the stage and have created different frames (which you'll learn to do in Chapter 3, "*Drawing and Color Tools*"), you can click and drag the playhead to move it to a specific frame. You can also scan through the Timeline (a process called **scrubbing**) to quickly preview animations. You will get a lot of practice doing this in the animation portions of this book.

Layer controls: This region lets you control the features of the layers, including adding, organizing, hiding, and locking layers, as well as displaying the content of layers as outlines. Because there are so many options here, they will be described in more detail later in this chapter.

Status bar: The status bar gives you feedback about the current frame, the number of frames per second (fps), and the elapsed time of your movie. It also contains other tools, such as onion skinning and editing multiple frames. All of these features will be addressed fully in Chapter 4, "*Animation Basics.*"

Frame view: This subtle drop-down menu lets you control the appearance of your Timeline. You can change the appearance of the individual frames and the entire size of the Timeline itself. As you will see in Chapter 13, "*Sound*," this can be helpful with certain projects.

Docking and Undocking the Timeline

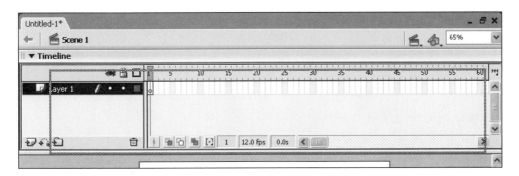

If you have the luxury of working with a large monitor or multiple monitors, you will be pleased to know that you can easily dock and undock the Timeline from the main document window. This feature allows you more flexibility in arranging your work environment. For example, you can place the stage on one monitor and stash all the Flash MX 2004 panels on your second monitor, giving you an uncluttered view of your work. By the way, if you find this feature annoying, you can disable it in the Preferences by choosing **Edit > Preferences**.

Docking and undocking the Timeline can be done in one or two easy steps: Move your cursor to the grid of dots in the upper-left corner of the Timeline until the cursor turns into either an icon with four arrows (Windows) or a Hand icon (Mac). Click and drag in that area to undock the Timeline. A thin outline will appear around the outline of the Timeline when you click, indicating that you have grabbed the Timeline and are moving it.

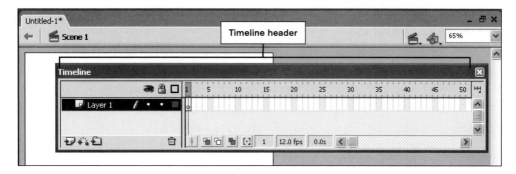

Release the mouse button and your Timeline will be undocked from the document window and will appear as its own window. Once it is undocked, you can click in the Timeline header, the bar that includes the panel name, to drag it around, as shown here.

If you want to redock the Timeline, you can choose from four locations:

- Its default position above the stage

- The right side of the document window

- The left side of the document window

- The bottom of the document window

To redock it, simply click in the Timeline header, drag it back to one of the four locations, and release the mouse button.

The Layer Controls

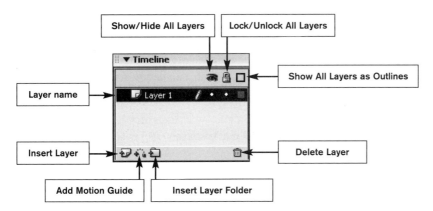

Flash MX 2004 allows you to use layers to organize your artwork, just like other graphics programs you might be familiar with, such as Macromedia Fireworks, Adobe Photoshop, and so on. The Timeline's Layer controls play an important role in your workflow. This is where you add, modify, delete, and organize layers. From here, you can also hide, lock, and control the appearance of the layer contents. As you add layers in Flash MX 2004, the artwork on the topmost layer in the Timeline will appear closest to you on the stage. At any time you can rearrange the stacking order of the artwork simply by dragging and dropping the layers higher or lower in the Timeline. The following list explains the Layer controls in detail:

Layer name: The default layer names are Layer 1, Layer 2, and so on. Double-click a layer name to rename it.

Insert Layer: Adding new layers to your projects is as easy as clicking this button. Each time you click, a new layer is added on top of the one that is currently selected.

Add Motion Guide: This button adds a guide layer on top of the currently selected layer. A guide layer allows you to animate objects by following a designated path that you draw. You will work with guide layers in Chapter 7, "*Motion Tweening and Timeline Effects.*"

Insert Layer Folder: This feature allows you to add a special layer folder that can hold other layers. This is helpful in organizing your layers into groups that can be easily expanded and collapsed.

Delete Layer: There's not much mystery to this trash can button. Clicking this button deletes the layer that is currently selected. Don't worry, though: If you click this button by accident, you can undo it by choosing **Edit > Undo Delete Layer.** Phew!!

Show/Hide All Layers: Clicking the Eye icon will temporarily hide the artwork on the stage and work area on all layers in the Timeline. **Note:** This will not hide your artwork in the published movie.

Lock/Unlock All Layers: Clicking the Padlock icon to lock the layer makes it impossible to edit anything on this layer. This control can be useful when you start working with multiple layers, especially ones with overlapping content. **Tip:** To lock all layers with the exception of the layer on which you are currently working in **Alt+click** (Windows) or **Option+click** (Mac) the padlock column of that current layer.

Show All Layers as Outlines: Clicking the Outline icon displays the contents of the layers in the Timeline in Outline view, in which solid shapes are represented as outlined shapes with no solid fill. This feature can be very helpful when you are working with multiple layers with overlapping content.

The Edit Bar

The **Edit Bar** is very useful for quick visual feedback as to where you are located in your movie. It contains buttons and a drop-down menu that provides quick access to the scenes and available zoom levels. Here is a brief description of each feature in the edit bar:

Current scene: The current scene readout on the left side of the edit bar displays the name of the scene that is currently open on the stage. You will learn about scenes in Chapter 11, "*ActionScript Basics and Behaviors.*"

Edit Scene menu: If your movie contains more than one scene, this drop-down menu displays a list of all the scenes in your project file. You will learn how to use multiple scenes in Chapter 11, "*ActionScript Basics and Behaviors.*"

Edit Symbols menu: This drop-down menu displays all of the symbols in your project. You'll learn about symbols in Chapter 6, "*Symbols and Instances.*"

Zoom box: It might seem like a little thing, and maybe it is in size, but the Zoom box is a handy drop-down menu that lets you quickly zoom into and out of the contents of your stage.

The Toolbar

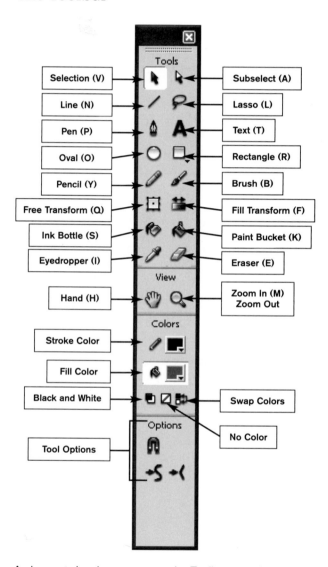

As in most drawing programs, the Toolbar contains tools that are necessary when creating and editing artwork. This long vertical bar gives you access to just about every tool you will need to create and modify objects in your Flash MX 2004 projects. Each of the main tools has an associated keyboard shortcut, which is listed in parentheses next to the tool name in the figure.

When you hover over a Toolbar icon, a small tooltip will appear with the name and keyboard shortcut for that option. You can disable this feature in the General Preferences by choosing **Edit > Preferences > General**.

WARNING | Docking the Toolbar on Windows Versus Macintosh

There is one minor difference between the Mac and Windows operating systems when it comes to docking the Toolbar. On the Macintosh, you can't dock the Toolbar. You can, however, click and drag to reposition the Toolbar freely around the screen. In the Windows operating system, the Toolbar can be docked only along either side of the document window.

The Panels

Panels are windows that contain tools and information to help you work in your project file more efficiently. You can also customize panels within the work area to streamline your workflow even further. Each of the panels can be used to view and modify elements within your project file. The options within the panels allow you to change settings such as color, type, size, rotation, and many others. You have the ability to display, hide, move, resize, group, and organize the panels so that you can customize the work area in any way you wish.

In the next few sections, you will learn the basic ins and outs of working with panels, including how to dock, resize, and work with panel sets. At the end of this section is a list that provides a quick reference to the panels in Flash MX 2004.

Undocking and Docking Panels

Don't think for a moment that you are stuck with the default panel layout. Just like the Timeline, mentioned earlier in this chapter, the panels can easily be undocked and docked to create new combinations that better fit your workflow.

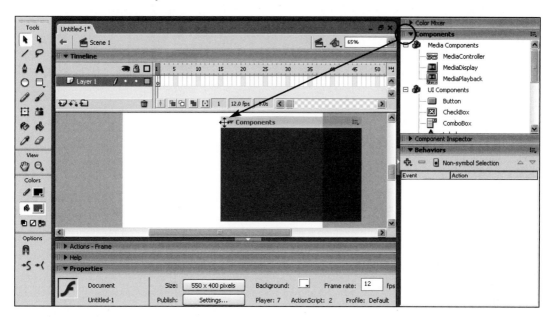

To undock a panel, move your mouse to the grid of dots in the upper-left corner of the panel title bar. You will notice that the pointer becomes either an icon with four arrows (Windows) or a Hand icon (Mac). Click and drag the panel away from its current docked position and let go of the mouse button to undock it.

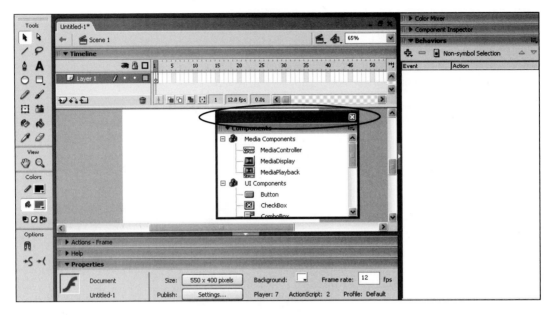

Once the panel is undocked, you can move it around the work area by clicking on the panel title bar and dragging.

To redock a panel or add it to another panel group, click the grid of dots in the upper left of the panel title bar (you will see the pointer change to arrows (Windows) or a hand (Mac) and drag the panel onto another panel. Once you are hovering over the other panel, you will see a dark outline appear over that panel, indicating that if you release your mouse, you will add the panel you are dragging to the panel group you are hovering over.

Tip: A few of the panels (such as the Properties inspector) will lose their dots once you undock them. In such cases, simply click the panel's solid bar and drag it over another panel until that panel is outlined and let go of the mouse to dock it again.

Resizing Panels

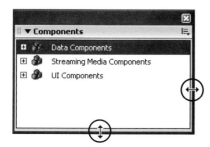

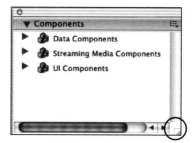

Windows panel.   *Macintosh panel.*

Flash MX 2004 not only allows you to completely customize the layout and arrangement of the panels, but it also lets you change the size of each panel. To resize a panel, either drag the panel's border (Windows) or drag the lower-right corner (Mac).

Note: A few of the panels, such as the Properties inspector and the Toolbar, cannot be resized. In these particular panels, the pointer will not turn into the resize arrows when you move it over the border (Windows), or you will not see the lines in the right corner of the panel (Mac).

Expanding, Collapsing, Hiding, and Closing Panels

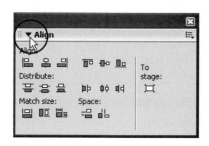

Panel expanded.   *Panel collapsed.*

To expand a panel when you see only its title, click the arrow next to the panel name once. Click the arrow again to collapse it. (You can also simply click the title bar of the panel to either expand or collapse the panel.)

To show or hide all of the panels in your document, press **F4** on the keyboard or choose **Window > Hide Panels** to close all of the panels.

Using the Panel Options Menu

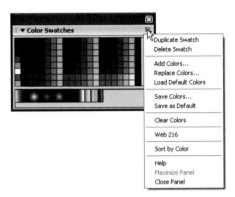

In addition to what you see in each panel, many of the panels have a control that displays a pop-up options menu when clicked. To display this menu, click the options menu control in the upper-right corner of the panel. You cannot access the pop-up options menu if the panel has been collapsed.

Creating and Saving Panel Sets

Flash MX 2004 gives you the flexibility to group panels in any combination you like. In addition, you can save these custom configurations. This means that with the click of the mouse, you can completely modify the arrangement of your panels. The following steps walk you through the process of saving a custom panel set.

Organize your panels in any way you want. For example, you can create different panel sets for different tasks, such as drawing, animation, and working with ActionScripts. This feature allows you to quickly organize your workspace for specific tasks.

1. Choose **Window > Save Panel Layout**. This opens the **Save Panel Layout** dialog box, which prompts you to assign a name for this arrangement.

2. Enter any name you want and click **OK**. That's all there is to it!

Switching to Another Panel Set

Changing from one panel set to another is as easy as selecting a menu option. Choose **Window > Panel Sets**, and select the name of the layout you want to display. Your panels will quickly be rearranged into that specific arrangement.

Note: To return the panels to their default positions, choose **Window > Panel Sets > Default Layout.**

TIP | Deleting Panel Sets

What do you do if you create a panel set that you just aren't happy with? Although there is no menu option for deleting them, you still can. All of the panel sets are stored in a folder on your hard drive:

(Windows) **Program Files/Macromedia/Flash MX 2004/en/First Run/Panel Sets**

(Mac) **Users/Username/Library/Application Support/Macromedia/Flash MX 2004/en/ Configuration/Panel Sets**

If you want to remove a panel set, just delete the appropriate file from this directory, and it will be gone forever.

The Panels Defined

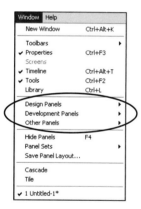

This section briefly describes each of the panels in Flash MX 2004. With this release of Flash, many of the panels have been categorized by **Design**, **Development**, and **Other**, so it may seem like a lot of new information. If so, just skim over it for now and then come back to it later as you read through the book. You will have several opportunities to work with each of the panels described here in depth as you navigate through the exercises in this book.

It is important to know before beginning that panels are accessed in one of two ways. First, you can display the **Window** menu (shown in the previous figure) and then choose the panel you want. Second, you can use the panel's associated keyboard shortcut. The method you use is a matter of personal preference, but it's a good idea to find one consistent way to work; it makes using Flash MX 2004 easier. A chart of the keyboard shortcuts to the various panels can be referenced in the "Panel Keyboard Shortcuts in Flash MX 2004" table later in this chapter.

Here is a description of each of the panels in Flash MX 2004.

Main: Allows you to perform simple tasks such as creating, saving, and opening Flash movies, as well as printing frames in your movie.

Note: The Main panel is only found on the Windows platform. To access it choose **Window > Toolbars > Main.**

Controller: Provides one way to preview your movie right inside the authoring environment. Although there are several ways to test your movie, the Controller panel contains features similar to those on a remote control, allowing you to stop, rewind, fast-forward, and play your movie using one panel.

Edit bar: Gives you quick visual feedback to your current location and allows you to go to different scenes in your Flash movie as well as zooming into or out of the contents on the stage.

Properties inspector: Acts as a one-stop shop for displaying and changing all of your most commonly used attributes of the current selection in one panel. This context-sensitive panel allows you to modify the current selection using only one panel, rather than having to open several panels.

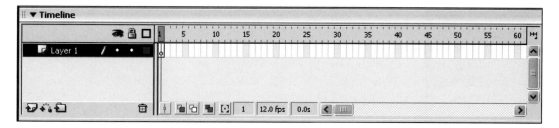

Timeline: Controls and displays all of the static and moving elements of your Flash MX 2004 projects. The layers represent the depth of the objects in your movie; the frames represent how they change over time.

Toolbar: Contains all the tools that are necessary to create and edit artwork, including drawing, painting, selection, and modification tools. The Toolbar is one of the most frequently used panels in the program. For a listing of the keyboard shortcuts to the various tools, refer to the "The Toolbar" section earlier in this chapter.

Library: Provides a location for you to store and organize specific assets within your project, including symbols, imported artwork, sound files, and video files. You will learn about the Library panel in Chapter 6, "*Symbols and Instances.*"

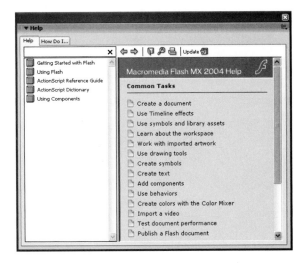

Help: Allows you to access all Help information within the program and provides in-context reference and tutorials. The Help panel is new to Flash MX 2004.

Align: Gives you access to several different alignment and distribution options.

Color Mixer: Allows you to create new colors in one of three different modes—RGB (red, green, blue), HSB (hue, saturation, brightness), or HEX (hexadecimal). The Color Mixer panel also lets you add alpha and work with different types of gradients.

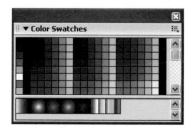

Color Swatches: Displays the default 216 Web-safe colors and lets you select, add, sort, replace, save, and clear colors.

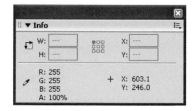

Info: Contains numerical information about the size, position, and color of the selected object. This panel is very helpful when you need pixel-specific positions and measurements.

Scene: Displays a list of all the scenes within your movie. This panel lets you quickly add, duplicate, delete, name, or rename scenes. The Scene panel also provides a way to jump to different scenes in your document.

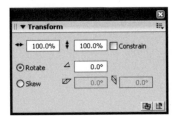

Transform: Allows you to numerically transform (rotate, scale, and skew) an object. This panel also lets you create a transformed copy of an object.

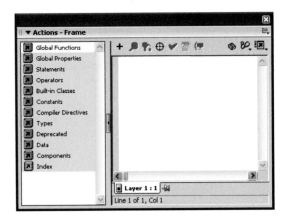

Actions: Allows you to add and modify actions for a frame, button, or movie clip. You will learn all about the Actions panel in Chapter 11, "*ActionScript Basics and Behaviors.*"

Behaviors: This panel is new to Flash MX 2004 and allows you to easily add interactivity to your Flash movie without the need for explicit coding in the Actions panel. You will learn more about behaviors in Chapter 11, "*ActionScript Basics and Behaviors*".

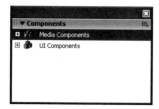

Components: This release of Flash has added several new components to the Components panel. You have access to media components, which are new to Flash MX 2004 and user interface (UI) components, which also contain a few new features. These components are essentially movie clips that contain complex ActionScript elements. As you will see in Chapter 14, "*Components and Forms*," the Components panel lets you add powerful functionality to your movie without requiring you to know advanced ActionScript.

Component Inspector: Allows you to set the parameters (attributes) of a component after you have added an instance of that component to your movie.

Debugger: Provides a way to check your movie for errors while it is playing in the Macromedia Flash Player.

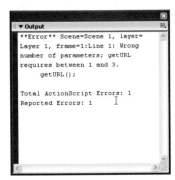

Output: Provides assistance during troubleshooting by displaying feedback information after you test your movie.

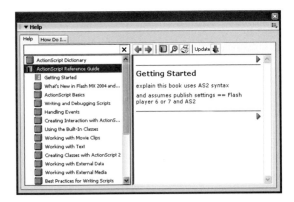

Reference: The Reference panel, found within the Help panel, displays detailed information about ActionScript usage and syntax. This panel is an essential tool for learning ActionScript; you will be working with it in Chapter 11, "*ActionScript Basics and Behaviors.*"

Accessibility: Gives you options that can help make your movies more accessible to people with seeing and hearing disabilities. Also, improved support for third-party plug-ins allows you to offer improved solutions for screen reading and closed captioning. You will learn more about creating accessible content in Chapter 18, "*Integration.*"

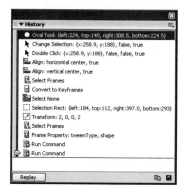

History: This new panel in Flash MX 2004 allows you to track the steps you've completed in your Flash document and convert those steps into reusable commands to automate repetitive tasks.

Movie Explorer: Displays the contents of your movie, organized in a hierarchical tree. You can use the Movie Explorer panel to search for specific elements within your project file so that you can quickly select and edit them with a few clicks of your mouse. You will learn about the Movie Explorer panel in Chapter 17, "*Putting It All Together.*"

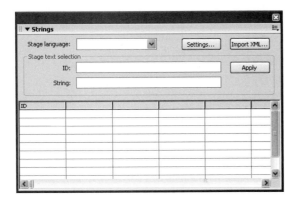

Strings: Aids you in deploying content into multiple languages by tracking strings for localization. The Strings panel is new to Flash MX 2004. This is an advanced feature and will not be covered in this book.

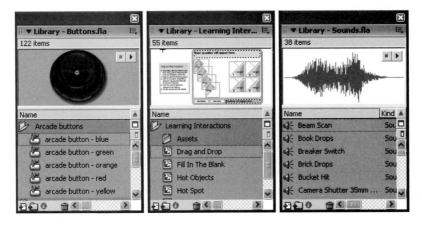

Common libraries: Provides access to sample libraries included with the program. These libraries contain premade buttons, learning interactions, and sounds, which you can use in your movies.

Shortcut Keys

Flash MX 2004 has lots and lots of shortcut keys, and if you are a keyboard shortcut junkie like me, then you'll want to add these shortcut keys to the various panels under your belt. For a listing of the shortcut keys to the different Flash MX 2004 tools, refer to the "The Toolbar" section earlier in this chapter.

Panel Keyboard Shortcuts in Flash MX 2004		
Panel	**Windows**	**Macintosh**
Properties inspector	Ctrl+F3	Cmd+F3
Timeline	Ctrl+Alt+T	Option+Cmd+T
Tools	Ctrl+F2	Cmd+F2
Library	Ctrl+L	Cmd+L
Align	Ctrl+K	Cmd+K
Color Mixer	Shift+F9	Shift+F9
Color Swatches	Ctrl+F9	Cmd+F9
Info	Ctrl+I	Cmd+I
Scene	Shift+F2	Shift+F2
Transform	Ctrl+T	Cmd+T
Help	F1	F1
Actions	F9	F9
Behaviors	Shift+F3	Shift+F3
Components	Ctrl+F7	Cmd+F7
Component Inspector	Alt+F7	Option+F7
Debugger	Shift+F4	Shift+F4
Output	F2	F2
Accessibility	Alt+F2	Option+F2
History	Ctrl+F10	Cmd+F10
Movie Explorer	Alt+F3	Option+F3
Strings	Ctrl+F11	Cmd+F11

Custom Keyboard Shortcuts

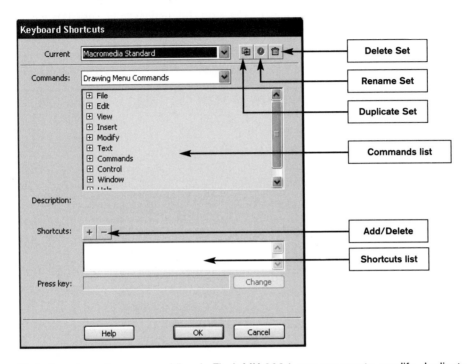

To further streamline your workflow in Flash MX 2004, you can create, modify, duplicate and delete sets of custom keyboard shortcuts. Macromedia has even designed an entire interface to make this process easy to do. One of its neatest features even allows you to assign keyboard shortcuts in Flash MX 2004 that match those used in other programs, such as Macromedia Fireworks, Macromedia Freehand, Adobe Photoshop, and even earlier versions of Macromedia Flash. You may think that this feature is only for power users, but you will be a power user in no time, right?!!?

The following steps outline the process of creating, modifying, and deleting custom keyboard shortcuts. This isn't an exercise that you have to complete; if you like, just make a mental note of it for later use.

Creating a New Shortcut Set

1. Choose **Edit > Keyboard Shortcuts** (Windows) or **Flash > Keyboard Shortcuts** (Mac) to open the **Keyboard Shortcuts** dialog box.

2. Click the **Duplicate Set** button to create a copy of the current set. This will ensure that you are working from a duplicate so you don't mess up the original set.

3. Enter a name for your custom set. You can name it anything you want, but it's best to stick to a meaningful name that you can recall later. Click **OK.**

4. Click to the left of any of the options in the **Commands** list to drill down and display the keyboard shortcuts for that menu. Select the option you want to change.

5. Click the **+** button to add a shortcut (click the **–** button to delete the selected shortcut). You can create multiple keyboard shortcuts for one option. (However, that may not be such a good idea.)

6. Press the keys you want to use as the keyboard shortcut to assign it to the option. Notice that the shortcut key appears in the **Press key** text box. Click the **Change** button to confirm your selection and assign it to the menu item.

Note: If the key combination you selected is already in use, you will get an error message at the bottom of the dialog box.

Well, that's the Flash MX 2004 interface for now. You should now feel a little more familiar with these interface elements. Next, you'll finally get a chance to work with some of them in the following chapter. So go ahead and turn the page to get started!

3.
Using the Drawing and Color Tools

Drawing Tools	Lines, Strokes, and Fills
Drawing with the Pencil Tool	Modifying Lines
Using the Oval and Rectangle Tools	Using the Brush Tool
Modifying Strokes and Fills	Working with Multiple Objects
Grouping Objects	Creating Gradients
Drawing with the Pen Tool	Modifying Paths

chap_03

Macromedia Flash MX 2004
H•O•T CD-ROM

When most people think of Macromedia Flash, they think of one thing: animation. What many people may not know is that the program comes complete with a good set of drawing and color tools that can help you create artwork for making cool and interactive animations.

You can also import existing artwork into Flash MX 2004 from other programs such as FreeHand, Fireworks, Photoshop, or Illustrator. Chapter 18, "*Integration*," shows you how to do this. The drawing and color tools inside Flash MX 2004 make it really easy and convenient to create artwork right inside the program. This chapter introduces you to the distinct characteristics and idiosyncrasies of the native drawing and color tools and shows how to use these tools within Flash MX 2004.

Drawing Tools Explained

Although the drawing tools in Flash MX 2004 are very powerful, and may be familiar to you from other programs, you'll find that some tools are unique as you try to understand their individual behaviors. This handy chart outlines the behavior of the tool and provides the keyboard shortcuts that should be familiar to you from Chapter 2, "*Interface*." Don't feel compelled to read through everything here. If you want to jump into the exercises, go right ahead. You will be comfortable drawing in Flash MX 2004 in a very short time!

Drawing Tools in Flash MX 2004		
Icon	**Name**	**What Does It Do?**
	Selection (V)	The Selection tool is the one tool that you'll use the most. It acts as your "hands" in the Flash MX 2004 environment by allowing you to select, move, and edit your artwork.
	Subselection (A)	The Subselection tool allows you to modify the anchor points and tangent handles of a shape's path, or outline.
	Line (N)	The Line tool creates straight lines. Holding down the Shift key with this tool will constrain the lines to 45-degree angles. The lines drawn with the Line tool can be modified with the Ink Bottle tool and/or by using the Properties inspector.
	Lasso (L)	The Lasso tool allows you to make odd-shaped selections of your artwork by drawing a freehand selection around it or by using the Lasso options to fine tune and adjust your selections.
	Pen (P)	The Pen tool creates straight or curved line segments and is the only Flash MX 2004 drawing tool capable of creating Bézier curves.
	Text (T)	The Text tool allows you to add static text or text fields to your movie. With text fields, you can accept user input and even display HTML formatted text that's been loaded from an external text file to your movie.
	Oval (O)	The Oval tool creates circles and ovals composed of fills and strokes, just fills, or just strokes. Holding down the Shift key while using this tool will allow you to create perfect circles. Holding down the Alt key (Windows) or the Option key (Mac) will start the shape from the center.

continues on next page

Drawing Tools in Flash MX 2004 *continued*		

Icon	Name	What Does It Do?
	Rectangle (R)	The Rectangle tool creates rectangles and squares composed of strokes and fills, just strokes, or just fills. Holding down the Shift key while using this tool will allow you to create perfect squares. Holding down the Alt key (Windows) or the Option key (Mac) will start the shape from the center.
	Pencil (Y)	The Pencil tool creates lines in one of three different modes: Straighten, Smooth, and Ink. These modes will allow you better control over how the lines are created.
	Brush (B)	The Brush tool creates shapes with fills only. You can adjust the size, style and behavior of the brush by adjusting the tool options or by using the Properties inspector.
	Free Transform (Q)	The Free Transform tool allows you to modify objects. You can use this tool to scale, rotate, flip, skew, or even change the center point of an object. Use the Shift key to maintain the aspect ratio while modifying the object.
	Fill Transform (F)	The Fill Transform tool allows you to change the size, direction, or center of a gradient or bitmap fill.
	Ink Bottle (S)	The Ink Bottle tool changes the color or width of a line or adds a stroke to a shape. The Ink Bottle will not change the fill of a shape. Instead, use the Paint Bucket tool.
	Paint Bucket (K)	The Paint Bucket tool adds a fill inside a shape and can change the color of a fill. The Paint Bucket will not change the stroke of a shape. Instead, use the Ink Bottle tool.
	Eyedropper (I)	The Eyedropper tool can be used to copy the fill or stroke attributes of one object and then apply them to another object. This tool is especially useful when you want to copy the exact color of one object to another object.
	Eraser (E)	The Eraser tool removes any unwanted image areas on the Stage. Holding down the Shift key permits you to erase in perfect horizontal and vertical lines.

Lines, Strokes, and Fills Explained

In addition to learning how each of the drawing tools behaves, you need to know the difference between **fills**, **strokes**, **lines**, and **shapes**. These differences can be confusing because the interface refers to both lines and strokes. The following chart gives an example and brief explanation of each.

Lines, Strokes, and Fills		
Lines and strokes		Lines are created with the Pencil, Pen, and Line tools. Strokes are the outlines that are created using the Rectangle and Oval tools. It is important to note that these terms are used interchangeably in the Macromedia documentation. We will also use both of these terms, since they both can be modified using the same tools. Lines and strokes are independent of any fills, and they are modified using the Ink Bottle, the Color and Tool modifiers in the Toolbar, the Color Mixer panel, or using the Stroke Color in the Properties inspector.
Fills		Fills are created using the Brush and Paint Bucket tools. Fills can be created with or without strokes around them. They are modified using the Paint Bucket, the Color and Tool modifiers in the Toolbar, the Color Mixer panel, or using the Properties inspector.
Strokes, lines, fills, and shapes		Strokes and lines can be attached to fills, as in the picture on the left, or they can be by themselves, as in the images in the top row. Strokes and lines are added to fills with the Ink Bottle and are modified using the Ink Bottle, the Color and Tool modifiers in the Toolbar, the Color Mixer panel, or using the Properties inspector. Flash MX 2004 refers to strokes, lines, fills, or a combination thereof as "shapes" when the selection appears as a dotted mesh and is displayed as a "Shape" in the Properties inspector.

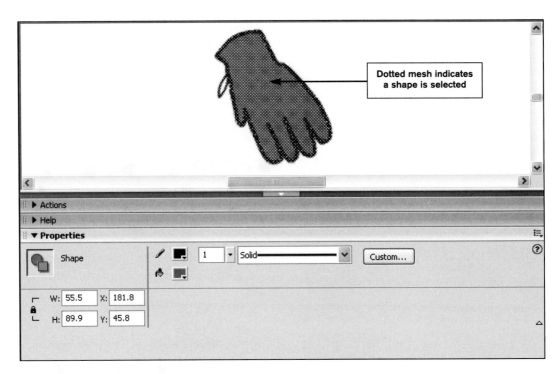

When you select a line, a stroke, a fill, or a combination thereof, and the selection appears as a dotted mesh, this is referred to as a shape inside of Flash MX 2004. The Properties inspector will also display the word "Shape" to indicate that a shape has been selected.

I. ——————————Drawing with the Pencil

The **Pencil** tool is one of the easiest drawing tools to use. It behaves much as you would expect a pencil to behave, drawing a line whenever you click and drag the mouse. By selecting one of the three modes (**Straighten**, **Smooth**, or **Ink**), you can control how the lines are created. In this exercise, you will draw a circle with the Pencil tool using each of the three modes, so you can better understand how each one behaves.

1. Copy the **chap_03** folder from the Macromedia Flash MX 2004 **H•O•T CD-ROM** to your hard drive. You must copy the files to your hard drive if you want to save changes to them.

2. Open **pencil.fla** file from the **chap_03** folder. This is just a blank file with the Stage dimensions set to 400 × 200 pixels. This should be enough space for you to draw some shapes.

The Pencil tool.

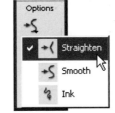

The Pencil Options appear at the bottom of the Toolbar when the Pencil tool is selected.

3. Select the **Pencil** tool from the **Toolbar.** By default, the **Pencil** tool is in **Straighten** mode.

Tip: If you leave your mouse over the tool long enough, a small tooltip will appear, with the keyboard shortcut for that tool in parentheses.

NOTE | About the Pencil Modes

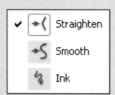

In Flash MX 2004, the Pencil tool works much the same as the pencil tools in other graphics programs. There are, however, some special drawing modes that can help you control the line's appearance: **Straighten**, **Smooth**, and **Ink**. For example, drawing a perfect circle might be really difficult for some of you (especially after that morning coffee!), but with Straighten mode, it's much easier to create perfect geometric circles.

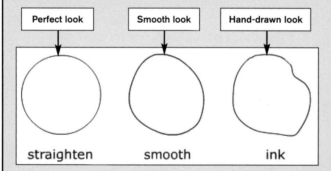

This example shows the result of a circle drawn with the Pencil tool, using each of the three modes.

The circle as you draw in Straighten mode.   *The circle when you release the mouse button.*

4. On the **Stage**, click and drag with the **Pencil** tool to create a circle. Release the mouse button when you are finished. Notice that the shape snaps to a circle when you release the mouse button. This is the effect of the **Straighten** mode as it tries to guess what shape you are trying to create.

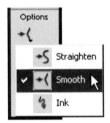

5. In the **Toolbar**, click the **Pencil Options** drop-down menu and select **Smooth**. This changes the mode of the **Pencil** tool to **Smooth**.

The circle as you draw in Smooth mode.   *The circle when you release the mouse button.*

6. Using the **Pencil** tool, draw another circle next to the one you just created. When you release the mouse button, notice that the circle gets smoother, but that the change is less significant than when you used **Straighten** mode.

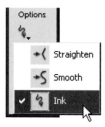

7. Click the **Pencil Options** drop-down menu and select **Ink**. This changes the mode of the **Pencil** tool to **Ink**.

The circle as you draw in Ink mode.   *The circle when you release the mouse button.*

8. Using the **Pencil** tool, draw a third circle next to the one you just created. When you release the mouse button, notice that there is very little change in the circle.

9. Tired of drawing circles? Go ahead and practice drawing other simple shapes, such as squares, triangles, polygons, and so on, with each of the different **Pencil** options. This will give you an even better idea of how each **Pencil** mode works and how they can help you create artwork in Flash MX 2004.

*Tip: If you want to clear the **Stage** area for more experimenting, press **Ctrl+A** (Windows) or **Cmd+A** (Mac) to select everything on the **Stage**. Then press the **Delete** key to delete the contents of the **Stage**.*

10. When you are done playing with the **Pencil** tool, save and close this file—you won't need it again.

2. ——————Modifying Lines

Now that you know how to use the Pencil tool, you need to know how to make changes to the lines you create. In this exercise, you will learn how to use the Properties inspector as well as the Ink Bottle to modify the appearance of lines. Both of these tools let you change an object either by adding a line or by modifying the existing line. In addition, you will learn some of the nuances involved in selecting lines and the reason why you would use the Ink Bottle versus the Properties inspector.

1. Open the **strokes.fla** file from the **chap_03** folder. This file contains some shapes created with lines and fills. You will use these shapes to learn to modify lines and add strokes to shapes.

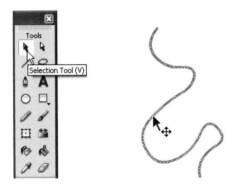

2. Select the **Selection** tool from the **Toolbar**, and then click on the squiggle drawing to select it. The line gets a bit thicker, and a dotted mesh appears over it, indicating that the line is selected.

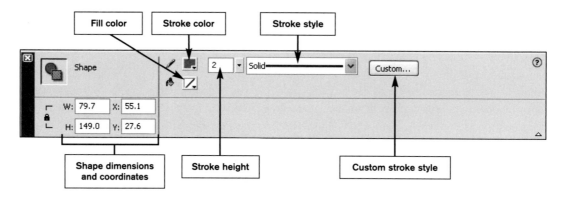

3. Make sure the **Properties inspector** is visible. If it's not, choose **Window > Properties** to make it visible. You must first select a line if you are going to use the Properties inspector to modify the stroke settings.

NOTE | The Properties Inspector

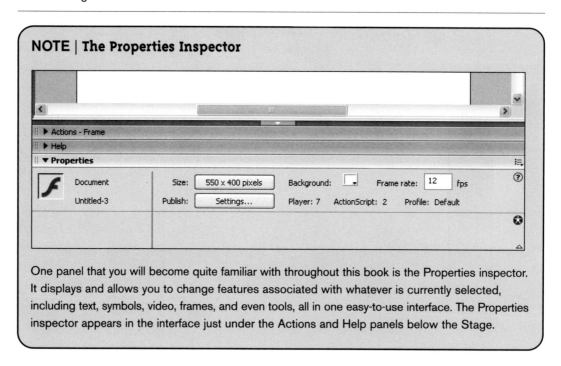

One panel that you will become quite familiar with throughout this book is the Properties inspector. It displays and allows you to change features associated with whatever is currently selected, including text, symbols, video, frames, and even tools, all in one easy-to-use interface. The Properties inspector appears in the interface just under the Actions and Help panels below the Stage.

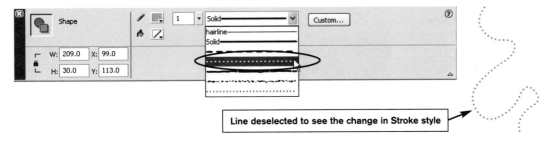

Line deselected to see the change in Stroke style

4. With the line still selected, click to see the **Stroke style** drop-down menu. Select the fourth style from the top, the dotted line, to change the style of the line from a solid line to a dotted line. Deselect the line by clicking on a blank area of the **Stage** to clearly see the changes.

You can use the Properties inspector as an easy way to modify artwork you select on the Stage. When you have a line selected, the Properties inspector displays the current settings for that line. This is helpful when you need to know what the line settings are for a particular object. The default stroke settings are a 1-point, solid black line.

TIP | Hiding Selections

When lines are selected, it can be very difficult to see the changes you've made. Press **Ctrl+H** (Windows) or **Shift+Cmd+E** (Mac) to temporarily hide the dotted mesh so you can see the changes better. Press the keyboard shortcut again to see the dotted mesh.

Line deselected to show the change in the Stroke height

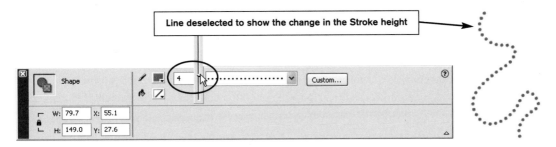

5. Make sure the line is selected on the **Stage** and, in the **Properties inspector**, click on the arrow next to the **Stroke height** to reveal the slider. Click and drag up on the slider until you reach a setting of **4**. This increases the thickness of the line. The total range of choices is from **0.25** to **10**. Deselect the line by clicking on a blank area of the **Stage** to clearly see the changes.

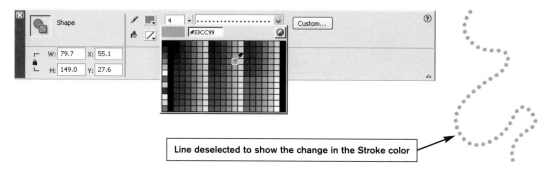

Line deselected to show the change in the Stroke color

6. Select the line on the **Stage** again, and from the **Stroke color** box in the **Properties inspector**, click and select another color. As you can probably guess, this will change the color of the line. Deselect the line by clicking on a blank area of the **Stage** to clearly see the changes.

TIP | Creating Custom Line Styles

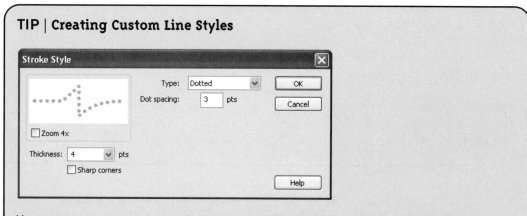

You can create your own custom line styles in the **Stroke Style** dialog box. With the line selected on the **Stage**, click the button named **Custom** in the **Properties inspector**. This will open the **Stroke Style** dialog box, where you can create your own line style using a number of different options. The changes you make to the settings here are temporary, and they will return to their default settings once you quit the program.

7. Using the **Selection** tool, move the cursor over the bottom line of the arrow shape in the middle of the Stage. (Don't click just yet.) Notice that as you move the cursor over the line, a small, curved line appears next to the **Selection** tool. This indicates that you are over a line segment.

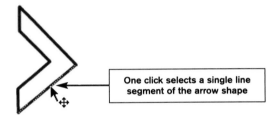

One click selects a single line segment of the arrow shape

8. Using the **Selection** tool, click on the lower-right line segment. Notice that a dotted mesh appears over the selection of the line segment only.

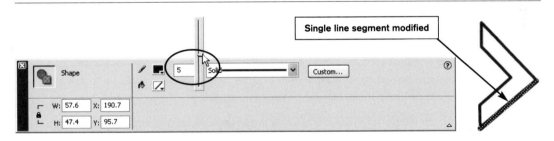

Single line segment modified

9. In the **Properties inspector**, use the **Stroke height** slider to change the line width to **5**. Notice that only the one selected line segment is changed. In order for a line to be modified, it must be selected before you change the settings in the **Stroke** panel, and in this case, only one of the six lines of this arrow shape was selected.

TIP | Selecting Lines in Flash MX 2004

Unlike other drawing programs, Flash MX 2004 breaks lines with hard angles into separate line objects. For example, clicking on the bottom line of the arrow shape selects only the bottom portion of the shape. That's because the shape has six hard angles, which have created six separate lines for this object. Double-clicking on one of the lines will select the entire arrow shape.

---

10. With the line still selected, change the line width back to **2.75**, the line's original width.

If you know the exact value you want to use, you can change the width of a line by entering a specific numeric value in the small box to the left of the slider.

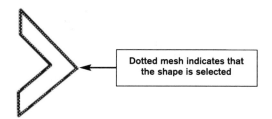

Dotted mesh indicates that
the shape is selected

11. Click away from the line to deselect it. Double-click on any part of the object and the entire shape will become selected. This shortcut is essential when you need to select entire shapes that are composed of multisegmented lines.

12. With the **Properties inspector**, practice changing the style, width, and color of the selected lines. You can choose any setting you like—the point here is to become more comfortable with selecting line styles and changing lines preferences using the Properties inspector.

Now you know how to modify an existing line using the Properties inspector, but what do you do when your object doesn't have a line? You add one using the Ink Bottle tool. You will learn how to do this in the following steps.

13. In the **Toolbar,** click to select the **Ink Bottle** tool. The Ink Bottle lets you add a stroke around a fill object that has no stroke or make changes to the color, width, and texture of existing lines.

With the Ink Bottle tool, you can set the stroke color using the Properties inspector or the Stroke Color options in the Toolbar. Since you have used the Properties inspector quite a bit in this exercise, you will have a chance to use the Toolbar color settings next.

NOTE | Properties Inspector or Toolbar?

In Flash MX 2004, there are often several ways to access and work with the same tools. You may find that using the Properties inspector will streamline your workflow, since it gives you quick access to the attributes of the object or tool selected, all in one panel.

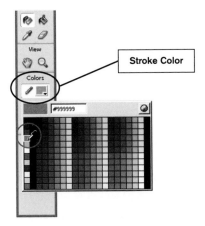

Stroke Color

14. In the **Toolbar,** click the **Stroke Color** icon, and in the **color palette** that pops up, choose a **light gray** color.

15. Using the **Ink Bottle**, click on the outer edge of the snowboard shape. This adds a stroke to the outside of the shape.

NOTE | The Ink Bottle

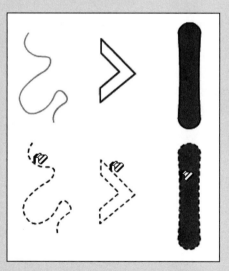

The Ink Bottle serves many purposes. You can add a stroke to an object, as you did in the last step, and you can modify the color, size and style of the stroke for several objects at once by **Shift+clicking** on multiple objects, rather than having to select each object and change its settings individually. This can save you a lot of time when you have several lines to add or modify.

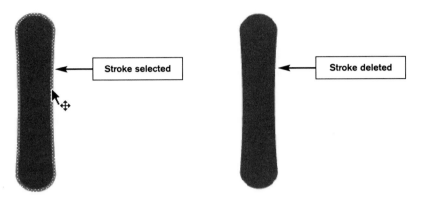

16. Using the **Selection** tool, double-click to select the stroke around the snowboard shape. The dotted mesh will appear, confirming that you have selected the stroke. Press the **Delete** key. This will remove the selected stroke. Now you know how to add strokes to objects and remove them—it's that easy!

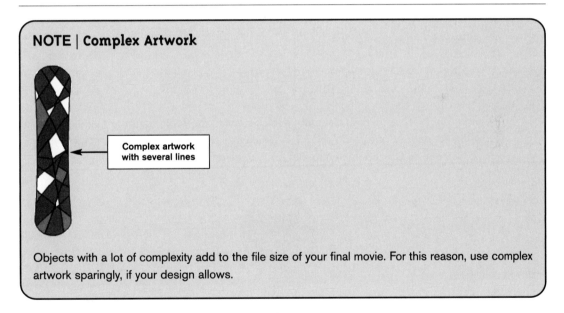

NOTE | Complex Artwork

Complex artwork
with several lines

Objects with a lot of complexity add to the file size of your final movie. For this reason, use complex artwork sparingly, if your design allows.

17. Save and close this file—you won't need it again.

---

3. _____ **Using the Oval and Rectangle Tools**

The **Oval tool** and **Rectangle tool** are ideal for creating geometric shapes such as circles and squares. You can create simple shapes with lines and/or fills that are independent of each other, quickly and effortlessly. In this exercise, you will learn how to use these tools.

1. Open the **shapes.fla** file located inside the **chap_03** folder. This is nothing more than a blank file that has been created for you.

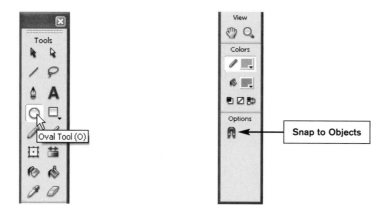

2. In the **Toolbar**, select the **Oval** tool. At the bottom of the **Toolbar**, notice that there is one option for this tool, **Snap to Objects**. This option aligns elements with one another. Single-click the **Snap to Objects** button to turn this feature on.

3. Press and hold down the **Shift** key. On the **Stage**, click and drag the crosshair cursor to the lower-right corner with the **Shift** key held down. As you do this, a large, thick circle will appear next to the crosshair. This indicates that you are drawing a perfect circle. Release the mouse button to draw the circle. Notice that Flash MX 2004 uses the current fill and stroke colors to create the circle.

TIP | Easy Perfect Shapes

When you are using the **Oval** tool or **Rectangle** tool, holding down the **Shift** key while you draw the shapes will force the tool to draw perfect circles or squares.

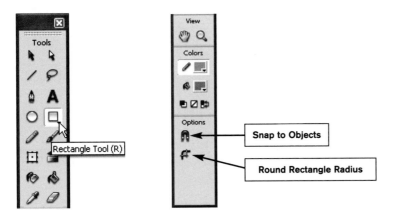

4. Using the same tool, draw an oval. When you use the **Oval** tool without holding down the **Shift** key, Flash MX 2004 doesn't constrain the shape to a perfect circle. Notice that the small circle around the crosshair is smaller and thinner. This indicates that you are drawing an oval, not a perfect circle.

5. In the **Toolbar**, select the **Rectangle** tool. At the bottom of the **Toolbar**, notice that there are two options for this tool: **Snap to Objects** and **Round Rectangle Radius**, which you will learn about in a few steps.

6. Hold down the **Shift** key and click and drag toward the lower-right corner of the **Stage**. As you do this, a rectangle preview will appear. Notice the "perfect shape" indicator. It's the same as the one you saw on the **Oval** tool. In this example, it indicates that you are drawing a perfect square. Release the mouse button to create the shape. Again, Flash MX 2004 uses the selected fill and line colors.

7. At the bottom of the **Toolbar**, click the **Round Rectangle Radius** button. This will open the **Rectangle Settings** dialog box.

8. Enter **25** for the **Corner radius** setting. Click **OK**. This will add rounded corners with a 25-point radius to the next rectangle you draw. You can enter any value between **0** and **999**.

9. Using the **Rectangle** tool, draw another rectangle on the **Stage**. Notice that the corners of the rectangle are rounded now. Nice!

TIP | Round Before You Draw

Creating rounded rectangles does require some forethought since you can't use the **Round Rectangle Radius** option to round the corners of a rectangle you have already drawn. Instead, you can adjust the points as you draw the rectangle. Pressing the up arrow key as you draw will decrease the corner radius points; pressing the down arrow key will increase the corner radius points. This is a very cool little shortcut.

---

10. Save and close this file, you won't be using it any more.

Using the Brush Tool

The **Brush** tool is used to paint shapes. You can create shapes with solid colors, gradients, and even bitmaps as fills. The Brush tool has several painting options that are unique to Flash MX 2004, such as **Paint Fills**, **Paint Selections**, **Paint Behind**, and **Paint Inside**. In this section, you will learn to use the Brush tool to create and modify shapes.

1. Open the **paint.fla** file located inside the **chap_03** folder. Once again, this is just a blank file that has been saved for you.

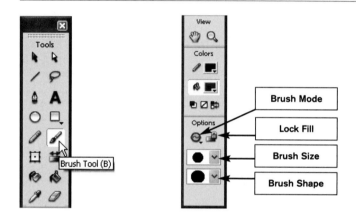

2. In the **Toolbar**, click to select the **Brush** tool. Notice that there are several options for this tool, **Brush Mode**, **Lock Fill**, **Brush Size**, and **Brush Shape**. You will learn about these options as you complete this exercise.

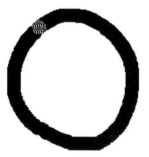

3. On the **Stage**, draw a circle with the **Brush** tool. Notice that it uses the fill color for this shape, rather than the stroke color. The Brush tool creates shapes that are fills and therefore uses the fill color.

4. At the bottom of the **Toolbar,** click on the **Brush Size** pop-up menu. Select the fourth size from the top. This will decrease the size of the next fill that you draw.

5. Draw a smaller circle inside the large one. Notice that the smaller brush size creates a fill shape that is narrower than the first one.

6. At the bottom of the **Toolbar**, click on the **Brush Shape** pop-up menu. Select the fifth shape from the bottom. This will change the shape of the next fill that you draw.

7. Draw another circle on the **Stage**. Notice that it uses the new brush shape to create the circle. You can produce some pretty cool calligraphy effects using these brushes.

TIP | Using Tablets

Flash MX 2004 offers support for most pressure-sensitive graphics tablets. Using a tablet can help you create natural-looking shapes that have a hand-drawn look. As you increase pressure on the tablet, the width of the shape will increase, whereas less pressure will create a thinner shape.

---

8. Experiment with the other brush shapes and sizes so that you are more comfortable with the **Brush** tool. If you have a graphics tablet, try out the pressure sensitivity with the **Brush** tool.

TIP | Adding Lines to Brush Shapes

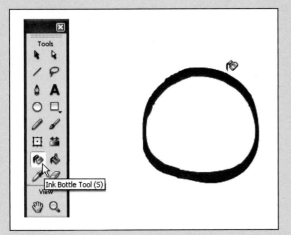

Because the Brush tool creates shapes that are fills, you can use the Ink Bottle to easily add a stroke to the shapes you create with the brush.

9. When you are done experimenting with the **Brush** tool, save and close this file—you won't need it again.

5.————————**Modifying Strokes and Fills**

There are several ways to change the fill of a shape. You can specify the fill color before you create the shape, or you can use the **Paint Bucket** tool to fill uncolored areas of a shape and to change an existing fill color. The Paint Bucket can also be used to modify bitmap and gradient fills. In addition, the Color Mixer panel lets you create solid, gradient, and bitmap fills, which you can apply to the shapes you create. In this exercise, you will learn how to use the Paint Bucket tool and the Fill color palette to modify the fill of a shape.

1. Open the **modifyFills.fla** file located inside the **chap_03** folder. This file contains one layer with a vector graphic of a snowboard.

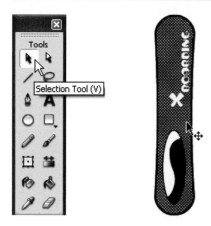

2. Using the **Selection** tool, select the blue background of the snowboard. When a shape is selected, a dotted mesh will appear over it. In this case, it's the background color of the snowboard.

3. Make sure the **Properties inspector** is visible. If it's not, choose **Window > Properties**, or use the shortcut **Ctrl+F3** (Windows) or **Cmd+F3** (Mac) to make it visible.

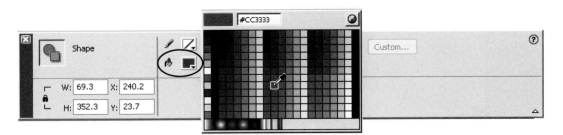

4. In the **Properties inspector**, click on the **Fill Color** box and select a shade of **red** you like from the **Fill color** palette. This changes the background color of the snowboard to red.

Some areas of the snowboard are still blue, like the insides of the letters. You will fix this next.

NOTE | Why Didn't Everything Turn to the Color I Selected?

Flash MX 2004 treats shapes that are one continuous color as one shape. Each time a new color appears, it is a new shape, which means it must be modified individually. In the previous step, the middle parts of the letters were treated as separate shapes because they were surrounded by white. You will learn how to quickly fill these remaining blue shapes with the **Paint Bucket** tool next.

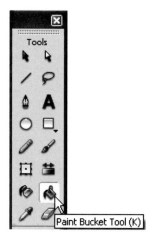

5. In the **Toolbar**, select the **Paint Bucket** tool and click on each of the blue shapes inside the letters to change the color to match the red background color you selected.

*Unlike the Properties inspector method, you do not need to select the artwork before you color it with the Paint Bucket tool. If you are having trouble clicking on the small blue regions inside the type, you may want to use the zoom feature. You can also use the shortcut keys to zoom in and out by pressing **Ctrl+** or **Ctrl−** (Windows) or **Cmd+** or **Cmd−** (Mac).*

*Tip: As a safeguard, you can always press **Ctrl+Z** (Windows) or **Cmd+Z** (Mac) to undo any mistakes you make.*

TIP | Applying Fills

Using the Fill Color box in the Properties inspector and using the Paint Bucket in the Toolbar are two ways to change the solid fill color of an object. Both methods will yield the same results; although using the Properties inspector can help speed up your workflow, since you can change and access many features of the selected object using only one panel. It is important to note that you must have the object selected first if you want to change the fill color using Properties inspector. You can also **Shift+click** to select multiple objects and change them all at once; this is a great way to make several changes quickly.

6. With the **Selection** tool, click the letter **B** on the snowboard. A dotted mesh will appear, indicating the area you have selected.

Rather than fill one letter at a time, you will fill all the letters at once next.

7. Shift+click on each of the remaining letters in the word **BOARDING** so that all the letters are selected at one time. If you make a mistake and want to start over, you can press the **Esc** key (Windows only), which will clear all selections, or click anywhere in a blank area of the **Stage** to deselect everything.

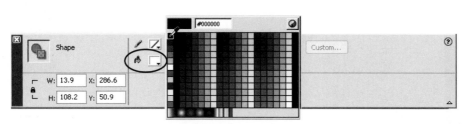

8. In the **Properties inspector**, select a new color for the letters by selecting the **Fill Color** box and choosing a new color from the **Fill color** palette. All the letters will change to the new color you selected! Click on a blank area of the Stage to clearly see the changes.

Up to this point, you have learned how to modify the fills on the snowboard shape. You will modify the strokes on the snowboard shape next.

9. Using the **Selection** tool, double-click the entire stroke of the snowboard to select it.

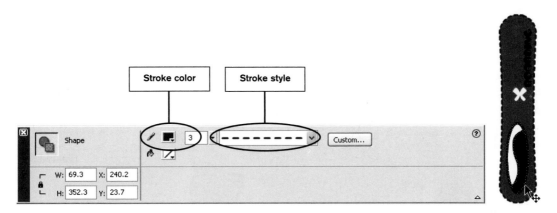

10. Using the **Properties inspector**, select a new **Stroke color** and **Stroke style** for the stroke of the snowboard. Click in a blank area of the **Stage** to deselect your artwork and see your changes clearly.

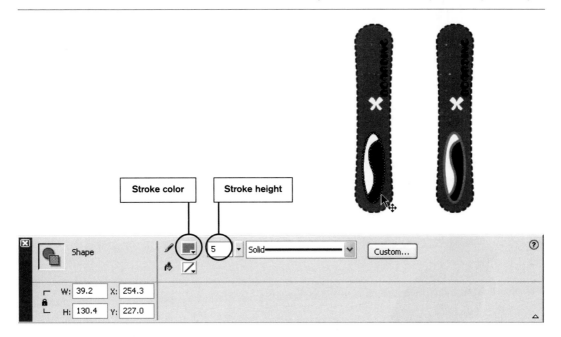

11. Using the **Selection** tool, double-click on the stroke of the yin and yang design on the snowboard to select it. In the **Properties inspector**, select a new **Stroke color** and **Stroke height** for the outline of the design. Deselect your artwork to clearly see your changes. This snowboard has come a long way since you started this exercise!

12. Save and close this file—you won't need it again.

6. ——————Working with Multiple Objects

By now, you should have a pretty good idea of how to draw in Flash MX 2004. This exercise will point out some of the nuances involved in drawing inside of Flash MX 2004 since it behaves differently than most other drawing programs. You will learn how it handles multiple and overlapping objects and how to protect artwork from being unintentionally modified.

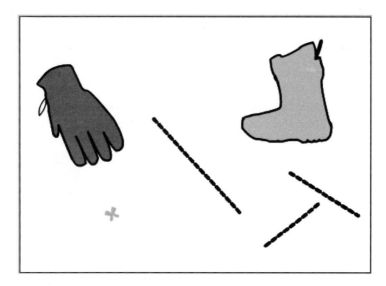

1. Open the **multiple.fla** file located inside the **chap_03** folder. This file contains simple shapes that you will work with to understand the unique behaviors of shapes inside of Flash MX 2004.

2. With the **Selection** tool, move the cursor over the stroke of the glove. Notice that a small, curved line appears at the end of the cursor. This curve indicates that you will select the stroke, rather than the fill, if you click.

3. Double-click to select the entire stroke around the glove. A dotted mesh will appear over the stroke once it has been selected. **Shift+double-click** on the black strap to select that also.

4. Click again on the stroke and drag it to the right. This will pull the stroke off the glove. As mentioned earlier, Flash MX 2004 treats the stroke and fill as separate objects. Because of this, you can easily separate the two.

5. Press **Delete** to permanently remove the stroke from the glove.

6. Move the cursor over the long line between the glove and the boot. The little curve will appear at the bottom of the cursor letting you know that you are about to select a line segment. Click once to select the line.

7. Click again on the line and drag it over the boot.

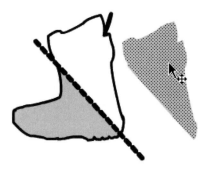

8. Click in the right section of the boot and drag to the right. Notice how the line you dragged on top of the boot has cut the fill into different objects.

Since the fill color of the boot is gray and the line is a different color (black), the line will cut the color into separate sections.

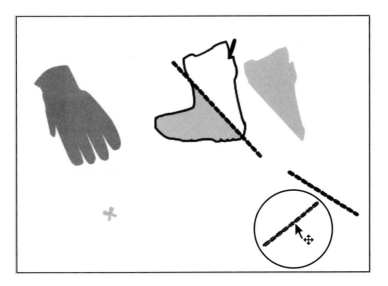

9. Click on one of the lines to the right of the boot to select it.

10. Click and drag that same line over so that it lies across the other line, then click in a blank area of the **Stage** to deselect the line.

11. Click to select the top-right line segment.

12. Click and drag to the right. Notice that the line was split into four segments simply by having two lines intersect. While this might seem counterintuitive, it's a great way to create interesting shapes in Flash MX 2004.

13. Click and drag the small X shape into the wristband of the glove.

14. Click on any blank area of the **Stage** to deselect the X shape.

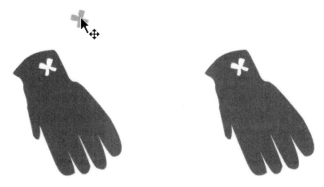

15. Click and drag the small X shape away from the glove. Notice that it has cut an X shape in the fill of the glove. Congratulations, you have just added a logo to the snowboarding glove! This technique is a quick and easy way of creating artwork inside of Flash MX 2004.

NOTE | What Happens if the Shapes are the Same Color?

If the X shape were exactly the same color as the glove, it would not have cut through the glove and made an X shape. Instead, it would have combined with the glove into one shape.

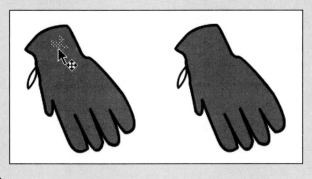

---

16. Save your file, but leave it open for the next exercise.

7.————————**Grouping Objects**

Now that you have a good idea of how the drawing features behave in Flash MX 2004, this exercise will show you how to create shapes that overlap without cutting into or combining with one another. As well, the following steps will show you how to create a **grouped object**.

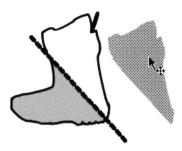

1. Using the **Selection** tool, click to select the top half of the boot you separated.

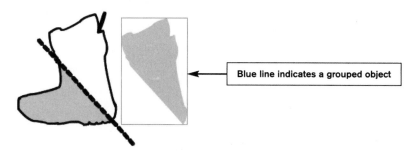

Blue line indicates a grouped object

2. Choose **Modify > Group**. When you do this, a thin blue line appears around the object, indicating that this is a grouped object, which protects it from intersecting with other objects on the Stage. You can also group an object by using the keyboard shortcuts, **Ctrl+G** (Windows) or **Cmd+G** (Mac).

3. Click and drag the gray half of the boot on top of the blue glove.

4. Deselect the gray half of the boot by clicking on any blank area of the **Stage**.

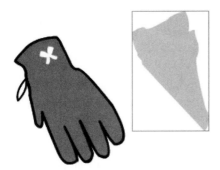

5. Click and drag the gray half of the boot off of the blue glove. Nothing happens. Phew! As you can see, grouping objects, even single objects, is a quick way of protecting them from being affected by or affecting other objects.

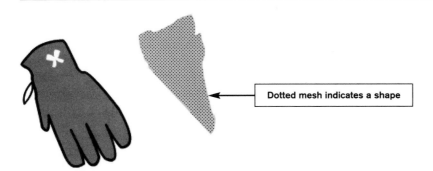

Dotted mesh indicates a shape

6. With the gray half of the boot still selected, choose **Modify > Ungroup**. This will ungroup the selected object. You can tell that this has been done because the thin blue line goes away and the dotted mesh returns, both telltale signs that this is a shape in its most primitive form. You can also use the keyboard shortcut keys to ungroup an object by pressing **Ctrl+Shift+G** (Windows) or **Cmd+Shift+G** (Mac).

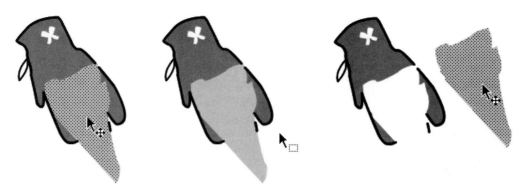

7. Now drag that ungrouped gray shape onto the blue glove, deselect it, and then drag it off again. Yikes! Look ma, no fingers! As you can see, grouping objects can be a quick and easy way to protect them from unwanted editing.

8. Save and close this file—you won't need it again.

What Is the Color Mixer Panel?

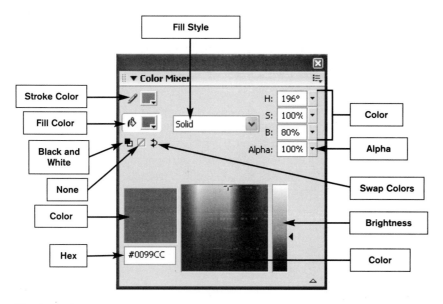

The **Color Mixer** panel gives you precise control over color, all in one panel. To access it choose **Window > Design Panels > Color Mixer**. The following exercise will show you how to use the Color Mixer panel to create gradient fills.

8. —————————**Creating Gradients**

Gradients can help you create lots of cool and interesting effects, such as glows, which you will learn more about in Chapter 5, "*Shape Tweening*." Flash MX 2004 lets you create two types of gradient fills: **linear** and **radial**. In this exercise, you will learn how to use the Color Mixer and Color Swatches panels to create, apply, and change the color of a linear and radial gradient with some shapes in Flash MX 2004.

1. Open the **newGradient.fla** file in the **chap_03** folder. This file contains one layer with two snowboards. You will be applying gradients to both of these shapes in this exercise.

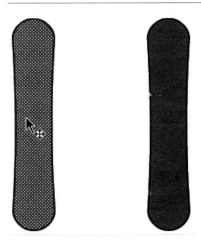

2. Using the **Selection** tool, click the fill in the snowboard on the left to select it.

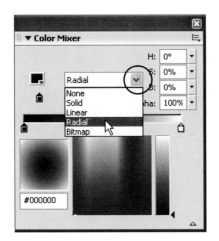 

3. Make sure the **Color Mixer** panel is open; if it is not, choose **Window > Design Panels > Color Mixer** to open it. Click the small down arrow to see the **Fill Style** pop-up menu. This drop-down menu displays the different types of available fills. Choose **Radial**. This fills the selected shape with a radial gradient, using black and white.

Tip: A radial gradient radiates outward from the center.

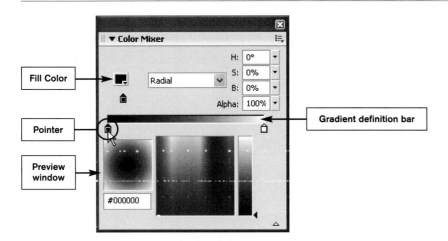

4. Click the **black pointer** in the **Color Mixer** panel. This selects the black color point of the gradient and causes the **Fill Color** box to display the color of the pointer. This box defines the fill color for the selected pointer.

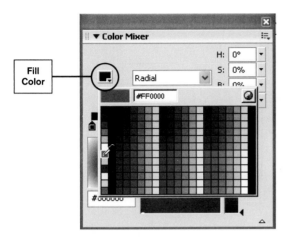

5. Click the **Fill Color** box and select a shade of **red** from the palette. This changes the appearance of the radial gradient to range from red to white instead of ranging from black to white.

You have just created your first custom gradient! Next you will make a linear gradient, in which the colors change horizontally or vertically.

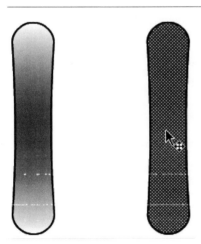

6. Using the **Selection** tool, click the fill in the snowboard on the right side of the **Stage**.

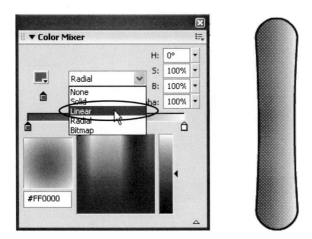

7. In the **Color Mixer** panel, choose **Linear** from the **Fill Style** menu. This creates a linear gradient, using the same color you used for the previous gradient.

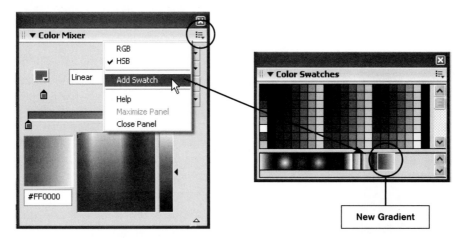

New Gradient

8. Click in the top right corner of the **Color Mixer** panel to reveal the **Color Mixer** pop-up menu, and choose **Add Swatch**. This saves the selected gradient in the **Color Swatches** panel so that you can access it easily. To open the **Color Swatches** panel, choose **Window > Design Panels > Color Swatches**.

9. Save and close this file—you won't need it again.

9. —————————Drawing with the Pen Tool

The **Pen tool** is found in many other vector graphics applications, including Macromedia FreeHand and Adobe Illustrator. If you are familiar with how the tool works in those programs, you'll know how to use it in Flash MX 2004.

If you haven't used the Pen tool before, it can take a little getting used to and will require a good amount of practice before you become really comfortable with it. The Pen tool allows you to precisely draw straight and curved lines to create more complex shapes. Shapes created with the Pen tool consist of paths, anchor points, and tangent handles, which you will learn how to modify with the Subselection tool in the following exercise. In this exercise, you will start by learning how to use the Pen tool to draw a few basic geometric shapes. When you are finished with this exercise, you should be a bit more comfortable working with the Pen tool to create more complex shapes of your own—not only in this program, but in other programs as well.

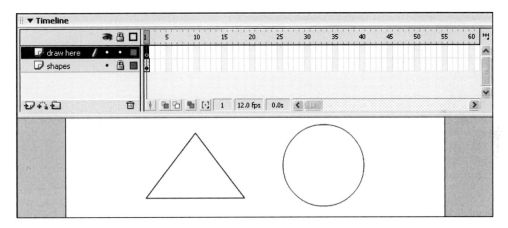

1. Open the **pen.fla** file located inside the **chap_03** folder. This document has two layers: one for the shape outlines, named **shapes**, and another named **draw here**, which is where you will draw these shapes using the **Pen** tool. The **shapes** layer is locked so you can't edit the artwork, but have fun drawing on the **draw here** layer.

*Note: Since you will be using the Pen tool in this exercise, it will be easier to see the results if you use the default settings for this tool. If you just completed the previous exercise, set the stroke settings back to their default values (**black**, **solid**, **1 point**), using the Properties inspector.*

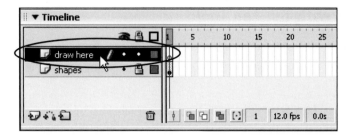

2. Make sure the **draw here** layer is selected in the **Timeline**. If the **shapes** layer is selected, and you try to draw on that layer, you will get an error message asking you to unlock and show that layer. To select the **draw here** layer, click on the layer name. A pencil appears next to the name of the layer, indicating that it is selected.

3. In the **Toolbar**, select the **Pen** tool.

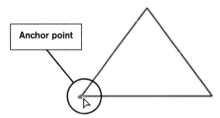

Anchor point

4. Move your mouse to the bottom-left corner of the triangle outline and click. A small circle appears. This is the first **anchor point**, indicating the beginning of your line. Line segments are created between pairs of anchor points to create shapes.

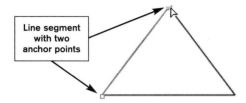

5. Click the top corner of the triangle to add the second anchor point, which creates a line segment that appears only after you click. The line segment will appear as a red line with two square anchor points. The line segment is the color currently set as the stroke color in the **Properties inspector** and in the **Toolbar**.

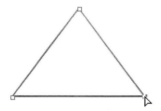

6. Click the lower-right corner of the triangle. This will create a second line segment between the upper- and lower-right anchor points.

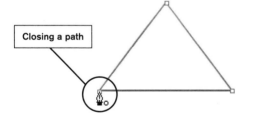

7. Move the cursor to the lower-left corner. A small circle appears at the end of the cursor indicating that the path will be closed if you click. Click to close the path and complete the shape. When you close a path, the shape automatically fills with whatever color you currently have selected for the fill color in the **Properties inspector** or the **Toolbar**.

Next you'll learn to draw a circle with the Pen tool. This can be a bit more complicated than drawing a square and may take some time to master. Don't worry if you have to do this exercise a few times before you get the hang of things.

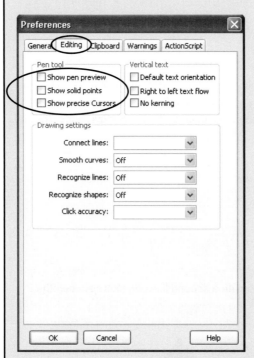

TIP | Pen Preferences

As you learn to work with the Pen tool, there are some preferences to be aware of that might make using the Pen tool a bit easier. Choose **Edit > Preferences** to access the **Preferences** dialog box. Click the **Editing** tab to see the Pen preferences, in the top-left corner. There are three preferences to consider here:

Show pen preview (off by default) lets you preview the line segments as you draw with the Pen tool. A stretchy line will appear as a preview of the line segment you will create when you click.

Show solid points (off by default) displays selected anchor points as solid points and unselected anchor points as hollow points when you use the Subselection tool.

Show precise Cursors (off by default) causes the Pen cursor to appear as a crosshair. This can be helpful for precise drawing and works great with the grid feature.

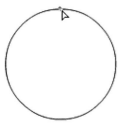

8. Using the **Pen** tool, click at the top center of the circle outline. This will create the first anchor point.

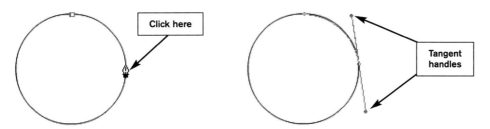

9. Click on the middle right edge of the circle and **drag down** to add another anchor point. As you drag, you will see two **tangent handles** appear. Move the mouse around and watch how the angle of the line changes as you do this. Don't release the mouse button just yet.

10. Drag down toward the bottom right until the line segment seems to match the outline of the circle. Now release the mouse button.

Note: *The circle you draw doesn't have to be perfect here; just try to get yourself comfortable working with the* **Pen** *tool.*

11. Click on the middle bottom edge of the circle to add another anchor point. The line will curve automatically when you add the third anchor point, and this will complete half of the circle shape.

12. Click and drag up on the middle-left edge of the circle to add another anchor point. As you drag, you will see two tangent handles appear. Don't release the mouse just yet.

13. Drag up toward the top left until the line segment seems to match the outline of the circle. Release the mouse button.

14. Move the cursor to the first anchor point you created at the top of the circle. Notice the small circle appearing at the end of the cursor, indicating that the path will be closed if you click. Click to close the path. This will complete the circle and fill it with whatever color you have selected for the fill color.

15. Save the changes you made to this file. After all that hard work, who wants to lose it? Go ahead and leave this file open for the next exercise. Don't worry if it isn't perfect because next you will learn how to modify lines using the shapes you just made.

10. _____Modifying Paths

Now that you know how to create shapes using the Pencil and Pen tools, it's a good time to learn how to reshape them. In this exercise, you'll use the **Subselection** tool to modify paths using their anchor points or tangent handles. The following steps will expose you to using both the Selection tool and the Subselection tool to give you a better understanding of how each of these tools works.

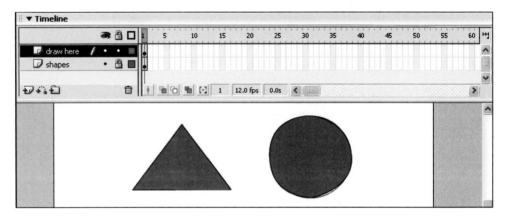

1. The file from the previous exercise should still be open. If it's not, open the **pen.fla** file located inside the **chap_03** folder.

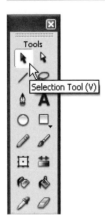

2. In the **Toolbar**, select the **Selection** tool.

3. Move your cursor over the left side of the triangle. Notice that a small curved line appears at the end of the cursor. This line indicates that you are over a line segment.

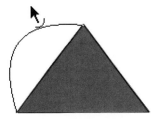

4. Click and drag the mouse to the left. The shape will start to distort and stretch as you continue to drag the mouse. (Hey, remember Silly Putty?) Release the mouse button. Notice that both the line and the fill have changed their shape.

The Selection tool offers a free-form way of transforming shapes, and although it can be fun, it can also lack the precision you sometimes need when creating complex shapes. When you do want pinpoint precision, you can use the Subselection tool, which lets you manipulate the anchor points and tangent handles of paths after you have added them.

TIP | What Do the Icons Associated with the Subselection Tool Mean?

The Subselection tool edits paths and anchor points created with the Pen tool. As you learn to edit paths, anchor points, and tangent handles with the Subselection tool, you will notice a few icons that appear below the Subselection tool as you work with it. This chart outlines the behaviors associated with the Subselection tool.

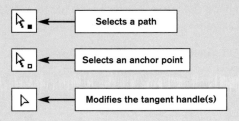

Selects a path

Selects an anchor point

Modifies the tangent handle(s)

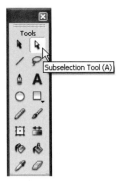

5. In the **Toolbar**, select the **Subselection** tool.

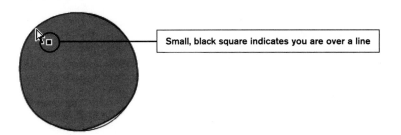

Small, black square indicates you are over a line

6. Move the cursor over the edge of the circle shape. A small black square will appear, indicating that you are over a line.

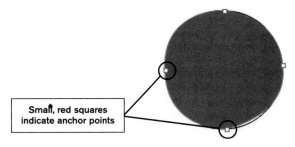

Small, red squares indicate anchor points

7. Click on the edge of the circle to select it. Notice that once the shape is selected, the anchor points become visible. The anchor points are represented by small red squares along the line of the circle.

Note: Flash MX 2004 adds anchor points, if necessary, to create the curve. That is why you might see more than the four anchor points on your artwork.

8. Using the **Subselection** tool, move the cursor over the middle-right anchor point. A small white square will appear next to the cursor when you are over the anchor point.

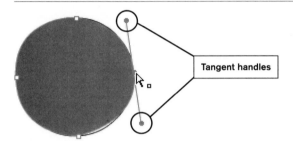

9. Click to select the middle right anchor point. When you do, the tangent handles for that anchor point appear.

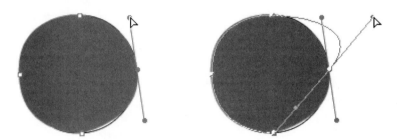

10. Click and drag the top tangent handle of the middle-right anchor point over to the right. Release the mouse button. Notice that the top and bottom portions of the curve change together. This is the normal behavior of tangent handles.

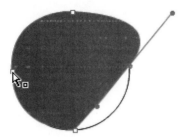

11. Click to select the middle-left anchor point.

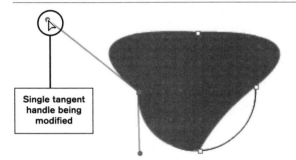

Single tangent handle being modified

12. Press and hold the **Alt** key (Windows) or **Option** key (Mac) as you click and drag the top tangent handle of the middle-left anchor point over to the left. Release the mouse button. Notice that only the top portion changes. This is how you modify one part of a curve without changing the other.

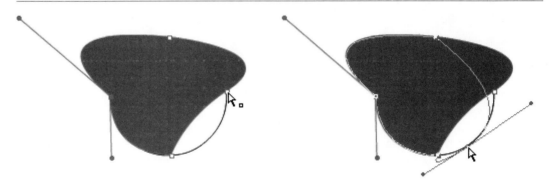

13. Using the **Subselection** tool, click on the anchor point on the middle right of the circle and drag down to try to match the circle image in the background. You can click and drag an anchor point to make the circle more perfect in shape.

Now you know how to use the Selection and Subselection tools to modify the lines you create in Flash MX 2004. With the Selection tool, you can reshape straight or curved lines by dragging the lines themselves. The Subselection tool lets you reshape by clicking on and moving the anchor points and tangent handles. Next you will learn how to add, remove, and convert anchor points. Knowing how to do this will give you more control when you are creating shapes in Flash MX 2004.

TIP | What Do the Icons Associated with the Pen Tool Mean?

As you learn to create paths, anchor points and tangent handles with the Pen tool you will notice varying icons that appear below the Pen tool as you work with it. This chart outlines each of the behaviors associated with the Pen tool.

Draws straight and curved paths to create objects

Adds anchor points to paths

Deletes anchor points from paths

Closes a path

Converts a corner point to a curve point and vice versa

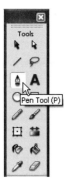

14. In the **Toolbar**, select the **Pen** tool. In addition to drawing shapes, the **Pen** tool lets you add anchor points to a line.

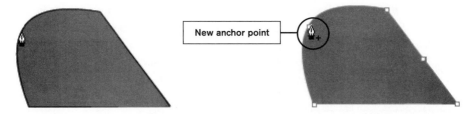

New anchor point

15. Move the **Pen** tool over the rounded side of the triangle shape. Click to select the path. Notice that when you move the **Pen** tool over the path a small **+** symbol appears next to the cursor. This symbol indicates that a new anchor point will be created if you click. Click to add a new anchor point here.

Converting curves to straight lines is a rather simple process and one you should know how to do. That's what you will do in the following steps.

16. With the **Pen** tool still selected, move the cursor over the newly added anchor point and notice that a small caret (**^**) symbol appears. This indicates that you will convert the curve point to a corner point if you click.

17. Click the anchor point. The curve point is converted to a corner point. This transforms the curve into a straight-edged shape, and it will look less like a curve. You will no longer have access to any tangent handles for this anchor point.

Converting a corner point to a curve point is even easier to do—you'll do that next.

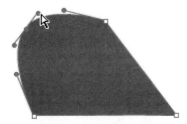

18. From the **Toolbar**, select the **Subselection** tool and click on the anchor point to select it. Now **Alt+click** (Windows) or **Option+click** (Mac) and drag the anchor point you just modified up a bit. When you do this, you will convert that corner point back to an anchor point.

Note: Make sure the anchor point is still selected before you drag it. Selected anchor points are red.

Tip: You can delete anchor points in a number of different ways. One of the easiest ways is to select the anchor point with the **Subselection** tool and press the **Delete** key.

19. With the anchor point still selected, press **Delete**. This removes the anchor point.

---

20. Save and close this file—you won't need it again.

By now, you should feel pretty comfortable working with the drawing and color tools inside Flash MX 2004. If you aren't quite there yet, feel free to take some time to practice and play with the different tools and color settings. You might try drawing some artwork for a project you want to create in Flash MX 2004. Nothing will ever replace good old-fashioned practice!

4.

Animation Basics

Timeline	Projects and Movies	Document Properties
Frame Types	Frame-by-Frame Animation	Frame Rate
Inserting and Deleting Frames	Copying and Reversing Frames
Onion Skinning	Free Transform Tool	Testing Movies

chap_04

Macromedia Flash MX 2004
H•O•T CD-ROM

Flash MX 2004 has a reputation as a powerful and robust animation tool. If you know other animation tools, such as Macromedia Director or Adobe After Effects, you might find yourself looking for similarities. It might surprise you that it's actually easier to learn the animation capabilities of Flash MX 2004 if you don't know other animation programs, because you have no preconceived notions of how you think it might work. If you've never used an animation tool before, you have an advantage over more experienced animators for this reason! This chapter introduces you to the Timeline, which plays a significant role in producing animation. This is the part of the interface where you will work with keyframes, blank keyframes, frame-by-frame animation, and onion skinning. If these are new terms to you, they won't be for long! This chapter also covers setting the frame rate and how the frame rate affects playback speeds. By the end of this chapter, things should really get moving for you, all puns intended!

The Timeline

Understanding and working with the Timeline is essential to creating animation in Flash MX 2004. This illustration identifies the elements of the Timeline you will be working with in this chapter. The following chart gives a detailed description of these features identified.

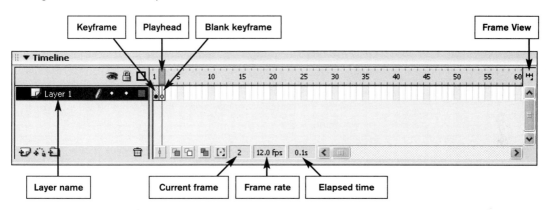

Timeline Features	
Feature	**Description**
Layers	Layers are a way of organizing the elements of your animation from front to back on the Stage, so that one object can move in front of or behind another or can make transitions that are independent of other objects. The Layer controls for your movie appear on the bottom-left side of the Timeline. Each layer has options for hiding or showing the layer, locking it, and displaying its contents as outlines. You will learn more about layers in Chapter 5, "*Shape Tweening.*"
Current frame	Displays the current position of the Playhead and the frame number of the frame that is currently visible.
Frame rate	Displays the number of frames per second (or fps) at which the movie attempts to play on the end user's browser or computer. Double-clicking here is a quick way to access the Document Properties dialog box.

continues on next page

Timeline Features *continued*	
Feature	**Description**
Elapsed time	Displays time elapsed from Frame 1 to the current Playhead location at the currently selected frame rate.
Frame View	This pop-up menu gives you several different options for specifying how the Timeline is displayed. The default view is usually just fine until you start creating a longer animation. At that point, it's great to be able to see more frames as you work. To see more or fewer frames on the Timeline, choose a view from the Frame View drop-down menu.
Blank keyframe	Blank keyframes are empty locations on the Timeline that are ready to have content placed into them. They can also be used to break up or make changes in your animation.
Keyframe	Keyframes define the moment in the Timeline when actions or animation changes occur. Keyframe content remains unchanged until another keyframe or a blank keyframe occurs in the Timeline.
Playhead	The Playhead—a red rectangle with a long, red line—indicates the current frame that you are viewing in the Timeline. You can click and drag (scrub) the Playhead back and forth in the Timeline to quickly preview your animation.

Projects and Movies

In Flash MX 2004, the term "movie" can be used to refer to three separate files—the authoring project file (with the extension .fla), the Flash MX 2004 content file that is published for the Internet (with the extension .swf), and the content published as a stand-alone file (projector). Calling these three different types of files "movies" can become rather confusing when you are learning Flash MX 2004. To help avoid this confusion, the term "project" will be used to identify the FLA file, "movie" to identify the SWF file, and "projector" to identify the projector files. A more comprehensive explanation of these different file types is available in Chapter 1, "*Background Information*." Here's a handy chart that illustrates the differences between these different types of files:

File Types		
Icon File	**Type**	**Description**
 Untitled.fla	**Project**	This file always has an extension of .fla and is the master authoring file used to create Flash MX 2004 content.
 Untitled.swf	**Movie**	This file always has an extension of .swf and is the file you will upload to be viewed on the Internet. It is a compiled version of the project file.
 Untitled.exe	**Windows projector**	Flash MX 2004 can produce stand-alone projector files for the Windows and Macintosh operating systems. Windows projector files have an extension of .exe. Macintosh projector files have the word "Projector" appended to the end of the file name.
 Untitled Projector	**Macintosh projector**	

I. Document Properties

The **Document Properties** are general specifications that affect your entire project. The first thing you should do when you start a new project in Flash MX 2004 is to set these properties, which include the Stage dimensions, background color, and frame rate. This exercise will show you how to set them.

1. Copy the **chap_04** folder, located on the Macromedia Flash MX 2004 **H•O•T CD-ROM**, to your hard drive. You need to have this folder on your hard drive in order to save files inside it.

2. Create a new file and save it as **movie.fla** in the **chap_04** folder.

3. The **Properties inspector** should be visible near the bottom of the document window. If it is not visible, choose **Window > Properties** to open it.

By default, the Stage dimensions will be 550 x 400 pixels, the movie will have a white background, and the frame rate will be 12 frames per second. You'll learn how to change each of these settings in the steps that follow.

4. In the **Properties inspector**, set the **Frame rate** to **24**. This sets the frame rate of your movie to 24 frames per second (fps). In other words, for every 24 frames in your animation, 1 second of time will elapse. You will learn more about frame rates in the next exercise.

5. In the **Properties inspector**, click the **Background** box. This will display the default color palette. Select a **light blue** color. This will change the background color of your movie to light blue.

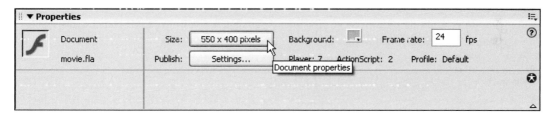

6. With the **Properties inspector** still open, click the **Size** button. This will open the **Document Properties** dialog box, which contains the frame rate preferences, movie dimensions, background color, and rule measurements that you can set for your entire movie.

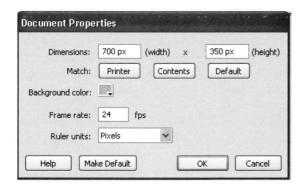

7. For the **Dimensions** settings, enter a width of **700** and a height of **350**. These options control the absolute pixel dimensions of your **Stage**. You will learn other ways to control the size of your movie when you get to Chapter 16, "*Publishing and Exporting*."

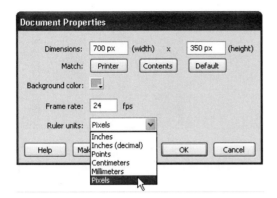

8. Click the **Ruler units** drop-down menu. This menu contains several ways to display the ruler units on your **Stage**. Make sure you leave this option set to the default of **Pixels**.

9. Click **OK**. Notice that the values in the **Properties inspector** (the dimensions, background color, and frame rate) are changed to your new specifications.

You can quickly use the Properties inspector at any point to change the movie's background color or frame rate. In addition, you can use the Size button to access the Document Properties dialog box, where you can change the dimensions and ruler units. However, you should avoid changing the dimensions of your movie once you have added content to your Stage. Changing the dimensions of your stage once you've started creating artwork and animation causes the position of all your art work to be offset, which can be difficult to fix.

10. When you are finished, save the changes you made to this file and keep it open for the next exercise.

TIP | Saving New Default Settings

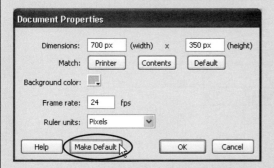

When you create a new movie, by default you will get a Stage that is 550 × 400 pixels with a white background and a frame rate of 12 fps. These settings may not be convenient when you are working on projects that require different property settings. But there's good news—you can redefine the default settings so they better fit your needs. Simply change the **Document Properties** to match the settings you need and click the **Make Default** button. Next time you create a new movie, it will already have all the properties you want. Pretty cool!

What Is a Keyframe?

The term **keyframe** has been used in animation since the early 1900s. It signifies a change in motion. In Flash MX 2004, keyframes are displayed on the Timeline. The Timeline represents the passing of time, with each slot representing an individual frame. If you have artwork in Frame 1, and you don't change it until Frame 20, the image in Frame 1 will persist until Frame 20. You would need to add a new keyframe in Frame 20 in order to make a change to the animation. If you have artwork in Frame 1 and you want to change it in Frame 2, you would need to add a new keyframe in Frame 2; therefore, you would end up with two keyframes, one in Frame 1 and the other in Frame 2.

This concept might seem abstract to you if you've never worked with keyframes before, but you will have lots of opportunities to work with keyframes in this chapter, so they won't be alien to you for long.

Keyframes in Flash MX 2004

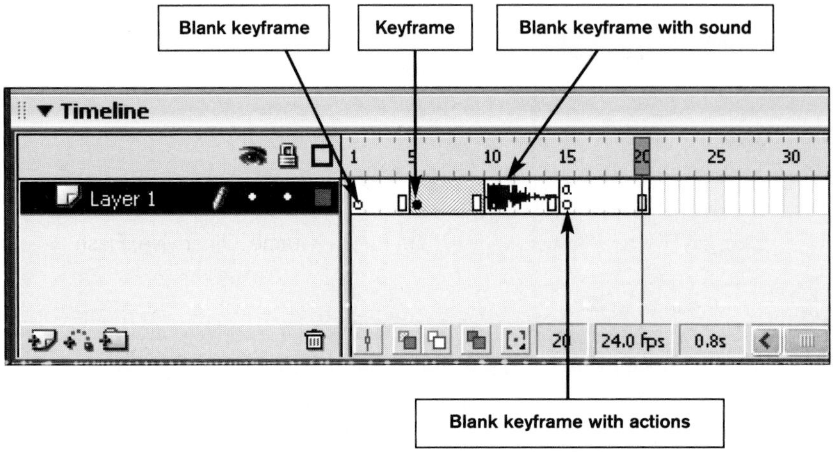

Keyframes are located in the Timeline. A keyframe that contains content displays a solid circle in the Timeline, and a blank keyframe that contains no content on the Stage is represented by a hollow circle in the Timeline. Subsequent frames that you add to the same layer will have the same content as the keyframe.

Flash MX 2004 also has different kinds of frames and keyframes. The following chart describes the different types and gives the keyboard shortcut for each in parentheses.

Frame Types	
Term	**Definition**
Blank keyframe (F7)	A blank or empty keyframe is represented by a hollow circle, which means that there is no artwork on the Stage on that frame. The Timeline, by default, opens with a blank keyframe. As soon as you put content on the Stage, the blank keyframe changes to a keyframe. From that point on, this artwork will be copied to all frames until you define another keyframe or blank keyframe and change the content on the Stage at that frame. Although a blank keyframe contains no artwork, it can contain sound and actions. To insert a blank keyframe, select a frame and press **F7** or choose **Insert > Timeline > Blank Keyframe.** You will learn more about sound in Chapter 13, "*Sound*," and more about actions in Chapter 11, "*ActionScript Basics and Behaviors*."
	continues on next page

Frame Types *continued*	
Term	**Definition**
Keyframe (F6)	A keyframe that contains content (meaning that artwork is on the Stage at that frame in the Timeline) is represented by a solid circle. By default, when you add a keyframe in Flash MX 2004, the content (except for actions and sounds) is copied from the previous keyframe. To make a change, you must alter the artwork on the Stage at the point on the Timeline where you have defined the new keyframe. Otherwise, Flash MX 2004 will simply copy the content from the previous change. In other words, simply adding a keyframe will not cause the artwork to change. To insert a keyframe, select a frame and press **F6** or choose **Insert > Timeline > Keyframe**
Frame (F5)	The Timeline in Flash MX 2004 looks as though it has lots of frames in each layer, which can be a bit deceiving! Although it has slots for frames, you have to specifically define them as frames (or keyframes, and so on). You can do this by clicking in any of the slots and pressing **F5** or by choosing **Insert > Timeline > Frame**. It's possible to have a different number of frames on different layers. For example, Layer 1 could have 10 frames while Layer 2 has one frame. It is up to you to set the frames for each layer.
Clear keyframe (Shift+F6)	To clear the content from a keyframe, you can use the clear keyframe keyboard shortcut **Shift+F6** or choose **Modify > Timeline > Clear Keyframe**. You do this when you want to erase the keyframe from the Timeline. Clearing a keyframe removes the content from the keyframe but leaves the frame. This will not reduce the number of frames on a layer but will simply remove the keyframe and change it to a regular frame. This command is usually used to fix (or clear) a mistake.
Remove frames (Shift+F5)	If you need to delete frames that you have set, select those frames and press **Shift+F5**, or **right-click** (Windows) or **Ctrl+click** (Mac) and choose **Remove Frames** from the context menu.

2. —————————Frame-by-Frame Animation with Keyframes

This exercise will teach you how to work with keyframes. A common animation technique is to make a word appear as though it is being written before your eyes. This is very simple to do using keyframes, because when you insert a keyframe, the program copies the content of the previous keyframe to the newly inserted keyframe. You will learn how to make the word "xboard!" animate on the stage using frame-by-frame animation in the following steps.

1. Open the **movieFinal.fla** file from the **chap_04** folder. This file has been created for you so that you can see the finished version of the exercise.

WARNING | Windows Users

If you don't see a file named **movieFinal.fla**, but you do see a file named **movieFinal**, your file extension display may be turned off on your computer. To learn how to make the file extension visible, see the "*Introduction*."

2. Press **Enter/Return** (Windows/Mac) on the keyboard to preview the animation on the **Stage**. You will notice the word "xboard!" being written right on the screen as it animates. You will be creating this same frame-by-frame animation with keyframes next.

---

3. Close the **movieFinal.fla** file.

4. You should still have the **movie.fla** file open from the last exercise, but in case you accidentally closed it, go ahead and open the **movie.fla** file you saved inside the **chap_04** folder in the last exercise.

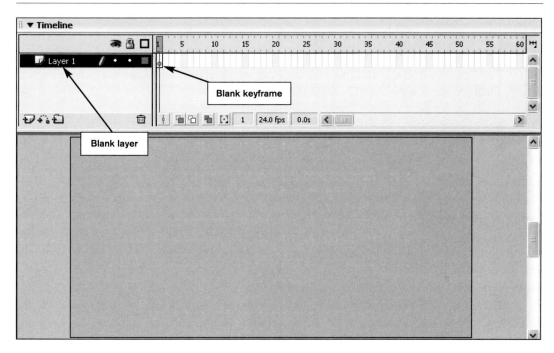

Notice that this document has a single layer containing a single blank keyframe. This is the minimum you need to start drawing, and this is the way all new documents appear by default.

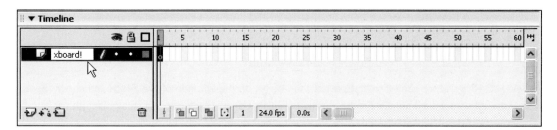

5. In the **Timeline**, double-click **Layer 1** to rename it as **xboard!**. Naming your layers is a good habit to practice and is especially helpful when your movie contains several layers.

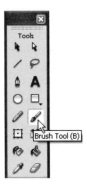

6. Select the **Brush** tool from the **Toolbar**. You can use any size, shape, and color (other than **white—** you will see why in Step 12) you want. You are going to write the word "xboard!" one letter at a time, in a series of keyframes.

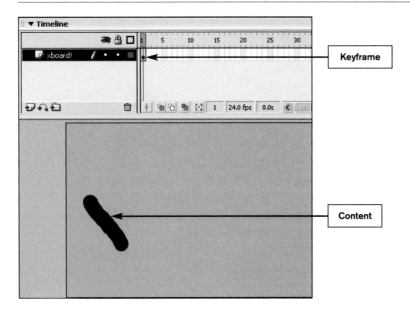

7. Using the **Brush** tool, draw the first part of the letter **x** on the left side of the **Stage**, as shown here. Notice that the blank keyframe in **Frame 1** now contains a small black dot, which signifies that it contains content. **Frame 1** is now referred to as a keyframe because it is no longer empty.

To make a change on the Timeline, you must have a keyframe where you want the change to occur. Now that you have filled in the first keyframe of Layer 1, you are going to add another keyframe after it so you can draw the second frame of your animation. Adding a new keyframe after the last one will copy all the content from the previous keyframe to this new keyframe. You will draw another stroke in this new keyframe in order to create a change in your animation.

8. Select **Frame 2** and choose **Insert > Timeline > Keyframe** or press **F6** (the shortcut key). This adds a new keyframe to the **Timeline** in **Frame 2**, copying all the artwork in **Frame 1** and allowing you to continue drawing.

Tip: F6 is a keyboard shortcut you should learn right away, because you will be using it often to insert keyframes.

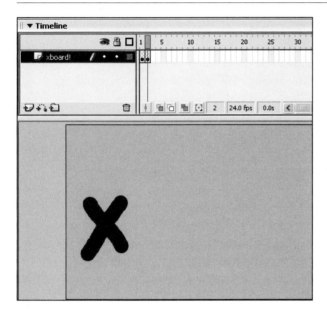

9. Using the **Brush** tool again, draw the second part of the **x** in the new keyframe, just like in the picture here.

10. Press **F6**.This adds a new keyframe to the **Timeline** in **Frame 3**, copying all the artwork from the previous keyframe, **Frame 2**.

11. Now draw a **b**, as shown here. Believe it or not, you have already created the beginning of your animation! You can click and drag (scrub) the **Playhead** back and forth in the **Timeline** to quickly preview the animation. You will see the **x** and the **b** being drawn directly on the **Stage**.

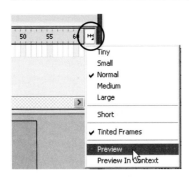

Looking at a Timeline with a bunch of black dots might seem somewhat abstract to you. The Frame View menu has several options that allow you to display the contents of your individual frames right in the Timeline.

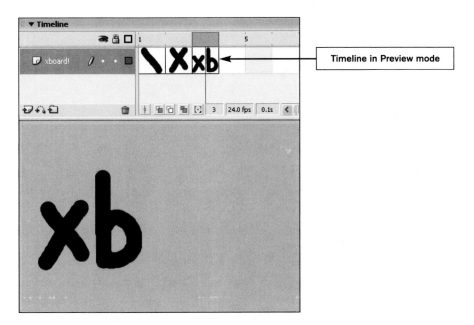

Timeline in Preview mode

12. From the **Frame View** drop-down menu, select **Preview**. This will change your **Timeline** so that you see a preview of what is on each frame instead of a bunch of black dots.

This view of the Timeline is very helpful when creating frame-by-frame animations.

Note: *If you had chosen white for the Brush color, you would not see the artwork in Preview mode since the Timeline frames are white also.*

---

13. Make sure the **Playhead** is on **Frame 3**. Press **F6** to insert another keyframe into **Frame 4** so you can continue to draw the pieces to spell out the word "xboard!."

---

14. Using the **Brush** tool, draw an **o** on the **Stage**. You should be able to see the contents of your fourth frame appear in the **Timeline** preview.

*As you continue to spell out the word "xboard!," you don't have to draw the whole letter in each keyframe. Instead, you can draw a part of the letter (just as you did with the "x") in one keyframe, press **F6** to insert the next keyframe, and draw the remaining parts of the letter in that keyframe for a more realistic drawing animation.*

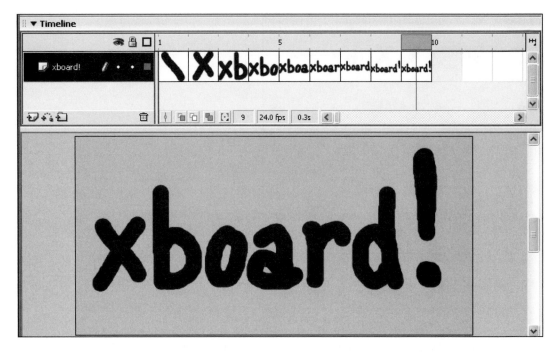

15. Go ahead and continue to spell out the word "xboard!" by pressing **F6** to add a new keyframe after the previous one and then adding more letters or parts of the letters in each one, using the **Brush** tool. When you are done, your **Timeline** should look like the one shown here.

You can get a quick preview of your animation right away using one of two methods. You can scrub the Playhead across the Timeline as mentioned in Step 11, or you can press Enter/Return and watch the animation play directly on the Stage. So get out the popcorn and watch your first animation!

---

16. Press **Enter/Return**. Your animation will play once on the **Stage** and stop at the last keyframe. Unlike scrubbing the **Playhead**, this time you are seeing an accurate preview of the frame rate for this movie, which you set in the previous exercise: 24 fps.

---

17. To see the animation repeat over and over, choose **Control > Loop Playback** and press **Enter/Return**. Notice how the animation plays fast? You will learn how to slow down the animation by adjusting the frame rate of the movie in the next exercise.

---

18. To stop the animation from playing and looping, press **Enter/Return** again.

---

19. Save this file and keep it open for the next exercise.

3. —————————Understanding Frame Rate

The frame rate defines how many frames your animation will try to play in one second. Due to the varying processor speeds of the computers that your end users might use, there is no guarantee that your movie will play back at the specified frame rate. In the following steps, you will test the animation to preview the current frame rate and then lower the frame rate to see the impact it has on playback speed.

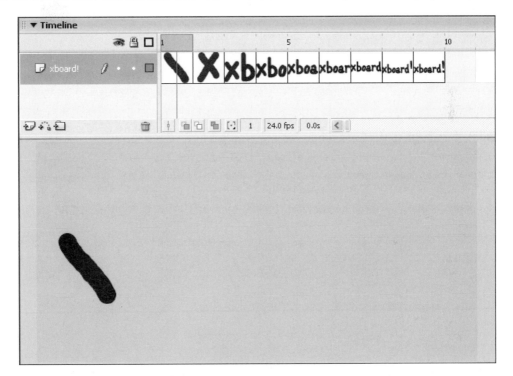

1. You should still have the **movie.fla** file open from the previous exercise. If not, go ahead and open the **movie.fla** file you saved inside the **chap_04** folder in the previous exercise.

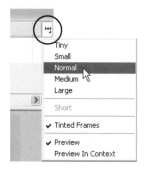
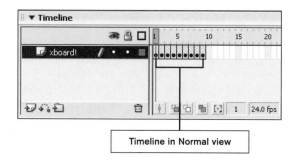

Timeline in Normal view

2. From the **Frame View** drop-down menu, select **Normal**. This will change your **Timeline** back to **Normal** view so that you see keyframes in the **Timeline** instead of a preview of the content on the stage.

3. Press **Enter/Return** to watch the "xboard!" animation play on the **Stage**. The animation plays at the frame rate of 24 fps, which you set in the **Properties inspector** of Exercise 1. Notice that the animation plays a bit fast. You are going to slow down the animation by changing the frame rate for the movie next.

4. Make sure the **Properties inspector** is open. If it is not, choose **Window > Properties** or press **Ctrl+F3** (Windows) or **Cmd+F3** (Mac) to open it.

5. In the **Frame rate** field, enter **12**. This will lower the frame rate to 12 frames per second, reducing the speed of the animation by half. A frame rate of 12 fps is also the default value when you create a new movie.

6. Press **Enter/Return**. Notice that the animation plays slower. The movie is taking twice the time to play the same number of frames. The lower the frame rate, the slower the animation will play and vice versa. Go ahead and experiment with other frame rates.

7. Save and close this file when you are done experimenting with different frame rates, you won't need it for the next exercise.

What Is the Frame Rate?

The frame rate determines the number of frames your movie plays per second. This rate corresponds directly to the length of time your animation takes to play.

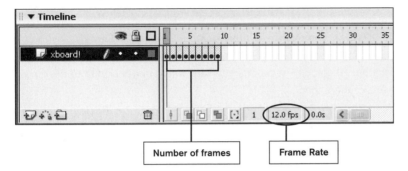

Number of frames   **Frame Rate**

Here's how to use the frame rate to calculate the playback time of your animation. Take the total number of frames in your Timeline and divide that by the frame rate; the result is the number of seconds it will take to view your movie.

For example, if your Timeline has 10 frames, and your frame rate is set to 6 fps (frames per second), your animation will display in 1.67 seconds. The following chart gives examples of how the frame rate affects the length of time an animation takes to play.

Number of Frames	÷	Frame Rate	=	Time
24 frames	÷	12 fps	=	2 seconds
36 frames	÷	12 fps	=	3 seconds
48 frames	÷	24 fps	=	2 seconds
72 frames	÷	24 fps	=	3 seconds

It is important to note that the frame rate affects all of the animations in your movie. In the next exercise, you will learn how to make animations play at different speeds in the same Timeline.

Recommended Frame Rates

When you set a frame rate in Flash MX 2004, you've set the maximum frame rate for your movie, or how quickly the movie "tries" to play. The actual playback frame rate depends upon several factors, including download speed and the processor speed of the computer viewing the movie. If the frame rate is set higher than the computer can display, the movie will play as fast as its processor will allow. So if you set your frame rate to 200 (which is really high), the average computer will not display the movie at that rate. Also, frames that have more objects, colors, or transparency than others take more time for the computer to render. Thus, the actual frame rate can vary during playback due to the rendering requirements from one frame to another.

Based on all this information, it is recommended that you use a frame rate of at least 12 fps and not more than 25 fps, so that the average computer can display your movie as you intended. A frame rate of 20 to 22 fps seems to work well most of the time. This rate is very similar to that used in motion pictures, which typically play at a frame rate of 24 frames per second.

4. —————————Inserting and Deleting Frames

As you learn to create frame-by-frame animation and other types of animation, at some point you will want to adjust the speed of your animations. In the previous exercise, you learned that adjusting the frame rate will do just that, but it affects the entire movie. What do you do if you want certain points in your movie to play faster or slower than other parts? That's just what you'll do in this exercise. You will learn how adding and removing frames in your Timeline can help control the timing of your animation. This means that you can have multiple animations playing at different tempos, even though they all share the same frame rate.

1. Open the **frames.fla** file from the **chap_04** folder. This file contains one layer with a simple frame-by-frame animation using text. You'll get a chance to work with text in Chapter 12, "*Working with Text.*"

2. Press **Enter/Return** to preview the animation on the **Stage**. The animation will play pretty quickly, so fast that you almost lose the effect of the text appearing one letter at a time.

If you adjust the frame rate to slow down this animation, it will also affect every other animation in this project. This could cause problems if you wanted other sections of your movie to play at a different speed. One way to remedy this is by inserting frames at strategic points to lengthen parts of the animation. That's exactly what the following steps will show you how to do.

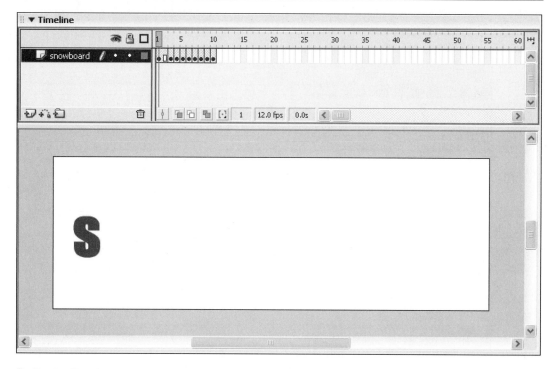

3. On the **Timeline**, click **Frame 1** of the layer named **snowboard**, and choose **Insert** > **Timeline** > **Frame** or use the shortcut key **F5**. This will insert an additional frame after **Frame 1**, extending the **Timeline** by one frame.

4. Press **F5** to insert another frame. Each time you choose **Insert** > **Timeline** > **Frame** or press **F5**, you will insert one frame and extend the **Timeline**.

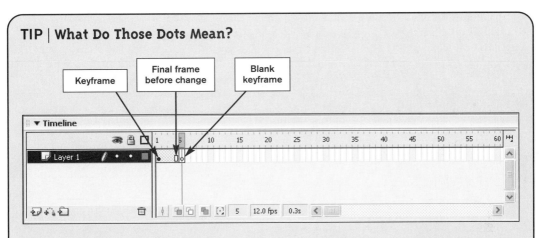

TIP | What Do Those Dots Mean?

As you start adding content to your Timeline, you will notice different icons appearing in your Timeline. The black dots indicate keyframes. The light gray frames after the keyframe indicate no change in content. The small white square inside a light gray frame indicates the ending point of a frame range, which also means that the next frame will be a blank keyframe or a keyframe. The white frame with a hollow circle, directly after the frame with a hollow square, is a blank keyframe.

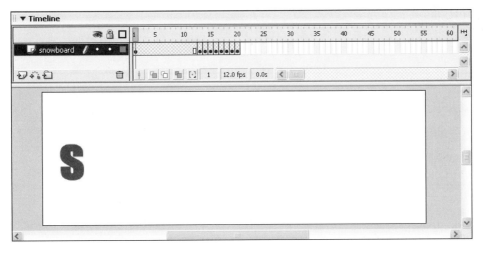

5. Press **F5** eight more times so that you have a total of 11 additional frames between your first two keyframes. By extending the space between the first two keyframes in the Timeline, you are able to control the timing of the animation, as your image will display for a longer period of time.

6. Press **Enter/Return** to preview the animation on the **Stage**. Now there is a noticeable delay between the letters **s** and **n**—about one second because 12 frames ÷ 12 fps = 1 second.

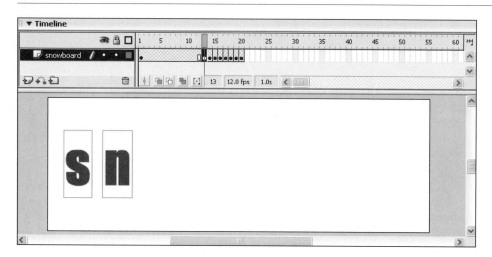

7. Click in **Frame 13** of the **Timeline**. This is where the second keyframe should be located.

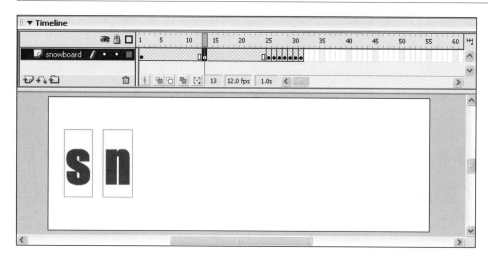

8. Press **F5** 11 times to insert 11 frames in the **Timeline**. This will create another pause between the letters **n** and **o**.

9. Repeat this process for the letters **o** and **w** in the word **snow**. When you are finished, your **Timeline** should look like the one shown here.

---

10. Press **Enter/Return** to preview your animation on the **Stage**. Notice how much slower the word **snow** animates on stage compared to **board**, which plays much faster.

You now know that you can control the timing of an animation without having to adjust the frame rate of your entire movie. You did that by inserting frames to slow down a specific point in the animation, so it should be no surprise that you can increase the timing of the animation by deleting frames. You will learn how to do this next.

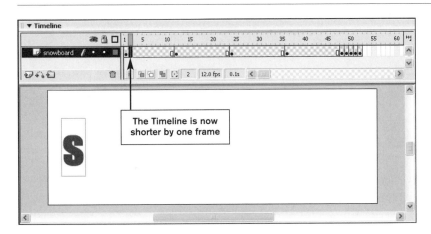

The Timeline is now shorter by one frame

11. Click **Frame 2** of the **Timeline** and **right-click** (Windows) or **Ctrl+click** (Mac) and choose **Remove Frames** from the context menu, or use the shortcut key **Shift+F5**. This will remove the selected frame, shortening your **Timeline** by one frame and decreasing the amount of time between the **s** and **n** letters in your animation.

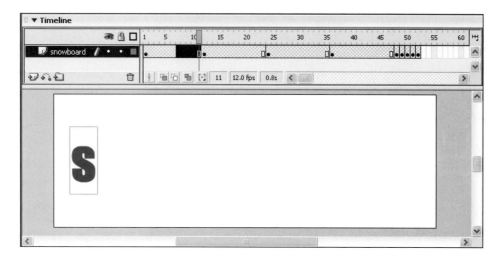

12. Click and drag **Frames 7** through **11** to select that range of frames.

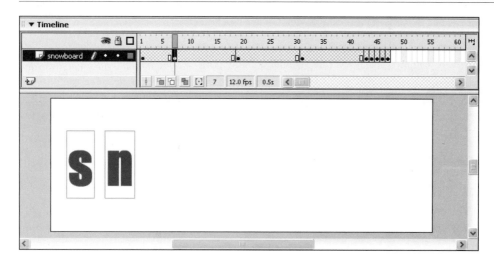

13. With **Frames 7** through **11** still selected, **right-click** (Windows) or **Ctrl+click** (Mac) and choose **Remove Frames** from the context menu, or use the shortcut key **Shift+F5**. This will remove the selected frames and shorten your **Timeline** by five frames.

14. Press **Shift+F5** to remove the frames between each of the keyframes in the **Timeline** so that there are only **five** frames between the **s**, **n**, **o**, and **w** keyframes. When you're finished, your **Timeline** should look like the one shown above.

15. Press **Enter/Return** to preview your animation on the **Stage**. The word **snow** will play faster than it did before, because there are fewer frames between the keyframes. Now you know how to speed up or slow down the timing of your animation without changing the frame rate of the entire movie.

16. Save and close this file.

5. —————————**Copying and Reversing Frames**

Creating a looping animation (one that repeats indefinitely) can be a lot of work if you have to draw all the frames over and over. In Flash MX 2004, you can quickly and easily copy, paste, and reverse a sequence of frames to create a looping animation. You will learn to do this in the steps that follow.

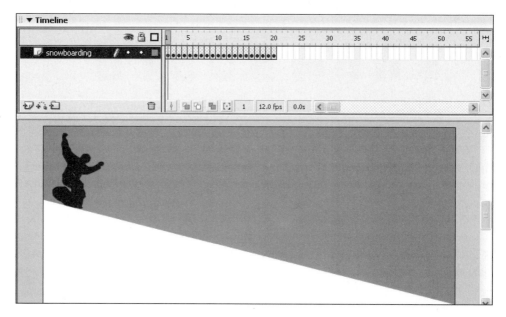

1. Open **loopingFinal.fla** from the **chap_04** folder. This is the completed version of the animation you are going to create.

2. Before you preview the animation, choose **Control > Loop Playback**. This will allow you to see the animation repeat over and over when you preview it.

3. Press **Enter/Return** on the keyboard to preview the animation on the **Stage**. You will see the snowboarder cruise down and up the mountain slope over and over. You will create this same animation technique without having to draw all the frames over again. To stop the looping, choose **Control > Loop Playback** again.

4. Close the **loopingFinal.fla** file

5. Open the **looping.fla** file from the **chap_04** folder. This file contains a single layer named **snowboarding** with a frame-by-frame animation of a snowboarder cruising down a mountain.

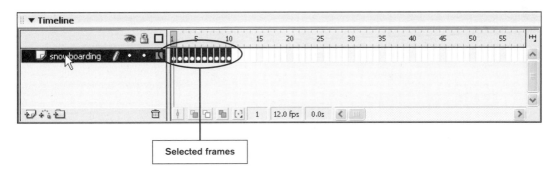

Selected frames

6. Click the layer name **snowboarding**. This is an easy way to select all of the frames on a layer. Before you can copy a range of frames, you need to select them first.

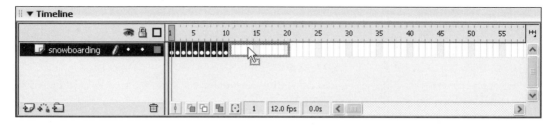

7. Move your cursor over the selected frames. Click and drag to the right. But don't release the mouse button just yet! **Note:** The light gray outline surrounding the frames indicates where they'll be moved when you release the mouse button.

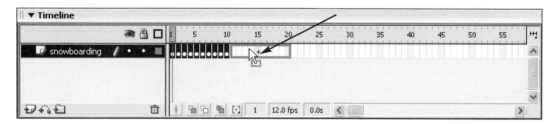

8. While still holding down the mouse button, press and hold down the **Alt** (Windows) or **Option** (Mac) key. Notice that a small plus sign appears to the right of the cursor. This indicates that you will duplicate, not move, the frames when you release the mouse button.

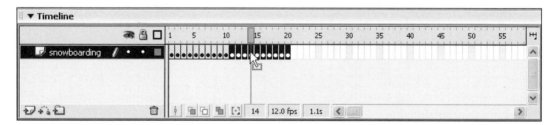

9. Release the mouse button. This will place a copy of the selected frames in **Frames 11** through **20**.

10. With **Frames 11** through **20** still selected, choose **Modify > Timeline > Reverse Frames**. You won't see a change in the **Timeline**, but you will notice the change on the **Stage** when you test the movie.

11. Press **Enter/Return** to preview your animation on the **Stage**. The snowboarder will race down the hill and then go backward up the hill, as if you were rewinding the film to view an instant replay! Neat! If you choose **Control > Loop Playback**, you can watch the animation preview loop endlessly.

12. Save and close this file.

6. ——————————Onion Skinning

Now that you have created a couple of frame-by-frame animations, it's a good time to add a few new tricks to your bag. First, you'll learn to use the **Onion Skinning** feature. This feature allows you to see a ghost image of the previous frame so you can see where you want to place the artwork on each frame in relation to the frames before it. You will also learn to use the **Free Transform** tool, which allows you to scale, rotate, skew, and distort your artwork.

1. Open **onionFinal.fla** file from the **chap_04** folder. This file has been created for you so that you can see the finished version of the exercise.

2. Before you preview the animation, choose **Control > Loop Playback**. This will allow you to see the animation repeat over and over when you preview it.

3. Press **Enter/Return** on the keyboard to preview the animation on the **Stage**. You will see the snowboarder catching some air! In the following steps, you will be creating this same animation technique. To stop the looping, choose **Control > Loop Playback** again.

4. Close the **onionFinal.fla** file.

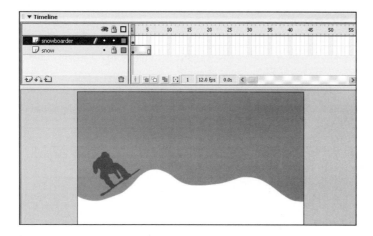

5. Open the **onion.fla** file from the **chap_04** folder. This file contains one keyframe with the snowboarder beginning his jump on the top layer and one keyframe with the snow on the bottom layer. The layer named snow has been locked so that you don't accidentally edit that layer. You will be modifying the artwork and creating the frame-by-frame animation on the snowboarder layer in the next few steps.

6. Select **Frame 2** and press **F6** to add a keyframe to the frame. Notice that **Frame 2** is now a keyframe because it contains a small black dot, which signifies that it contains content.

If you press F6 without first selecting the frame where you want to add a keyframe, nothing happens. Why? When you have more than one layer in your document, you have to select the frame first in order for Flash MX 2004 to know where you want to place the keyframe.

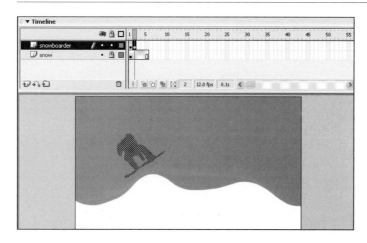

7. With the Playhead on **Frame 2**, click the snowboarder artwork on Stage to select it, and move it up and to the right, as though he is advancing in his jump.

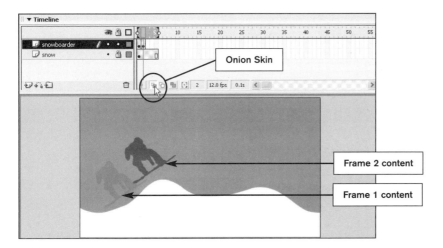

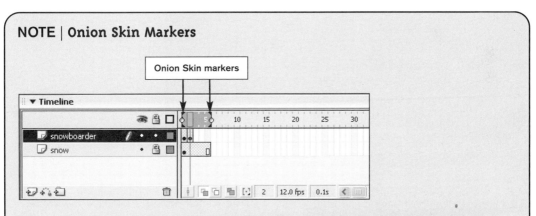

8. At the bottom of the Timeline is a row of five buttons. Click the second button from the left. This is the **Onion Skin** button. You will be able to see a faint ghost image of the content in **Frame 1** on the **Stage**. This convenient feature allows you to see the artwork in the previous keyframes and change the artwork relative to the ghost images.

NOTE | Onion Skin Markers

After you click the Onion Skin button, a gray bar with a draggable bracket on each end appears at the top of the Timeline. These are called **Onion Skin markers**. The **Start Onion Skin** marker (the one on the left) is on Frame 1 (the first frame of your animation), and the **End Onion Skin** marker (the one on the right) is on Frame 5 (the last frame of your animation). If you click and drag your Playhead to the right or left and let go, the Start Onion Skin marker will move along with it. You can always drag one of the Onion Skin markers to include more frames if it is spanning fewer keyframes than you have in the Timeline.

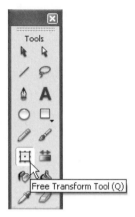

9. With onion skinning turned on, select the **Free Transform** tool in the **Toolbar**. This tool allows you to modify your artwork by changing the size, rotation, skew, and distortion of the selected artwork. The chart at the end of this exercise illustrates the functions of the **Free Transform** tool.

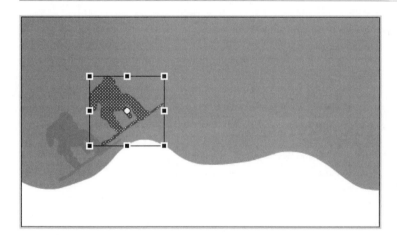

10. Make sure the **Playhead** is on **Frame 2**. With the **Free Transform** tool, click the snowboarder on the **Stage** to select the shape, if it is not already selected. Notice the bounding box that appears around the artwork. This box indicates that you can transform the artwork.

If you move the cursor over different parts of the selected artwork, the cursor will change to indicate what transformation function is available.

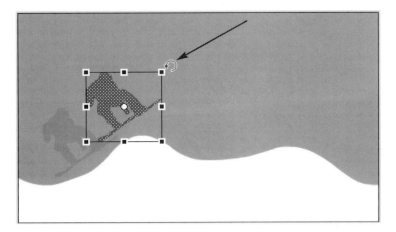

11. Move your cursor just outside the upper-right corner of the bounding box until it changes to a round arrow, as shown in this picture. This icon indicates that you can rotate the artwork. Click and drag to the right to rotate the snowboarder a bit and make the jump look more realistic.

12. Select **Frame 3** and press **F6** to insert another keyframe. You will modify the keyframe in Frame 3 next.

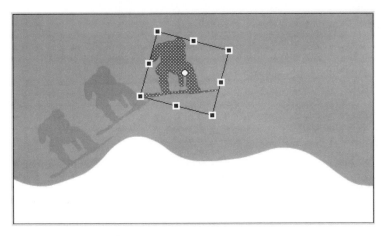

13. With onion skinning still turned on, select the snowboarder artwork in **Frame 3** and move it to the right. Select the **Free Transform** tool and rotate the snowboarder again, just as you did in Step 11.

14. Finish off the snowboarder jump by repeating Steps 12 and 13 twice more, adding two more keyframes to **Frames 4** and **5** and modifying the artwork in each keyframe.

15. Choose **Control > Loop Playback** so that you can see the animation repeat over and over.

16. Press **Enter/Return** to test the movie. You will see the snowboarder catching some air!

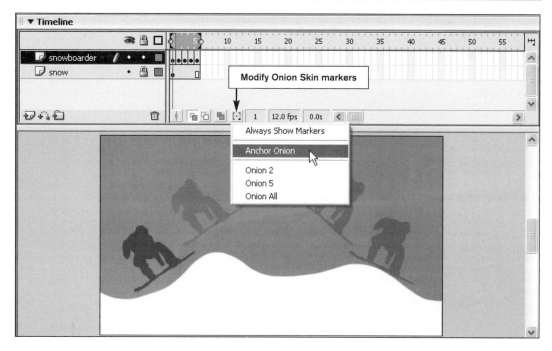

If you do not want the Onion Skin markers to move when you move the Playhead or click a frame in the Timeline, you can choose **Anchor Onion** from the menu that appears when you click the **Modify Onion Skin Markers** button at the bottom of the **Timeline**. This will lock the Onion Skinning span where it is until you unlock it again or manually drag the **Start** or **End Onion Skin** markers.

17. Go ahead and play with the **Free Transform** tool to create more effects. When you are done experimenting save and close this file. You will have the chance to work with the other features of the **Free Transform** tool in Chapter 6, "*Symbols and Instances*."

MOVIE | onion.mov

To see this exercise performed, play **onion.mov** located in the movies folder on the **H•O•T CD-ROM.**

NOTE | The Free Transform Tool

You can use the Free Transform tool to modify objects in several ways. As you move the cursor over the bounding box around a selected object, it will change to indicate what type of transformation is available to you. As you drag, you will see a preview of the transformation you are about to make. The following chart lists the features of the Free Transform tool.

Free Transform Tool Functions

	Clicking and dragging up or down on a corner transform handle will rotate the object. The cursor icon will change to a round arrow, as shown in the image at left. This arrow indicates that you can rotate the object.
	Clicking and dragging diagonally on one of the corner transform handles will modify the scale of the object. The cursor icon will change to a diagonal double-pointed arrow when you can perform this transformation.
	Clicking and dragging on one of the middle side transform handles will modify the width or height of the object. The cursor icon will change to a horizontal (or vertical depending on which side you are on) double-pointed arrow when you can perform this transformation.
	Clicking and dragging between any two transform handles will skew the object. The cursor icon will change as shown at left. This icon indicates that you can skew the object.
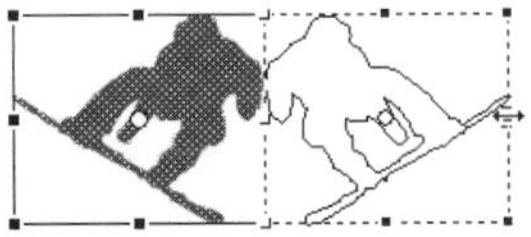	Clicking and dragging one of the middle side transform handles to the other side of the object will flip the object. The cursor will change to a horizontal or vertical double-pointed arrow depending on which side you are on.
	Clicking and dragging the center registration point will modify the center point of the object. After you alter the center point, all transformations will rotate or move in relation to the new center point location.

7. ————————**Testing Movies**

So far, you've been testing your movies by pressing **Enter/Return** and watching them play on the **Stage**. This is a great way to test the frame rate, but there are other ways to test your work. In this exercise, you will learn how to preview the movie file (SWF) with the **Test Movie** feature and how to preview your movie in a browser with the **Preview in Browser** feature. You will also learn a really easy way to produce the HTML file needed to hold your SWF file. More in-depth instruction on publishing Flash MX 2004 content is provided in Chapter 16, "*Publishing and Exporting.*"

1. Open the **frames.fla** file from the **chap_04** folder.

You should have the **frames.fla** file saved inside the **chap_04** folder from Exercise 4. It is important to know where your project file (FLA) has been saved before you use the Test Movie and Preview in Browser features since Flash MX 2004 automatically generates new files and saves them in the same location that your project file (FLA) resides. If you saved your file in a different location, make sure you know where it is.

Resize handle

2. Choose **Control > Test Movie** or press the shortcut keys **Ctrl+Enter** (Windows) or **Cmd+Return** (Mac). This will open a new window with a preview of the movie file (SWF) that would be exported if you chose to publish your movie right now.

Tip: You can click the resize handle of the Preview window and drag to make your window larger. Although the size of the window will change, the snowboard letters will stay the same size. You will learn how to make the content scalable, also using the publish settings, in Chapter 16, "Publishing and Exporting."

TIP | Loop-de-Loop

At this point, you're probably wondering why your animation is looping (playing over and over). This is the default behavior of all movies in Flash MX 2004, although you don't see it when you simply press **Enter/Return** to preview your work (unless you've set the file to **Loop Playback**). If you uploaded your published file to the Web, it would loop. You will learn to control the looping in your final movie (SWF) file in Chapter 11, "*ActionScript Basics and Behaviors*," when you learn how to add actions to frames. If all this looping is making you dizzy, you can select **Control > Loop Playback** to deselect this feature and turn it off temporarily.

3. With the SWF file still open, choose **Window > Toolbars > Controller**. You'll see a small toolbar on your screen that looks like the front of a VCR or other media players. This handy little gadget helps you control the playing of your animation.

4. Click the **Stop** button. As you probably guessed, this stops your animation.

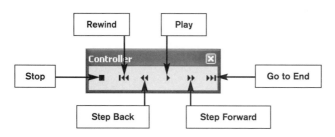

5. Click the **Play** button. Yes, you guessed it; this plays your animation. Go ahead and take a few minutes to try the other buttons on the **Controller**.

Something else happened, behind the scenes, when you chose **Control > Test Movie**. *Flash MX 2004 automatically created the SWF file for this movie and saved it in the same location as your project (FLA) file. You'll locate this file next.*

6. Open the **chap_04** folder from your **Desktop**. Notice that there is a **frames.swf** file inside this folder. This file was automatically generated by Flash MX 2004. Also notice that the SWF file has a different icon than the FLA files. This can be helpful visual feedback, especially if your file extensions are turned off. The SWF file is the file that you would add to an HTML page, same as you would a GIF or JPG file.

7. Return to Flash MX 2004 and close the **Preview** window.

8. Choose **File > Publish Preview > Default – (HTML)** or use the shortcut key **F12**. This will launch your default browser with a preview of your movie file (SWF) inside the browser window. This command provides a quick and easy way to see what your movie files will look like in a browser. You will learn a more appropriate and formal way of publishing your Flash MX 2004 movies later in Chapter 16, "*Publishing and Exporting*."

Again, something extra is happening behind the scenes. When you preview your movie in a browser, Flash MX 2004 will automatically create an HTML file, as well as the SWF file if there isn't one already, in the same location as the project file (FLA). So make sure you always know where you're saving your project files.

NOTE | How Does Flash MX 2004 Know Which Browser to Use?

If you have several browsers installed on your system, you can specify which one Flash MX 2004 uses as the default browser. You can change the default browser to your preferred browser in a few steps. There's a great explanation of how to do this for either a Windows machine or a Macintosh on Macromedia's Web site: **http://www.macromedia.com/support/flash/ts/ documents/browser_pref.htm**.

9. Hide Flash MX 2004 for a moment and look inside the **chap_04** folder on your **Desktop**. Notice that there is a **frames.html** file inside this folder. Flash MX 2004 generated this file automatically to hold your **frames.swf** file.

At this point, all the files necessary to publish to the Web have been generated automatically. More thorough instructions and details are provided in Chapter 16, "Publishing and Exporting." This exercise simply demonstrated a quick and easy way to generate files.

10. Return to Flash MX 2004 and save the changes you made to this file. You can close this file—you are finished with this chapter! Congratulation on completing a long but essential part of your animation training!

The next three chapters deal with more complex and specific issues, such as symbols and instances, motion tweening, shape tweening, and Timeline Effects. Now would be a great time for a break—you've worked through a lot of material, and you deserve one!

5.

Shape Tweening

What Is Shape Tweening?	Shape Tweening Text
Shape Hinting	Multiple Shape Tweening
Layer Folders	Layer Properties	Animating Gradients

chap_05

Macromedia Flash MX 2004
H•O•T CD-ROM

Most of you have seen animations on the Web or on television that show an object transforming (or morphing) from one shape into another. You can create this same effect in your Flash MX 2004 movies through a technique called **shape tweening**.

The exercises in this chapter offer a thorough introduction to shape tweening. By working through them, you will expand your Flash MX 2004 skill set to include shape tweening, hinting, animating gradients, and multiple shape tweening.

What Is Shape Tweening?

Shape tweening works like this. If you wanted to create an animation that showed a square transforming into a circle, you could create the starting point of the animation—the square—and the ending point—the circle—by placing them on separate keyframes, leaving empty frames between them. You could then set up a shape tween and have Flash MX 2004 automatically generate the art for the empty frames between the two images.

Before describing shape tweening in more detail, a few terms need to be defined—shape, keyframes, and tweening. Here's a handy chart to refer to if these terms are new to you:

Shape Tweening Definitions
Shape
In Flash MX 2004, a shape is a vector-based object or series of objects. You can create shapes in Flash MX 2004 using any of the drawing tools, or you can bring shapes into Flash MX 2004 from other vector-creation programs, such as FreeHand or Illustrator. In order for a shape to be suitable for shape tweening, it cannot be composed of grouped objects, bitmaps, or symbols. (You will learn about symbols in Chapter 6, "*Symbols and Instances*.") Type can be the subject of a shape tween if it is first converted to a shape. The process of converting text to a shape is called "breaking apart." You will learn how to break type apart later in this chapter.
Keyframes
In traditional animation, a "key" or "lead" animator would draw "extremes," or the important frames of artwork that define what the motion should look like. If, for example, you needed an animation of a circle turning into a square, a key artist would draw two keyframes, the first with a circle and the second with a square.
In Flash MX 2004, a keyframe is symbolized in the Timeline by a gray frame with a filled black circle at the bottom. In this example, the circle would be inside the first keyframe and the square would reside in the next keyframe.
Tweening
The term "tweening" is borrowed from traditional cel animation terminology, and is slang for "in-betweening." In cel animation, a person called an "in-betweener" would take the keyframes that a lead animator creates and draw all the frames that go between them that describe the motion. For example, the in-betweener would take the two keyframes just described and would use them to draw a series of images of the shapes in various stages of morphing from one object, the circle, into the other object, the square.

Flash MX 2004 lets you use shape tweening to animate between lines and shapes and to animate the colors and gradients that are applied to them. This process is often referred to as morphing. The illustrations that follow are a good example of a shape tween:

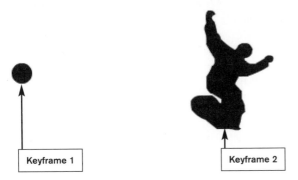

The first step in creating a shape tween is to create two unique keyframes.

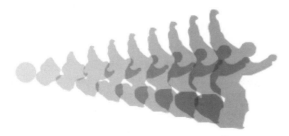

The next step is to apply a shape tween to the frames with a few clicks of the mouse. Flash MX 2004 will then interpolate the difference between the keyframes and automatically generate all of the frames in-between.

Shape tweening is the only process in Flash MX 2004 that lets you quickly animate from one distinct shape to another. It can also be used to animate from one gradient to another, from one color to another, and/or from one position to another. As you might imagine, creating this kind of animation by drawing each frame of the artwork would be rather tedious. The shape tweening feature in Flash MX 2004 automates this process.

The lists that follow outline some of the things that you can and can't do with shape tweens in Flash MX 2004.

What Shape Tweening Can Do

- Tween the shape of an object

- Tween the color of an object (including a color with transparency)

- Tween the position of an object on the Stage

- Tween the transformation (scale, rotation, skew) of an object

- Tween text that has been broken apart

- Tween gradients

What Shape Tweening Can't Do

- Tween grouped objects

- Tween symbols

- Tween text that has not been broken apart

 _____Shape Tweening Text

In the steps that follow, you will create an animation of a snowboard changing into the letter "X." This will introduce you to the basics of shape tweening.

1. Copy the **chap_05** folder, located on the **H•O•T CD-ROM**, to your hard drive. You will need to have this folder on your hard drive in order to save changes to the files inside it.

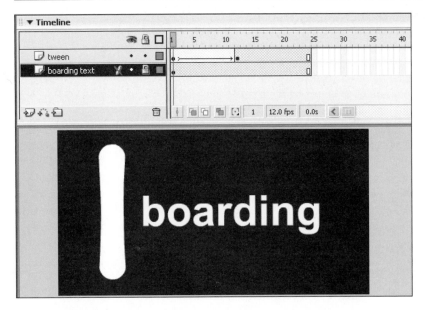

2. Open the **textTween_Final.fla** file from the **chap_05** folder. This is a finished version of the animation you will create in the following steps.

3. Press **Enter/Return** to preview the shape tweening animation. Notice the animation of the snowboard turning into the letter "X." You will create this shape tween next.

4. Close the **textTween_Final.fla** file.

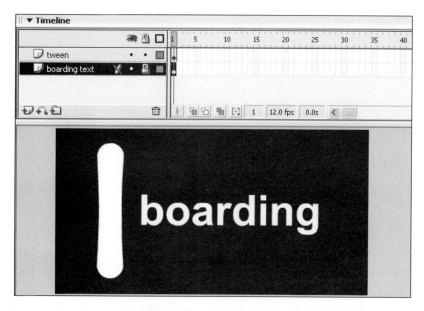

5. Open the **textTween.fla** file from the **chap_05** folder. This file contains two layers: one named **boarding text** with the word "boarding" on it and one named **tween** with the snowboard shape on it. You will be working on the **tween** layer.

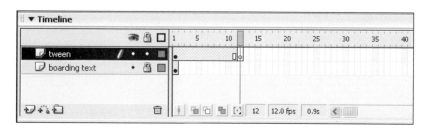

6. On the **tween** layer, press **F7** on **Frame 12**. This adds a blank keyframe to **Frame 12**. You are adding a blank keyframe rather than a keyframe because you want to add new artwork on **Frame 12**, not copy the artwork from **Frame 1**.

7. Notice that after the first frame, the word "boarding" disappears. This happens because the **boarding text** layer has only one frame, and the **tween** layer now has 12 frames. In order for the word "boarding" to appear throughout the entire animation, the **boarding text** layer must also contain 12 frames. Click **Frame 12** and press **F5** in the **boarding text** layer to add frames up to **Frame 12** on that layer.

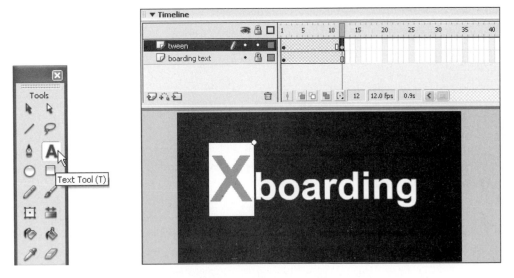

8. In the **Toolbar**, select the **Text** tool. Select **Frame 12** on the **tween** layer, click on the **Stage**, and type the capital letter **X** in **Frame 12** just before the letter "b" in the word "boarding," as shown here.

Note: *I used the Arial font, size 96, white, and bold to type the "X," but you can use whatever font and size you like. You will learn more about the text options in Flash MX 2004 in Chapter 12, "Working with Text."*

9. Using the **Selection** tool, click to select the large "X" on the **Stage**. Drag the "X" to position it before the letter "b," with a little space so that the "X" is aligned with the middle of the "b."

When you type text using the Text tool, the "X" is still in an editable format, which means you can double-click on it at any time and change the letter to something else. If you deselect the text and use the Selection tool to select it again, you will see a blue bounding box and no dotted mesh, indicating that it is not a shape. To use text in a shape tween, you have to make it a shape by breaking it apart. The act of breaking text apart converts it from editable text into an editable shape. You must do this because editable type cannot be the source of a shape tween. It's one of the rules of shape tweening—you can't use grouped objects or symbols either. Although you might not think of type as a grouped object, by Flash MX 2004's definition it must be broken apart to become a shape. You will learn more about working with text tools in Chapter 12, "Working with Text."

Dotted mesh indicates selection is a shape

10. With the "X" still selected, choose **Modify > Break Apart**, or **Ctrl+B** (Windows) or **Cmd+B** (Mac). The text is broken apart and converted into a shape, ready to be shape tweened. The dotted mesh over the "X" indicates that you are now working with a shape. This will be the last keyframe of your animation.

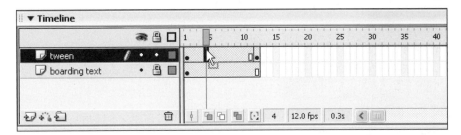

11. Click anywhere between the two keyframes to select a frame in the middle of that range of frames.

12. Make sure the **Properties inspector** is open. If it is not, choose **Window > Properties**.

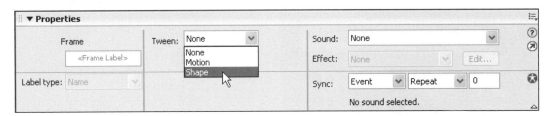

13. In the **Properties inspector**, select **Shape** from the **Tween** drop-down menu to apply a shape tween between the two keyframes.

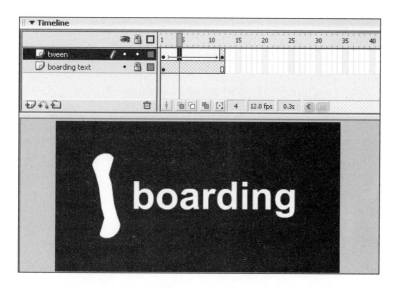

Once you have applied a shape tween between two keyframes, the Timeline will be shaded green, and a long arrow will appear between the keyframes. This is a visual indication that a shape tween is active.

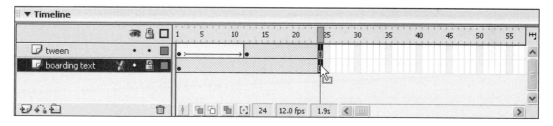

14. Hold down the **Shift** key, and click on both layers on **Frame 24** to select them both. With both frames selected, press **F5**, which will add more frames up to **Frame 24**. This will add one more second to the animation before it loops again, making the entire animation about two seconds.

15. Choose **Control > Test Movie** to test your tween. You will see the snowboard turning into the letter "X". If it looks unattractive to you, you'll learn how to smooth it out with shape hints in the upcoming exercise.

16. When you are finished testing, close the **Preview** window and return to Flash MX 2004. Save your project file and keep it open for the next exercise.

WARNING | Spotting Broken Tweens

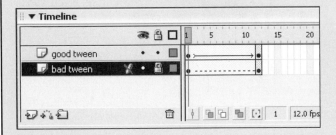

As you work more with shape tweens (and motion tweens in Chapter 7, "*Motion Tweening and Timeline Effects*"), you may see a broken (dashed) line appear in your Timeline instead of a solid line. Any time you see a broken line in your Timeline, it means that the shape tween (or motion tween) is not working properly. This makes it easy to spot problems in your animations. If you do see a dashed line in the Timeline when you are trying to create a shape tween, make sure that each of the objects in each of the keyframes is in fact a shape and not a grouped object or text that hasn't been broken apart. You'll learn more about the causes of broken shape tweens when you learn about symbols in future chapters.

2. —————————Shape Hinting

When working with shape tweening, Flash MX 2004 will automatically determine how to change from one shape to the next. Because this is an automatic process, you don't have complete control over how the tween occurs. Shape hinting is a feature that helps you regain some control over a tween. It is used primarily to fix a shape tween that doesn't look good, which can happen easily. In this exercise, you will take the shape tween that you created in the previous exercise and add shape hints to better control how the snowboard morphs into the "X."

1. You should still have the file **textTween.fla** open from the previous exercise. If you don't, go ahead and open it now.

2. Press **Enter/Return** to preview this shape tween.

Notice that, as the shape tween progresses, the snowboard appears to crumple up like a piece of paper and then all of a sudden pop into the letter "X." That is how Flash MX 2004 decided to create this shape tween. What if you want the tween to appear more fluid? You'll learn how to do this using shape hinting in the steps that follow.

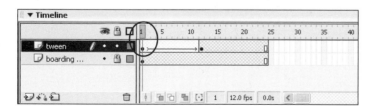

3. Make sure the **tween** layer is selected and that the **Playhead** is over **Frame 1**. When you add shape hints, you must start on the first keyframe of your animation.

4. Choose **Modify > Shape > Add Shape Hint**.

5. A red circle with an "a" in it will appear in the middle of the snowboard. This is a shape hint. Click and drag the shape hint to the upper-left corner of the snowboard shape. **Note:** You must use the **Selection** tool from the **Toolbar** to do this.

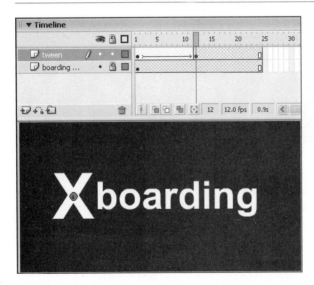

6. Move the **Playhead** to the last keyframe (**Frame 12**) of your animation. This is the last frame of the shape tween. The shape hint appears on this frame as well, and it needs to be positioned, which you'll do next.

7. Click and drag the shape hint (the small "a") to the upper-left, inside corner of the "X," as shown here. Moving the shape hint will make sure that the upper-left corner of the snowboard ends up as the upper-left corner of the letter "X."

When you let go of your mouse, notice that the shape hint changes from red to green. Why? This is how you know that the shape hint has been accepted. When your shape hint doesn't turn green on the ending keyframe, it means that it was not placed in the same (or in a similar) location as the first shape hint. The Macromedia documentation states that shape hints are yellow in the starting keyframe, green in the ending keyframe, and red when they are not on a curve. However, this is not always the case, as shown in this exercise, where the "X" shape has no curves, but the hints still turn green. In order for shape hints to work properly, your best bet is to place them in similar locations on each keyframe and to pay more attention to how the tween animates than to the color of the hints. If necessary, try repositioning your shape hint for a better tween effect. Sometimes it takes just a small adjustment for Flash MX 2004 to get the hint (pun intended)!

8. Move the **Playhead** back to **Frame 1** and press **Enter/Return** to preview the effect of changing the shape tween by using a shape hint. Notice that the shape tween looks better. You will make the transition even smoother by adding more shape hints next.

9. In the **Timeline**, make sure the **Playhead** is over **Frame 1**. Choose **Modify > Shape > Add Shape Hint** to add another shape hint.

10. The second shape hint will appear as a small "b" in the middle of the snowboard. Click and drag the second shape hint to the upper-right corner of the snowboard shape, as shown here.

TIP | Multiple Shape Hints

After you add a second shape hint, it appears as a red circle with the letter "b" rather than an "a" in the middle of it. The next shape hint after that will be "c," and so on. I think you see the pattern here. When you get to "z," that's it! You're all out of shape hints. You're given a total of 26 shape hints per shape tween. But don't worry; 26 shape hints should be far too many for most animations. If you find yourself needing more than 26 shape hints, you might want to rethink the complexity of your animation, because by then it is probably going to put a lot of strain on the end user's computer processor.

11. Move the **Playhead** to the last keyframe (**Frame 12**) of your animation. Click and drag the second shape hint ("b") to the upper-right, outside corner of the "X," as shown here.

12. Move the **Playhead** back to **Frame 1** and press **Enter/Return** to preview the effect of changing the shape tween by adding another shape hint. Notice that the shape tween transition is getting better.

13. In the **Timeline**, make sure the **Playhead** is over **Frame 1**. Repeat Steps 9, 10, and 11 two more times to add two more shape hints, moving them to the remaining corners of the "X." When you are finished, **Frame 1** and **Frame 12** should look like the pictures shown here.

14. Press **Enter/Return** to test the shape tween with four shape hints.

Try experimenting by moving the shape hints around. Moving them even slightly can give a completely different look to your shape tween. Now that you know how to add shape hints, you should learn how to remove them as well. The following steps show you how to remove a shape hint.

15. Click and drag the **Playhead** back to **Frame 1**.

16. Right-click (Windows) or **Ctrl+click** (Mac) on the shape hint with the "d" on it. Choose **Remove Hint** from the pop-up menu. This will remove the selected shape hint and return the animation back to the point of using just three shape hints.

17. Press **Enter/Return** to test the shape tween animation again. Go ahead and experiment by removing another shape hint and notice how it affects the animation.

18. When you are finished, save and close this file—you won't need it to complete the next exercise.

TIP | Quickly Removing Shape Hints

If you add too many shape hints and really mess up your animation, don't worry. You can remove them all with just a few clicks. **Right-click** (Windows) or **Ctrl+click** (Mac) on any shape hint and select **Remove All Hints** from the pop-up menu. You can also select **Modify > Shape > Remove All Hints**. Either option will remove every shape hint from your animation. Thank goodness for this feature!

3. —————————**Multiple Shape Tweening**

So far, you have learned how to create single shape tweens. There will likely come a time, however, when you will want to create more than one shape tween in your project. In this exercise, you will learn how to create multiple shape tweens by placing them on separate layers using the Distribute to Layers feature. Working with multiple layers is the only way to choreograph animations with multiple tweens. This exercise will also introduce the layer folder feature, which is a wonderful way to organize and consolidate animations that contain many different layers.

1. Open the **mutplShpTwn_Final.fla** file from the **chap_05** folder. This file contains a finished version of the shape tween animation you are about to create.

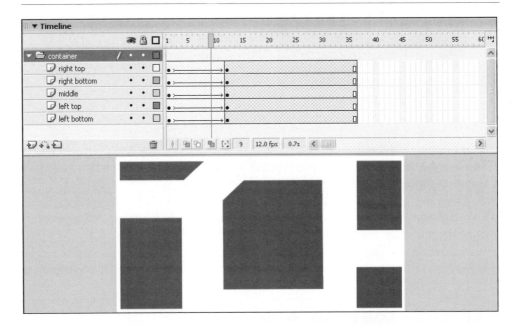

2. Press **Enter/Return** to preview this file. If you can't see the entire **Stage**, choose **View > Magnification > Show All** so that you can see the whole multiple shape tween animation. In this exercise, you will shape tween the alpha and size of multiple shapes. In the **Timeline**, notice the folder icon with all the layers in it. This designates a layer folder, which you'll learn about near the end of this exercise.

3. When you are finished previewing, close the file. You will learn to create this same animation in the steps that follow.

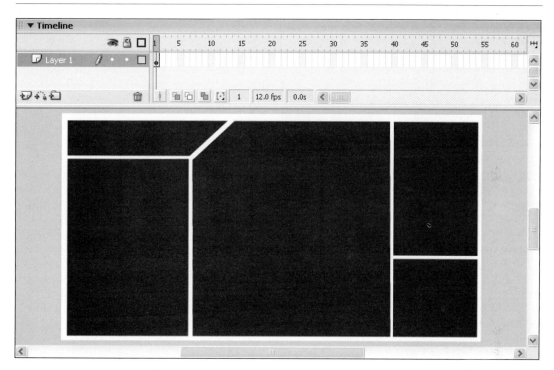

4. Open the file named **mutplShpTwn.fla** located inside the **chap_05** folder. Currently, this file has one layer with five different shapes on it.

Up to this point in the chapter, you have been creating shape tweens in which one shape turns into another on one layer. Although it is possible to tween one shape into many shapes using only one layer, some effects require you to place your shapes on separate layers. The following steps show a good example of when it's necessary to put your shapes on separate layers.

5. Click on **Frame 1** to select all the shapes on **Frame 1**, and choose **Modify > Timeline > Distribute to Layers**.

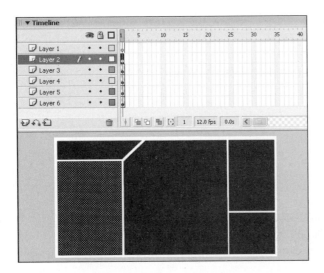

The Distribute to Layers feature will take each selected shape and place it on its own layer. You can click on any of the shapes on the Stage, and you will see the corresponding layer become highlighted in the Timeline, as shown here.

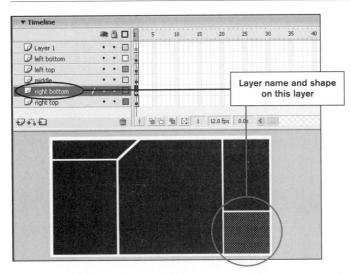

Layer name and shape
on this layer

6. Starting with **Layer 2**, double-click on each of the layer names in the **Timeline** to give them new, more descriptive names. Change **Layer 2** to **left bottom**, **Layer 3** to **left top**, **Layer 4** to **middle**, **Layer 5** to **right bottom**, and **Layer 6** to **right top**, just as you see in the picture here. Make sure that the name you give to each layer matches the shape's location on the **Stage**. This makes it easier to know what shapes are on each of the layers.

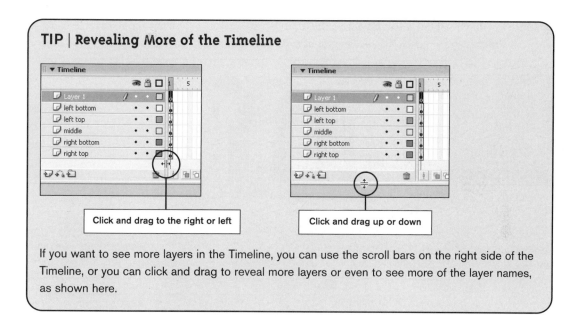

TIP | Revealing More of the Timeline

Click and drag to the right or left

Click and drag up or down

If you want to see more layers in the Timeline, you can use the scroll bars on the right side of the Timeline, or you can click and drag to reveal more layers or even to see more of the layer names, as shown here.

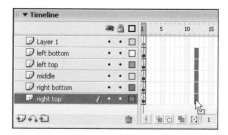

7. Starting with **Frame 12** on the **left bottom** layer, click and drag down to select **Frame 12** on all the layers below the **left bottom** layer, as shown here.

8. Press **F6** to add a keyframe on **Frame 12** of each layer you selected. Inserting a keyframe will copy the artwork from **Frame 1** of each layer in the **Timeline**. This will serve as the ending keyframe of your shape tween animation.

9. Move the **Playhead** back to **Frame 1**. In the following steps, you will be altering the size of each shape in **Frame 1**, to serve as the beginning point of the shape tween animation.

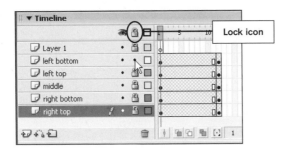

10. In the **Timeline**, click the **Lock** icon, next to the **Eye** icon, to lock all the layers at once. Click the **Lock** icon for the **left bottom** layer to unlock just that layer. This makes it much easier to work on just the shapes on the **left bottom** layer without affecting any of the other shapes.

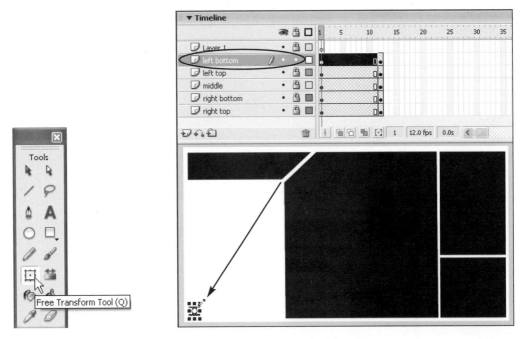

11. Click on **Frame 1** on the **left bottom** layer to select it. In the **Toolbar**, select the **Free Transform** tool, and then click and drag the upper-right resize handle toward the lower-left portion of the **Stage**. This will scale the shape down to create the starting point of the animation for the **left bottom** layer.

Tip: To scale the shape proportionately, ***Shift+click*** and drag the resize handle.

12. Click on the dot in the **Lock** column on the **left bottom** layer to lock that layer. Then click on the **Lock** icon for the **middle** layer to unlock that layer. You will be altering the size of the shape on this layer next.

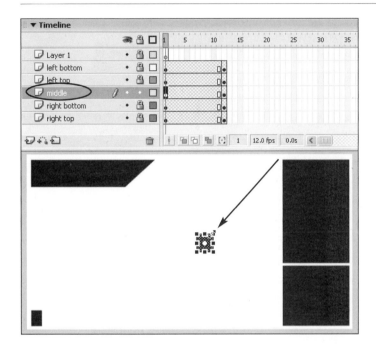

13. Click on **Frame 1** on the **middle** layer to select it. In the **Toolbar**, select the **Free Transform** tool, and then click and drag the upper-right resize handle down and toward the lower left of the **Stage**, just as you see in the picture here. This will scale down the shape to create the starting point for the animation in the **middle** layer.

*Tip: To scale the shape from its center, press **Shift+Alt** (Windows) or **Shift+Option** (Mac) and click and drag the resize handle.*

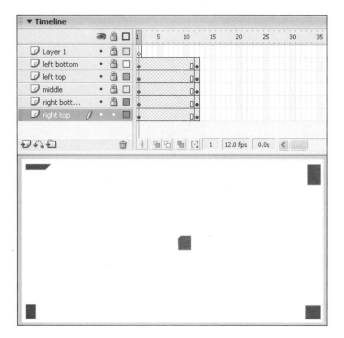

14. Repeat Steps 11 and 12 for the **left top**, **right bottom**, and **right top** layers. When you are finished, the shapes on all the layers on **Frame 1** should look like the image shown here. You may need to use the **Selection** tool to reposition the middle shape near the center of the **Stage**.

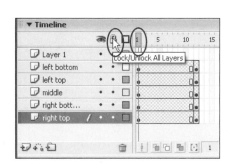

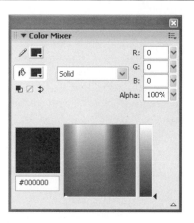

15. Unlock all the layers in the **Timeline**. Make sure the **Playhead** is on **Frame 1**; this is the beginning point of the animation where you will set all the keyframes to an alpha of **0%** using the **Color Mixer**. If the **Color Mixer** panel is not open, choose **Window > Design Panels > Color Mixer**.

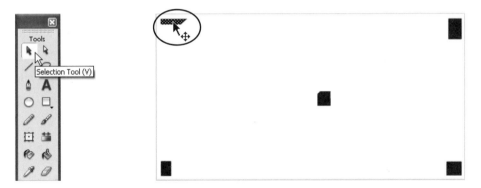

16. With the **Selection** tool, click the shape on the upper-left corner of the Stage to select it. You will change the **alpha** of this shape using the **Color Mixer** panel next.

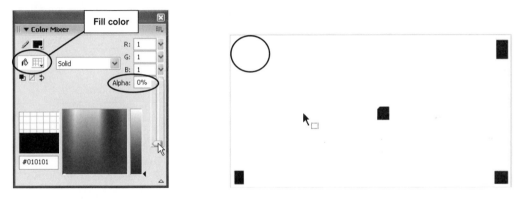

17. In the **Color Mixer** panel, make sure the **Fill color** button is selected. For the **Alpha**, enter a value of **0%**, or click and drag the slider down to **0%**. To see your changes, deselect on a blank area of the **Stage**. The shape should now be invisible.

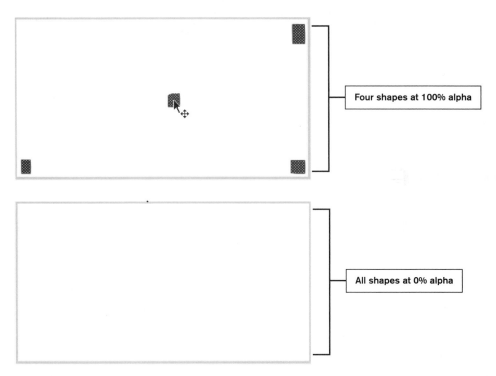

Four shapes at 100% alpha

All shapes at 0% alpha

18. Shift+click the remaining shapes on **Stage—left bottom**, **middle**, **right top**, and **right bottom—** to set the **Alpha** to **0%** all at once. When you are finished, your **Stage** should appear as though it is blank. Don't worry, the shapes are still there. You will add the tween to make them fade up to 100% alpha next.

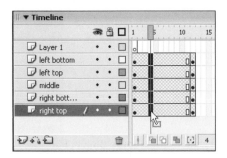

19. Starting with the **left bottom** layer, click and drag down between the two keyframes to select all the layers, as shown here. You will add the shape tween next.

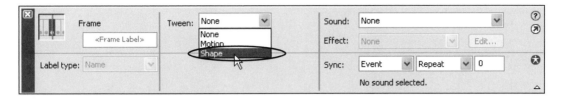

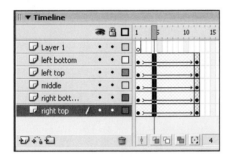

20. Make sure the **Properties inspector** is open. If it is not, choose **Window > Properties**. Select **Shape** from the **Tween** drop-down menu. This will automatically generate a shape tween between each of the two keyframes on all the layers. Notice the solid arrow and the green tint between the keyframes, which signifies that the tween is active.

21. Press **Enter/Return** to see the shape tween in action! Cool! Notice the shapes fade up from invisible to visible while tweening the size at the same time. Next, you will add frames to the animation to extend the last set of keyframes for two more seconds.

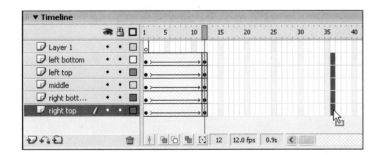

22. Starting with **Frame 36** on the **left bottom** layer, click and drag to select **Frame 36** on all the layers below the **left bottom** layer, as shown here.

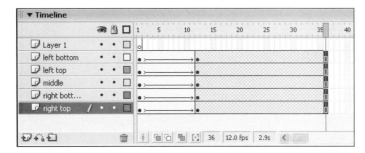

23. Press **F5** to add frames up to **Frame 36** to extend the **Timeline**. The animation will be about 3 seconds: 36 frames ÷ 12 fps = 3 seconds. One second for the shapes to tween from 0% to 100% alpha, and then the shapes will remain on **Stage** for another two seconds before looping again.

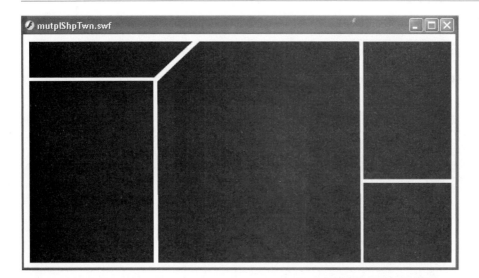

24. Choose **Control > Test Movie** to view the movie file (SWF) to see the shape tweens in action again! Notice the shapes in the animation fade up from 0% to 100% alpha and then remain on **Stage** for about two more seconds before looping again. By using a multiple shape tween, you can have different animations on different layers all happening at the same time.

What about that layer folder you saw in the finished version of this file? All you have left to do is to put your shape tween layers into a layer folder, which you will learn how to do next.

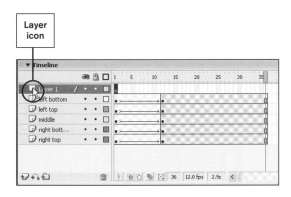

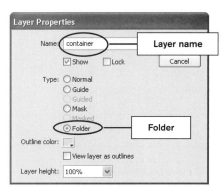

25. Double-click on the **Layer 1** icon. This opens the **Layer Properties** dialog box. For the **Name**, type **container** and for the **Type**, select **Folder**. This changes **Layer 1** into a layer folder and names the folder **container**. Click **OK**. A chart describing all the layer properties found in this dialog box is provided at the end of this exercise.

NOTE | What Is a Layer Folder?

A layer folder is a special kind of layer that can hold other layers inside of it. It is important to note that you cannot have artwork on a layer folder—the layer folder's sole purpose is to hold multiple layers so that you can keep your Timeline compact and organized.

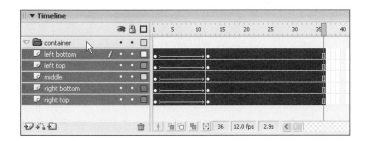

26. In the **Timeline**, hold down the **Shift** key and click the layers named **left bottom** and **right top**. This will select all the layers except the layer folder named **container**. With all the layers selected, drag the layers onto the **container** layer. This will place all the layers in the layer folder. After you do this, notice that the layers are all indented under the layer folder.

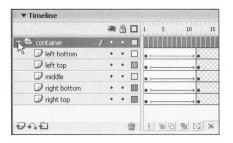

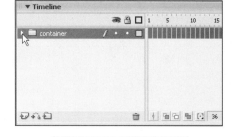

Layer folder expanded	Layer folder collapsed

27. Click on the arrow to the left of the **container** layer name to collapse the folder. Now you see the layers, now you don't! This is organization! You will really come to appreciate this feature when you work on projects that have tons of layers.

28. Choose **Control > Test Movie** to view the movie file (SWF) of your multiple shape tween animation again. Although you've moved the layers into a layer folder, the animation is left untouched.

29. When you are finished, save and close this file.

MOVIE | mutplShpTwn.mov

To see this exercise performed, play **mutplShpTwn.mov** located in the **movies** folder on the **H•O•T CD-ROM**.

Layer Properties Defined

The Timeline offers a number of ways of controlling layers, but other options are available in the Layer Properties dialog box that aren't visible in the Timeline. The following chart covers these additional options.

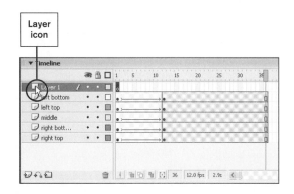

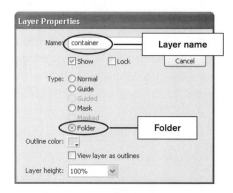

Layer Properties	
Option	**Description**
Guide	This option enables you to use the contents of a layer as a tracing image (or guide), which helps you create artwork on other layers. Guide layers are the only layers that are not exported with the movie. You will work with a Guide layer in Chapter 7, "*Motion Tweening and Timeline Effects*."
Guided	A Guided layer is a layer that is linked to a Guide layer. The artwork on this layer can follow the path of the Guide layer it is linked to. Chapter 7, "*Motion Tweening and Timeline Effects*," will give you hands-on experience working with Guided layers.
Mask	Selecting this option will turn the layer into a Mask layer. You will learn more about this layer type in Chapter 8, "*Bitmaps*."
Masked	Selecting this option will cause the layer to be masked by the Mask layer above it. You will learn how to work with this option as well in Chapter 8, "*Bitmaps*."
Folder	Choosing this option will turn the layer into a layer folder so that you can organize your layers.
Outline color	This option specifies the color that will be used if you select the **View layer as outlines** option. By default, each layer will have a different color. This just gives you an extra bit of organizational control. You will get a chance to work with outlines in the following exercise.
Layer height	This option makes a layer's Timeline display "taller" when you increase the line height of a specific layer. You can choose 100% (the default), 200%, or 300%. This feature is especially useful for working with sounds on the main Timeline. Allowing the layer containing the sound to be taller makes it easier to work with the waveforms and to synchronize the sound with your animation. You will try this later in Chapter 13, "*Sound*."

4. ———————Animating Gradients

Shape tweening can be used to create additional effects besides morphing one shape into another. You can also use the shape tween process to animate **gradients**. This can produce dramatic lighting effects, such as glows and strobes. In this exercise, you will learn how to modify and animate a gradient as well as use the View Outlines feature in the Timeline. You will also get a chance to work with rulers and guides to help you place your keyframes on the Stage.

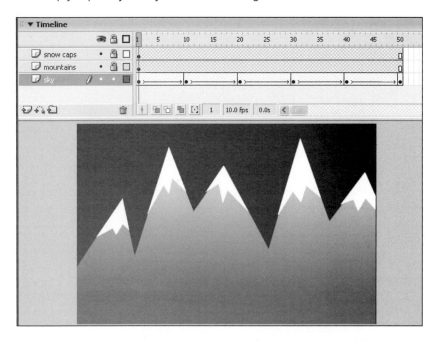

1. Open the **animatedGradient_Final.fla** file from the **chap_05** folder.

2. Press **Enter/Return** to preview the animation. Notice that the gradient appears to move from left to right. This is a finished version of the animated gradient effect you will create in the following steps.

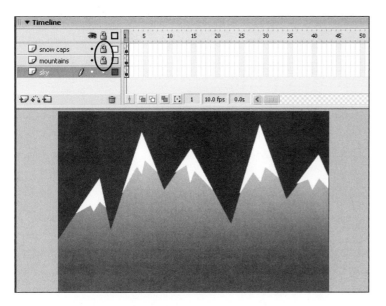

3. Close the **animatedGradient_Final.fla** file and open the **animatedGradient.fla** file from the **chap_05** folder. This file contains three layers: **snow caps**, **mountains**, and **sky**, which is where you will create the gradient tween. The layers **snow caps** and **mountains** are locked so that you don't edit them accidentally.

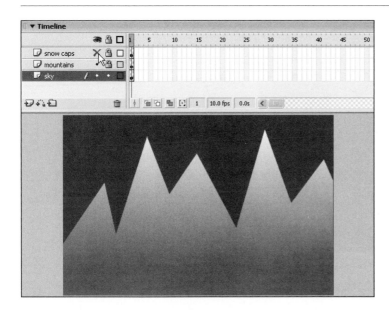

4. Check out the individual layers by turning on and off the **Show/Hide layers** icon to see the content on the individual layers. When you are done examining the layers, make sure all the layers are visible.

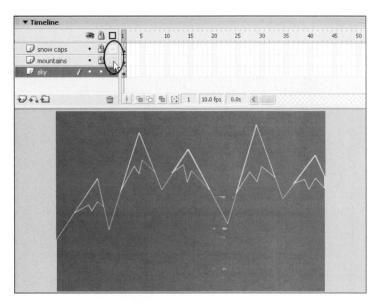

5. Click on the **View Outlines** icon of the **snow caps** layer and the **mountains** layer. By viewing the outlines of these layers, the fills will not be displayed, only their outlines will be seen allowing you to view the artwork on the **sky** layer. In the following steps, you will be adding a gradient and moving the gradient by adding keyframes to make it appear as if it's moving across the sky. But first you will add guides to help you position the keyframes.

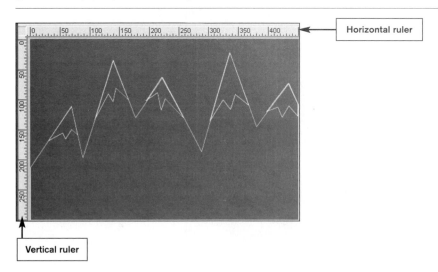

6. Choose **View > Rulers** to view the rulers. Next you will create guidelines to help you position your keyframes.

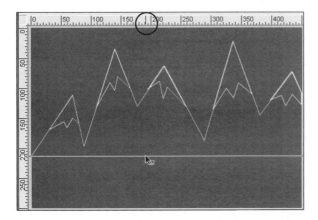

7. Click in the top horizontal ruler and drag a guide down to where the first mountain begins on the left side, as shown here. This guide will help you position the last keyframe of the gradient fill.

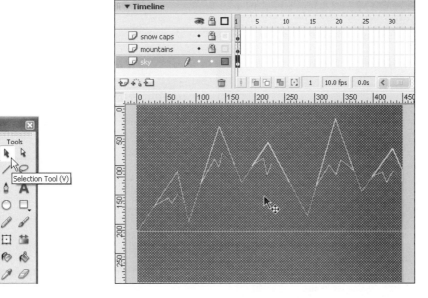

8. With the **Selection** tool, click on the solid blue fill on the **Stage**. You are going to add a gradient fill next.

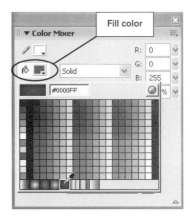

9. Make sure the **Color Mixer** panel is open. If it's not, choose **Window > Design Panels > Color Mixer**. Make sure the solid blue fill on the **Stage** is still selected and click on the **Fill Color** box to open the **Fill Color** palette. At the very bottom of this palette are some gradients. Choose the **black** and **blue** radial gradient; it is fifth from the left.

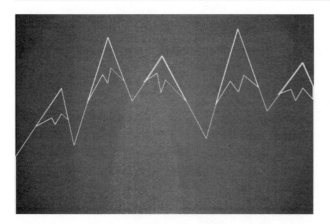

As soon as you select the black and blue radial gradient, the shape on the Stage will change to reflect the new gradient fill color because it was already selected. You can click anywhere away from the Stage to deselect the shapes and see the gradient fill better. To create the effect of the gradient moving from one side of the word to the other, you will change the center of the gradient next.

10. Click on **Frame 1** of the **sky** layer to select the shape on **Stage** again.

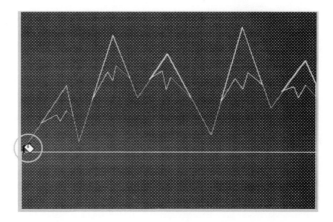

11. In the **Toolbar**, select the **Paint Bucket** tool and click on the left side of the shape where the mountain begins, as shown here. The spot where you click defines the center of the radial gradient. Because the radial gradient is blue in the center and black on the outside, the place where you click is where the blue point of the gradient will be.

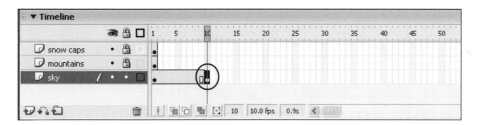

12. On the **sky** layer, press **F6** on **Frame 10** in the **Timeline** to add a new keyframe to the frame.

*As you might remember from Chapter 4, "Animation Basics," pressing **F6** copies the content from the previous keyframe and places it on the new keyframe. This can save you from having to re-create entire pieces of artwork, and it's especially useful when you want to make only minor changes.*

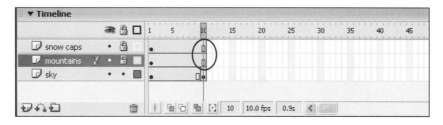

13. On the **snow caps** and **mountains** layers, press **F5** on **Frame 10** to add frames up to **Frame 10** on these layers. This will allow the content on these layers to be visible through **Frame 10**.

Tip: Even though the snow caps and mountains layers are locked, you can still add and delete frames in the Timeline—you just can't select the artwork or objects on the Stage in a locked layer.

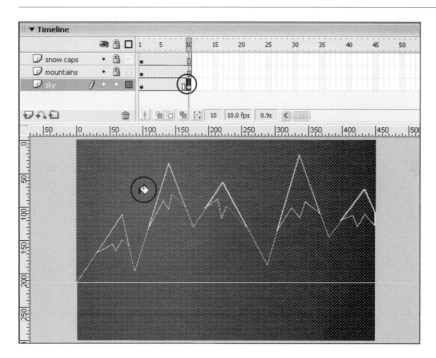

14. Click on **Frame 10** in the **sky** layer to select it. In the **Toolbar**, make sure the **Paint Bucket** tool is still selected, and this time click between the first two mountain peaks on the left side of the **Stage**, as shown here. Now it appears as though a light source is moving across the horizon.

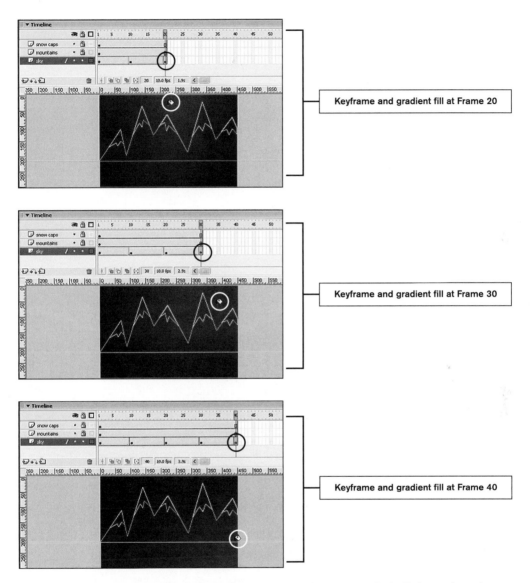

Keyframe and gradient fill at Frame 20

Keyframe and gradient fill at Frame 30

Keyframe and gradient fill at Frame 40

15. Repeat Steps 12 through 14 for **Frames 20**, **30**, and **40**, respectively. Refer to these images to set the keyframes for the **sky** layer.

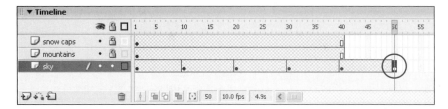

16. You're almost done—just one last detail. You are going to make the blue moonlit sky turn to midnight. On the **sky** layer, press **F6** on **Frame 50** in the **Timeline** to add a new keyframe to the frame.

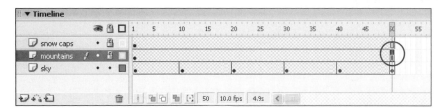

17. On the **snow caps** and **mountains** layers, press **F5** on **Frame 50** to add frames.

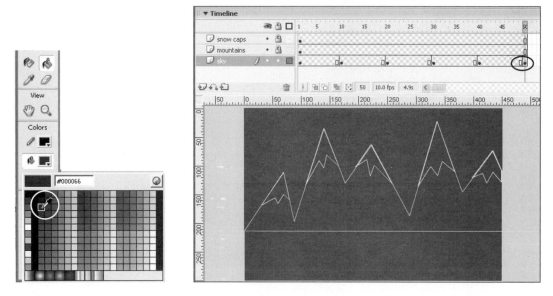

18. Click on **Frame 50** in the **sky** layer to select it. In the **Toolbar**, make sure the **Paint Bucket** tool is selected and in the **Fill Color** box, select a dark **blue**. Click anywhere away from the **Stage** to see the changes. This is the last keyframe of the animation and will make the blue moonlit sky turn to midnight. You will add the tween to the **sky** layer next.

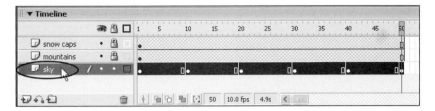

19. Click the **sky** layer name to select all the frames in that layer.

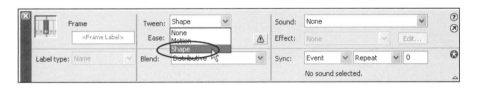

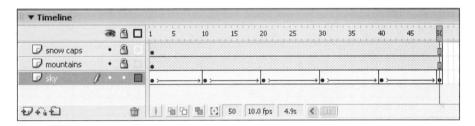

20. In the **Properties inspector**, choose **Shape** from the **Tween** drop-down menu to create a shape tween between all the keyframes. Notice the green tint and the solid black arrow between the keyframes, letting you know that the tween is active. Before your test your shape tween, you will turn off the guides and layer outlines first.

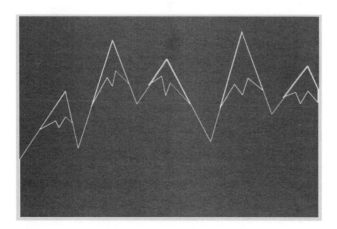

21. Choose **View > Guides > Show Guides** to turn the guides off.

Tip: *If you want to clear all guides, you can choose* ***View > Guides > Clear Guides*** *or drag the guides back to the ruler units.*

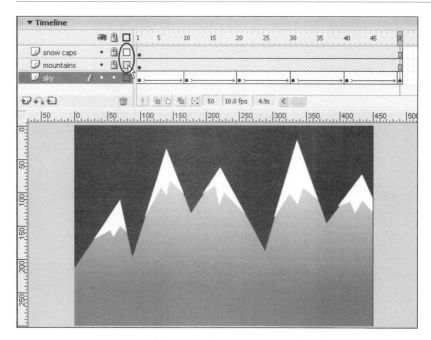

22. To see the **snow caps** and **mountains** layers in the **Normal** mode, click the **Outline** icon in each layer. Notice that you can see the mountains and their snow caps clearly now.

23. Choose **Control > Test Movie** to test your shape tween. Now it looks as though the blue sky is moving across the horizon and changing to night!

Don't be deceived by the word "shape" in "shape tweening." As you've just seen, shape tweens can be used to create animations that don't involve changing one shape into another. In this example, shape tweening was used to animate a gradient.

---

24. When you are finished, save and close this file—you won't need it anymore.

I hope this chapter uncovered the many secrets and nuances of shape tweening. As you gain experience in Flash MX 2004, shape tweening will likely become a technique you use often for many different types of effects. If you have the stamina, keep pressing forward to the next chapter, where you will learn about symbols and instances.

6.

Symbols and Instances

Symbol and Instance Structure	Creating Graphic Symbols
Library	Registration Point	Creating Symbol Instances
Editing Symbols	Editing Symbol Instances	Color Styles
Animating Graphic Symbols	Alpha Transparency
Animating Instances by Modifying the Registration Point

chap_06

Macromedia Flash MX 2004
H•O•T CD-ROM

Effective Flash MX 2004 movies, even very simple ones, often rely on symbols and instances. So, what are symbols and instances and what can they do for you? Symbols are built around the idea of creating content once that you can use over and over in your Flash MX 2004 movies. This very powerful feature has several benefits. Symbols enable you to create complex movies at small file sizes that are faster to download. How? Symbols are downloaded only once, regardless of how many copies (called **instances**) you have in your movie. For example, if you had a symbol of a snowflake, and you added 50 instances of that snowflake to the Stage, the file size would be not be that much larger. However, if you were to instead draw 50 separate snowflakes, the user would have to download all 50 snowflakes, and the file size would increase dramatically.

The concept of symbols and instances takes practice to fully comprehend since it is unique compared to other common graphics, animation, or interactive programs. This chapter will give you a better understanding of how to create and work with symbols and instances than if you just read about them. For many, trying something and gaining firsthand experience is the key to understanding!

The Symbol and Instance Structure

Think of a Flash MX 2004 symbol as a master object of sorts. You create a symbol once—it can be a simple shape or something very complex—and use it multiple times throughout your movie. Each time you reuse a symbol in your project file, it is called an instance, which is a copy of a symbol.

The concept of symbols and instances is the key to reducing the file size and download weight of your Flash MX 2004 documents, because the symbol is downloaded only once, whereas the instances are simply described in a small text file by their attributes (scale, color, transparency, animation, and so on). That is why instances add very little to the file size of your final movie. To reduce the file size of your movie, you should create symbols for any object that you plan to reuse in your projects. Besides reducing the final file size and download time, symbols and instances also help you make quick updates to objects across your entire project file—this is a real time-saver! Later in the book, as you learn about more advanced animation techniques, you'll see that symbols and instances play another dramatic role. But first you'll focus on how to create and manipulate symbols and instances in this chapter.

There are three types of symbols in Flash MX 2004: graphic symbols, button symbols, and movie clip symbols. In this chapter, you will be working with graphic symbols. Hands-on exercises for creating button and movie clip symbols are covered in later chapters.

Here's a handy chart that explains some of the terms found in this chapter:

Symbol Definitions	
Term	**Definition**
Symbol	A reusable object that serves as a master from which you can create copies (instances). Once a symbol is created, it automatically becomes part of the project file's Library. You will learn about the Library later in this chapter.
Instance	A copy of the original symbol. You can alter the color, size, shape, and position of an instance without affecting the original symbol.
Graphic symbol	One of the three types of symbols. It consists of artwork that can be either static or animated. The Graphic Symbol Timeline is dependent on the Main Timeline—it will play only while the Main Timeline is playing. You'll learn more about this behavior as you work through the exercises in this book.

Symbol Naming Conventions

As you learn to create symbols and instances in this chapter, you'll need to create names for them. In past versions of Macromedia Flash, it didn't matter what name you gave to symbols or instances. With changes to ActionScript in Flash MX 2004 (which you will learn about in later chapters), naming conventions are more important than they used to be. This is especially true for movie clip symbols. For this reason, you should get used to naming all your symbols in Flash MX 2004 following the same rules, so you don't develop bad habits that haunt you down the road. Here's a handy chart that explains the rules.

Naming Symbols	
Convention	**Explanation**
No spaces	Don't use any spaces. Instead, string the words together or add underscores. For example, instead of my first symbol, use the name myFirstSymbol or my_first_symbol.
No special characters	Special characters—such as ! @ # $ % ^ & * ( ) - + = { } [ ] \ ; : ' " < > ? , . /—are forbidden. Some special characters have specific meaning to the Flash MX 2004 Player and can mess up the ActionScript in the future, so be sure to avoid them.
No forward slashes	Forward slashes are often misinterpreted as path locations on a hard drive, instead of as the name of an object. So, for example, don't use the name my/first/symbol.
Begin with a lowercase letter	Symbol names that begin with numbers and capital letters can cause confusion in the ActionScript. For this reason, always start your symbol names with a lowercase letter. Names can contain numbers, but the first character should be a lowercase letter.
No dots	Don't put dots in your file names, such as snow.boarder—dots are reserved for ActionScripting syntax.
Use a descriptive name	It is good practice to use descriptive names for symbols. Rather than symbol6, you should choose a name that is more easily recognized, like gfxLogoBkgd. When you use multiword names for symbols, capitalize the first letter of all words except the first so that you can read it more easily. When you refer to an object in ActionScripting (which you'll get to try in later chapters), you must refer to the symbol with the same capitalization you used in its name.

Important Timeline Vocabulary Terms

This chapter reintroduces you to the Timeline. In the following exercises, you will learn that a symbol has a Timeline, too, and therefore you may have one Flash MX 2004 project that contains several different Timelines. The following chart will help you further understand the distinctions among the various types of Timelines.

Timeline Definitions	
Term	**Definition**
Main Timeline	When you open a Flash MX 2004 project (FLA), it always defaults to showing the Timeline of Scene 1. This is also called the Main Timeline in the Flash MX 2004 documentation. The Main Timeline is the Timeline that is visible when you're inside a scene. (You will learn more about scenes in Chapter 11, "*ActionScript Basics and Behaviors*.")
Graphic Symbol Timeline	Each symbol has its own Timeline. The Timeline for a graphic symbol and the scene in which the symbol is placed must have the same number of frames, or the symbol's animation will not play properly. This is a unique behavior of the graphic symbol; button and movie clip symbols do not behave the same way. You'll learn about button and movie clip symbols in later chapters.
Scene's Timeline	Every Flash MX 2004 project (.fla) has a Main Timeline in the form of Scene 1's Timeline. You'll see in later chapters that Flash MX 2004 projects can have multiple scenes. In those cases, each scene is considered part of the Main Timeline. Learning the difference between a scene's Timeline and a symbol's Timeline is one of the key foundations to working successfully with Flash MX 2004.

I. _____ **Creating Graphic Symbols**

Symbols are used for many purposes in Flash MX 2004. Before you learn hands-on what they're good for, you'll need to know how to create them. This first exercise shows you how to create a graphic symbol. Later in the book, you'll learn to work with the two other symbol types—Buttons and Movie Clips.

1. Copy the **chap_06** folder, located on the **H•O•T CD-ROM**, to your hard drive. You need to have this folder on your hard drive in order to save changes to the files inside it.

2. Open the **graphicSymbol.fla** file from the **chap_06** folder. This file contains one layer with a snowflake shape in Frame 1. You will convert this shape into a graphic symbol in the steps that follow.

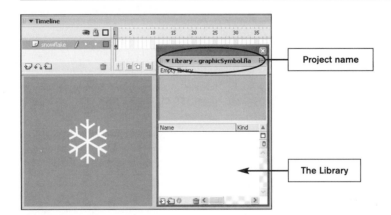

3. Choose **Window > Library**, or press **Ctrl+L** (Windows) or **Cmd+L** (Mac) to open the **Library** panel. Notice that the project file name is displayed at the top of the Library panel.

NOTE | What Is the Library?

The Library is a container where Flash MX 2004 stores and organizes symbols, bitmap graphics, sound clips, video clips, and fonts. Since each media has a different icon associated with it, it's easy to identify the different assets inside the Library at a glance. For designers, it can be one of the most useful and frequently used interface elements in the program. The Library is attached to the movie that you're working with. If you give your project file (FLA) to someone else, and that person opens it, he or she will see the same Library that you see when you have that file open.

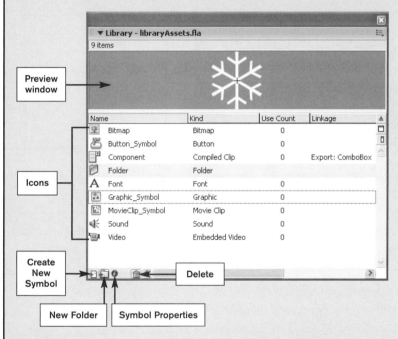

Inside the Library, you can sort the contents by name, kind, use count, and linkage. As your files become more complex, you will find it useful to create folders within your Library to help separate your symbols into different categories. Since you will frequently work with the Library in Flash MX 2004, it's useful to learn the shortcut to open the Library: **Ctrl+L** (Windows) or **Cmd+L** (Mac). You will get an in-depth look at the Library and all its functions in later chapters.

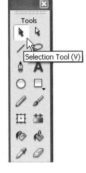

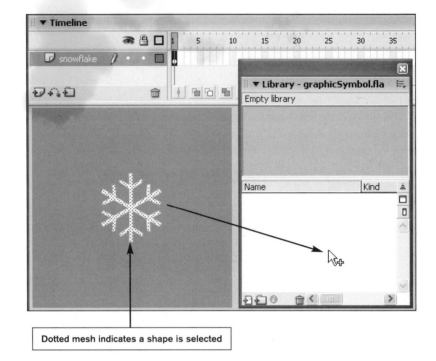

Dotted mesh indicates a shape is selected

4. Using the **Selection** tool, select the **snowflake** on the **Stage**. Notice the dotted mesh when you select the snowflake, which indicates that you have selected a shape. Drag the **snowflake** into the lower half of the **Library** panel to convert it into a symbol. This will open the **Convert to Symbol** dialog box.

*Note: Instead of dragging the shape into the **Library**, you can also select the shape and choose **Modify > Convert to Symbol** or press **F8** to open the **Convert to Symbol** dialog box.*

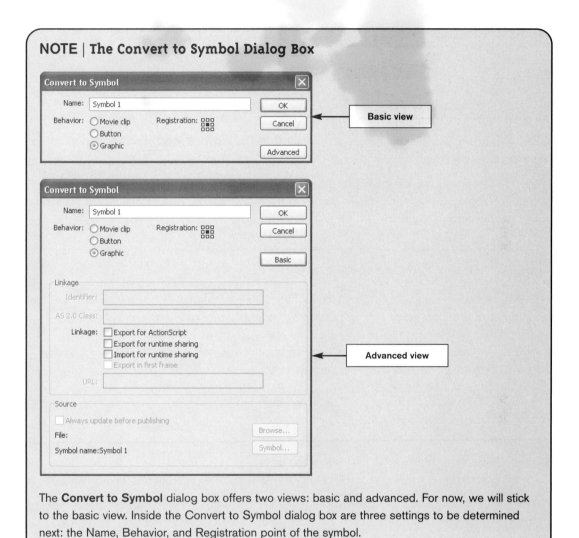

NOTE | The Convert to Symbol Dialog Box

The **Convert to Symbol** dialog box offers two views: basic and advanced. For now, we will stick to the basic view. Inside the Convert to Symbol dialog box are three settings to be determined next: the Name, Behavior, and Registration point of the symbol.

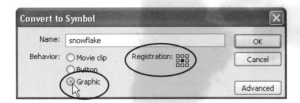

5. For **Name**, type **snowflake**; for **Behavior**, select **Graphic**; and for **Registration**, make sure the box in the middle of the square is selected. Click **OK**.

Note: You'll learn about movie clip and button symbols in later chapters. They are more complex to explain and require that you understand graphic symbols first. For this reason, this chapter focuses exclusively on graphic symbols.

NOTE | What Is a Registration Point?

When you convert a shape into a symbol, Flash MX 2004 needs to know where you want the center point to be located on that shape. Why? It becomes very important when you create animation using rotation because the symbol will rotate around its registration point. If this seems a bit abstract to you, it will make more sense once you have completed Exercise 6 later in the chapter. For now, make sure the registration point is in the middle.

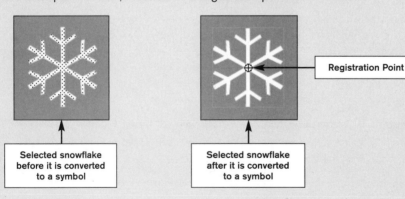

Selected snowflake
before it is converted
to a symbol

Selected snowflake
after it is converted
to a symbol

Registration Point

Once you click OK, the snowflake on the Stage will change slightly. Notice the bounding box and the circle with a crosshair in the middle of the snowflake. This provides visual feedback that your snowflake is now a graphic symbol. The circle and crosshair in the middle of the snowflake act as a marker, telling you where the center (or registration point) of the symbol is. This is an important indicator because it affects how all of the instances (which you will learn about in the next exercise) of this symbol are rotated and scaled. You will also learn how to rotate and scale instances later in this chapter.

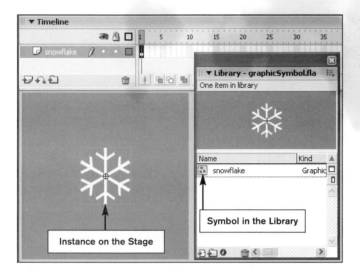

6. After you click **OK** in the **Convert to Symbol** dialog box, notice that you now have two snowflakes in your project file: the **snowflake symbol**, which is located in the **Library**, and an **instance** (a copy of the original symbol) on the **Stage**. Instances are copies of symbols from the Library brought to the Stage.

Congratulations! You have just made your first graphic symbol.

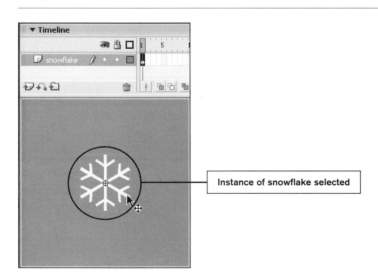

7. With the **Selection** tool, click the **snowflake** instance on the **Stage** to select it.

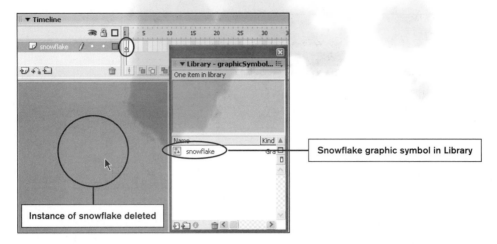

Snowflake graphic symbol in Library

Instance of snowflake deleted

8. Press the **Delete** key to delete it from the **Stage**. Notice that the snowflake is no longer on Stage and that on Frame 1 of the snowflake layer there is a blank keyframe instead of a keyframe. Did the symbol get deleted from the project file, too? No, fortunately the snowflake graphic symbol is safely saved in the Library.

*Note: Don't worry if you delete an instance from the Stage; you can still find it in the Library. However, if you delete a symbol from the Library, it may be gone forever. If you accidentally do this, quickly undo the deletion by choosing **Edit > Undo Library Item(s)** or **Ctrl+Z** (Windows) or **Cmd+Z** (Mac). You can also choose **File > Revert** to return the project file back to the last time you saved it.*

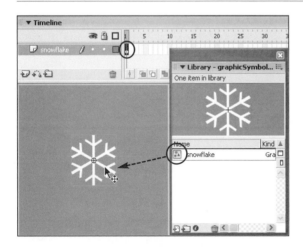

9. In the **Library**, click on the **snowflake** graphic symbol icon, and drag it onto the **Stage** to add it back to the **Stage** again. When you release the mouse button, an instance of the **snowflake** is placed on the **Stage**. Notice also that a keyframe is placed in **Frame 1** of the **snowflake** layer.

10. Save and close the file.

In the next exercise, you will learn to work with symbol instances.

TIP | Five Ways to Create a Symbol

There are five different ways to create a symbol when you are working with Flash MX 2004. You can create a symbol using artwork that already exists on the Stage or create a new symbol from scratch on a blank Stage. The five ways are explained here:

1. Select the artwork on the **Stage** and drag it into the **Library**, as you did in Step 4 of the previous exercise. This will turn the artwork you select into a symbol.

2. Select the artwork on the **Stage** and choose **Modify > Convert to Symbol**, or use the shortcut key **F8**. This will also turn the artwork you select into a symbol.

3. Choose **Insert > New Symbol** or use the shortcut key **Ctrl+F8** (Windows) or **Cmd+F8** (Mac). This places you in symbol editing mode with a blank canvas ready for you to add or create artwork.

4. Choose **New Symbol** from the **Library Options** menu in the upper-right corner of the **Library**. This places you in symbol editing mode with a blank canvas ready for you to add or create artwork.

5. Click the **Create New Symbol** button in the lower-left corner of the **Library**. This will place you in symbol editing mode with a blank canvas ready for you to add or create artwork.

2. <u>_____</u>**Creating Symbol Instances**

In the last exercise, you learned how to create a symbol. In this exercise, you will learn how to create and modify instances of a symbol. Instances are copies of the original symbol that can be modified individually without affecting the symbol in the Library. You will learn to do this in the following steps.

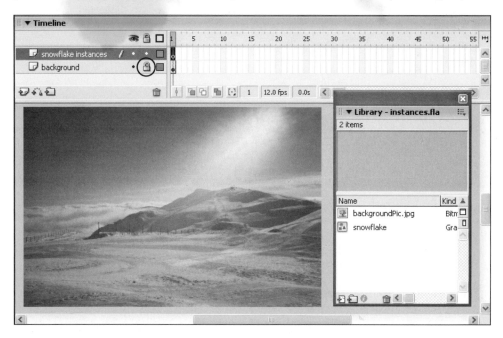

1. Open the **instances.fla** file from the **chap_06** folder. This file contains two layers: a layer named **background**, which contains a bitmap image, and a layer named **snowflake instances**, where you will place instances of the **snowflake** graphic symbol you created in the last exercise. The **background** layer has been locked so that you don't accidentally edit that layer.

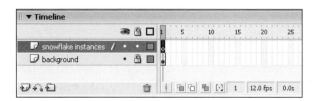

2. Select the **snowflake instances** layer.

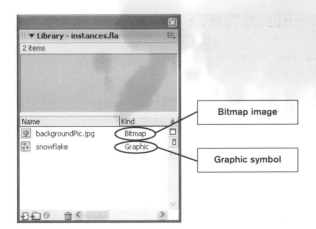

3. Make sure the **Library** is open. If it's not, choose **Window > Library**, or press **Ctrl+L** (Windows) or **Cmd+L** (Mac). Notice that there are two items in the Library: the **snowflake** symbol and something called **backgroundPic.jpg**. You might be wondering how those elements got there. The snowflake was saved as a symbol in this project file, and it automatically appears in the Library whenever you open this project file, just like the snowflake symbol you created in Exercise 1. The backgroundPic item is a bitmap that was also saved as a Library element and is used for the background layer.

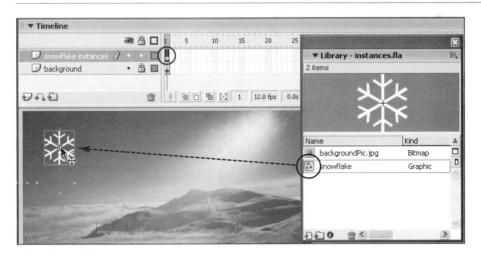

4. In the **Library**, click the **snowflake** graphic symbol icon, and drag it onto the **Stage**. When you release the mouse button, an instance of the **snowflake** is placed on the **Stage**. Notice also that a keyframe is placed in Frame 1 of the **snowflake instances** layer.

One point to remember is that symbols are stored in the Library and instances are located on the Stage. From every symbol, you can create as many instances as you want.

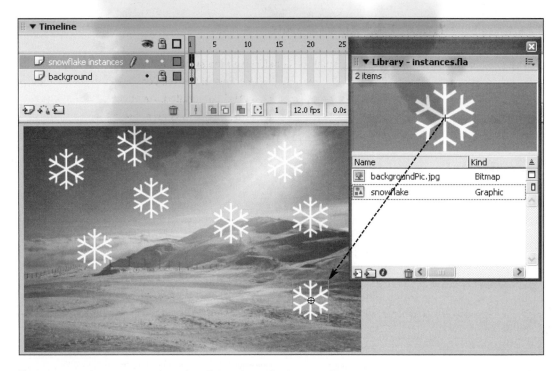

5. Click and drag **seven** more **snowflakes** from the **Library**. This will create a total of eight instances on your **Stage**. You can also insert instances by clicking in the Library's **Preview** window and dragging an instance onto the **Stage**.

*Clicking and dragging from the **Library** is one way to create instances on your **Stage**, but you can also **Ctrl+drag** (Windows) or **Option+drag** (Mac) an instance on the **Stage** to create a duplicate of it without opening the **Library**.*

6. Save the changes you made to this file. Keep this file open for the next exercise. You will learn how to edit symbols next.

3. ————————**Editing Symbols**

The instances on your Stage have a special relationship with the symbol in the Library. This is often referred to as a parent/child relationship. One of the advantages of this relationship is that if you change a symbol in the Library, all of the instances on your Stage will be updated. As you can imagine, this can save you a lot of time when you need to make large updates across an entire project. This ability to make quick—and sometimes large—updates is one of the powerful advantages of using symbols and instances. In this exercise, you will modify the appearance of the snowflake symbol to change all eight instances on the Stage.

1. The file from the previous exercise should still be open. If you closed it, go ahead and open the **instances.fla** file from the **chap_06** folder.

2. Make sure the **Library** is open. If it's not, press **Ctrl+L** (Windows) or **Cmd+L** (Mac) to open it now.

Your Stage should look similar to the one shown here. If for some reason it does not, refer to the previous exercise to learn how to create multiple instances of the snowflake symbol.

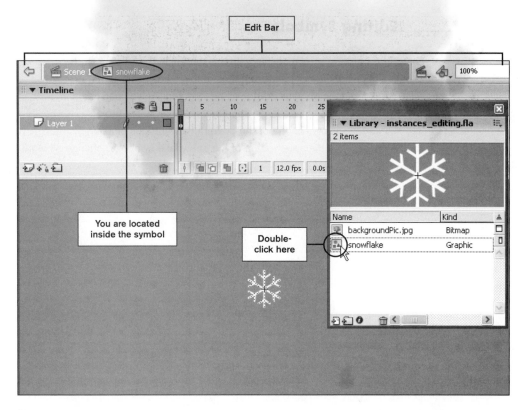

3. In the **Library**, double-click on the **graphic symbol** icon to the left of the **snowflake** symbol name. Your **Stage** will change, because you are now editing the **Timeline** for the symbol, where you can create or modify its contents. At this point, you are no longer working in the Main Timeline. Notice that the gray (work) area around your Stage is gone, as is the blue bounding box around the symbol. When you're in symbol editing mode (inside a symbol), you will not see the work area, unless you are using the Edit in Place feature, which you will learn about later in this exercise. Notice also that the edit bar above the Stage shows two names: Scene 1 and snowflake. This is another indicator that you are no longer working on the Main Timeline. Instead, you are inside the edit mode and Timeline for the snowflake graphic symbol.

TIP | Know Your Location

There are several ways to get into symbol editing mode. It's so easy to get into and out of this mode that you may not even be aware that you have switched views, so be constantly aware of where you are while you work. Keep an eye on the edit bar and make sure that you are drawing, animating, or creating in the correct location of your project.

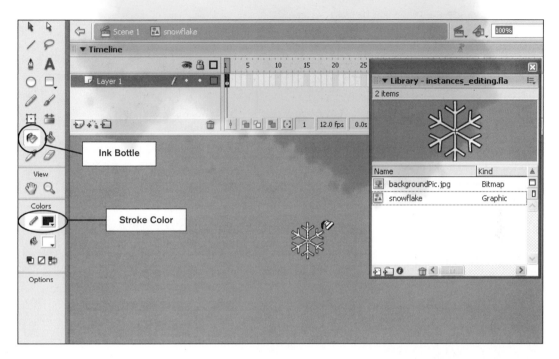

4. In the **Toolbar**, select the **Ink Bottle** tool, and select **black** for the **Stroke Color**. Click on the **snowflake** to add a stroke to the snowflake shape. Notice that as soon as you click on the shape with the Ink Bottle tool, the Preview window in the Library is updated instantly to reflect the change you made.

Note: *In the Flash MX 2004 documentation, the terms "outline" and "stroke" are at times used inter-changeably. As you may recall from Chapter 3, "Drawing and Color Tools," you can add strokes (sometimes called outlines) to objects that don't already have a stroke applied to them with the Ink Bottle, as you did in the previous step. You can also modify an existing stroke by selecting it and then changing its width and appearance using the Properties inspector.*

5. In the edit bar, click on the **Scene 1** link to return to the **Main Timeline**. You should see the bitmap with the snow and sky again.

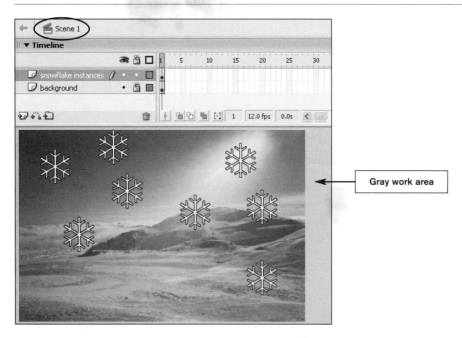

Gray work area

As soon as you click on the Scene 1 link, the gray work area appears again, and you see only the Scene 1 name, without the snowflake name next to it. Notice also that all of the instances of the snowflake now have a black stroke around them. Every time you modify a symbol, it affects all of the instances you have in your project file, just as you saw here. This can be a very powerful way to make changes throughout your project.

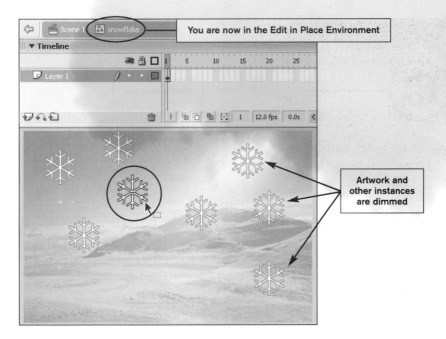

6. With the **Selection** tool, select a **snowflake** instance on the **Stage** and double-click on it. This will allow you to edit the symbol in place, which means in the context of the other instances on the Stage. When you edit a symbol in place, all the other objects on the Stage are dimmed to differentiate them from the symbol you are editing. You can also edit the symbol in place by choosing **Edit > Edit in Place**.

TIP | Techniques for Editing Symbols

Editing an instance in place (double-clicking on the instance on the Stage) will produce the same end result as editing the symbol in the Library (double-clicking on the graphic symbol icon to the left of the symbol name in the Library). Both techniques change the appearance of the master symbol as well as all of its instances. The difference between the two techniques is that when you edit the symbol in the Library, you cannot see the Main Timeline. When you edit an instance in place, you see a dimmed version of the Stage, and you can preview your changes in context with the rest of the Stage on the Main Timeline before returning to the Main Timeline.

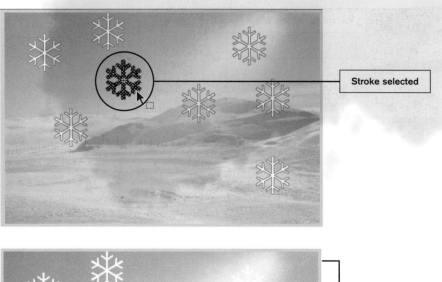

Stroke selected

Stroke deleted from all
snowflake instances

7. Using the **Selection** tool, double-click on the **stroke** around the **snowflake** to select it. Press the **Delete** key to remove it. Notice that the strokes on all the other snowflake instances have been deleted as well. Again, each time you edit a symbol, all the other instances of that symbol get updated as well. Next, instead of the stroke, you'll make a change to the fill this time.

8. Use the **Selection** tool to select a **snowflake** shape on the Stage.

9. In the **Properties inspector**, click on the **Fill Color** box and choose a shade of **blue**. Because the snowflake was already selected, Flash MX 2004 automatically updates the color of the snowflake as soon as you select a color. Again, notice that all the other instances of the snowflake change color as well!

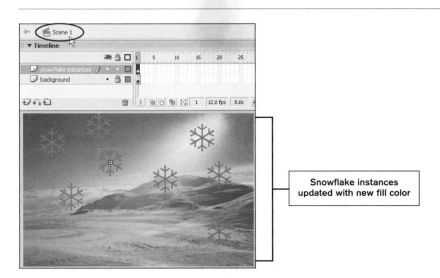

Snowflake instances updated with new fill color

10. In the edit bar, click on the **Scene 1** link to return to the **Main Timeline**. You should see the background bitmap and the snowflake instances in full color.

11. Save the changes you made to this file and keep it open for the next exercise.

4. ————————Editing Symbol Instances

In the previous exercise, you learned how to modify a symbol to make changes to all of the instances on the Stage. But what do you do if you want to change the color of only one instance or of each instance individually? You can do this by selecting the instance on the Stage in the Main Timeline and modifying the Color setting in the Properties inspector. The Properties inspector will let you change the tint, brightness, and alpha settings of symbol instances. This is the only way to change the color values of an instance because the Paint Bucket and Brush tools work only on shapes, not on symbol instances. In this exercise, you will use the Properties inspector and the Free Transform tool to change the appearance of individual snowflakes.

1. The file from the previous exercise should still be open. If it's not, open the **instances.fla** file from the **chap_06** folder.

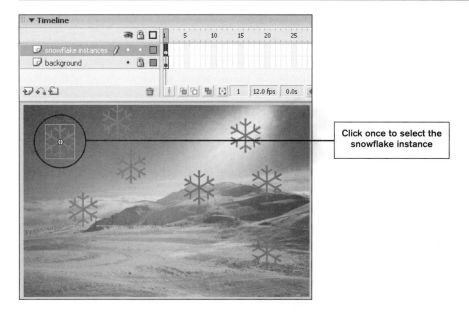

Click once to select the snowflake instance

2. Click to select the **snowflake** instance in the upper-left corner of the **Stage**.

It's very important that you select the snowflake instance by clicking on it only once. If you double-click it accidentally, you will be in symbol editing mode to edit the symbol, not the instance. If this happens, go back to the Main Timeline by clicking on the Scene 1 link in the edit bar.

3. Make sure the **Properties inspector** is open. If it's not, choose **Window > Properties** or use the shortcut **Ctrl+F3** (Windows) or **Cmd+F3** (Mac) to open it.

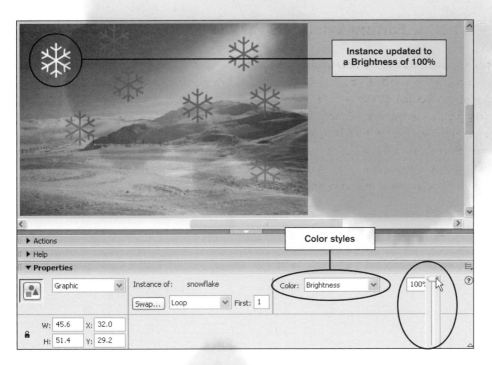

4. From the **Color** box in the **Properties inspector**, choose **Brightness**. Click the slider to the right of the menu and drag it up to **100%**. This will increase the brightness level of the selected object as you drag up.

Note: The Brightness option controls the brightness value of the instance and has a range of −100% to 100%, with −100% being completely black and 100% being completely white.

5. Click to select a different **snowflake** instance on the **Stage**. You can choose any snowflake you want.

6. From the **Color** box in the **Properties inspector**, choose **Tint**. The Tint option applies a tint to the base color of your instance.

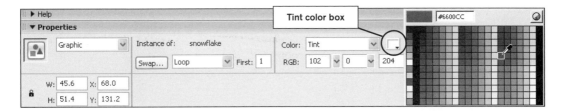

7. Click inside the **Tint color** box, and from the pop-up color palette, select a shade of **purple**.

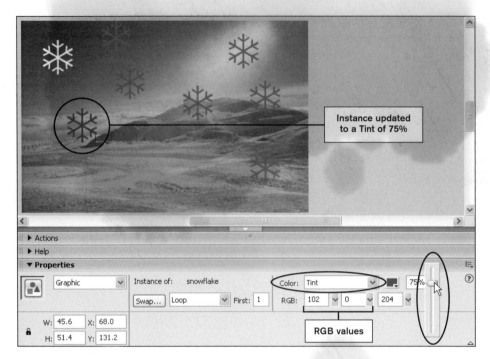

8. Click and drag the **Tint** slider to **75%**. As you drag the slider up, notice how the color becomes brighter. The Tint option has a range of 0% (no tint) to 100% (fully saturated). Basically, this changes the amount of color that is applied to the instance. It also changes the RGB values in the Properties inspector.

Note: *You control the color of the instance by modifying the percentage of the tint being applied and the individual RGB (red, green, and blue) values. The Tint option is the only way you can change the color of an instance, other than using the advanced settings, where you can set the RGB values. This option also changes both the Fill and Stroke settings to the value you specify. You cannot change these settings separately when editing the instance; this can be done only by editing the symbol.*

9. Click to select another **snowflake** instance on the **Stage**. Select one that has not been modified yet.

10. From the **Color** box in the **Properties inspector**, choose **Alpha**. This option, which has a range of 100% (opaque) to 0% (transparent), lets you control the transparency value of the selected instance.

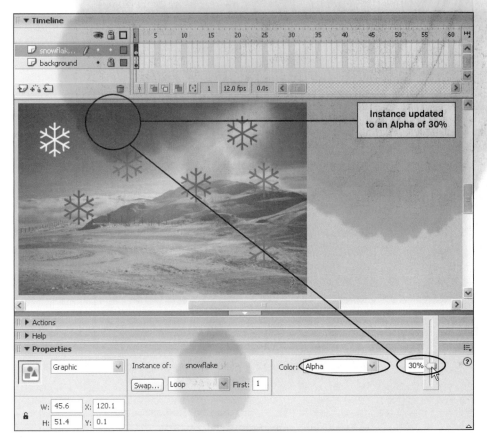

11. Click and drag the **Alpha** slider down to **0%**. Watch the selected snowflake disappear as you drag the slider down. Return the **Alpha** slider to **30%**.

In the next few steps, you will learn about the Advanced option in the Color Styles drop-down menu. This option lets you modify multiple settings for a selected object. For example, you can use this option to adjust the Tint and Alpha settings of the selected instance. The best way to learn about it is by using it, and that's exactly what you are going to do.

12. Click to select another unmodified **snowflake** instance on the **Stage**.

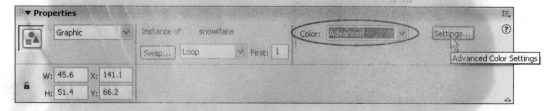

13. From the **Color** box in the **Properties inspector,** choose **Advanced** from the drop-down menu. Click the **Settings** button.

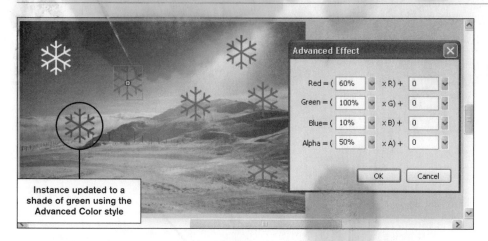

Instance updated to a shade of green using the Advanced Color style

14. In the **Advanced Effect** dialog box, click the arrow and drag the **Red** slider to **60%**. Click and drag the **Blue** slider down to **10%**. Click and drag the **Alpha** slider to **50%**. The end result should be a snowflake that is a nice shade of green.

The left column of fields in the Advanced Effect dialog box allows you to manipulate the colors using percentages, and the right column of fields allows you to manipulate the colors using numbers that correspond with color values.

15. Go ahead and practice changing the **Brightness, Tint, Alpha,** or a combination of these using the **Advanced** feature for the remaining snowflakes. It never hurts to practice! For your reference, a chart is provided at the end of this exercise that outlines all of the options in the Color drop-down menu.

NOTE | Removing Color Styles

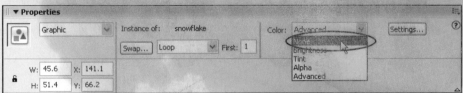

Up to this point in the exercise, you have added many different color styles to the instances on your Stage. If you want to remove the styles you have applied to an instance, you can simply select the instance and choose **None** from the **Color** drop-down menu. This will turn off any color styles you have applied and restore the instance to its original condition.

So far, you've gained some experience in changing symbol instances by modifying their brightness, tint, and alpha. You can also rotate, scale, and skew instances. In the following steps, you will use the Free Transform tool to modify the instances on your Stage.

16. Click to select another unmodified **snowflake** on the **Stage**. It doesn't really matter which one you select because you will eventually select them all.

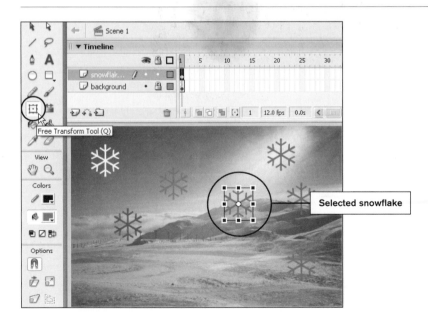

Selected snowflake

17. In the **Toolbar**, select the **Free Transform** tool.

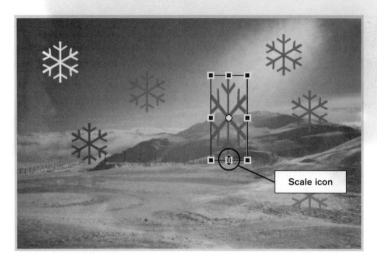

Scale icon

18. Click on the middle handle on the bottom of the **snowflake** and drag down. This will increase the height of the snowflake.

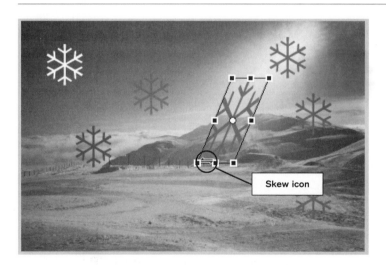

Skew icon

19. Move your cursor between the bottom left and middle handles (slightly above the handles) until you see the **skew cursor** icon, as shown in the picture here. Once you see the icon, click and drag to the left. This will skew the selected snowflake.

Selected snowflake

20. Click to select another unmodified **snowflake** instance on the **Stage**.

Scale icon

21. With the **Free Transform** tool, click and drag diagonally on one of the corner handles. This will scale the snowflake to a larger size.

*Tip: If you hold down the **Shift** key while you drag one of the handles, the snowflake will scale proportionally on all sides.*

Selected snowflake

22. Click to select another unmodified **snowflake** instance on the **Stage**.

Rotate icon

23. With the **Free Transform** tool, move your cursor over a corner handle until the **rotate** icon appears, as shown in the picture here. Click and drag down. This will rotate the selected snowflake.

NOTE | Changing the Registration Point

When using the Free Transform tool, you might have noticed that the circle in the center of an instance serves as an anchor from which position, rotation, and scale originate. It is possible to move the center point (registration point) if you want to.

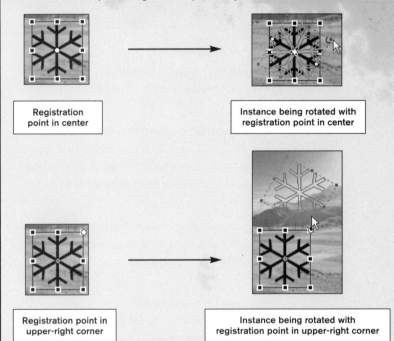

Registration
point in center

Instance being rotated with
registration point in center

Registration point in
upper-right corner

Instance being rotated with
registration point in upper-right corner

To change the registration point, select the instance with the **Free Transform** tool and then click and drag the center circle to a new location. From then on, any transformations you make will originate from this new position. Use this technique when you want to rotate from a corner; you can even move the registration point off the image to rotate on a distant axis. You will learn how to create an animation by changing the registration point of an instance in the last exercise of this chapter.

24. Go ahead and select the last **snowflake** on the **Stage**. Using the **Free Transform** tool, apply any transformation you like. Remember, practice makes perfect, so have some fun creating your own transformation to the last unchanged snowflake instance.

25. When you are finished, save your changes and close this file. You won't need it again.

Color Styles

The following chart explains the different options available in the Color drop-down menu in the Properties inspector. As you learned in this exercise, the color styles options can be used to change the color and alpha properties of an instance.

Color Styles Options	
Option	**Description**
Brightness	Controls the brightness (lightness or darkness) of the selected symbol. The percentage slider goes from −100% (black) to 100% (white).
Tint	Allows you to tint a selected symbol a specific RGB color. You can choose a color from the Tint color palette and use the slider to modify the percentage of that specific color. You can also choose a color by moving the R, G, and B color sliders up and down.
Alpha	Allows you to change the transparency of a selected instance. Using the slider, you can have a completely opaque instance (100%) or a completely transparent instance (0%), or any value in-between.
Advanced	A complex option that lets you adjust the tint and alpha of an instance. The *Using Macromedia Flash MX 2004* manual has a good explanation of the complex mathematical equations involved with this panel. You may find it easier to just play with the different settings to get the right look.

5. ———————————Animating Graphic Symbols

Up until now, you have been working with static graphic symbols. Now you will learn how to create a graphic symbol that contains animation. When you use animated graphic symbols in Flash MX 2004, it's important to understand that the number of frames inside the symbol have to relate to the number of frames that are set on the Main Timeline. This will make more sense to you after you try it.

In this exercise, you will modify the snowflake graphic symbol and add a simple shape tween animation to its Timeline to convert it into an animated graphic symbol. The end result will be a snowflake that turns into a small snowball and fades away.

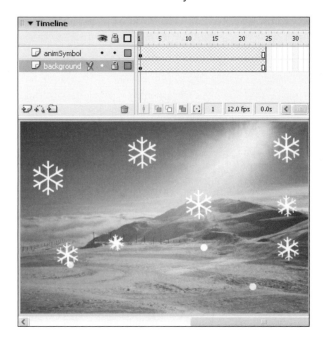

1. Open the **animSymbol_Final.fla** file from the **chap_06** folder. Choose **Control > Test Movie** to preview the animation. It's snowing! You will play Mother Nature and create the snowing animation next.

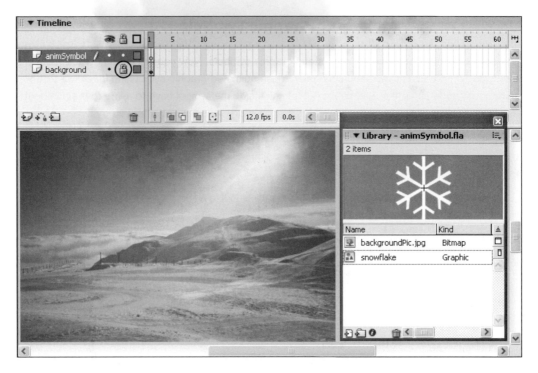

2. Close **animSymbol_Final.fla** and open the file named **animSymbol.fla** from the **chap_06** folder. This file is similar to the one you started with in Exercise 2. It contains two layers: one named **background**, which contains a bitmap background image, and one named **animSymbol**, where you will place the animated graphic symbol you are about to create. The background layer has been locked so that you don't accidentally modify that layer.

3. Make sure the **Library** is open. If it's not, press **Ctrl+L** (Windows) or **Cmd+L** (Mac) to open it. The Library contains two items: **backgroundPic.jpg**, which is the background image, and a **snowflake** graphic symbol, which you will animate next.

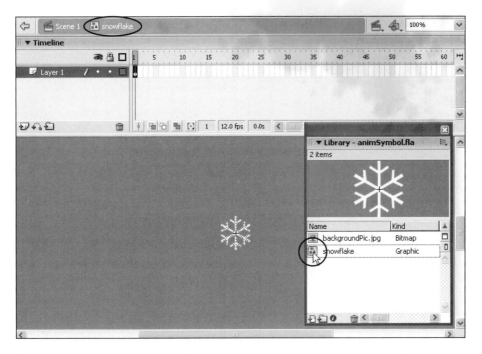

4. In the **Library**, double-click on the small **graphic symbol** icon to the left of the word **snowflake**. This will take you into editing mode for this symbol. Notice that the contents of the Stage have changed and that the snowflake graphic symbol icon appears in the edit bar. These are two clues to indicate that you are in symbol editing mode.

In the following steps, you will create a shape tween animation that will make the snowflake look as though it is falling as it changes into a small snowball and fades away. Keep in mind that you are creating this animation of your snowflake on the Graphic Symbol Timeline, which is different from the Main Timeline in Scene 1. This means that the animation will affect all the instances of this symbol, because you are editing the master symbol.

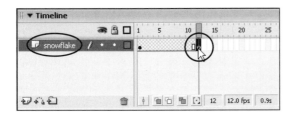

5. In the **Timeline**, rename **Layer 1** to **snowflake** and press **F7** on **Frame 12** to add a blank keyframe.

Remember, a blank keyframe identifies a change and does not copy any artwork from the previous keyframe.

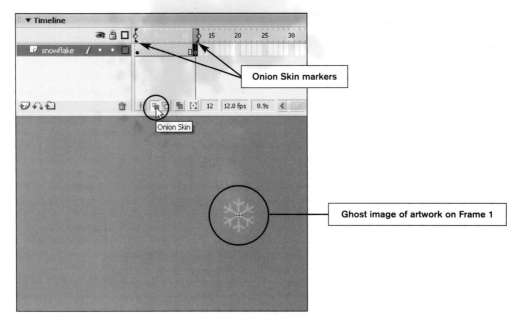

Onion Skin markers

Onion Skin

Ghost image of artwork on Frame 1

6. At the bottom of the **Timeline**, click on the **Onion Skin** icon. Make sure that the **Start Onion Skin** marker is anchored at **Frame 1** and the **End Onion Skin** marker is anchored at **Frame 12**. By turning on onion skinning, you will be able to see a faint ghost image of the artwork in Frame 1 and add artwork relative to it.

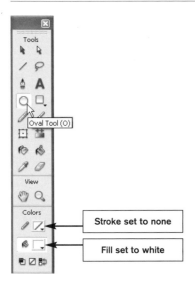

Oval Tool (O)

Stroke set to none

Fill set to white

7. In the **Toolbar**, select the **Oval** tool and set the **Stroke** to **none** and the **Fill** to **white**.

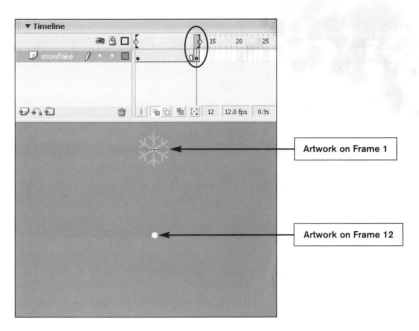

Artwork on Frame 1

Artwork on Frame 12

8. Make sure the playhead is on **Frame 12**. With the **Oval** tool, draw a small **snowball** just below the ghost image of the **snowflake**. Notice the new keyframe on Frame 12. You will create the tween between the two keyframes in the following steps.

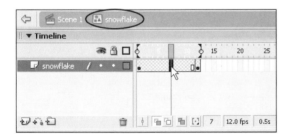

9. In the **snowflake Graphic Symbol Timeline**, click anywhere between **Frame 1** and **Frame 12** to select one of the frames.

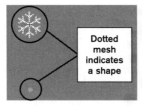

10. Make sure the **Properties inspector** is open. If it is not, press **Ctrl+F3** (Windows) or **Cmd+F3** (Mac). Since the snowflake and the snowball are both shapes, choose **Shape** from the **Tween** drop-down menu.

11. Press **Enter** (Windows) or **Return** (Mac) to get a quick preview of what your animation will look like. Notice that the snowflake turns into a snowball in about 1 second (12 frames ÷ 12 fps = 1 second).

You just have one more tween to add.

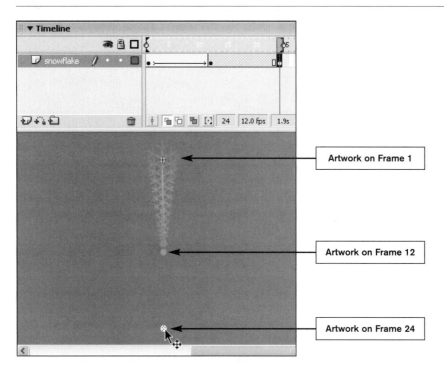

12. Press **F6** on **Frame 24** to add a keyframe. With the **Selection** tool, move the **snowball** circle on **Frame 24** down, as shown in the picture here.

Remember, a keyframe identifies a change in the Timeline and copies the artwork of the previous keyframe. In this case, you copied the artwork of the snowball on Frame 12 to Frame 24 and then moved the artwork down. You will make the snowball invisible next.

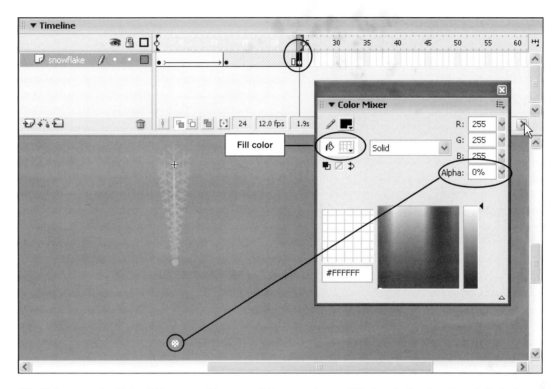

13. Make sure the **Color Mixer** panel is open. If it's not, choose **Window > Design Panels > Color Mixer** or press **Shift+F9**. With the **snowball** still selected on **Frame 24**, make sure the **Fill color** is selected in the **Color Mixer** panel and set the **Alpha** to **0%**. This will make the **snowball** in **Frame 24** transparent. Click anywhere off the **snowball** to deselect it, and you will see it disappear!

The snowflake will turn into a snowball from Frame 1 to 12, and then the snowball will disappear from Frame 12 to 24. You will add the second tween next.

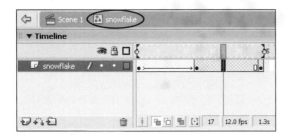

14. In the **snowflake Graphic Symbol Timeline**, click anywhere between **Frame 12** and **Frame 24** to select one of the frames.

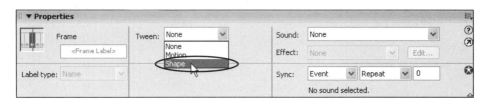

15. Choose **Shape** from the **Tween** drop-down menu. This adds the tween to make the animation of the snowball fall and disappear. Before you preview your animation, you will turn onion skinning off next.

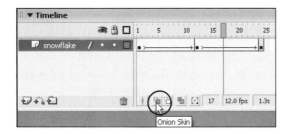

16. At the bottom of the **Timeline**, click the **Onion Skin** icon to turn off onion skinning. Notice that the Onion Skin markers have disappeared.

17. Move the playhead to **Frame 1** and press **Enter/Return** to preview the entire animation. As the snowflake falls, it should turn into a snowball, and then the snowball should fade away, all in about 2 seconds (24 frames ÷ 12 fps = 2 seconds). Neat!

TIP | Where Do I Change the Alpha Transparency?

To change the Alpha transparency of an instance, you need to use the Properties inspector, which you learned in Exercise 4 of this chapter.

To change the Alpha transparency of a shape (dotted mesh), you need to use the Color Mixer panel, which you learned in Step 13 of this exercise.

Changing the Alpha transparency for an instance

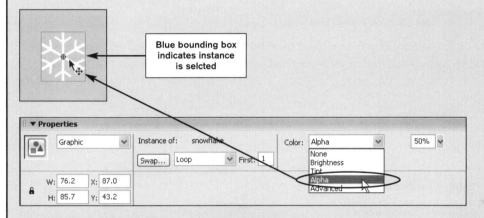

Changing the Alpha transparency for a shape

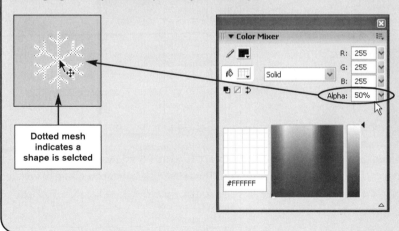

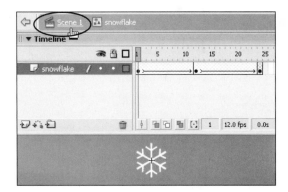

18. When you are happy with your animation, click the **Scene 1** link in the edit bar to return to the **Main Timeline**. You will add the snowflake animated graphic symbol to the Main Timeline next.

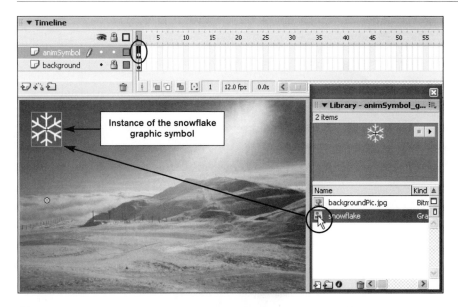

Instance of the snowflake graphic symbol

19. Select **Frame 1** of the **animSymbol** layer. From the **Library** (**Ctrl+L** [Windows] or **Cmd+L** [Mac]), drag the **snowflake** graphic symbol onto the **Stage**. This will add an instance of the animated snowflake graphic symbol to the Main Timeline, Scene 1. Notice that there is a keyframe in Frame 1 of the **animSymbol** layer now.

20. Choose **Control > Test Movie** to preview your movie. But wait, the snowflake is not animating! Why? Close the **Preview** window to return to the **Main Timeline**. You will learn how to fix this next.

The Timeline of the animated graphic symbol is directly related to the Main Timeline (the current scene—in this case, Scene 1) of the project. This means that if the animated graphic symbol is 24 frames in length, the Main Timeline also needs to be at least 24 frames in length. Currently, the Main Timeline is 1 frame in length; therefore, only one frame is being displayed. To fix the animation, you need to extend the Main Timeline to be at least as long as the Timeline of the animated graphic symbol, which is 24 frames long.

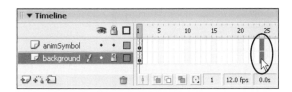

21. Click in **Frame 24** of the **animSymbol** layer and drag down to **Frame 24** of the **background** layer. This will select the range of frames between the layers.

22. Press **F5** to insert frames and extend the **Timeline** of both layers to **24** frames in length. Notice that Frames 2 through 24 in both layers are now shaded in gray because you added frames. Now the Main Timeline is at least as long as the Timeline of the animated graphic symbol, which means that you will see the entire animation play. Your snowflake is about to animate!

Note: You just extended both layers so that the content of these layers is displayed for the same length of time. For example, extending just the animSymbol layer would cause the background layer to disappear when the playhead reached Frame 2. Extending both layers to Frame 24 ensures that all of the layers are displayed for the same length of time.

23. Choose **Control > Test Movie** again to preview your movie. Cool—this time your snowflake is animating! Notice that the animation starts out as a snowflake, turns into a snowball, and disappears as it falls towards the ground. You will add more instances of the snowflake graphic symbol to the Stage to create the effect of falling snow next.

24. Close the **Preview** window.

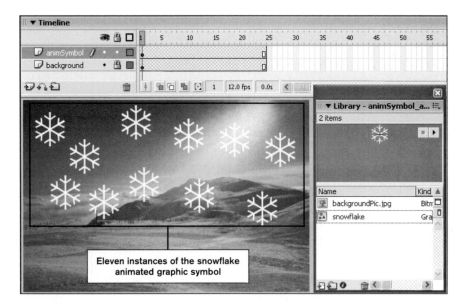

Eleven instances of the snowflake animated graphic symbol

25. On the **Main Timeline**, make sure the Playhead is over **Frame 1**. Drag **10** more instances of the animated **snowflake** symbol onto the **Stage**, to make a total of **11 snowflakes** on the **Stage**.

26. Choose **Control > Test Movie**. This will open a new window with a preview of your movie.

Notice that the snowflakes are all falling in unison, which doesn't look very natural. The following steps will show you how to change the starting frames of each animated graphic symbol to create a more realistic looking snowfall.

27. Close the **Preview** window.

28. Click to select a **snowflake** instance on the **Stage**.

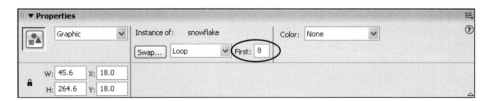

29. In the middle of the **Properties inspector**, enter any number between **1** and **24** in the **First** field. This field sets the frame on which the animation begins. Since the snowflake animated graphic symbol has a total of 24 frames, you can enter a number between 1 and 24.

30. Repeat this process for all of the **snowflakes** on your **Stage**, entering a different **First** value for each one. By changing the starting frame of each animation, you will change the starting point of each animation, and that will produce a more realistic snowfall effect.

---

31. Choose **Control > Test Movie** to preview your movie. It's snowing! When you are done previewing your movie, go ahead and close the **Preview** window.

Could you have achieved this same effect using a different method? The answer is "yes." In Flash MX 2004, you can often produce the same effect in a number of different ways. However, some ways are more efficient than others. The exercise you just completed outlines an efficient way of using one symbol to create several instances that look and behave very differently. You could have created and animated each of the snowflakes separately to produce the same effect, but that would require much more work.

---

32. Save the changes you made to this file and close it.

> ### NOTE | Looping
>
> You might have noticed that the 24-frame animation of the falling snowflakes played over and over again when you tested the movie. This type of behavior is called a loop, which is an animation sequence that repeats over and over. Flash MX 2004 defaults to looping whatever is on the Stage, unless you tell it not to through the use of ActionScript. You will learn about ActionScript in Chapter 11, "*ActionScript Basics and Behaviors.*"

Great job! You've made it this far; now you have only one more exercise to go. Next, you will learn how to modify the registration points of an object to create some interesting animation effects.

6. ———**Animating Instances by Modifying the Registration Point**

Now that you know how to create animations using symbols and instances, you will learn how to create more interesting animations by changing the registration point of an object. By default, the registration point of an object is located in the center. When the registration point of an object is moved, any transformations will rotate or move in relation to the new registration point or axis. This technique can create some interesting effects.

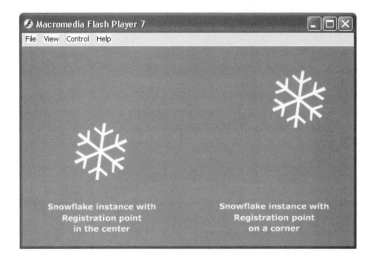

1. Open the **registrationPoint_Final.fla** file from the **chap_06** folder. Choose **Control >Test Movie** to preview the animation. Notice that the two snowflakes are animating round and round but each is rotating on a different axis.

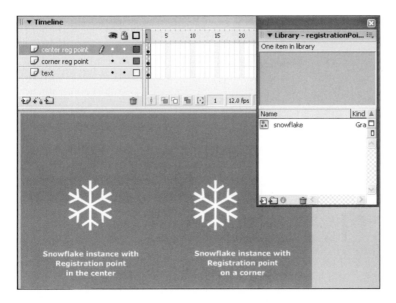

2. Close **registrationPoint_Final.fla** and open the file named **registrationPoint.fla** from the **chap_06** folder. This file contains three layers: **center reg point**, which contains an instance of the snowflake graphic symbol that will rotate around its center axis; **corner reg point**, which contains another instance of the snowflake graphic symbol that will rotate on a corner axis; and a layer named **text**, which just contains a description of the two snowflake instances.

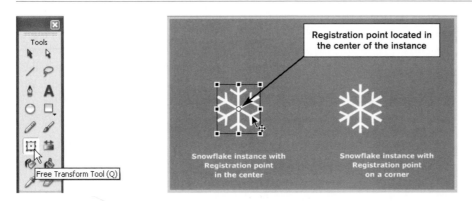

3. Select the **Free Transform** tool from the **Toolbar** and click the **left snowflake** instance to select it. Notice that its registration point is already in the center of the snowflake instance. You do not have to move the center point for this instance. Instead you will create a motion tween that will make the snowflake rotate on its center axis clockwise two times.

Note: *In order to modify the registration point of a symbol you must use the Free Transform tool.*

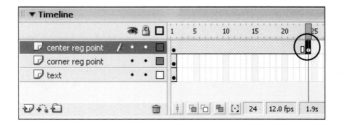

4. In the **Timeline**, on the layer named **center reg point**, select **Frame 24** and press **F6** to insert a keyframe. You will add a motion tween next.

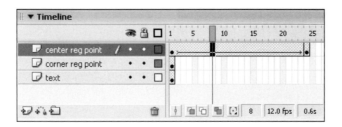

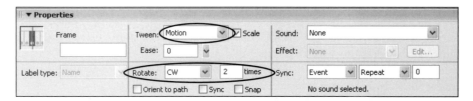

5. Make sure the **Properties inspector** is open. If it's not, choose **Window > Properties**. In the layer named **center reg point**, select anywhere between the two keyframes to select a frame. In the **Properties inspector**, choose **Motion** from the **Tween** drop-down menu, choose **CW** from the **Rotate** drop-down menu, and enter **2** for the **times** field. This will make the snowflake instance on the left side of the Stage rotate on its center axis counter clockwise (CW) two times.

*Note: Why select **Motion** instead of **Shape** from the **Tween** drop-down menu? In this exercise, you are working with symbols on the Stage, rather than shapes. Tweening symbols requires that you select Motion, whereas if you were tweening shapes, you would select Shape from the Tween drop-down menu. You will learn more about Motion Tweening in the next chapter.*

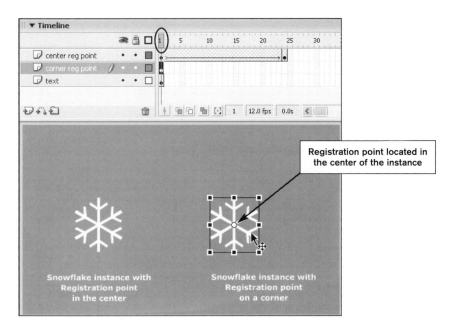

Registration point located in the center of the instance

Snowflake instance with Registration point in the center

Snowflake instance with Registration point on a corner

6. Bring the playhead to **Frame 1**. With the **Free Transform** tool, select the instance of the **snowflake** on the **right side** of the **Stage**. Notice that the registration point of the snowflake instance is in the center. You will move the registration point to the top-right corner next.

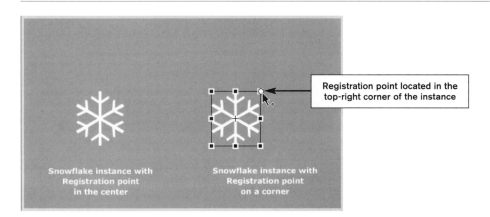

Registration point located in the top-right corner of the instance

Snowflake instance with Registration point in the center

Snowflake instance with Registration point on a corner

7. With the **Free Transform** tool, click and drag the **registration point** to the top-right corner of the snowflake instance.

Note: *The registration point is the axis on which the instance will rotate.*

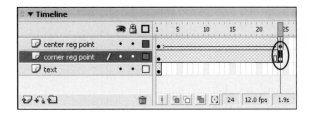

8. In the **Timeline**, on the layer named **corner reg point**, select **Frame 24** and press **F6** to insert a keyframe. You will add a motion tween next.

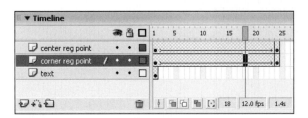

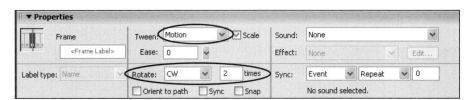

9. In the layer named **corner reg point**, select anywhere between the two keyframes to select a frame. In the **Properties inspector**, choose **Motion** from the **Tween** drop-down menu, select **CW** from the **Rotate** drop-down menu, and enter **2** for the **times** field. This will make the snowflake instance on the right side of the Stage rotate around its top-right corner registration point two times. You are almost done—you will add frames to the **text** layer next.

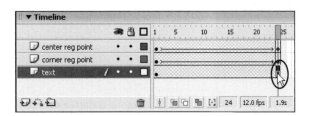

10. In the **text** layer, select **Frame 24** and press **F5** to add frames up to **Frame 24**. This will ensure that the text layer is seen throughout the entire movie.

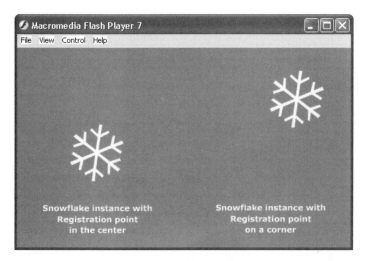

11. Choose **Control > Test Movie** to preview the snowflakes. Notice that the two snowflakes are animating round and round and that each is rotating on different axis! When you are done previewing your movie, go ahead and close the **Preview** window.

12. Save the changes you made and close this file. You won't need it again.

Congratulations, you made it! By now, you should feel a lot more comfortable working with symbols and instances and understand the role they can play in your projects. But you aren't finished yet. Future chapters on buttons and movie clips will continue this learning process. So don't stop now—you are just getting to the good stuff.

7.

Motion Tweening and Timeline Effects

Basic Motion Tweening	Tweening Effects
Editing Multiple Frames	Using a Motion Guide
Easing In and Easing Out	Exploding Text	Timeline Effect Assistants
Transition and Blur Timeline Effects

chap_07

Macromedia Flash MX 2004
H•O•T CD-ROM

Similar to shape tweening, **motion tweening** is a method of animation that takes the position and attributes of an object in a start keyframe, and the position and attributes of an object in an end keyframe, and calculates all the animation that will occur between the two. However, unlike shape tweening, motion tweening requires that you use symbols, groups, and text blocks, rather than shapes, to create animation. In addition to position, motion tweens can animate scale, tint, transparency, rotation, and distortion. Throughout the following exercises, you will learn much more than simple motion tweening, including how to edit multiple frames, how to use motion guides, and how to use Timeline Effects, which is new to Flash MX 2004.

Flash MX 2004 ships with several Timeline Effects grouped into three categories: Assistants, Effects, and Transform/Transition. These Timeline Effects help make automating Timeline tasks much easier. You will get a chance to work with some of these effects later in the chapter, but first it's important to understand the intricacies of shape tweening and motion tweening, so that you can create more complicated animations that Timeline Effects is not able to do.

Shape Tweening Versus Motion Tweening

When you start working in Flash MX 2004, you might be confused about which type of tween to choose: motion or shape. You may spend unnecessary time trying to figure out why your animation is not working when the solution turns out to be that you simply selected the wrong type of tween. The basic distinction between the two types of tweening is that with shape tweening, you use shapes to morph one simple shape into another, for example turning a red square into a blue circle or the shape of a snowboard into the letter X where the letter X is broken apart into a shape first. With motion tweening, you use groups, text, or symbols to create the effect. Use the following chart as a reference tool when deciding on the type of tween to use.

Tween Types Simplified					
	Shape	Group	Symbol	Text Blocks	Broken-Apart Text
				Xboard **X**board	**X**board
Shape tween	Yes	No	No	No	Yes
Motion tween	No	Yes	Yes	Yes	No

I. Basic Motion Tweening

This exercise demonstrates how to create a basic motion tween using a graphic symbol. You will create a motion tween from scratch starting with creating a graphic symbol first, because a motion tween works only with symbols, grouped objects, and editable text. Motion tweening is very simple, especially once you've learned shape tweening. The big difference is not in the technique but in understanding when to use which type of object among shape, group, symbol, text, or broken-apart text. You may find yourself referring back to the "Tween Types Simplified" chart often, since remembering the rules of objects and tweening is harder than the process itself.

1. Copy the **chap_07** folder, located on the **H•O•T CD-ROM**, to your hard drive. You need to have this folder on your hard drive in order to save changes to the files inside it.

2. Open the file **motionTween_Final.fla** inside the **chap_07** folder. Choose **Control > Test Movie** to preview the motion tween animation you are about to create. Notice that the snowboard that begins on the left side of the Stage travels up to the peak of the mountain and then does a jump off the lip of the peak and flips counterclockwise down to the bottom of the mountain on the right side of the Stage. You should also notice that the snowboarder changes in size and color as well. In the next two exercises, you will create this same animation of the snowboarder that tweens its position, size, and color.

3. When you are finished previewing the animation, close the **Preview** window as well as the **motionTween_Final.fla** file. Open the **motionTween.fla** file located inside the **chap_07** folder. Notice that this file contains two layers: a layer named **snowboarder**, which will contain the motion tween you are about to create in the following steps, and a layer named **background**, which contains a bitmap image of the little mountain. The **background** layer is locked to prevent you from editing it. In the **Library** (**Ctrl+L** [Windows] or **Cmd+L** [Mac]), there is only a bitmap image of the mountain called **jump.jpg**. Since motion tweening does not work on shapes, you will convert the shape of the snowboarder on the Stage to a graphic symbol next.

Note: You will learn all about bitmaps in Chapter 8, "Bitmaps."

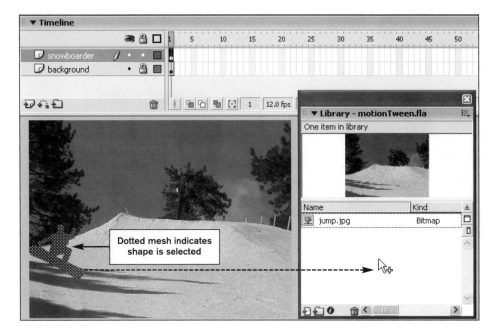

4. With the **Selection** tool, click the snowboarder to select it. Notice the dotted mesh when the snowboarder is selected, indicating that you have selected a shape. Drag the snowboard shape to the bottom half of the **Library**, which will open the **Convert to Symbol** dialog box.

5. In the **Convert to Symbol** dialog box for the **Name** field, type **snowboarder**. For the **Behavior**, select **Graphic**. For the **Registration Point**, make sure the **middle square** is selected. Click **OK**.

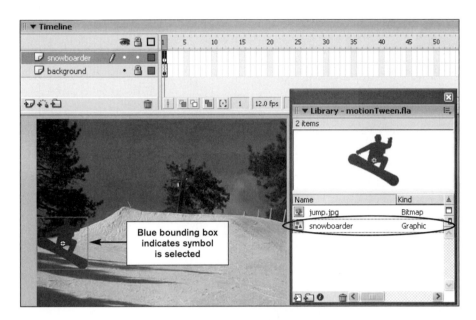

6. After you convert the shape of the snowboarder into a symbol, notice that there is a blue bounding box around the snowboarder instead of the dotted mesh, and in the Library, there is a graphic symbol called **snowboarder**. You are ready to create your first motion tween where the snowboarder will ride up to the mountain peak.

7. With the **Selection** tool, click the snowboarder and drag the instance offstage into the lower-left corner of the work area (the gray area surrounding the Stage), as shown here. This will make the snowboarder enter the **Stage** from the left.

Note: Artwork placed in the work area will not be seen in the SWF (published movie).

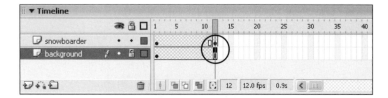

8. In the **Timeline**, select **Frame 12** of the **snowboarder** layer and press **F6** to add a keyframe. This will copy the contents of **Frame 1** to **Frame 12**. On the layer named **background**, select **Frame 12** and press **F5** to add frames up to **Frame 12**. You will move the position of the **snowboarder** instance on **Frame 12** next.

9. In the **Timeline**, select the keyframe on **Frame 12** of the **snowboarder** layer. Move the instance of the snowboarder from the lower-left side of the work area to just above the mountain peak on the **Stage**, as shown here. You will add the motion tween in the following steps.

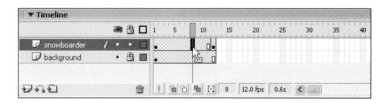

10. In the **Timeline**, click anywhere between **Frame 1** and **Frame 12** to select a frame.

11. Make sure the **Properties inspector** panel is open. If it's not, choose **Window > Properties** or press **Ctrl+F3** (Windows) or **Cmd+F3** (Mac). Choose **Motion** from the **Tween** drop-down menu. This sets a motion tween for the range of frames between **Frame 1** and **Frame 12** of the **snowboarder** layer. Notice the blue tint and the solid arrow between those frames, indicating that a motion tween is active.

12. Move the **playhead** back to **Frame 1** and press **Enter/Return** to view the motion tween. You should see the snowboarder enter from the left of the Stage and animate up to the mountain peak. All you had to do was set up the beginning and ending keyframes and turn on motion tweening, and Flash MX 2004 did the rest. You will add the ending keyframe to the animation next.

Note: You can also scrub (move) the playhead back and forth to view the motion tween or press the less than (<) or greater than (>) signs on the keyboard to advance the playhead forward or backward one frame at a time.

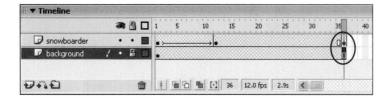

13. In the **Timeline**, select **Frame 36** of the **snowboarder** layer and press **F6** to add a keyframe. This will copy the contents of **Frame 12** to **Frame 36**. On the **background** layer, select **Frame 36** and press **F5** to add frames up to **Frame 36**. You will move the position of the **snowboarder** instance on **Frame 36** next.

14. In the **Timeline**, select the keyframe on **Frame 36** of the **snowboarder** layer. Move the instance of the snowboarder from the mountain peak to the lower-right corner of the work area, as shown in the picture here. You will add the last motion tween in the following steps.

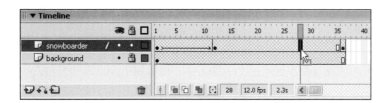

15. In the **Timeline**, click anywhere between **Frame 12** and **Frame 36** to select a frame.

16. In the **Properties inspector** panel, choose **Motion** from the **Tween** drop-down menu. This sets another motion tween in the **snowboard** layer for the range of frames between **Frame 12** and **Frame 36**. Again, notice the blue tint and the solid arrow between those frames, indicating that a motion tween is active.

17. Press **Enter/Return** to view the motion tween. You should see the snowboarder enter from the bottom left of the Stage, animate up to the mountain peak, and then slide down the slope to the lower-right corner of the work area.

Congratulations, you have created your first motion tween—two motion tweens to be exact!

18. Save this file and leave it open. You will need it for the next exercise.

2. _____Tweening Effects

Surprisingly, a motion tween isn't used solely for tweening motion, as its name implies. You can also tween the alpha, tint, brightness, size, position, and skew of a graphic symbol. This exercise will show you how to do just that and will open the door for you to create a wide range of animated effects—far beyond simply moving an object from one location to another.

1. You should have the file open from the previous exercise. If you closed it, open the **motionTween.fla** file from the **chap_07** folder.

2. Make sure the **playhead** is over **Frame 1** in the **Timeline**. To make this animation a bit more realistic, you will rotate and scale the instance of the snowboarder in the following steps.

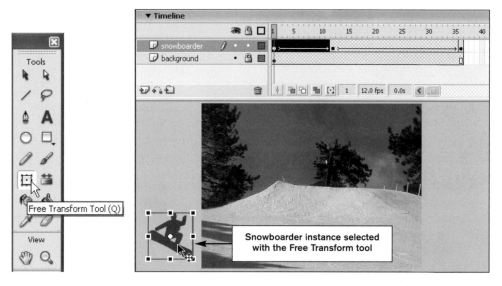

Snowboarder instance selected with the Free Transform tool

3. Select the **Free Transform** tool from the **Toolbar** and click the **snowboarder** instance on the **Stage** to select it. You will scale the **snowboarder** instance next.

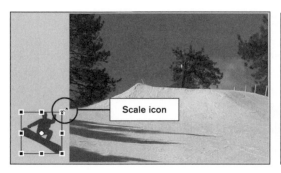

4. With the **Free Transform** tool, move the cursor over the top-right corner handle until the scale icon appears. Click and drag diagonally to scale the snowboarder to a smaller size. You will rotate the **snowboarder** instance next.

Tip: *If you hold down the* **Shift** *key while you drag one of the handles, the snowboarder will scale proportionally on all sides.*

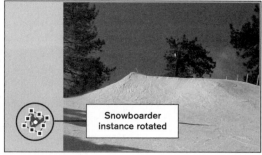

5. Move the cursor over the top-left corner handle of the **snowboarder** instance until the rotate icon appears. Click and drag down until the board in the **snowboarder** instance is pointing upwards, as shown here. You will rotate the **snowboarder** instance on **Frame 12** next.

6. In the **Timeline**, select the keyframe in **Frame 12** of the **snowboarder** layer. With the **Free Transform** tool, move the cursor over the top-left corner handle of the **snowboarder** instance until the rotate icon appears. Click and drag down until the board in the **snowboarder** instance is pointing upwards, as shown here. You will make the **snowboarder** instance do a jump in the following steps.

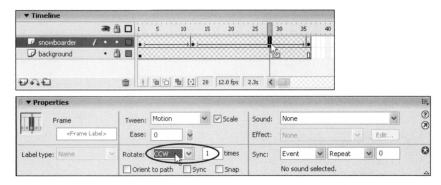

7. In the **Timeline**, select anywhere between **Frame 12** and **Frame 36** of the **snowboarder** layer to select the second motion tween. In the **Properties inspector** panel (**Window > Properties**), choose **CCW** for the **Rotate** option. This will make the snowboarder rotate counterclockwise (CCW) one time during the last motion tween.

8. Press **Enter/Return** to preview the animation.

Now that's a jump! You're almost done—you will scale and change the tint of the snowboarder instance on the last keyframe in the following steps.

9. In the **Timeline**, select the keyframe on **Frame 36**. With the **Free Transform** tool, move the cursor over the top-right corner handle until the scale icon appears. Click and drag diagonally to scale the snowboarder to a smaller size. Remember, holding down the **Shift** key while you drag will maintain the original aspect ratio of the image. You'll change the tint color of the **snowboard** instance next.

10. Make sure the Playhead is still on **Frame 36** of the **snowboarder** layer. With the **Selection** tool, click the **snowboarder** instance on the **Stage**.

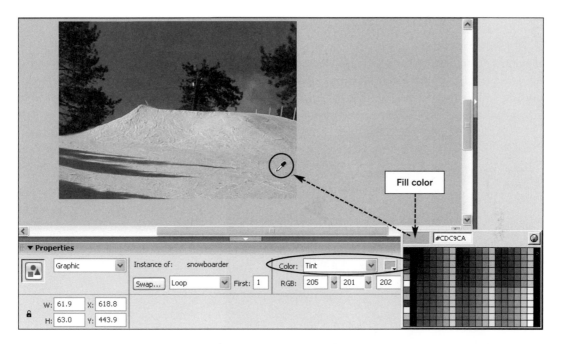

11. In the **Properties inspector** panel (**Window > Properties**), set **Color** to **Tint**. Click the **Fill Color** box and notice that the cursor changes into an eyedropper. Move the **eyedropper** to the background image to sample a color from the snow. You'll see the snowboarder update to the color you have sampled—in this case a shade of gray.

Tip: As you just learned, you can sample a color from the artwork on the Stage rather than choosing a color from the Fill Color box. Also, If you already know the RGB or hexadecimal value you want, you can also simply type it in the appropriate field.

12. Choose **Control > Test Movie** to preview your animation. Notice the snowboarder enters the Stage from the left side, starts off small, and gets larger as it moves toward the peak of the mountain. When it reaches the peak of the mountain, the snowboarder jumps the lip and rotates counterclockwise once until it reaches the bottom of the slope. At the same time that the size is tweening, the tint of the snowboarder is also changing as it moves! You are now tweening the tint and scale (not to mention the position) in a motion tween!

13. Go ahead and experiment by making more changes to any of the keyframes in the motion tween by using the **Free Transform** tool or modifying the **Color** in the **Properties inspector** panel and see how it changes your animation.

14. When you are finished, save and close this file.

3. ———————— **Editing Multiple Frames**

Suppose you created a motion tween but then decided you would rather have the animation occur in a different position on the Stage. Can you imagine repositioning the items one frame at a time? With the Edit Multiple Frames feature, you can bypass that tedious work. The following exercise will show you a method to move the entire animation with ease.

1. Open the file named **editMultipleFrames.fla** from the **chap_07** folder. This file contains one layer with a background image. The **background** layer is locked so that you don't accidentally edit it.

*Tip: If you can't see the whole background image, choose **View > Magnification > Show All** to see the whole image.*

2. In the **Timeline**, click the **Insert Layer** button to add a new layer to the **Timeline**. Double-click the **Layer 2** name, and rename this layer **tween**.

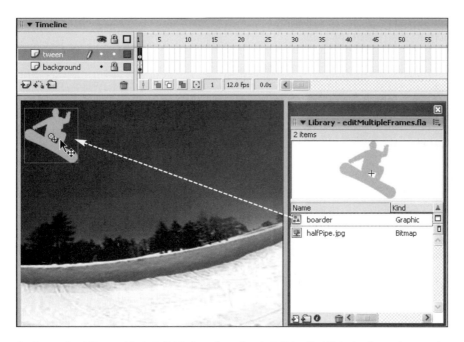

3. Open the **Library** (**Ctrl+L** [Windows] or **Cmd+L** [Mac]). Click the **boarder** graphic symbol in the **Library** and drag it to the upper-left corner of the sky in the background image, as shown in the picture here. This is where the boarder is going to start its animation.

4. In the **Timeline**, on the layer named **tween**, select **Frame 12** and press **F6** to add a keyframe. This will copy the contents of **Frame 1** to **Frame 12**. Select **Frame 12** on the **background** layer and press **F5** to add frames to that layer too. This way, the background image will be visible throughout the motion tween.

5. With the **playhead** over **Frame 12**, drag the boarder to the right side of the **Stage** in the sky. This will serve as the end point of your animation.

6. In the **Timeline**, click anywhere between the two keyframes to select one of the frames between **Frame 1** and **Frame 12**.

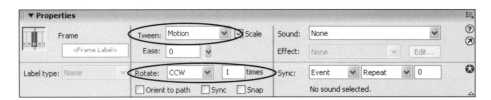

7. In the **Properties inspector** panel, from the **Tween** drop-down menu, choose **Motion**. Set the **Rotate** option to **CCW** to make the boarder rotate counterclockwise one time during the motion tween.

8. Press **Enter/Return** to preview the motion tween. Notice that it looks good, but for a more realistic look, the animation should occur in the snow rather than in the sky. You will change this next.

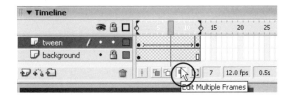

9. At the bottom of the **Timeline**, turn on the **Edit Multiple Frames** feature by clicking the **Edit Multiple Frames** button located in the status bar of the **Timeline**.

Note: When you click the Edit Multiple Frames button, you'll see two markers at the top of the Timeline that look identical to the Onion Skinning markers, which you learned about in Chapter 4, "Animation Basics." Don't be fooled by the similarities, though. Editing multiple frames is quite different from onion skinning. When working with onion skinning, the Onion Skinning bar represents the range of frames you are seeing at the same time on your Stage. With Edit Multiple Frames, however, the bar represents the range of keyframes you will be editing at the same time.

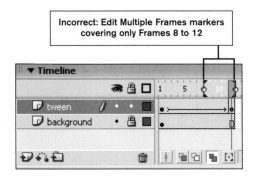

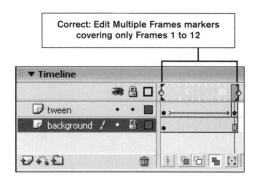

10. Position the starting point and ending point of the markers (representing your Edit Multiple Frames range) to span from **Frame 1** to **Frame 12**. If either the starting point or ending point is not over the correct frame, click and drag the bar over the correct frame. By doing this, you are defining which keyframes you are going to edit simultaneously.

In the following steps, you will be moving your entire animation to the bottom part of the Stage, so you want to make sure all of the frames are covered by the Edit Multiple Frames bar. Since your animation is composed of two keyframes (Frame 1 and Frame 12), these are the frames that you want the bar to cover.

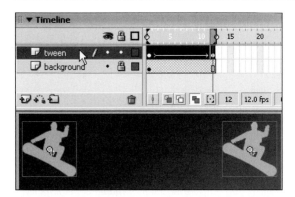

11. Click the **tween** layer name to select the entire layer. Notice that you can see the boarder on the first keyframe and the boarder on the last keyframe. Unlike with onion skinning, however, you won't see ghosted representations of all of the frames between the two keyframes. Also notice that both boarders are selected (they have a border around them), which means that you can move them together at one time.

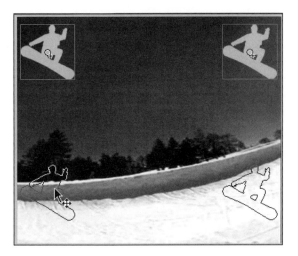

12. Click either one of the boarders on the **Stage** and drag downward. Notice that as you drag, both boarders move.

---

13. Turn off **Edit Multiple Frames** by clicking the **Edit Multiple Frames** button again.

It's very important that you turn off Edit Multiple Frames once you have completed your task. If you leave Edit Multiple Frames turned on and continue to work in your movie, Flash MX 2004 will become confused as to which frame you're working in, and your movie will produce unexpected results. If you do make this mistake, remember that by default, you can undo the previous 100 actions!

---

14. Preview the animation by pressing **Enter/Return**. Now the whole animation has been moved to the bottom of the **Stage**, and the boarder is moving across the snow rather than in the air!

Note: The Edit Multiple Frames feature is a great technique to use when you need to move the contents of many frames all at once. It is also the only way to move an entire animation together at one time.

---

15. Save this file and close it. You won't need it again.

Using a Motion Guide

This exercise shows you how to create a motion tween using a motion guide. A motion guide is a type of layer on which you can draw a path. This type of guide layer allows the symbol used in the motion tween to follow the path, rather than traveling a straight line between two keyframes. This is the only way in Flash MX 2004 to make a motion tween follow a curved path, so it is an important technique to understand.

1. Open **motionGuide_Final.fla** from your **chap_07** folder. This file is a finished version of the file you are about to create. Choose **Control > Test Movie** to view the movie (SWF) file. Notice how the snowflake moves from side to side in a downward direction before reaching the bottom of the screen. Using a motion guide, you will create this same effect next.

---

2. When you are finished, close the **Preview** window and then close the project file.

3. Now open **motionGuide.fla** from your **chap_07** folder. Notice that this file contains one layer with the background image. The **background** layer is locked to prevent you from editing that layer. You'll be adding the falling snowflake in the following steps.

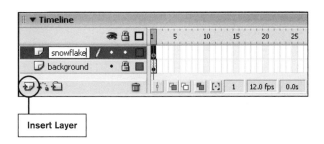

4. In the **Timeline**, click the **Insert Layer** button to add a new layer to the **Timeline**. Double-click the **Layer 2** name and rename this layer **snowflake**.

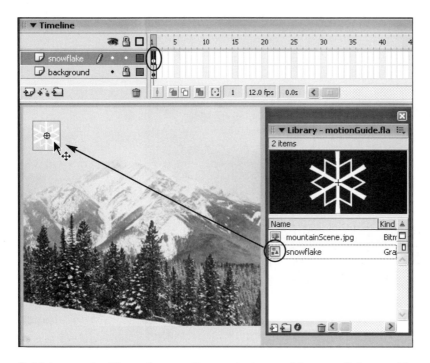

5. Make sure the **Library** is open. Drag an instance of the **snowflake** graphic symbol onto the **Stage** in the top-left corner. This will be the beginning of the animation—notice the keyframe in **Frame 1** of the **snowflake** layer. Close the **Library** by pressing **Ctrl+L** (Windows) or **Cmd+L** (Mac) to make your workspace less cluttered.

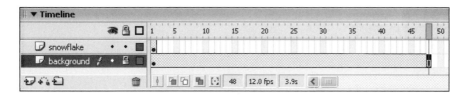

6. In the **Timeline**, click **Frame 48** of the **background** layer and press **F5** to add frames up to **Frame 48**. This will make sure the background shows throughout the snowflake animation, which you will create next.

7. On the **snowflake** layer, click **Frame 48** and press **F6** to add a new keyframe. This will copy the contents of **Frame 1** to **Frame 48**. With the **playhead** over **Frame 48**, click the **snowflake** instance and drag it to the lower-right corner of the screen. This will be the end point of the animation.

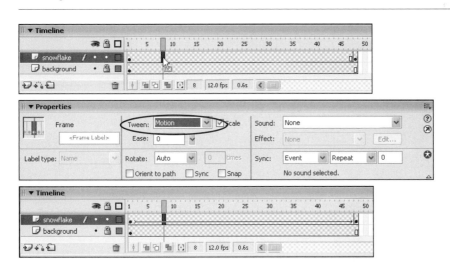

8. On the **Timeline**, click anywhere between **Frame 1** and **Frame 40** to select a frame between the two keyframes. In the **Properties inspector** panel (**Ctrl+F3** [Windows] or **Cmd+F3** [Mac]), choose **Motion** from the **Tween** drop-down menu. Notice the blue tint and the solid arrow between **Frame 1** and **Frame 48** of the **snowflake** layer, indicating that a motion tween is active.

9. Press **Enter/Return** to test the motion tween animation. Notice the snowflake move from the top-left corner of the **Stage** down to the bottom-right corner of the **Stage** in a linear motion. You will make the snowflake follow a motion guide so that it moves across the Stage from right to left in a side-to-side fashion before reaching the ground. But first you will add the motion guide.

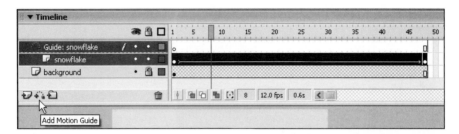

10. Click the **snowflake** layer to select it. At the bottom of the **Timeline** to the right of the **Insert Layer** button, click the **Add Motion Guide** button once. This will add a motion guide layer above the **snowflake** layer. This new layer has automatically been named **Guide: snowflake**.

Notice the icon in front of the guide layer. This icon is visual feedback that this layer is now a guide layer. Something else has happened that you haven't seen before: The snowflake layer is indented below the guide layer. This means that the snowflake layer is taking instructions from the guide layer. The snowflake layer contains your motion tween, and the guide layer will contain the trail or path that the tween will follow. Before it can follow the path, however, you will have to draw one. That's coming up soon, so keep following along.

11. Lock the **snowflake** layer to avoid editing it and click the **Guide: snowflake** layer once to select it.

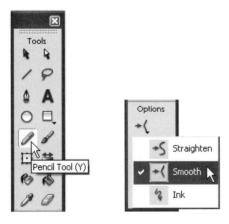

12. In the **Toolbar**, select the **Pencil** tool. For the **Pencil Mode** option, choose **Smooth**. That way, when you draw the path for the snowflake to follow, Flash MX 2004 will smooth out any irregularities for you.

13. On the **Stage**, draw a curved line to serve as the path that the snowflake will follow (as shown here). It doesn't matter what color or stroke width you choose. Flash MX 2004 is concerned only with the path of the line.

Note: *The path drawn on the motion guide layer will not be seen in the published file.*

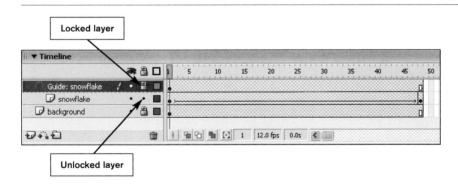

14. Unlock the **snowflake** layer and lock the **Guide: snowflake** layer since you're done with it and you want to avoid moving or editing it accidentally.

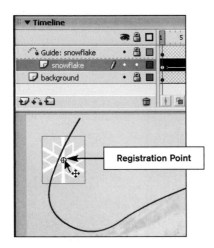

15. Move the **playhead** so that it is over **Frame 1**. Using the **Selection** tool, click the **snowflake** instance to select it. Click the **Registration Point** in the center of it and drag the snowflake to the beginning of the path that you drew in the guide layer. When you get close to the path, the snowflake will "snap" to it, and the **Registration Point** will turn into a small circle. This is where the snowflake will start following the path.

Note: It is very important that you grab the snowflake symbol instance from the Registration Point in order for the motion guide to work properly. You will know if you have done this correctly if the Registration Point turns into a circle, as shown in the previous illustration.

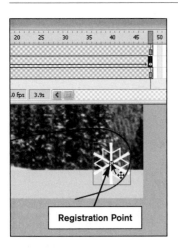

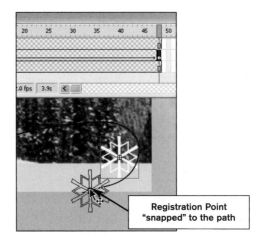

16. Move the **playhead** to **Frame 48**, the last keyframe of the animation. Again, click the **Registration Point** of the **snowflake** instance, and drag the snowflake to the bottom of the path that you drew on the guide layer. This is where the snowflake will stop following the path. That's it!

17. Press **Enter/Return** to preview the snowflake animation. Notice that the snowflake now follows the path that you drew on the guide layer! Now choose **Control > Test Movie**. Notice that now you don't see the line at all! That is because the contents of your motion guide layer will not be seen in the final movie (SWF) file, but your snowflake will still continue to follow the path.

Wouldn't it be nice if the snowflake rotated in the direction of its movement, instead of always facing in the same direction? In other words, if the snowflake is moving down, it should be pointing down, don't you think? You're going to do that next.

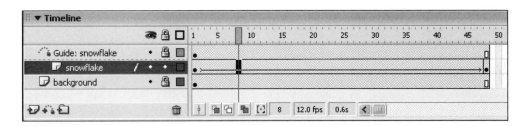

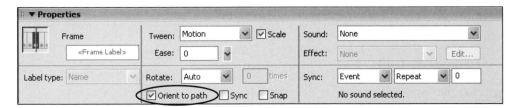

18. Click anywhere in the motion tween of the **snowflake** layer. In the **Properties inspector** panel, click the check box next to **Orient to path**. When it is selected, Flash MX 2004 will do its best to make the snowflake face the direction that the path is going.

19. Choose **Control > Test Movie** to view the snowflake animation. Notice that as the snowflake falls it faces the direction of the path. Nice! To make this animation a bit more realistic, you will make the snowflake gradually speed up as though it gets windier as it reaches the ground.

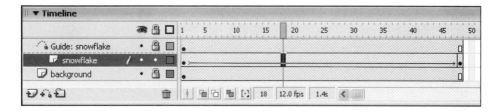

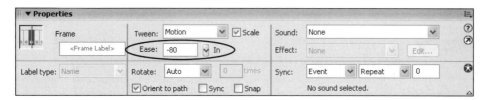

20. Click anywhere in the tween of the **snowflake** layer to select the motion tween. In the **Properties inspector** panel, move the **Ease** slider to **–80** to make the snowflake start off slow and then gradually speed up as it follows the path.

TIP | Easing In and Easing Out

The terms "easing in" and "easing out" have to do with the speed of animation. If you leave the Ease setting at its default of None, animation in Flash MX 2004 will occur in a linear motion, meaning that all the frames will move at the same speed. Easing out means that the animation gradually slows to the last keyframe. Easing in means that the animation gradually speeds up to the last keyframe.

---

21. Preview your animation again by pressing **Enter/Return** on your keyboard.

Just by selecting one check box, Flash MX 2004 points the snowflake symbol instance in the direction the path is moving, as though the wind was blowing it along. Altering the speed of the snowflake and adjusting the amount of easing have also given a more realistic feel to the snowflake's movement. This is a great (and easy) way to add the visual effect that your graphic is actually following the path.

22. Save and close this file. You won't be using it again.

MOVIE | motionGuide.mov

To see a movie of making this motion guide, play **motionGuide.mov** which is located in the **movies** folder on the **H•O•T CD-ROM**.

5. _____**Exploding Text**

In this exercise, you will create the effect of a word exploding on the screen. In the process, you'll get to practice creating a symbol from text, breaking apart the letters, distributing them to layers, and adding a Folder layer.

1. Open the **explode_Final.fla** file from the **chap_07** folder.

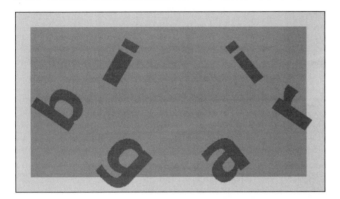

2. Choose **Control > Test Movie** to test the animation. The words explode before your eyes! When you are finished previewing, close the file. You will create this animation next.

3. Open the **explode.fla** file from the **chap_07** folder. This file was created for you; it has a blue background, and the frame rate has been set to 20 frames per second.

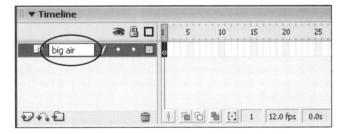

4. In the **Timeline**, select **Layer 1** and rename it **big air**. You will add the text to this layer in the following steps.

5. Select the **Text** tool from the **Toolbar** and click the Stage to bring focus to it. In the **Properties inspector** panel, set the **Font** to **Verdana**, set the **Font Size** to **96**, choose a **dark blue** from the **Fill Color** box, and select **Bold**.

6. Type the words **big air** on the **Stage**. Notice there is now a keyframe in **Frame 1** of the **big air** layer.

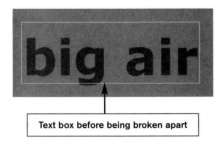

Text box before being broken apart

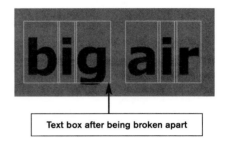

Text box after being broken apart

7. With the **big air** text selected, choose **Modify > Break Apart**. This will break the text box into six individual text boxes, one box for each letter.

8. With all six text boxes still selected, choose **Modify > Timeline > Distribute to Layers**. Notice that this technique places each letter on a separate layer. This step is important because in order to create several motion tweens occurring at once, each tween must reside on its own layer. Likewise, each symbol (which you will create next) must reside on a separate layer.

9. With the **Selection** tool, click anywhere off the **Stage** to deselect all six letters. Select the letter **b** and press **F8** to convert it into a symbol. In the **Convert to Symbol** dialog box, name the symbol **letter_b** and set **Behavior** to **Graphic**. Make sure the **Registration Point** is in the **center**. Click **OK**.

NOTE | Motion Tweening Text

You don't have to convert a regular text block to a symbol in order to use it as the artwork for a motion tween. However, you are limited in the effects that you can apply to text boxes. With a text block, you can animate the position and scale, rotation, skew, and flip. However, with a graphic symbol with text inside, you can animate color styles such as color, brightness, alpha, and tint. With a symbol, you have more options for creating effects in your motion tween than you have using a regular text block.

---

10. With the **Selection** tool, select the letter **i**. Press **F8** to convert it into a symbol. In the **Convert to Symbol** dialog box, name the symbol **letter_i** and set the **Behavior** option to **Graphic**. Make sure the **Registration Point** is in the **center**. Click **OK**.

11. Repeat Step 10 three more times to make three more symbols: **g**, **a**, and **r**. Name the symbols **letter_g**, **letter_a**, and **letter_r**, respectively, in the **Convert to Symbol** dialog box. Do not convert the letter **i** in the word **air**. You will learn to replace it with an instance of the graphic symbol **letter_i** by using the **Info** panel next.

Note: You might be wondering why you didn't have to convert the letter i in the word "air" into a symbol. Since you already created a letter_i graphic symbol in Step 10, you will use that same graphic symbol to create another instance of the letter_i on the Stage for a total of two instances. This is the beauty of symbols: you have to create only one symbol, and from that symbol, you can create several instances on the Stage without increasing the file size or download time.

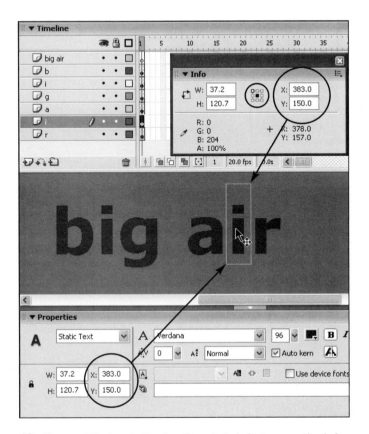

12. Choose **Window > Design Panels > Info** to open the **Info** panel. With the **Selection** tool, click the letter **i** in the word "air" on the **Stage** to select it. In the Info panel make sure the Registration Point is in the center. Notice the **X** and **Y** coordinates in the **Info** panel are set to **383.0** and **150.0**, respectively. With 0,0 being the coordinates for the top-left corner of the Stage, this means that where **X = 383.0** pixels, the letter **i** is **383.0** pixels from the left side of the **Stage**; where **Y = 150.0** pixels, the letter **i** is **150.0** pixels down from the top of the **Stage**.

Note: The X and Y coordinates in your file may be different from what is shown here, depending on where you placed your artwork on the Stage. The point is to make sure you take note of where the X and Y coordinates of the letter i in the word air are in your file.

Note: You can also get the X and Y position of an element in the Properties inspector panel as well. With the Info panel, however, you can access additional information such as the Registration Point and the RGB and Alpha transparency values.

13. Delete the letter **i** in the word "air" from the **Stage**. Notice also that the keyframe in **Frame 1** of the second **i** layer is now a blank keyframe. You will place an instance of the **letter_i** graphic symbol on the **Stage** next.

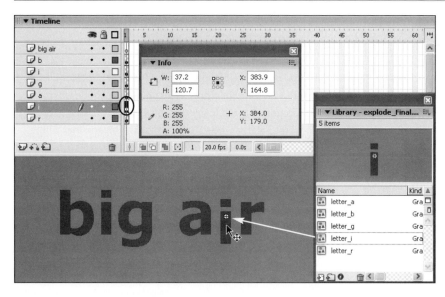

14. Open the Library (**Ctrl+L** [Windows] or **Cmd+L** [Mac]) and drag and instance of the **letter_i** graphic symbol to the **Stage**. Notice **Frame 1** of the second **i** layer now has a keyframe. Don't worry about positioning it precisely. You will use the **Info** panel to do that next.

15. Make sure the letter **i** in the word **air** is still selected. In the **Info** panel, change the **X** and **Y** values to what you noted in Step 12. Notice that the letter **i** in the word **air** is now in its original position. Now you have two instances of the **letter_i** graphic symbol instead of one! You can close the **Info** and **Library** panels if you'd like.

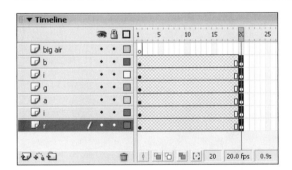

16. On the **Timeline**, click **Frame 20** and drag down over all six layers that have a symbol on them to select those frames. Press **F6** to add a keyframe to **Frame 20** on all six layers.

17. Add a keyframe on **Frame 40** of all six layers in the same way you did in the previous step. This is where the letters are going to finish their animation.

18. Click anywhere off the **Stage** to deselect all the symbols. Making sure the **playhead** is over **Frame 40**, click and drag the **letter_b** instance off the left side of the **Stage** onto the work area. When the **b** explodes, it will end up in this position.

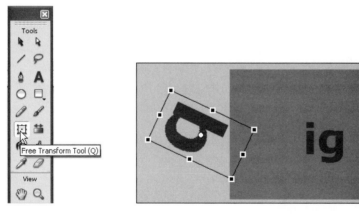

19. In the **Toolbar**, select the **Free Transform** tool. Use this tool to rotate and scale the **letter_b** instance. The degree of rotation and scale are completely up to you.

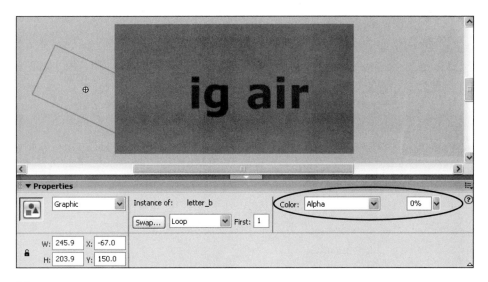

20. Make sure the **Properties inspector** panel is open; if it is not, choose **Window > Properties**. For **Color**, choose **Alpha** and set the amount to **0%** to make the letter **b** fade out completely as the words "big air" explode into space.

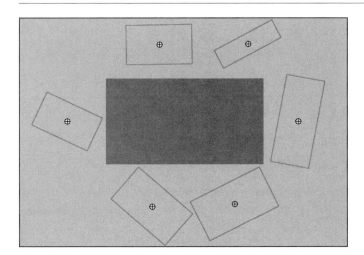

21. Repeat steps 18, 19, and 20 to modify the positions of the other graphic symbols on **Frame 40**, scaling, rotating, and adding an alpha effect to each one. Feel free to move the symbols and then use the **Free Transform** tool to scale, rotate, or even flip and skew each letter in any way you want, but make sure to keep the **Alpha** setting at **0%** in the last keyframe to ensure that the words "big air" explode and disappear at the same time.

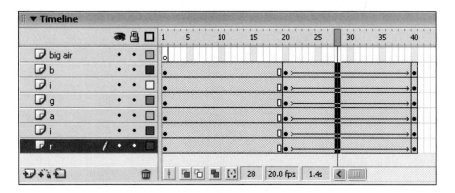

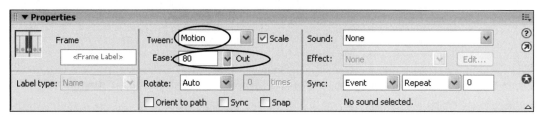

22. Click anywhere between **Frames 20** and **40** on the **b** layer and drag down to the **r** layer to select all the layers on that frame. In the **Properties inspector** panel, choose **Motion** from the **Tween** drop-down menu and drag the Ease slider up until it reads 80 Out. This will add a motion tween to all the layers at once and will cause the motion tween animation to start off fast and then slow down as it nears the end of the animation! Nice workflow shortcut, don't you think?

23. That's it! Choose **Control > Test Movie**, or use the shortcut **Ctrl+Enter** (Windows) or **Cmd+Return** (Mac) to preview the animation. Notice that the animation is a total of about two seconds and that the words "big air" stay on the **Stage** for about one second before exploding and fading away.

You are almost done. Just a little housekeeping left to do...

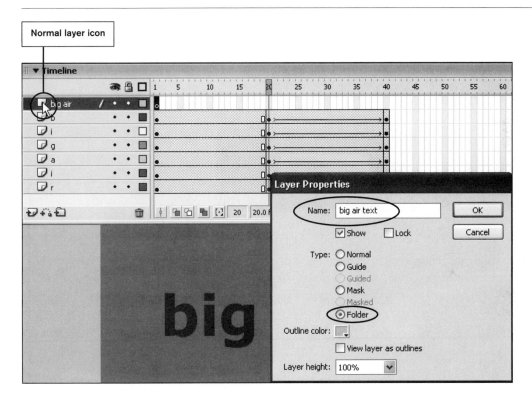

24. In the **Timeline**, on the layer named **big air**, double-click the **normal layer** icon to open the **Layer Properties** dialog box. Name the layer **big air text** and set the **Type** option to **Folder**. This will turn the normal layer into a folder layer, which you learned about in Chapter 5, "*Shape Tweening*."

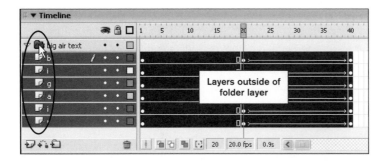

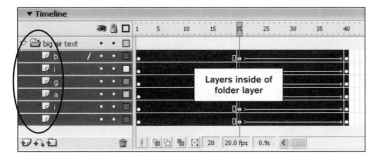

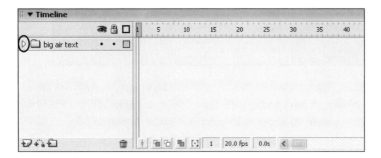

25. In the **Timeline**, notice that the **normal layer** icon is now a **folder** icon. Click the **b** layer and then **Shift+click** the **r** layer to select all the layers. Drag the layers on top of the layer folder to place the layers inside the folder. Notice that all the layers are now indented inside the folder layer.

26. Click the arrow to the left of the **layer folder** icon to collapse the folder. Much better—everything is neat and put away now!

27. You can save and close this file. You will not need it again.

Motion Tweening Options and Limitations

There are many additional options for creating animation using motion tweens. For your reference, here is a list of the things that motion tweening can and can't do.

What Motion Tweening Can Do

Symbol Instances

- Tween position
- Tween brightness
- Tween tint
- Tween alpha
- Tween scaling
- Tween rotation
- Tween skew

Grouped Objects

- Tween position
- Tween scaling
- Tween rotation
- Tween skew
- Tween a text block (editable text)

What Motion Tweening Can't Do

- Tween a shape
- Tween broken-apart text
- Tween multiple items on the same layer

Through these exercises, you learned how to use symbols to create motion tween animation and that motion tweening can produce many different effects beyond simply moving a symbol from one location to another. The exercises showed you how to use motion tweening to animate the scale, rotation, tint, and alpha of symbol instances. You also learned how to create a motion guide and make text appear as though it were exploding! In the next section, you will learn to use a feature new to Flash MX 2004 called Timeline Effects.

NOTE | What Are Timeline Effects?

Flash MX 2004 includes prebuilt Timeline Effects that allow you to create common Timeline animations with just one step, reducing the need for excessive keyframing. Timeline Effects can be edited so you can modify them repeatedly or undo them. Effects include Copy to Grid, Distribute Duplicate, Blur, Drop Shadow, Expand, Explode, Transition, and Transform. You can apply Timeline Effects to text and graphics, including shapes, groups, and graphic symbols, bitmap images (which you will learn about in Chapter 8, "*Bitmaps*"), button symbols (which you will learn about in Chapter 9, "*Buttons*"), and movie clips (which you will learn about in Chapter 10, "*Movie Clips*").

---

6. _____Timeline Effect Assistants

This exercise will show you how to use Timeline Effects to create elements in an interface that normally would take much planning and time. You will learn how to use the Timeline Effect assistants, **Distributed Duplicate** and **Copy To Grid**, to duplicate and distribute an object multiple times on the Stage, as well as how to create a grid of lines painlessly and in little time.

1. Open the file called **assistants_Final.fla** from the **chap_07** folder. This is the finished version of the project you'll be building in this exercise.

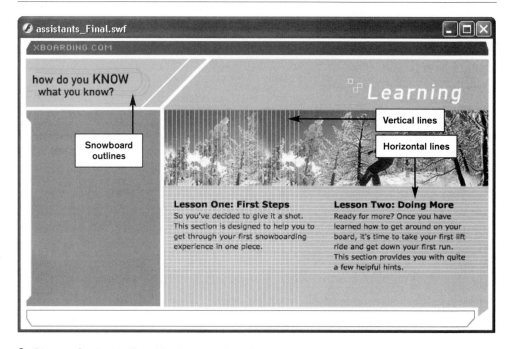

2. Choose **Control > Test Movie** to preview the interface of the movie.

Although nothing plays in the movie, notice the vertical and horizontal lines as well as the snowboard outlines. You will draw each line once and learn how to use the new Timeline Effect assistants to quickly duplicate the lines and distribute them across the Stage effortlessly in the following steps.

3. When you are done examining the interface, close the **Preview** window and the file.

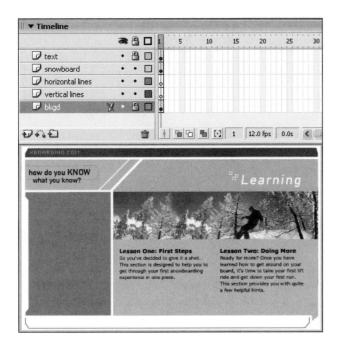

4. Open the file **assistants.fla** from the **chap_07** folder. Notice there are five layers and that the **text** and **bkgd** layers are locked so that you don't accidentally edit those layers. You will learn how to duplicate and distribute the snowboard outline using the **Distributed Duplicate** Timeline Effect in the following steps.

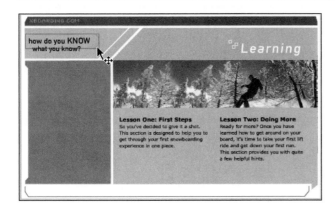

5. Select the snowboard outline on the **Stage** and choose **Insert > Timeline Effects > Assistants > Distributed Duplicate**. This will open up the **Distributed Duplicate** window. You will configure the settings next.

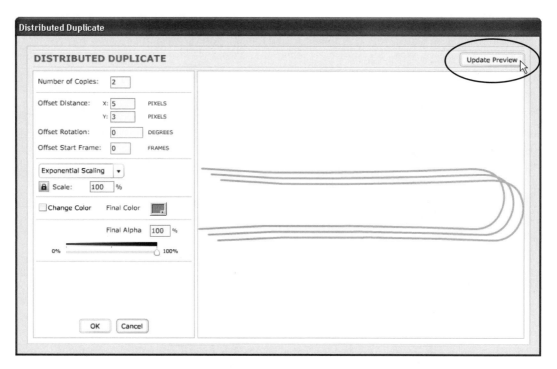

6. In the **Distributed Duplicate** window, for **Number of Copies**, enter **2**. This will duplicate the snowboard outline two more times, for a total of three snowboard outlines on the **Stage**. For **Offset Distance X**, enter **5**, for **Y**, enter **3**. This will offset the outlines of the snowboard five pixels to the right and three pixels down in relation to each other. Leave **Offset Rotation** and **Offset Start Frame** to **0** and make sure **Change Color** is unchecked. Your settings should match the settings shown here. When you are done configuring your settings, click the **Update Preview** button to update the preview screen with the settings you applied. If you are satisfied with your results, click **OK**.

The Distributed Duplicate Timeline Effect allows you to quickly duplicate an object on the Stage as well as change the scale, color, rotation, and alpha transparency while animating it over a specified number of frames. In this example, each copy of the snowboard outline is offset five pixels horizontally (X) and three pixels vertically (Y) from the previous snowboard outline. The Offset Start Frame specifies the number of frames to play before the next object appears.

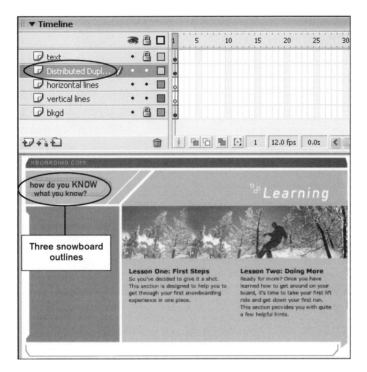

7. Notice that there are now three snowboard outlines on the **Stage** and in the **Timeline**. Also, notice that the **snowboard** layer was renamed **Distributed Duplicate 37**, since that is the name of the effect you applied to it. That's all there is to it! You will examine what Flash MX 2004 actually did to the shape next.

Note: The number 37 in the Distributed Duplicate layer may be different in your project file. The number represents the order in which the effect is applied out of all effects in your document. The layer name in my file is appended with a larger number because I created several Timeline Effects previous to this one. What's important to note is that it was renamed with the effect you applied, in this case, the Distributed Duplicate Timeline Effect.

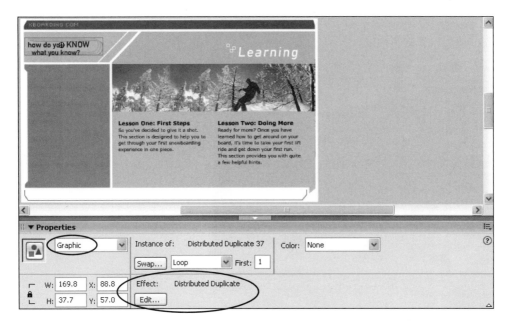

8. Make sure the **Properties inspector** is open; press **Ctrl+F3** (Windows) or **Cmd+F3** (Mac) if it's not. Select the snowboard outlines on the **Stage** and notice that it has been turned into a graphic symbol. The **Properties inspector** also displays the name of the Timeline effect you applied and an **Edit** button. Clicking the **Edit** button will allow you to open the **Distributed Duplicate** dialog box again with your settings intact, and you can configure your settings again if you'd like.

Note: *If you want to change the stroke color of the snowboard lines, you can click the Edit button in the Properties inspector to reconfigure your settings again; change the instance of the graphic symbol on the Stage by selecting it and modifying the Color field in the Properties inspector; or you can double-click the graphic symbol in the Effects folder, inside the Library, to open it in Symbol Editing Mode.*

You will examine the Library next.

NOTE | What Happens When I Add a Timeline Effect?

When you add a Timeline Effect to an object, Flash MX 2004 creates a layer and transfers the object to the new layer. The object is placed inside the effect graphic symbol, and all tweens and transformations required for the effect reside in the graphic symbol on the newly created layer. The new layer automatically receives the same name as the effect, appended with a number that represents the order in which the effect is applied, out of all effects in your document. When you add a Timeline Effect, a folder with the effect's name is added to the Library, containing the elements used in creating the effect.

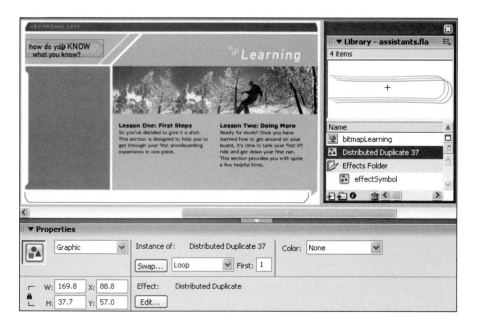

9. Open the **Library** and notice that there is an **Effects** folder. Inside that folder is the original shape. There is another symbol, **Distributed Duplicate 37**, which contains the snowboard outline with the settings you applied in the **Distributed Duplicate Timeline Effects** dialog box.

Note: If you double-click the Distributed 37 symbol, which contains the Timeline Effects you applied, a dialog box will appear warning you that if you decide to proceed, you will lose the ability to edit the settings.

10. Save your file, and keep it open to continue the exercise.

Now that you have an understanding of how Timeline Effects work, you'll learn the Copy to Grid Timeline Effect in the following steps.

Note: The Copy to Grid Timeline Effect is used to copy the selected item in a matrix formation based on the settings you specify. This tool is useful for creating repeating patterns.

TIP | Editing Timeline Effects

You cannot double-click a symbol on the Stage that has a Timeline Effect applied to it. To edit a symbol with a Timeline Effect, you can modify it in one of three ways:

- **Properties inspector:** Select the symbol on the **Stage** and click the **Edit** button in the **Properties inspector**.

- **Menu bar:** Select the symbol on the **Stage** and choose **Modify > Timeline Effects > Edit Effect**.

- **Contextual menu:** Select the symbol on the **Stage** and **right-click** (Windows) or **Ctrl+click** (Mac) and choose **Timeline Effects > Edit Effect**.

Whichever method you use will open up the dialog box of the Timeline Effect applied.

NOTE | Editing Symbols That Have Timeline Effects

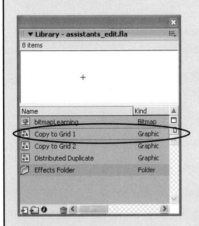

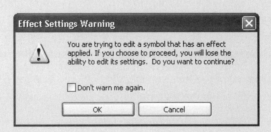

As noted earlier, when you use a Timeline Effect, Flash MX 2004 creates a layer and transfers the object to the new layer. The object is placed inside the effect graphic symbol, and all tweens and transformations required for the effect reside in the graphic symbol on the newly created layer.

When you double-click a symbol with a Timeline Effect applied to it, such as the Copy to Grid 1 symbol shown here, you will be presented with an **Effect Settings Warning**. Basically, the warning lets you know that if you decide to proceed with editing the symbol, it will no longer offer you the ability to adjust the effect you applied earlier.

continues on next page

NOTE | Editing Symbols That Have Timeline Effects *continued*

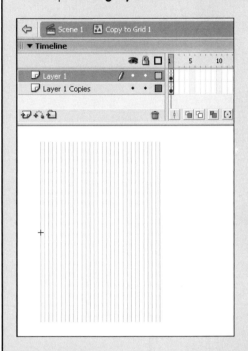

However, beyond the effects themselves, another useful way to use Timeline Effects is to apply them to an object and then edit the symbol. In the example shown here, I clicked OK (agreeing to the fact that I will no longer be able to adjust the Timeline Effect) in the Effects Setting Warning dialog box. The Copy to Grid effect created two layers: The first layer contains the original shape, which has been turned into a symbol, and the second layer contains the symbol duplicated several times in the grid formation specified in the Copy to Grid dialog box. Now that Flash MX 2004 has done the work of duplicating a symbol 30 times in a grid for me, I can now continue to build upon this and create some more interesting and unique results than just with the Timeline Effects alone.

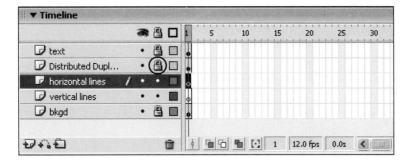

11. In the **Timeline**, lock the **Distributed Duplicate** layer to avoid accidentally editing it and click the **horizontal lines** layer to select it. You will draw a horizontal line on the **Stage** with the **Line** tool in the following steps.

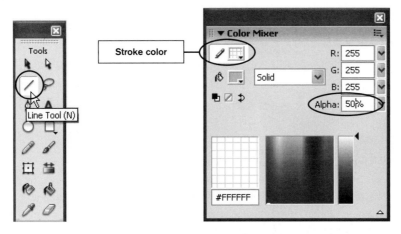

12. Choose **Window > Design Panels > Color Mixer** to open the **Color Mixer** panel, if it is not already open. Select the **Line** tool from the **Toolbar**, and in the **Color Mixer** panel, select **white** for the **Stroke color** and set the **Alpha** to **50%** and press **Enter/Return**.

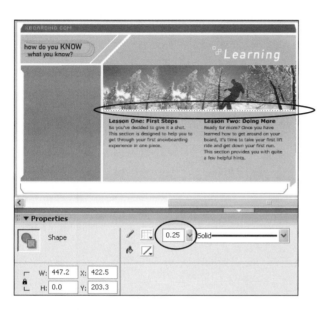

13. On the **Stage**, draw a horizontal line where the photo meets the solid gray area, as shown here. To draw a straight line, hold down the **Shift** key while you draw the line. After you've drawn your line, select it with the Selection tool, and in the **Properties inspector** set the **Stroke** to **0.25**. You will add the **Copy to Grid Timeline Effect** next.

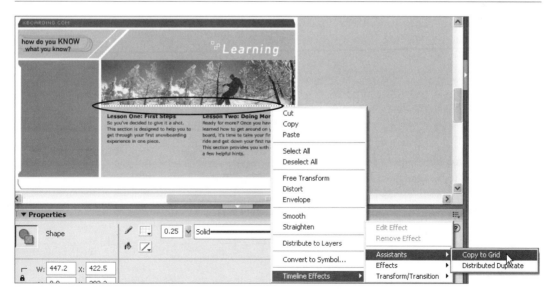

14. With the line still selected on the **Stage**, **right-click** (Windows) or **Ctrl+click** (Mac) to bring up the contextual menu and choose **Timeline Effects > Assistants > Copy to Grid**.

15. In the **Copy To Grid** dialog box, for the **Grid Size**, enter **Rows: 24** and **Columns: 1**. For the **Grid Spacing**, enter **Rows: 5** pixels and **Columns: 1** pixel. These settings will create a grid of 24 lines that are in 1 column. The spacing between each line will be five pixels above and below. When you are finished entering these values, click the **Update Preview** button. Notice that when you click the **Update Preview** button, you can't see anything in the **Preview** window. That is because the lines that you are drawing are white. You will learn how to get around this next.

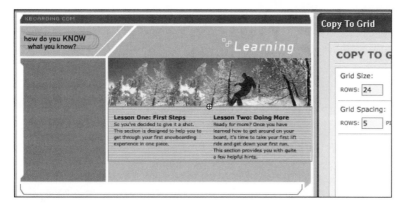

16. Move the **Copy To Grid** dialog box over so that you can see the **Stage**. Notice the **Stage** has been updated with rows of horizontal lines. Neat! Back in the **Copy To Grid** dialog box, click **OK** to accept these settings.

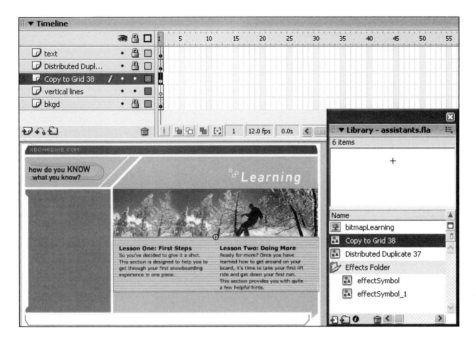

17. Notice the changes in the **Timeline** and in the **Library**. In the **Timeline**, the layer named **horizontal lines** was renamed **Copy to Grid 38**. This layer contains the grid of horizontal lines you just created. In the **Library**, in the **Effects** folder, notice there are now two graphic symbols, the original snowboard outline and the original horizontal line. Also in the **Library** is the **Copy to Grid 38** graphic symbol, which contains the setting you applied to the horizontal line in the **Copy To Grid** dialog box in Step 15. You will draw a vertical line on the **Stage** with the **Line** tool in the following steps.

Note: The numbers appended to the symbols in the Library may be different in your project file.

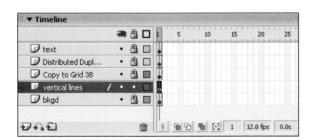

18. In the **Timeline**, lock the **Copy to Grid 38** layer and click the **vertical lines** layer to select it.

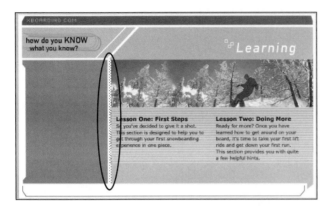

19. Select the **Line** tool from the **Toolbar,** and on the **Stage,** draw a vertical line where the photo meets the solid dark gray area, as shown here. To draw a straight line, hold down the **Shift** key while you draw the line. You will add the **Copy to Grid Timeline Effect** next.

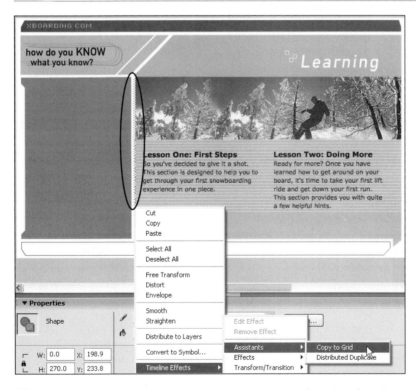

20. With the line still selected on the **Stage, right-click** (Windows) or **Ctrl+click** (Mac) to bring up the contextual menu and choose **Timeline Effects > Assistants > Copy to Grid.**

21. In the **Copy To Grid** dialog box, for the **Grid Size**, enter **Rows: 1** and **Columns: 30**. For the **Grid Spacing**, enter **Rows: 1** pixel and **Columns: 5** pixels. These settings will create a grid of 30 lines that are in 1 row. The spacing between each line will be five pixels on either side of the line. When you are finished entering these values, click the **Update Preview** button and slide the **Copy To Grid** dialog box out of the way for a moment so that you can see your changes on the **Stage**.

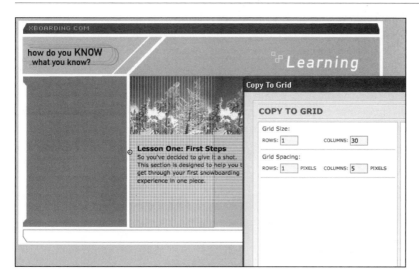

22. When you are satisfied with your settings, click **OK** in the **Copy To Grid** dialog box to accept the settings.

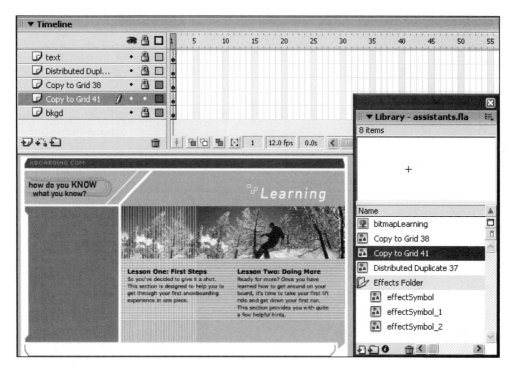

23. Notice the changes in the **Timeline** and in the **Library** again. In the **Timeline**, the layer named **vertical lines** was renamed **Copy to Grid 41**. This layer contains the grid of vertical lines you just created. In the **Library**, in the **Effects** folder, notice there are now three graphic symbols, one for each original shape (snowboard outline, horizontal line, and vertical line). Also in the **Library** is the **Copy to Grid 41** graphic symbol, which contains the setting you applied to the vertical line in the **Copy To Grid** dialog box in Step 21.

Note: Again, the numbers appended to the layer names in the Timeline and the numbers appended to the symbol names in the Library may be different in your project file.

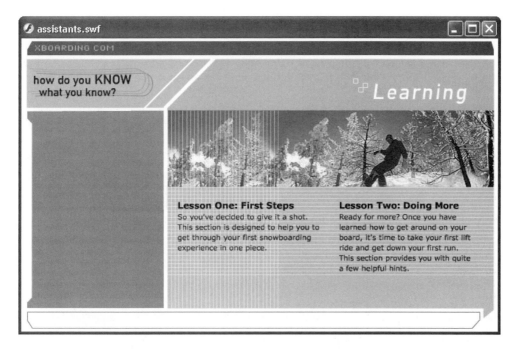

24. Choose **Control > Test Movie** to check out your new interface design.

Nice! Instead of creating the shape, turning it into a graphic symbol and laying out all the instances of that symbol on the Stage in a repeating pattern, you learned to use the Timeline Effect Assistants, Copy to Grid, and Distributed Duplicate, to save you the time and energy of doing it yourself!

Note: *If you want to change the stroke color of the lines, you can change the instance of the graphic symbol on the Stage by selecting it and modifying the Color field in the Properties inspector, or you can double-click the graphic symbol in the Effects folder (inside the Library) to open it in symbol editing mode.*

---

25. When you are done previewing your interface design, close the **Preview** window, and save and close the file.

In the next exercise, you will learn how to use the Transition and Blur Timeline Effects.

---

7. —————————Transition and Blur Timeline Effects

Oftentimes, when creating Flash content, you will want to make an object fade in or fade out. You may even want titles in your Flash movie to have a blurred effect. In this exercise, you will learn how to do just that with the Transition and Blur Timeline Effects.

1. Open the file called **transitionBlur_Final.fla** from the **chap_07** folder. This is the finished version of the project you'll be building in this exercise.

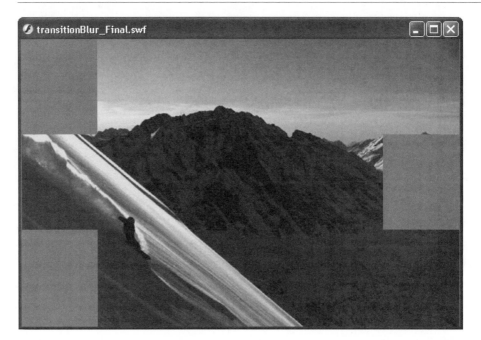

2. Choose **Control > Test Movie** to preview the movie. Notice the photo breaks into three segments and transitions off the **Stage**, revealing the text "xboarding," which starts out normal and then becomes blurred. You will learn how to create these techniques using the **Transition** and **Blur Timeline Effects** in the following steps.

3. When you are done previewing the movie, close the **Preview** window and the file.

4. Open the file **transitionBlur.fla** from the **chap_07** folder. In the **Timeline**, notice there are three layers: **top**, **middle**, and **bottom**. Go ahead and examine the content of the layers by clicking the **Show/Hide** icon for each layer. You will notice the image on Stage is divided into three parts: top, middle and bottom. In the **Library**, there is a graphic symbol and a bitmap image. You will learn more about bitmaps in the next chapter.

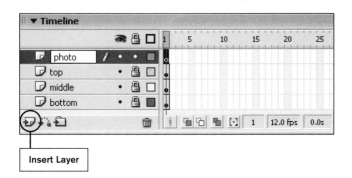

Insert Layer

5. Click the **Insert Layer** button to create a new layer. Name it **photo**. Make sure the **photo** layer is above all other layers, as shown here. You will add the bitmap image from the **Library** to this layer next.

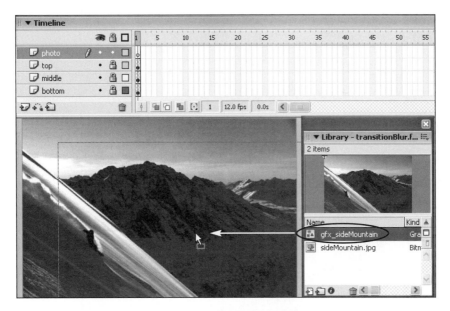

6. In the **Library**, select the graphic symbol **gfx_sideMountain** and drag it to the **Stage**. You will reposition it using the **Align** panel next.

7. Choose **Windows > Design Panels > Align** to open up the **Align** panel. In the **Align** panel, select **To stage** and then click the **Align horizontal center** button and the **Align vertical center** button. This will center the graphic symbol to the **Stage** horizontally and vertically.

8. In the **Timeline**, select **Frame 10** of the **photo** layer and press **F5** to add frames.

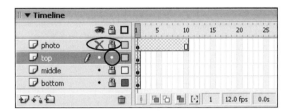

9. Lock and hide the **photo** layer and unlock the **top** layer. You will add the **Transition Timeline Effect** to the **top** layer next.

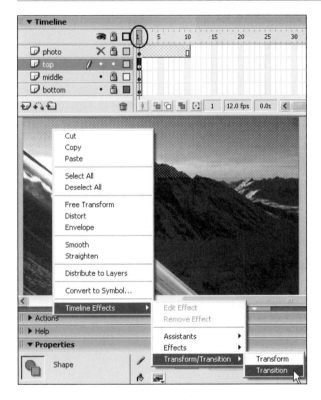

10. Make sure the **playhead** is on **Frame 1** and click the top portion of the **Stage** to select the shape in the top layer. **Right-click** (Windows) or **Ctrl+click** (Mac) and choose **Timeline Effects > Transform/Transition > Transition**. You will configure the **Transition** dialog box next.

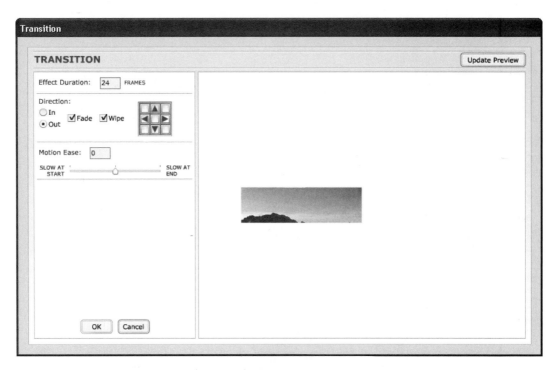

11. In the **Transition** dialog box, for **Effect Duration**, enter **24** frames. For **Directions**, select **Out**, **Fade**, and **Wipe** and make sure the **right arrow** is selected, as shown here. Leave **Motion Ease** at its default settings. Click the **Update Preview** button to preview your settings. Notice that the image fades out from left to right. Click **OK** when you are satisfied with your settings.

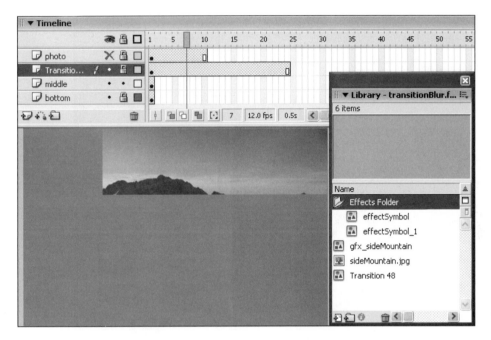

12. Press **Enter/Return** to play your movie. Notice that only the top portion of the image fades out from left to right. In the **Timeline**, also notice that the **top** layer was renamed **Transition 48**, and in the **Library** there is an **Effects** folder that contains the graphic symbols needed to create the effect and a graphic symbol called **Transition 48**, which is the original shape. You will add the **Transition Timeline Effect** to the middle and bottom shapes in the following steps.

Note: Depending on the number of Timeline Effects you have created, the numbers appended to the layer names in the Timeline and the numbers appended to the symbol names in the Library will be different in your project file compared to my project file.

13. Repeat Steps 9, 10, and 11 to the **middle** and **bottom** layers. In the **Transition** dialog box for the **middle** layer, keep the settings the same as shown in Step 11, except make sure the **left arrow** is selected in the **Direction** field.

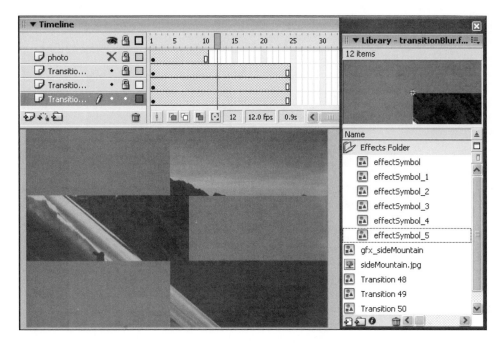

14. When you have finished adding the **Transition Timeline Effect** to the middle and bottom segments, press **Enter/Return** to play your movie. The top, middle, and bottom segments wipe off the **Stage**, revealing an empty **Stage**, where the next Timeline Effect will appear in the following steps. In the **Timeline**, notice that the **middle** and **bottom** layers have been renamed, and in the **Library** are the additional graphic symbols in the **Effects** folder, as well as the original shapes that have been converted into graphic symbols.

15. Save your file but don't close it. You will create another animation using the **Blur Timeline Effect** in the following steps.

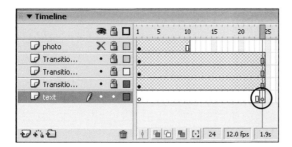

16. In the **Timeline**, click the **Insert Layer** button to add a new layer and rename it **text**. Make sure the **text** layer is at the bottom of all layers. Select **Frame 24** of the **text** layer and press **F7** to add a blank keyframe. Lock all layers except the **text** layer. You will add text to this layer next.

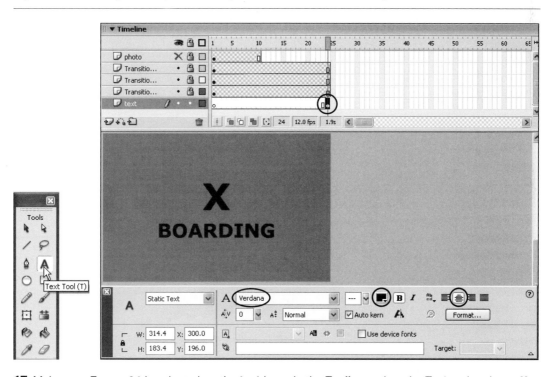

17. Make sure **Frame 24** is selected on the **text** layer. In the **Toolbar**, select the **Text** tool and type **X BOARDING** in all caps. With the text selected on the **Stage**, in the **Properties inspector**, set the **Font** to **Verdana**, the **Text Color** to **Black**, and select the **Align Center** button. For the "**X**," set the **Font Size** to **96**, and for the "**BOARDING**" text, set the **Font Size** to **50**. You will blur this text next.

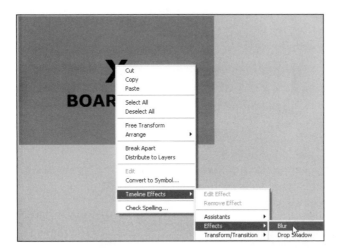

18. With the **Selection** tool, select the text block. **Right-click** (Windows) or **Ctrl+click** (Mac) to open the contextual menu and choose **Timeline Effects > Effects > Blur**. You will configure the **Blur** dialog box next.

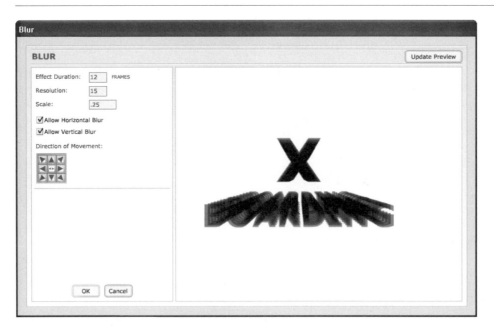

19. In the **Blur** dialog box, go ahead and experiment with the different settings, just make sure to click the **Update Preview** button to see your results. Configure the settings to your liking or use the settings I have entered, as shown here. Click **OK** when you are finished entering your settings.

The settings I entered will make the text blur over 12 frames, horizontally and vertically from the center.

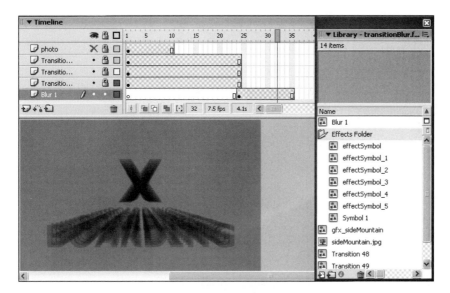

20. Press **Enter/Return** to play your movie. The top, middle, and bottom segments wipe off the **Stage**, revealing the blurred text. Nice! In the **Timeline**, notice that the **text** layer has been renamed, and in the **Library** are the additional graphic symbols in the **Effects** folder, as well as the original shapes that have been converted into graphic symbols. You have just completed another movie using the new Timeline Effects in Flash MX 2004.

*Note: If you want to change the Text color of the text, you can change the instance of the graphic symbol on the Stage by selecting it and modifying the Color field in the Properties inspector. Or you can double-click the graphic symbol in the **Effects** folder (inside the Library) to open it in **Symbol Editing** mode.*

21. Save this file but don't close it yet. You will move frames in the Timeline so that the graphic symbol of the mountain photo in the **photo** layer is seen on the **Stage** for a short while before it wipes off the **Stage**.

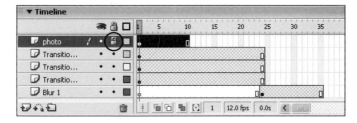

22. In the **Timeline**, show all the layers and unlock all the layers except the **photo** layer, as shown here. You will reposition the **Transition** layers in the Timeline in the following steps.

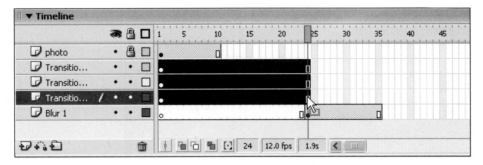

23. In one motion, select **Frame 1** in the first **Transition** layer and drag down to the last frame in the last **Transition** layer to select those frames, as shown here.

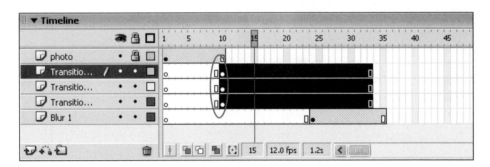

24. With the frames still selected, click and drag the range of frames over to the right so that the keyframes are on **Frame 10**, as shown here. You will move the frames on the **Blur** layer next.

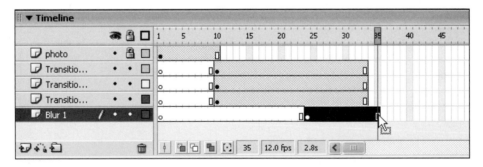

25. In one motion, on the **Blur** layer, select the keyframe on **Frame 24** and drag over to the last frame at **Frame 35**, as shown here.

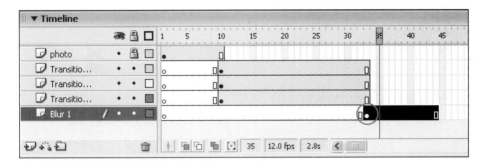

26. With the frames still selected, click and drag the range of frames over to the right so that the beginning keyframe is on **Frame 33**, as shown here. You will preview your animation next.

27. Choose **Control > Test Movie** to preview your animation. Notice the image of the mountain stays on the **Stage** for a short while before breaking up into three segments that wipe off the **Stage**, to reveal the blurred text.

Great work! You completed another movie with the use of the new Timeline Effects.

28. Save and close this file.

In this chapter, you learned how to create motion tween animations with symbols, as well as the new Timeline Effects that save you time and ease the task of creating effects and animation. This should give you a good starting point for experimenting with them, so go ahead and experiment with the other Timeline Effects or create your own animations with shape tweening and/or motion tweening. Otherwise, take a break and then get ready for the next chapter, where we'll cover bitmaps.

8.

Bitmaps

Benefits of Bitmaps	Compression
Importing and Compressing Bitmaps	Importing Bitmap Sequences
Converting Bitmaps to Vectors	Basic Masking
Animated Masks	Breaking Apart Bitmaps	Stroking a Bitmap
Combining Bitmaps and Vectors

chap_08

Macromedia Flash MX 2004
H•O•T CD-ROM

So far, even though you have used bitmap images as background images in several of the exercise files, you've mostly worked with vector images. Although many people think of Flash MX 2004 as simply a vector-editing and animation program, you will soon learn that it has some pretty impressive bitmap-editing features as well. This chapter concentrates on bitmap files, examining how Flash MX 2004 treats them differently from vectors. You will learn how to import bitmaps and how to optimize them. You'll also learn the art of breaking apart bitmaps to edit or crop them, and how to create a static and animated mask of a bitmap. At the end of this chapter, you will learn how to create interesting animation effects using bitmaps, including how to convert them to vectors.

Benefits of Bitmaps

Vector graphics are probably best known for their crisp appearance, small file size, and flexibility in scaling. Their efficient file size makes your movie play faster, which makes your site visitors happier. However, vectors do have a few negative aspects. Complex vector artwork made up of many individual vector objects can actually generate large files, making it harder for the computer to process, and thereby slowing the playback speed of the movie. Also, a photographic look is hard to achieve with vector artwork. In these cases, you'll want to work with bitmap files.

Bitmap graphics (also known as raster graphics) are stored in the computer as a series of values, with each pixel taking a set amount of memory. Because each pixel is defined individually, this format is great for photographic images with complex details.

Conveniently, Flash MX 2004 has the capability to import bitmap graphics of many different formats, including JPEG, GIF, and TIFF. If you have QuickTime 4 or later installed on your machine, the list of files available for import increases even further. The following chart lists the bitmap file formats that can be imported into Flash MX 2004. For a chart describing the vector file types supported by Flash MX 2004, see Chapter 18, "*Integration.*"

Bitmap File Types				
File Type	**Extension**	**Windows**	**Mac**	**QuickTime 4 or Later Needed?**
Bitmap	.bmp	X	X	No with Windows, yes with Mac
GIF and animated GIF	.gif	X	X	No
JPEG	.jpg	X	X	No
PICT	.pct, .pict, .pic	X	X	Yes with Windows, no with Mac
PNG	.png	X	X	No
MacPaint	.pntg	X	X	Yes
Photoshop	.psd	X	X	Yes
QuickTime Image	.qtif	X	X	Yes
Silicon Graphics	.sai	X	X	Yes
TGA	.tgf	X	X	Yes
TIFF	.tif, .tiff	X	X	Yes

Note: Flash MX 2004 will honor the transparency settings of graphics that can have a transparency applied, such as GIF, PNG, and PICT files.

Compression in Flash MX 2004

One of the most important issues to understand when working with bitmap files is that unless you tell it otherwise, Flash MX 2004 will always apply its own default compression settings to your bitmap graphics when the movie is exported from the project file. The graphics compression settings can be changed in two locations. You can set a single compression method and amount for every graphic in the project using the global Publish settings (covered in Chapter 16, "*Publishing and Exporting*"), or you can use the Bitmap Properties dialog box to set and preview individual compression settings for each file. Any changes you make in the Bitmap Properties dialog box will affect the graphic in the Library and all the instances of the bitmap within the project file.

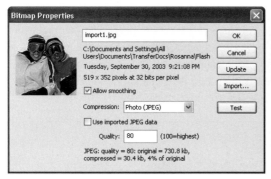

Lossy (JPEG) compression

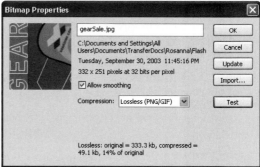

Lossless (PNG/GIF) compression

In the following exercise, you will learn how to compress bitmap images by changing the compression settings in the Bitmap Properties dialog box. There are two choices for compression: Photo (JPEG), also known as lossy; or Lossless (PNG/GIF). Generally, a photographic image will compress better with Lossy (JPEG) compression, and images that have a lot of solid colors will compress better as Lossless (PNG/GIF). What's nice is that you'll be able to see a preview within this dialog box to determine which choice is best.

When Flash MX 2004 outputs your finished movie, it takes this individual image compression into account and overrides its default compression settings.

Importing and Compressing Bitmaps

This first exercise will teach you how to import a bitmap into Flash MX 2004 and then how to adjust its compression settings.

> **1.** Copy the **chap_08** folder from the Macromedia Flash MX 2004 **H•O•T CD-ROM** to your hard drive. You must copy the files to your hard drive in order to save changes to them.

> **2.** Open a new document in Flash MX 2004. Save the file as **import.fla** in the **chap_08** folder.

> **3.** Choose **File > Import > Import to Stage**, or press **Ctrl+R** (Windows) or **Cmd+R** (Mac). This will open the **Import** dialog box. Browse to the **import1.jpg** file located inside the **chap_08** folder. Select the file, and click **Open**.

> *Note: The file **import1.jpg** may or may not have the .jpg extension, depending on which platform you are using (Windows or Mac) and whether you have the extensions turned on or off. Either way is fine, since the file name, import1, is what is important to locate this file. See the Introduction to learn how to hide or reveal the file name extensions. When you add a bitmap file to your project using the Import dialog box, you might wonder where the file goes. The file is automatically placed in three locations: on the Stage, in the Timeline, in the Library, and in the Bitmap Fill of the Color Mixer panel.*

> **4.** Press **Ctrl+L** (Windows) or **Cmd+L** (Mac) to open the **Library** panel.

5. Select the **import1** image inside the **Library**. Click the **Properties** button at the bottom of the **Library** window. The **Bitmap Properties** dialog box will open.

TIP | Additional Ways to See the Bitmap Properties

In this exercise, you used the Properties button in the Library window to display the Bitmap Properties dialog box. There are three additional ways to access this dialog box.

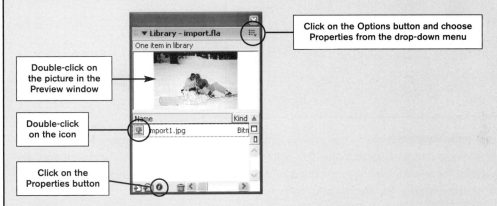

Double-click on the picture in the Preview window

Click on the Options button and choose Properties from the drop-down menu

Double-click on the icon

Click on the Properties button

You can double-click the picture in the Library Preview window, double-click the icon next to the image's name in the Library, or click the Options button in the upper-right corner of the Library and choose Properties from the drop-down menu.

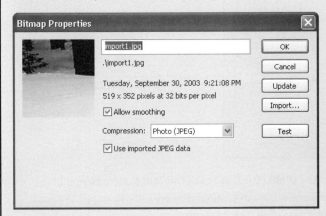

The Bitmap Properties dialog box is where you can set compression for individual images. A chart that describes all of the settings in this dialog box is located at the end of this exercise.

6. In the **Bitmap Properties** dialog box, move your cursor over the **Preview** window. Notice that your cursor changes to a hand. Click and drag the picture until you see the snowboarders in the **Preview** window. Since the snowboarders are the focus of the image, this will give you a much better view of the compression changes you are about to make.

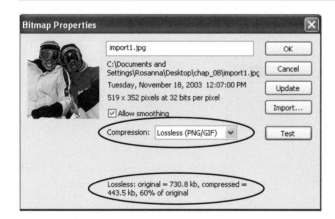

7. Set the **Compression** option to **Lossless (PNG/GIF)** and click the **Test** button. Notice that the new compression information appears at the bottom of the dialog box. You have just changed the compression settings for the **import1** image. The new compressed image size is 443.5 Kb, compared to the original, which was 730.8 Kb. If you click **OK**, this setting will alter the bitmap in the **Library** and the instance on the **Stage**. However, don't click **OK** just yet–you are going to make a couple more changes.

NOTE | Why Is File Size Important?

As you build project files in Flash MX 2004, you may have to keep your total SWF file size below a certain number, so that playback is optimal for all users viewing a Web site, including people using dial-up connections. With this in mind, it is important to find a good balance between image quality (check the Preview window after you click the Test button) and file size. You may have to experiment with several settings, but the file-size savings will be well worth the time spent!

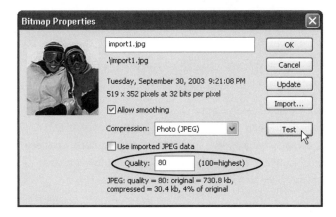

8. In the **Bitmap Properties** dialog box, change the **Compression** setting back to JPEG by choosing **Photo (JPEG)**. Uncheck the **Use imported JPEG data** check box, and add your own quality setting by typing **80** (100 is best; 0 is worst) in the **Quality** box. Click the **Test** button again. Notice that the new compression information appears at the bottom of the dialog box. The new compressed image size is 30.4 Kb, significantly smaller than the size obtained using PNG/GIF compression, which was 443.5 Kb. Additionally, the image still looks great in the **Preview** window. A good rule of thumb is that most photographic content will compress best with the **Photo (JPEG)** setting, and imported images that have more graphical content (solid colors, graphic shapes, text, and so on) will do better with the **Lossless (PNG/GIF)** setting.

9. Click **OK** to keep the last settings you applied.

10. Save and close this file.

Bitmap Properties Dialog Box	
Option	**Description**
Preview window	Shows the current properties of the bitmap and allows you to preview any changes applied to the settings in the dialog box.
File Name	Displays the bitmap's Library item name. Clicking in the File Name field and typing a new name will change the bitmap's name.
Image path	Displays the path for the image.
File information	Shows the date the bitmap was last modified, the file's dimensions, and the color depth.
Allow smoothing	Smoothes or dithers the image when checked. If this box is unchecked, the image will appear aliased or jagged.
Compression	Allows you to choose between **Photo (JPEG)** or **Lossless (PNG/GIF)** for that particular bitmap in the Library. Photo compression (JPEG) is best used for complex bitmaps with many colors or gradations. Lossless compression (PNG/GIF) is best used for bitmaps with fewer colors and simple shapes filled with single colors.
Use imported JPEG data	Allows you to use the original compression settings and avoid double compression when checked. If this box is not checked, you can enter your own values—between 1 and 100—for the **Quality** of the image.
Update button	Allows you to update the bitmap image if it has been changed outside of Flash MX 2004. It uses the image path to track the original image's location and will update the image selected in the Library with the file located in the original location.
Import button	Enables you to change the actual file the image path points to. Clicking this button will change the current image to the new file chosen, and all instances in the project file will reflect the new bitmap.
Test button	Allows you to see the changes you make to the settings of the Bitmap Properties dialog box in the Preview window and displays the new compression information at the bottom of the dialog box.

2. ——————————**Importing Bitmap Sequences**

One way to create a "mock" video effect in Flash MX 2004 is to use a sequence of photographs in which each image is just slightly different from the previous image. When these images are placed in keyframes, one right after another, and you test the movie, it will appear as if the camera is rolling! The following exercise demonstrates Flash MX 2004's capability to create frame-by-frame animations (or mock video) by importing a series of bitmap graphics all at once.

1. Open **bitmapSequence_Final.fla** in the **chap_08** folder.

2. You will see a series of images in **Frames 1** through **14**. Press **Enter/Return** to preview the movie. It seems as though you are watching a video of a snowboarder making a jump. You will create this animation sequence next.

3. Close the file.

4. Open the **bitmapSequence.fla** file from the **chap_08** folder. This is a blank file with a black background.

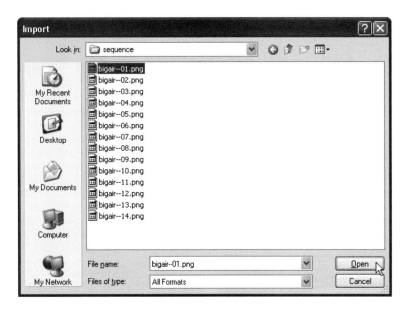

5. Choose **File > Import > Import to Stage**, or press **Ctrl+R** (Windows) or **Cmd+R** (Mac). In the **chap_08** folder, open the **sequence** folder. Notice that there are 14 numbered files named **bigair--xx**. Select the file **bigair--01.png** and click **Open**.

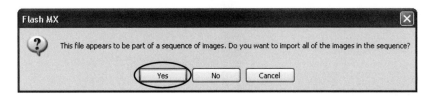

6. Flash MX 2004 will automatically detect that the image you are trying to import is part of a sequence of images, and you will be asked if you want to import the whole series of images. Click **Yes** to import all of the images into Flash MX 2004.

If you ever want to import a sequence of images as successive frames and have Flash MX recognize it as a sequence, be sure to number the images in the order you want the sequence to appear, such as image01, image02, and so on. Whenever Flash MX 2004 sees sequentially numbered images in the same folder, it will ask you whether the images should all be imported at once in a sequence.

When you clicked Yes in the last step, Flash MX 2004 imported all 14 files in the sequence, placed them on the Stage, and created a new keyframe for each one in the Timeline. Notice that the imported images are not centered on the Stage. Why? By default, Flash MX 2004 will place the imported sequence in the upper-left corner of the Stage. You will change this next.

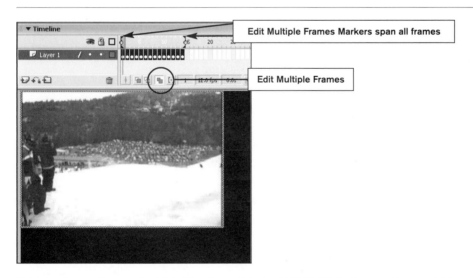

7. In the Status Bar on the Main Timeline, click the **Edit Multiple Frames** button. Make sure that the **Edit Multiple Frames** bar in the **Timeline** spans all the frames. If it doesn't, drag the markers so that it covers all 14 frames. Click the layer name to select all the frames on the layer. Next, click and drag the bitmap image into the center of the **Stage**. This allows you to reposition all the frames at once. When you are finished repositioning all the frames, click the Edit Multiple Frames button to turn it off.

8. Test the movie (**Control > Test Movie**). Notice that even though each frame holds a separate image, when you test the movie, it appears that you're watching video footage! When you are finished, close the **Preview** window.

Note: If your movie doesn't look very realistic, you can make a change that will fix that. You will do that next.

9. In the **Properties inspector**, type **16** for the **Frame rate**. This will speed up your movie to make the bitmap sequence animation seem more realistic. Choose **Control > Test Movie** to preview it. When you are finished, close the **Preview** window. Back in the project file, change the **Frame rate** to **6** and preview the movie again.

Tip: You may have to experiment with the frame rate a few times to make your movie appear the most realistic.

10. When you are satisfied with your movie, save this file and keep it open for the next exercise.

Converting Bitmaps to Vectors

When you import bitmaps, you are not limited to using the files as they exist in their original form. You can convert imported bitmaps into vector art by using the **Trace Bitmap** feature. This feature traces the shapes of a bitmap graphic and creates a new set of vector shapes that simulate the appearance of the bitmap file. Trace Bitmap is not an exact science, though; it requires a little experimentation to get it just right. This exercise will teach you how to use this feature to turn a bitmap into a vector.

1. You should still have the **bitmapSequence.fla** file open from the last exercise. Make sure the **Edit Multiple Frames** button is not selected.

2. In **Frame 1**, select the image on the **Stage** and choose **Modify > Bitmap > Trace Bitmap**. This will open the **Trace Bitmap** dialog box. You are going to turn the bitmap into a vector next.

NOTE | What Is Trace Bitmap?

The Trace Bitmap feature allows you to convert imported bitmaps into vector art. You might want to do this to create a neat animation effect, reduce the file size of a photographic image, or zoom into a photographic image during an animation. (Vectors scale when you magnify them; bitmaps get blurry.) The Trace Bitmap feature traces the outlines and internal shapes of a bitmap graphic and simulates the appearance of the bitmap file by creating a new set of vector shapes. You can use the settings in the Trace Bitmap dialog box to control how closely the new vector shapes match the original image.

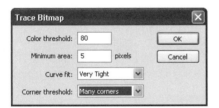

3. To produce a vector that closely resembles the original bitmap, decrease the **Color threshold** to **80** and the **Minimum area** to **5**. For **Curve fit**, choose **Very Tight**, and for the **Corner threshold**, choose **Many corners** to create a vector that has outlines with sharp edges that closely match the original bitmap. Click **OK**.

Be aware that the more detail a bitmap contains and the lower your settings in the Trace Bitmap dialog box, the longer it will take to convert the bitmap to a vector. This can increase the file size of the movie. A reference chart describing all the settings found in the Trace Bitmap dialog box is at the end of this exercise.

| Original bitmap | Vector image after using the Trace Bitmap feature |

4. When the conversion process completes, click anywhere outside of the image to deselect it. Notice that the traced bitmap looks very similar to the original.

Note: When you use the Trace Bitmap function, the changes will affect only the selected image on the Stage. The bitmap in the Library will remain unchanged. When you publish your movie, the vector image will appear instead of the original image.

5. Move the **playhead** to **Frame 14**. On the **Stage**, select the bitmap on **Frame 14** and choose **Modify > Bitmap > Trace Bitmap** to open the **Trace Bitmap** dialog box. You will modify the last image in the sequence next.

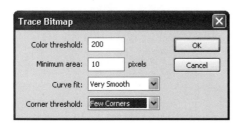

6. In the **Trace Bitmap** dialog box, enter **Color threshold: 200** and **Minimum area: 10**. For **Curve fit**, choose **Very Smooth**, and for the **Corner threshold**, select **Few Corners**. Click **OK**. This will turn the bitmap into a vector shape that has little detail and does not closely resemble the bitmap.

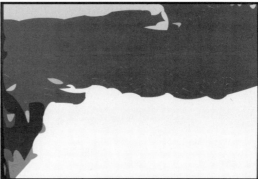

| Original bitmap | Vector image after using the Trace Bitmap feature |

7. When the conversion process completes, you will have an image that is more abstract and does not resemble the original image as closely as the settings you used on the image in **Frame 1**.

8. Repeat Steps 5 through 7, using the **Trace Bitmap** command to trace the remaining 12 images. Go ahead and experiment by applying different settings to each image to see how they change the original image.

*Tip: By using the Undo function—**Ctrl+Z** (Windows) or **Cmd+Z** (Mac)—you can always return the vector art to the original bitmap version and try it again if you don't like how the new image turned out.*

9. When you are finished, choose **Control > Test Movie** to preview the animation.

You are now watching vector-simulated video footage! This effect produces a stylized version of the video in which the artwork is all vectors. This technique is used often for aesthetic reasons. If you zoom into vectors, they remain crisp, whereas if you scale a bitmap, it will look blurry.

Note: Tracing works best on bitmaps with few colors and gradients. Tracing a bitmap with many colors will not only tax the computer's resources, but can also result in a vector graphic that is larger in file size than the original bitmap. To achieve the best results, experiment with different settings and take note of the file sizes.

10. Save and close the file. This exercise taught you quite a few things. First, you learned how to import a series of bitmap images, and how to change the position of multiple images spanning multiple frames. This is a skill that you can use independent of whether you convert the images to vectors using Trace Bitmap. Next, you learned how to use Trace Bitmap to multiple images. You can use Trace Bitmap on a single image or hundreds of images, depending on what effect you desire.

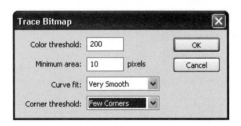

Trace Bitmap Dialog Box	
Option	**Description**
Color threshold	Sets the amount by which the color of each pixel can vary before it is considered a different color. As the threshold value increases, the number of colors in the image decreases, and the resulting traced bitmap image will have fewer colors than the original. The Color Threshold range is **1** to **500.**
Minimum area	Determines the number of surrounding pixels to consider when calculating the color of a pixel. The Minimum area range is **1** to **1000.**
Curve fit	Determines how smooth the outlines in the traced shape are drawn and how closely they match the original image.
Corner threshold	Determines whether to use sharp edges (**Many Corners**) or smoother edges (**Few Corners**).

Note: If the desired result of using the Trace Bitmap feature is to conserve file size or create a more abstract image, rather than to match the original image as closely as possible, you can choose a higher Color threshold, higher Minimum area, Smooth Curve fit, and Few Corners. These settings will decrease the final file size.

4. ———————Basic Masking

Masking is another great technique that can be created using bitmaps. A mask is a special layer that defines what is visible on the layer below it. Only layers that are beneath the shapes in the mask layer will be visible. In this exercise, you will create a text mask that masks a bitmap background.

> **1.** Open the **mask.fla** file from the **chap_08** folder. This file contains a blue background and one symbol in the **Library**.
>
> ---
>
> **2.** Choose **File > Import > Import to Stage**. In the **chap_08** folder, double-click the **sideMountain** file to open it. This places the bitmap on the **Stage**.
>
> ---
>
> **3.** In the **Main Timeline**, double-click the **Layer 1** name and rename the layer **mountain**. This layer will become the layer that is masked in the next few steps.
>
> ---

> **4.** Lock the **mountain** layer by clicking the **Lock** icon for the layer. This way, you won't accidentally move or select the bitmap on the **mountain** layer.
>
> ---

5. Click the **Insert Layer** button to add a new layer and rename it **xboarding**. Make sure the **xboarding** layer is above the **mountain** layer, as shown here.

6. Open the Library (**Ctrl+L** [Windows] or **Cmd+L** [Mac]). Notice the symbol named **siteName**. This is a graphic symbol that has been created for you. Drag an instance of the symbol onto the **Stage** and position the **X** over the snowboarder in the bitmap image, just as you see in the picture here.

This symbol instance of the xboarding.com name is going to end up as the mask for the bitmap. You can think of the text inside the symbol instance as a cookie cutter that will allow you to see what you cut out of the mountain image.

Tip: *It does not matter what color the mask is—Flash MX 2004 treats artwork of all colors as solid mask shapes.*

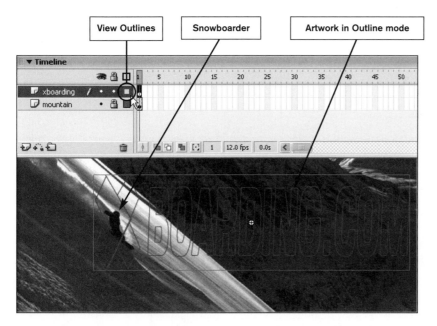

Tip: *To better see where the snowboarder is in relation to the xboarding graphic, click the **View Outlines** icon for the **xboarding** layer, as shown here.*

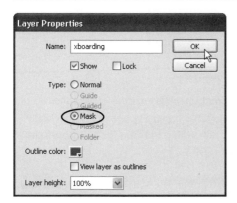

7. With the **xboarding** layer selected, choose **Modify > Timeline > Layer Properties**. This will open the **Layer Properties** dialog box. For **Type**, select **Mask**. Click **OK**. This will turn the **xboarding** layer into a **Mask** layer.

Note: *You can also select the layer icon in the Timeline and **right-click** (Windows) or **Ctrl+click** (Mac) to access the **Layer Properties** dialog box.*

Up to this point, you have a mask layer (xboarding) with a defined mask area. Now you need to create the Masked layer—that is, the layer connected to the Mask layer.

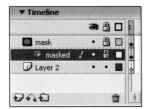

Note: *You can tell whether or not a layer is a mask layer or a masked layer by its icon and indentation. An unmasked (normal) layer has a standard layer icon: a white sheet of paper with the bottom-right corner turned up. A mask layer has a blue square with a checkerboard oval inside it, and a masked layer is indented under the mask layer and displays a checkerboard square with the bottom-right corner turned up. Additionally, the lines that separate masked layers from the mask layer are dotted rather than solid.*

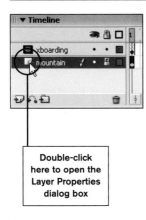
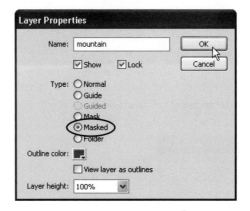

8. To make the **mountain** layer become masked by the **xboarding** mask layer, double-click the **mountain** layer icon to the left of the mountain name. This opens the **Layer Properties** dialog box. For **Type**, select **Masked** and click **OK**. In the **Main Timeline**, notice that the icon for the **mountain** layer has changed.

*There are three different ways to access the Layer Properties dialog box. You can choose **Modify > Timeline > Layer Properties**, as you did in Step 7, or you can double-click the icon next to the layer name, as you did here. Additionally, you can **right-click** (Windows) or **Ctrl+click** (Mac) the layer's name and choose **Properties** from the drop-down menu. Any of these options will allow you to declare the layer as a mask, so you can decide which method works better for you!*

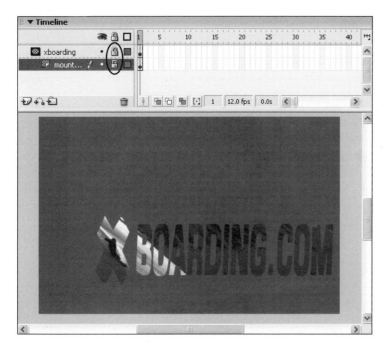

9. Lock the **xboarding** layer so that both layers are locked. You will see the bitmap showing through the text shapes!

*Tip: In order to preview what your mask will look like on the Stage, you must have both of the layers locked. To lock the layer, you can either click the **Lock** column in the layers or **right-click** (Windows) or **Ctrl+click** (Mac) the layer's name and choose **Show Masking** from the drop-down menu, which will lock both layers for you.*

You have just created your first mask! In the next exercise, you are going to animate the mask.

10. Save this file and keep it open for the next exercise.

5. —————————Animated Masks

In the previous exercise, you learned how to create a basic mask out of text. But masks do not have to be static! This exercise will teach you how to create a text mask that moves over a bitmap background.

1. You should still have the **mask.fla** file open from the previous exercise. If you accidentally closed it, open the **mask.fla** file you saved in the **chap_08** folder on your hard drive.

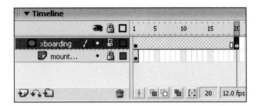

2. On the **xboarding** layer, click **Frame 20** and press **F6** to add a keyframe.

3. On the **mountain** layer, click **Frame 20** and press **F5** to add frames.

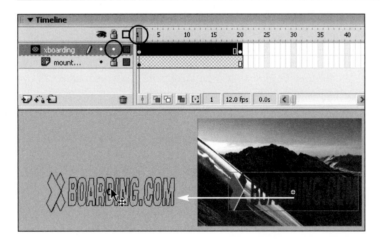

4. Unlock the **xboarding** layer by clicking on the **Lock** icon. Make sure the Playhead is on Frame 1. Select the xboarding symbol instance and move it off the Stage to the left, as shown here.

5. With the instance still selected in **Frame 1**, choose **Modify > Transform > Flip Vertical**. This will turn the **xboarding** symbol instance upside down, to serve as the beginning of the mask animation.

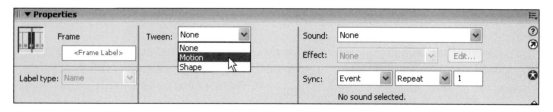

6. In the **Timeline**, select one of the frames in the **xboarding** layer between **Frame 1** and **Frame 20**. In the **Properties inspector**, select **Motion** from the **Tween** drop-down menu. This will add a motion tween to the mask.

7. Click the **Lock** icon to lock the **xboarding** layer. Notice that you can immediately see the masked image on the **Stage**.

8. Press **Enter/Return** to test your movie. Great job! In just a few steps, you have changed the basic mask from the previous exercise to an animated mask.

9. Save and close this file.

6. _____**Breaking Apart Bitmaps**

When you import bitmaps, you have many options for how you use the resulting image in your Flash MX 2004 movie. Often, you may want to use only part of a picture and delete the rest, although with bitmaps, this is not as simple as it sounds. Conveniently, Flash MX 2004 offers a feature that allows you to convert a bitmap into one simple shape so that you can crop and resize a specific portion of the original bitmap. The following exercise will teach you how to do this.

1. Open the **effects_Final.fla** file from the **chap_08** folder. This is a finished version of the file you will create over the next three exercises.

2. Choose **Control > Test Movie**, or press **Ctrl+Enter** (Windows) or **Cmd+Return** (Mac) to preview the SWF file.

You will see a pencil outline being drawn, the outline being filled with a bitmap that fades in from invisible to visible, and then a background image fading in. In the next three exercises, you will create this effect.

3. Close this file.

4. Open the **breakApart.fla** file from the **chap_08** folder. This is a blank file with a black background that has been created ahead of time to get you started.

5. Choose **File > Import > Import to Stage** or press **Ctrl+R** (Windows) or **Cmd+R** (Mac). In the **chap_08** folder, browse to the file named **boarderCloseUp.jpg** and double-click it to import it. You will see a photo of a snowboarder on the **Stage**.

*Tip: If you can't see the whole picture, choose **View > Magnification > Show All.***

6. *In the **Timeline**, rename **Layer 1** to **boarder**.*

Original bitmap

Broken-apart bitmap

7. Select the **snowboarder** bitmap on the **Stage** and choose **Modify > Break Apart**, or use the keyboard shortcut **Ctrl+B** (Windows) or **Cmd+B** (Mac). This option will turn the bitmap into a vector so you can edit it inside Flash MX 2004.

Note: Breaking apart a bitmap will affect only the instance on the Stage and not the original in the Library.

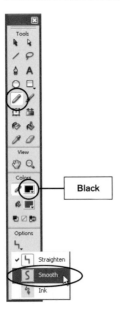

8. In the **Toolbar**, select the **Pencil** tool. Make sure the **Stroke Color** is set to **black**, and choose **Smooth** from the **Pencil Mode** options.

9. Using the **Pencil** tool, draw an outline around the snowboarder similar to the picture above. Make sure that you start and end in the same spot so that the outline is a continuous line, without breaks.

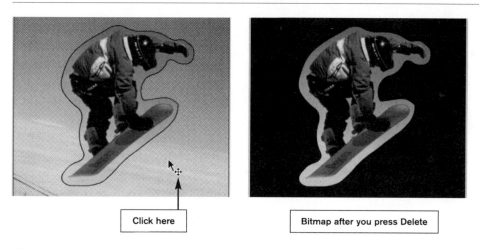

Click here

Bitmap after you press Delete

10. With the **Selection** tool, click anywhere off the **Stage** to deselect the bitmap. Next click the area outside the outline you drew. This will select the portion of the bitmap that is outside the line. You will see a selection mesh on the image, outside the outline, but notice that there is no selection mesh over the boarder. The mesh indicates the area that has been selected. Press **Delete**. Presto! You have cropped your bitmap!

In this exercise, you were able to crop your bitmap because once a bitmap is broken apart, it is considered a shape or a fill. Since a stroke will cut though a fill, as you learned in Chapter 3, "Drawing and Color Tools," you can use a stroke to cut the broken-apart bitmap and then separate the shapes. Neat!

11. Save this file and keep it open for the next exercise.

Stroking a Bitmap

Once you have broken apart the bitmap, you can use the stroke you drew with the Pencil tool to create some neat animation effects. This exercise will show you how.

1. You should still have the **breakApart.fla** file open from the last exercise.

2. Save this file as **strokeAnim.fla** in the **chap_08** folder.

3. Remember the outline you drew around the snowboarder? It is still there—you just can't see it because it is black like the background of the movie. Move your cursor over the edge of the snowboarder shape and double-click to select the entire outline stroke.

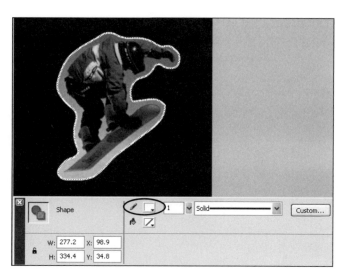

4. In the **Properties inspector**, change the **Stroke Color** to **white**. Now you will be able to see the stroke better.

5. With the stroke still selected, choose **Edit > Cut**, or press **Ctrl+X** (Windows) or **Cmd+X** (Mac) to cut the stroke out of the frame. You will be pasting the stroke into a different layer in a few steps.

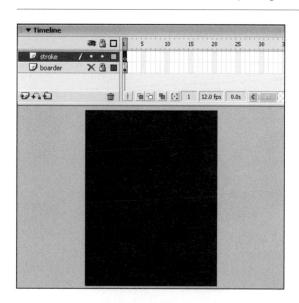

6. In the **Timeline**, lock the **boarder** layer and click the **Insert Layer** button to add a new layer. Rename the new layer **stroke**. Hide the **boarder** layer by clicking on the dot below the **Eye** icon so you can concentrate on the **stroke** layer for the next few steps.

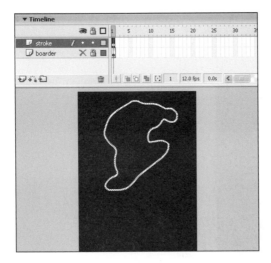

7. With the **stroke** layer selected, choose **Edit > Paste In Place**. This will position the stroke exactly where it used to be, just in a different frame, so you can work with it separately in the following steps.

Note: Was only part of your outline pasted? If you drew the original outline back in Exercise 6 without selecting the Smooth option for the Pencil mode, or if you drew the outline in several different segments rather than in one continuous segment, you may need to double-click to select all of the outline before you cut it in Step 5.

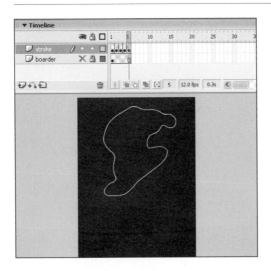

8. Press **F6** four times to add four more keyframes to the stroke layer. This will automatically add frames to the **boarder** layer to match the **stroke** layer. You are going to create a frame-by-frame animation that simulates a pencil drawing next.

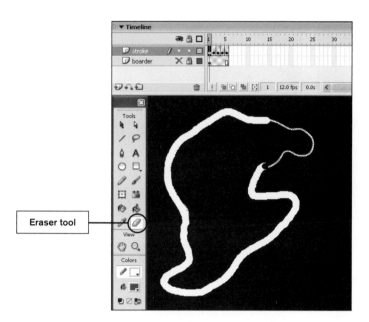

Eraser tool

9. In the **Timeline**, move the **playhead** back to **Frame 1**. Using the **Eraser** tool, draw over the stroke, leaving only a small portion of the outline, as shown here. When you release the mouse, only the portion of the stroke that you did not draw over will remain.

Tip: You can change the size of the **Eraser** tool if you prefer a larger erasing area by clicking on the **Eraser Shape** drop-down menu.

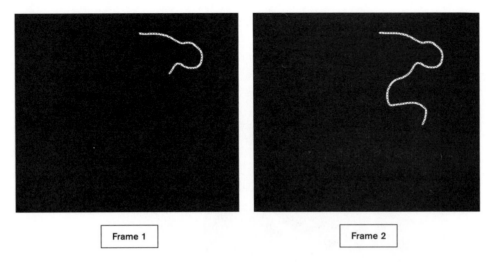

Frame 1 Frame 2

10. Move the **playhead** back to **Frame 2**. Using the **Eraser** tool again, draw over the stroke in **Frame 2**, but this time, allow more of the stroke to remain, as shown here. The idea here is to give the illusion that a pencil is drawing the outline, so in each frame, you want to reveal a little more of the outline until you see the full outline in **Frame 5**.

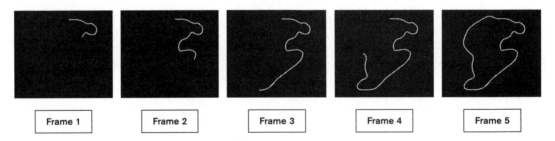

Frame 1 Frame 2 Frame 3 Frame 4 Frame 5

11. Repeat Step 10 for **Frames 3**, **4**, and **5**, leaving more of the outline each time. When you are finished, the content in each frame should look similar to the pictures here.

12. Press **Enter/Return** to preview the animation. The outline will draw itself.

13. When you are finished, save this file and keep it open for one last exercise.

8. Combining Bitmaps and Vectors

When you are working with bitmaps, you can make them fade in from invisible to visible or vice versa. This handy technique can be accomplished by turning the bitmap into a symbol, creating a motion tween, and applying an alpha to one of the symbols at the end or beginning of the tween. You will learn how to do this in the following steps.

1. You should still have the **strokeAnim.fla** file open from the last exercise.

2. Save this file as **effects.fla** in the **chap_08** folder.

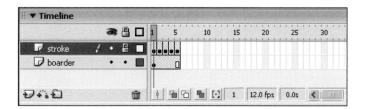

3. Lock the **stroke** layer, and unlock and unhide the **boarder** layer.

You will be creating a motion tween of the boarder changing from invisible to visible in the following steps.

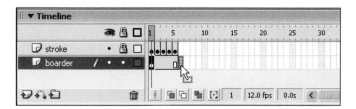

4. On the **boarder** layer, click the keyframe on **Frame 1** to select it. Next, click and drag the keyframe from **Frame 1** to **Frame 6**. This is how you move frames in the **Timeline**.

5. Select the boarder on the **Stage** and press **F8** to convert the boarder shape to a symbol. In the **Convert to Symbol** dialog box, name the symbol **boarder**, and choose **Graphic** for the **Behavior**. Click **OK**. This will be the beginning of the tween animation.

Why am I using a symbol? In the next few steps, you will be using alpha to create the fade effect, and you can't apply an alpha effect to an object that is not a graphic or movie clip symbol (which you will learn about in Chapter 10, "Movie Clips").

6. On the **boarder** layer, select **Frame 20** and press **F6** to add a keyframe to **Frame 20**. This will be the end of the tween animation.

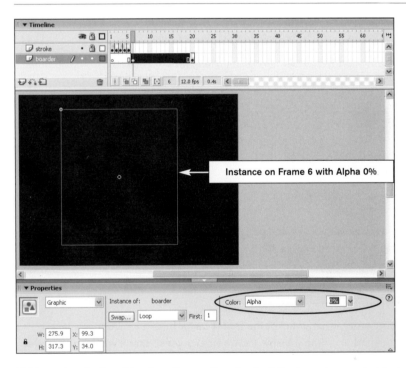

Instance on Frame 6 with Alpha 0%

7. Move the **playhead** back to **Frame 6** and select the **boarder** symbol instance on the **Stage**. (Be careful to select the instance on the **Stage** and not the frame so that the **Properties inspector** shows you the right attributes.) In the **Properties inspector**, set **Color** to **Alpha 0%**.

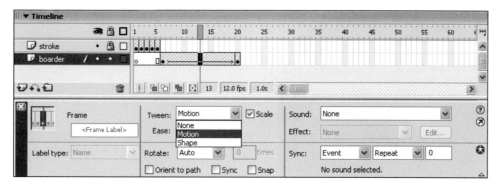

8. Click anywhere between **Frames 6** and **20** to select one of the frames. In the **Properties inspector**, choose **Motion** from the **Tween** drop-down menu.

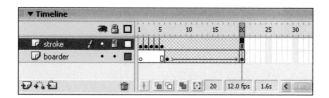

9. In the **stroke** layer, select **Frame 20** and press **F5** to add frames to match the number of frames on the **boarder** layer. This will make the outline draw itself and remain visible on the **Stage** during the tween animation.

10. Press **Enter/Return** to preview the animation. The outline will draw itself, and then the **boarder** layer will fade from invisible to full color.

You have one more tween animation to create.

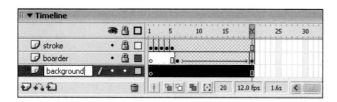

11. In the **Timeline**, lock the **boarder** layer and click the **Insert Layer** button to add a new layer. Rename the new layer **background** and drag it below the **boarder** layer so that it is the bottom layer in the **Timeline**.

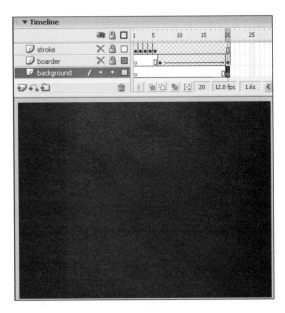

12. Select **Frame 20** and press **F7** to add a blank keyframe to **Frame 20** of the **background** layer. Hide the **stroke** and **boarder** layers so that you can see only the **background** layer for the next few steps.

13. Press **Ctrl+L** (Windows) or **Cmd+L** (Mac) to open the **Library**. Drag an instance of the **boarderCloseUp** bitmap graphic onto the **Stage**.

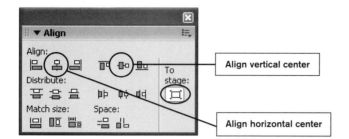

Align vertical center

Align horizontal center

14. Using the **Align** panel (**Ctrl+K** [Windows] or **Cmd+K** [Mac]), center the bitmap on the **Stage** by clicking the **To Stage** button and selecting the **Align vertical center** and **Align horizontal center** buttons.

*Note: The **Align** panel allows you to position selected objects relative to the **Stage** if the **To stage** button is selected or relative to one another if several objects are selected.*

15. With the snowboarder bitmap still selected on the **Stage**, press **F8** to convert the bitmap to a symbol. In the **Convert to Symbol** dialog box, name the symbol **origImage**, and for **Behavior** select **Graphic**. Click OK. This will convert the bitmap to a symbol so that you can create a motion tween in the following steps.

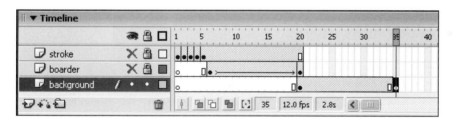

16. Select **Frame 35** on the **background** layer and press **F6** to add a keyframe to **Frame 35**. This will be the end of the tween animation.

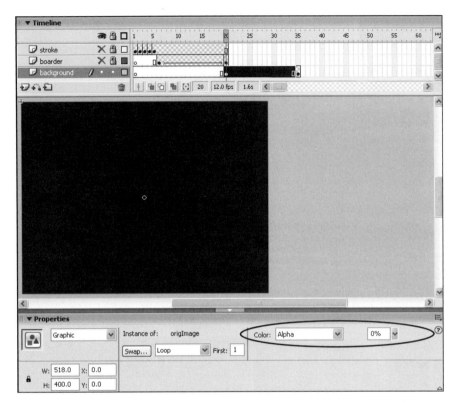

17. Move the **playhead** back to **Frame 20** and select the **origImage** symbol instance on the **Stage**. (Be careful to select the instance on the **Stage** and not the frame so that the **Properties inspector** shows you the right attributes.) In the **Properties inspector**, set **Color** to **Alpha 0%**. This will be the beginning of the animation on the **background** layer.

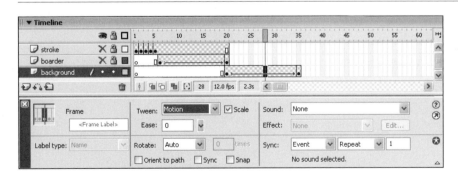

18. Click anywhere between **Frames 20** and **35** to select one of the frames. In the **Properties inspector**, choose **Motion** from the **Tween** drop-down menu.

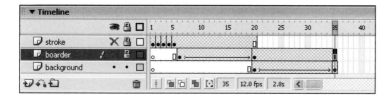

19. In the **boarder** layer, select **Frame 35** and press **F5** to add frames to match the number of frames on the **background** layer. This will make the boarder layer remain visible on the **Stage** during the background tween animation.

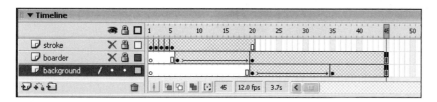

20. Click and drag down on **Frame 45** in the **boarder** and **background** layers to select **Frame 45** in both layers. Press **F5** to add frames up to **Frame 45**. This will add frames so that once the background fades up, it will remain for **10** frames before the animation starts over again.

21. Choose **Control > Test Movie** to preview the final animation. The outline will draw itself, the boarder layer will fade from invisible to full color, and then the background will fade in. Great work!

*Note: When you press **Enter/Return**, it is only a preview of the animation inside the editing environment and may not be exactly true to form. A more realistic test of the animation is to choose **Control > Test Movie** so that you can see the actual SWF file inside the Macromedia Flash Player. In Chapter 16, "Publishing and Exporting," you will learn the most reliable way to see how the file will look in a browser, which is using the Publish command.*

22. When you are finished, save and close this file.

That's it! You have conquered another chapter! Take a much-deserved break and get ready to learn about buttons next.

9.

Buttons

| Button States | Button Types |
| Rollover Buttons | Rollover Buttons with Text |
| Duplicating and Aligning Buttons |
| Adding Sound to Buttons | Invisible Buttons |

chap_09

Macromedia Flash MX 2004
H•O•T CD-ROM

There are three types of symbols in Flash MX 2004: graphic symbols, button symbols, and movie clip symbols. You learned about graphic symbols in Chapter 6, and this chapter will introduce you to the button symbol. In the next chapter, you'll learn about movie clip symbols.

Buttons are a special type of symbol in Flash MX 2004. They can include rollover states and even animated rollover states (which you'll learn about in Chapter 10, "*Movie Clips*"). What you might not realize is that there's more to making buttons than creating the artwork for them. Buttons can also be programmed to accept "actions" written in ActionScript (covered in Chapter 11, "*ActionScript Basics and Behaviors*"). Through actions, buttons can be made to play, stop, rewind, fast forward, change artwork, and numerous other things in your Flash movies! Before you will learn how to program the ActionScript for them, you have to learn how to create button symbols. Learning Flash MX 2004 involves putting a lot of puzzle pieces together, and button symbols are an extremely important part of the puzzle. In this chapter, you will build a solid foundation for working with buttons, including how to create, add sound to, test, and preview them.

Button States

When you create or edit a **button symbol**, you will see that it has its own Timeline, just as graphic symbols do. The difference with a button symbol's Timeline is that it displays four premade frames that are prelabeled: **Up**, **Over**, **Down**, and **Hit**. The first three frames of the button Timeline determine the appearance of the button during three different kinds of mouse interactions. The fourth frame, Hit, determines the clickable area of the button. The terms Up, Over, Down, and Hit are also called **states**, which are described in the upcoming chart. You've already learned that a Timeline must contain keyframes in order to contain changing content. Even though there are slots for the Up, Over, Down, and Hit states, you must insert keyframes in these slots in order to place artwork that changes within each or some of these states.

When you create a button symbol, Flash MX 2004 automatically adds a blank keyframe in the first frame—the Up state—of the button.

Button States	
State	**Description**
Up	The Up keyframe holds artwork that defines what the button looks like before the user's mouse interacts with the button.
Over	The Over keyframe is what the button looks like when the user positions the mouse over the Hit area of the button. This is also referred to as the rollover state of the button.
Down	The Down keyframe defines what the button looks like when it is clicked. This state is usually seen for only a split second, but it can be seen for longer periods of time if the user holds down the mouse.
Hit	The Hit keyframe of the button is always invisible to the user. It defines the area of the button that is reactive to the mouse. This is what makes the button clickable.

Button Types

Fundamentally, all button symbols are constructed alike. However, you can significantly change their appearance and behavior by altering the frames you use and the keyframes you set to contain artwork. The possibilities are nearly endless, but they will generally fall into the four categories listed in the following chart.

Button Types	
Type	**Description**
Basic	A basic button has the same content in the Up, Over, and Down states. Users can click it, and it can contain actions, but it provides no visual feedback during the user's interaction with it.
Rollover	A rollover button has different content in the Up state than in the Over state (and sometimes the Down state). It gives visual feedback about the user's mouse position by changing when the cursor moves over it.
Animated Rollover	An animated rollover button is similar to a rollover button, but one or more of its keyframes (usually the Over state) contains a movie clip instance. Whenever that keyframe is displayed, a movie clip animates. You will learn how to make animated rollover buttons and movie clips in the next chapter.
Invisible	Invisible buttons contain a blank keyframe in the Up state and a keyframe in the Hit state. They can also contain artwork in the Over or Down state, although they never contain artwork in the Up state. Because there is no artwork in the Up state, the button is invisible to users until they mouse over it. You will learn how to make an invisible button in Exercise 5.

I. ————————•**Rollover Buttons**

This first exercise will teach you how to create a basic rollover button. You will see how the button's Timeline is different from the Main Timeline, and you will learn about the four different states of buttons. This exercise will also show you how to test and preview the button you created.

1. Copy the **chap_09** folder, located on the **H•O•T CD-ROM**, to your hard drive. You need to have this folder on your hard drive in order to save files inside it.

2. Open **rollOverButton.fla** from the **chap_09** folder. This is a blank file with a gray background that has been created for you.

3. Choose **Insert > New Symbol** to create a new button symbol. This will open the **Create New Symbol** dialog box. Name the symbol **btnRollo** and set the **Behavior** to **Button**. Click **OK**.

> ## **NOTE | Button Naming Conventions**
>
> When developing Flash content, I prefer to give symbols names that begin with an abbreviation indicating the type of symbol it is, followed by a meaningful name for the symbol, such as "btnRollo." This way, when I have many symbols in the Library, I can sort my symbols alphabetically and have all the buttons grouped together, all the graphic symbols grouped together, and all the movie clip symbols (which you will learn about in the next chapter) grouped together. You will have a chance to work with the Library in many of the upcoming chapters.

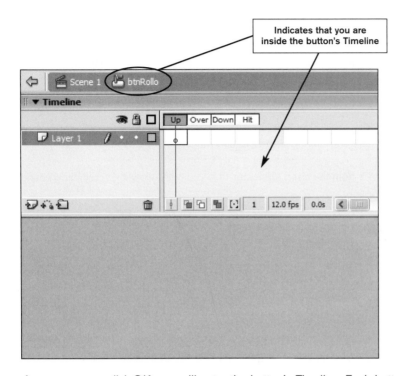

Indicates that you are inside the button's Timeline

As soon as you click OK, you will enter the button's Timeline. Each button symbol has its own Timeline, which is independent of the Main Timeline. This means that you can place the finished button on the Stage, and even though it contains multiple button states, it will occupy only one frame in the Main Timeline. Notice that the button Timeline contains four frames: Up, Over, Down, and Hit. Buttons do not automatically "play" as the Main Timeline does or as animated graphic symbols do. Rather, the button's Timeline remains paused at the first keyframe (or Up state), showing only the content in the Up state until the cursor comes into contact with the button. The other keyframes in the button symbol (Over and Down) are shown only in reaction to the cursor position.

4. Choose **View > Grid > Show Grid**. This will cover the Stage with a grid temporarily—the grid will not be exported with your movie. It is visible only in the Flash MX 2004 editing environment.

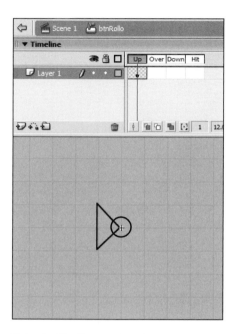

5. In the **Toolbar**, select the **Line** tool. Make sure the **Stroke Color** is set to **black**, and draw a small triangle that spans about two grid boxes in height. The right point of the triangle should be on the center crosshair on the **Stage** (which is actually the **Registration Point** of the button), as shown here. Placing the triangle on the center crosshair will ensure that the triangle is set to pivot on this point. If you choose to rotate, scale, transform, or position the triangle button, it will always pivot from the **Registration Point**, as you learned to do in Chapter 4, "*Animation Basics.*"

This will serve as the Up state of the button before the user interacts with it.

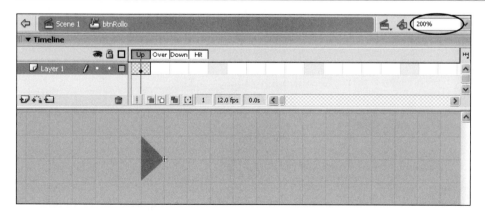

Tip: *To make it easier to draw the triangle, you can change the view to **200%** in the Edit Bar.*

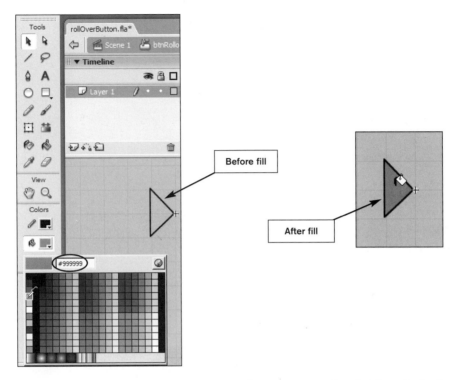

Before fill

After fill

6. Select the **Paint Bucket** tool. Set the **Fill Color** to the fourth color down in the first column of the **Fill Color** palette in the **Toolbar**, with the value of **#999999**, as shown here. Click once inside the triangle to fill the triangle with gray.

Why do you have to choose that specific gray? The next three exercises will build on one another, and it is important to use the right color in this first exercise so that by the time you get to Exercise 3, the colors will match the interface you will be working with.

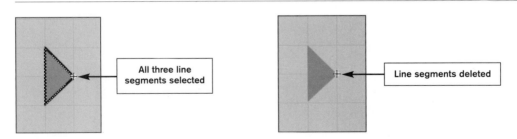

All three line segments selected

Line segments deleted

7. Select the **Selection** tool and move the cursor over the black stroke of the triangle; double-click it to select all three line segments. Press **Delete** on the keyboard to delete the black stroke. You will now have a solid gray triangle without a stroke around it.

8. Press **F6** to add a keyframe to the **Over** frame of the button. This will copy the content—the triangle—from the last keyframe into the **Over** frame.

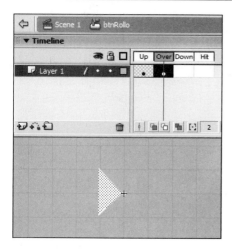

9. Select the **Paint Bucket** tool again, and this time choose **white** for the **Fill Color**. This will fill the triangle with white.

10. Press **F6** to add a keyframe to the **Down** state of the button. Set the **Fill Color** to the same color you used in Step 6: the fourth **gray** color swatch down from the top-left corner of the **Fill Color** palette in the **Toolbar**. This will fill the triangle with gray.

11. Move (or scrub) the **playhead** to see the different states of the button. The **Up** state triangle should be gray, the **Over** state triangle should be white, and the **Down** state triangle should be gray again.

To complete the button symbol, you need to define the Hit state of the button. You will do this next.

12. Press **F6** to add a keyframe to the **Hit** frame of the button. This will define the "hot" area of the button, or the area that will react to the mouse, which in this case is the exact same shape as the button. This is what makes the button clickable.

The Hit state is always invisible to the user. Therefore, it does not matter what color the content in the Hit keyframe is. The Hit state defines what area of the Stage will be used to activate the button rollover.

NOTE | Hit Me!

The Hit state of the button has one objective: to define an area that will be active when the cursor comes into contact with it. Because the Hit keyframe defines the area of the button that is reactive to the mouse, it is important that it cover the entire area of the button that you want to be active. If the button is tiny and the Hit area is small or smaller, it may be difficult for the user to interact with the button at all. For tiny buttons or buttons that are text only, I suggest using a solid shape that is slightly larger than the button's Up or Over states. You will learn to do this in the next exercise!

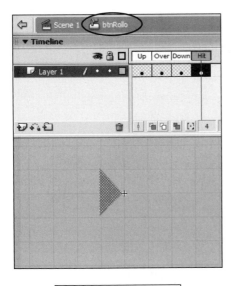

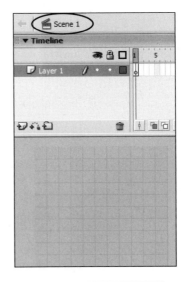

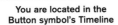
You are located in the
Button symbol's Timeline

You are located in Scene 1
of the Main Timeline

13. In the edit bar, click **Scene 1** to return to Scene 1 of the **Main Timeline**.

NOTE | Where's the Button?

When you choose **Insert > New Symbol** (as you did in back in Step 3), Flash MX 2004 automatically places the new button symbol in the Library, so you will not see the button on the Stage of the Main Timeline. If you want to use the new button in your movie, you must drag an instance of the button onto the Stage. In order to test the button you have three options: You can test it in the Library, on the Stage, or by using **Control > Test Movie**. You will try each option next.

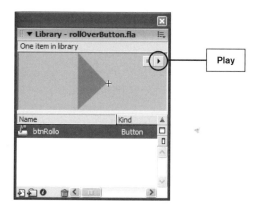

Play

14. Press **Ctrl+L** (Windows) or **Cmd+L** (Mac) to open the **Library**. Click the **btnRollo** symbol in the **Library**. Click the **Play** button on the **Controller** in the **Preview** window to preview the button in the **Library**.

Notice that the button will play one frame right after the next (Up, Over, Down, and Hit). Although this will give you a quick preview, it may not be very realistic. The following steps will teach you how to preview the button on the Stage.

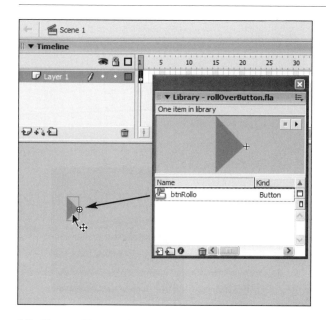

15. Choose **View > Grid > Show Grid** to hide the grid on the **Stage**. Drag an instance of the button you created onto the **Stage**.

16. Choose **Control > Enable Simple Buttons**. This will allow you to test the button right on the Stage.

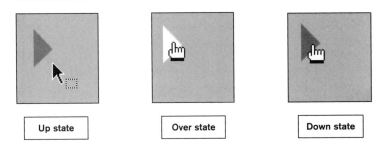

| Up state | Over state | Down state |

17. Go ahead and move your mouse over the button to see the **Over** state. Click the button to see the **Down** state.

18. Choose **Control > Enable Simple Buttons** again to deselect this option. The button will not be active on the **Stage** anymore.

Although you can still select enabled buttons, it is easier to work with them if they are disabled. You can always enable the buttons again when you want to test their behavior on the Stage.

19. Choose **Control > Test Movie**. This will produce the SWF file (you'll learn more about this in Chapter 16, "*Publishing and Exporting*") that will let you test any of the buttons in the movie. This method of testing will yield the same visual results as choosing **Enable Simple Buttons**; it's just another way to test your work. Go ahead and move the mouse over the button to trigger the Over state to see it working. When you are finished, close the SWF file to return to the editing environment.

20. Save this file and keep it open for the next exercise.

2. ————————Rollover Buttons with Text

In the previous exercise, you learned to create and test a button. This exercise will show you how to alter that button by adding text and altering the Hit state of the button. In the steps that follow, you will learn the difference between using text to define the Hit state and using a solid shape to define the Hit state of the button.

1. You should still have the file **rollOverButton.fla** open from the previous exercise. Save this file as **textButton.fla** in the **chap_09** folder.

2. In the **Library**, double-click the button symbol's icon to open the button's **Timeline**.

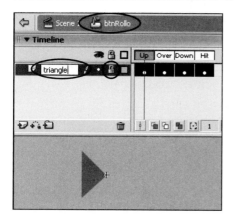

3. Inside the button symbol's **Timeline**, rename **Layer 1** to **triangle**, and lock the **triangle** layer.

4. Click the **Insert Layer** button to add a new layer to the button's **Timeline**. Rename the new layer **text**.

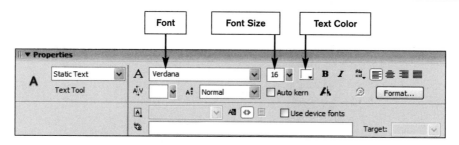

5. In the **Toolbar**, select the **Text** tool and click on the Stage to bring focus to it. In the **Properties inspector**, choose **Verdana** for the **Font**, **16** for the **Font Size**, and **white** for the **Text Color**.

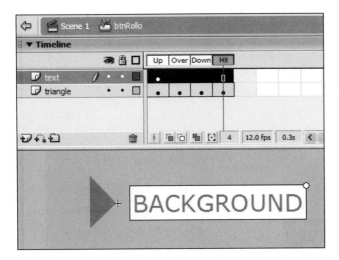

6. On the **Stage**, click to the right of the triangle and type the word **BACKGROUND** in capital letters. This will automatically add frames so that the word **BACKGROUND** appears across the **Up**, **Over**, **Down**, and **Hit** states.

7. Press **F6** to add a keyframe to the **Over** state of the button.

8. Select the text block on the **Stage** in the **Over** frame. In the **Properties inspector**, click the **Text Color** box and choose the **dark gray** color, three from the top, as shown here. This will change the text color for the text in the **Over** frame.

9. Choose **Control > Test Movie** to test the button.

NOTE | Using Text in the Hit State

| Button not activated | Button not activated | Button activated |

Notice that, depending on where you click, the button may or may not work. This is because you used text in the Hit state, and therefore the button will not be active until the mouse passes directly over the actual text itself (not in between the characters), as shown in these pictures. This can be confusing, because the button will not work unless the user places the mouse cursor directly over a solid part of a letter. A hole in an "O" or even the space between letters can cause the button to flicker on and off. This is why using text to define the Hit state of your buttons is not a good idea. You will learn how to use a solid shape to define the Hit state next.

10. Close the **Preview** window to return to the project file. Move the **playhead** to the **Hit** frame.

*To trigger the button, the mouse must move over the area that is defined as the Hit state. In this case, the Hit frame is defined by the content inside it, which consists of the triangle and the text, **BACKGROUND**. As noted in the "Using Text in the Hit State" sidebar, the current Hit state causes the button to be triggered only when the mouse rolls exactly over the text or the arrow. This is not the correct way to create a Hit state.*

You will modify the button's Hit state next.

11. In the button's **Timeline**, click and drag down on both layers in the **Hit** frame to select the layers. **Right-click** (Windows) or **Ctrl+click** (Mac) the selected layers to access the shortcut menu. Choose **Remove Frames** to remove both keyframes in the **Hit** state of the button. You will be adding new content to define the **Hit** area in the next few steps.

12. Lock the **text** layer and click the **Insert Layer** button to add a new layer to the button's **Timeline**. Drag the new layer below the **triangle** layer and rename it to **hit**.

13. Click in the **Hit** frame on the **hit** layer, and press **F7** to add a blank keyframe to the **Hit** state of the button.

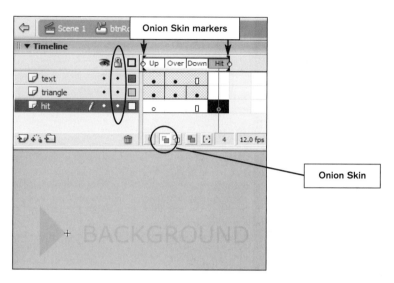

14. Unlock all the layers and select the **Onion Skin** button. Make sure the **Onion Skin** markers span all four states of the button, as shown here. You will be creating the new **Hit** state next, and you need to be able to see the artwork in the other frames.

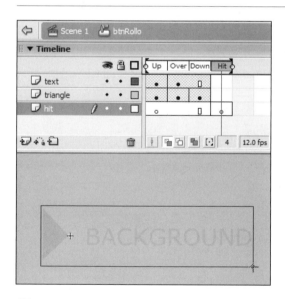

15. In the **Toolbar**, select the **Rectangle** tool. On the **Stage**, draw a **rectangle** that covers both the **triangle** and the **text**. This way, the mouse will only need to move over the rectangle in order for the button to be triggered. After you are finished drawing the rectangle, deselect the **Onion Skin** button to turn off onion skinning.

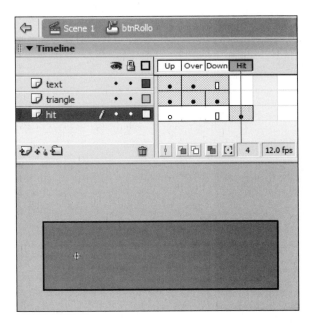

After you draw the rectangle, you will end up with a solid shape that will define the new Hit state for the button symbol. It doesn't matter what color the Hit state is or if it contains a stroke and a fill. You need to stay focused only on making sure that it covers the appropriate area. The "Understanding the Hit State" sidebar details more about the Hit state.

You have just modified the Hit state of your rollover button symbol! You will test it again next.

---

16. In the edit bar, click **Scene 1** to leave the button symbol's **Timeline** and return to the **Main Timeline**.

Notice the button instance you placed on the Stage in the previous exercise. Since you modified the actual symbol itself in this exercise, the button instance on the Stage will automatically be updated with the text and the new Hit state.

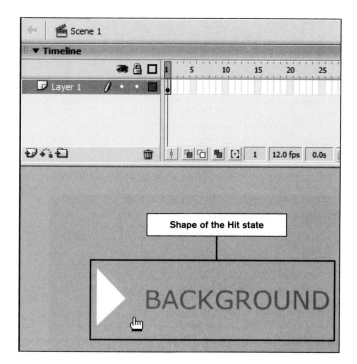

17. Choose **Control > Enable Simple Buttons** to test the button on the **Stage**. Move your mouse over the button to see the **Over** state, and click the button to preview the **Down** state.

Notice how much easier it is to interact with the button now that you've changed the Hit state. This is because you've defined the Hit state as a solid shape that covers the whole Up state of the button (the arrow and the text). Therefore, when you test the button, as soon as you touch the edge of the invisible rectangle shape (the Hit state), the Over state of the button is triggered.

18. Choose **Control > Enable Simple Buttons** again to deselect this option. The button will not be active on the **Stage** anymore.

19. Save and close this file.

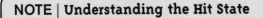

NOTE | Understanding the Hit State

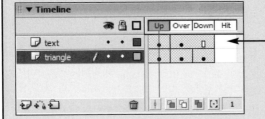

No frame or keyframe in the Hit state:
Rollover button will work using the currently
displayed frame as the Hit state

If there is no frame or keyframe in the specified Hit state, the Hit shape of the button is set by the currently displayed keyframe of the button. This means that if the Up and Over keyframes contain different shapes, the Hit state will change when the user rolls over the button. This is not an ideal way to create buttons.

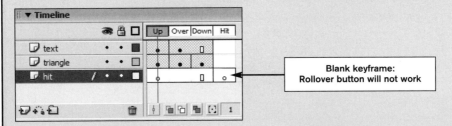

Frame in the Hit state:
Rollover button will work using the
previous frame as the Hit state

If a frame is specified in the Hit state, it will use the contents of the last set keyframe.

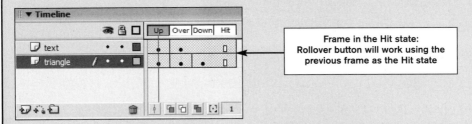

Blank keyframe:
Rollover button will not work

Setting a blank keyframe in the Hit state will disable the rollover, since a Hit state is required to trigger the Over and Down states.

If the shape for the button is large enough for the Hit state, you don't have to create a keyframe or new artwork in that frame. In this exercise, however, the text was not an adequate shape or size for the user to trigger the rollover consistently. The best method is to test your rollovers first, to ensure that the Hit state is an adequate shape for the job.

Duplicating and Aligning Buttons

In the last two exercises, you have learned how to create buttons, how to preview the results, and why the Hit state is important. Now that you know how to make a rollover button, another handy skill is to make copies of the button in the Library. For example, you can change the text in each copy of the button symbol to create a navigation bar in little time. This exercise will show you how to duplicate buttons in the Library and how to align them on the Stage. You will also learn how to use Library items from other movie projects. This exercise demonstrates a practical workflow for reusing and modifying an existing button design.

1. Open the file named **duplicateAlign.fla** from the **chap_09** folder. This file contains one layer with a background image.

*Tip: Choose **View > Magnification > Show All** to see the whole background image.*

2. Press **Ctrl+L** (Windows) or **Cmd+L** (Mac) to open the **Library**. Notice that there are three items in the Library: the interface graphic symbol and two bitmaps.

3. Choose **File > Import > Open External Library** and select the **textButton.fla** file from the **chap_09** folder. This will open only the **Library** (with the button symbol you created from the last exercise) from the **textButton.fla** file. You will be using the button from that file inside the **duplicateAlign.fla** file in the following steps.

The Open External Library technique can come in handy when you want to use assets such as symbols from one project in another project. This command allows you to open only the Library that is attached to a Flash project file. This will keep your computer screen less cluttered than if you had to open a different project file just to use its Library assets.

4. Notice that now the **Library** looks longer than normal. This is because there are two **Libraries** in the panel window. On the top is the **Library** from the **duplicateAlign** movie you are currently working on, and below is the **Library** from the **textButton** movie, which you opened in Step 3.

As you can see, using the Open External Library technique makes it easier to use Library assets from one project to another, rather than opening up the project file (FLA) that contains the Library items. So, instead of having several project files and their Libraries open, you can use the Open External Library technique to open the Libraries from as many project files as you need, without opening up their FLAs. This will save you time, keep your computer screen less cluttered, and help you avoid the headache of managing several open projects at the same time.

Note: *In some cases, the Libraries may be on top of each other but in the reverse order, which is fine. This will not affect the exercise in any adverse way. The important point is that both Libraries are there.*

5. In the **Main Timeline**, insert a new layer and name it **buttons**. Make sure the **buttons** layer is above the **background** layer.

6. In the **textButton Library**, drag an instance of the **btnRollo** symbol onto the **Stage**, and place it over the gray box on the left side of the **Stage**, as shown here.

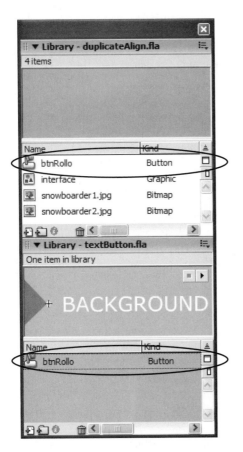

After you place the instance on the Stage, something interesting happens. The btnRollo symbol is now located in the duplicateAlign Library also. This is because you have added the symbol from the textButton movie to the duplicateAlign movie, and Flash MX 2004 adds the symbol to the Library for you.

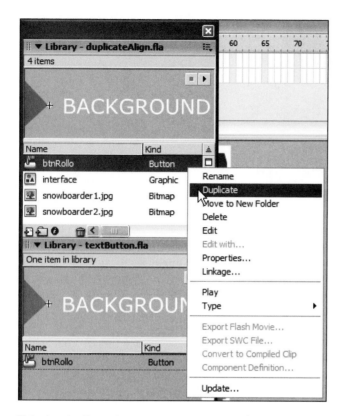

7. In the **duplicateAlign Library**, **right-click** (Windows) or **Ctrl+click** (Mac) on the **btnRollo** symbol to access the shortcut menu. Choose **Duplicate** to make a copy of the button symbol. This opens the **Duplicate Symbol** dialog box.

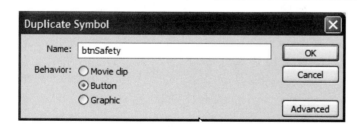

8. In the **Duplicate Symbol** dialog box, type **btnSafety** in the **Name** field and make sure **Behavior: Button** is selected. Click **OK**. You have just made an exact duplicate of the button you previously created. Notice the new **btnSafety** symbol in the **Library**.

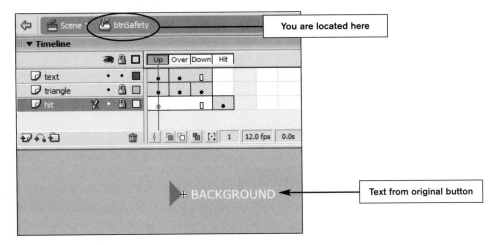

9. Double-click **btnSafety** in the **Library** to open the button symbol's **Timeline**. Notice that the **Timeline** looks identical to the original button you created. Lock the **triangle** and **hit** layers so you don't accidentally edit anything on those layers. You will be changing the text of this button next.

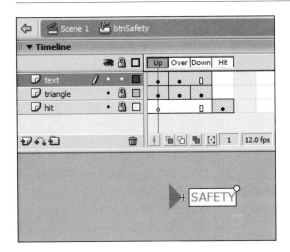

10. On the **text** layer, click in **Frame 1** (the **Up** state of the button). Double-click the **text block** on the **Stage**, highlight the **text**, and type the word **SAFETY** in capital letters. This will replace the existing text in the first frame with the word **SAFETY**.

11. Click **Frame 2** in the **text** layer (the **Over** state of the button). Double-click the **text block** on the **Stage**, highlight the **text**, and type the word **SAFETY** in capital letters. This will replace the existing text in the second frame with the word **SAFETY**.

NOTE | Changing the Hit State

The most important things to remember about the Hit state are that it should cover the entire area you want to designate as reactive to the mouse and that it should cover the entire area of the artwork/text.

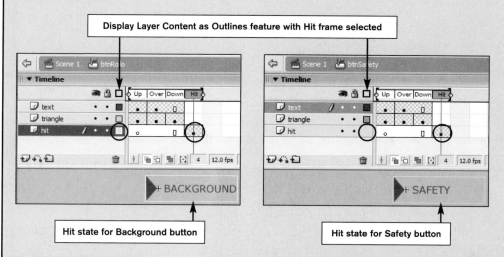

Display Layer Content as Outlines feature with Hit frame selected

Hit state for Background button

Hit state for Safety button

In the last step, the Hit frame contained a rectangle that completely covered the Safety button's triangle and text. Therefore, you did not need to make the rectangle in the Hit state bigger. It is okay if the Hit state is a bit longer than the button text. It is important to make sure that it is not shorter, though. I have turned on onion skinning and the Display Layer Content as Outlines feature in the Timeline to illustrate this point. This feature allows you to view the content on the Stage as outlines rather than solid shapes for any layer that is selected. Here it allows you to see the outline of the rectangles in relation to the button text.

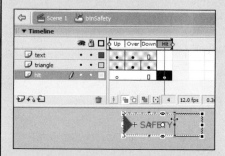

You can, however, resize the rectangle in the Hit frame if you want to for any reason by selecting the Free Transform tool and resizing the shape to your liking—just make sure that it covers the entire artwork and text area.

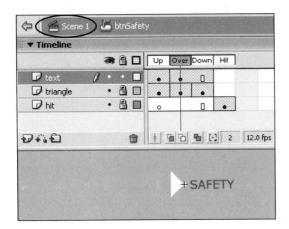

12. In the edit bar, click **Scene 1** to leave the button symbol's **Timeline** and return to the **Main Timeline**.

13. Drag an instance of the new button, **btnSafety**, onto the **Stage**, just below the **background** button. Choose **Control > Enable Simple Buttons** and test it. When you are finished testing it, choose **Control > Enable Simple Buttons** again to deselect this feature.

14. Repeat Steps 7 through 11 to create three more duplicate buttons. Name them **btnLearning**, **btnGear**, and **btnWhatsNew**, respectively. Inside each button, the text should read **GEAR**, **LEARNING**, and **WHAT'S NEW**.

15. When you are finished duplicating and editing the buttons, click **Scene 1** in the edit bar to return to the **Main Timeline**.

Click and drag to resize

Collapse arrow

16. Click the collapse arrow in the **textButton Library** to collapse that **Library**, and click and drag down diagonally on the right corner of the **Library** panel to resize the entire panel. This way you will be able to see all the buttons you created at the same time.

NOTE | Closing the Additional Library

In addition to collapsing the textButton Library, you can permanently close the textButton Library by following two easy steps:

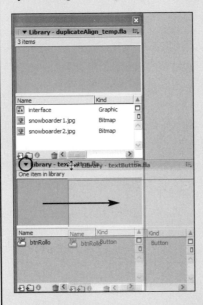

In the **textButton Library** panel, click the series of dots in the upper-left corner and drag the **Library** to the right to undock the two **Libraries** from each other.

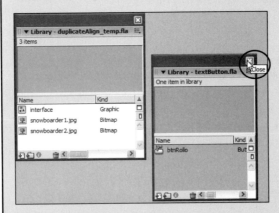

Once the **Library** is undocked, you can close it by clicking the **Close** button in the upper-right corner of the **textButton Library** window (Windows) or in the upper-left corner of the **textButton Library** window (Mac).

*Warning: Once you close a Library that was opened using the Open As Library command, you cannot press **Ctrl+L** (Windows) or **Cmd+L** (Mac) to open it again. **Ctrl+L** (Windows) and **Cmd+L** (Mac) are reserved for the currently open project file (FLA). To open the textButton Library again after you close it, you would need to select **File > Import > Open External Library** to open it again.*

17. Drag the **btnLearning**, **btnGear**, and **btnWhatsNew** buttons onto the **Stage** below the other two buttons.

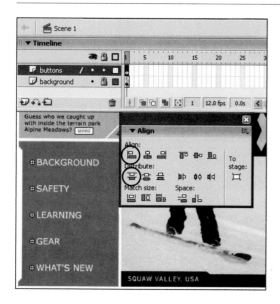

18. Press **Ctrl+A** (Windows) or **Cmd+A** (Mac) to select all five buttons on the **Stage**. Open the **Align** panel (**Window > Design Panels > Align**) and make sure the **To Stage** button is not selected. Select **Align Left Edge** and **Distribute Vertical Center** to make all the buttons align to the left and be equally spaced.

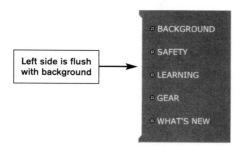

Left side is flush with background

19. Make sure all the buttons are still selected. Using the **right arrow** key on the keyboard, nudge the buttons to the right so that the left side of each button is flush with the gray background, as shown here.

20. Choose **Control > Test Movie** to test your rollover buttons. Rather than creating five separate buttons, one at a time, and creating all the artwork inside each button, you have streamlined the process. You have created this simple navigation system by creating the artwork for only one button, duplicating it four more times, and changing only the text inside each button.

21. Save this file and keep it open for the next exercise.

NOTE | Duplicate Versus Instance

In the last exercise, you duplicated the Library item of one button, and created four new buttons based off that original. You might wonder why you couldn't simply drag the button from the Library to the Stage three times and modify the instances. Since the original symbol contains text, you would have to go into the symbol itself to modify the text. In general, you can change the shape, size, rotation, skew, and color of any instance, but you are unable to change actual artwork or text without going back to the original symbol. Think of it like this: Any time you have to actually go inside the symbol's Timeline to modify something, you are changing the symbol. Any time you change an instance on the Stage in the Main Timeline, you are modifying an instance of the original symbol.

4. ———————Adding Sound to Buttons

The different states of the buttons you create can each hold a different sound to give feedback to the user. This exercise shows you how to add a simple sound to a button.

1. You should still have the **duplicateAlign.fla** file open from the last exercise.

2. Choose **File > Import > Open External Library** and select the **buttonSounds.fla** file from the **chap_09** folder.

*This will open only the Library of the **buttonSounds.fla** file. You will be using the sound files inside this Library in the following steps.*

Note: A list of supported sound formats in Macromedia Flash MX 2004 is in Chapter 13, "*Sound.*"

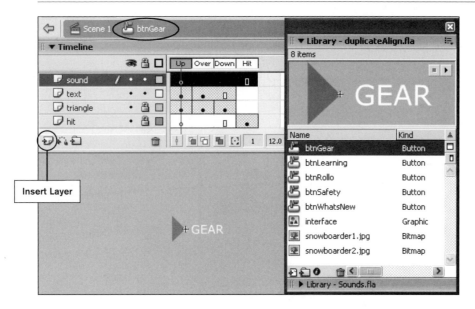

3. In the **duplicateAlign Library**, double-click the **btnGear** button icon to open the button's **Timeline**. Click the **Insert Layer** button to add a new layer, and make sure it is the topmost layer. Name this layer **sound**.

4. In the **sound** layer, press **F7** on the **Over** frame to add a blank keyframe. You will be adding a sound to this frame next.

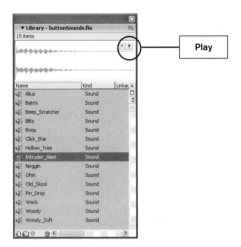

5. In the **buttonSounds Library**, select any of the sound files, and preview the sounds by clicking the **Play** button in the **Library Preview** window.

Note: *A list of supported sound formats in Flash MX 2004 is in Chapter 13, "Sound."*

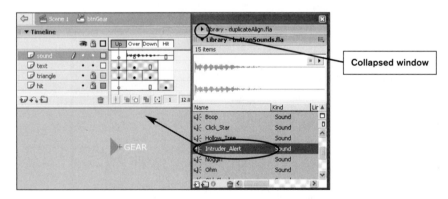

6. Collapse the **duplicateAlign Library** window so you have more room to work. With the **Over** frame selected in the **sound** layer, select the **Intruder_Alert** sound from the **buttonSounds Library** and drag an instance of it onto the **Stage**. That's it! You have just added a sound to the button.

Note: *You will not see a visual representation of the sound on the Stage. Instead, you will see sound waves in the Over frame of the Timeline. It is okay if the sound extends into the Hit frame in the button's Timeline, because the Hit state is determined by artwork on the Stage, not sound in the Timeline. Therefore, having a sound in the Hit frame will have no effect on the button.*

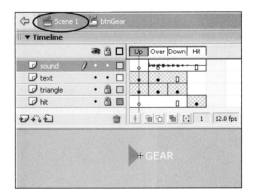

7. In the Edit Bar, click **Scene 1** to return to the **Main Timeline**.

Since you modified the button in the Library, it will update all of the instances on the Stage as well as include the sound you added.

8. Choose **Control > Enable Simple Buttons**. This will allow you to test the button on the **Stage**. You should hear the sound play when you move the mouse over the **btnGear** button, because you added the sound to the **Over** state of that button. When you are finished testing it, choose **Control > Enable Simple Buttons** again to deselect this feature. You will add a sound to the **Down** state of the **What's New** button next.

Tip: This is a very brief introduction to working with sound. You will learn about sound in depth, including compressing and testing, in Chapter 13, "Sound."

9. In the **Library** panel, expand the **duplicateAlign Library** to see all its contents. Double-click the **btnWhatsNew** button icon to open the button's **Timeline**. Collapse the **duplicateAlign Library** to hide it temporarily.

10. Lock the **text** layer, and click the **Insert Layer** button to add a new layer, making sure it's the top-most layer. Name this layer **sound**.

11. In the **sound** layer, press **F7** to add a blank keyframe on the **Down** frame. You will be adding a sound to this frame next.

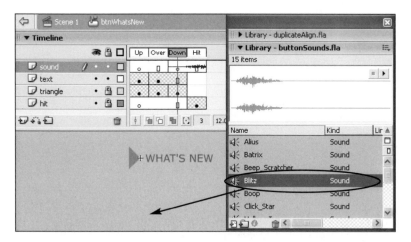

12. With the **Down** frame selected in the **sound** layer, select the **Blitz** sound from the **buttonSounds** **Library** and drag an instance of it onto the **Stage**. Notice the sound wave appear in the **Down** frame of the **Timeline**.

13. Choose **Control > Test Movie** to test your buttons. Notice that the sound in the **Gear** button will play when the mouse rolls over the button and that the sound in the **What's New** button will play when you click the button (because you placed the sound in the **Down** state).

*Tip: You can also choose **Control > Enable Simple Buttons** in the editing environment to hear the button sounds on the **Stage**. One method is not better than the other; I just wanted to give you practice using both!*

14. Open the **duplicateAlign Library** and notice that the sounds you added to the **Gear** and **What's New** buttons are in the **Library**.

15. Repeat Steps 9 through 12 to add sounds of your choice to the remaining buttons: **btnSafety**, **btnLearning**, and **btnRollo** (the **Background** button).

16. Save and close the file.

Invisible Buttons

In previous exercises, you learned about the importance of the Hit state for rollover buttons. The Hit state can also be used to create what are known as **invisible buttons**. This kind of button comes as an unexpected surprise, because there's no visible display of the button object until the end user passes the mouse over an invisible region. You will learn to change regular buttons into invisible buttons in this exercise.

1. Open the **invisButton_Final.fla** file from the **chap_09** folder. This is the finished version of the movie you are going to create in this exercise.

2. Choose **Control > Test Movie** to preview this movie. Move your cursor over the **lodges** in the picture. Notice how the descriptions magically appear. You will be creating this same effect next. When you are finished looking at this movie, close the file.

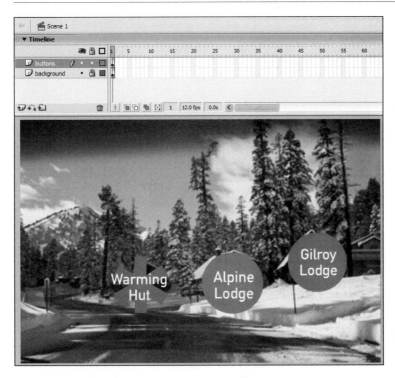

3. Open the **invisible.fla** file located inside the **chap_09** folder. This file was created ahead of time to get you started. Notice that the file contains two layers—one with a background image on it and the other with three buttons on it.

4. Choose **Control > Test Movie** to preview the buttons. Move your mouse over the buttons and notice that they are not invisible. They behave just like normal rollover buttons, with the text changing color when you roll over them with the mouse—not very exciting. You will turn them into invisible buttons to create a surprise rollover effect next.

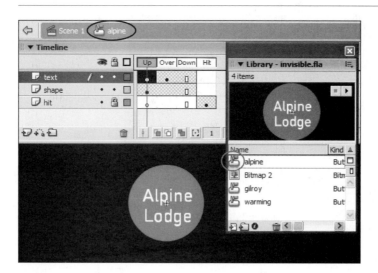

5. Close the **Preview** window. Back in the project file, open the **Library**. Double-click the **alpine** button's icon to open the button's **Timeline**. Notice that the button has three layers. Scrub the **playhead** to preview the **Up, Over, Down,** and **Hit** states of the button.

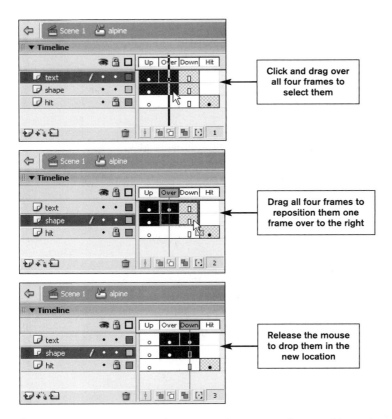

Click and drag over
all four frames to
select them

Drag all four frames to
reposition them one
frame over to the right

Release the mouse
to drop them in the
new location

6. Click a blank area of the **Stage** to make sure you have nothing selected. In one motion, click and drag to select the first two frames in the **text** and **shape** layers. Drag the four selected frames one frame to the right and release the mouse. This is how you reposition a block of frames at one time.

Why did you move the frames out of the Up state? When you create an invisible button, the Up state needs to be empty so that the user will not know that any button even exists until the mouse moves over the area that is defined in the Hit state. You will test the button next.

7. In the edit bar, click **Scene 1** to return to the **Main Timeline**.

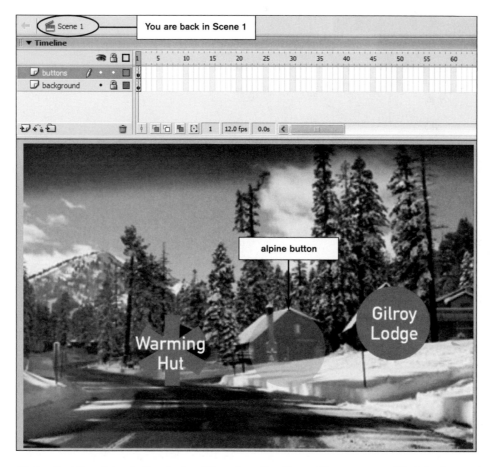

Notice that the alpine button looks different on the Stage. Since you modified the button in the Library, any instance on the Stage will be updated. Since the button has no Up state, Flash MX 2004 will display the shape of the Hit frame in a transparent blue color as visual feedback for where the button is located.

Why not just use a shape with a transparent fill for the Up state when you create a button? That would certainly work as an invisible button, but then it would be hard to see the instances of the button in your work area. When you build an invisible button with a Hit state, Flash MX 2004 displays the button as a translucent blue, which represents the hot spot of the button. This allows you to easily position and work with the button in the work area.

Up state = invisible

Over state = white text

Down state = black text

8. Choose **Control > Test Movie** to test the invisible button you just created. Notice the three different states of the button. Since you moved the frames to the right by one frame in Step 6, the old **Up** state of the button (white text, graphic background) is now the **Over** state, and the old **Over** state (black text, graphic background) is now the **Down** state. Test the **gilroy** button and the **warming** button to see the difference between the invisible button and the normal buttons.

You will change the other two buttons into invisible buttons next.

9. Repeat Step 6 for the other two buttons in the **Library**: the **gilroy** and **warming** buttons.

10. Choose **Control > Test Movie** to test all three buttons. Neat!

11. When you are finished, save and close this file.

That's it! I hope this chapter gave you a good foundation for working with and understanding the different button states and different kinds of buttons in Flash MX 2004. The next chapter will introduce you to movie clips. Knowing how to make a movie clip will help you learn to make an animated rollover button and so much more!

10.

Movie Clips

| What Is a Movie Clip? | Creating a Movie Clip |
| Animated Graphic Symbols Versus Movie Clip Symbols |
| Creating an Animated Rollover Button |
| Animated Rollover Button in Action |

chap_10

Macromedia Flash MX 2004
H·O·T CD-ROM

Understanding movie clip symbols is key to producing interactive Flash MX 2004 movies. This understanding is the last step in building a foundation that will prepare you for Chapter 11, "*ActionScript Basics and Behaviors*." As you will see, ActionScripting often requires a movie clip symbol, so don't underestimate the importance of this chapter.

Up to this point in the book, you've learned how to create both graphic and button symbols. At last, you will be introduced to movie clip symbols and gain a solid understanding of how they are created and used, compared to—or in combination with—the other two types of symbols you already know.

What Is a Movie Clip?

I saved movie clip symbols for last because they can be the most difficult type of symbol to learn to use in Flash MX 2004. Let's start with a few vocabulary terms.

Vocabulary Definitions	
Term	**Definition**
Main Timeline	The Main Timeline, introduced in Chapter 6, "*Symbols and Instances*," is the Timeline of the scene (or scenes) in your project file. If you have more than one scene, Flash MX 2004 will consider them part of the same Main Timeline and will simply add the number of frames inside each scene together to make up one Main Timeline. For example, if Scene 1 contains 35 frames and Scene 2 contains 20 frames, Macromedia Flash will consider the Main Timeline to span 55 frames. You will learn more about managing and naming scenes in Chapter 11, "*ActionScript Basics and Behaviors*." As you've seen, graphic symbols have their own Timeline that has a relationship to the Main Timeline. For example, if your graphic symbol contains 10 frames of animation, the Main Timeline must also contain 10 frames for the graphic symbol to play.
Timeline	As you have learned, graphic (and animated graphic) symbols have a direct relationship to the Main Timeline. Button and movie clip symbols do not have a direct relationship to the Main Timeline. They are referred to as "Timeline independent" objects. Why? Because they can function (play animation, sounds, and so on) regardless of how many frames the Main Timeline contains. For example, if you have a movie clip that contains a 10-frame animation of a chair lift moving up a hill, and you place this on the Stage inside the Main Timeline, the chair lift will continue to move up the hill even if the Timeline contains only a single frame. This ability to have different animations and actions occur independently of the Main Timeline is what makes movie clips so powerful.
Movie clips	Movie clip symbols can contain multiple layers, graphic symbols, button symbols, and even other movie clip symbols, as well as animations, sounds, and ActionScripting. Movie clips operate independently of the Main Timeline. They can continue to play even if the Main Timeline has stopped, which, as you will learn, is important when you start to work with ActionScript in the following chapter. A movie clip requires only a single keyframe on the Main Timeline to play, regardless of how long its own Timeline is. It's helpful to think of movie clips as movies nested in the Main Timeline.

Although movie clips are extremely powerful and flexible, they cannot be previewed simply by pressing **Enter/Return**, as is done with button and graphic symbol instances. Movie clips can be previewed only in the **Library** (out of context of the main movie), by selecting **Control > Test Movie**, or by publishing the final movie (which you will learn about in Chapter 16, "*Publishing and Exporting*"). This is a very important point, because you will find yourself unable to view your work unless you remember this!

I. ——————**Creating a Movie Clip**

This exercise will start you off by showing how to make a simple movie clip.

1. Copy the **chap_10** folder, located on the **H•O•T CD-ROM**, to your hard drive. You need to have this folder on your hard drive in order to save files inside it.

2. Open the **movieClip_Final.fla** file from the **chap_10** folder. Notice that there is only one keyframe in the Main Timeline.

3. Choose **Control > Test Movie** to preview the movie clip. Notice how the fill of the movie clip fades in and out repeatedly. This is the xboarding logo that you are going to animate and convert into a movie clip in the following steps. When you are finished previewing this movie, close the file.

4. Open the **movieClip.fla** file from the **chap_10** folder. This file has been created ahead of time to get you started. Notice that it has two layers: one named **outline**, which contains the outline of the "X," and the other named **text**, which contains the boarding.com letters. You are going to create a simple motion tween next.

5. Click the **Insert Layer** button to add a new layer to the **Timeline**. Name this layer **fillTween**.

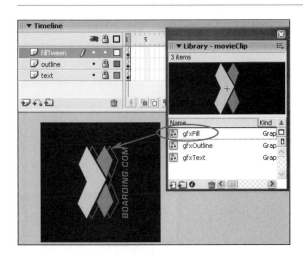

6. Press **Ctrl+L** (Windows) or **Cmd+L** (Mac) to open the **Library**. Drag an instance of the **gfxFill** graphic symbol onto the **Stage** in the **fillTween** layer. Using the arrow keys on the keyboard, position the **gfxFill** instance so that it covers the X outline exactly. You will be creating an animation of this outline filling in with color in the next few steps, so it is important that the **gfxFill** symbol is positioned directly on top of the outline artwork on the **Stage**.

*Tip: You may want to change the magnification in the **Edit Bar** to **200%** so that you can better see the placement of your artwork.*

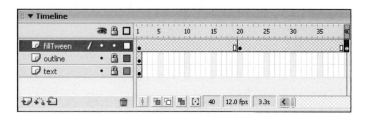

7. In the **fillTween** layer, add a keyframe to **Frame 20** and **Frame 40** by selecting each frame and pressing **F6**.

In the following steps, you will be creating a motion tween in which the gfxFill instance starts off invisible in Frame 1, becomes completely visible in Frame 20, and fades to invisible again in Frame 40.

8. Make sure the **playhead** is over **Frame 40**, and select the instance on the **Stage**. Using the **Properties inspector**, set the **Color Styles** options to **Alpha** and **0%**.

9. Move the **playhead** to **Frame 1** and select the instance on the **Stage**. Using the **Properties inspector**, set the **Color Styles** options to **Alpha** and **0%**.

10. In the **Timeline**, click the **fillTween** layer to select all the frames on the layer. In the **Properties inspector**, choose **Tween: Motion**. This will add a motion tween across all of the frames.

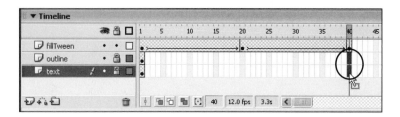

11. In the **outline** layer, click **Frame 40** and drag down to **Frame 40** of the **text** layer to select **Frame 40** in both layers, as shown here. Press **F5** to add frames up to **Frame 40**. This way, the artwork on the outline and text layers will be visible throughout the motion tween on the **fillTween** layer.

12. Press **Enter/Return** to test the animation. The "X" outline fills in with color, and then the fill fades away.

You may be thinking…"What does this all have to do with movie clips?" You are going to create a movie clip using this animation next.

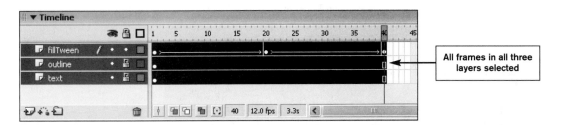

All frames in all three layers selected

13. Click the **text** layer to select all the frames on that layer. **Shift+click** the **outline** and **fillTween** layers to select all the frames on both of those layers as well. With all the frames in all three layers selected, choose **Edit > Timeline > Cut Frames**. This will cut all the frames you have selected from the **Main Timeline**.

Don't worry—they won't be gone for long. You will be pasting the frames inside a movie clip next. **Note:** *It's important that you choose* **Cut Frames**, *and not* **Cut**. **Cut Frames** *allows you to cut multiple frames and layers, but a simple* **Cut** *command does not.*

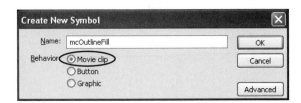

14. Choose **Insert > New Symbol** and type **Name: mcOutlineFill**. Make sure **Behavior: Movie clip** is selected. Click **OK** when you are finished. This will create a movie clip symbol. As soon as you click **OK**, you will be located inside the movie clip symbol's **Timeline**.

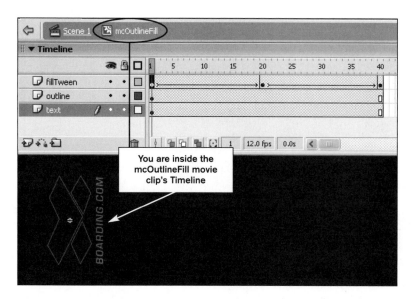

15. After you click **OK**, notice that you are inside **mcOutlineFill's Timeline**. Select the first keyframe and choose **Edit > Timeline > Paste Frames**. This will paste all the frames and all the layers right inside the movie clip, maintaining all the layers and layer names just as you had them in the **Main Timeline**, as shown here.

You have just created your first movie clip! You will be able to test it in the next steps.

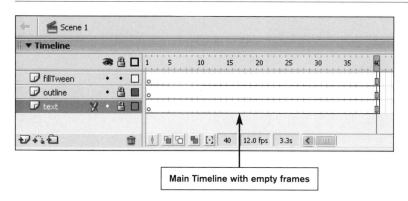

16. Click the **Scene 1** button in the **Edit Bar** to return to the **Main Timeline**. Notice in the **Main Timeline** the three layers you originally had are still there, although they have no content on them. This is because you cut the frames and pasted them into the movie clip symbol.

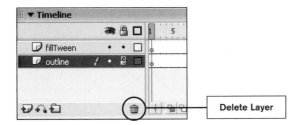

Delete Layer

17. Select the **text** layer and click the **Trash** icon in the **Timeline**. This will delete the **text** layer, since you will not need it anymore. Repeat this process to delete the **outline** layer.

What's with all this cutting and pasting and copying? Wouldn't it be easier to just create the content inside the movie clip in the first place? Although that would be easier, it may not always be a realistic workflow. Oftentimes, you will find that you create artwork on the Main Timeline first and later decide to turn it into a movie clip. Since creating artwork inside a movie clip is the easier of the two work-flows, I thought it would help to give you experience in the other method, which is to copy and paste artwork from the Main Timeline into a movie clip symbol's Timeline.

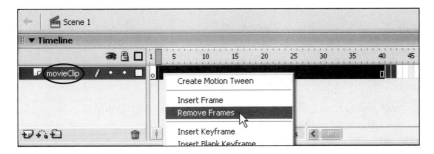

18. Double-click the **fillTween** layer name and rename this layer **movieClip**. In the **Timeline**, click **Frame 42** and drag backward to **Frame 2** to select **Frames 2** through **40**. (Since there are no frames on **Frame 41** or **42**, only the frames up to **Frame 40** will be selected. However, this method of "overselecting" makes sure you select all the frames and don't miss any.) **Right-click** (Windows) or **Ctrl+click** (Mac) on the selected frame to access the context menu. Choose **Remove Frames**. This will remove all the frames you have selected.

*Note: When you use **Cut Frames**, it cuts the content of the layers and frames, but the **Timeline** still contains the frames. The only way to remove them is to use the **Remove Frames** command.*

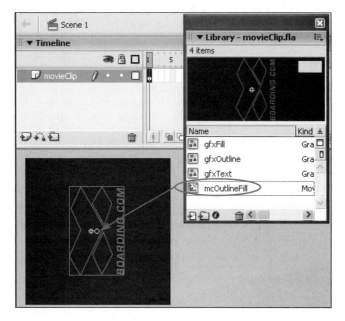

19. Open the **Library** (**Ctrl+L** [Windows] or **Cmd+L** [Mac]), and notice the **mcOutlineFill** movie clip symbol you created. Drag an instance of the movie clip onto the **Stage**.

20. Choose **Control > Test Movie** to preview the movie clip you just made.

Notice that the movie clip plays even though there is only one frame in the Main Timeline. This is because the movie clip's Timeline is independent from the Main Timeline. Movie clips need only one keyframe in the Main Timeline in order to play.

21. Save this file and keep it open. You will need it for the next exercise.

TIP | Modifying Movie Clip Instances

Not only do movie clips have a Timeline that is independent from the main movie, but, just as you learned with graphic symbols in Chapter 6, "*Symbols and Instances*," you can apply effects to movie clip instances on the Stage as well. You have to create the movie clip just once, and then you can change the attributes (such as scale, alpha, skew, and rotation) of each instance on the Stage to achieve different visual effects. By adding transformations or effects to the instances on the Stage, you can change the appearance of the movie clip with just a few clicks of the mouse. The original movie clip, however, will remain unchanged in the Library.

2.————Animated Graphic Symbols Versus Movie Clip Symbols

In this exercise, you will learn the differences between animated graphic symbols and movie clip symbols. You'll see that the animated graphic symbol requires multiple frames in the Main Timeline; a movie clip does not. Here you will learn firsthand why I have placed so much emphasis on the Timeline independence of movie clips.

1. You should still have the **movieClip.fla** file open from the last exercise. Using **File > Save As**, save another version of this file as **mcVsGfx.fla** in the **chap_10** folder. This way you will have two copies of the file: one with everything you have completed up to this point (**movieClip.fla**) and one that will have everything you will do in this exercise (**mcVsGfx.fla**).

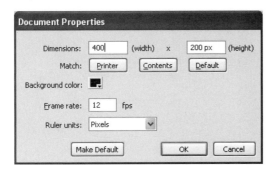

2. Click the **Stage**. In the **Properties inspector**, click the **Size** button to open the **Document Properties** dialog box. For **Dimensions**, change the width to **400** pixels. This will change the width of the **Stage** to 400 pixels, which will give you a little more room to work.

To understand the difference between an animated graphic symbol and a movie clip symbol, you need to have one of each type in your project file. Since you already created a movie clip symbol in the last exercise, you can use that same symbol, duplicating it and changing its behavior, to make an animated graphic symbol, rather than building a new animated graphic symbol from scratch. You will do this in the steps that follow.

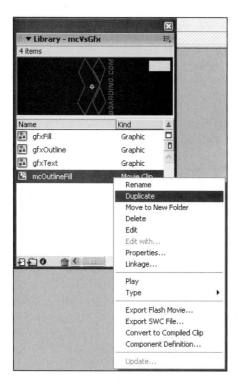

3. Press **Ctrl+L** (Windows) or **Cmd+L** (Mac) to open the **Library** if it isn't already open. **Right-click** (Windows) or **Ctrl+click** (Mac) on the **mcOutlineFill** movie clip symbol in the **Library** to access the context menu. Choose **Duplicate** to make a copy of the symbol.

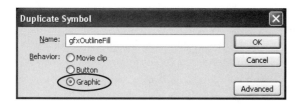

4. In the **Duplicate Symbol** dialog box that opens, name the symbol **gfxOutlineFill** and select **Graphic** for the **Behavior** option. Click **OK**. This will take all the contents of the movie clip symbol and make an exact copy of that symbol. The only difference is that by setting the **Behavior** option to **Graphic**, you have changed the way this new symbol functions. Since it contains animation (the fill tween), this kind of symbol is often referred to as an animated graphic symbol.

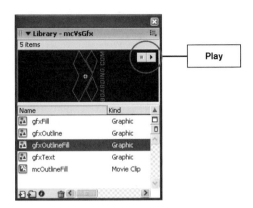

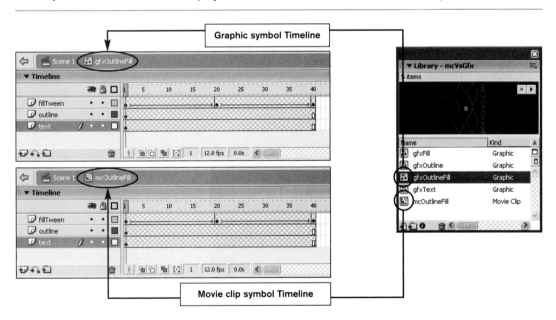

5. In the **Library**, select the **gfxOutlineFill** symbol and click the **Play** button in the **Preview** window to test the graphic symbol in the **Library**. Next, select the **mcOutlineFill** symbol in the **Library** and click the **Play** button to test the movie clip symbol. Notice how the animations are exactly the same?

6. Double-click the **gfxOutlineFill** graphic symbol icon to open the symbol's **Timeline**. Notice that it looks exactly like the **mcOutlineFill** movie clip symbol you created in the last exercise. Double-click the **mcOutlineFill** movie clip icon to view the movie clip's **Timeline**. You will see that the two symbols do, in fact, have the same elements in their **Timelines**. The only difference between the two symbols is that one is a movie clip and the other is a graphic symbol.

Tip: Double-clicking on the movie clip symbol icon in the Library automatically switches the "view" to the Library item you just double-clicked on. No closing of windows necessary!

7. In the **Edit Bar**, click **Scene 1** to return to the **Main Timeline**.

Edit Scene button

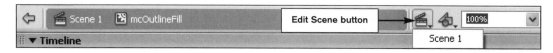

*Tip: You can also return to **Scene 1** by clicking the **Edit Scene** button in the **Edit Bar** and choosing **Scene 1** or by choosing **Edit > Edit Document**.*

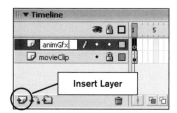

8. In the **Timeline**, lock the **movieClip** layer. Add a new layer by clicking the **Insert Layer** button in the **Timeline**. Rename the new layer **animGfx**. This layer will hold the animated graphic symbol that you will create.

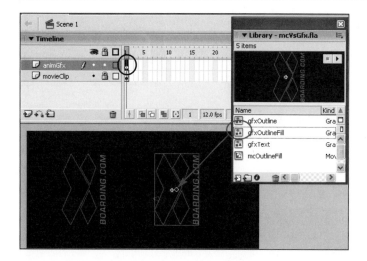

9. Drag an instance of the **gfxOutlineFill** symbol onto the **Stage**, and position it to the right of the **mcOutlineFill** movie clip symbol. This adds the animated graphic symbol to the **Main Timeline**.

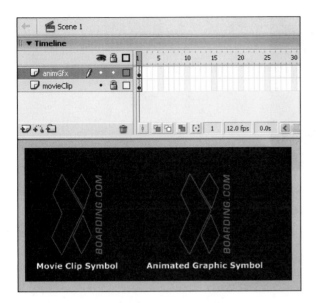

10. In the **Toolbar**, select the **Text** tool. Below the **gfxOutlineFill** instance, click the **Stage** and add the text **Animated Graphic Symbol**, as shown here. Lock the **animGfx** layer, unlock the **movieClip** layer, and add the text **Movie Clip Symbol** below the **mcOutlineFill** instance. When you are testing the movie in the following steps, this will help you remember which instance is which.

11. Press **Enter/Return** to test the movie. Notice that nothing happens.

Why? When you press Enter/Return to test the movie, Flash MX 2004 automatically moves the playhead across all the frames in the Main Timeline of the movie. In this movie, you have only one frame, so the playhead has nowhere to go. Therefore, you will see both symbols in their static states only.

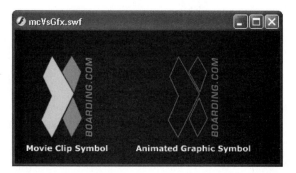

12. Choose **Control > Test Movie** to preview the movie. This time, notice that the movie clip symbol plays and the animated graphic symbol does not. Why?

The main difference between an animated graphic symbol and a movie clip symbol is that the movie clip's Timeline is completely independent of the main movie's Timeline. So a movie clip's Timeline can play regardless of how many frames the Main Timeline contains. Animated graphic symbols, on the other hand, play in sync with the Main Timeline. The Timeline of an animated graphic symbol is tied to the Main Timeline, and therefore, at least the same number of frames in the graphic symbol's Timeline must exist in the Main Timeline in order for the graphic symbol to play.

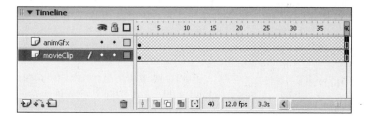

13. Close the **Preview** window and return to the project file. Back on the **Main Timeline**, click and drag to select **Frame 40** in both layers and press **F5** to add frames up to **Frame 40**.

Why 40 frames? This is the same number of frames that exist in both the graphic symbol's Timeline and the movie clip's Timeline, as you saw in Step 6.

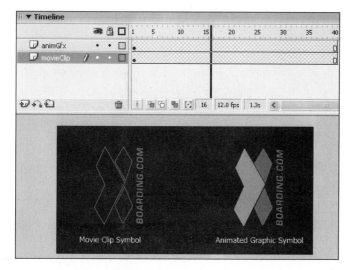

14. Press **Enter/Return** to test the movie.

*This time, the animated graphic symbol will play, although the movie clip symbol will not play. This is because there are now enough frames in the Main Timeline so that the animated graphic symbol can play. However, you will not be able to see the movie clip play on the Stage because, as you learned in Exercise 1, in order to preview a movie clip, you must view it either in the **Library** or using **Control >Test Movie**. This is one of the "rules" of movie clips. They don't preview in the editing environment.*

15. Choose **Control > Test Movie**. Notice that now both symbols are animating.

To summarize, the animated graphic symbol will play if there are enough frames in the Main Timeline, but the movie clip will play regardless in the Preview window.

16. Save this file, but leave it open for the next exercise.

NOTE | Why Is Timeline Independence Important?

At this point, you probably understand that the movie clip can play in its entirety, even though it takes up only one frame in the Main Timeline, whereas the graphic symbol needs all 40 frames inserted into the Main Timeline in order to play. You also probably understand that a movie clip cannot be previewed inside the editing environment of Flash MX 2004, and that you must choose Control > Test Movie in order to see the movie clip play. Keep in mind that having a symbol be independent of the Timeline is extremely important when programming interactive presentations. ActionScripting, which you'll learn about in the next chapter, can refer to movie clips because they have the capacity to be "named" and referenced in scripts, whereas graphic symbols do not.

3. ———————————**Creating an Animated Rollover Button**

This exercise will demonstrate how to turn a normal rollover button into an animated rollover button by nesting a movie clip in the Over state of a button symbol. If you've been wondering why Timeline independence is important, this example will drive the point home. As you learned when you created buttons in Chapter 9, "*Buttons*," there are only four frames in each button symbol—Up, Over, Down, and Hit. The only way to put an animation into a single frame for one of these states is to use a symbol that can contain animation yet has an independent Timeline. A movie clip symbol will do just that.

1. You should still have the **mcVsGfx.fla** file open from the last exercise. Choose **File > Save As** to save it as **animRolloBtn.fla** to the **chap_10** folder on your hard drive.

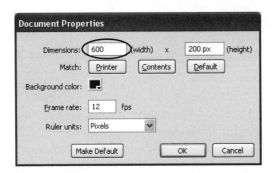

2. In the **Properties inspector**, click the **Size** button to open the **Document Properties** dialog box. For **Dimensions**, change the **width** to **600** pixels. This will change the width of the **Stage** to 600 pixels, which will give you more room to work with this exercise. Click **OK**.

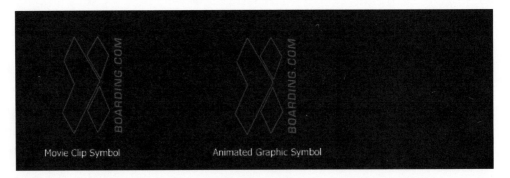

When you change the document dimensions, your Stage should look like this.

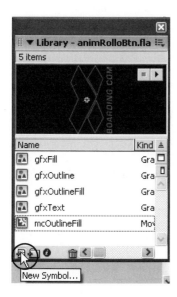

3. Make sure the **Library** is open (**Ctrl+L** [Windows] or **Cmd+L** [Mac]). To create a new symbol, click the **New Symbol** button in the bottom-left corner of the **Library**. This is another way to open the **Symbol Properties** dialog box.

You will be creating an animated button symbol in the following steps.

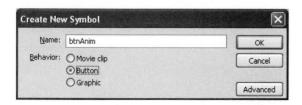

4. In the **Symbol Properties** dialog box, name the symbol **btnAnim**, and set its **Behavior** to **Button**. Click **OK**.

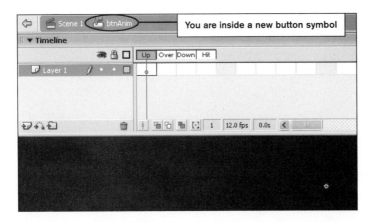

*After you click **OK**, you will be inside the editing environment for the button symbol's **Timeline**.*

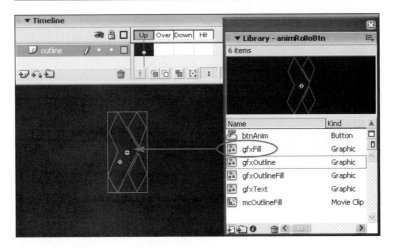

5. Rename **Layer 1** to **outline**. Drag an instance of the **gfxOutline** symbol onto the **Stage**. This symbol is static and contains only the outline of the "X."

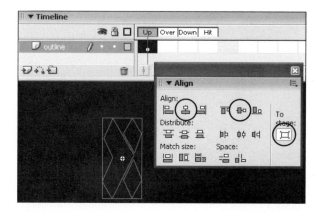

6. With the **gfxOutline** instance still selected on the **Stage**, choose **Window > Design Panels > Align** to open the **Align** panel. Click the **To Stage** button, and then click the **Align vertical center** and **Align horizontal center** buttons (all circled in the picture) to perfectly align the instance in the center of the **Stage**.

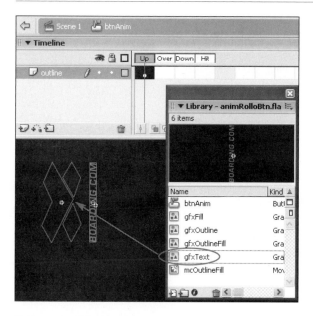

7. From the **Library**, drag an instance of the **gxfText** symbol onto the **Stage**, just to the right of the "X" outline, as shown here. This symbol is static and contains the word "boarding.com" on only one frame. The **Align** panel should still be open. If it is not, press **Ctrl+K** (Windows) or **Cmd+K** (Mac). Make sure the **To Stage** button is selected, and click **Align vertical center** in the **Align** panel. You have now created the **Up** state of the button.

8. Press **F5** in the **Down** frame to add frames in the **Over** and **Down** states of the button. Lock this layer so you don't accidentally select anything on it. You will be adding a movie clip symbol to the button in the following steps.

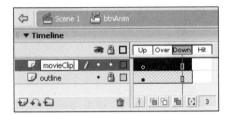

9. Click the **Insert Layer** button to add a new layer and rename it **movieClip**.

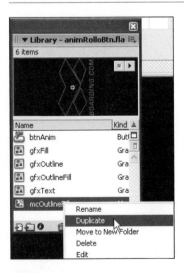

10. In the **Library, right-click** (Windows) or **Ctrl+click** (Mac) on the **mcOutlineFill** movie clip symbol to access the shortcut menu. Choose **Duplicate** to make a copy of the symbol.

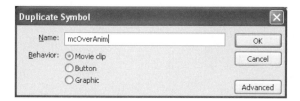

11. In the **Duplicate Symbol** dialog box that opens, name the symbol **mcOverAnim** and select **Movie clip** for **Behavior**. Click **OK**. This will take all the contents of the movie clip symbol and make an exact copy of that symbol. This movie clip will be used for the **Over** state of the button, but first you have to make a modification to the **mcOverAnim** symbol. You will do this next.

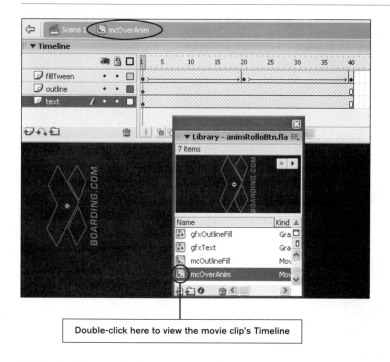

Double-click here to view the movie clip's Timeline

12. In the **Library**, double-click the **mcOverAnim** movie clip icon. This will take you into the movie clip's **Timeline**. Notice that it looks exactly like the **Timeline** for the **mcOutlineFill** movie clip symbol you created in Exercise 1. You will modify this movie clip next.

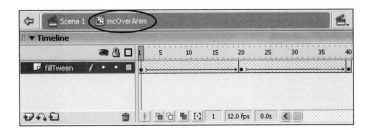

13. Select the **text** layer and click the **Trash** icon to delete the **text** layer. Repeat this step for the **outline** layer to delete it also. When you are finished, the **Timeline** for the **mcOverAnim** movie clip should have only one layer with the fill tween on it, as shown here.

*You deleted these extra layers because you need only the "X" artwork for the animated **Over** state you are creating for the button.*

14. Scrub the **playhead** to see the motion tween animation. This movie clip will serve as the **Over** state of the button (once you add it to the button's **Timeline**).

*Tip: You can also preview the motion tween inside the movie clip by pressing **Enter/Return** or by selecting **mcOverAnim** in the **Library** and clicking the **Play** button in the **Library Preview** window.*

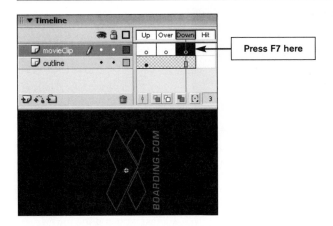

15. In the **Library**, double-click the **btnAnim** icon to open the button symbol's **Timeline**. On the **movieClip** layer, press **F7** in the **Over** frame and again in the **Down** frame to add blank keyframes to both the **Over** and **Down** states of the button.

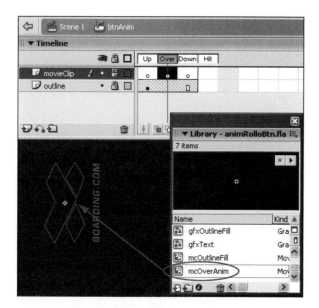

16. With the **Over** state of the button selected, drag an instance of the **mcOverAnim** movie clip onto the **Stage**. Use the **Align** panel to center the movie clip in the middle of the **Stage**, just as you did in Step 6. When you are finished, lock the **movieClip** layer.

*You have just added the movie clip to the **Over** state of the button. You will add the **Hit** state to the button next to complete the exercise.*

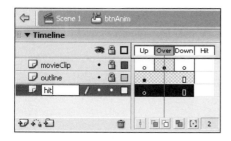

17. Click the **Insert Layer** button to add a new layer to the button symbol's **Timeline**. Rename the new layer **hit** and place it at the bottom of the **Timeline**.

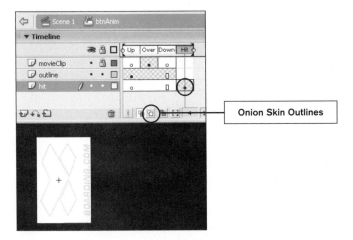

Onion Skin Outlines

18. On the **hit** layer, press **F7** in the **Hit** frame to add a blank keyframe. Unlock the outline layer and click the **Onion Skin Outlines** button to turn onion skinning outlines on. This will help you make sure the rectangle covers the X outline and the boarding.com text. In the **Toolbar**, select the **Rectangle** tool and draw a rectangle that covers the X outline and the boarding.com text. When you are done drawing your rectangle, click the **Onion Skin Outlines** button again to turn it off.

*The rectangle will serve as the **Hit** state of the button, so when the user's mouse touches any part of the rectangle, the **Over** state will be triggered.*

19. You are finished with the button. Click **Scene 1** to return to the **Main Timeline**.

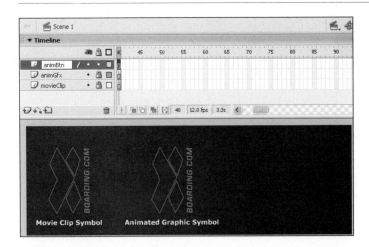

Movie Clip Symbol   Animated Graphic Symbol

20. In the **Main Timeline**, lock both the **animGfx** and **movieClip** layers. Click the **Insert Layer** button to add a new layer, and rename the layer **animBtn**. You will be placing the button you just created on this layer next.

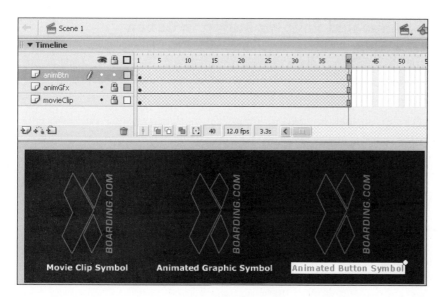

21. Drag an instance of the **btnAnim** button symbol onto the **Stage**, to the right of the animated graphic symbol. In the **Toolbar**, select the **Text** tool. Below the **btnAnim** instance, click the **Stage** and add the text **Animated Button Symbol**, as shown in the picture.

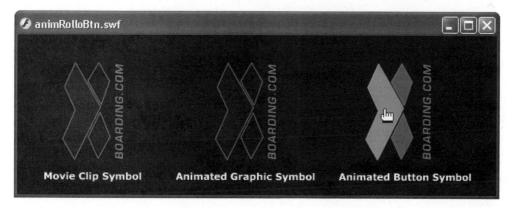

22. Choose **Control > Test Movie** to preview and test all of the symbols.

Notice that the movie clip and animated graphic symbol continue to animate on their own, while the button symbol waits for you to move the mouse over it in order for the animation to begin. By adding movie clips to different states of a button, you can take the rollover button to the next level.

23. Save this file, but keep it open for one last exercise.

4. ————— Animated Rollover Button in Action

In the previous exercise, you learned how to use a movie clip in a button's Over state to create an animated rollover button. In this exercise, you will learn how to use that same button in a different project file and place it in a Web page interface.

1. You should still have the **animRolloBtn.fla** file open from the last exercise. Press **Ctrl+L** (Windows) or **Cmd+L** (Mac) to open the **Library** if it is not already open. It is important that you keep this file (including the **Library**) open and that you don't close it during the next few steps. You will be taking the animated button symbol you made in the last exercise from the **Library** and using it in another file next.

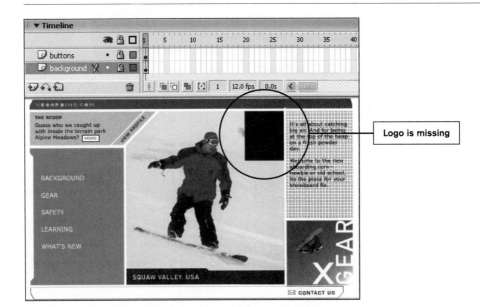

Logo is missing

2. Open the **animBtnLive.fla** from the **chap_10** folder. Notice that this file is similar to one you worked on in the last chapter. It contains two layers that are locked, but in this file, the logo is missing from the interface. You will be adding the logo in a few steps.

3. Open the **Library** (**Ctrl+L** [Windows] or **Cmd+L** [Mac]) if it is not open. Notice that there are two Libraries in the panel window. On the top is the **Library** from the **animRolloBtn** movie, and below is the **Library** from the **animBtnLive** movie.

*Since you never closed the **animRolloBtn** project, and you made sure the **Library** was open before you opened the **animBtnLive** file, the **Library** for the **animRolloBtn** project will stay open until you either close the file or close the **Library** for that project. In addition to the **File > Import > Open External Library** workflow you learned in Chapter 9, "Buttons," this is another way you can use assets such as symbols from one project in another project. You will add the movie clip symbol from the **animRolloBtn** movie to the **animBtnLive** movie next.*

4. In the **Main Timeline** of the **animBtnLive** move, insert a new layer and name the layer **logo**. Make sure the **logo** layer is above all the other layers, as shown here.

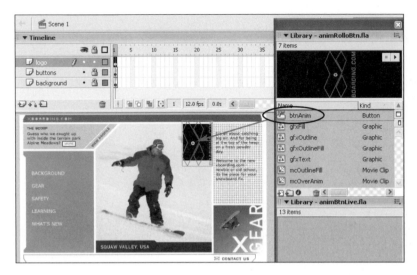

5. In the **animRolloBtn Library**, drag an instance of **btnAnim** onto the **Stage** and place it over the black box, as shown here.

*After you place the instance on the **Stage**, the **btnAnim** symbol is also located in the **animBtnLive Library**. This is because you have added the symbol from the **animRolloBtn** movie to the **animBtnLive** movie, and Flash MX 2004 adds the symbol to the **Library** for you.*

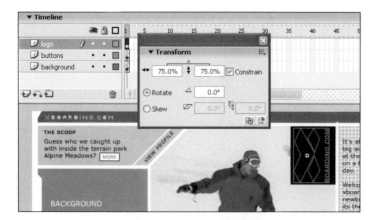

6. Choose **Window > Design Panels > Transform** to open the **Transform** panel. With the instance still selected, make sure the **Constrain** box is checked, and enter **75.0%** in either the **width** or **height** field. This will change the size of the instance so that it fits in the box in the interface.

7. Choose **Control > Test Movie** and roll the mouse over the logo to test the animation!

8. When you are finished, save and close all the files. You are finished with this chapter.

Congratulations! You have made it through an essential chapter. You now know how to create, modify, and nest movie clips inside buttons. In the next chapter, you will use movie clips in more advanced ways. Make sure you are well rested before you take on the next chapter, "ActionScript Basics and Behaviors." It's one of the most challenging chapters in the book.

II.

ActionScript Basics and Behaviors

| Controlling the Timeline | Controlling Movie Clips |
| The goto Action to Create a Slideshow |
| Go to Web Page Behavior | Targeting Scenes |
| Creating a Drop-Down Menu | Loading Movies |

chap_11

Macromedia Flash MX 2004
H•O•T CD-ROM

So far, you've learned how to draw, mask, animate, and create symbols in Flash MX 2004. The last step in learning how to make fully interactive presentations is to add ActionScript to your projects. ActionScript is an internal programming language that Flash MX 2004 uses, and its format is similar, but not identical, to JavaScript. The good news is that you do not have to know JavaScript or be a programmer to add ActionScript to your movies. The Flash MX 2004 Actions panel assists you so that it is not necessary to write the code from scratch. What's even better is the new Behaviors panel in Flash MX 2004, which simplifies adding ActionScript to your movies for simple and repetitive tasks such as navigation controls.

Why is ActionScript important? On a basic level, ActionScript enables you to create buttons that control the Main Timeline or movie clips, make slideshows with Forward and Back buttons, link to other URLs on the Internet, or load other movies into a Flash MX 2004 movie. This is a short list, and covers only some of the possibilities that ActionScript offers. By the time you are finished with this chapter, you will have a solid understanding of how to add ActionScript to objects and frames and why you would choose one over the other. You will also learn many of the basic ActionScripts to apply in your own projects.

Working with ActionScript code is one of the most technically challenging aspects of Flash MX 2004. This chapter will give you a solid foundation on which to build later on your own.

Where Do I Place ActionScript?

ActionScript can be attached to a button instance, a movie clip instance, or a keyframe in the Timeline. However, ActionScript cannot be attached to an instance of a graphic symbol. This chapter will give you a chance to attach ActionScript to each of these elements. You will use the Actions panel and the Behaviors panel to add ActionScript to your project file.

The Actions Panel Defined

In Flash MX 2004, you use the Actions panel to build ActionScripts that can control your movie. The Actions panel is where you create and edit object actions or frame actions, which you'll learn about in great detail later in this chapter.

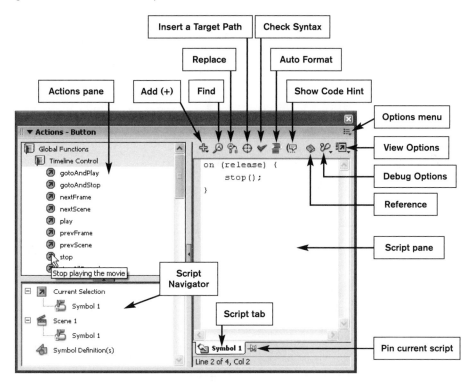

The Actions panel, shown here, allows you to create ActionScript by choosing from the list of code found within the Actions pane, by using the Add (+) button, or by typing code manually into the Script pane. When you roll over an item in the Toolbar, the description of the item appears as a tooltip. For example, in this picture, the mouse has been rolled over the **stop** action in the Script pane, and the tooltip reads, "Stop playing the movie." When an item is double-clicked in the Actions pane or selected using the (+) button, it will appear in the Script pane on the right side of the Actions panel. Additionally, you can drag and drop an item from the Toolbar into the Script pane.

You can also enter parameters for actions inside the Script pane, change the order of statements inside the Script pane, delete actions, and keep a script available when you click off of the frame or object by using the Pin button. In the exercises of this chapter, you will have a chance to work with many of these features.

The Actions panel also allows you to type ActionScript code from scratch directly into the Script pane. It is important to learn how to hand code actions, because many things can't be done without at least some manual scripting. Writing code by hand represents a change in workflow since this release of Flash MX 2004 has done away with Normal mode. This mode offered ways to add ActionScript by selecting items from the Actions pane, and then Flash MX would prompt you to fill in the parameters (arguments) needed for each action. In Flash MX 2004, you can still use the Actions pane to add ActionScript to your projects, but you will need to manually fill in the parameters for each action. Flash MX 2004 will no longer prompt you with parameter selections from which to choose from as it has in past versions. Because this book is targeted at beginners, hand coding ActionScript will be kept to a minimum whenever possible. Once you're finished with this book, you will have a solid understanding of ActionScript basics, and you will be better prepared to go deeper into ActionScript.

The Behaviors Panel

New to Flash MX 2004 is the Behaviors panel, which gives you the ability to add specific functionality to movies quickly and easily. There are several categories of behaviors: Data, Embedded Video, Media, Movieclip, Sound, and Web. Each of these provides menu options for adding scripts that will perform various tasks. For example, the **Web > Go to Web Page Behavior** creates a script that tells a button to open up another Web page when clicked. Because this is a common task in movies, this behavior can save you the trouble of writing the script each time you need it.

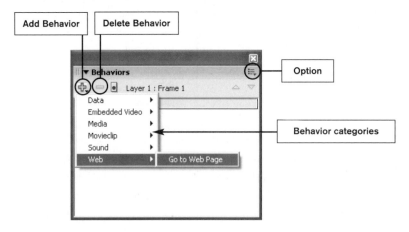

To use the Behaviors panel to create a script, simply locate the menu option you want in the panel, click it, and then fill out the options in the resulting window. You'll see examples of this later on in the chapter.

I. ————————Controlling the Timeline

In Flash MX 2004, once a movie starts, it will play in its entirety until it reaches the last frame of the Timeline, unless you tell it otherwise. Using ActionScript, you can control when a movie stops and when it starts. This exercise will teach you how to assign stop and play actions to button instances in order to control animation on the Main Timeline. As well, you will learn to apply actions to frames on the Main Timeline to further control the movie.

1. Copy the **chap_11** folder, located on the **H•O•T CD-ROM**, to your hard drive. You need to have this folder on your hard drive in order to save files inside it.

2. Open the file called **stopAndPlay_Final.fla** from the **chap_11** folder. This is the finished version of the project you'll be building in this exercise.

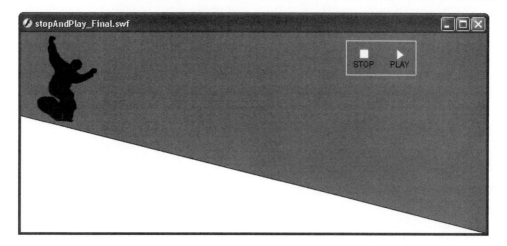

3. Choose **Control > Test Movie** to preview the movie. In the SWF file, click the **Play** button to set the boarder in motion, moving down the mountain. Click the **Stop** button to stop the boarder. You will learn how to add the same functionality to this movie in the following steps.

4. When you are finished stopping and playing this movie, close the **Preview** window and this file.

5. Open the **stopAndPlay.fla** file from the **chap_11** folder. This is an unfinished version of the movie you just previewed. It contains everything except the ActionScript, which you will add in this exercise.

6. Choose **Control > Test Movie** to preview the movie. Click the **Stop** and **Play** buttons. Notice how nothing happens and the movie continues to play. Why? No actions have been added to these buttons yet, and therefore, the buttons do not control the movie. You will learn to do this next.

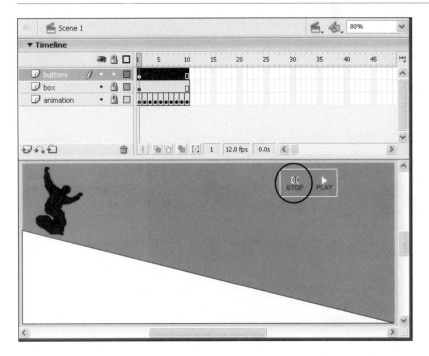

7. Close the **Preview** window and return to the project file. Click the **Stop** button instance on the **Stage** to select it.

NOTE | Object or Frame Action Instruction

To add an action to an object, as you will do in the following steps with the Stop and Play buttons, you must select the object and then add the action. **Note:** When you add actions to an object, the object must either be a movie clip symbol or a button symbol. To add an action to a frame in a Timeline, you must place an action in a keyframe. You will have a chance to do this later in the exercise.

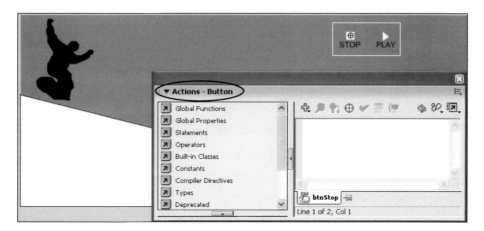

8. Choose **Window > Development Panels > Actions (F9)** to open the **Actions** panel. Notice how the top of the **Actions** panel reads "Actions – Button." Because you have selected the button instance, Flash MX 2004 knows that you will be adding actions to the button instance on the **Stage**.

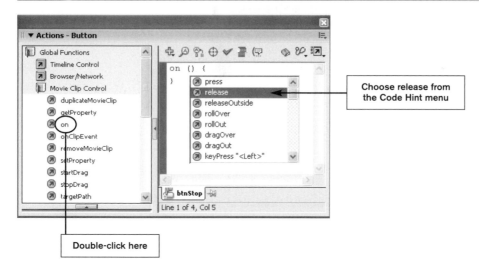

Choose release from the Code Hint menu

Double-click here

9. In the **Actions** panel, click the **Global Functions** category in the **Actions pane** to access a list of all the actions that fall under that category. Click on **Movie Clip Control** to expand that category. Double-click the **on** action to add it to the **Script** pane. From the **Code Hint** menu that appears, choose **release** for the mouse event.

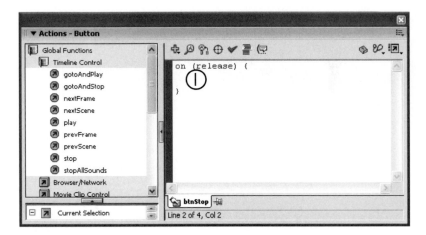

10. In the **Script** pane, place your cursor after the open curly brace and press **Enter/Return** to bring the cursor down to the second line, as shown here.

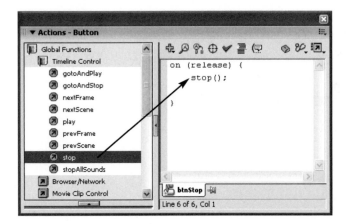

11. In the **Actions** pane, choose **Global Functions > Timeline Control** and double-click the **stop** action to add it to the **Script** pane. You have just added your first action to the project. The **Stop** button instance now has the power to stop the **Timeline** once you test the movie, which you will get to do shortly!

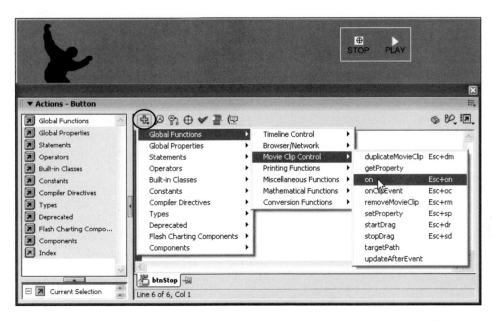

*You can also add an action to the list by dragging it from the **Actions pane** to the **Script** pane or by selecting the **Add (+)** button and choosing the action from the pull-down menus, as shown here.*

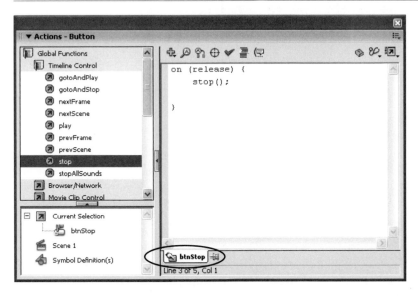

*When you double-clicked the **stop** action in the Actions pane, ActionScript appeared in the Script pane on the right. This Script pane of the Actions panel holds the ActionScript statements and displays all the code for the actions that are applied to an object.*

Located below the Script pane is a tab that shows you which instance you're attaching code to. The script tab will display the name of the object or frame the code is attached to, which is great feedback so you can make sure you are adding the ActionScript to the right item.

In this case, you have applied the script to an instance of the btnStop button on the Stage, and since you have not named the instance (which is not necessary in this exercise), the script tab states the name of the symbol itself. If you had named the instance in the Properties inspector, the instance name would appear here instead. The reason you would name an instance is so you can use ActionScript to directly refer to ("talk to") that instance. Unless you need to refer to an instance by its name via ActionScript, it is not necessary to name each instance in your project file. In later exercises in this chapter, you will need to name an instance in order for the ActionScript to work; this name will be reflected in the Script tab.

12. Choose **Control > Test Movie** and try out the **stop** action you just added to the button instance. When you click the **Stop** button, the movie will stop!

Once a movie is stopped, it must be explicitly started again in order to play. You can do this with the ***play*** *action, which you will do next.*

13. Close the **Preview** window when you are finished. On the **Stage**, click the **Play** button instance to select it. In the **Actions** panel, add the **on** handler again by choosing **Global Functions > Movie Clip Control** and then double-clicking the **on** action to add it to the **Script** pane. From the **Code Hint** menu that appears, choose **release** for the mouse event.

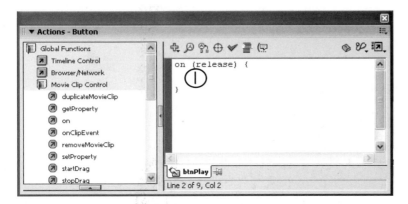

14. In the **Script** pane, place your cursor after the open curly brace and press **Enter/Return** to bring the cursor down to the second line, as shown here.

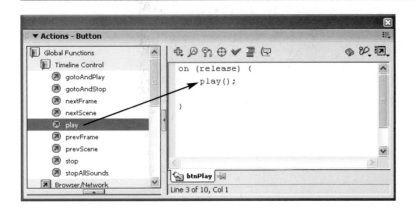

15. In the **Actions** pane, choose **Global Functions > Timeline Control** and double-click the **play** action to add it to the **Script** pane.

You have just added a play action to the button instance on the Stage.

16. Choose **Control > Test Movie** and test the movie again. Click the **Stop** button to stop the movie. Click the **Play** button to make the movie play again! When you are finished, close the **Preview** window.

Notice that the movie immediately plays as soon as the Preview window opens. You'll learn to change this using frame actions next.

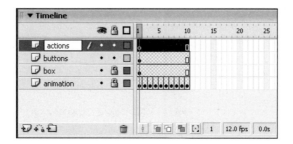

17. Back in the **Main Timeline**, click the **Insert Layer** button to add a new layer to the **Timeline**, and name it **actions**. Make sure the **actions** layer is above all other layers, as shown here.

By default, the Main Timeline in the movie will automatically begin to play unless you tell it otherwise. You can keep a movie from playing automatically by adding an action to the Timeline to tell the movie to stop before it begins to play. The movie will then start in a stopped position, and it will not play until the Play button is clicked. You will do this next.

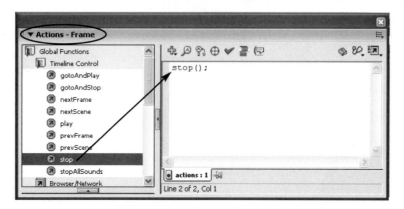

18. In the **Main Timeline**, select **Frame 1** of the **actions** layer, which contains a blank keyframe. In the **Actions** panel, double-click the **stop** action to add it to the **Script** pane.

Notice that the Actions panel no longer reads "Actions – Button," but instead it reads "Actions – Frame". This gives you immediate feedback as to where the action is located and whether you are applying the action to an object, such as a button or movie clip, or to a keyframe.

NOTE | Adding a Layer for the Frame Action

I strongly recommend that you get in the habit of placing all frame actions on their own separate layers in the Timeline. I also recommend that this layer always be located on top of all the other layers in your movie and that you consistently give it the same name: **actions**. As the movies you create become more and more complex, it will be significantly easier to troubleshoot and debug a movie if you know you can always find the frame actions in the same place: on the first layer of the movie, on the layer named actions.

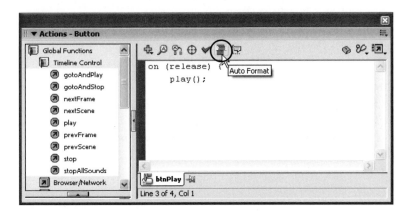

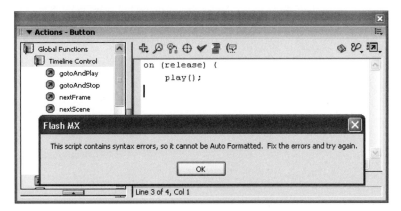

*Tip: You can use the **Auto Format** button in the **Actions** panel to quickly format your code. This will not work if the code has syntactical errors in it, so it's also a great way to make sure you're writing your code correctly.*

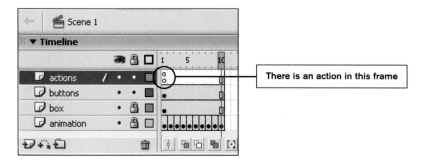

Once you have added an action to a keyframe, the Timeline will display a small "a" inside the frame as further feedback that there is an action in the keyframe.

---

19. Test the movie again (**Control > Test Movie**). The movie will now begin in a stopped position, waiting for the user to click the **Play** button. Click the **Stop** and **Play** buttons to control the animation.

*Notice that once the boarder reaches the end of the mountain, it stops. Why? This is because you added a **stop** action to the first keyframe, so the movie will begin in a stopped state since the first thing the playhead encounters is a **stop** action in the first frame, which will stop the movie. When a user clicks on the Play button, it sets the playhead in motion. The playhead will play through all the frames and will automatically loop by default, going back to the first frame, where it will encounter that **stop** action again, which will stop the movie. You can choose to bypass the movie stopping each time it tries to start again; you will do this next.*

---

20. Close the **Preview** window. In the **Main Timeline**, on the **actions** layer, select **Frame 10**, and press **F6** to add a keyframe. You will be adding actions to **Frame 10** next; in order to add an action to a frame, the frame must first be set as a keyframe.

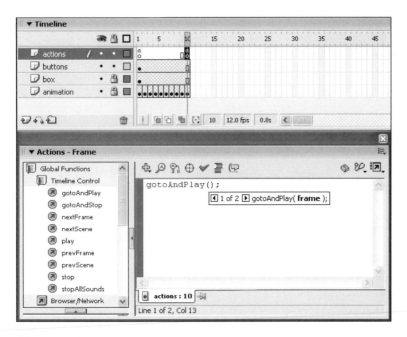

21. Make sure **Frame 10** is selected in the **actions** layer. In the **Actions** panel, double-click the **gotoAndPlay** action to add it to the **Script** pane. You should see **gotoAndPlay();** appear in the **Script** pane, along with a code hint that tells you to specify the frame you want to play.

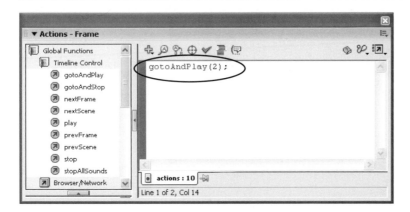

22. In the parentheses, type the number **2**. This tells Flash MX 2004 that when the **playhead** hits **Frame 10**, send the playhead to **Frame 2** and play. This creates a small loop because each time the **playhead** hits **Frame 10**, it will go to **Frame 2**, play the rest of the frames, and then return to **Frame 2**, and so on, each time bypassing **Frame 1**, which has the **stop** action on it.

23. Choose **Control > Test Movie** and test the movie again. The movie will begin in a stopped state. As soon as you click the **Play** button, the movie will play and continue to play over and over, without stopping, until you click the **Stop** button.

24. When you are finished, save and close this file.

 MOVIE | stop_play_actions.mov

To see a movie demonstration of this exercise, view **stop_play_actions.mov** located in the **movies** folder on the **H•O•T CD-ROM**. **Note:** The movie playback will perform best if you copy this file to your hard drive.

Interactivity and Actions: Events and Event Handlers

When a movie plays, certain actions, such as a user releasing the mouse on a button, are considered events in Flash MX 2004. The events fall into one of the following categories: mouse events, movie clip events, keyboard events, and Timeline events. For every event, there must be something that manages the event. In Flash MX 2004, this is known as an event handler. You can think of the event handler as the event's manager because the event handler is in charge of (manages) the event. The four types of basic events are described in the following sections.

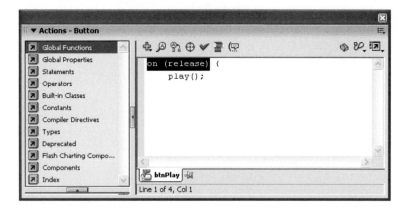

When you add an action to an object (either a button symbol or a movie clip symbol) in Flash MX 2004, you must introduce an event. In this illustration, the event is a mouse event. It states **on (release)**, meaning that when the user clicks the button, the action is triggered after the mouse has been released. The event handler is the **on** action, which handles button events.

Mouse Events

Mouse events occur when the user interacts with a button instance. When an action (such as a **stop** action) is added to a button instance, an **on** event handler is automatically added, as you saw in Exercise 1. The default **on** event is **release**.

The following table defines each possible mouse event.

Mouse Events Defined	
Event	**When It Occurs**
press	When the mouse pointer is moved over the Hit area of the button, and the mouse is pressed.
release	When the mouse pointer is moved over the Hit area of the button, and the mouse is pressed and then released.
releaseOutside	When a press occurs on the Hit area of a button, and then the mouse pointer is moved outside of the Hit area and released.
rollOver	When the mouse pointer moves over the Hit area of a button.
rollOut	When the mouse pointer moves off the Hit area of a button.
dragOver	When the mouse is pressed on the Hit area of a button, then rolls out of the Hit area, and reenters the Hit area with the mouse still pressed.
dragOut	When the mouse is pressed on the Hit area of a button, and then the mouse pointer rolls out of the Hit area with the mouse still pressed.
keyPress	When the specified key is pressed on the keyboard.

Keyboard Events

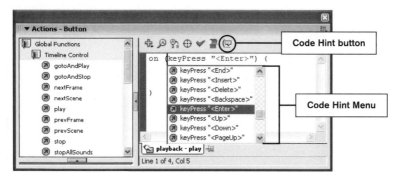

Keyboard events are similar to mouse events, except that they occur when the user presses a key on the keyboard rather than interacting with the mouse. For example, you might want to make a slideshow move forward and backward by pressing the arrow keys on your keyboard instead of having physical buttons on your Stage. This kind of functionality is great when using Flash MX 2004 as a substitute for a PowerPoint presentation. To change the mouse event to a keyboard event, click the **Code Hint** button to open the **Code Hint Menu** and double-click a keyboard even to add it to the Script pane. In this example, Flash MX 2004 will execute the **play** action when the user presses the **Enter** key.

Note: Use caution when assigning a keyboard event to a movie that will be displayed on the Web: Keypresses will not be executed in a browser unless the user has already clicked inside the movie at some point. And further, your end users might not intuitively know to use their keyboards unless they are instructed to do so.

Movie Clip Events

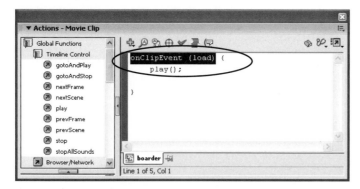

Movie clip events occur when something happens with a movie clip instance. When an action (such as **play**) is added to a movie clip instance, an **onClipEvent** event handler will need to be added. The default **onClipEvent** is **load** (shown here). **Note:** You can also create a movie clip that receives button events; this will automatically have the **on** (rather than the **onClipEvent**) event handler.

The following table defines each possible movie clip event.

Movie Clip Events Defined	
Event	**When It Occurs**
load	When the movie clip is inserted and appears in the Timeline.
unload	When the movie clip is removed from the Timeline.
enterFrame	When the playhead hits a frame, the action is triggered continually at the frame rate of the movie.
mouseDown	When the mouse button is pressed.
mouseMove	Every time the mouse is moved.
mouseUp	When the mouse button is released.
keyDown	When a key is pressed.
keyUp	When a key is released.
data	When data is received in a **loadVariables** or **loadMovie** action.

Timeline Events

Unlike mouse events, keyboard events, and movie clip events, Timeline events occur when the playhead reaches a keyframe containing actions in the Timeline.

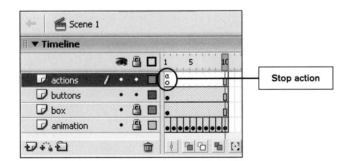

In the last exercise, you added a Timeline event by adding the **stop** frame action to the first keyframe in the project file so that when the movie begins, the playhead will come across the **stop** frame action located on Frame 1 and do just that—stop at Frame 1. Timeline events can exist on the Main Timeline or in any graphic or movie clip instance's Timeline.

2.——————————**Controlling Movie Clips**

In the last exercise, you attached the **stop** and **play** actions to button instances to control an animation on the Main Timeline. You can also use the **stop** and **play** actions to control the Timeline of any movie clip or loaded movie. In order to control a movie clip, you must give it an instance name, and it must be present in the Timeline. This exercise will show you how.

1. Open the file called **stopAndPlayMC.fla** from the **chap_11** folder. This file was created to get you started.

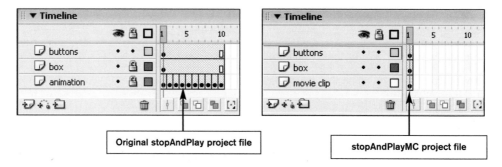

Original stopAndPlay project file

stopAndPlayMC project file

2. Notice that this project file looks very similar to the original project file from Exercise 1, with two exceptions: In the **stopAndPlayMC** project file, there is a **boarder** movie clip rather than an animation layer in the **Main Timeline**, and there is only one frame in the **Main Timeline**.

*Because this exercise will show you how to use actions to control a movie clip rather than the Main Timeline, the frames from the animation layer in the **stopAndPlay** project file were converted into a movie clip, which was placed inside the **stopAndPlayMC** project file for you.*

3. Choose **Control > Test Movie** to preview the movie. Click the **Stop** and **Play** buttons. Notice that nothing happens and the movie continues to play. This is because no actions have been added to these buttons yet, and therefore, the buttons do not control the movie. You will add actions to control the movie clip in the steps that follow. When you are finished previewing the movie, close the **Preview** window.

The Power of Movie Clips

Many exercises in this chapter use movie clip symbols. Movie clips are addressed differently in ActionScript than other kinds of symbols. You might be asking yourself, "Why should I create a movie clip symbol when I can create the same animation on the Main Timeline?" Although there is no right or wrong answer to this question, the question really is, "Which method is more effective?" As you learned in Chapter 10, "*Movie Clips*," movie clip symbols are the most powerful and flexible of all symbols since they can contain multiple layers, graphic symbols, button symbols, even other movie clip symbols, as well as animations, sounds, and ActionScript. Since movie clip symbols can contain all of these things and be represented on the Timeline in just one keyframe, your Timeline will be more organized and less cluttered. And, don't forget that movie clip symbols are Timeline independent, meaning that the movie clip will continue to play even though the playhead in the Main Timeline has stopped.

Let's say, for example, that you have a company logo that you want to subtly animate throughout your entire movie. In this example, it is far more effective to create a movie clip symbol than to create all the animation on the Main Timeline, for several reasons. By creating a movie clip symbol for your company logo, you can have it animate throughout your entire movie in just one keyframe, which also makes for a cleaner, less cluttered Timeline. Also, if you need to edit your logo, you could simply open up the movie clip symbol and edit it without affecting the work you have on the Main Timeline. Since it is a symbol, you could reuse the movie clip of your company logo in other presentations as well!

On the flip side, if you were to create your company logo animation on the Main Timeline, you would have to keep repeating the animation throughout the project to ensure that it plays throughout the entire movie, which would also end up making the file size larger. And if you wanted to edit your animation, you would have to locate each place in your project file that needs to be changed– yikes! So, although movie clip symbols are more complex to learn, with practice you will find that they actually make creating your Flash projects easier!

But, there's one more thing–as you learned in Chapter 10, "*Movie Clips*," movie clip symbols are Timeline independent. So, how do you control them if they have a mind of their own? You will find out next! In the following steps, you will learn how to control a movie clip symbol by giving it an instance name so that you can refer to it in ActionScript.

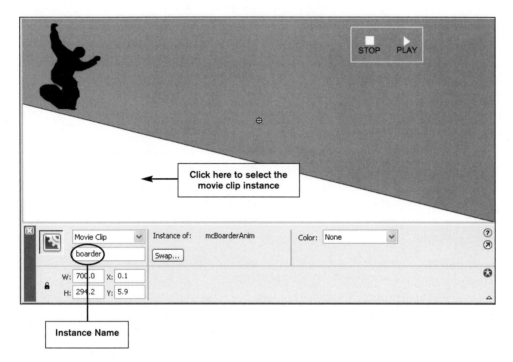

Click here to select the movie clip instance

Instance Name

4. In the **Timeline,** unlock the **boarder** layer. On the **Stage,** click the **snow** to select the movie clip instance. In the **Properties inspector (Window > Properties),** type **boarder** in the **Instance Name** field. This will assign an instance name to the movie clip on the **Stage.**

In Exercise 1, the **stop** *and* **play** *actions you added to the buttons automatically controlled the Main Timeline. Conversely, in order to control a movie clip, (make it start or stop, for example) you have to refer to the movie clip by its instance name when you apply actions to the buttons in the next steps.*

5. Select the **Stop** button instance on the **Stage** to select it.

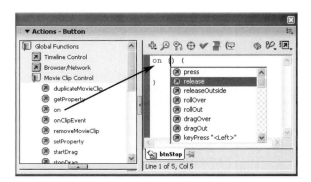

6. In the **Actions** panel (**F9**), choose **Global Functions > Movie Clip Control** and double-click the **on** action to add it to the **Script** pane. From the **Code Hint** menu that appears, choose **release** for the mouse event.

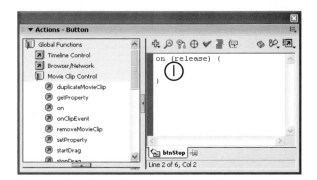

7. In the **Script** pane, place your cursor after the open curly brace and press **Enter/Return** to bring the cursor down to the second line, as shown here.

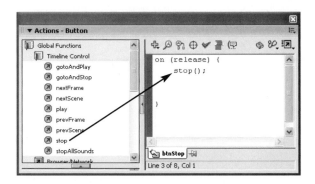

8. In the **Actions** pane, choose **Global Functions > Timeline Control** and double-click the **stop** action to add it to the **Script** pane.

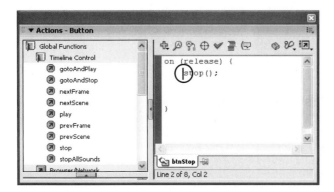

9. Place your cursor before the **stop** script. You will add the instance name of the movie clip to tell it to stop playing next.

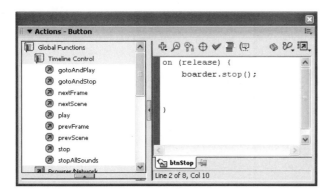

10. Type **boarder.** before the **stop** script, as shown here. This tells the movie clip **boarder**, which you named in Step 4, to stop playing when the user clicks the **Stop** button.

*This is slightly different than choosing **Timeline Control > stop** as you did in Exercise 1, because this time, you want to use an action that controls a movie clip, rather than the Main Timeline.*

NOTE | Controlling Movie Clips

In Flash MX 2004, movie clips can be controlled using either actions or methods. In ActionScript, methods are functions that are assigned to an object. Because some actions and methods yield the same behavior, you can control a movie clip by either one. For example, to make a movie clip stop, you need the instance name, a dot, and then the method, such as **boarder.stop();**, as you did in the last step. In other words, the **stop** method halts the playhead in the boarder movie clip instance.

11. Choose **Control > Test Movie** and try out the **stop** action you just added to the button instance. When you click the **Stop** button, the boarder movie clip will stop in its tracks! When you are finished previewing, close the **Preview** window. You will add the ActionScript that will tell the **boarder** movie clip to play when the user clicks the **Play** button in the following steps.

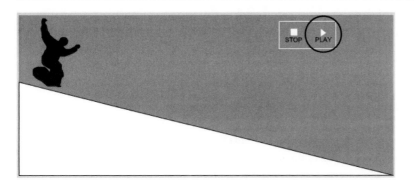

12. Back in the project file, click the **Play** button on the **Stage** to select it.

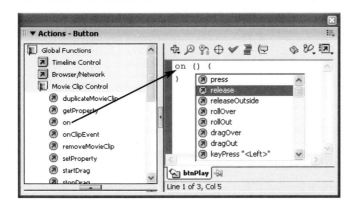

13. In the **Actions** panel (**F9**), choose **Global Functions > Movie Clip Control** and double-click the **on** action to add it to the **Script** pane. From the **Code Hint** menu that appears, choose **release** for the mouse event.

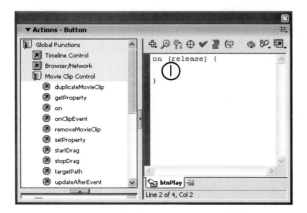

14. In the **Script** pane, place your cursor after the open curly brace and press **Enter/Return** to bring the cursor down to the second line, as shown here.

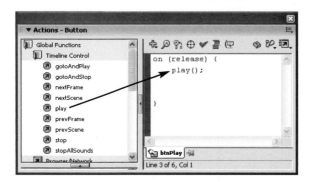

15. In the **Actions** pane, choose **Global Functions > Timeline Control** and double-click the **play** action to add it to the **Script** pane.

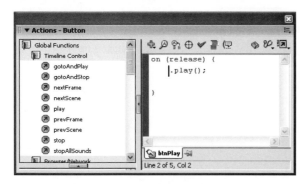

16. Place your cursor before the **play** script and type a period (.). Then place the cursor before the period, as shown here. You will add the instance name of the movie clip by inserting a **target path** next.

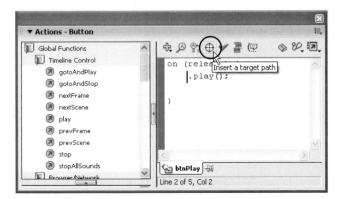

17. Above the **Script** pane, click the **Insert a target path** button.

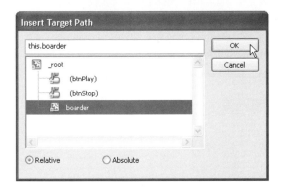

18. In the **Insert Target Path** dialog box, select **boarder** and click **OK**.

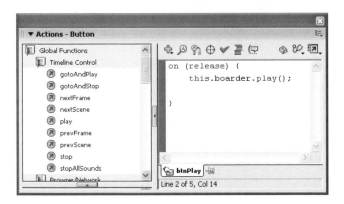

19. In the **Script** panel, notice the ActionScript now reads `this.boarder.play();`. This tells the **boarder** movie clip to begin playing when the user clicks the **Play** button.

20. Choose **Control > Test Movie** and try out the **Stop** and **Play** buttons. When you click the **Stop** button, the **boarder** movie clip will stop in its tracks again, and when you click the **Play** button, the **boarder** movie clip will begin playing where it left off! When you are finished previewing, close the **Preview** window. You will add a frame action to the **Main Timeline** to make the movie begin playing in a stopped position in the following steps.

NOTE | What Are Target Paths?

Target paths are hierarchical addresses that display movie clip instance names, variables, and objects inside your movie. After you name a movie clip instance in the **Properties inspector**, as you did in Step 4, you can use the **Insert a target path** button to find all the movie clip instance names in the movie (you have only one movie clip instance name in this exercise) and select the one you want to direct the action to. Using the **Insert a target path** button to find the boarder instance name is the same as typing the **boarder** name in the **Script** pane, as you did in Step 10. Oftentimes, you may forget exactly how you spelled an instance name; the target path feature is a quick and surefire way to find the instance you want to refer to.

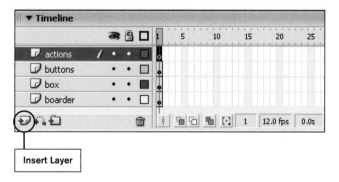

Insert Layer

21. Click the **Insert Layer** button to add a new layer to the **Timeline** and name it **actions**. Make sure the **actions** layer is above all other layers, as shown here.

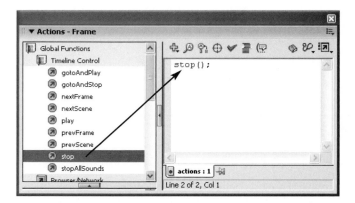

22. Select **Frame 1** of the **actions** layer and in the **Actions** panel (**F9**), choose **Global Functions >
Timeline Control** and double-click the **stop** action to add it to the **Script** pane.

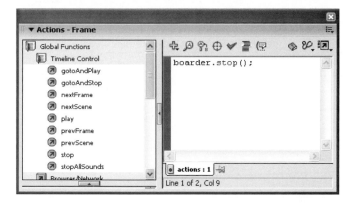

23. In the Script pane, type **boarder**. before the **stop** action, as shown here. This tells the **boarder**
movie clip to stop, so that it begins in a stopped position.

*In Step 18 of Exercise 1, you added a **stop** frame action that read: **stop();**. This tells the Main
Timeline to stop playing.*

*In the previous step, you added a stop frame action that read: **boarder.stop();**. This tells the movie
clip with the instance name of **boarder** to stop playing.*

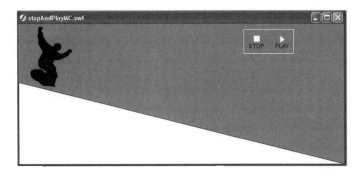

24. Choose **Control > Test Movie**. Notice that the movie begins playing in a stopped position. Go ahead and click the buttons to make your movie play and stop.

NOTE | Starting the Movie in a Stopped Position in the Movie Clip Symbol

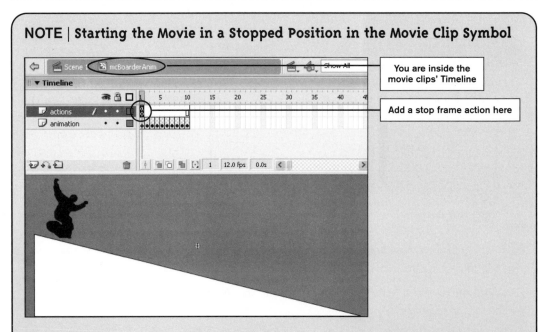

As you learned in Chapter 10, "*Movie Clips*," movie clips play independently of the Main Timeline, so in order for the movie clip to start in a stopped state, another way is to add a **stop** frame action to the first frame inside the movie clip's Timeline.

To access the movie clip's Timeline, you can either double-click the movie clip on the **Stage**, double-click the movie clip in the **Library**, or select the movie clip symbol on the **Stage** and use the menu commands **Edit > Edit Symbols**, **Edit > Edit Selected**, or **Edit > Edit in Place**, all of which will open the movie clip symbol's Timeline. Also, in this example, in **Frame 10** you can add the **gotoAndPlay Frame 2** ActionScript to send the **playhead** to **Frame 2** to create a loop.

25. When you are finished, save and close this file.

 MOVIE | controlMC.mov

To see this exercise performed, play the **controlMC.mov** located in the **movies** folder on the **H•O•T CD-ROM**.

What Is Dot Syntax?

You may have noticed that there was a dot (.) added between the instance name and the **stop** and **play** methods in the last exercise: **boarder.stop();**. In ActionScript, the dot indicates the properties or methods that relate to a movie clip or other objects. This is part of the ActionScript syntax, also referred to as **dot syntax**.

You may have heard of dot syntax before. In Flash MX 2004, dot syntax simply refers to the formatting convention that is used to create ActionScript that refers to movie clips or other objects. Dot syntax is used to construct statements that consist of objects, properties, methods, and variables. Each dot syntax statement begins with the name of the object followed by a dot (.) and ends with the property, method, or variable you want to identify. For example, in the statement **this.boarder.play ( );**, *this* is the Main Timeline, the object is the movie clip named *boarder*, and the method is *play*. The parentheses hold the parameters (called **arguments**) that apply to an action; in this case, no parameters are required. The semicolon (;) marks the end of a statement (just as a period marks the end of a sentence).

3. ——————————The goto Action to Create a Slideshow

In addition to the **stop** and **play** actions, you can be even more specific and add actions that tell the playhead not just to play, but exactly where to start and stop on the Timeline. This exercise will demonstrate how ActionScript can be used to create a Flash MX 2004 movie that can be navigated one frame at a time, similar to a slideshow. You will use the **goto** action—which can be used to send the playhead to a frame you specify—to do this.

1. Open the **slideShow_Final.fla** file from inside the **chap_11** folder. This is the finished version of the slideshow you are going to create.

2. Choose **Control > Test Movie** to preview the movie. Click the **Next** button to advance the slideshow forward. Click the **Back** button to display the previous slide. You will be creating this same slideshow in the steps that follow.

3. When you are finished, close the **Preview** window and **slideShow_Final.fla** file.

4. Open the **slideShow.fla** file from the **chap_11** folder. This is an unfinished version of the movie you just previewed, containing only the slideshow images. You will add new layers, buttons, and the necessary ActionScript in this exercise.

5. Choose **Control > Test Movie** to preview the movie. Notice that the frames go by very fast, one after another. This is because, by default, the movie will automatically play through the frames unless you tell it otherwise. You will add a **stop** action to **Frame 1** so that the movie starts in a stopped state. Close the **Preview** window when you are finished.

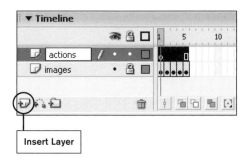

Insert Layer

6. In the **Main Timeline**, click the **Insert Layer** button to add a new layer to the **Timeline**. Name the new layer **actions**. Make sure the **actions** layer is above the **images** layer, as shown here.

7. Select **Frame 1** in the **actions** layer and open the **Actions** panel (**F9**).

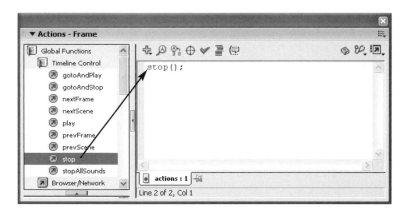

8. In the **Actions** pane, choose **Global Functions > Timeline Control** and double-click **stop** to add a **stop** action to the **Script** pane. Because you are adding the **stop** action to the **Main Timeline**, this will cause the movie to begin playing in a stopped position.

9. Choose **Control > Test Movie** to preview your movie. Notice the movie begins in a stopped position. Close the **Preview** window and return back to the project file. You will add the buttons to your movie in the following steps.

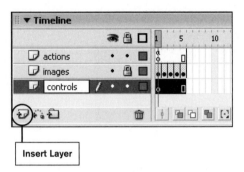

Insert Layer

10. Click the **Insert Layer** button to add another new layer to the **Timeline**. Name the new layer **controls**. Drag the **controls** layer below the other two layers, as shown here.

11. Lock the **actions** and **images** layers so that you don't accidentally select anything in either of those layers. Select **Frame 1** of the **controls** layer.

12. Open the **Library** (**Ctrl+L** [Windows] or **Cmd+L** [Mac]). Drag an instance of **btnNext** and **btnBack** onto the **Stage**. Position them side by side. Select both of the button instances using **Ctrl+A** (Windows) or **Cmd+A** (Mac), then choose **Ctrl+K** (Windows) or **Cmd+K** (Mac) to open the **Align** panel and align the bottom edge of the buttons.

13. Click the **btnNext** instance and make sure that the **Actions** panel is open (**F9**). You will be adding actions to the button instance **Next**. (You may have to click off the **Stage** to deselect both buttons and then click the **btnNext** instance to select only that instance.)

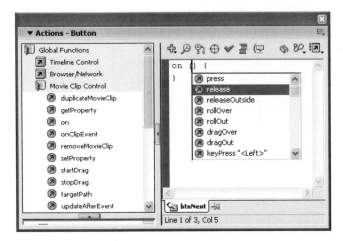

14. Choose **Global Functions > Movie Clip Control** and double-click the **on** action to add it to the **Script** pane. From the **Code Hint** menu, choose **release** for the mouse event.

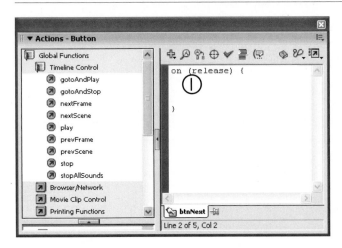

15. In the **Script** pane, place your cursor after the open curly brace and press **Enter/Return** to bring the cursor down to the second line, as shown here.

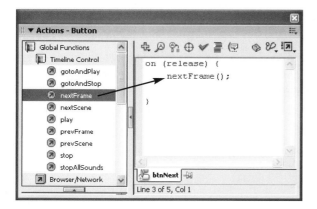

16. From the **Actions** pane, choose **Global Functions > Timeline Control** and double-click **nextFrame** to insert it into the **Script** pane.

You have just added ActionScript to the Next button. Now when the user clicks on the Next button and releases the mouse, the playhead will advance to the next frame and stop.

Tip: *Part of the description in the* **nextFrame** *action will send the playhead to the next frame and automatically stop, so you do not need to add an additional* **stop** *action.*

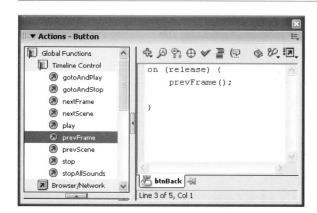

17. Click the **Back** button instance on the **Stage** to select it. Choose **Global Functions > Movie Clip Control** and double-click the **on** action to add it to the **Script** pane. In the **Code Hint** menu, choose **release** from the list. Then, insert a line break after the opening curly brace, choose **Global Functions > Timeline Control**, and double-click the **prevFrame** action.

This time, you have added ActionScript to the Back button. Now when the user clicks on this button and releases the mouse, the playhead will move to the previous frame and stop.

18. Choose **Control > Test Movie** to test your movie. Click the **Next** arrow button several times to advance the slideshow to the next picture and click the **Back** arrow button to reveal the previous picture.

Neat! Notice that when you continue to click the Next arrow, the slideshow stops at boarder 5 (the last frame) and never starts over at Frame 1. Likewise, notice that when you continue to click the Back arrow, the slideshow stops at boarder 1 (the first frame) and never loops to Frame 5. You can fix this to make the slideshow loop back to the beginning or to the end by adding a few keyframes and changing some of the ActionScript, which you will do next.

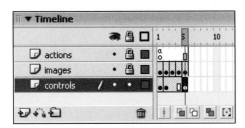

19. On the **controls** layer, add keyframes to **Frames 2** and **5** by selecting each frame and then pressing **F6**. Your **controls** layer should look like the picture here. Adding a keyframe will copy all the contents of **Frame 1**, including the actions attached to the buttons, to **Frames 2** and **5**.

20. Move the playhead so that it is over **Frame 1** of the **controls** layer. On the **Stage**, select the **Back** button instance. (You may have to click off the **Stage** to deselect both buttons first and then select the **Back** button.) You are going to change the ActionScript in this button next.

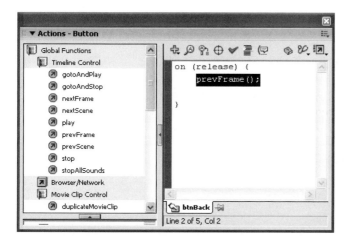

21. In the **Actions** panel, highlight the line in the **Script** pane that reads **prevFrame ();**. This line needs to be changed to direct the **playhead** to the last frame of the slideshow, **Frame 5**.

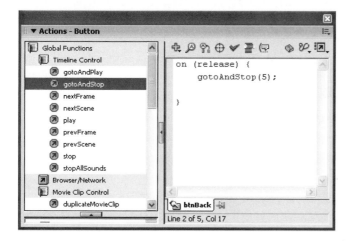

22. With the script still highlighted, choose **Global Functions > Timeline Control** and double-click the **gotoAndStop** action to add it to the **Script** pane. Between the parentheses, type 5.

You have just changed the ActionScript on the Back button instance appearing in the first keyframe of the movie. Instead of the script telling the playhead to go to the previous frame (which it can't do because this is Frame 1, the first frame), you have now changed the script to tell Flash MX 2004 the following: When the user releases the mouse on this button in the first frame of the movie, just go to Frame 5 and stop there!

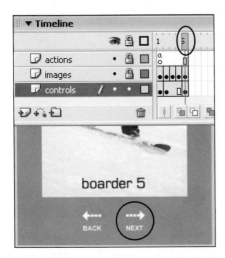

23. Move the **playhead** so that it is over the last keyframe of the **controls** layer. On the **Stage**, select the **btnNext** instance. You are going to change the ActionScript in this button and then you are done!

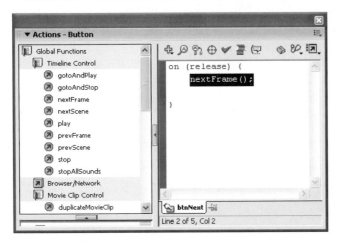

24. In the **Actions** panel, highlight the line in the **Script** pane that reads **nextFrame ();**. This line needs to be changed to direct the **playhead** to the first frame of the slideshow, **Frame 1**.

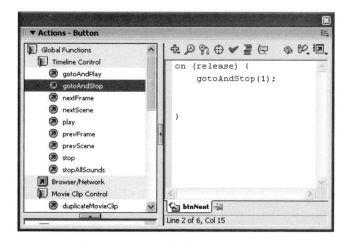

25. With the script still highlighted, choose **Global Functions > Timeline Control** and double-click the **gotoAndStop** action to add it to the **Script** pane. Between the parentheses, type **1**.

You have just changed the ActionScript on the Next button instance appearing in the last keyframe of the movie. Instead of the script telling the playhead to go to the next frame (which it can't do because this is Frame 5, the last frame), you have now changed the script to tell Flash MX 2004 the following: When the user releases the mouse on this button in the last frame of the movie, just go to Frame 1 and stop there!

26. Choose **Control > Test Movie** to preview the movie again. This time, the movie should never be "stuck" on **boarder 1** or **boarder 5**. Instead, it should loop when either the first or last frame is reached.

27. When you are finished testing the movie, save and close this file.

Go to Web Page Behavior

You can also open other Web sites from within a Flash MX 2004 movie. This exercise will introduce the **Behaviors** panel, new to Flash MX 2004, and the **Go to Web Page** behavior, which is used to create links to other documents on the Web. The following steps will teach you how to use the Go to Web Page behavior to link to an external Web page and to generate a pre-addressed email message.

1. Open the **getURL.fla** file from the **chap_11** folder. This file has been created to get you started.

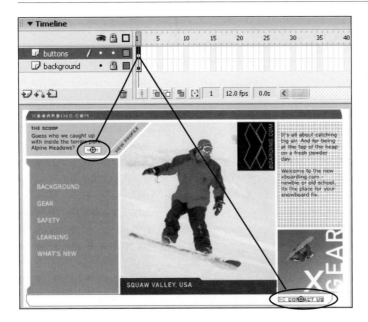

There are two button instances on the Stage. First, you will add the Go to Web Page behavior to the More button that will open up an HTML page in a new browser window. Later in the exercise, you will add the same behavior to the Contact Us button to create an email message.

2. Choose **Window > Development Panels > Behaviors** to open the **Behaviors** panel. On the Stage, select the **More** button to add a behavior to it. In the **Behaviors** panel, click the **Add Behavior** button and choose **Web > Go To Web Page**.

3. In the **Go to URL** dialog box that appears, type "**thescoop.html**" in the **URL** field and choose "**_blank**" in the **Open in** field. Click **OK**. When the user clicks on the **More** button, the HTML file **thescoop.html** will open in a Web browser. The HTML file **thescoop.html** is located in the **chap_11** folder. Additionally, the "**_blank**" setting tells Flash MX 2004 to open the link in a new browser window.

*You have the ability to control the window or frame that displays the linked file by changing the parameters in the **Open in** field. The following chart explains each of the four options: **_blank**, **__self**, **_parent**, and **_top**.*

Note: *The **thescoop.html** file has been provided for you and is in the same directory as your project file. If you want to keep your HTML files in another directory, separate from the project file, you would simply define the directory it is in followed by a forward slash (/), like so: newdirectory/thescoop.html.*

NOTE | Relative and Absolute Addresses

The addresses that you use in the **Go to URL** dialog box can be either relative or absolute addresses. Relative addresses describe the file's location in relation to another. Relative addresses can refer to local HTML files that are located in the same directory as the SWF file, such as **thescoop.html**. Absolute addresses are the complete addresses that specify the names of the servers on which the files reside. Absolute addresses can refer to files located on other Web servers, such as **http://www.xboarding.com**.

Go to URL Window Parameter Options	
Option	**Description**
_blank	Opens the link in a new browser window.
_self	Opens the link in the same browser window that is occupied by the current Flash MX 2004 movie.
_parent	Opens the link in the parent window of the current window.
_top	Opens the link in the same browser window and removes any existing framesets.

4. Choose **Control > Test Movie** and click the **More** button to preview the link you just created. Notice when you click the **More** button, the **Go to Web Page** behavior will automatically launch your machine's default browser and load the HTML Web page you specified into a new window. When you are finished, close the browser window and the **Preview** window.

Like an HREF tag in HTML, the Go to Web Page behavior can be used as an email link by adding "mailto" to an email address. In the steps that follow, you will add the Go To Web Page behavior to the second button to create an email link that will produce a pre-addressed email message, ***mailto:fl04hot@lynda.com.***

5. Back in the project file, select the **Contact Us** button on the **Stage**. In the **Behaviors** panel, click the **Add Behavior** button and choose **Web > Go to Web Page** behavior again.

6. In the **Go to URL** dialog box, type **mailto:fl04hot@lynda.com** in the **URL** field and choose "**_blank**" from the **Open in** field. These settings will pre-address the email message to **fl04hot@lynda.com** when the user clicks the **Contact Us** button and open the email message in a new window, leaving the Flash MX 2004 movie still visible in the background.

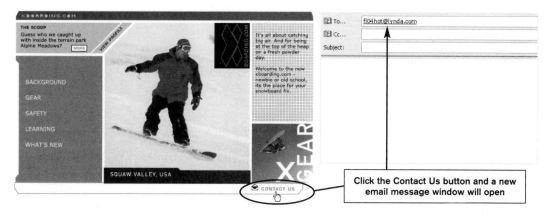

Click the Contact Us button and a new
email message window will open

7. Choose **File > Publish Preview > HTML.** This will open the SWF file in a browser window so that you can test the email link. Once the browser window opens, click the **Contact Us** button to test the link. A new email message window will open when you click the button!

*Note: On some computers, you may be able to choose **Control > Test Movie** and have this file work, although I have found this not always to be the case. Therefore, if you test it in a realistic environment by viewing the SWF file inside a browser, it will work on all machines. You will learn about the Publish settings in depth in Chapter 16, "Publishing and Exporting."*

8. When you are finished, close the open windows and save and close this file.

What Are Scenes?

In Flash MX 2004, you are not limited to only the frames in the Timeline of the main movie. You can have several timelines, which play one right after another. Flash MX 2004 calls these multiple Timelines scenes. Scenes allow you to break up large projects into smaller, more manageable pieces, similar to the way in which many Web sites are broken up into individual Web pages. By default, Flash MX 2004 will play all the scenes in order, unless you use ActionScript to tell it otherwise. If no ActionScript is present in the Main Timeline to stop the movie, the playhead will continue on to the next scene and continue to play the frames until the end is reached or a **stop** action is encountered. The Macromedia Flash Player treats all the scenes in a movie as one long Timeline. Therefore, if the first scene contains 30 frames and the second scene contains 20, the Macromedia Flash Player will see that as one Timeline of 50 consecutive frames and will play the scenes in the order in which they appear in the Scene panel. You can use scenes to break up a Web site into different sections, to structure a project where many smaller movies get loaded on demand, or even as a way to organize different stages of a project. The next exercise will teach you how to work with scenes.

Targeting Scenes

Up to this point in the book, you have been working with one scene, Scene 1, in the Main Timeline. In the following exercise, you will learn how to create additional scenes in Flash MX 2004 as well as how to rename, duplicate, and target them using ActionScript.

1. Open the **gotoScene_Final.fla** file from the **chap_11** folder. This is the finished version of the file you are going to create. At first glance, the interface may look similar to the file you created in the last exercise, although as you will see in the next step, this is an entire Web site.

NOTE | Missing Fonts

When you open **gotoScene_Final.fla**, you may see a dialog box that reads, "One or more of the fonts used by this movie are not available. Substitute fonts will be used for display and export. They will not be saved to the Macromedia Flash authoring document." This simply means that your computer does not have some of the fonts that were used to create the artwork in this file. Go ahead and click **Use Default** so that your computer will pick a default font to replace the unrecognizable fonts in the movie.

2. Choose **Control > Test Movie** to preview the movie. Click each of the navigation buttons to view a different section of the Web site. What is happening behind the scenes (pun intended) is that when you click the button, the playhead is moving to the appropriate scene in the movie. You will learn how to re-create this Web site next. When you are finished previewing the movie, close the **Preview** window and then close the project file.

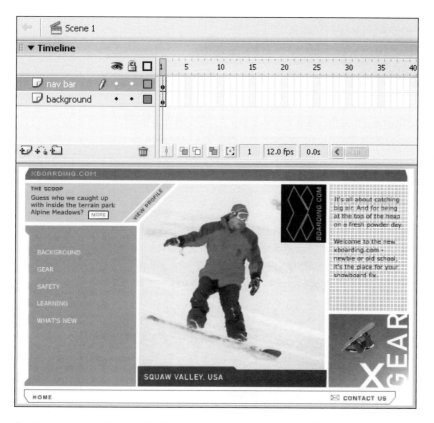

3. Open the **gotoScene.fla** file from the **chap_11** folder. This is an unfinished version of the movie that you just previewed; you just need to add the ActionScript to re-create the movie.

4. Choose **Control > Test Movie** to preview the movie. Notice that the navigation buttons don't go anywhere when you click on them. This is because there are no actions on the buttons telling them where to go. You will be adding ActionScript to the buttons in the steps that follow. When you are finished previewing the movie, close the **Preview** window.

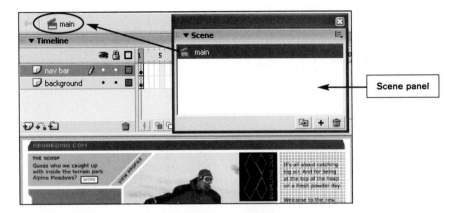

5. In the **Main Timeline**, choose **Window > Design Panels > Scene** to open the **Scene** panel. The **Scene** panel displays a list of the scenes in this movie. At this point, you have only one scene named **Scene 1** by default. Double-click inside the **Scene 1** name in the **Scene** panel and rename the scene **main**. As soon as you press **Enter/Return**, the name will change to **main** in the **Scene** panel and also in the **Edit Bar** of the project window.

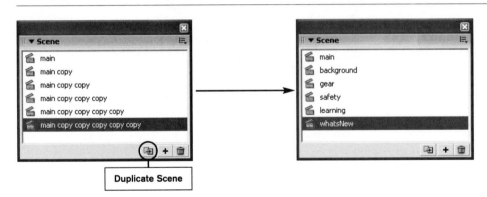

6. In the **Scene** panel, click the **Duplicate Scene** button five times to duplicate the **main** scene five times. Next, double-click on each of the duplicate scenes in the **Scene** panel and rename them to match the navigation buttons on the **Stage**: **background**, **gear**, **safety**, **learning**, and **whatsNew**, as shown here.

Note: *When you name the scenes in your movie, try to keep the names short and descriptive. Because you will be using ActionScript to target the scenes, it is important that scene names reflect the content inside them.*

You have just added five new scenes to the movie, although they will all look exactly the same because you just duplicated the main scene. You will change the content inside each scene next. You'll soon realize the value of duplicating scenes as you learn to align new artwork from scene to scene.

7. Click the **Edit Scene** button on the right side of the **Edit Bar**. A menu will appear with the list of scenes that you just made in this project. From the menu, select the scene named **background**. This will take you into the **Timeline** of that scene. Notice that the scene name changed in the **Edit Bar**, the **background** scene is highlighted in the **Scene** panel, and there is a checkmark next to the **background** scene in the **Edit Scene** button's drop-down menu. These are all cues that tell you which scene you are currently inside within the project. When you are finished, close the **Scene** panel.

Note: The Edit Scene button is useful to move quickly from scene to scene. The Scene panel can also be used to jump from scene to scene, but additionally, this is where you can add, delete, name, and copy scenes in your movie.

8. Click anywhere on the **Stage** to select the artwork. Open the **Properties inspector**, if it isn't already open (**Window > Properties**), and notice that it says, "Instance of: mcMain." This means that the artwork on the **Stage** is contained in an instance of the **mcMain** movie clip. Because you are now located in the background scene, you need to change the artwork to reflect the correct scene; you can do this with a few clicks of the mouse. Make sure the **mcMain** instance is still selected, and in the **Properties inspector**, click the **Swap Symbol** button.

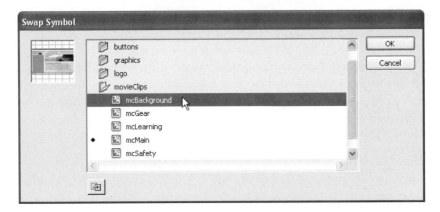

9. In the **Swap Symbol** dialog box, select the **mcBackground** movie clip and click **OK**. This will swap (or change) the **mcMain** movie clip with the **mcBackground** movie clip.

Tip: In the Swap Symbol dialog box, you can also double-click the symbol you want to swap rather than selecting it and clicking OK. By swapping a symbol, you keep it in perfect alignment with the symbol that was there before. Keep in mind that this is true only if both symbols have the same dimensions, which is the case in this exercise.

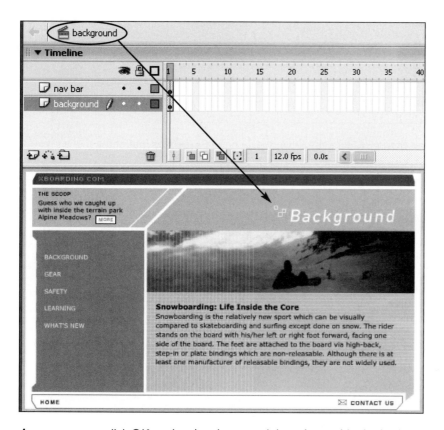

As soon as you click OK, notice that the artwork has changed in the background scene. This artwork was created ahead of time and saved as a movie clip. It is the same size as the main scene movie clip; the difference is in the colors, the photo, and the text. Swapping symbols is a good technique to use, for example, when you mock up several pages for a Web site and need to show a client how the Web site will work. You can create the artwork, save each page as a movie clip or graphic symbol in Flash MX 2004, make one scene, duplicate it, and switch out the artwork in each scene. This helps keep all the artwork registered in the same place. It's not easy to register artwork from scene to scene any other way, because you don't have onion skinning between scenes, only between frames on the Timeline.

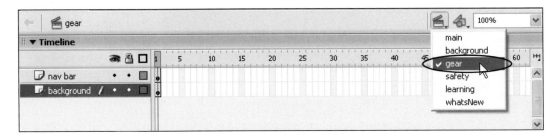

10. Using the **Edit Scene** button again, choose the scene named **gear** to open the **gear** scene's **Timeline**.

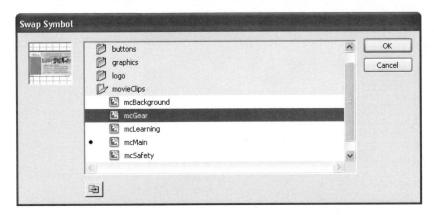

11. Select the artwork on the **Stage**, and in the **Properties inspector**, select the **Swap Symbol** button again. This time double-click the **mcGear** movie clip in the **Swap Symbol** dialog box.

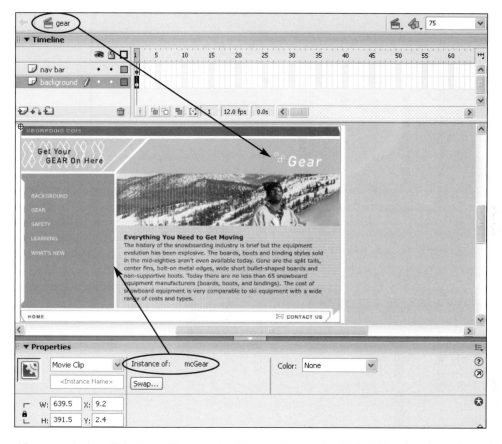

After you double-click the mcGear movie clip, your Stage should look like the picture here. Notice also that the Properties inspector reflects the name of the new movie clip you chose.

12. Repeat Steps 10 and 11 for the remaining scenes: in **safety**, swap the **mcSafety** movie clip; in **learning**, swap the **mcLearning** movie clip; in **whatsNew**, swap the **mcWhatsNew** Movie clip. When you are finished, you can use the **Edit Scene** button to quickly check each scene and make sure the scene name in the **Edit Bar** matches the artwork.

Next, you will add the ActionScript to the buttons to tell Flash MX 2004 to go to a specific scene when the user clicks on a button.

13. In the **Edit Bar**, click the **Edit Scene** button and choose **main** to open the **main** scene's **Timeline**. You will add ActionScript to the buttons in the following steps.

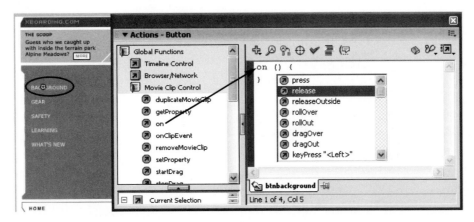

14. Select the **Background** button on the **Stage** and open the **Actions** panel (**F9**). Using the **Actions** pane, choose **Global Functions > Movie Clip Control** and double-click **on** to add it to the **Script** pane. Choose **release** from the **Code Hint** menu.

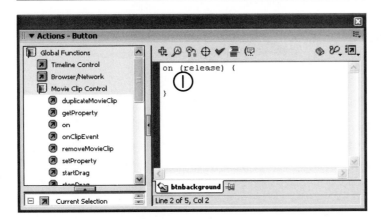

15. In the **Script** pane, place your cursor after the open curly brace and press **Enter/Return** to bring the cursor down to the second line, as shown here.

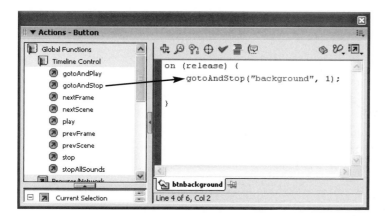

16. In the **Actions** pane, choose **Global Functions > Timeline Control** and double-click **gotoAndStop** action to add it to the **Script** pane. In the parentheses for the **gotoAndStop** action, type **"background"**, 1. This ActionScript will tell Flash MX 2004 that as soon as the user releases the mouse on the **Background** button, it should go to the scene named **background** and stop at **Frame 1**.

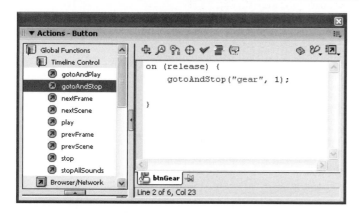

17. Repeat Steps 14, 15, and 16 for the **Gear**, **Safety**, **Learning**, and **What's New** buttons on the **main** scene. The only differences are these: In the parentheses for the **gotoAndStop** action, type **gear** for the **Gear** button; **safety** for the **Safety** button; **learning** for the **Learning** button; and **whatsNew** for the **What's New** button.

You now have five buttons on the main scene, each with ActionScript that instructs Flash MX 2004 to go to the appropriate scene when the user releases the mouse on each button. You will copy and paste the buttons and the ActionScript in each of the scenes next.

18. Select **Frame 1** in the **nav bar** layer to select all the content in **Frame 1**. Choose **Edit > Timeline > Copy Frames**.

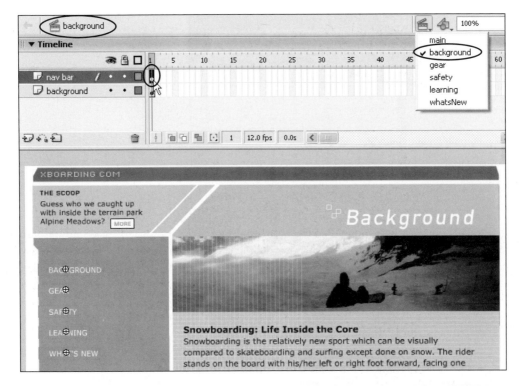

19. Using the **Edit Scene** button again, choose the **background** scene to open its **Timeline**. Select **Frame 1** in the **nav bar** layer and choose **Edit > Timeline > Paste Frames**. This will paste the buttons and all the ActionScript, from the **main** scene in **Frame 1** of the **nav bar** layer into **Frame 1** of the **nav bar** layer in the **background** scene, replacing any content that was previously in that frame.

Why I am copying the buttons into a scene that already has buttons? There are many ways to do this, but the idea is to be efficient as possible in your workflow. So rather than recode each button in every scene, copying and pasting frames is a quick and easy way to copy all the buttons with their attached ActionScript into another scene.

20. Repeat Step 19 for the remaining scenes: **gear**, **safety**, **learning**, and **whatsNew**.

*Be sure to select **Frame 1** in the **nav bar** layer inside each scene before you paste the frames so that you paste the buttons into the right location!*

21. Choose **Control > Test Movie** to test the movie. Notice that all the scenes play, one right after another. By default, the movie will continue to play, one scene after another, unless you tell the **playhead** to stop by adding a **stop** action to a frame in the **Timeline**. You will do this next. When you are finished testing the movie, close the **Preview** window.

22. Back in the project file, using the **Edit Scenes** button, choose the **main** scene. Inside the **main** scene's **Timeline**, click the **Insert Layer** button to add a new layer, and rename it **actions**. Make sure the **actions** layer is above all the other layers; if it is not, click the layer name and drag it above all the other layers.

Note: Ideally, as you create projects that use scenes to separate pages of a Web site, you will want to do as much work as possible on the main scene before duplicating it. This will save you from having to edit sections of each scene as you continue to work on the project file. This exercise is the ideal situation, so you may find that you still have to go back and alter parts of each scene, but the more you do in the beginning, the more efficient your workflow will be.

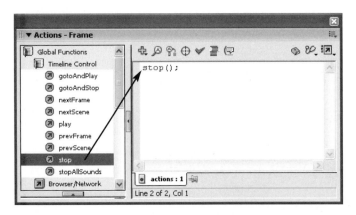

23. Select **Frame 1** in the **actions** layer, and in the **Actions** pane, choose **Global Functions >
Timeline Control** and double-click **stop** to add it to the **Script** pane. This will cause the movie to
stop when the **playhead** reaches the first frame in the **main** scene.

24. Repeat Steps 22 and 23 to add a **stop** frame action to **Frame 1** of the **background**, **gear**, **safety**,
learning, and **whatsNew** scenes. This will force the **playhead** to stop as soon as it reaches **Frame 1**
in each of the scenes.

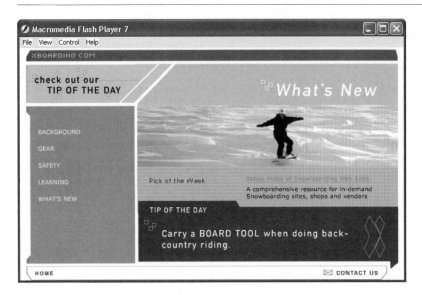

25. Choose **Control > Test Movie** to test the movie. Preview the scenes by clicking on each navigation button. Notice that once you click on a button to advance to a different scene, there is no visual
feedback on the button to let you know which scene you are in. You will change this last element of the
movie next. When you are finished, close the **Preview** window.

26. Back in the project file, use the **Edit Scene** button and choose the **background** scene. Click the **Background** button on the **Stage** to select it.

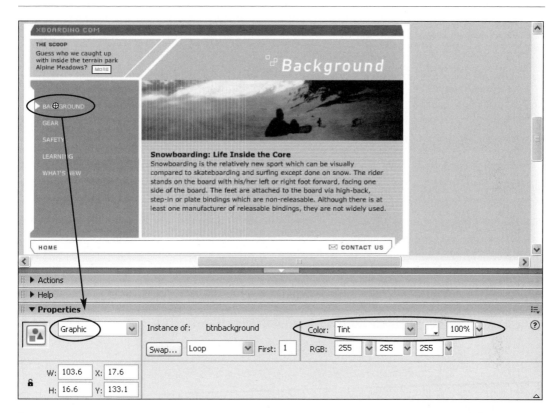

27. In the **Properties inspector**, choose **Graphic** from the **Symbol Behavior** drop-down list. You may get a warning that converting the symbol will delete the ActionScript. If you do, just click **OK**. This will convert the behavior of the **Background** button instance in this scene to become a graphic symbol, which cannot be clicked on and cannot have actions applied to it. From the **Color** drop-down menu, choose **Tint**, select **white** for the **Tint** color, and choose **100%**.

Because the Up state of this button contains a triangle next to the word "Background," changing the tint to white will turn the triangle white and provide visual feedback to the user regarding where he or she is located. So when you are in the background scene, the Background button will be white, and you will not be able to click on it because you are already in the background scene. Cool!

NOTE | Why Do I Need to Change the Behavior and Color of My Button?

There are many different ways to give the user visual feedback that a button has been selected. In good user interface design, you should make it as easy as possible for the user to know where he or she is at all times. By changing the behavior of the button to a graphic, the button instance (not the original button symbol in the Library) will turn into a graphic symbol, using the button's Up state as the graphic. When the button is a graphic, the user will not be able to click on it because it is no longer a button. Further, by also changing the color of the button-turned-graphic, you provide the user with extra visual feedback that he or she is located in a particular section of the Web site.

28. Repeat Steps 26 and 27 for the remaining scenes: **gear**, **safety**, **learning**, and **whatsNew**. Inside the **gear** scene, select the **Gear** button and change its **Symbol Behavior** to **Graphic** and **Tint** to **white** at **100%**. Likewise, inside the **safety** scene, select the **Safety** button; inside the **learning** scene, select the **Learning** button; and in the **whatsNew** scene, select the **What's New** button. In the **Properties inspector**, make the same changes for each button.

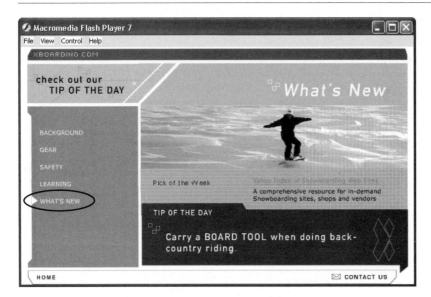

29. Choose **Control > Test Movie** to test the movie one last time! Click each button to go to the appropriate scene. Notice that once you are inside a scene, the button with the same name of the scene will now reflect the current scene by showing the white arrow and will not allow you to click on it. By using scenes, you can separate different sections of the project and target those sections on demand using ActionScript.

30. When you are finished testing the movie, save and close the file.

In this exercise, you learned that scenes are a way to divide your project file into more manageable sections, and how to link to them via ActionScript. In the next exercise, you will learn how to break down your project file even more by dividing up the Timeline through the use of frame labels.

NOTE | What Is a Frame Label?

Frame labels identify a frame by a name, rather than by a number. As you add and delete frames in the movie, the frame numbers will change, which can cause problems if you are referring to a frame number in your ActionScript. When you reference a frame label, if frames are added or deleted, the frame label will remain constant, and Flash MX 2004 will be able to find the correct frame.

Just like ActionScript that has been added to the movie, frame labels are also exported with the rest of the movie, so it is a good idea to keep the frame labels short in order to minimize overall file size. Also, shorter frame labels are much easier to work with.

NOTE | Why Use Frame Labels Instead of Scenes?

As you learned in the previous exercise, scenes are a way to break up large projects into smaller, more manageable pieces, much like a Web site is broken up into individual Web pages. In this exercise, rather than break up the navigation into separate scenes, you will keep all the work contained in a movie clip and divide the movie clip's Timeline into different sections, much like anchor links on a Web page.

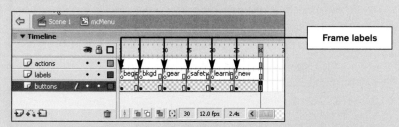

All the content is contained in its own Timeline, but divided out into sections using frame labels so that when you click on a button, the ActionScript will tell the playhead to go to the appropriate frame label within its Timeline. Although you will be adding frame labels to the movie clip's Timeline in this exercise, frame labels are not restricted to movie clips only; you can include frame labels in the Main Timeline as well.

6. ————————Creating a Drop-Down Menu Using Frame Labels

There are many ways to create interactive menus in Flash MX 2004. From scrolling menus to animated menus to draggable menus, all you need is a little creativity and a few bits of ActionScript to develop all kinds of different navigation systems for your users. This exercise will provide you with additional hands-on exercises with the Behaviors panel and start you on your way to creating interactive navigation schemes by teaching you how to develop a basic drop-down menu using frame labels.

1. Open the **menu_Final.fla** file from the **chap_11** folder. This is the finished version of the menu you are going to create.

2. Choose **Control > Test Movie** to preview the movie. Click on the different navigation buttons and notice that some of them will reveal a drop-down menu. When you are finished, close the **Preview** window and **menu_Final.fla**.

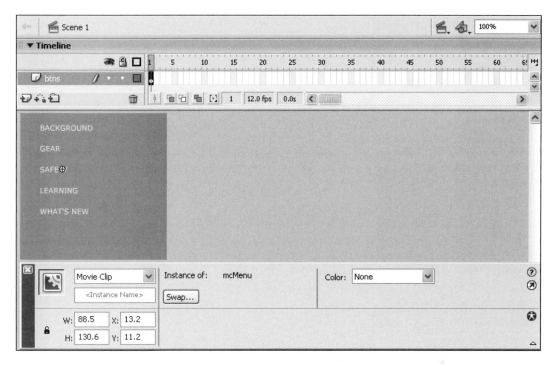

3. Open the **menu.fla** file from the **chap_11** folder. This is an unfinished version of the movie you just previewed, containing everything you need to create a drop-down menu. Notice there is one layer named **btns**, which is a movie clip symbol.

In this exercise, you will expand the navigation to include a drop-down menu using frame labels and behaviors to make this drop-down menu work. In the following exercise, you will build upon what you have learned and take your project a step further by using the same movie clip symbol and adding functionality to the buttons on the menu to load different SWF files into the interface by using the **loadMovieNum** *action.*

As you may have guessed by now, this movie clip contains buttons symbols and graphic symbols and will require ActionScript. It will be used over and over throughout the completed project in this book, which is why a movie clip symbol was used over a button symbol or graphic symbol.

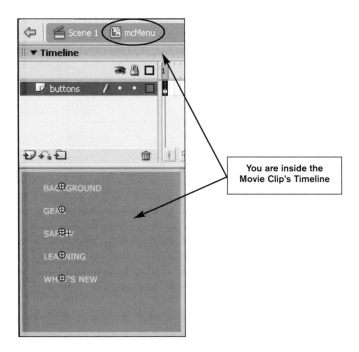

4. Double-click the menu on the **Stage** to open the movie clip's **Timeline**. Notice that there is one layer with five buttons. Choose **Control > Test Movie** to preview the menu. As you click each button, you will see that there are no drop-down menus. You will be creating them next. When you are finished previewing the menu, close the **Preview** window.

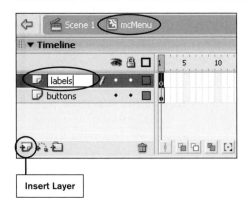

Insert Layer

5. Back in the project file, inside the **mcMenu** movie clip, click on the **Insert Layer** button to add a new layer to the **Timeline**. Rename this layer **labels**. Make sure this layer is above the **buttons** layer.

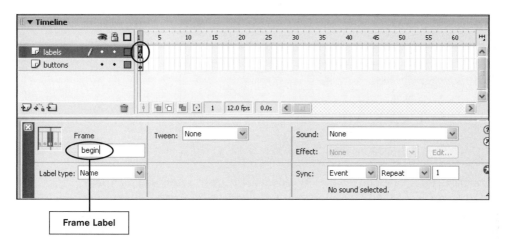

Frame Label

6. In the **Timeline**, select **Frame 1** in the **labels** layer. In the **Properties inspector**, type the name **begin** in the **Frame Label** field. This will add the frame label **begin** to **Frame 1**, where the menu is in the starting position.

As soon as you add the label name, notice the hollow circle and the flag in the Timeline. This is feedback to show you that a label exists on this frame. **Note:** *You will not be able to see the* **begin** *frame label name just yet, because there are not enough frames in the Timeline, but you will see it after the next step.*

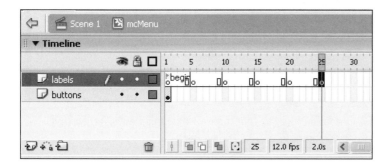

7. On the **labels** layer, select **Frames 5**, **10**, **15**, **20**, and **25**, one at a time, and press **F7** on each of them to add a blank keyframe to each of the frames, as shown here.

8. In the **Properties inspector**, add the **Frame Labels bkgd**, **gear**, **safety**, **learning**, and **new** to **Frames 5**, **10**, **15**, **20**, and **25**, respectively. Select **Frame 30** and press **F5** to add frames up to **Frame 30** so that you can see the **new** label. When you are finished, your **Timeline** should look like the picture here.

*Tip: In order for a frame label to be visible in the Timeline, there must be enough frames to display the entire name; so by pressing **F5**, you can add frames and see the name. **Note:** Even if you can't see the whole name, the label is still there; you can always tell that by looking for the flag on the frame in the Timeline or by looking at the Frame Label in the Properties inspector.*

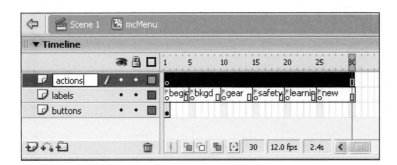

9. Click the **Insert Layer** button to add another layer to your movie. Name this new layer **actions**. Make sure the **actions** layer is above all the other layers, as shown here.

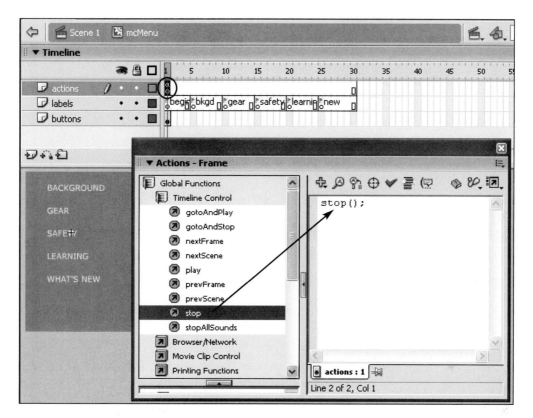

10. Select **Frame 1** in the **actions** layer and open the **Actions** panel (**F9**). In the **Actions** pane, choose **Global Functions** >**Timeline Control** and double-click the **stop** action to add it to the **Script** pane. This action will tell the **playhead** to stop on **Frame 1** when the movie begins. You will add behaviors to the buttons in the following steps.

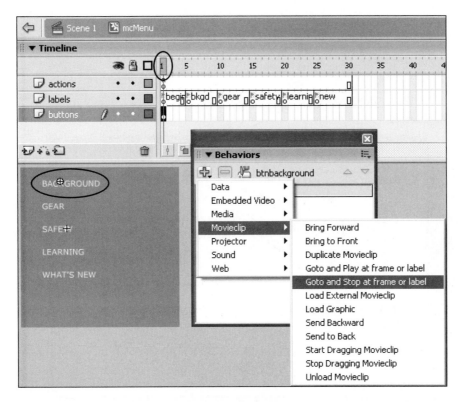

11. Choose **Window > Development Panels > Behaviors** to open the **Behaviors** panel. In the **Timeline**, make sure the **playhead** is on **Frame 1** and click on the **Background** button instance on the **Stage** to select it. In the **Behaviors** panel, click the **Add Behavior** button and choose **Movieclip > Goto and Stop at frame or label** from the drop-down menu.

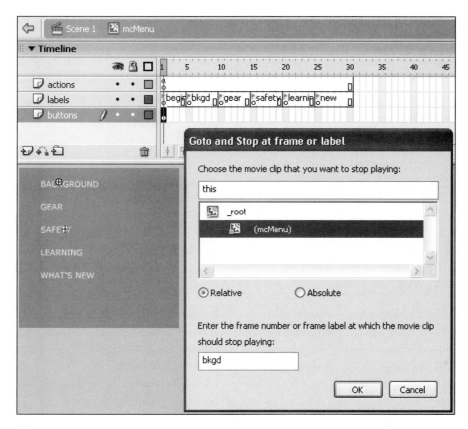

12. In the **Goto and Stop at frame or label** dialog box that appears, make sure **mcMenu** is selected and type **bkgd** in the **Enter the number or frame label at which the movie clip should stop playing** field. Click OK.

*This behavior will tell Flash MX 2004 that as soon as the user releases the mouse on the Background button, it should go to the frame label **bkgd** and stop there.*

13. Make sure the **playhead** is on **Frame 1** and repeat Steps 11 and 12 to add behaviors to the four remaining navigation buttons. For the **Gear** button, type **gear** for the frame label; for the **Safety** button, type **safety** for the frame label; for the **Learning** button, type **learning** for the frame label; and for the **What's New** button, type **new** for the frame label in the **Goto and Stop at frame or label** dialog box.

*Notice that the names you type in the **Enter the number or frame label at which the movie clip should stop playing** field correspond to the frame labels you added in Step 8.*

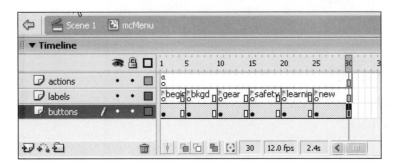

14. In the **Timeline**, on the **buttons** layer, add a keyframe to **Frames 5, 10, 15, 20,** and **25** by pressing **F6** on each of those frames one at a time. This will copy the buttons, including the behaviors, into each frame. Select **Frame 30** and press **F5** to add frames up to **Frame 30** on the **buttons** layer. Your **Timeline** should look like the one pictured here.

15. Choose **Control > Test Movie** to test the buttons. Notice that nothing much happens.

By pressing F6 in the previous step, you copied all the contents of the last keyframe into the next keyframe; although the behaviors are working to send the playhead to a different frame label, all the content will look the same. In the steps that follow, you will slightly modify the buttons in each keyframe so that the menu changes at each keyframe.

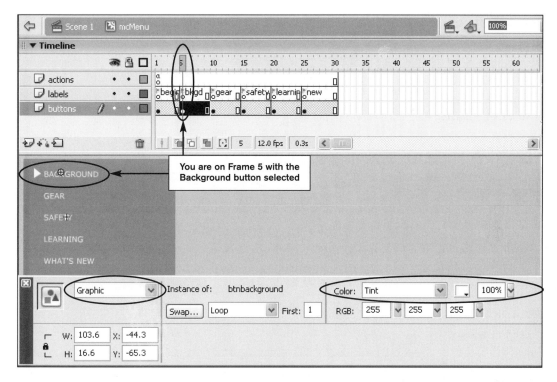

16. Move the **playhead** to **Frame 5** and select the **Background** button on the **Stage**. In the **Properties inspector**, just as you did in the last exercise, choose **Graphic** from the **Symbol Behavior** drop-down menu. **Note:** You may get a warning that converting the symbol will delete the ActionScript. If you do, just click **OK**. For **Color Styles**, choose **Tint**, select **white** for the **Tint** color, and choose **100%**.

This will change the behavior of the Background button instance in this frame only to a graphic symbol, which cannot be clicked on and cannot have behaviors applied to it. So when the playhead hits the background label, the Background button will be white, and you will not be able to click on it because you are already in the Background section.

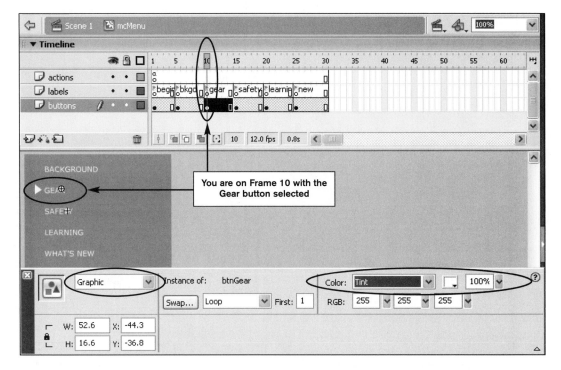

17. Move the **playhead** to **Frame 10**. Select the **Gear** button on the Stage, and in the **Properties inspector**, choose **Graphic** from the **Symbol Behavior** drop-down menu. For **Color Styles**, choose **Tint**, select **white** for the **Tint** color, and choose **100%**.

This will change the behavior of the Gear button instance in this frame only to a graphic symbol, which cannot be clicked on and cannot have behaviors applied to it. So when the playhead hits the gear label, the Gear button will be white and you will not be able to click on it because you are already in the Gear section.

18. Repeat Step 17 and modify the **Safety** button on **Frame 15**, the **Learning** button on **Frame 20**, and the **What's New** button on **Frame 25**.

Make sure you move the playhead to the correct frame first, select the appropriate button on the Stage next, and then make the changes in the Properties inspector to make sure you are changing the right button on the right frame.

19. Test the movie (**Control > Test Movie**). Click on each of the buttons. Notice that when you do, the arrow will appear to indicate where you are located. All you have left to do is to add the subnavigation menus, which you will do next. When you are finished testing the movie, close the **Preview** window.

20. In the project file, move the **playhead** to **Frame 10**. Open the **Library** (**Ctrl+L** [Windows] or **Cmd+L** [Mac]) and notice two buttons named **btnGearSub1** and **btnGearSub2**. These are subnavigation buttons that have been created for you.

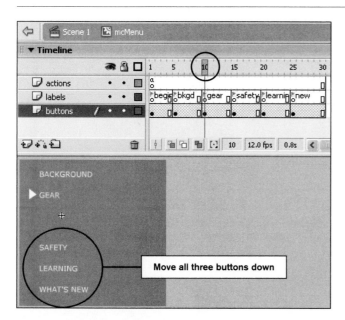

Move all three buttons down

21. On **Frame 10**, **Shift+click** to select the **Safety**, **Learning**, and **What's New** buttons on the **Stage** all at once. With those three buttons selected, use the **down arrow** key on your keyboard to move them down toward the bottom of the **Stage** to make room for two subnavigation buttons, which you will add next, under the **Gear** button.

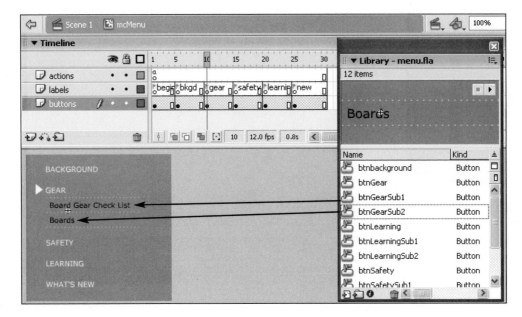

22. Drag an instance of **btnGearSub1** and **btnGearSub2** from the **Library** onto the Stage and position them, as shown here.

These will serve as the subnavigation buttons for the Gear section.

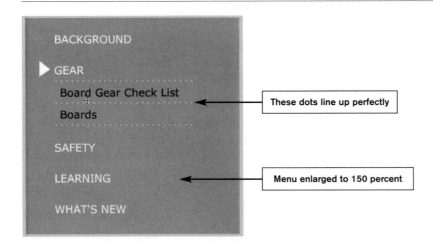

*Note: In this example, the two subnavigation buttons are positioned so that the bottom dotted line of one button lines up and overlaps the top dotted line on the other button, so that it appears as if there is only one dotted line between the two buttons. You can use the **Zoom** button in the **Edit Bar** to get a close-up view to make lining up the buttons easier.*

23. Choose **Control > Test Movie**. When you click the **Gear** button, the arrow and the subnavigation buttons will appear. When you are finished, close the **Preview** window.

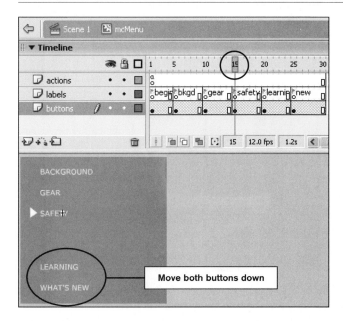

Move both buttons down

24. In the project file, move the **playhead** to **Frame 15** and **Shift+click** to select the **Learning** and **What's New** buttons on the **Stage**. With those two buttons selected, use the **down arrow** key on your keyboard to move them down toward the bottom of the **Stage** to make room for two subnavigation buttons, which you will add next.

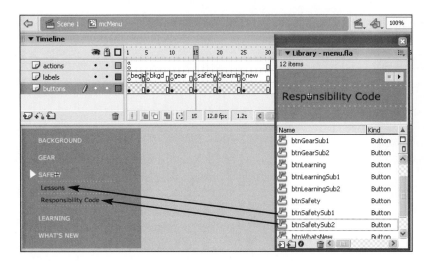

25. From the **Library**, drag an instance of **btnSafetySub1** and **btnSafetySub2** onto the **Stage** and position them, as shown here.

These will serve as the subnavigation buttons for the Safety section. You have one last subnavigation section to add next.

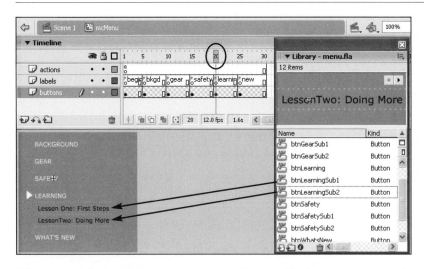

26. Move the **playhead** to **Frame 20** and select the **What's New** button on the **Stage**. Use the **down arrow** key on your keyboard to move the **What's New** button down toward the bottom of the **Stage** to make room for two subnavigation buttons under the **Learning** button. From the **Library**, drag an instance of **btnLearningSub1** and **btnLearningSub2** onto the **Stage** and position them, as shown here.

These will serve as the subnavigation buttons for the Learning section.

27. Choose **Control > Test Movie** to test your drop-down menu! Click on each of the buttons to make sure they are all working correctly. When you are done testing the menu, close the **Preview** window.

28. When you are finished, save and close this file.

In the next exercise, you are going to use a menu similar to the one you just created, and you will add ActionScript to create a finished Web site using a new technique with the **loadMovieNum** *action.*

 MOVIE | menu.mov

To see this exercise performed, play the **menu.mov** located in the **movies** folder on the **H•O•T CD-ROM.**

What Is loadMovieNum?

In earlier chapters, the differences between the project file (FLA) and the movie file (SWF) were described. In this chapter, you will learn that the SWF file has the capability to load other SWF files into itself. This idea is similar to links on an HTML page, which replace content with other HTML pages when clicked.

Why would you want to do this in Flash MX 2004? If you have a large project with lots of graphics and navigation, it can take a long time to download all the content to the user's browser before he or she can access the finished result. If you instead learn to structure your projects so that many smaller movies are loaded on demand, it can create a better user experience for your audience. This process is called **Load Movie** in Flash MX 2004, because it requires the **loadMovieNum** action.

As you begin to stack SWF files on top of one another, their arrangement simulates layers. In ActionScript, the layers are called **levels**. The Main Timeline (named Scene 1 by default) is always located at Level 0, and when you load an additional movie, you can specify a level number for that movie, such as 5 or 20. The number of levels is infinite, and as you load movies into different levels, any movies that are currently in different levels will still be visible, and the movies that are loaded into higher levels will be placed in front of movies in lower levels. If this sounds abstract, it will become more clear as you work through the next exercise. The stacking order of **loadMovieNum** is similar to the stacking order of layers in the Timeline. Additionally, if you load a movie into a level that is already occupied by another movie, the new movie will replace the previous one. You will learn to program the **loadMovieNum** action in the following exercise.

7.————————Loading Movies

Loading multiple SWFs into the main SWF is an efficient way to present large Flash MX 2004 documents, because the visitor doesn't have to download the entire Flash MX 2004 movie. Instead, with the Load Movie ActionScript, multiple SWFs can be downloaded in the Macromedia Flash Player on demand. This exercise will show you how this is done.

1. Open the **loadMovieNum** folder inside the **chap_11** folder. Inside you will see many SWF files and one FLA file.

2. Double-click on any of the SWF files to open and preview the artwork inside them. These are the SWF files that you will be loading into the FLA file holding the main interface in the steps that follow. When you are finished, close the SWF files.

3. Open the file named **loadMovieNum.fla** from the **loadMovieNum** folder. This file has been created to get you started.

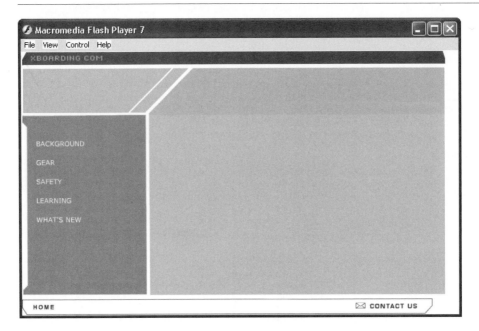

4. Choose **Control > Test Movie** to preview the movie. Notice that all you see is an empty interface with the navigation menu. This will serve as the main movie file. You will load the external movies (the SWF files that you previewed in Step 2) into levels above the main movie, using the `loadMovieNum` action in the steps that follow. When you are finished previewing the movie, close the **Preview** window.

*Note: If you get an error message telling you to check if the file destination is locked, or to check if the file name is not too long, try removing the **Read-only** option to both **chap_11** and its subfolder,* **loadMovieNum.**

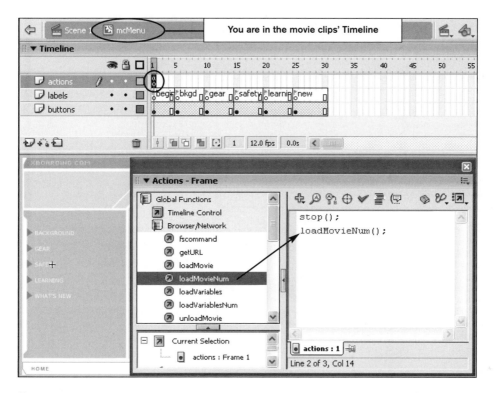

5. In the project file, double-click the menu to open the movie clip's Timeline. (This menu is identical to the one you built in the last exercise.) Select **Frame 1** of the **actions** layer in the **Timeline** and open the **Actions** panel (**F9**). In the **Actions** pane, choose **Global Functions > Browser/Network** and double-click the **loadMovieNum** action to add it to the **Script** pane.

TIP | Why Add the Actions to a Frame Rather Than an Object?

You can add the **loadMovieNum** action to either a frame or an object. Which one you choose will largely depend on how you set up your movie. By adding the actions to a keyframe, as you did in the previous step, the ActionScript will be executed as soon as the playhead hits the keyframe with the action in it. In the following steps, you will also add the **loadMovieNum** ActionScript to objects as well.

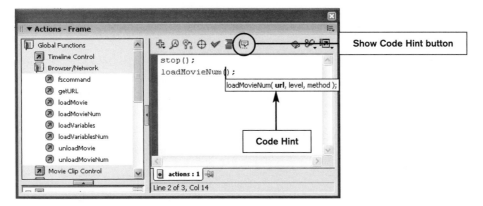

6. In the **Script** pane, place your cursor between the parentheses and click the **Show Code Hint** button to give you a hint of the information you need to type in: **url**, **level**, and **method**.

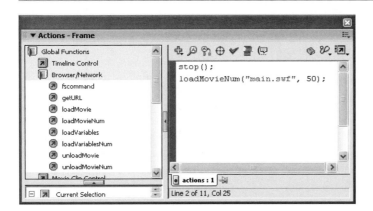

7. Between the parentheses, type **"main.swf", 50**. (**Note:** You must type the ActionScript exactly as shown here for the script to work.) This will tell Flash MX 2004 to load the SWF file you specified (**main.swf**) into **Level 50**, above the main movie.

NOTE | Movie Levels

Why Level 50? Because you can specify any level (up to an infinite amount) to load a movie into, I choose 50 so that you have plenty of other "open" levels under 50 and over 50 that you can load additional content into. The Main Timeline is always located at Level 0; when you load an additional movie at a level higher than 0, it will appear above the Main Timeline. As you load movies into different levels, any movies that are currently in other levels will still be visible, and the movies that are loaded into higher levels will be placed in front of movies in lower levels.

> ### NOTE | Load Movie and Addressing
>
> When you use the **loadMovieNum** ActionScript, the URL path can be either relative or absolute. In this example, a relative path is used; it is simply **main.swf**. Therefore, all the SWF files you will be loading into levels above the main movie must be located in the same folder or directory as the main movie; otherwise, Flash MX 2004 will not know where to find these files.
>
> Use caution! Whenever you use a relative address for the **loadMovieNum** command, Flash MX 2004 will always look for the files in the same folder as the main project file.

8. Choose **Control > Test Movie** to test the ActionScript you added. You will now see content inside the interface. Notice that you added the **main.swf** file, but the menu is still visible on the left side. This is because you loaded the **main.swf** file into **Level 50**, which is above the original interface, so **main.swf** will be above the original interface, and anywhere there is no artwork in the loaded movie, those sections will be transparent, allowing the original interface to show through. When you are finished, close the **Preview** window.

The Main Timeline is always located at Level 0, and as additional movies are loaded above it, their corresponding level counts upward. Because there is no such thing as a negative level, you can't load movies below Level 0. When you load movies into different levels, any movies that are currently in other levels will still be visible, and the movies that are loaded into higher levels will be placed above movies in lower levels. Further, the loaded movies will have transparent Stages. So here, the original interface is at Level 0 (the lowest level) and all other movies with their transparent backgrounds will stack above the original interface.

NOTE | The File Cabinet Analogy

As you begin to stack SWF files on top of one another, their arrangement simulates layers. In ActionScript, the layers are called levels. The concept of loading movies into layers can be a bit confusing, so I will use the likeness of a file cabinet to explain this more clearly.

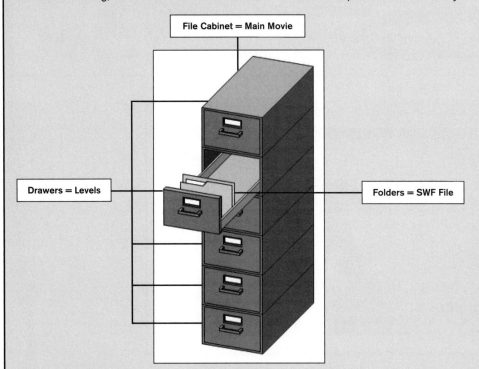

File Cabinet = Main Movie

Drawers = Levels

Folders = SWF File

Imagine a file cabinet. This file cabinet is analogous to the main movie. Inside the cabinet, you have empty drawers, which are similar to levels within the main movie. Let's say that each drawer can contain only one thing, a folder, which is analogous to the SWF file. You can place one folder (SWF file) into any drawer (level) that you want to, but each drawer can hold only one folder. If you want to place a purple folder (SWF file) into a drawer (Level 4) that already has a green folder (SWF file) in it, you have to take out the green folder first before you put the purple one in, because you can have only one folder (SWF file) in a drawer (level) at a time. However, if you have the green folder (SWF file) already in a drawer (Level 4), you can add a blue folder (SWF file) to a drawer above it (Level 5, for example). If you did this, you would have the file cabinet, a green folder in drawer 4, and a blue folder in drawer 5. Or, in Flash MX 2004 terminology, you would have the main movie at Level 0, with the SWF file loaded into Level 4, above both the main movie and another SWF file loaded into Level 5, above both the main movie and the SWF file in level 4.

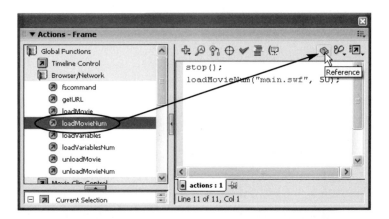

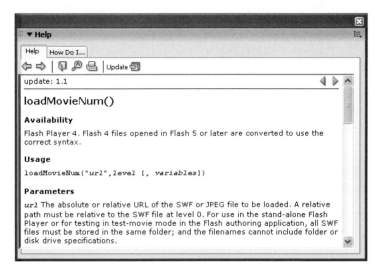

9. In the project file, select the **loadMovieNum** action in the **Actions** pane. Click the **Reference** button to open the **ActionScript Reference Guide** within the **Help** panel. Notice that the **Help** panel automatically displays information about the **loadMovieNum** action. If you select an action or a line of code, the **Help** panel will display information about that action.

*Tip: You can also access the **Help** panel by choosing **Help** >**Help** (F1).*

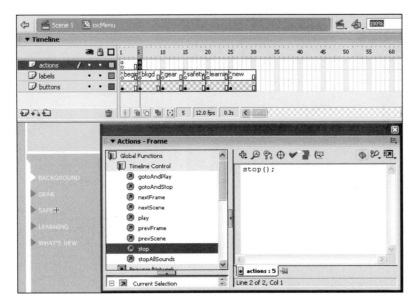

10. You should still be inside the menu movie clip's **Timeline**. Select **Frame 5** of the **actions** layer and press **F7** to add a blank keyframe. Open the **Actions** panel (**F9**) and in the **Actions** pane, choose **Global Functions > Timeline Control** and double-click the **stop** action to add it to the **Script** pane.

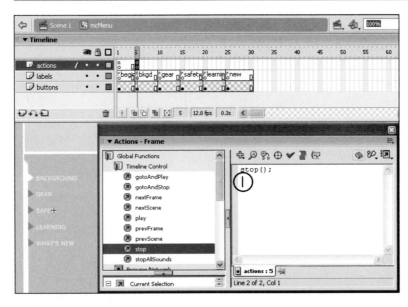

11. In the **Script** pane, place your cursor after the semicolon and press **Enter/Return** to bring the cursor down to the second line, as shown here. You will add the **loadMovieNum** action next.

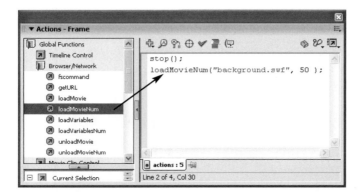

12. In the **Actions** pane, choose **Global Functions > Browser/Network** and double-click **loadMovieNum** to add it to the **Script** pane. Between the parentheses, type **"background.swf", 50**, as shown here. This will tell Flash MX 2004 to load the SWF file you specified (**background.swf**) into **Level 50**, above the main movie.

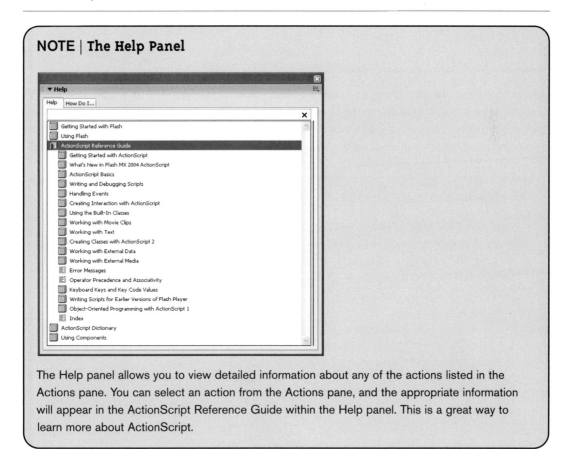

NOTE | The Help Panel

The Help panel allows you to view detailed information about any of the actions listed in the Actions pane. You can select an action from the Actions pane, and the appropriate information will appear in the ActionScript Reference Guide within the Help panel. This is a great way to learn more about ActionScript.

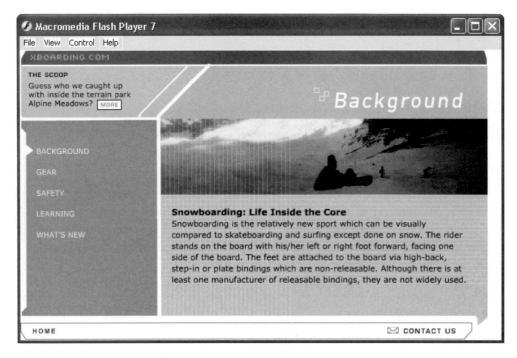

13. Choose **Control > Test Movie** and click the **Background** button. As soon as you do, notice that the main content is switched out for the background content. How did this happen? Each time you use the `loadMovieNum` command to load a movie into a level (such as **50**) that already had content in it, the new content will replace the old content. When you are finished previewing the file, close the window.

TIP | Loading into an Already Occupied Level

A movie doesn't have to be loaded into the next empty level; you can load a movie to any level you wish. However, if a movie is loaded into a level that is already occupied by another file, the old file is kicked out and replaced by the new movie.

14. Repeat Steps 10, 11, and 12 for **Frames 10, 15, 20,** and **25**. For **Frame 10**, type **"gear.swf", 50** between the parentheses; for **Frame 15**, type **"safety.swf", 50** between the parentheses; for **Frame 20**, type **"learning.swf", 50** between the parentheses; and for **Frame 25**, type **"whatsNew.swf", 50** between the parentheses. This will load the appropriate content into **Level 50**, kicking out any content that was previously loaded into that level, each time the **playhead** hits the appropriate frame.

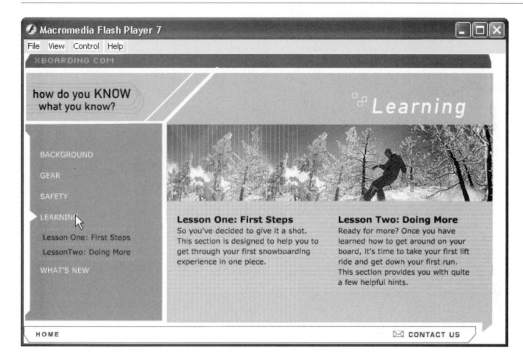

15. Choose **Control > Test Movie**. Click on each of the top-level navigation buttons to test the movie. When you are finished, close the **Preview** window. You will add ActionScript to the subnavigation buttons in the steps that follow.

16. Back in the project file of the **mcMenu Timeline**, move the **playhead** to **Frame 10**. On the **Stage**, select the **Board Gear Checklist** button.

You will be adding the `loadMovieNum` *action to this button next.*

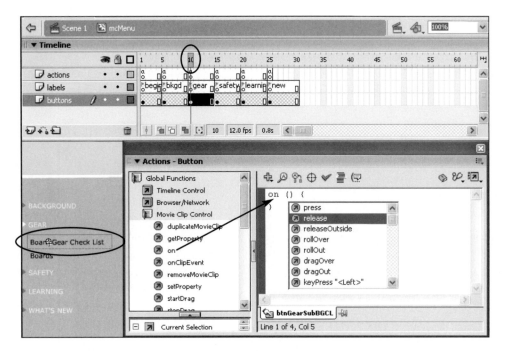

17. In the **Actions** pane, choose **Global Functions > Movie Clip Control** and double-click the **on** action to add it to the **Script** pane. Choose **release** from the **Code Hint** menu for the mouse event. You will add the **loadMovieNum** action in the following steps.

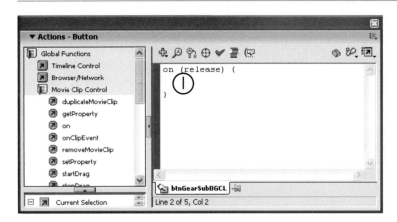

18. In the **Script** pane, place your cursor after the open curly brace and press **Enter/Return** to bring the cursor down to the second line, as shown here.

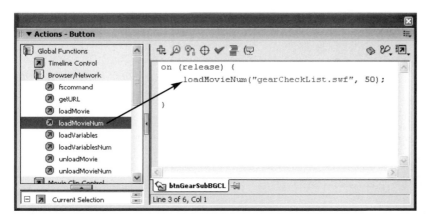

19. From the **Actions** pane, choose **Global Functions > Browser/Network** and double-click the **loadMovieNum** action to add it to the **Script** pane. Between the parentheses, type **"gearCheckList.swf"**, **50**. This will tell Flash MX 2004 to load the **gearCheckList.swf** file into **Level 50** when the user clicks on this button.

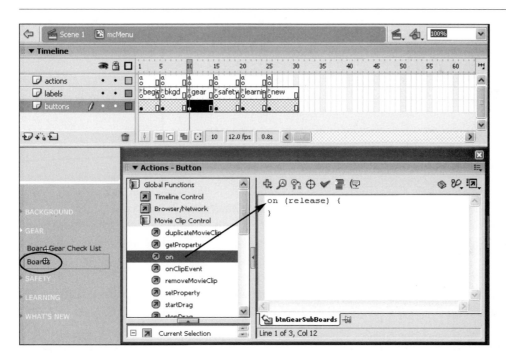

20. On the **Stage**, select the **Boards** button. In the **Actions** pane, choose **Global Functions > Movie Clip Control** and double-click the **on** action to add it to the **Script** pane. Choose **release** from the **Code Hint** menu for the mouse event.

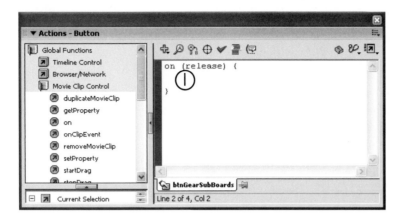

21. In the **Script** pane, place your cursor after the open curly brace and press **Enter/Return** to bring the cursor down to the second line.

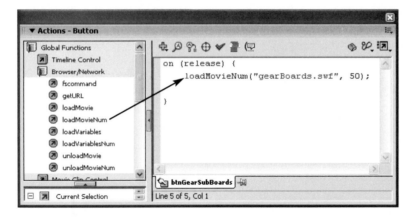

22. In the **Actions** pane, choose **Global Functions > Browser/Network** and double-click the **loadMovieNum** action to add it to the **Script** pane. Between the parentheses, type **"gearBoards.swf", 50**. This will tell Flash MX 2004 to load the **gearBoards.swf** file into **Level 50** when the user clicks on this button.

23. Repeat Steps 20, 21, and 22 for the four remaining subnavigation buttons: two buttons on **Frame 15** and two buttons on **Frame 20**. This will add the **loadMovieNum** action to each of the subnavigation buttons.

For each of the buttons, the ActionScript should look like the following:

Frame 15—Lessons button:
```
on (release) {
    loadMovieNum("safetyLessons.swf", 50);
}
```

Frame 15—Responsibility Code button:

```
on (release) {
    loadMovieNum("safetyRC.swf", 50);
}
```

Frame 20—Lesson One: First Steps button:

```
on (release) {
    loadMovieNum("learningL1.swf", 50);
}
```

Frame 20—Lesson Two: Doing More button:

```
on (release) {
    loadMovieNum("learningL2.swf", 50);
}
```

You have one last button to add. In the following steps, you will copy the ActionScript on the Lesson Two: Doing More button and paste it into the Home button on the Main Timeline. Since the code will be the same for the two buttons, with the exception of the name of the SWF you will load, copying and pasting the code is an efficient way of adding ActionScript to your buttons, rather than going through the various Action books in the ActionScipt panel.

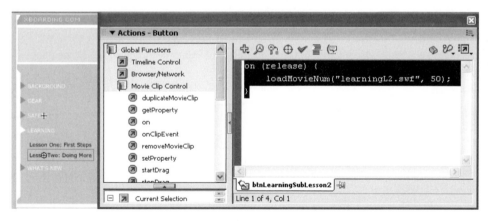

24. Select the **Lesson Two: Doing More** button and in the **Script** pane, highlight the ActionScript, as shown here, and press **Ctrl+C** (Windows) or **Cmd+C** (Mac) to copy the ActionScript. In the following steps, you will paste the ActionScript to the **Home** button on the **Main Timeline**.

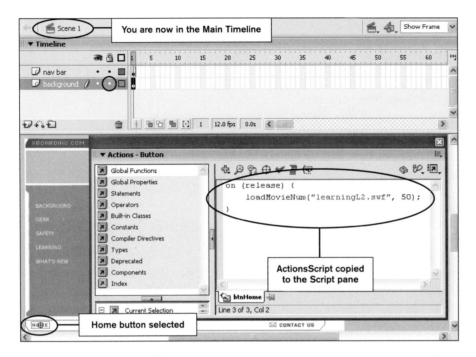

25. In the **Edit Bar**, click **Scene 1** to return to the **Main Timeline**. Unlock the **background** layer and select the **Home** button in the bottom-left corner of the **Stage**. In the **Actions** panel, click the **Script** pane and press **Ctrl+V** (Windows) or **Cmd+V** (Mac) to paste the ActionScript into the **Script** pane. You will modify the code next to load the appropriate movie.

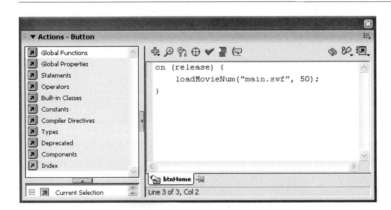

26. In the **Script** pane, replace **learningL2.swf** with **main.swf**, as shown here.

Once you are familiar with the nuances of ActionScript, copying and pasting the ActionScript rather than navigating through the ActionScript toolbar is one way to speed up your production time.

27. Choose **Control > Test Movie** to preview your movie! Try all the buttons, including the subnavigation buttons, to see how they work. When you are finished, close the **Preview** window.

Now that you are intimately familiar with loading movies into the same level, you have a chance to see the results of loading a movie into a different level next.

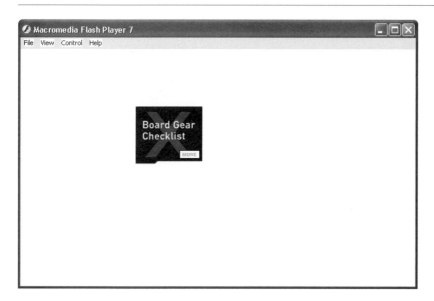

28. Open the **loadMovieNum** folder inside the **chap_11** folder again. Double-click the **gearExtra.swf** file to preview the file. Notice that there is only one small button in the **Preview** window. You will be loading this file in the main movie next. When you are finished, close the SWF file.

Why is there so much extra space around the button? When you load movies into levels, Flash MX 2004 automatically places the loaded movie flush top left in the Macromedia Flash Player. Up to this point in the exercise, you have loaded movies into levels that all had the same dimensions. If you load a new movie that has much smaller dimensions into a level, it will automatically be registered in the top-left corner and therefore might not be placed where you want it.

*There are two ways around this issue. In this case, the button in the **gearExtra.swf** has been strategically placed where it should "land" in the interface, but the movie dimensions in the **gearExtra.swf** file match each of the other SWF files you have worked with in this exercise. Because all loaded movies will be transparent except for the content, you will see the button only when you load it in. Another way to have precision control over where a movie lands when it is loaded is to load it into a target that would be a movie clip, rather than a level. You will concentrate on loading movies into levels, and you will load the **gearExtra.swf** file into a different level in the next steps.*

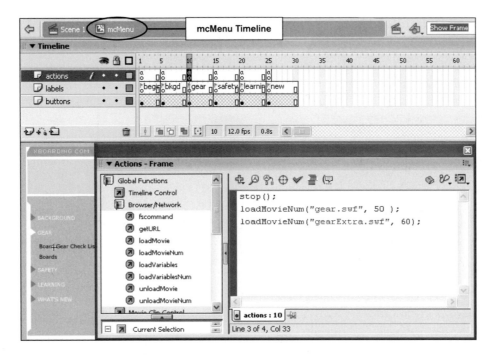

29. Back in the project file, double-click the **mcMenu** movie clip on the Stage to open the movie clip's **Timeline**. Select **Frame 10** of the **actions** layer in the **Timeline**. Notice the previous frame actions you added in earlier steps are still there. In the **Actions** panel, choose **Global Functions > Browser/Network** and double-click the **loadMovieNum** action to add it to the **Script** pane. Between the parentheses, type **"gearExtra.swf", 60**, as shown here.

You just added a new script below the previous **loadMovieNum** *script you created earlier. This new script will tell Flash MX 2004 to load the SWF file you specified (**gearExtra.swf**) into Level 60, above the main movie (at Level 0) and also above the **gear.swf** file in Level 50.*

*What is really going on behind the scenes? When the user clicks on the Gear button, the playhead will be sent to the gear label inside the menu movie clip's Timeline. (You already programmed this ActionScript when you built the menu in the last exercise.) When the playhead hits the gear label in the Timeline (which is Frame 10), first it will stop (because you have a stop action) and then it will load the **gear.swf** file into Level 50 and then load the **gearExtra.swf** file into Level 60.*

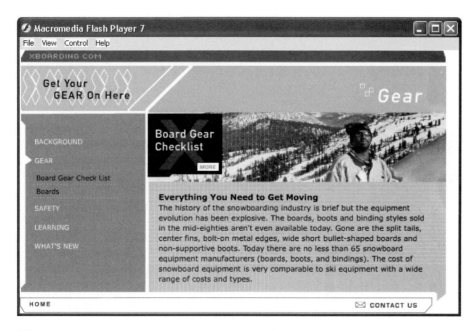

30. Choose **Control > Test Movie** and click the **Gear** button in the menu. Notice that the button from **gearExtra.swf** file is there! This is because you loaded the **gearExtra.swf** file into **Level 60**, above any content loaded into **Level 50**. As far as stacking order goes with loaded movies in Flash MX 2004, the higher the level number, the closer to the top of the stacking order; so in this case, the **gearExtra.swf** file is loaded just above the **gear.swf** file. Close the **Preview** window when you are finished.

*When you click any of the other buttons in the menu, notice that the **gearExtra.swf** file appears, no matter what section you are in. Why? This is because the **gearExtra.swf** file has been loaded into Level 60, and it will stay there (no matter what else is going on in other levels, such as Level 50) until you tell it otherwise, which you will do next.*

Note: *You may have noticed that if you click the gearExtra button, the Board Gear Checklist page shows up. Why? This is because inside the project file that created the **gearExtra.swf**, there is a button with the following ActionScript attached to it:*

```
on (release) {
loadMovieNum("gearCheckList.swf", 50);
}
```

*This means that when a user clicks on the button, it should load the **gearExtra.swf** file into Level 50.*

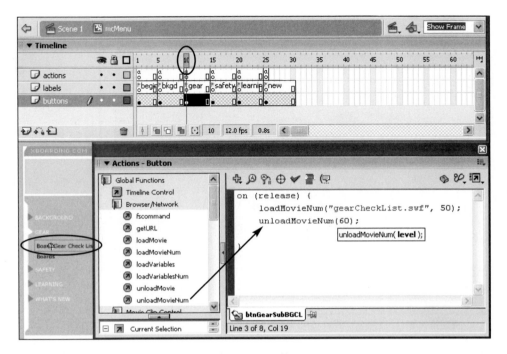

31. In the project file, the **playhead** should still be over **Frame 10**. This time, select the **Board Gear Checklist** button on the **Stage** and in the **Script** pane after `loadMovieNum ("gearCheckList.swf", 50);`, press **Enter/Return** to bring your cursor to the next line. In the **Actions** pane, double-click **unloadMovieNum** to add it to the **Script** pane. Between the parentheses, type **60**, as shown here.

*This ActionScript tells Flash MX 2004 that when a user clicks on the Board Gear Checklist button, it should unload whatever movie is currently in Level 60 (this happens to be **gearExtra.swf**).*

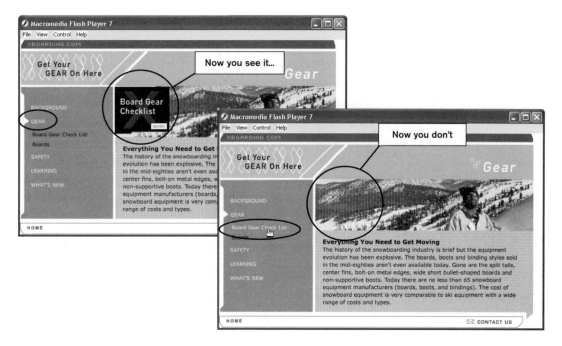

32. Choose **Control > Test Movie** and click the **Gear** button in the menu. Notice that the button from the **gearExtra.swf** file is there! Click the **Safety** and **Learning** buttons and notice that the **gearExtra.swf** content remains in place. Now click the **Board Gear Checklist** button and notice that the **gearExtra.swf** content is gone. This is because you unloaded the **gearExtra.swf** file from **Level 60** when the user clicks on the button.

In summary, by using the `loadMovieNum` action, you can keep the main movie small, and you can load additional movies into levels above the main movie as you wish or as they are needed.

---

33. When you are finished, save and close this file.

 MOVIE | loadMovieNum.mov

To see this exercise performed, play the **loadMovieNum.mov** located in the **movies** folder on the **H•O•T CD-ROM**.

That's a wrap on this chapter. A lot of information was covered in the exercises, and if anything isn't crystal clear, you can always go back and do a review. Take a well-deserved break and then get ready for the "Working with Text" chapter, which comes next.

I2.
Working with Text

| Text Field Types | Text Options |
| Static Text and Device Fonts | Small Type and Alias Text |
| Loading a Text File into a Dynamic Text Field |
| Dynamic Text and HTML | Scrollable Dynamic Text Fields |
| Dynamic Text and CSS | Input Text |

chap_12

Macromedia Flash MX 2004
H•O•T CD-ROM

When working with text, you have many options that go far beyond simply selecting the Text tool and typing on the Stage. In Flash MX 2004, you can create horizontal or vertical text, you can change the text attributes such as kerning (spacing between characters) and line spacing, and you can apply transformations such as rotation and skew. However, that is only the beginning. As you go through this chapter, you will learn to create text fields that bring in text from external documents, make text scroll, and create text fields where users can input their information. Additionally, you will take your Flash project skills a step forward by combining HTML tags within a loaded external text document. And it doesn't stop here! Flash MX 2004 now includes a spell check feature and supports Cascading Style Sheets (CSS), which allows you to create text styles that can be applied to HTML, making design across HTML and Flash MX 2004 content more consistent.

Flash MX 2004 allows you to create three different types of text elements: Static text, Dynamic text, and Input text. You'll learn about these different types of text elements and try them out with hands-on exercises.

Text Field Types

When you select the Text tool in Flash MX, you can choose from three types of text fields: **Static text**, **Dynamic text**, or **Input text**.

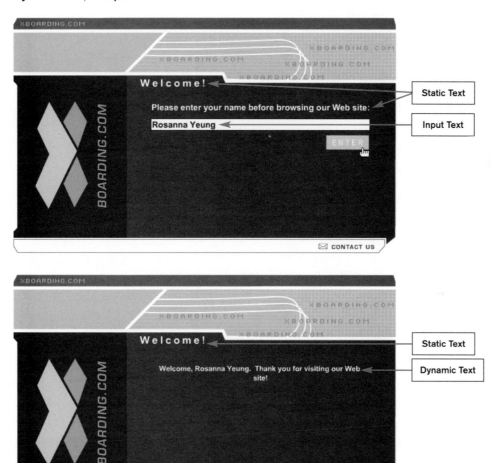

Static text is text that you would use to display information or to label buttons, forms, or navigation. Use Static text when you want to simply display text. Dynamic text is used to show up-to-date information that Flash MX 2004 can generate automatically from an external text file or a database. Use Dynamic text when you want to automatically show information that is updated often. Input text is text that the end user is required to input such as a user name and password, forms, and surveys. As you go through the exercises in this chapter, you will get hands-on experience with each of these text types.

Text Field Boxes

When you add a text field to the Stage, a text block is created with a corner handle to identify the type of text field you are creating. A chart follows to identify the different types of text fields. Later in this chapter, you will learn what each type can be used for.

Types of Text Blocks					
Text Type	**Orientation**	**Defined or Extending**	**Handle Shape**	**Handle Position**	
Static	Horizontal	Extending	Round	Upper-right corner	xboarding.com
Static	Horizontal	Defined	Square	Upper-right corner	xboarding.com
Static	Vertical (right to left)	Extending	Round	Lower-left corner	x b o a r d
Static	Vertical (right to left)	Defined	Square	Lower-left corner	x b o a r d
Static	Vertical (left to right)	Extending	Round	Lower-right corner	x b o a r d
Static	Vertical (left to right)	Defined	Square	Lower-right corner	x b o a r d
Dynamic or Input	Horizontal only	Extending	Round	Lower-right corner	xboarding.com
Dynamic or Input	Horizontal only	Defined	Square	Lower-right corner	xboarding.com

TIP | Changing the Text Field Box

You can switch a text field from an extending text field to a defined text field and back again simply by double-clicking the handle.

TIP | Fixing a Text Field Box That Extends Too Far

If, by accident, you create a text field that continues off the Stage, don't worry: You can choose **View > Work Area** (which is selected by default) and reduce the magnification to make the entire line of text visible. You can then force the text to wrap downward by either placing the cursor inside the text block and adding your own line breaks, or by dragging the text field handle to create a defined text field that will fit within the Stage area. When you create a defined text field, the text within that field will wrap to fit the field size.

Creating, Modifying, and Formatting Text

In Flash MX 2004, you have a lot of control over the attributes of type. By using the Properties inspector, you can change, preview, and adjust text in a few easy clicks of the mouse. The next section will give you a close look at each of the available settings.

Text Options in the Properties Inspector

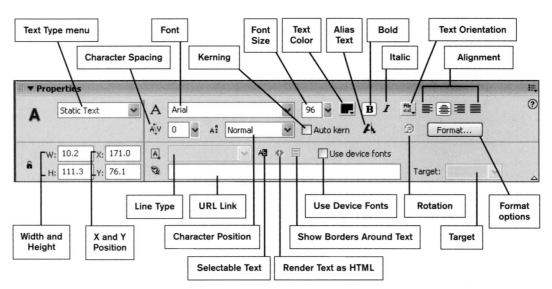

As soon as you select the Text tool, the Properties inspector will display the available text attributes. A chart follows detailing each of the items labeled in the previous illustration.

Text Attributes Defined	
Attribute	**Description**
Text Type menu	Allows you to choose from one of three text fields (**Static**, **Dynamic**, or **Input text**). Each text type has its own associated options that will appear in the Properties inspector when that text field type is selected. **Static text** is the default text field.
Font	Displays the name of the current font. Click the arrow to the right of the font name to view a list of all the available fonts. As you scroll through the font list, Flash MX 2004 displays a preview of what each font will look like.
Character Spacing (tracking/kerning)	Allows you to adjust the space between characters in selected text. Click the arrow next to the Character Spacing field and use the slider to increase or decrease the amount of space between characters.

continues on next page

Attribute	Description
Text Attributes Defined *continued*	
Character Position (Baseline Shift)	**Normal:** Resets characters to the baseline. **Superscript:** Shifts characters above the baseline. **Subscript:** Shifts characters below the baseline.
Font Size (Font Height)	Displays the current font size in points. Click the arrow to the right of the Font Size field and use the slider to adjust the size of the font.
Auto Kern	Controls the spacing between pairs of characters. Checking this box will automatically use the font's built-in kerning information. (See the sidebar following this table for more information on kerning.)
Alias Text	New feature in Flash MX 2004. By default, text in Flash MX 2004 is anti-aliased, meaning that the edges of the text are smoothed. Although this looks great with larger type, the anti-aliasing can make the text look blurry when text is small. With the new Alias Text button, you can hide the anti-aliasing to make small text sharper and easier to read.
Text (Fill) Color	Allows you to change the color of the type by presenting you with a palette of available colors. **Note:** For text blocks, you can use only solid colors, not gradients. If you want to use gradients, you have to break the text apart, which will convert it to a shape, and then you can apply a gradient.
Bold	Bolds the selected type.
Italic	Italicizes the selected type.
Text Orientation	Changes the direction of the text. You can choose from **Horizontal**; **Vertical, Left to Right**; and **Vertical, Right to Left**.
Alignment	Controls how the selected text will be aligned: **Left Justified**, **Center Justified**, **Right Justified**, or **Full Justified**.

continues on next page

Text Attributes Defined *continued*	
Attribute	**Description**
Rotation	Allows you to have more control over vertical text and change its rotation. x b o a r d i n g This option is available only for vertical text.
Format options	Launches a pop-up window with options for formatting text blocks where you can specifically set the values. For horizontal text, the options are **Indent, Line spacing, Left margin,** and **Right margin.** For vertical text, the options are **Indent, Column spacing, Top margin,** and **Bottom margin.** **Format Options** Indent: `0 px` OK Line spacing: `2 pt` Cancel Left margin: `0 px` Right margin: `0 px` **Format Options for horizontal text** **Format Options** Indent: `0 px` OK Column spacing: `2 pt` Cancel Top margin: `0 px` Bottom `0 px` **Format Options for vertical text** **Indent** controls the distance between the margin of a paragraph and the beginning of the first line of a paragraph. **Line/Column spacing** (Leading) controls the spacing between lines of type (horizontal text) or between vertical columns (vertical text). **Left/Top margin** determines the amount of space between the characters and the left side (horizontal text) or top (vertical text) of the text box. Even if text is centered or right-aligned, increasing the amount of space in the left/top margin will create the space you specify from the left side/top of the text box to the leftmost/first character within the text box. **Right/Bottom margin** determines the amount of space between the characters and the right side (horizontal text) or bottom (vertical text) of the text box.

continues on next page

Text Attributes Defined *continued*	
Attribute	**Description**
Width and Height	Displays the width and height of a selected text field.
X and Y Position	Displays the X and Y position of the top left of a selected text box, relative to the Stage, where 0, 0 is the top left of the Stage.
URL Link	Creates a hyperlink that is attached to selected text. In effect, this creates a button that will link to an internal or external HTML file, without the need to create a button symbol. Using this option will automatically add a dotted line under the linked text in the FLA file. Note, however, that hyperlinks created using this feature will not carry any visual feedback (such as an underline) in the SWF file, although when previewed in a browser, the hand icon will appear when the user moves his or her mouse over the linked text. You learned a better way to create a hyperlink in Chapter 11, "*ActionScript Basics and Behaviors.*"
Line Type	Allows you to choose from **Single line** (displaying the text on one line), **Multiline** (displaying the text in multiple lines with word wrap), **Multiline No Wrap** (displaying the text in multiple lines), and **Password**. This option is available only for Dynamic and Input text.
Selectable text	Allows a user to select your text and copy it.
Render as HTML	Preserves Rich Text Formatting, including fonts, hyperlinks, and bold with the appropriate HTML tags. You will learn to use this option in Exercise 4 of this chapter.
Show Border	When selected, displays a white background with a black border for the text field. This option is only available for Dynamic and Input text fields.
Use Device Fonts	By default, this box is not checked in the Properties inspector, which means that Flash MX 2004 will embed font information for any fonts used within a Static text field. When the movie is exported, this font will appear anti-aliased (smooth edge). If this box is checked, Flash MX will prevent the font information from being embedded. You will learn more about device fonts in Exercise 1 of this chapter.

continues on next page

Text Attributes Defined *continued*	
Attribute	**Description**
Variable	You can specify a variable name for the selected Dynamic or Input text field here. Variables will be discussed later in this chapter.
Target	Used in conjunction with the URL link feature. When assigning a hyperlink to selected text, you can also specify a target. Choosing a target allows you to specify the URL to load in a new window or to a specific Web page layout that utilizes framesets.
Character options	Visible only when using Dynamic or Input text fields. This allows you to choose how the font will be embedded into your Flash MX 2004 SWF file. Font embedding will be discussed later in this chapter.

NOTE | To Kern or Not to Kern?

When font sets are created, the individual characters might look great all by themselves, but some letters might not look very good next to each other or may not be spaced very well. To solve this issue, many fonts are created with additional instructions about spacing between specific characters. This is known as **kerning** information.

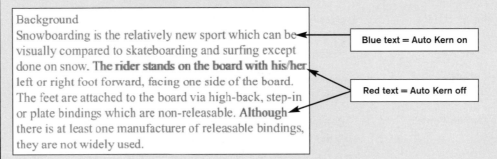

To illustrate this point, two text blocks (one blue and one red) were created and placed in the exact same position, with the blue text on top of the red text. The Auto Kern feature in the Properties inspector was selected for the blue text, and the red text was left alone with its default spacing. Notice how the red text shows through in some spots. This indicates that the Auto Kern feature has changed the spacing of the blue text.

continues on next page

NOTE | To Kern or Not to Kern? *continued*

When you create horizontal text, kerning sets the horizontal distance between characters. As you may have guessed, when you create vertical text, kerning sets the vertical distance between characters.

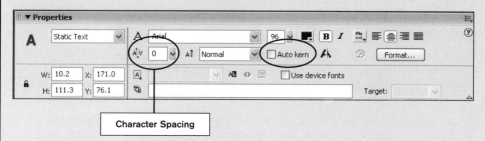

Character Spacing

Flash MX 2004 will not automatically add this special kerning information to your text unless you tell it to by checking the **Auto kern** check box in the Properties inspector. Use this option, especially when typing paragraphs of text, to achieve the best-looking text Flash MX 2004 is capable of producing.

You can also select the **Character Spacing** option if you wish to adjust the space between selected individual characters or blocks of characters.

WARNING | Text in Flash MX 2004 and Search Engines

When you create text in Flash MX 2004, it is important to note that unlike HTML, Flash MX 2004 text is not searchable by search engines. Therefore, if you need keywords within your movie to be seen by search engines, I suggest you add Meta tags to the HTML document that the SWF file resides in. You will learn more about embedding SWF files in HTML documents in Chapter 16, "*Publishing and Exporting*." For further information about Meta tags, a good resource book is *HTML 4 for the World Wide Web Visual QuickStart Guide*, from Peachpit Press.

I. —————————Working with Static Text and Device Fonts

Static text is display text that doesn't change onscreen, such as displaying the information in an interface that the end user will read or for labeling buttons, forms, and navigation. When you add Static text to your movie, by default Flash MX 2004 will embed the font outlines in the SWF file for the font you're using. Depending on the font you choose and how much text you use, this can add a measurable amount to the overall file size of the SWF. If your goal is to achieve a small file size, one way to do that is by using a device font. A device font is a type of font that won't embed itself in the SWF file. Instead, you choose a device font for the end users' machines to display—_serif, _sans, or _typewriter—and the end users' machines will display that device font for the Static text. This reduces the file size of the SWF because the font outlines are not embedded in the SWF file when you use a device font. At the end of this exercise, the pros and cons of using Static text and device fonts will be discussed but first you'll begin with learning how to spell check your projects, a feature new to Flash MX 2004.

1. Copy the **chap_12** folder, located on the **H•O•T CD-ROM**, to your hard drive. You need to have this folder on your hard drive in order to save files inside it.

2. Open the **staticText.fla** file from the **chap_12** folder. This file has been created to get you started.

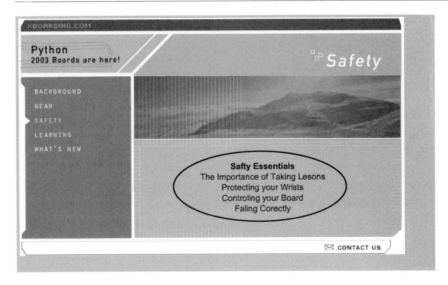

3. Read the copy in the interface. Notice any misspelled words? You will check your project file for any spelling errors and correct them with the new spell check feature in Flash MX 2004 next.

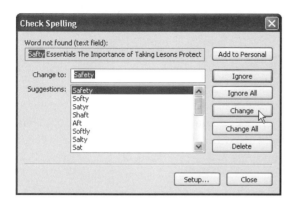

4. Choose **Text > Check Spelling** to open the **Check Spelling** dialog box. Click **Change** to correctly spell the words **Safety, Lessons, Controlling, Falling,** and **Correctly.** Click **OK** when you are prompted with the **Flash MX** dialog box.

Note: The spell check feature only works with editable text. Since it does not work with text that has been broken apart, be sure to spell check your movie before you break apart any text. You learned how to break apart text in Chapter 5, "Shape Tweening."

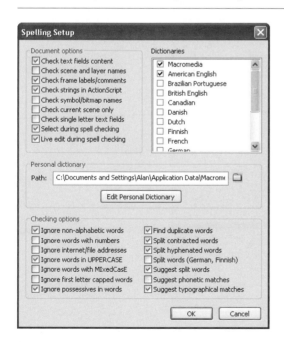

*You can modify the spelling setup by choosing **Text > Spelling Setup** or by clicking **Setup...** in the* ***Check Spelling*** *dialog box.*

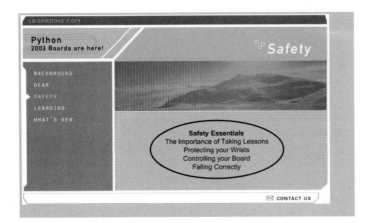

5. Read the copy in the interface again and notice that all the misspelled words are now spelled correctly! Now that your movie is free of spelling errors, you will learn about static text and device fonts in the following steps.

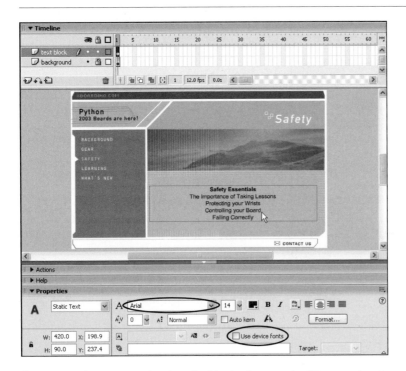

6. With the **Selection** tool, select the block of text on the **Stage** and make sure the **Properties inspector** is open (**Window > Properties**). In the **Properties inspector**, notice that the **Font** setting applied to that text block is **Arial** and that the **Use device fonts** check box is unchecked.

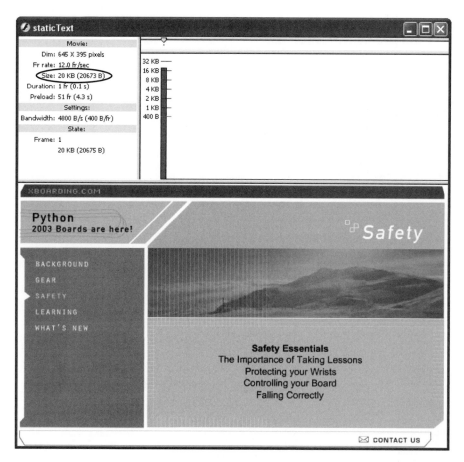

7. Choose **Control > Test Movie** to preview the text. When the **Preview** window opens, choose **View > Bandwidth Profiler**. The **Bandwidth Profiler** will appear at the top of the **Preview** window and, among other things, will tell you the file size of your SWF file. Currently, the file size is 20 KB. This file size accounts for all the graphics and font outlines being used in this movie.

In the following steps, you will modify the text block by using a device font to make the file size smaller.

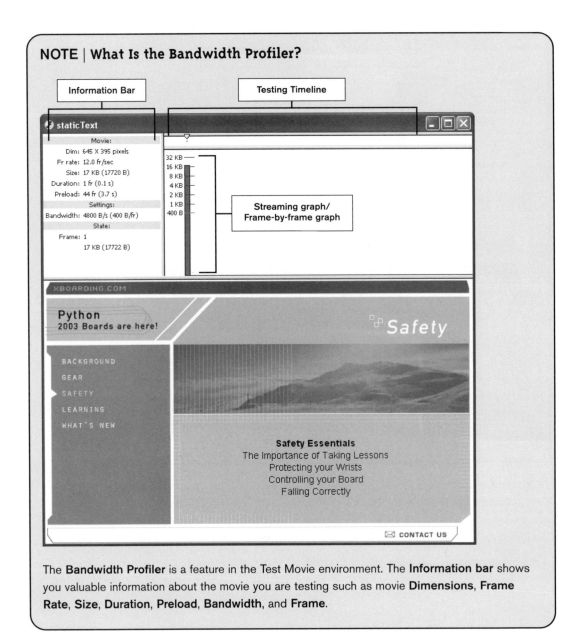

The **Bandwidth Profiler** is a feature in the Test Movie environment. The **Information bar** shows you valuable information about the movie you are testing such as movie **Dimensions**, **Frame Rate**, **Size**, **Duration**, **Preload**, **Bandwidth**, and **Frame**.

The Bandwidth Profiler Edit Bar

Term	Description
Dim	The width and height (dimensions) of the movie.
Fr rate	The speed at which the movie plays based on the frames per second.
Size	The file size of the movie or scene you are testing. The number in parentheses represents the total amount.
Duration	The total number of frames in your movie or scene. The number in parentheses represents the length of your movie or scene in seconds rather than frames.
Preload	The number of frames and seconds at which the movie begins to download, and the point at which the movie is ready to begin playing. You will create a Preloader in Chapter 17, "*Putting It All Together.*"
Bandwidth	The speed used to simulate an actual download when used with the Simulate Download command. You will learn more about the Simulate Download command in Chapter 17, "*Putting It All Together.*"
Frame	This area shows two numbers. The top number shows the frame at which the playhead is positioned in the Test Movie Preview window. The bottom number shows the file size for the frame where the playhead is positioned. The number in parentheses represents the total file size. You can get individual frame information by moving the playhead in the Bandwidth Profiler Timeline. This is especially helpful in detecting frames that have a lot of content.

8. When you are done viewing the **Bandwidth Profiler**, close the **Preview window** and return to the project file.

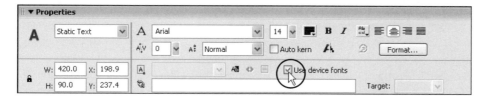

9. With the **Selection** tool, click the **text block** to select it. In the **Properties inspector**, check the **Use device fonts** box.

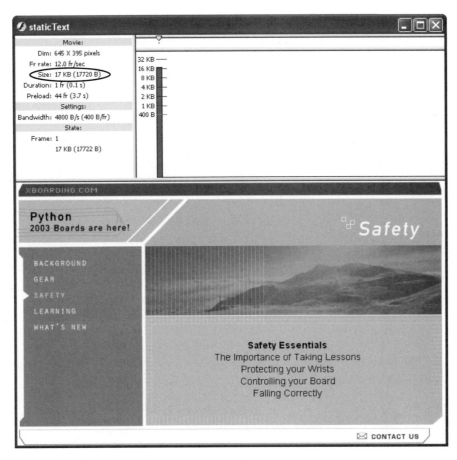

10. Choose **Control > Test Movie** to preview the text. The **Bandwidth Profiler** should still be visible above the **Preview** window. If not, choose **View > Bandwidth Profiler**. In the **Bandwidth Profiler**, notice the size is now 17 KB. Before the text field was set to a device font, the file size of the SWF was 20 KB. By using a device font for that paragraph of text you saved 3 Kilobytes!

Three Kilobytes might not sound like much, but if you're designing a banner ad, and your target file size is a measly 12 KB, 3 KB is 25 percent of the total file size!

11. Hide the **Bandwidth Profiler** by choosing **View > Bandwidth Profiler**, and close the **Preview** window.

12. Save and close this file.

NOTE | Embedded Fonts Versus Device Fonts

When you select a specific font for a text block in the Properties inspector, Flash MX 2004 automatically takes all the font information (the font's description, kerning, leading, and so on) and embeds it in the exported movie. This is what is known as an **embedded font**. The capability to embed fonts makes Flash MX 2004 a great platform for using unusual fonts in movies because the end user doesn't have to have the fonts installed on his or her computer to see the results. Flash MX 2004 automatically embeds all the necessary information.

The downside to using embedded fonts is that they will increase the file size of the SWF. Also, it is important to know that some fonts, while still displayed in your project file, cannot be exported with the movie because Flash MX 2004 cannot embed the font's outline. This may happen because the font was not installed properly or because the computer has only the screen font. The font may display properly in the production file (FLA) yet falter when the movie is exported (SWF) because the actual font to which the screen font refers cannot be found when the movie is published. You can select **View > Preview Mode > Anti-Alias Text** (which is already enabled by default) to preview the text. If it appears rough or jagged, this indicates that the text will not be exported when the SWF file is published. If this happens, it's a good idea to choose another font.

Because the font outlines will be embedded in the SWF file when you publish your movie, you need to have all the fonts that are being used in the Flash MX 2004 document installed on your computer to be able to properly publish your movie. If you receive a FLA from a friend or colleague that uses a font that you don't have installed on your computer, you will get an error message (shown here) informing you that a substitute font will be used in its place. At this point, you have two options. You can allow Flash MX 2004 to replace the font with its default replacement font by clicking the **Use Default** button, or you can click the **Choose Substitute** button and replace the font with a font you have installed on your computer.

Device fonts were created as a way around this issue. They are special fonts that will not be embedded in the exported movie and therefore will create a SWF file with a smaller file size. Rather than use an embedded font, the Flash Player displays the text using the closest match on the end user's computer to the device font.

continues on next page

NOTE | Embedded Fonts Versus Device Fonts *continued*

The drawback to device fonts is that if a user doesn't have a font installed on his or her system that is similar to the device font, he or she might see text that bears little resemblance to the text you see on your machine. To combat this concern, Flash MX 2004 includes three built-in device fonts to help produce results closer to what you expect. These are all available under the Type pull-down menu, along with the other fonts:

- **_sans**–Similar to Helvetica or Arial

- **_serif**–Similar to Times Roman

- **_typewriter**–Similar to Courier

NOTE | Alias Text Versus Anti-Alias Text

Anti-aliasing is a term that refers to blurring of the edges to make the text appear smooth. Most digital artists prefer the way anti-aliasing text looks, but at small sizes, it can appear fuzzy and become hard to read due to the blurred edges. For text that is 10 point or smaller, alias text is sharper and easier to read because the edges of the text are not blurred.

Alias Text	Anti-Alias Text
# xboard	# xboard
Alias text at large sizes appears jaggy. The edges of the text lack the smoothing effect.	Anti-alias text at large sizes appears smooth because the edges are blurred to smooth the text. Anti-alias text works best with large font sizes.
xboard	xboard
Alias text at small sizes is sharper and easier to read. Alias text works best on sizes 10 point or smaller.	Anti-alias text at small sizes is fuzzy and hard to read because the smoothing effect on the edges causes the text to become too blurry.

2. —————————Small Type and Alias Text

When working with small type (10 point or smaller), the text might become difficult to read because of the anti-aliasing that is automatically applied to vector shapes in Flash MX 2004, which includes type. Anti-aliasing is a blurring, or "smoothing," of the edges of vector shapes and text. In most cases, anti-aliasing adds to the quality of the shape because it gives its edges a nice, smooth appearance. However, anti-aliasing can be a drawback when attempting to use small text and trying to keep it readable. Now, in Flash MX 2004, Macromedia has added a new **Alias Text** button that allows you to alias blocks of type, thereby greatly increasing readability at small point sizes.

1. Open the **aliasText.fla** file from the **chap_12** folder. This file has been created to get you started. Notice the two text blocks side by side. Both of these text blocks have the same text attributes.

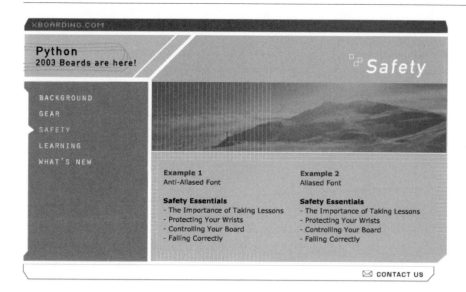

2. Choose **Control > Test Movie** to preview the text blocks. When the **Preview** window opens, notice that both text blocks look the same. Also notice that the text looks a little blurry. This blurriness is caused because the text is set in a small font size. The anti-aliasing, which is usually helpful, is actually causing the text to become blurry and difficult to read.

3. Close the **Preview** window.

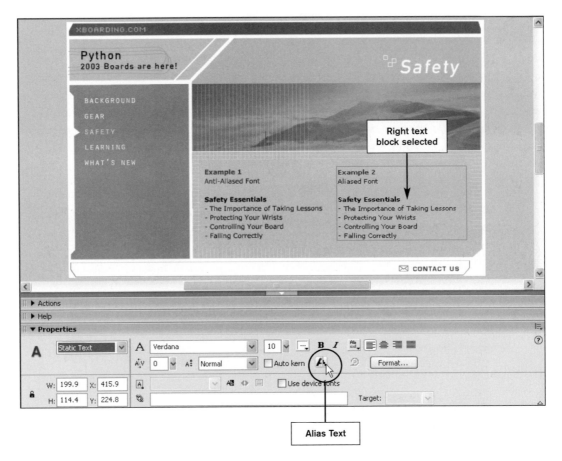

4. Select the **text block** on the right and in the **Properties inspector**, click the **Alias Text** button. Notice how the text block on the right is sharper, cleaner, and easier to read compared to the text block on the left. This is because the anti-aliasing has now been turned off for the selected text.

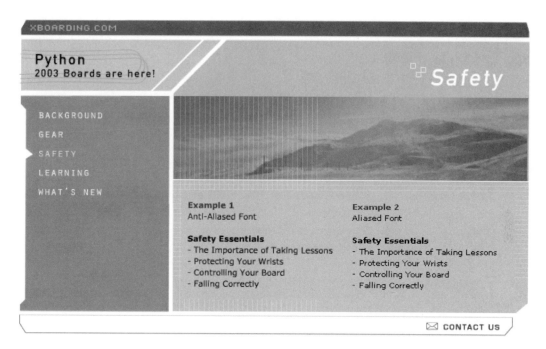

5. Test the movie once more by choosing **Control > Test Movie**. Notice that the text block on the right is much easier to read!

Note: The Alias text feature can be applied to Static, Dynamic, and Input text fields. However, if a visitor to your Flash Web site does not have version 7 or newer of the Flash plug-in, they will only see Static text aliased. If you are using any Dynamic or Input text fields with the Alias text feature, viewers with earlier versions of the Flash plug-in will see that text as anti-aliased.

3. ————————Loading a Text File into a Dynamic Text Field

Oftentimes, you may want to display current information such as news, weather reports, or company information that will need to be updated in your movie often. Flash MX 2004 allows you to do this by establishing a Dynamic text field, storing an external file that holds the text, and employing a little bit of ActionScript. Flash MX 2004 is a robust program for handling data-driven content that comes from a database or an external file that you can update without opening the Flash MX 2004 production file (FLA). The following exercise will take you through these steps and teach you how to load a text file (TXT) right into a Dynamic text field.

1. Open the **chap_12** folder, and double-click the **textFileLearning.txt** file to open it. Notice this is not a Flash MX 2004 file, it is a TXT file, and it will open in the default text editor on your computer. (You might need to turn on word wrapping so you can see all the text at once.) This TXT file has been created to get you started.

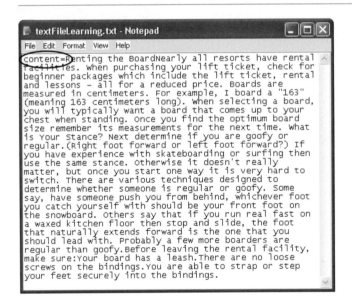

2. In order for Flash MX 2004 to recognize the information in this file, you need to give it a variable name. Place your cursor at the very beginning of the paragraph and type **content=** , as shown here. You have now declared that the text within the text file will be assigned to the variable name **content**.

NOTE | What Is a Variable?

A variable is simply a container that holds information, such as a name or number.

For example, in the following ActionScript,

`author="Rosanna";`

the variable name (or container) is **author** and everything after the equal sign is the value of the variable, which, in this example, is **"Rosanna."**

NOTE | URL-Encoded Text

When you use the `loadVariables` action (which you will add in Step 11) to load an external text file, the data in the text file must be in a special format called **URL-encoded**. This format requires that each variable travel in a pair with its associated value. The variable and the associated value are separated by the = symbol. In Step 2, the variable name is **content** and the associated value is all the text that immediately follows the = symbol.

3. Save and close the text file. Make sure you save it in the **chap_12** folder, because Flash MX 2004 will be referring to this file in later steps.

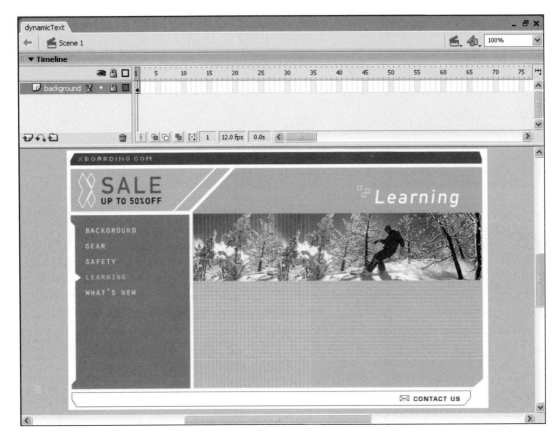

4. In Flash MX 2004, open the **dynamicText.fla** file from the **chap_12** folder. Notice that this file contains one layer with a background image.

You will add the Dynamic text box next.

5. In the **Timeline**, add a new layer by clicking the **Insert Layer** button, and rename this layer **holder**. Make sure the **holder** layer is above the **background** layer.

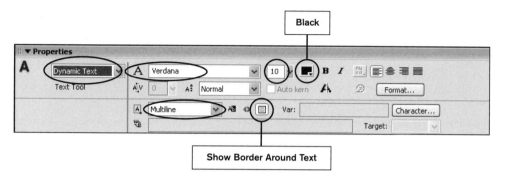

Black

Show Border Around Text

6. Select the **Text** tool from the **Toolbar** and click the **Stage** to bring focus to it. In the **Properties inspector**, choose **Dynamic Text**, **Multiline**, and **Show Border Around Text**. Make sure the **Font Color** is set to **black** and the **Font Type** is set to **Verdana** with a **Point Size** of **10**.

When you draw the text field on the Stage (which you will do next), these settings will create a Dynamic text field with a white background and a black border that can support multiple lines of text that will wrap.

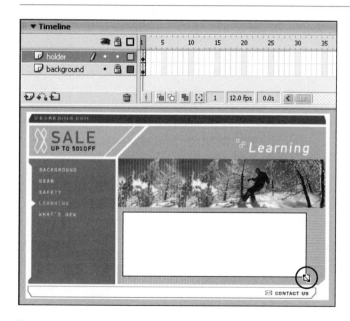

7. With the **holder** layer selected, click and drag on the **Stage** to create a text field that looks just like the picture here.

Tip: After you draw the text field, you can drag the handle of the Dynamic text field to resize the text field, if necessary.

8. In the **Properties inspector**, type the word **content** in the **Var** (variable) field. This will be the variable name that is assigned to the text field. This has to be the same variable name you assigned to the text inside the TXT file in Step 2.

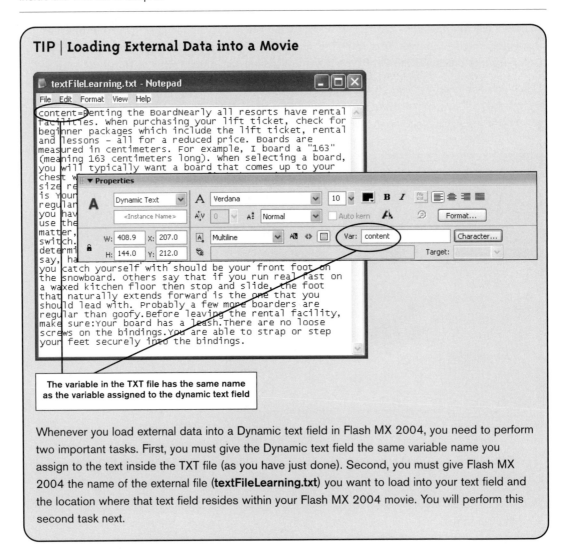

TIP | Loading External Data into a Movie

The variable in the TXT file has the same name as the variable assigned to the dynamic text field

Whenever you load external data into a Dynamic text field in Flash MX 2004, you need to perform two important tasks. First, you must give the Dynamic text field the same variable name you assign to the text inside the TXT file (as you have just done). Second, you must give Flash MX 2004 the name of the external file (**textFileLearning.txt**) you want to load into your text field and the location where that text field resides within your Flash MX 2004 movie. You will perform this second task next.

9. On the **Main Timeline**, click the **Insert Layer** button to add one last layer, and rename the layer **actions**. Make sure the **actions** layer is above all other layers.

10. In the **Timeline**, select **Frame 1** in the **actions** layer. Open the **Actions** panel (**F9**).

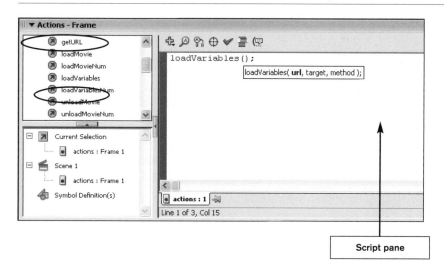

Script pane

11. Inside the **Actions** panel, make sure it reads **Actions – Frame**. In the **Actions** pane, choose **Global Functions > Browser/Network** and double-click the **loadVariables** action to add it to the **Script** pane.

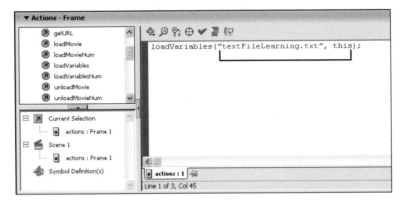

12. Click in-between the parentheses **( )** and type **"textFileLearning.txt", this**. It's very important that you include the quotation marks around the name of the text file you're loading the variables from (**textFileLearning.txt**). If you forget to use the quotation marks, it won't work properly. This ActionScript command tells Flash MX 2004 to look for **textFileLearning.txt** and to load the variables from that file into the current (Scene 1) Timeline (this). Since you assigned the variable name **content** to both the Dynamic text field and the text within the **textFileLearning.txt** file, the text field will dynamically generate the text from the TXT file.

Note: Since the TXT file is in the same folder as the project file (FLA) and the SWF file, you can simply type the name of the file (the relative address) in the URL field. If, however, the TXT file was located in a different folder, you would have to specify the path to that folder (the absolute address) in the URL field, such as ../projectSnow/learning/textFileLearning.txt.

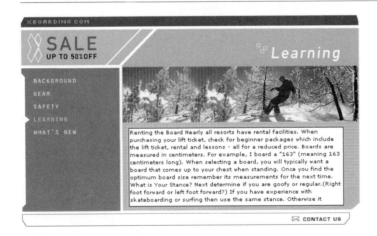

13. Choose **Control > Test Movie** to test your movie! Notice how the text is dynamically generated inside the Flash movie (**dynamicText.swf**) without actually typing anything inside the Flash MX 2004 project file (**dynamicText.fla**)!

Troubleshooting tip: If you don't see any text when you test the movie, select the Dynamic text field back in the project file and make sure the **Font Color** is set to black. Also click **Frame 1** on the **actions** layer, and in the **Actions** panel, check the spelling of the TXT file name to make sure you have the name spelled exactly as the document is named. Although the TXT file name (**textFileLearning.txt**) within the `loadVariables` action isn't case sensitive, to adhere to proper ActionScript guidelines, you should make sure that you're using the same case (upper- or lowercase) in the ActionScript as you are using in the TXT file name. Also make sure that in the `loadVariables` line of code, you have quotation marks around the name of the TXT file.

14. Close the **Preview** window and the **dynamicText.fla** file, making sure to save any changes you've made.

*Next, you will make changes to the **textFileLearning.txt** file and see that Flash MX 2004 will automatically update the content in the Dynamic text field without opening the production file (**dynamicText.fla**). If you want to change the content inside the text file, all you need to do is open the TXT file, make the changes, and open the SWF file again. You will do this in the following steps.*

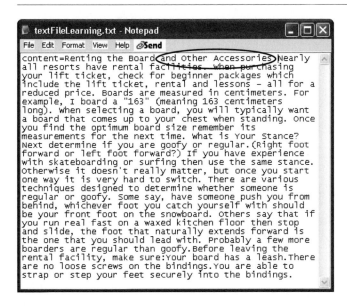

15. Open **textFileLearning.txt** from the **chap_12** folder. After the text **Renting the Board**, type the text **and Other Accessories**. When you are finished, save the **textFileLearning.txt** file.

16. Hide Flash MX 2004 for a moment and look inside the **chap_12** folder on your desktop. Notice the **dynamicText.swf** file inside this folder.

17. Double-click the **dynamicText.swf** file to open it in the **Flash Player**. Notice the changes you made to the TXT file in Step 15 have been updated in the SWF file (**dynamicText.swf**) without opening up the production file (**dynamicText.fla**)! When you are done viewing the **movie**, close **dynamicText.swf**.

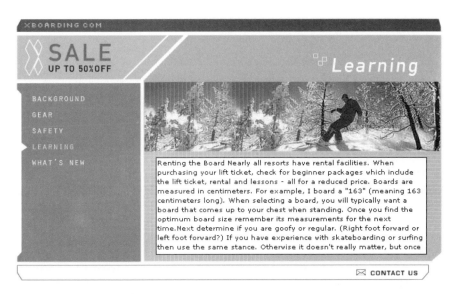

18. Back in the **textFileLearning.txt** file, delete the text **and Other Accessories** you entered in Step 15 and save your changes. Open the **dynamicText.swf** file located in the **chap_12** folder and notice that the changes have been updated again without opening the production file (**dynamicText.fla**).

19. Go ahead and make more changes if you'd like. When you are done, close the **dynamicText.swf** file and keep the **textFileLearning.txt** file open. You will format the text in the following exercise.

As you can see, the text loaded into the Dynamic text field is unformatted (no paragraph breaks, bolding, and so forth). You will learn how to format the loaded text with HTML next.

NOTE | Changing Character Attributes

The text that loads into the Dynamic text field will take on all the character attributes that are applied to the field within the Properties inspector. You can quickly change the way the text is displayed in the SWF file by making some slight modifications to the text field by using the Properties inspector. First, select the Dynamic text field. Then change the font name, the font height, and the font color. You can even deselect the Show Border Around Text option to remove the white background from the text. Test the movie again, and you will see a completely different look for your text field!

4.————————Working with Dynamic Text and HTML

In the last exercise, you created a Dynamic text field in your project file that displayed the data of an external text file. In this exercise, you will take it one step further and change one setting of the Dynamic text field to allow Flash MX 2004 to recognize and preserve HTML formatting applied to the content inside the external text file.

1. You should have the **textFileLearning.txt** file open from the last exercise. If not, go ahead and open it from the **chap_12** folder.

NOTE | Dynamic Text HTML Support

Flash MX 2004 supports the following HTML tags in Dynamic and Input text fields:

<a> = anchor, **<b>** = bold, **<font color>** = font color, **<font face>** = typeface, **<font size>** = font size, **<i>** = italic, **<img>** = image, **<li>** = list item, **<p>** = paragraph, **
** = line break, **<u>** = underline, and **<a href="…">** = hyperlinks.

Flash MX 2004 also supports the following HTML attributes in Dynamic and Input text fields:

leftmargin, rightmargin, align, indent, and **leading**.

You will add some of these tags in the next few steps.

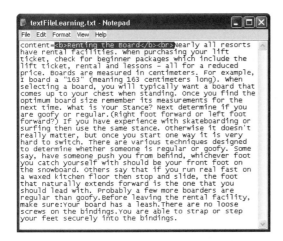

2. Add bold HTML tags around the words **Renting the Board** and add one line break tag. It should read **Renting the Board
**. Save your changes and keep the file open.

*All you need to do is change one setting in the Properties inspector of the **dynamicText.fla file** and you will see the HTML-based text file loaded into the same Dynamic text box. You will do this next.*

3. Open the **dynamicText.fla** file from the **chap_12** folder. This is the same FLA file you worked with in the last exercise.

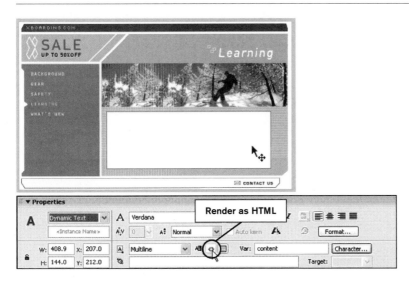

4. With the **Selection** tool, select the Dynamic text field on the **Stage**. In the **Properties inspector**, click the **Render as HTML** button. This will allow the Dynamic text block to interpret the HTML code and dynamically display any of the supported HTML tags within the external text file.

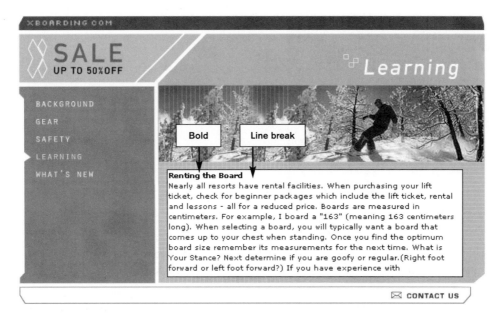

5. Choose **Control > Test Movie** to test your movie. Notice that Flash MX 2004 recognized the HTML formatting you made in the text file.

*Note: In the last exercise, you previewed the changes you made to the **textFileLearning.txt** file by opening the **dynamicText.swf** file located in the **chap_12** folder. For ease of workflow, you will preview your changes using **Control > Test Movie** by creating the SWF file again from the production file (**dynamicText.fla**). This minimizes going back and forth from the Flash MX 2004 application to the desktop and vice versa.*

---

6. Close the **Preview** window when you are done viewing your changes. You will add more HTML formatting to the **textFileLearning.txt** file next.

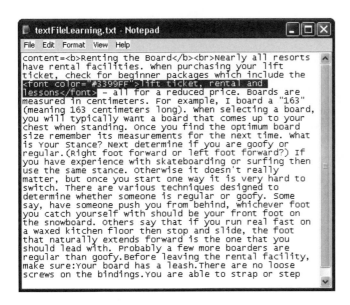

7. Back in the **textFileLearning.txt** file, add font color HTML tags around the words **lift ticket, rental and lessons**. It should read **<font color="#3399FF">lift ticket, rental and lessons</font>**.

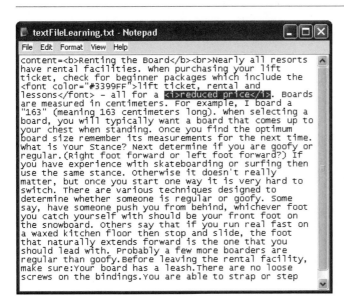

8. Add italic HTML tags around the words **reduced price**. It should read **<i>reduced price</i>**. Save your changes and keep the file open. You will preview your new changes next.

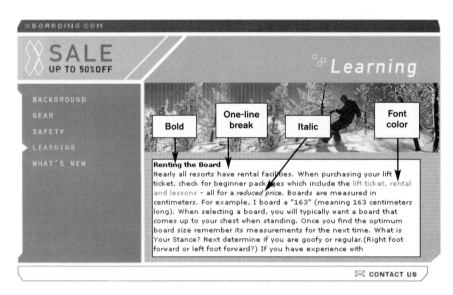

9. Choose **Control > Test Movie** to test your movie again. Notice that Flash MX 2004 recognized the additional HTML formatting you made in the text file again. Close the **Preview** window when you are done viewing your changes. You will add more HTML formatting to the **textFileLearning.txt** file next.

10. To break this large block of text up into smaller, more readable chunks, you're going to add five more line breaks (just as you did in Step 2 after the text **Renting the Board**). Add the line breaks (**
**) to the locations in the text that you see in this image.

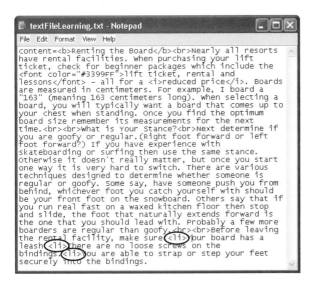

11. To make the last three sentences of the copy more readable, you will add list item HTML tags to them. Add list item (**<li>**) tags to the locations in the text that you see in this image. Save your changes and close the file. You will preview your new changes next.

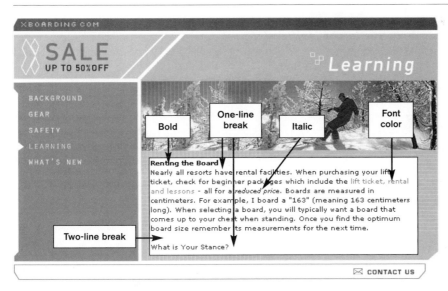

12. Choose **Control > Test Movie** to test your movie. You will notice that Flash MX 2004 recognized all the HTML formatting you made in the text file! But where is the rest of the content? You will add buttons to make the content scroll up and down in the next exercise.

13. Save this file and keep it open for one more exercise.

5. —————————————**Scrollable Dynamic Text Fields**

In the previous two exercises, you have been working with Dynamic text fields. This exercise will take the project file one step further: You will add buttons to the interface and learn how to make the Dynamic text scroll up and down within the Dynamic text field box. In the last version of Flash MX, there was a component for adding a scroll bar. This version does not include a scroll bar component, so you will learn to program the up and down arrow buttons with the scroll function using ActionScript.

1. You should still have the **dynamicText.fla** file open from the last exercise. If not, go ahead and open it from the **chap_12** folder.

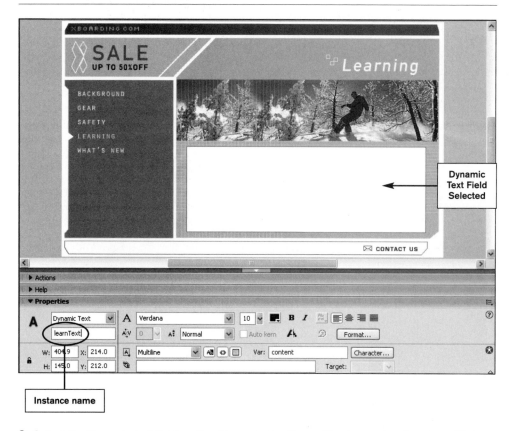

2. Select the Dynamic text field on the **Stage**. In the **Properties inspector**, type **learnText** in the **Instance Name** box. This will assign the instance name **learnText** to the Dynamic text field.

NOTE | Why Do I Need an Instance Name and a Variable Name?

In Flash MX 2004, text is its own ActionScript object, so a text field (Dynamic and Input) can have both a variable name and an instance name. As you learned in Exercise 3, you need a variable name to be able to load the external text file into a Dynamic text field. In this exercise, you need to give the text field an instance name so that the ActionScript on the buttons can control the text field. You will do this next.

3. In the **Timeline**, lock the **holder** layer and click the **Insert Layer** button to add a new layer. Rename the layer **buttons**. Position the **buttons** layer below the **actions** layer.

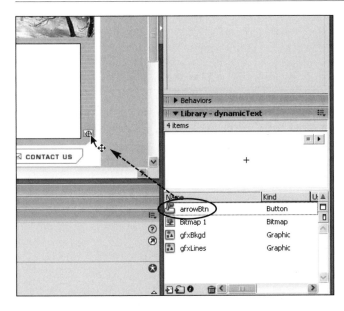

4. Open the **Library** (**Ctrl+L** [Windows] or **Cmd+L** [Mac]) and notice the button **arrowBtn**. Drag an instance of **arrowBtn** onto the **Stage**. Position it toward the bottom right of the Dynamic text field, as shown here.

5. Select the **arrowBtn** button on the **Stage** and press **F9** to open the **Actions** panel.

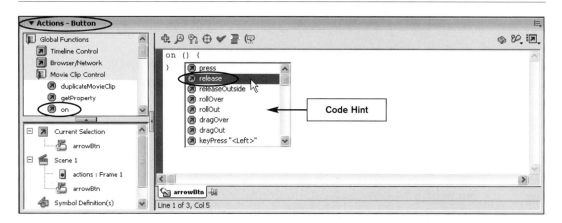

6. Make sure the **Actions** panel reads **Actions – Button**. From the **Actions** pane, choose **Global Functions > Movie Clip Control** and double-click **on** to add it to the **Script** pane. From the **Code Hint** menu that will automatically pop up, double-click **release**.

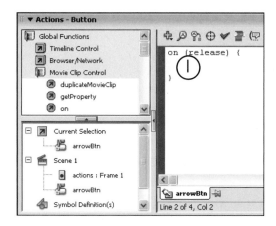

7. In the **Script** pane, place the cursor after the open curly brace and press **Enter/Return** to bring the cursor down to the second line, as shown here.

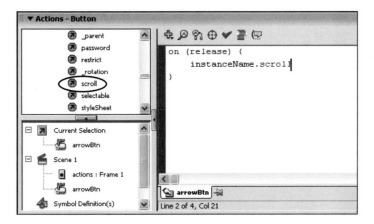

8. In the **Actions** pane, choose **Built-in Classes > Movie > TextField > Properties**. Double-click **scroll** to add it after the **on (release) {** line.

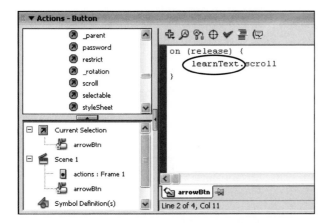

9. In the **Script** pane, replace the text **instanceName** (it's there just as a placeholder for you) with the instance name **learnText**, which you assigned to the Dynamic text field in Step 2. Make sure that you don't accidentally remove the period between **learnText** and **scroll**.

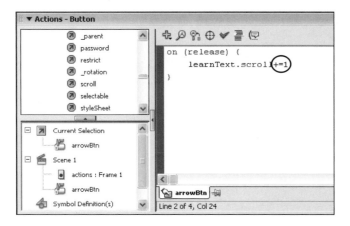

10. After the word **scroll**, type **+=1**. The action should now read `learnText.scroll+=1`. This tells Flash MX 2004 that when a user clicks this down button, it should take the **learnText** instance (the Dynamic text field) and scroll it up one line.

*Tip: You can change the number of lines that scroll at one time by changing the number after the **+= 1**. For example,* `learnText.scroll+=5` *will scroll the Dynamic text field up five lines for each click of the button.*

11. Hide the **Actions** panel for a moment by pressing **F9**. You will add the up arrow button to the interface by making a copy of the down button next.

12. While holding down your **Alt** (Windows) or **Option** (Mac) and **Shift** keys, click and drag the **arrowBtn** up towards the top of the text field. Then, once you have it in place, choose **Modify >** **Transform > Flip Vertical** to flip the arrow so it is pointing up.

Copying the down arrow to use for the up arrow accomplishes two things. One, because both arrows are instances of the same original symbol, arrowBtn, you're not increasing the file size of your movie by adding another graphic to your project. And two, by copying the down arrow, you're also copying the ActionScript that you applied to that arrow. This means you won't have to type all that ActionScript in again, thank goodness! You only have to make one, small modification to the ActionScript on the up button, which you will do next.

13. Select the up button on the **Stage** (the one you just copied) and press **F9** to open the **Actions** panel.

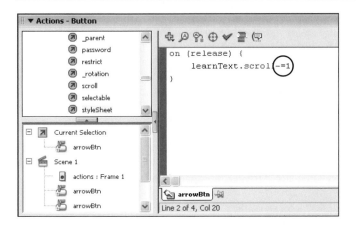

14. Change the **+=** to now read **-=**. The action should now read **learnText.scroll-=1**. This will tell the Flash Player that, when a user clicks the up button, it should take the **learnText** instance (the Dynamic text field) and scroll it down one line.

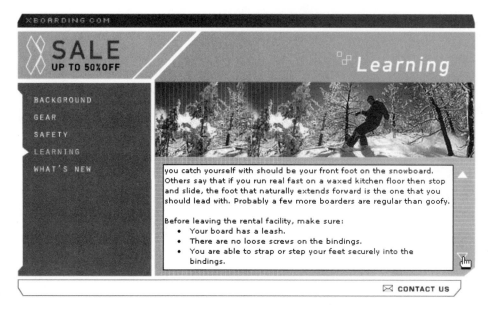

15. Choose **Control > Test Movie** to try out your new scroll buttons! Notice that Flash MX 2004 recognized the additional HTML formatting you made in the text file again. The last 3 sentences are now presented in a bulleted list. Nice!

Troubleshooting tip: *If your scroll buttons don't work, go back and check the ActionScript on the buttons and make sure that the instance name is spelled correctly and that you used the correct lowercase and uppercase letters, since the ActionScript you applied to the buttons is case-sensitive.*

16. When you are finished, save and keep this file open. You will take this project file another step forward and link a Cascading Style Sheet (CSS) to this file next.

NOTE | What Are Cascading Style Sheets?

Cascading Style Sheets allow you to describe how structured content, like HTML, should be presented. Whereas HTML describes what a document's elements are, such as paragraphs or images, CSS describes how a document's elements should be styled in terms of appearance. For example, CSS could be used to specify that a selected portion of the text be in a particular font, at a particular size, and that other portions of the text be in a particular font color and style. For further information about Cascading Style Sheets, two good resources are *Cascading Style Sheets: The Designer's Edge* by Molly E. Holzschlag and *Cascading Style Sheets: The Definitive Guide* by Eric A. Meyer.

6. _____Dynamic Text and CSS

Flash MX 2004 now supports Cascading Style Sheets (CSS), which allow you to create text styles that can be applied to HTML—and that is exactly what you'll do in this exercise. The following steps will take your project file one more step forward and show you how to add a Cascading Style Sheet to the HTML formatted text file that you loaded into a Dynamic text field from the previous exercise.

1. You should still have the **dynamicText.fla** file open from **chap_12**. If not, go ahead and open it now.

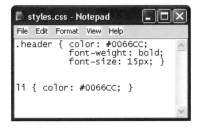

2. Open the **styles.css** file located inside the **chap_12** folder in a text editor such as WordPad for Windows or TextEdit for Mac. Double-clicking the file on your hard drive should launch whatever text editor is installed on your machine. Don't work with this file in Microsoft Word, which might introduce formatting that is not allowed in HTML or CSS. This file has been created for you to get you started. Notice that there are two style rules. Text that is styled with **.header** will be blue for the font color, bold for the font weight, and 15 point for the font size. The rule **li** will style all the text with the HTML tag **<li>** in a font color of blue. Close **styles.css** when you are done viewing it. You will add the **.header** style to the **textFileLearning.txt** file next.

NOTE | What Is a CSS Rule?

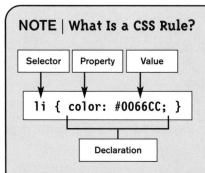

A **CSS rule** specifies how to format HTML elements and is made up of a selector, a property, and a value. A **selector** is how you specify exactly what should be styled. In this example, the HTML tag **<li>** is the selector. A **property** controls which stylistic attribute is being set. In this example, the property is color. The **value** is what the property is being set to. In this example, the color property is being set to a value of blue (#0066CC). It's important to note that a colon always separates the property and value. The property and value pair together are called a **declaration**. You can have multiple declarations associated with each selector; you just have to separate them with semicolons.

3. You should still have the **textFileLearning.txt** file open from the last exercise. If not, go ahead and open it from **chap_12**.

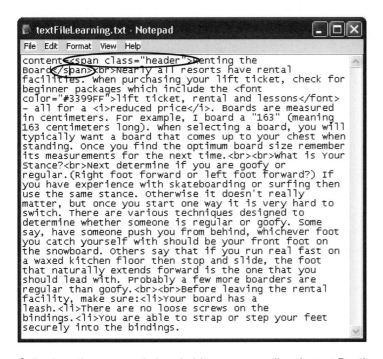

4. Replace the open and close bold tags surrounding the text **Renting the Board** with **<span class = "header">** and **</span>** as shown here. This will add the **.header** style to text. You will add this style one more time to the text file next.

*Adding the .header style will complete three tasks for the selected text: blue for the font color, bold for the font weight, and 15 point for the font size all accomplished with the **<span>** tag. Using CSS cuts down on the additional HTML you would have to add to format the text this way. Additionally, if you wanted to change the way the HTML is presented, you could do so by editing the CSS file, which will then update all the styles in the HTML formatted text.*

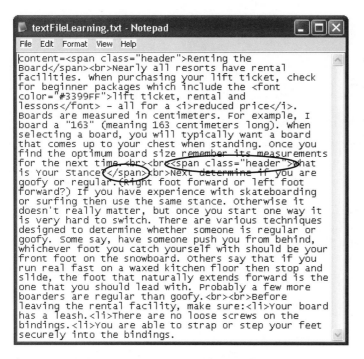

5. Wrap the **<span class = "header">** and **</span>** tags around the sentence **What is Your Stance?** as shown here. This will add the **.header** style to text.

6. Save and close this file. You will add the ActionScript that will call the style sheet and attach it to the text file in the following steps.

NOTE | Formatting Text with Cascading Style Sheets

Cascading Style Sheets are represented in ActionScript by the **TextField.StyleSheet** class. It is important to note that this feature is only available for SWF files that target the **Flash Player 7**. To add styles to a style sheet object, you can either load an external CSS file into the object, which you will learn to do in this exercise, or define the styles in ActionScript.

To load an external CSS file, use the **load()** method of the **TextField.StyleSheet** class. You can create styles that redefine built-in HTML formatting tags (such as **<p>** and **<li>**), create style "classes" that can be applied to specific HTML elements using the **<p>** or **<span>** tag's **class** attribute, or define new tags. For example, the following code creates a style sheet object named **style_sheet** that loads into a Dynamic text block and formats the HTML text file in the Dynamic text block:

```
var style_sheet = new TextField.StyleSheet();
var css_url = "styles.css";
style_sheet.load(css_url);
learnText.styleSheet = style_sheet;
loadVariables("textFileLearning.txt", this);
```

Loading an external style sheet is an efficient way to incorporate CSS into your Flash MX 2004 movies since the external style sheet can be shared among your Flash MX 2004 movies. Additionally, as with making changes to an external text file that loads into a Dynamic text field, you can edit the CSS file and the changes will take place without opening up the production file (FLA).

To define styles in ActionScript, use the **setStyle()** method of the **TextField.StyleSheet** class. This method takes two parameters: the name of the style and an object that defines that style's properties. For example, the following code creates a style sheet object named **styles** that defines two styles:

```
var styles = new TextField.StyleSheet();
styles.setStyle("bodyText",
    {fontFamily: 'Verdana, Trebuchet,sans-serif',
    fontSize: '12px'}
styles.setStyle("header",
    {fontFamily: 'Verdana, Trebuchet,sans-serif',
    fontSize: '24px'}
;
```

continues on next page

NOTE | Formatting Text with Cascading Style Sheets *continued*

Remember, when loading data, the file should reside in the same directory as the SWF that is loading the file.

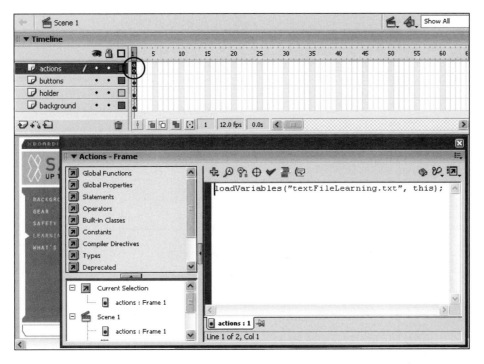

7. Select **Frame 1** of the **actions** layer and open the **Actions** panel (**F9**). Notice the ActionScript you added in Exercise 3. You will add more ActionScript to **Frame 1** of the **actions** layer in the following steps.

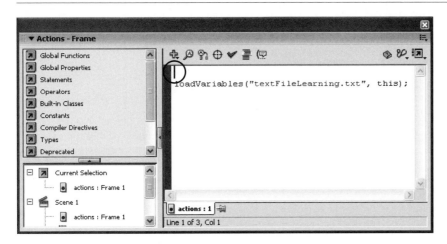

8. In the **Actions** pane, place the cursor before the text **loadVariables** and press **Enter/Return** to bring the line of code down to the next line. Then place the cursor at the empty line at the top of the **Script** pane as shown here. You will declare a variable for a new style sheet object in the following steps.

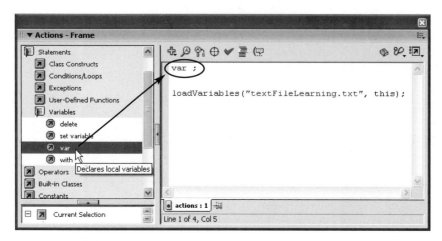

9. In the **Actions** pane, choose **Statements > Variables** and double-click **var** to add it to the **Script** pane. You will give a name to this variable next.

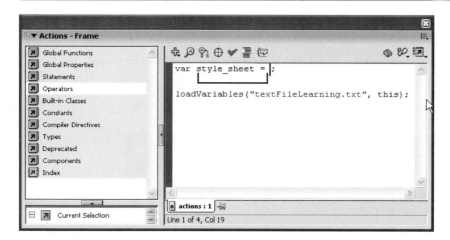

10. Place the cursor before the semicolon (;) and type **style_sheet =** . The name of this variable is now style_sheet.

To add styles to a style sheet object, you can define the styles in ActionScript, or you can load an external CSS file into the object, which you will do in the following steps.

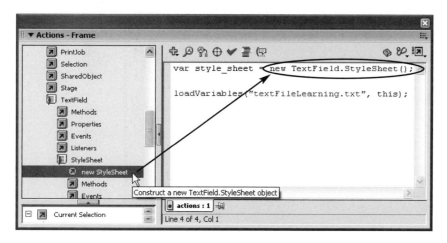

11. In the **Actions** pane, choose **Built-in Classes > Movie > TextField > StyleSheet** and double-click **new StyleSheet** to add it to the **Script** pane. In the following steps, you will define the location of the CSS file.

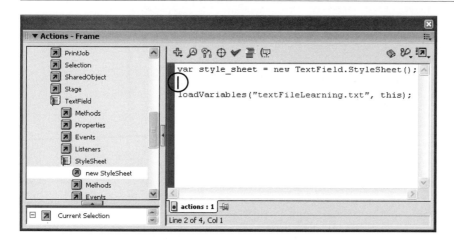

12. In the **Script** pane, place the cursor in the next empty line, as shown here. You will declare another variable next.

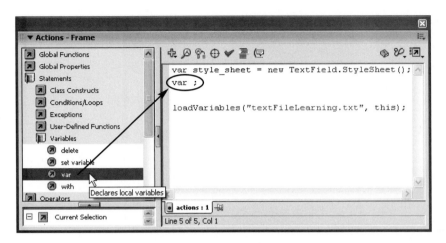

13. In the **Actions** pane, choose **Statements > Variables** and double-click **var** to add it to the **Script** pane. You will give a name to this variable next.

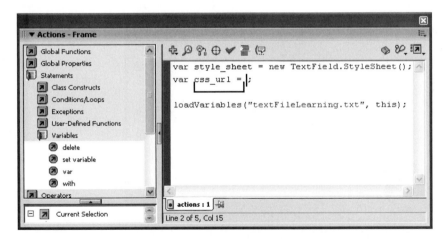

14. Place the cursor before the semicolon and type **css_url =** . The name of this variable is now **css_url**. You will attach the name of the style sheet to the variable **css_url** next.

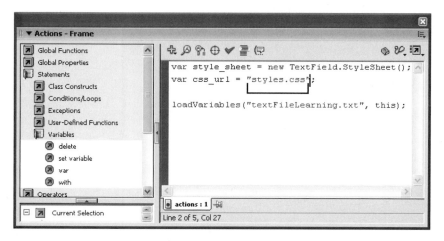

15. After the equals sign (=), type **"styles.css"**, which is the name of the external style sheet found in the **chap_12** folder on your hard drive. In the following steps, you will load the CSS file into the style sheet object.

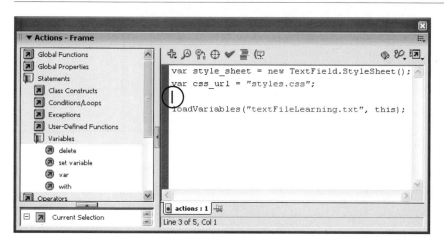

16. In the **Script** pane, place the cursor in the next empty line, as shown here.

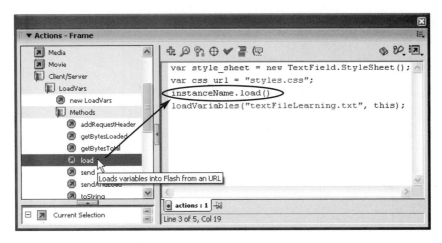

17. In the **Actions** pane, choose **Built-in Classes** > **Client/Server** > **LoadVars** > **Methods** and double-click **load** to add it to the **Script** pane. You will type in the instance name next.

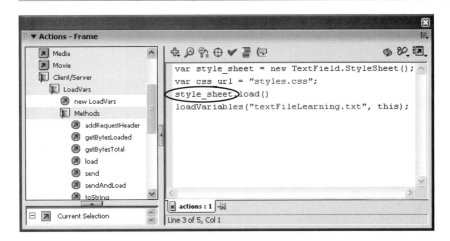

18. Replace the placeholder text **instanceName** with **style_sheet**, which is the variable name of the style sheet object you defined in Step 10. You will assign the style sheet to the text object next.

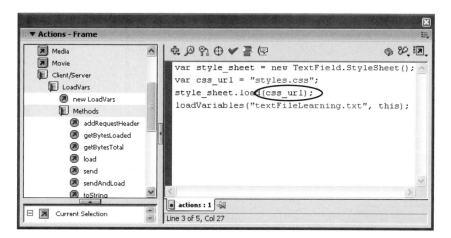

19. Click between the parentheses after **load**, and type **css_url**. After the closing parenthesis, type **;**, as shown here.

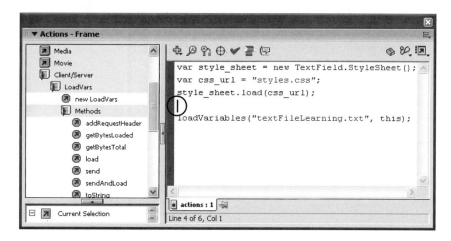

20. Press **Enter/Return** to bring your cursor to the next line. You will assign the style sheet to the Dynamic text field in the following steps.

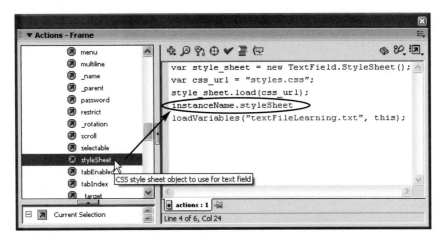

21. In the **Actions** pane, choose **Built-in Classes > Movie > TextField > Properties** and double-click **styleSheet** to add it to the **Script** pane. You will type in the instance name next.

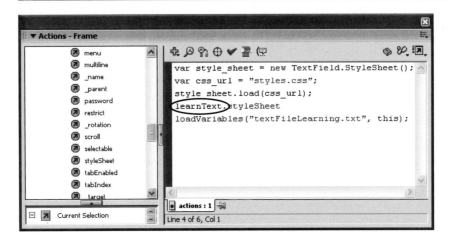

22. Replace the text **instanceName** with **learnText**, which is the instance name of the Dynamic text field you defined in Step 2 of Exercise 5.

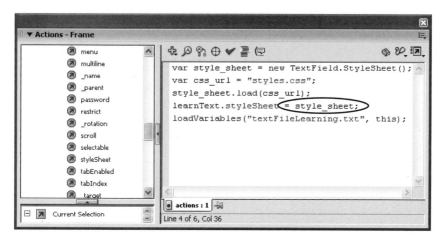

23. After the word **stylesheet**, type **= style_sheet;**. This assigns the style sheet to the Dynamic text field. You are just about to test your movie, but first you'll verify your code.

24. Your code should look like the following:

```
var style_sheet = new TextField.StyleSheet();
var css_url = "styles.css";
style_sheet.load(css_url);
learnText.styleSheet = style_sheet;
loadVariables("textFileLearning.txt", this);
```

Here's an explanation of each line:

```
// This creates a new style sheet object
var style_sheet = new TextField.StyleSheet();
```

```
// This is the location of the CSS file that defines the styles
var css_url = "styles.css";
```

```
// This loads the CSS file with the onLoad handler
style_sheet.load(css_url);
```

```
// This assigns the loaded style sheet to the Dynamic text block
learnText.styleSheet = style_sheet;
```

```
// This loads the external HTML formatted text file into the Dynamic text block
loadVariables("textFileLearning.txt", this);
```

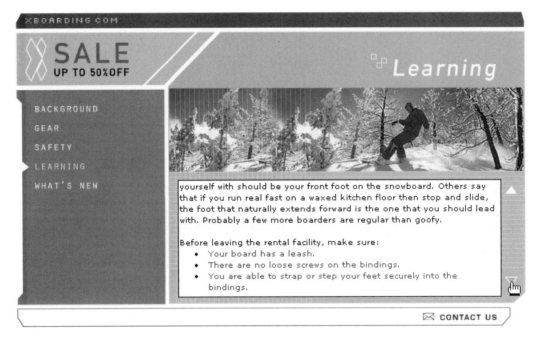

25. Choose **Control > Test Movie** to preview your movie. Notice that the text **Renting the Board** and **What is Your Stance?** now display the **.header** style. Additionally, when you scroll down to the bottom of the text field, notice that the bulleted list items are now blue, too!

26. Save and close this file.

Whew! You just progressed to a new level of ActionScript—and you thought this chapter was only about text! If anything isn't crystal clear, you can always go back and do a review. Otherwise, if you have the stamina, press forward to the next exercise, where you'll learn about Input text.

7. ———————Working with Input Text

Now that you've learned how to use Static and Dynamic text fields, it's time to explore the last remaining text field type: **Input text**. Input text fields, as the name implies, allow you to input text into them, much like an HTML form. If you've ever purchased a product online, you had to give the vendor your name, address, credit card number, and so forth. You entered that information in an Input text field. In this exercise, you will learn how to use an Input text field to create an area for visitors to enter in their names. Later, you will use that name, in combination with some other text, to populate a Dynamic text field.

1. Open the **inputText.fla** file from the **chap_12** folder. Notice that this file has one layer with a background image on it.

2. Click the **Insert Layer** button four times to add **four** new layers above the **background** layer. You will be adding the Input text field, some text, a button, and actions to these layers in the following steps.

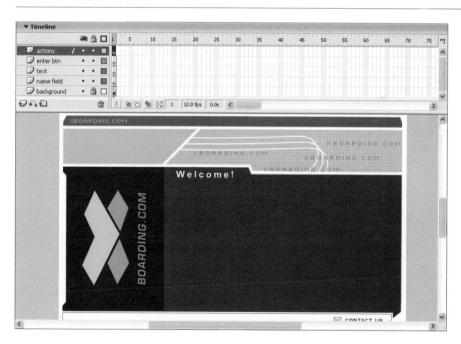

3. Starting from the top, name the four new layers **actions**, **enter btn**, **text**, and **name field**, as shown here.

Below the text "Welcome!," you will enter in a little bit of text and create an Input text field. The Input text field is where the visitor to your Web site will enter in his or her name. Later in this same exercise, you will use that name in a Dynamic text field by adding some ActionScript.

4. In the **Timeline**, select the **text** layer. From the **Toolbar**, select the **Text** tool and click the **Stage** to bring focus to it. In the **Properties inspector**, set the **Text Type** to **Static Text, Font** to **Arial, Font Size** to **14**, **Text Color** to **white** and **bold**. **Text Alignment** should be set to **Align left**, and **Auto kern** should be checked. Your **Properties inspector** settings should match the screen shot here.

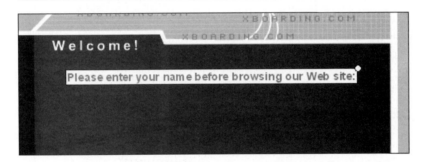

5. Click the **Stage** to create a text block, and type **Please enter your name before browsing our Web site:**. After you've typed the text, reposition the text block with the **Selection** tool if you need to.

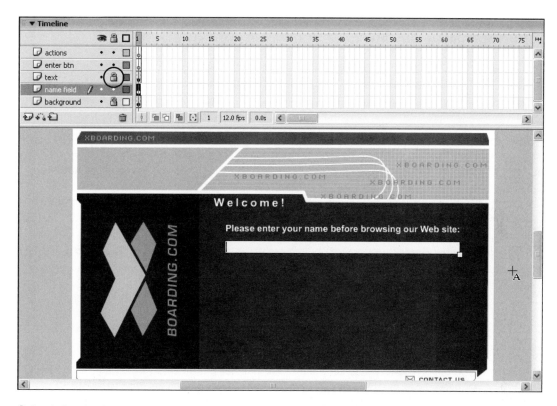

6. Lock the **text** layer and select the **name field** layer. Select the **Text** tool and click the **Stage** to bring focus to it. In the **Properties inspector**, choose **Input Text** for the **Text Type**. Create a text box (by clicking and dragging) below the **Please enter your name before browsing our Web site:** text on the **Stage**.

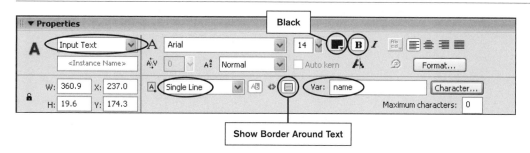

7. With the **Selection** tool, select the Input text field (that you've just drawn) on the **Stage**. In the **Properties inspector**, make sure the **Text Type** is set to **Input Text**, **Font** to **Arial**, **Font Size** to **14**, **Font Color** to **Black** and **Bold**. Set the **Line Type** to **Single Line**, select the **Show border around text** button, and in the **Var** field, type the word **name** to give this Input text field the variable name of **name**. The **Properties inspector** should match the image shown here.

NOTE | Naming Variables

According to the ActionScript Coding Standards, variable names can contain only letters, numbers, and underscores. However, when you name variables in Flash MX 2004, they should begin with a lowercase letter and cannot begin with numbers or underscores. Additionally, words that are used by ActionScript, such as "scroll," should not be used as variable names. For more information on ActionScript Coding Standards, visit **http://www.macromedia.com/devnet/mx/ flash/whitepapers/actionscript_standards.pdf**.

NOTE | Input Text Options

Clicking the **Show Border Around Text** button creates a border and background around the Input text box. If Show Border Around Text is not enabled, a dotted line will surround the text box in the FLA file, although when you publish the movie, there will be no border or background.

The **Maximum characters** setting allows you to set the maximum number of characters that can be typed in the text box. The default is set to 0, meaning that there is no maximum number of characters.

The **Line Type** option allows you to set the text box to either **Single Line** (displaying the text on one line), **Multiline** (displaying the text in multiple lines), **Multiline no wrap** (displaying the text on one line unless a line break [Enter/Return] is used), or **Password** (automatically turns all characters into asterisks as they are typed in the field of either the SWF file or the executable).

The **Var** setting (variable) enables you to assign a variable name to the text field.

NOTE | Embedding Font Outlines

When using a Static text field, as explained earlier, the font outlines for all the text you used will be embedded in the SWF file. That way, you're able to use any font you want in your project, and the end user will see the font you chose whether they have the font installed or not.

When using a Dynamic or Input text field, however, Flash MX 2004 does *not* embed the font outline for the font you've chosen. Because of the nature of Dynamic and Input text fields, where any text and any character can appear in those fields, Flash MX 2004 won't automatically embed the font outlines. Instead, you must manually specify what part of the font face (upper case characters, lower case, numerals, and so forth) you want to embed in the SWF file. If you don't set, for *each* Dynamic and/or Input text field, the font embedding settings, the viewer's computer will treat the text in that field like a Device font. Unless the end user has the same font face you've chosen for the text field, his or her computer will substitute it for whatever serif or sans-serif type face that comes closest to the one you've picked and will be displayed as aliased (jagged edge) instead of anti-aliased (smooth edge). So unless you're trying to save file size by not embedding font outlines in your SWF file, make sure you specify your font embedding settings for each Dynamic and/or Input text field in your project.

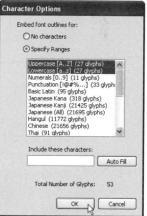

8. In the **Properties inspector**, click the **Character** button. This will open the **Character Options** dialog box where you specify what **range** of the type face you've chosen (Arial, in this example) to be embedded in the SWF file. Select the **Specify Ranges** radio button, and in the list box, **Shift+click** to select **Uppercase** and **Lowercase**. Since the visitor to your Web site will only be entering his or her name, the uppercase and lowercase characters should be all that you'll need to embed. Click **OK** to accept these changes.

NOTE | Including Specific Characters

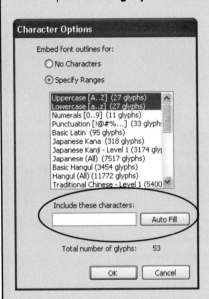

If you want to embed only a few characters, and not an entire range, you can type specific characters into the **Include these characters** field. For example, if you only wanted to embed letters and numbers a, b, c, d, e, f, 1, 2, 3, 4, 5, and 6, you would type those characters into this box, without commas or spaces—unless you want to embed those as well.

NOTE | Embedding Multiple, Identical Font Outlines

Say you have two Input text fields, for instance, and each text field is using the Arial font. As I've mentioned, you need to specify the font embedding options for *all* Dynamic or Input text fields individually. So if you embed the upper- and lowercase characters for both Input text fields, does that mean that the font outlines for Arial upper- and lowercase will be embedded twice, increasing your file size even more? No, thankfully it doesn't. Whew!

9. In the **Timeline**, lock the **name field** layer, and select the **enter btn** layer.

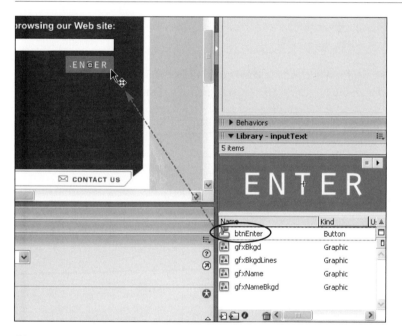

10. Open the **Library** by pressing **Ctrl+L** (Windows) or **Cmd+L** (Mac). Drag the **btnEnter** button symbol onto the **Stage** and position it below the bottom-right corner of the name field, as shown here.

11. Make sure the **btnEnter** button is selected and open the **Actions** panel by pressing **F9**.

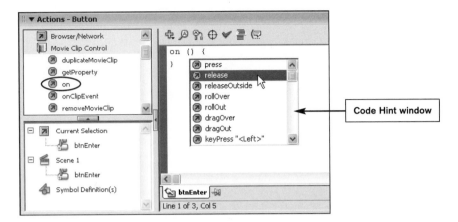

12. In the **Actions** pane, choose **Global Functions > Movie Clip Control** and double-click the **on** action to add it to the **Script** pane. From the **Code Hint** menu, choose **release** for the mouse event.

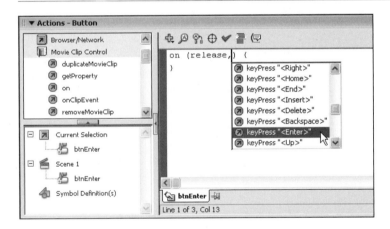

13. After **release**, type a comma (,). A new **Code Hint** menu will automatically open. Scroll down the **Code Hint** window and double-click **keyPress "<Enter>"**. You have just specified a mouse event to be triggered by the end user when they click the Enter button, or press the Enter/Return key on the keyboard.

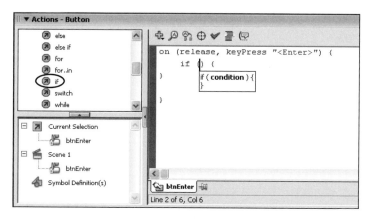

14. In the **Script** pane, place your cursor after the open curly brace and press **Enter/Return** to bring the cursor down to the second line. In the **Actions** pane, choose **Statements > Conditions/Loops** and double-click **if** to add it to the **Script** pane.

*Later in this exercise, on Frame 2, you will create a Dynamic text field where the user's name will be displayed along with some additional text. By entering his or her name and clicking the Enter button, the visitor will successfully go to the next frame. However, if the visitor doesn't enter any information into the name field, he or she won't be allowed to go to the next frame. This **if** action you are about to create will verify that the viewer enters something into the **name** field.*

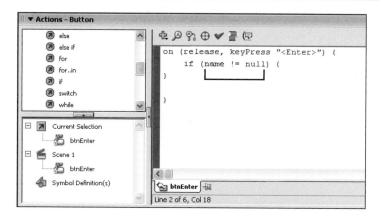

15. Between the parentheses after **if**, type **name != null**.

name *is the variable name of the Input text field where the viewer enters his or her name. != means "does not equal," and* **null** *means no value. So, in plain English, this* **if** *action essentially says "If the Input text field **name** is not empty (meaning, someone has typed* something *into it), then…".*

In the next few steps, you will complete the rest of that statement.

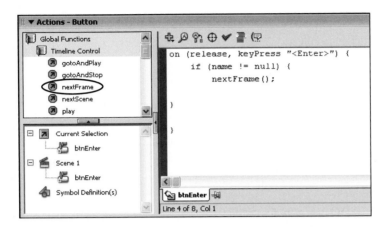

16. Click after the line of scripting `if (name != null) {` and press **Enter/Return** to bring the cursor to the next line. Then choose **Global Functions > Timeline Control** and double-click `nextFrame`. `nextFrame` instructs Flash MX 2004 to go to the next frame in the Timeline.

*Essentially, this script reads, "When the end user clicks the Enter button, or presses Enter/Return on his or her keyboard, if the **name** field has some text in it, go to the next frame in the Timeline." There's no need, in this case, to tell Flash MX 2004 what not to do if the viewer hasn't entered anything in the **name** field. If the viewer has not entered any text into the **name** field, Flash MX 2004 simply won't go to the next frame (because you've told it only to go to the next frame if the viewer has entered something in the **name** field). Next, you will create the message, on the next frame, that the viewer will see once he or she enters a name into the **name** field and clicks the Enter button or presses Enter/Return.*

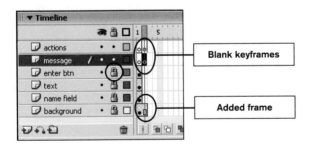

17. Lock the **enter btn** layer, and create a new layer. Rename the new layer **message**. On **Frame 2** of the **message** and **actions** layers, press **F7** to create a blank keyframe. On the **background** layer, press **F5** to add a frame to **Frame 2**.

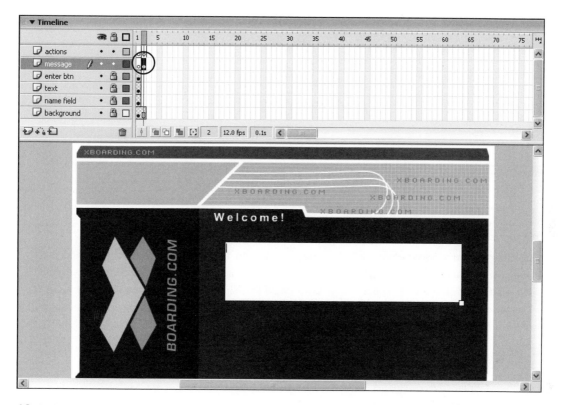

18. Make sure **Frame 2** of the **message** layer is selected. From the **Toolbar**, select the **Text** tool and click the **Stage** to bring focus to it. In the **Properties inspector**, set the **Text Type** to **Dynamic Text**, and then draw out a large rectangle below the "Welcome!" text. This will be the Dynamic text field, where the message, incorporating the visitor's name, will be displayed. You will set the remaining options in the **Properties inspector** next.

19. With the **Selection** tool, select the Dynamic text field that you just created on the **Stage**. In the **Properties inspector**, make sure the **Text Type** is still set to **Dynamic Text**. Set the **Font** to **Arial**, **12** point, **White**, and **Bold**. Make sure the **Text Alignment** is set to **Center** and **Line Type** is set to **Multiline**, and **Show Border Around Text** button is delected. In the **Var** (variable) field, type **message**. You will set the **Character Options** for the Dynamic text field next.

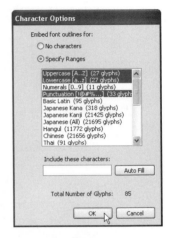

20. In the **Properties inspector**, click the **Character** button. In the **Character Options** dialog box, make sure the radio button for **Specify Ranges** is selected. In the list box, select **Uppercase**; then while holding down the **Ctrl** (Windows) or **Cmd** (Mac) key, single-click **Lowercase** and **Punctuation** to select all three options at the same time. Since it's only going to be a simple message that also includes the name that the visitor gave, these three ranges will do fine. Click **OK**.

Now that you have all the pieces in place, it's time to put it all together with a little bit of ActionScript.

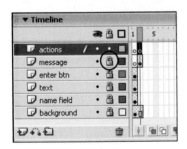

21. Lock the **message** layer, click **Frame 2** in the **actions** layer, and open the **Actions** panel (**F9**).

*At this point, what you're trying to accomplish with ActionScript is to write a little bit of text that will be combined with the **name** the visitor entered in the Input text field, and then place that name inside a Dynamic text field (which you gave a variable name of **message**).*

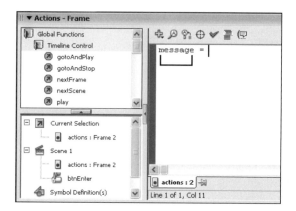

22. Click in the **Script** pane, and type **message =**. Remember, **message** is the variable name that you assigned to the Dynamic text field on **Frame 2**.

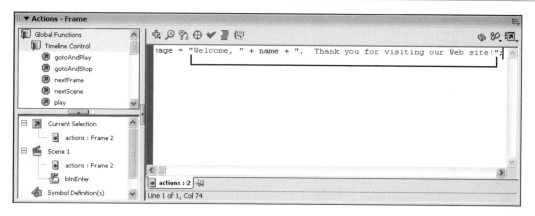

23. After **message =**, type "Welcome, " + name + ". Thank you for visiting our Web site!";.

NOTE | String Literal Versus Expression

In the text that you just entered, you'll notice how some are in quotes, and some (like **name**) are not. The bits of text in quotes are called **string literals**. If you want Flash MX 2004 to display some text, you put it in quotes. Anything that is not in quotes (in this case, **name**), Flash MX 2004 will treat as an **expression**. An expression, essentially, is a bit of ActionScript that represents a value. You don't *literally* want to put the text "name" in the Dynamic text field, you instead want Flash MX 2004 to go get the *value* of the **name** variable (which is whatever the visitor to your site enters in the Input text field) and insert it into a sentence. To combine string literals with expressions, use the + (addition operator).

*Lastly, to prevent the movie from initially playing, you need to add a **stop** action to the first keyframe.*

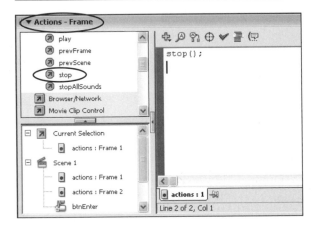

24. Select **Frame 1** in the **actions** layer, and open the **Actions** panel by pressing **F9**. Make sure the **Actions** panel reads **Actions – Frame**. In the **Actions** pane, choose **Global Functions > Timeline Control** and double-click **stop** to add it to the **Script** pane.

Congratulations! You're done! Now it's time to test your handiwork, so cross your fingers...;-)

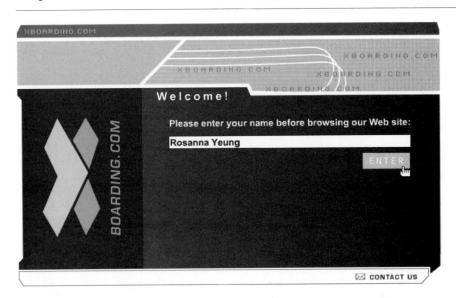

25. Choose **Control > Test Movie**. When the **Preview** window appears, type your name in the name field and click **Enter**.

You should now see a simple block of text that incorporates your name into it! Little does the visitor to your site realize the hard work you put into making that block of text seem so simple.

26. When you are finished, save and close this file.

*Troubleshooting tip: If you don't see your name in the Dynamic text field when you test the movie, go back to the project file and in the message layer, select the Dynamic text field in **Frame 2** and make sure the **Show Border Around Text** button is deselected; otherwise, you won't be able to see the white text. Also click **Frame 2** of the **actions** layer, and in the **Actions** panel, check the ActionScript to make sure you have correctly inserted the code for the frame action. Refer to Steps 22 and 23 for accuracy.*

You have successfully made it through the text chapter! Time to take a quick break and get amped up (pun intended) for the sound chapter next!

13.
Sound

| Importing Sounds | Compressing Sounds |
| Creating Background Sound | Controlling Sound |
| Compression Settings for Narration |
| Synchronizing Sound to Narration Cues |
| Controlling Animation and Sound | Creating a Simple Music Selector |

chap_13

Macromedia Flash MX 2004
H•O•T CD-ROM

In Flash MX 2004, sound can be used for many purposes—including narration, background soundtracks, rollover noises, and for sound effects that complement animation effects. You also have the ability to work with a variety of sound formats, including WAV files (Windows users), AIFF files (Mac users), and MP3 files (which work on both the Windows and Macintosh platforms). The advantage of MP3 files is that they allow the file size to be small while providing high sound quality.

This chapter will give you a solid understanding of how to work with sounds in Flash MX 2004, including how to import sounds and compress sound files. You will learn how to change the format of a sound using MP3 compression settings, how to create background sounds, and how to control sound using buttons. The last three exercises are also set up and designed to provide real work flow scenarios, where you will also learn how to synchronize voice sound clips with animation and how to dynamically load MP3's into your Flash MX 2004 movie.

Importing Sounds

In this exercise, you will learn how to import sound files into Flash MX 2004. The following steps will teach you which kinds of sounds can be imported into Flash MX 2004 and will show you where the sound files go when you import them.

1. Copy the **chap_13** folder, located on the **H•O•T CD-ROM**, to your hard drive. You need to have this folder on your hard drive in order to save files inside it.

2. Open a new file and save it as **basicSound.fla** inside the **chap_13** folder.

3. Choose **File > Import > Import to Library**. Navigate to the **sounds** folder (also inside the **chap_13** folder) and browse to the folder named **soundsPC** if you are using a Windows machine or **soundsMac** if you are using a Macintosh.

*Note: If you choose **File > Import > Import to Stage**, the sound files will not be imported to the Stage. They will be imported to the Library.*

TIP | I Don't See Any Files!

If you don't see any sounds in the list, make sure you select **Files of Type: All Files** in the **Import** dialog box rather than **Files of Type: All Formats**.

NOTE | What Kinds of Sounds Can I Import?

In Flash MX 2004, you can import a variety of sound files, depending on which platform you use and whether you have QuickTime 4 or later installed on your machine. If you have QuickTime 4 or later installed on your system, you can import additional sound file formats. The chart that follows lists the types of files you can import. You will learn about compressing sounds in the next exercise.

Sound File Types Supported by Flash MX 2004		
Sound File Format	**Windows**	**Mac**
WAV	Yes	Yes, with QuickTime 4 or later installed
AIFF	Yes, with QuickTime 4 or later installed	Yes
MP3	Yes	Yes
Sound Designer II	No	Yes, with QuickTime 4 or later installed
Sound Only QuickTime Movies	Yes, with QuickTime 4 or later installed	Yes, with QuickTime 4 or later installed
Sun AU	Yes, with QuickTime 4 or later installed	Yes, with QuickTime 4 or later installed
System 7 Sounds	No	Yes, with QuickTime 4 or later installed

---

4. To import the sound files from inside the **soundsPC/soundsMac** folder:

Windows users:
Ctrl+click the files to select **Free.wav, Lektropolis.wav,** and **Space_Jam.wav,** and click **Open** to import the sounds into Flash MX 2004.

Mac users:
Cmd+click the files named **Free.aif, Lektropolis.aif,** and **Space_Jam.aif,** and click **Import.** The sound files will be imported into Flash MX 2004.

TIP | Where Did the Sounds Go?

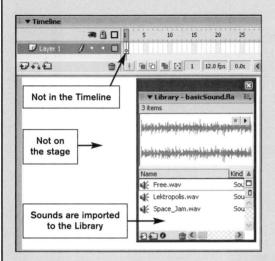

When you import an image, you will see the image on the Stage as soon as you click Import. When you import a sound, however, it is not visible on the Stage. Instead, you must open the Library to view the sound files. You will do this next.

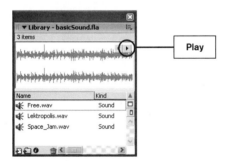

5. Open the **Library** (**Ctrl+L** [Windows] or **Cmd+L** [Mac]). You will see the three sounds you just imported. Select each sound, one at a time, and click the **Play** button to listen to each one.

That's all there is to it! Importing sounds is the simple part. Working with them in the Timeline can be a bit more challenging. By the end of this chapter, you will have experience working with sounds, the Timeline, and sound integration in Flash MX 2004.

6. Save this file and keep it open for the next exercise. You will learn how to compress sounds inside of Flash MX 2004 next.

2. ——————Compressing Sound

Now that you know how to import sounds into Flash MX 2004, the next step is to learn how to compress them. Compressing sounds is especially important to keep your file size down, because uncompressed sounds will increase your file size drastically. In this exercise, you will learn how to compress sound by using the Sound Properties dialog box and how to alter one of the sounds using the MP3 compression setting.

1. You should still have the **basicSound.fla** file open from the last exercise.

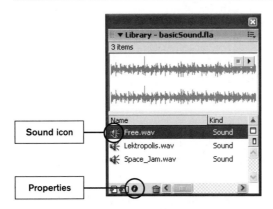

2. In the **Library**, click the **Free.wav** sound to select it. Click the **Properties** button, located at the bottom of the **Library** panel, to open the **Sound Properties** dialog box. You can also open the **Sound Properties** dialog box by double-clicking on a file's **sound** icon in the **Library**.

Note: *The sounds provided here were generously donated by Patrick Miko for use in your own projects. Visit **http://www.ultrashock.com** for access to even more sounds to use in your projects and **http://www.session12.com** to hear more of his work.*

NOTE | Sound Compression: Moviewide or Individual?

In Flash MX 2004, you have two general options for sound compression: You can set the moviewide compression settings in the Publish Settings dialog box, or you can set the compression settings for each sound file individually in the Library, which you will learn next. You will learn about the Publish settings in Chapter 16, "*Publishing and Exporting.*" Since all sounds are not alike, I recommend setting the compression settings individually to ensure the best fidelity and lowest file size for each sound.

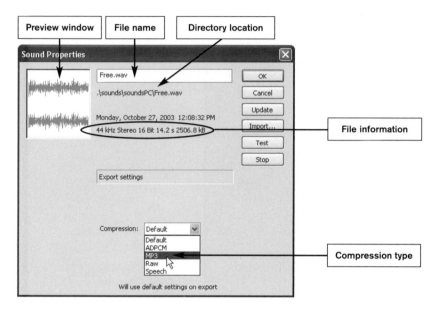

3. Notice that the sound is large at its default compression setting: **2506.8 kB**. Click to see the **Compression** drop-down menu. You'll see five settings: Default, ADPCM, MP3, Raw, and Speech. Choose **MP3**.

The MP3 compression setting offers the best compression rates and sound fidelity and can be heard by users with the Macromedia Flash 4 and later players.

Sound Compression Defined	
Option	**Description**
Default	This option uses the global compression settings in the Publish Settings dialog box. You will learn about the Publish settings in Chapter 16, "*Publishing and Exporting.*"
ADPCM	This compression model is the "old" method of compression from Macromedia Flash 3. It sets compression for 8-bit and 16-bit sound data. You may want to consider using this format if you need to author back to the Flash 3 Player.
MP3	This compression model can be heard by users with the Macromedia Flash 4 and later Players. It offers the best compression rates and sound fidelity.
Raw	This format will resample the file at the specified rate but will not perform any compression.
Speech	This option uses a compression method designed specifically for speech sound files. You will work with this compression type in Exercise 5 of this chapter.

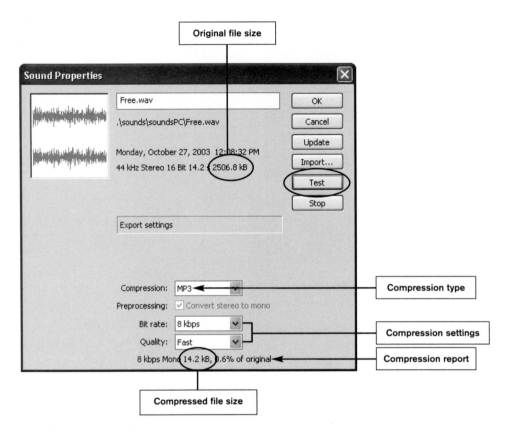

4. Choose **Bit Rate: 8 kbps**. Click the **Test** button to hear the sound with the new compression applied. Notice that the file size has drastically decreased from the original **2506.8 kB** to **14.2 kB** with the compression settings you applied.

Note: *The lower the bit rate, the lower the sound quality and the lower the file size. The higher the bit rate, the higher the sound quality and the larger the file size.*

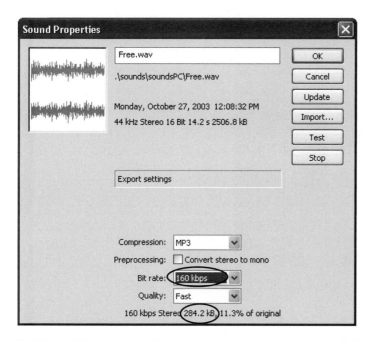

5. Choose **Bit Rate: 160 kbps** and uncheck the **Preprocessing: Convert stereo to mono** box. Click the **Test** button to hear the sound again. Notice how much better the sound quality is at 160 kbps. However, look at the file size: It has increased to **284.2 kB**. Although this is smaller than the original **2506.8 kB**, it is more than 20 times the size of the file at the 8 kbps bit rate.

Note: The Preprocessing option is available only for bit rates of 20 kbps or higher. This feature converts mixed stereo sounds to mono sound if selected.

---

6. Choose **Bit Rate: 24 kbps** and make sure the **Preprocessing: Convert stereo to mono** box is unchecked. Click the **Test** button to preview the sound. Notice that the sound quality is acceptable and the file size has dropped to **42.6 kB**.

When you are working with sound files in Flash MX 2004, you will want to test several bit-rate settings to determine which one offers the lowest file size without sacrificing sound quality.

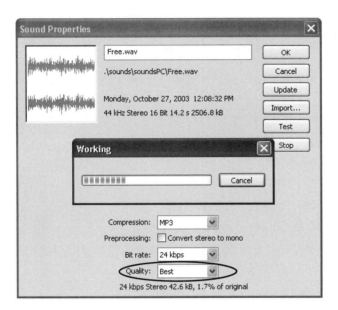

7. Choose **Quality: Best**. Click the **Test** button and notice that it takes a bit longer to convert the file to an MP3. The sound file will sound better, and the file size will be the same; the only trade-off is that it will take longer to convert the file inside Flash MX 2004. That's not a bad price to pay for better sound.

Note: The longer conversion time for the Best setting occurs inside the Flash MX 2004 project file, and since the file size is the same (between Best and Fast), you will not notice a difference in download time on a user's computer, although the Best sound will sound better.

8. When you are finished, click **OK** to accept the settings and close the **Sound Properties** dialog box.

To summarize, you will find that choosing the best compression settings is often a process of selecting and testing several different options before you settle on the best setting to meet your needs. I recommend using the MP3 compression setting whenever possible because of its superior compression capabilities. You have the best of both worlds using this compression method: small file size with good sound quality.

9. Save and close this file. You just learned how to import and compress sounds in Flash MX 2004. Next, you will apply these techniques in a more applicable exercise.

Note: Once you produce the SWF file, the sound in your Flash MX 2004 movie can be heard by users on both Windows and Mac machines, and it will not matter which format the sound was in when it was originally imported. This is because the sound is compressed as either ADPCM, MP3, Raw, or Speech when you create the SWF file, and these options are platform independent.

3.————————**Creating Background Sound with Sound Effects**

As you develop certain projects in Flash MX 2004, you may find that adding background sound will help the interface come to life. This exercise will show you how to add background sound, including how to use one of the sound effects in the Properties inspector. You will also be introduced to the **Edit Envelope** dialog box, which can be used to customize effects applied to the sound files.

1. Open the file named **bkgdSound.fla** from the **chap_13** folder. Choose **View > Magnification > Show All** to see the whole image on the **Stage**. Notice that it contains one layer with a background image.

2. Open the **Library** (**Ctrl+L** [Windows] or **Cmd+L** [Mac]). Notice that there are bitmaps, a graphic symbol, and some buttons but no sounds… yet.

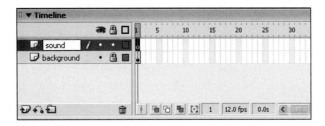

3. On the **Main Timeline**, click the **Insert Layer** button to add a new layer. Rename the layer **sound** and make sure it is above the **background** layer.

TIP | Why Am I Making a New Layer for the Sound?

Ideally, sound files, like frame actions, should be placed on their own separate layer. This will separate the sound from other artwork and animation, allowing you to view the waveform (the picture of the sound) better and to work with the sound more easily.

---

4. Choose **File > Import > Import to Library**. Inside the **sounds** folder (inside the **chap_13** folder), open the **mp3** folder and select the sound file named **Hype.mp3**. Click **Open** (Windows) or **Import** (Mac) to import the MP3 sound file.

MP3 sounds will work on both Macintosh and Windows machines, so no matter which platform you are using, this file will work for you.

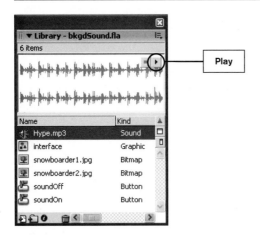

5. After you import the sound, notice that the sound is added to the **Library**. Click the **Play** button to test the sound. You will be adding this sound to the **Timeline** next.

> **NOTE** | **When Sound Exists**
>
> Although the sound file has been successfully imported into the Flash MX 2004 project file, it does not officially exist in the movie yet—it exists only in the Library. In order for the sound to be a part of the movie, you must add it to a keyframe in the Timeline.

6. With the first frame in the **sound** layer selected, drag the **Hype.mp3** sound out of the **Library** and drop it anywhere on the **Stage**. After you drop the sound, you will not see a representation of that sound anywhere on the **Stage**. However, the sound will appear in the **Timeline** in the form of a blue waveform. This is visual feedback to you that the sound is located there.

NOTE | Adding Sounds to Keyframes

Each sound file must be tied to a keyframe. The simplest way to do this is to drag a sound out of the Library and drop it onto the Stage at the point in your Timeline that you want it to start play-ing. Make sure that you have a keyframe at the point where you want your sound to begin, and that you have selected that keyframe. Otherwise, you will not be able to add the sound at all, or the sound will attach itself to the last keyframe prior to the location of the playhead at the time you drag and drop.

---

7. Choose **Control > Test Movie** to preview the movie with the new sound added. You will hear the sound play once and stop. When you are finished, close the **Preview** window.

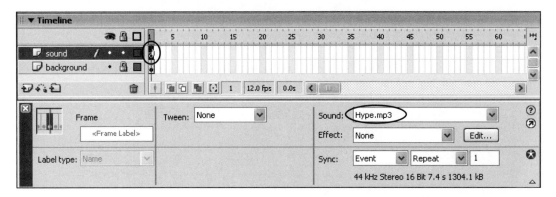

8. Click **Frame 1** in the **sound** layer to select the sound. Notice the settings in the **Properties inspector**, including the name of the sound displayed in the **Sound** drop-down menu. This section of the **Properties inspector** is where you control the behavior of the sound.

9. In the **Properties inspector**, notice that the **Sync** option is set to **Event**. This setting causes the sound to start playing when the **playhead** hits the frame that contains it. The sound will continue to play all the way to the end, independently of whatever is happening on the **Main Timeline**—even if the **Main Timeline** stops or is only one frame in length, as you tested in Step 7.

10. In the **Properties inspector**, choose **Sync: Stream**.

11. Choose **Control > Test Movie** to preview the movie with the **Stream** sound setting. You will not hear the sound at all. Why? Unlike the **Event** setting, the **Stream** setting stops the sound when the movie stops. So if you have only one frame in your movie, and you apply a **Stream** setting to a sound in the **Main Timeline**, the sound will not play. Stream sounds play only within the frames they occupy. Close the **Preview** window when you are done previewing your movie.

Stream sounds have many benefits. These will be discussed in the chart at the end of this exercise and again in Exercise 6, where you will synchronize Stream sounds to animation.

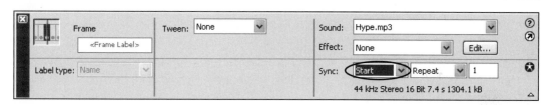

12. In the **Properties inspector** choose **Sync: Start**. This setting is most often used for background sounds. The **Start** setting is very similar to the **Event** setting: It causes the sound to begin playing as soon as the keyframe holding it is reached, and the sound will play to the end, independently of the **Main Timeline**, just as an **Event** sound will. The difference between the **Event** and **Start** settings is that if a **Start** sound is already playing, no new instance of the sound can be played. With the **Event** setting, if an instance of the sound is playing and another instance is triggered, the sounds will overlap.

If the previous description seems a little abstract, you might be wondering when you would use the Start sound setting. This setting is often used if you have a layer with a sound that is already playing, and you don't want the new sound to begin until the currently playing sound has stopped. The Start setting prevents the sound from overlapping itself. For a detailed explanation of all the sound settings available to you, see the "Modifying Sound Settings" section following this exercise.

13. Choose **Control > Test Movie** to preview the movie with the **Start** sound setting. The sound will play just as it would with the **Event** setting. When you are finished, close the **Preview** window. You will add basic sound effects in the following steps.

NOTE | Testing Sounds

All sounds can be tested using **Control > Test Movie**, since you are creating the SWF file when you use that method. You can also test sounds in the editing environment by pressing **Enter/Return**, but this method has its limitations, since certain conditions must be met in order for the sound to play. The list that follows defines when you can test sounds in the editing environment.

• When the Main Timeline has only one frame, no sound can be tested using Enter/Return.

• When the Main Timeline has more than one frame, you can test Event and Start sounds using Enter/Return, and they will play in their entirety (even if there are two frames in the Timeline, but the sound takes 100 frames to play). Event and Start sounds play independently of the Main Timeline. (You will see what Event, Start, and Stream sounds are as you follow the steps of the exercise.)

• When the Main Timeline has more than one frame, Stream sounds can be tested using Enter/Return. Use caution, however, because if the number of frames in the Timeline is fewer than the length of the sound, or if another keyframe is encountered before the sound finishes, the sound will stop (it will be cut short) when the Timeline stops or encounters another keyframe. Stream sounds are tied directly to the Main Timeline.

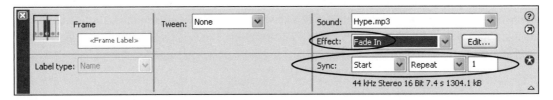

14. In the **Properties inspector**, choose **Effect: Fade In**. This will make the sound start out soft and gradually become louder. For the **Sync** setting, make sure **Start** is selected and choose **Repeat** and enter **1** for the number of times the sound will repeat.

---

15. Choose **Control > Test Movie** to preview the sound settings you applied. Notice that the sound fades in. Keep listening—the sound will repeat once and then stop. When the sound has stopped playing, close the **Preview** window.

16. In the **Properties inspector**, choose **Loop** instead of **Repeat**. This will make the sound play continuously throughout the movie. The **Start** setting will not affect the overall file size, since Flash MX 2004 downloads the file only once.

17. Choose **Control > Test Movie** to listen to the sound settings you applied. Notice that the sound fades in, and continues to play over and over again (**Loop**) for as long as you have the **Preview** window open. When you are done previewing the sound, close the **Preview** window.

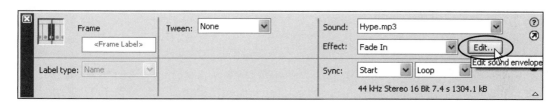

18. Click the **Edit** button in the **Properties inspector**. This opens the **Edit Envelope** dialog box.

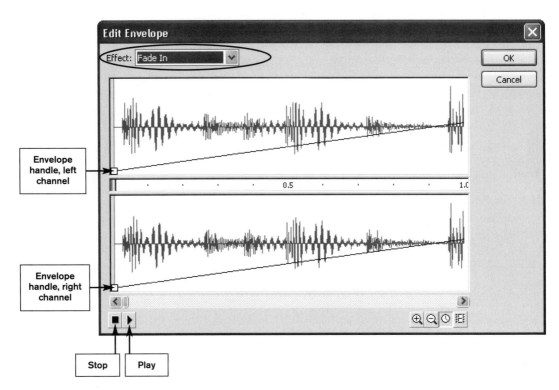

*When you click the **Edit** button in the **Properties inspector**'s Sound panel, Flash MX 2004 will open the **Edit Envelope** dialog box, where you can edit your sound. Notice that the **Effect** option shows **Fade In** selected. This effect was created when you chose it from the drop-down list in the **Sound** panel of the **Properties inspector**.*

19. In the **Edit Envelope** dialog box, click the **Play** button to test the sound. Notice that the sound starts out softly and gradually becomes louder. Click the **Stop** button. Experiment and move the right and left **Envelope** handles. This will change the way the sound fades into the right and left speakers. Click the **Play** button again to test it.

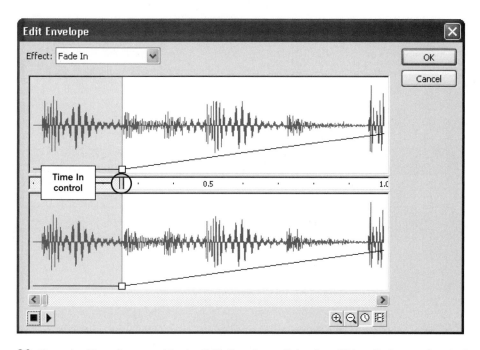

20. Drag the **Time In** control in the **Edit Envelope** dialog box. This will change the **start point** of the sound. Click the **Play** button again to test it. When you are happy with the way your adjustments sound, click **OK** in the **Edit Envelope** dialog box to accept the settings.

21. Choose **Control > Test Movie** to preview the movie again. You will hear the sound with your custom effects applied to it.

*Tip: If you don't like the custom effects you created, rather than clicking **OK** in the **Edit Envelope** dialog box, you can either click **Cancel** or you can choose an **Effect** option other than **Custom** in the **Properties inspector** to reset the sound to the effect you choose.*

22. Save this file and keep it open for the next exercise. You will learn how to control the sound with On and Off buttons in the next exercise.

Modifying Sound Settings

After you place an instance of a sound in the Timeline, you can use the settings in the Properties inspector to control the behavior of the sound, as you learned in this exercise. The following sections provide an in-depth look at the sound settings options.

Effect Option

The Effect option in the Properties inspector allows you to choose from a drop-down list of preset effects that you can apply to your sound. Choosing the Custom setting will allow you to create your own sound effects.

Effect Options Explained	
Option	**Description**
Left Channel	Plays only the left channel of a stereo sound.
Right Channel	Plays only the right channel of a stereo sound.
Fade Left to Right	Creates a panning effect by playing a stereo sound from the left channel to the right channel (or left speaker to right speaker).
Fade Right to Left	Creates a panning effect by playing a stereo sound from the right channel to the left channel (or right speaker to left speaker).
Fade In	Makes the sound gradually become louder as it begins to play.
Fade Out	Makes the sound gradually become softer as it nears the end.
Custom	Allows you to create your own effects for the sound.

Sync Option

The Sync option in the Properties inspector allows you to set the synchronization of the sound file in the movie. Each option controls the behavior of the sound in the Timeline. The following chart explains the various Sync options.

Sync Options Explained	
Option	**Description**
Event	Begins playing the sound when the playhead reaches the frame that holds the sound in the Timeline. Event sounds will continue to play independently, even if the Timeline stops. If a different instance of the same sound is started, the sounds will overlap. This option is good for button sound.
Start	Behaves similarly to an Event sound, except that a second instance of the sound cannot be started until any currently playing instances have finished. This prevents the sound from overlapping itself. This option is good for background sound.
Stop	Stops the indicated sound. You might use this feature, for example, if you have a sound in the Main Timeline that spans 50 frames and is set to Start. The sound will play in its entirely no matter what happens in the Main Timeline. If you need the sound to stop at Frame 30, you can add the same sound to a keyframe in Frame 30 and set that sound to Stop. This will stop the Start sound (or an Event sound) from playing.
Stream	Forces the movie to keep pace with the sound. If the movie cannot download its frames fast enough to keep pace, the Flash Player forces it to skip frames. Stream sounds stop when the Timeline stops or when another keyframe is encountered on the same layer. One advantage to Stream sounds is that they begin to play before the entire sound file is downloaded. This is not the case for Event and Start sounds. Stream sounds are great for narration and animation.

Repeat/Loop Option

The Repeat option in the Properties inspector sets the number of times that the sound will repeat. The Loop option sets the sound to play continuously. Repeating or Looping Event or Start sounds have no effect on file size. However, use caution when you have Sync: Stream selected because repeating or looping a Stream sound will cause Flash MX 2004 to add frames for each loop, thereby increasing the file size significantly.

Edit Button

When you click the Edit button in the Properties inspector, Flash MX 2004 will open the Edit Envelope dialog box, where you can edit your sound.

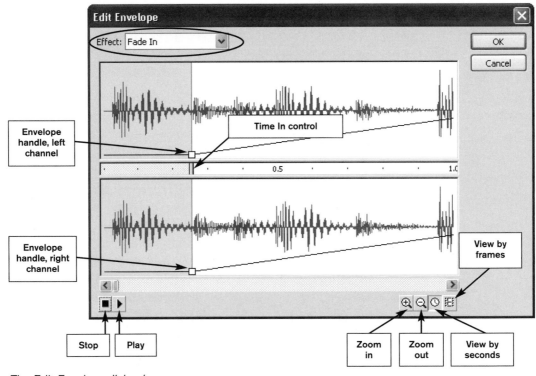

The Edit Envelope dialog box

Inside the Edit Envelope dialog box, you can change the effect of the sound, change the start and end points of a sound, modify the Envelope handles to change the volume of the sound, test the sound, view the sound using seconds or frames, and zoom in and out to see more or less of the sound wave.

4. ————————Controlling Sound with On/Off Buttons

Even though you might choose a sound that you love for the background sound of your movie, certain users may simply not want to listen to it. This exercise will teach you how to add sound controls to your movie so that others can stop and play the sound.

1. Open the **soundOnOff_Final.fla** file from the **chap_13** folder.

2. Choose **Control > Test Movie** to preview the movie. Click the **sound off** button to stop the sound. Click the **sound on** button to start it again. You will be creating this movie in the steps that follow. When you are finished, close this file.

3. You should still have the **bkgdSound.fla** file open from the last exercise. Save the file as **soundOnOff.fla** inside the **chap_13** folder.

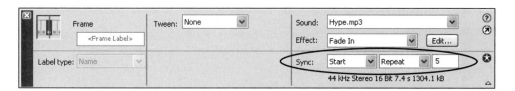

4. Select the **sound** in the **Timeline**. In the **Properties inspector**, make sure **Sync** is set to **Start**, choose **Repeat**, and type **5**. These settings will make the sound fade in, play independently of the Timeline, and repeat five times.

Tip: *If you want the sound to play continuously, looping over and over, select* **Loop** *instead of* **Repeat**.

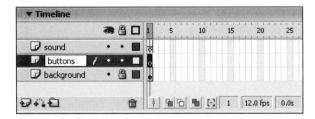

5. In the **Timeline**, click the **Insert Layer** button to add a new layer and rename it **buttons**. Make sure the **buttons** layer is below the **sounds** layer, as shown here.

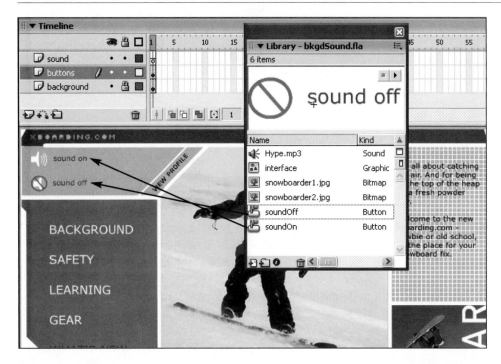

6. Open the **Library** and notice that there are two buttons inside: one named **soundOn** and one named **soundOff**. These are basic rollover buttons that have been created ahead of time for you. Select **Frame 1** of the **buttons** layer and drag an instance of each button onto the **Stage**, as shown here.

Now that you have added the buttons to the movie, you will add ActionScript and behaviors to the buttons that make the sound stop playing or begin playing.

7. Choose **Window > Development Panels > Behaviors** to open the **Behaviors** panel. Select the **sound off** button on the **Stage**, and in the **Behaviors** panel, click the **plus** sign and choose **Sound > Stop All Sounds**. The **Stop All Sounds** dialog box will appear next.

8. In the **Stop All Sounds** dialog box, click **OK** to accept that this behavior will stop all sounds from playing.

This behavior will stop any sounds that are currently playing in the Timeline.

9. Choose **Control > Test Movie** to test the **sound off** button. Notice that the sound stops playing after you click the **sound off** button. Nice!

10. Close the **Preview** window when you are finished previewing your movie.

*Now that you have the **sound off** button working, you will make the **sound on** button work. Since there is no **playAllSounds** behavior, getting the sound to play again is a little more tricky, but the following steps will get your **sound on** button working in no time!*

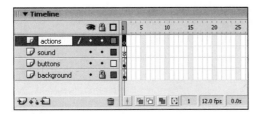

11. In the **Timeline**, add a new layer and name it **actions**. Make sure the **actions** layer is above all layers. You are going to add a **stop** action to the **Timeline**, but first you will add frames to the **Timeline**.

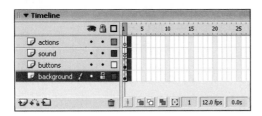

12. In the **Timeline**, click and drag down on **Frame 2** to select it on all the layers at once. Press **F5** to add a frame to each layer in the **Timeline**. You need to have a least two frames in the **Timeline** for this technique to work.

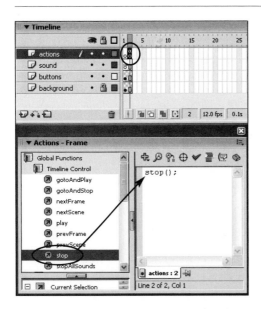

13. In the **Timeline**, select **Frame 2** of the **actions** layer and press **F7** to add a blank keyframe. In the **Actions** panel (**F9**), choose **Global Functions > Timeline Control** and double-click the **stop** action to add it to the **Script** pane. This action tells the **playhead** to stop when it hits **Frame 2**.

*Why add the **stop** action in the Timeline? Even though you have added ActionScript to stop all sounds, the Main Timeline is still going to loop by default. To prevent it from doing this, you added a **stop** action to Frame 2. Keep in mind that the sound file will not stop, since event and start sounds are independent of the Main Timeline. So even though you stop the Timeline at Frame 2, the sound will keep playing until you click the sound off button. You will add ActionScript to the Play button next.*

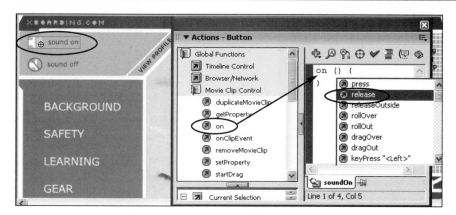

14. On the **stage**, click the **sound on** button to select it. In the **Actions** panel (**F9**), choose **Global Functions > Movie Clip Control** and double-click the **on** action to add it to the **Script** pane. In the **Code Hint** menu that appears, choose **release** for the mouse event.

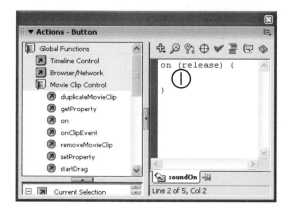

15. In the **Script** pane, place your cursor after the open curly brace and press **Enter/Return** to bring the cursor down to the second line.

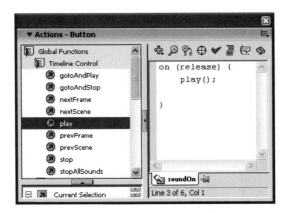

16. In the **Actions** pane, choose **Global Functions > Timeline Control** and double-click the **play** action to add it to the **Script** pane. This will tell the **playhead** to move to the next frame, which is **Frame 1**, and the sound will begin to play again from **Frame 1**.

*When the movie begins, the sound also starts playing because the sound starts on Frame 1. The playhead moves on to Frame 2 and encounters a **stop** frame action, which tells the playhead to stop. Since the Sync is set to Start, the sound will continue to play although the Timeline has stopped at Frame 2. When you click the sound off button, the sound will stop playing, and the playhead will continue to stay at Frame 2 until you click the sound on button. This is why you needed to add frames in Step 12. When you click the sound on button, the ActionScript instructs the playhead to play. The playhead will move on to the next frame, and in this case, since there are only two frames, the playhead will loop back to Frame 1 and play the sound again.*

17. Choose **Control > Test Movie** to preview the movie again. Click the **sound off** button and then click the **sound on** button. Notice how the sound immediately stops when you click the **sound off** button and starts over again when you click the **sound on** button. You have successfully added a background sound to your movie with Stop and Play controls!

18. Save and close this file.

5. ————————**Compression Settings for Narration**

Sound in Flash MX 2004 can also be controlled so that it synchronizes with animation, such as narration or a sound effect that is synchronized with a character's movement. This exercise will show you how to import and compress sounds using Speech compression and how to set the Stream Sync option so that voice sound files synchronize with animation. You will also learn how to modify the Timeline for easier editing.

1. Open the **soundSync_Final.fla** file inside the **chap_13** folder. This is a finished version of the file you will create in the next two exercises.

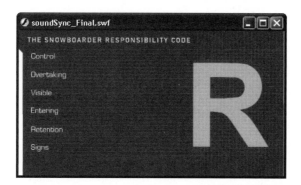

2. Choose **Control > Test Movie** to preview the movie. Notice that the narration voice is synchronized perfectly with the animation. You will create this same effect in the following steps. When you are finished previewing the movie, close this file.

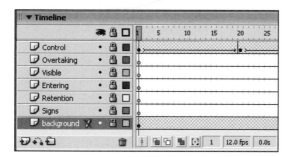

3. Open the **soundSync.fla** file from the **chap_13** folder. This file has been created to get you started. Notice the seven layers in the **Main Timeline**. The top six layers hold different parts of the animation, and the bottom layer holds a background image. Scrub the **playhead** back and forth to see the letters animate. In a few steps, you will be adding the voice sound clips to the **Timeline**, and you'll decide where each sound should begin.

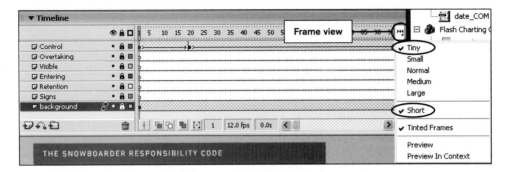

*Tip: Since there are a lot of frames in the Main Timeline, you can change the frame view temporarily by clicking on the **Frame View** pop-up menu and choosing **Tiny** and **Short**. This will allow you to see more frames at once on the Timeline.*

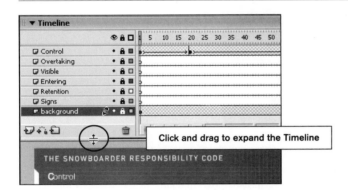

You can also expand the Timeline by clicking and dragging on the bottom of the Timeline so that you can view all the layers.

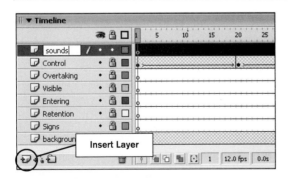

4. On the **Main Timeline**, click the **Insert Layer** button to add a new layer. Rename the layer **sounds**. Drag the **sounds** layer so that it is on top of all the other layers. You will import the sound files next.

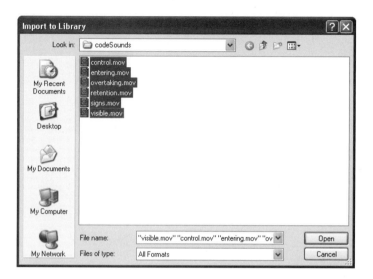

5. Choose **File > Import > Import to Library**. Open the **chap_13** folder. Inside the **sounds** folder, open the **codeSounds** folder. **Shift+click** to select all the sounds and click **Open** to import them.

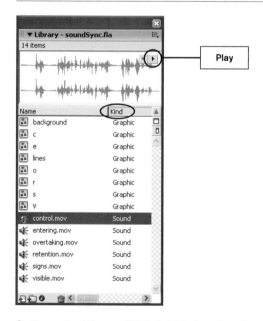

6. Open the **Library**, (**Ctrl+L** [Windows] or **Cmd+L** [Mac]). Click **Kind** to organize the **Library** assets by type instead of alphabetical order. Notice that the six sounds are now in the **Library**. Select the **control** sound and click the **Play** button to test it. Select the other sounds in the **Library** and click the **Play** button to test those as well. You will change the compression setting of the sounds next.

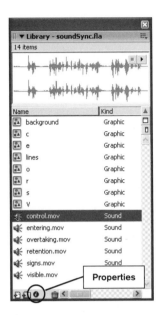

7. Select the **control** sound again and click the **Properties** button, located at the bottom of the **Library** panel, to open the **Sound Properties** dialog box.

*Tip: You can also double-click a file's **sound** icon to open the **Sound Properties** dialog box.*

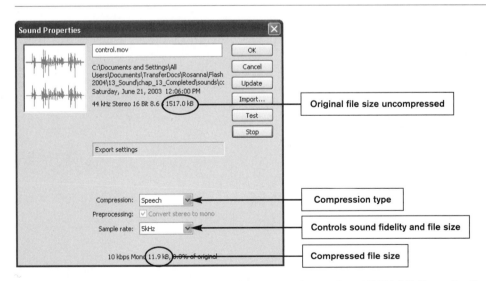

8. Notice that the sound is large at its default compression setting: **1517.0 kB**. From the **Compression** drop-down menu, choose **Speech**. From the **Sample rate** drop-down menu, choose **5kHz**. Click the **Test** button to test the sound. Notice that it does not sound acceptable.

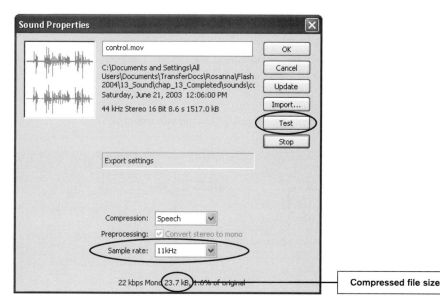

9. Choose **Sample rate: 11kHz** and click the **Test** button again. Notice that the sound is much better, and the file size has been reduced to only **23.7 kB**! Click **OK** to accept the settings.

Speech compression is specifically adapted to speech sounds. The sample rate controls sound fidelity and file size. The lower the sample rate is, the lower the file size and the lower the sound quality. However, 11 kHz is the recommended sample rate for speech.

10. In the **Library**, (**Ctrl+L** [Windows] or **Cmd+L** [Mac]), choose each of the remaining five sounds, one at a time, and change each sound's compression settings using the **Sound Properties** dialog box. For each sound, select **Compression: Speech** and **Sample rate: 11kHz**. Click **OK**.

Note: If you have multiple sounds in your project that will all have the same compression settings, you can set them globally all at once using Flash MX 2004's Publish settings, which you will learn about in Chapter 16, "Publishing and Exporting." A drawback to setting sounds globally is that you can't test (listen to) the different sound settings when you use Publish settings. For that reason, I showed you how to set them individually in this exercise.

11. Save this file and keep it open for the next exercise.

6. ———————————**Synchronizing Sound to Narration Cues**

In the previous exercise, you learned to compress sounds using the Speech compression setting. This exercise will show you how to use the **Stream** option and to work with the Main Timeline so that voice sound files synchronize with animation.

1. You should still have the **soundSync.fla** file open from the last exercise.

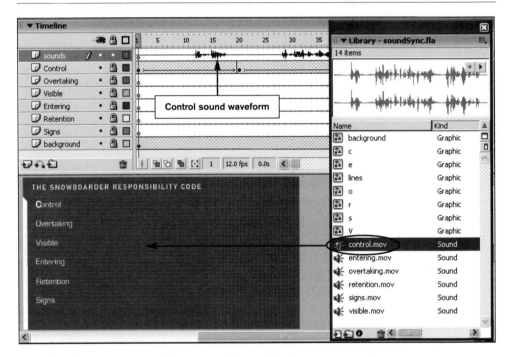

2. In the **Timeline**, select **Frame 1** in the **sounds** layer. From the **Library**, drag an instance of the **control** sound onto the **Stage**. Notice the waveform in the **Timeline**. You will adjust the height of the **sounds** layer to make it easier to work with next.

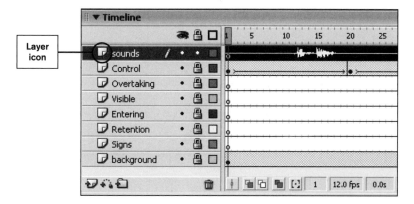

3. Double-click the **Layer** icon next to the **sounds** layer name. This will open the **Layer Properties** dialog box.

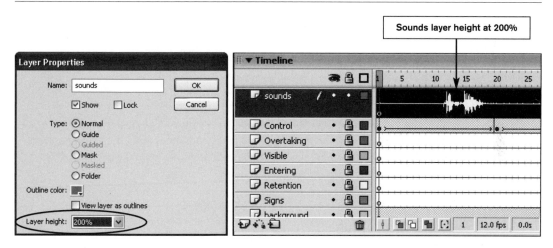

4. In the **Layer Properties** dialog box, choose **200%** from the **Layer height** drop-down menu, and click **OK**. This will make the **sounds** layer taller than all the rest of the layers in the **Timeline**. Increasing the layer height allows you to view the waveform more easily. Notice that you can see the waveform in more detail now.

Tip: *You can also access the* ***Layer Properties*** *dialog box by choosing* ***Modify > Timeline > Layer Properties.***

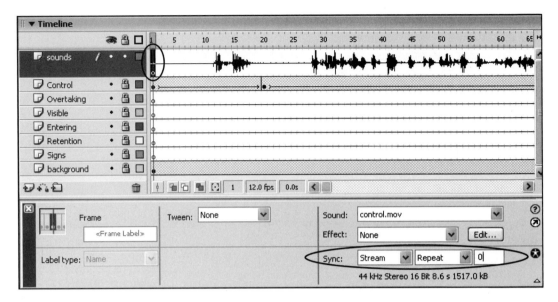

5. Click **Frame 1** of the **sounds** layer to select it. In the **Properties inspector**, select **Sync: Stream** and **Repeat: 0**. The **Stream** setting forces the movie to keep pace with the sound. If the movie cannot download its frames fast enough to keep pace, Flash MX 2004 forces it to skip frames.

6. Choose **Control > Test Movie** to test the sound and the animation. The sound will play in synchronization with the animation. You will add the remaining sounds to the **Timeline** in the following steps, but first you'll learn how to change the appearance of the **Timeline** to see more layers. Close the **Preview** window when you are finished previewing your movie.

TIP | Streaming and Looping

Be careful about setting your sound's Sync to Stream and adding loops. Unlike the Event and Start settings, Stream causes the file size to increase for each loop you specify. If you can avoid it, try not to loop sounds that are set to the Stream setting.

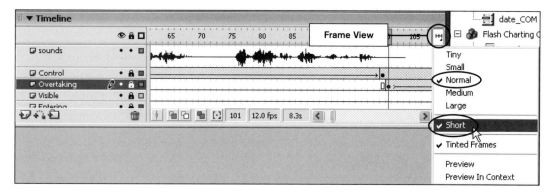

7. Click the **Frame View** pop-up menu on the right side of the **Timeline**, and choose **Normal** and **Short**. This will allow you to see more of the layers in the **Timeline**.

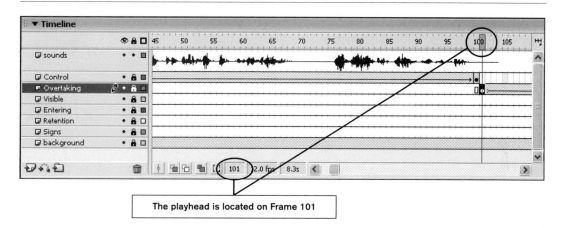

The playhead is located on Frame 101

8. Scrub the **playhead** back and forth to identify where the **O** animation begins on the **Overtaking** layer. Notice that this happens at about **Frame 101**. You want the **overtaking** sound clip to start where the **O** animation begins. You will do this next.

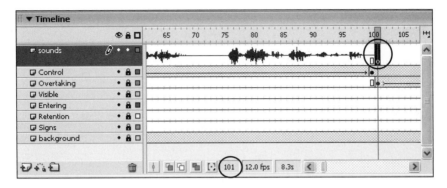

9. On the **sounds** layer, select **Frame 101** and press **F7** to add a blank keyframe. You will add the **overtaking** sound next.

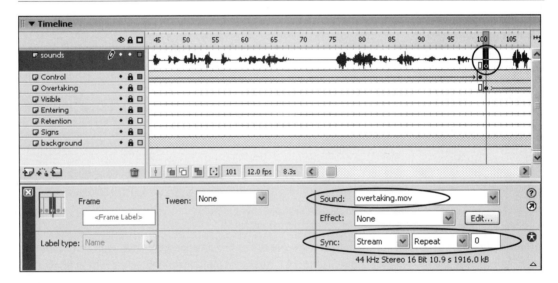

10. In the **Properties inspector**, choose **overtaking** from the **Sound** drop-down menu. This will add the **overtaking** sound to **Frame 101**. For **Sync**, choose **Stream**, **Repeat**, and **0**.

Flash MX 2004 automatically allows you to access all the sounds inside the movie's Library from the Sound drop-down list in the Properties inspector. This way, you can access all the sounds in your Library quickly and can even switch the sound located in a keyframe by selecting a different sound from the drop-down list.

NOTE | Adding Sound to the Timeline

In this chapter, you have learned two ways to add sounds to the Timeline. You can drag an instance of the sound onto the Stage, or you can select the frame in the Timeline and then choose a sound from the drop-down Sound list. Both workflow methods yield the same result—you can decide which is best for you!

---

11. Repeat Steps 8 and 9 to add blank keyframes on the **sounds** layer where each new letter animation begins.

*Hint: Each animation is 100 frames long, so place a blank keyframe at the beginning of each new animation: **Frames 201, 301, 401,** and **501.***

---

12. Repeat Step 10 for each of the blank keyframes you just added to attach the appropriate sound.

*Hint: Frame 201 (**visible** sound), Frame 301 (**entering** sound), Frame 401 (**retention** sound), and Frame 501 (**signs** sound).*

---

13. Test the movie again. Notice that some of the sounds are cut short when a new animation begins. Why? This is because some sound files are longer than others. As you can hear, **Stream** sounds will stop as soon as another keyframe or blank keyframe is encountered in the same layer. Close the **Preview** window when you are finished previewing your movie.

In the following steps, you will fix the sound files so they don't get cut short. Now here's where real workflow issues come in to play. Depending on how you plan out your project, you can either lay out the animation in the Timeline first (as this file has been prepared), or you can lay out the sound in the Timeline first. Either way, you will still have to figure out just where the animations should start and end according to the sounds. So, from this point forward, not only will you become more acquainted with sounds and their settings, but you will be much more comfortable and confident at moving frames around in the Timeline.

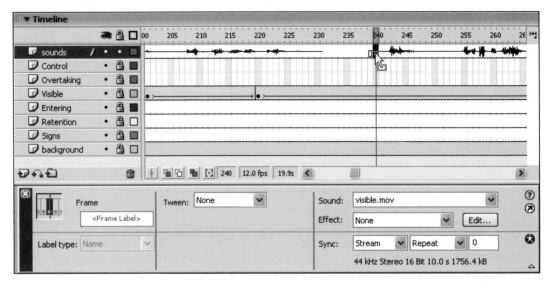

14. In the **Timeline**, on the **sounds** layer, click and drag **Frame 201** (with the **visible** sound) to the right to **Frame 240**. Notice that as you do, the sound wave in the previous frame (the **overtaking** sound) continues until **Frame 231**. This means that the **overtaking** sound is not 100 frames long, as the animation is. Instead, it is 131 frames long. Therefore, in order for the animation and the sound file to span the same duration, you need to make them match. You will do this next by moving the frames in the **Timeline**.

Note: As you learned in Exercise 3, Stream sounds play only within the frames they occupy. So, in order to hear the sound in its entirety, you will extend the Timeline for each sound.

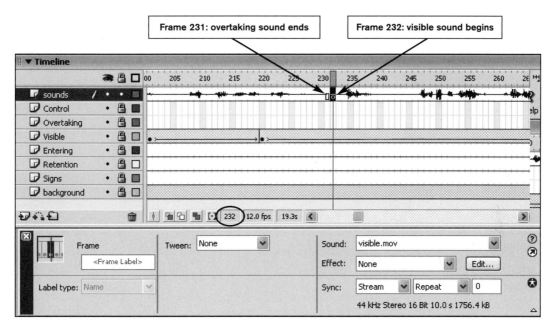

Frame 231: overtaking sound ends

Frame 232: visible sound begins

15. Click and drag **Frame 240** back to **Frame 232**, just after the **overtaking** sound wave ends in the **Timeline**. This will start the next sound (**visible**) after the **overtaking** sound ends, without cutting it off. You will move the frames in the **overtaking** layer so the animation and sound are in sync next.

Note: As soon as the playhead encounters another Stream sound in the Timeline, the previous Stream sound will stop, and the new Stream sound will play.

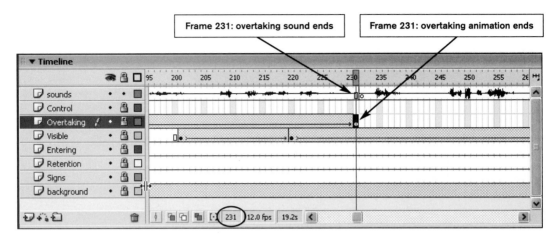

Frame 231: overtaking sound ends

Frame 231: overtaking animation ends

16. Click and drag the last keyframe in the **Overtaking** layer to **Frame 231**. This will make the overtaking animation and the sound narration end together. You will synchronize the **visible** animation to the **visible** sound in the following steps

Note: Even though you can move the frames in the Overtaking layer while it is locked, you cannot move the artwork on the Stage.

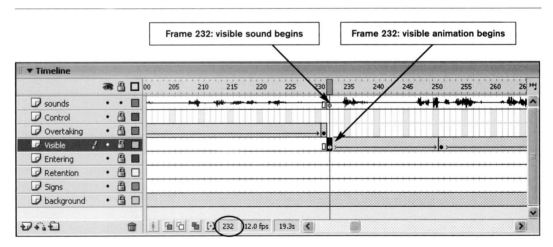

Frame 232: visible sound begins

Frame 232: visible animation begins

17. Notice that the **visible** sound begins on **Frame 232**. Click the **Visible** layer to select all the frames on that layer. Click and drag all the frames to the right at once, so that the tween now begins on **Frame 232**, at the same point that the **visible** sound begins, as shown here. You will move the last keyframe in the **Visible** layer so that the animation and sound end together next.

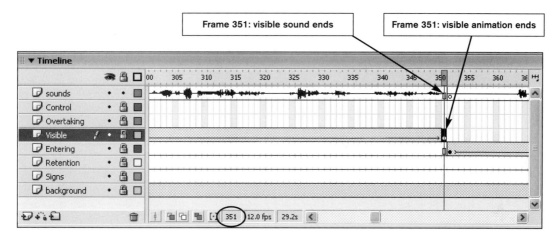

18. Notice that the **visible** sound ends on **Frame 351**. Click the last keyframe in the **Visible** layer and drag it to **Frame 351**, at the same point that the **visible** sound ends, as shown here. This will make the visible animation and **visible** sound end together. You will synchronize the **entering** animation to the **entering** sound in the following steps.

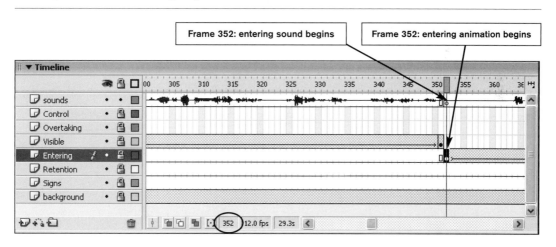

19. Notice that the **entering** sound begins on **Frame 352**. Click the **Entering** layer to select all the frames on that layer. Click and drag all the frames to the right at once, so that the tween now begins on **Frame 352**, at the same point that the **entering** sound begins, as shown here. You will move the last keyframe in the **Entering** layer so that the animation and sound end together next.

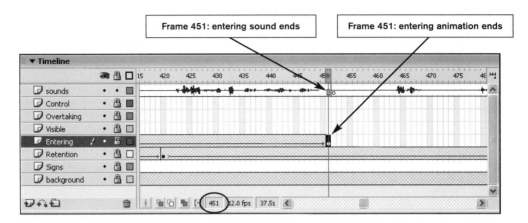

Frame 451: entering sound ends

Frame 451: entering animation ends

20. Notice that the **entering** sound ends on **Frame 451**. Click the last keyframe in the **Entering** layer and drag it to **Frame 451**, at the same point that the **entering** sound ends, as shown here. This will make the **entering** animation and **entering** sound end together. You will synchronize the **retention** animation to the **retention** sound in the following steps, but first you'll test your movie.

21. Choose **Control > Test Movie**. Notice that the sounds and the animations to the first few letters are now harmonized, and the sounds are not cut short! You will complete the rest of the movie in the following steps.

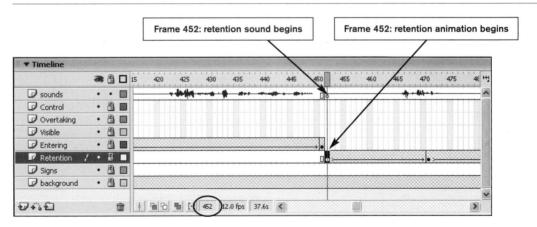

Frame 452: retention sound begins

Frame 452: retention animation begins

22. Notice that the **retention** sound begins on **Frame 452**. Click the **Retention** layer to select all the frames on that layer. Click and drag all the frames to the right at once, so that the tween now begins on **Frame 452**, at the same point that the **retention** sound begins, as shown here. You will move the last keyframe in the **Retention** layer so that the animation and sound end together next.

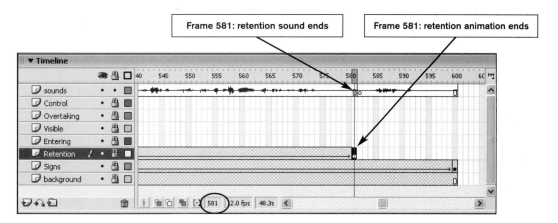

Frame 581: retention sound ends

Frame 581: retention animation ends

23. Notice that the **retention** sound ends on **Frame 581**. Click the last keyframe in the **Retention** layer and drag it to **Frame 581**, at the same point that the **retention** sound ends, as shown here. This will make the **retention** animation and **retention** sound end together. You will synchronize the **signs** animation to the **signs** sound in the following steps.

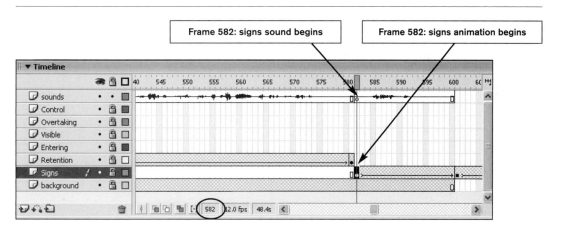

Frame 582: signs sound begins

Frame 582: signs animation begins

24. Notice that the **signs** sound begins on **Frame 582**. Click the **Signs** layer to select all the frames on that layer. Click and drag all the frames to the right at once, so that the tween now begins on **Frame 582**, at the same point that the **signs** sound begins, as shown here. You will move the last keyframe in the **Signs** layer so that the animation and sound end together next.

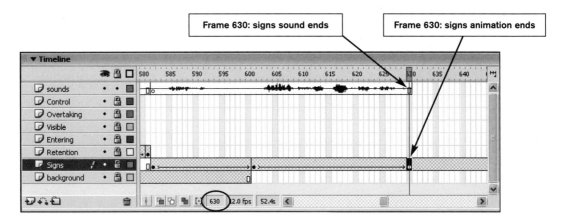

Frame 630: signs sound ends

Frame 630: signs animation ends

25. Notice that the **signs** sound ends on **Frame 630**. Click the last keyframe in the **Signs** layer and drag it to **Frame 630**, at the same point that the **signs** sound ends, as shown here. This will make the **signs** animation and **signs** sound end together. You will clean up the **Timeline** next. When you are done, you will have a movie with perfectly synchronized narration and animation!

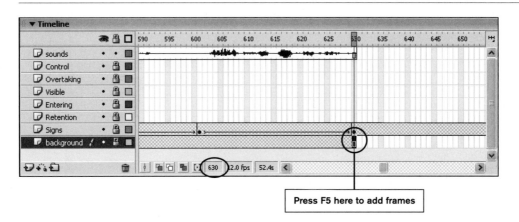

Press F5 here to add frames

26. In the **Timeline**, select **Frame 630** on the **background** layer and press **F5** to add frames. This will make the **background** layer visible throughout the entire movie. You will delete the extra frames in the **Signs** layer next.

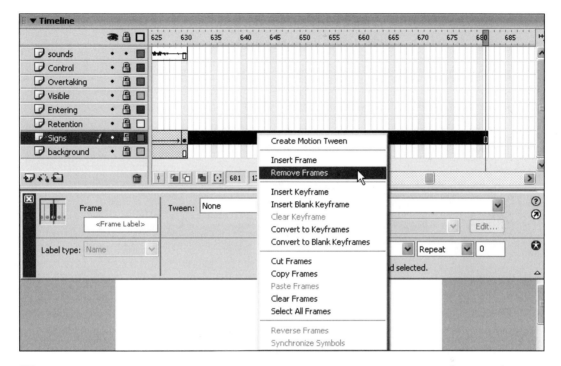

27. In the **Signs** layer, select any remaining frames after **Frame 630** and **right-click** (Windows) or **Ctrl+click** (Mac) and choose **Remove Frames** from the contextual menu.

Note: You can also choose **Edit > Timeline > Remove Frames** or press **Shift+F5** to remove frames.

28. Choose **Control > Test Movie** again to preview the animations and sounds all synced together!

29. When you are finished, save this file and keep it open for one more exercise.

Controlling Animation and Sound
with Stop and Play Buttons

In the previous exercise, you learned how to sync the sound with the animation. This exercise, will take the project file one step further. You will add Stop and Play buttons from the Common Libraries that ship with Flash MX 2004, and make the animation and the sound stop at the same time.

1. You should still have the **soundSync.fla** file open from the last exercise. Choose **File > Save As** to rename the file as **SoundAnimCtrl.fla** to the **chap_13** folder.

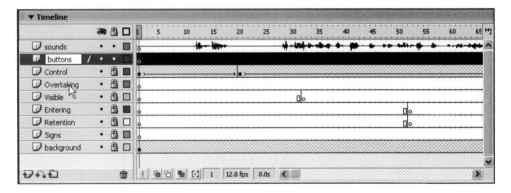

2. In the **Main Timeline**, click the **Insert Layer** button to add a new layer. Rename the new layer **buttons** and place it below the **sounds** layer, as shown here. You will add **Stop** and **Play** buttons to the **Stage** from the **Common Libraries** in the following steps.

3. Choose **Window > Other Panels > Common Libraries > Buttons** to open the buttons library that ships with Flash MX 2004. Double-click the **Playback** folder to expand and view the buttons in this folder.

Note: In the Common Libraries that ship with Flash MX 2004, you will find premade Buttons, Classes, and Learning Interactions that you can quickly add to your Flash movies.

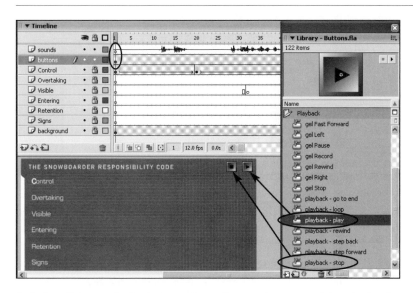

4. Select **Frame 1** in the **buttons** layer. Drag an instance of the **playback – stop** and **playback – play** buttons from the **Buttons Library** to the **Stage**, as shown here.

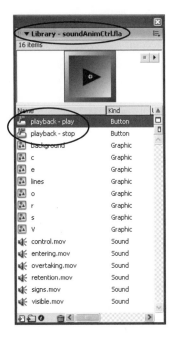

5. Open the **Library** (**Ctrl+L** [Windows] or **Cmd+L** [Mac]) and notice the two buttons you just added from the **Buttons Library** are now in the **Library** of your project file. You will add the ActionScript to the **Stop** button on the **Stage** next.

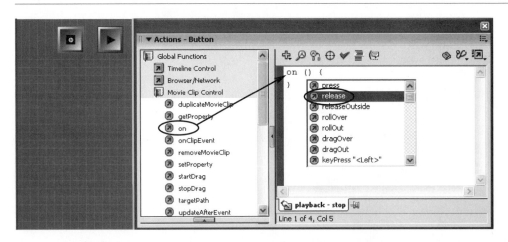

6. On the **Stage**, click the **Stop** button instance to select it. In the **Actions** panel (**F9**), choose **Global Functions > Movie Clip Control** and then double-click the **on** action to add it to the **Script** pane. From the **Code Hint** menu that appears, choose **release** for the mouse event.

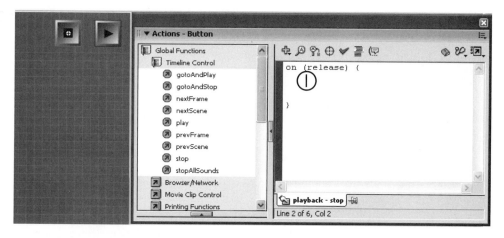

7. In the **Script** pane, place your cursor after the open curly brace and press **Enter/Return** to bring the cursor down to the second line.

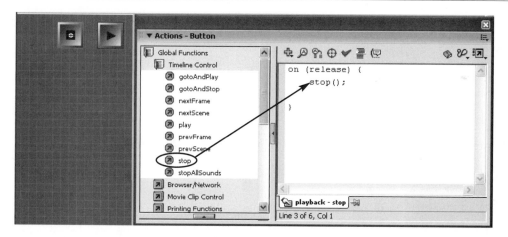

8. In the **Actions** pane, choose **Global Functions** > **Timeline Control** and double-click the **stop** action to add it to the **Script** pane. This tells the **playhead** to stop when the user clicks the **Stop** button.

9. Choose **Control** > **Test Movie** to test the **Stop** button. Notice that when you click the **Stop** button, the sound and the animation stop at the same time. Cool! You will add the ActionScript to the **Play** button next. Close the **Preview** window when you are finished previewing your movie.

10. With the **Stop** button still selected on the **Stage**, select the ActionScript for the **Stop** button in the **Script** pane and **right-click** (Windows) or **Ctrl+click** (Mac) and choose **Copy** from the contextual drop-down menu.

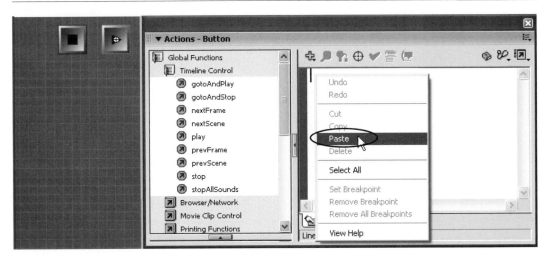

11. Select the **Play** button on the **Stage** In the **Actions** panel, **right-click** (Windows) or **Ctrl+click** (Mac) and choose **Paste** from the contextual drop-down menu.

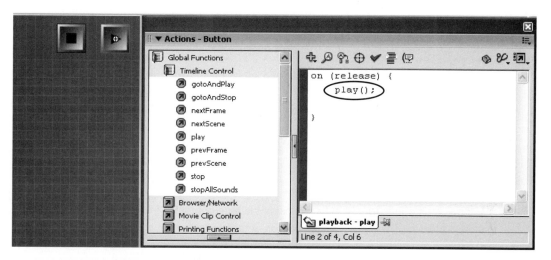

12. In the **Script** pane, change **stop** to **play**, as shown here.

13. Choose **Control > Test Movie** to test the movie again. Click the **Stop** button and notice that the sound and animation stop at the same time. Click the **Play** button and notice that the sound and animation begin playing at the same time and pick up where they last ended.

*The ActionScript you added to the buttons in this exercise instructs the playhead to either stop or play, and since the sound **Sync** is set to **Stream**, the sounds will stop any time the playhead stops. Stream sounds are dependent on the Timeline.*

14. When you are finished, save and close this file.

8. _____ Creating a Simple Music Selector

Now that you know how to add sound to your Flash MX 2004 movies and how to stop and play them, you will expand your Flash MX 2004 skills further and learn how to dynamically load MP3 files into your movies through ActionScript. This exercise is a bit similar to the Dynamic Text and CSS exercise you completed in Chapter 12, "*Working with Text*." However, in this exercise, you will be dynamically loading sound. The **loadSound** ActionScript allows you to include sound in your Flash movies without having to actually place them in the Timeline. This is an easy, yet powerful, technique to make your Flash movies more engaging. In addition, you will gain experience with preplanning and laying out the Timeline, as you would in a real workflow.

1. Open **musicSelector_Final.fla** file inside the **MusicSelector** folder (also inside the **chap_13** folder). This is the finished version of the movie you are going to create.

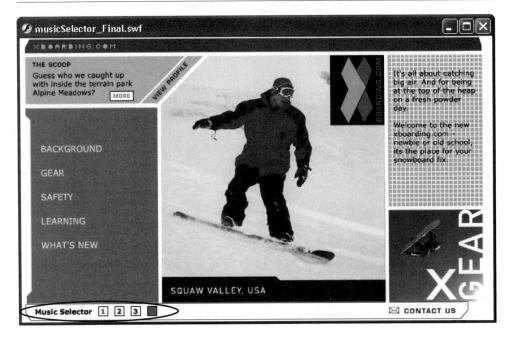

2. Choose **Control > Test Movie** to preview the movie. Notice the **Music Selector** at the bottom of the interface. Click the buttons to hear the background sounds. Notice that when you click another button, the new sound plays and the previous sound stops playing. To stop the sounds from playing, click the red **Stop** button. When you are finished, close the **Preview** window and the file.

3. Open the file **musicSelector.fla** inside the **MusicSelector** folder, also inside the **chap_13** folder. Notice that it contains one layer with a background image. Open the **Library** (**Ctrl+L** [Windows] or **Cmd+L** [Mac]), and expand the folders to view their contents. The **background** folder contains all the assets needed to create the **background** layer. The **music selector** folder contains all the assets needed to create artwork for the **Music Selector**, which you will do in the following steps. But where are the sounds? You will find out next.

4. Hide Flash MX 2004 for a moment and browse to the **music** folder inside the **MusicSelector** folder (also inside the **chap_13** folder). Notice the three MP3 files. Double-click each one to hear the music. You will dynamically load each of these MP3 files into your movie, but first you will continue to set up your **Timeline** in the steps that follow. Return to the project file.

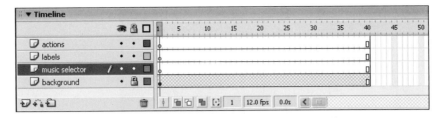

5. Back in the project file, in the **Timeline**, click the **Insert Layer** button to add three more layers to the **Timeline**. Rename these layers **actions**, **labels**, and **music selector**, as shown here. You will add the ActionScript that will make the movie begin in a stopped position next.

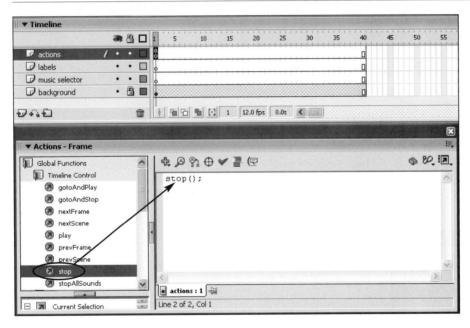

6. In the **Timeline**, select **Frame 1** in the **actions** layer. Open the **Actions** panel (**F9**), choose **Global Functions > Timeline Control**, and double-click the **stop** action to add it to the **Script** pane, as shown here. This will ensure that the movie begins in a stopped position since the first frame the **playhead** encounters is a **stop** frame action.

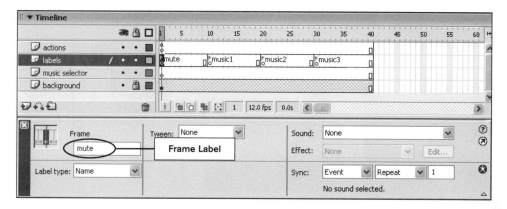

7. In the **labels** layer, press **F7** to add blank keyframes to Frames **10**, **20**, and **30**. In the **Properties inspector**, add the **Frame Labels mute**, **music1**, **music2**, and **music3** to **Frames 1, 10, 20,** and **30,** as shown here. You will add the artwork to the **music selector** layer in the following steps.

Note: The frames in the Timeline are spread apart so that you can see the names for the frame labels.

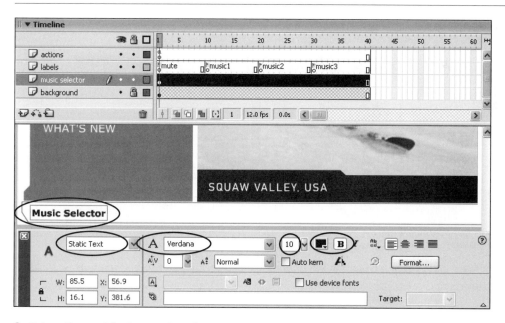

8. Select **Frame 1** in the **music selector** layer. From the **Toolbar**, select the **Text** tool and type **Music Selector** on the **Stage**, as shown here. In the **Properties inspector**, make sure the text is set to **Static Text**, the **Font Type** is set to **Verdana**, and the **Font Color** is set to **Black** with a **Point Size** of **10** and **bold**.

9. Make sure **Frame1** of the **music selector** layer is still selected. From the **Library**, drag an instance of each button—**music1**, **music2**, **music3**, and **stopMusic**—next to the **Music Selector** text, as shown here. In the following steps, you will add the ActionScript to the buttons that will load the MP3s when the user clicks on any of the buttons.

*Tip: Use the **Align** panel or use **Ctrl+K** (Windows) or **Cmd+K** (Mac) to align the buttons.*

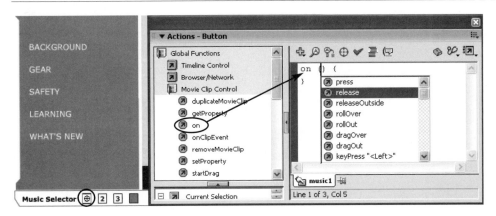

10. Select the **1** button on the **Stage**. In the **Actions** panel (**F9**), choose **Global Functions > Movie Clip Control** and double-click the **on** action to add it to the **Script** pane. Choose **release** from the **Code Hint** menu for the mouse event.

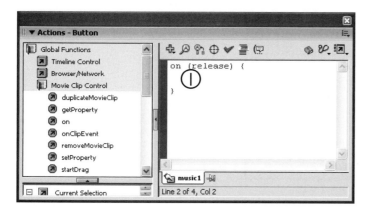

11. In the **Script** pane, place your cursor after the open curly brace and press **Enter/Return** to bring the cursor down to the second line.

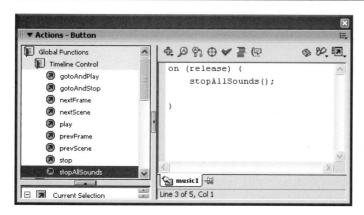

12. In the **Actions** panel, choose **Global Functions > Timeline Control** and double-click **stopAllSounds** to add it to the **Script** pane. This ActionScript will stop any sounds from playing. You will create a new sound object next.

Note: In Exercise 4 of this chapter, you learned how to stop all sounds from playing with the behavior **stopAllSounds***. As you can see, you can also execute the same command in the ActionScript panel. Rather than toggle back and forth between the Behaviors panel and the ActionScript panel, you will work in the ActionScript panel for a fluid workflow.*

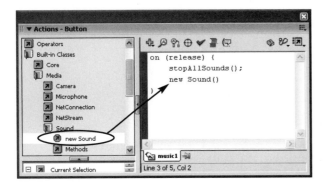

13. In the **Actions** panel, choose **Built-in Classes > Media > Sound** and double-click **new Sound** to add it to the **Script** pane, as shown here. You will name your new sound object next.

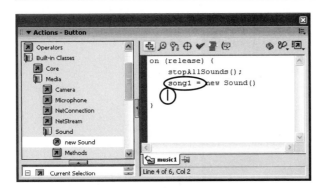

14. In the **Script** pane, before **new Sound ()**, type **song1 =**, then bring the cursor to the next line, as shown here. You will add the **loadSound** action next.

15. In the **Actions** panel, choose **Built-in Classes > Media > Sound > Methods** and double-click the **loadSound** action to add it to the **Script** pane.

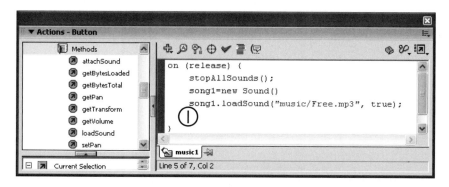

16. In the **Script** pane, change **instanceName** to **song1** and between the parentheses after **loadSound**, type **"music/Free.mp3", true**. After the closing parenthesis type a semicolon (;) and bring the cursor to the next line. Your **Script** pane should match the one shown here. You will add one more line of ActionScript.

Note: What does `"music/Free.mp3", true` mean? This entry defines the name and location of the MP3 file you want to load into your movie. As you discovered in Step 4, the MP3 files are located in the **music** directory. The **true** parameter sets whether the sound should behave as an event sound or a streaming sound. By setting it to **true** (Streaming), the sound will begin to play. If you set it to `false` (Event), the entire file must be downloaded before it will play.

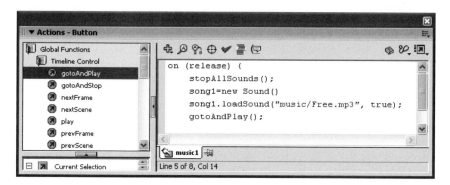

17. In the **Actions** panel, choose **Global Functions > Timeline Control** and double-click the **gotoAndPlay** action to add it to the **Script** pane.

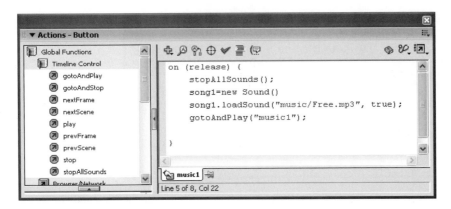

18. Between the parentheses after **gotoAndPlay**, type **"music1"**. This will tell the **playhead** to go to and play to the frame label named **music1**. You are done adding the ActionScript. What about the other buttons? You will copy and paste the code into the remaining buttons in the steps that follow.

Here's an explanation of each line:

```
on (release) {
```

```
// This instructs all sounds to stop playing when the user releases the mouse
stopAllSounds();
```

```
// This creates a new sound object
song1 = new Sound()
```

```
// This defines the location of the MP3 file, sets it to Stream, and loads into the sound object
song1.loadSound("music/Free.mp3", true);
```

```
// This instructs the playhead to go to and play the frame label named "music1" where the artwork and
behavior of the button has changed to give the user a visual indicator of which button was selected.
gotoAndPlay("music1");
}
```

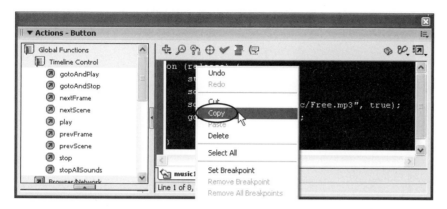

19. Select the ActionScript in the **Script** pane. **Right-click** (Windows) or **Cmd+click** (Mac) and choose **Copy** from the contextual drop-down menu. You will paste the ActionScript into the **2** button on the **Stage** next.

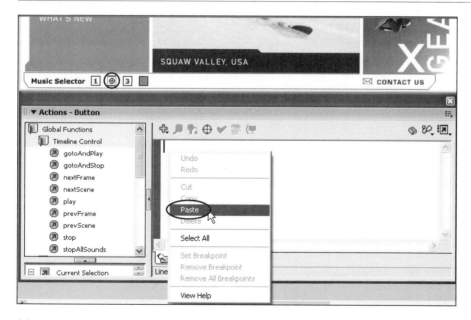

20. On the **Stage**, select the **2** button. In the **Script** pane of the **Actions** panel, **right-click** (Windows) or **Ctrl+click** (Mac) and choose **Paste** from the contextual drop-down menu. You will change the code to reflect the **2** button next.

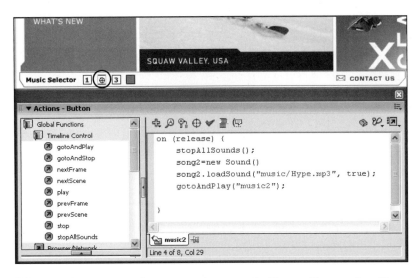

21. In the **Script** pane, change **song1** to **song2**. Change **Free.mp3** to **Hype.mp3**. Lastly, change **music1** to **music2**. Your changes should reflect the **Script** pane shown here. You will add the ActionScript to the last two buttons next.

22. Repeat Steps 19 and 20 to copy and paste the ActionScript to the **3** button and the **Stop** button.

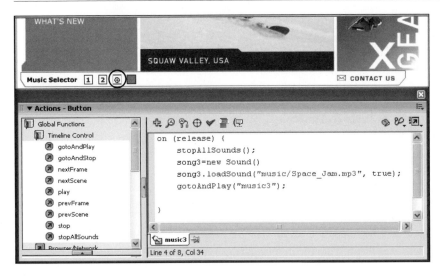

23. Select the **3** button on the **Stage**. In the **Script** pane, change **song2** to **song3**. Change **Hype.mp3** to **Space_Jam.mp3**. Lastly, change **music2** to **music3**. Your changes should reflect the **Script** pane shown here. You will modify the ActionScript in the **Stop** button next.

24. Select the **Stop** button on the **Stage**. In the **Script** pane, delete the code on the third and fourth lines. Change **gotoAndPlay** to **gotoAndStop** and change **music3** to **mute**. This will make the play-head go to and stop at the frame label named **mute**. Your changes should reflect the **Script** pane shown here.

25. In the Timeline, on the **music selector** layer, press **F6** on **Frames 10**, **20**, and **30** to add keyframes. By adding keyframes, you are copying the artwork as well as the ActionScript to Frames 10, 20, and 30. It's time to test your movie.

26. Choose **Control > Test Movie** to preview the music selector. Click each of the buttons and notice that the sound changes each time you click a different button and that the sound stops when you click the **Stop** button. But how do you know which button you've just clicked? You will change the appearance of the button so the user has a visual indication of which one they selected in the following steps. Close the Preview window when you are finished previewing your movie.

Note: *If you listen to each song long enough, you may notice that it doesn't continue to loop. You will fix this later in the exercise, too.*

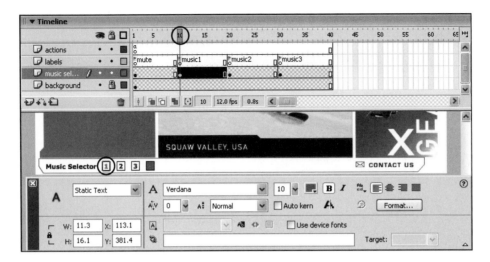

27. In the **Timeline**, move the **playhead** to **Frame 10**. Select the **1** button on the **Stage** and press **Ctrl+B** (Windows) or **Cmd+B** (Mac) to break it apart so that it is no longer a button. In the **Properties inspector**, change the color of the number **1** from **black** to **red**. This will give the user a visual indicator of the button they just clicked.

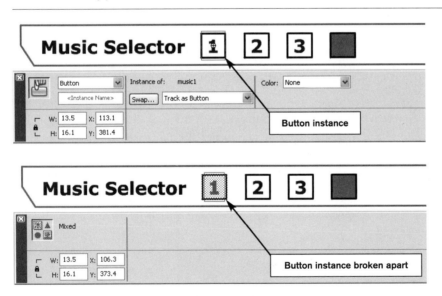

When you select the button instance on the Stage, you will see blue bounding box. After breaking it apart, you will see the dotted mesh, indicating that it is no longer a symbol. Now you can change the color of the number without affecting the symbol in the Library, because it is no longer a button symbol.

28. Repeat Step 27 for button **2**, making sure the **playhead** is on **Frame 20**; repeat Step 27 again for button **3**, making sure the **playhead** is on **Frame 30**.

In the following steps, you will add ActionScript to the Timeline so that the sound continues to loop.

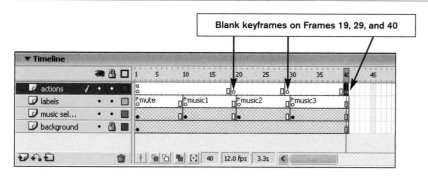

Blank keyframes on Frames 19, 29, and 40

29. In the **actions** layer of the **Timeline**, press **F7** to add a blank keyframe to Frames **19**, **29**, and **40**, as shown here. You will add ActionScript to each of these frames to tell Flash MX 2004 to start playing the current song again when it ends.

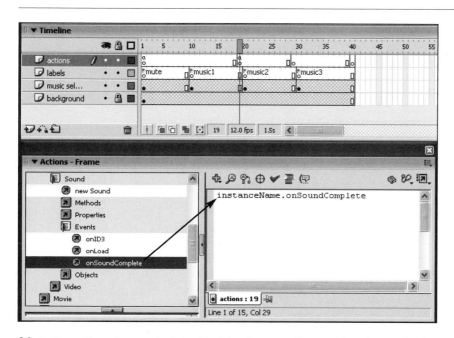

30. In the **actions** layer, select the blank keyframe on **Frame 19** and open the **Actions** panel (**F9**). In the **Actions** pane, choose **Built-in Classes** > **Media** > **Sound** > **Events** and double-click **onSoundComplete** to add it to the **Script** pane. You will assign the instance name next.

31. Change the **instanceName** placeholder to **song1**, as shown here.

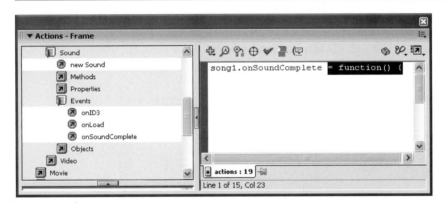

32. After **onSoundComplete**, type **= function() {**, as shown here.

*Note: A **function** allows you to assign a name to a section of code that has a specific purpose. Once you have defined and named a function, you can use it in other scripts by referencing its name. You will finish defining this function in the next few steps.*

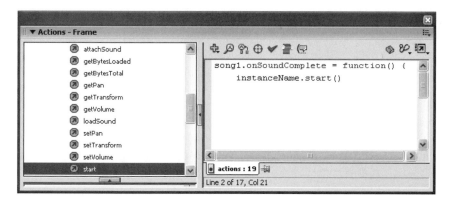

33. Press **Enter/Return** to bring your cursor to the second line. In the **Actions** pane, choose **Built-in Classes** > **Media** > **Sound** > **Methods** and double-click **start** to add it to the **Script** pane.

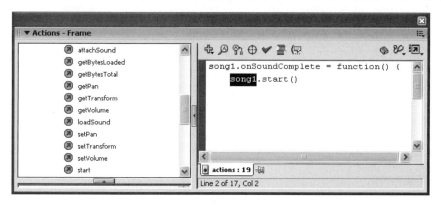

34. Change **instanceName** to **song1**, as shown here.

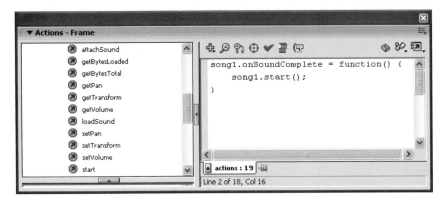

35. To complete the function, type a semicolon (;), and press **Enter/Return** to bring the cursor to the next line. On the new line, type a closing curly brace (}).

Note: This function instructs the song to begin playing again after it has completed playing.

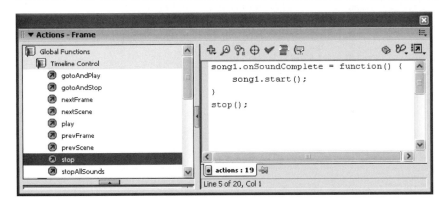

36. Press **Enter/Return** to bring the cursor to the next line. In the **Actions** pane, choose **Global Functions > Timeline Control** and double-click **stop** to add it to the **Script** pane, as shown here. You will copy and paste the code into the blank keyframes on **Frames 29** and **40** in the following steps.

*Note: The **stop** action tells the playhead to stop, not the sound. The playhead will stop but the sound will continue to play until the user clicks any of the other buttons on the music selector on the Stage.*

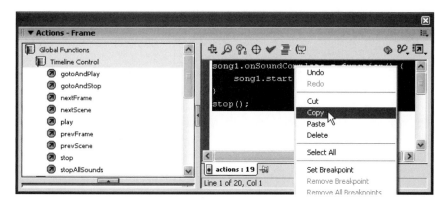

37. Select the ActionScript in the **Script** pane. **Right-click** (Windows) or **Cmd+click** (Mac) and choose **Copy** from the contextual drop-down menu. You will paste the ActionScript into the blank keyframe on **Frame 29** of the **actions** layer next.

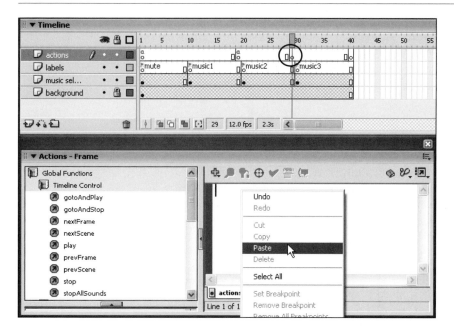

38. In the **Timeline**, select the blank keyframe on **Frame 29** of the **actions** layer. In the **Script** pane of the **Actions** panel, **right-click** (Windows) or **Cmd+click** (Mac) and choose **Paste** from the contextual drop-down menu. You will change the code to reflect the **2** button next.

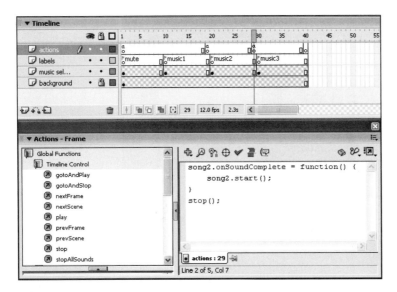

39. In the **Script** pane, change **song1** to **song2**, as shown here. You will add the ActionScript to the blank keyframe on **Frame 40** of the **actions** layer next.

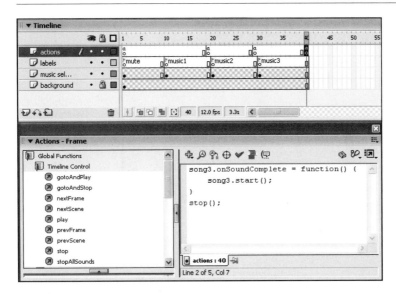

40. In the **Timeline**, select the blank keyframe on **Frame 40** of the **actions** layer. In the **Script** pane of the **Actions** panel, **right-click** (Windows) or **Cmd+click** (Mac) and choose **Paste** from the contextual drop-down menu. In the **Script** pane, change **song1** to **song3**, as shown here.

It's time to preview your movie.

41. Choose **Control > Test Movie** to test your sounds. Click the buttons and notice that the sounds continue to loop and that the button of the sound you are listening to is highlighted in red. Click the red **Stop** button to stop all sounds. Cool! You have created a music selector through the ActionScript **loadSound**.

---

42. When you are finished, save and close this file.

Congratulations! You have conquered another chapter. You should now feel comfortable working with sound in Flash MX 2004. If you feel you need more practice, you can always review the exercises again. Working with components and forms is next!

I4.

Components and Forms

| What Are Components? | Creating a Form |
| Configuring Components | Modifying Component Themes |
| Macromedia Exchange |

chap_14

Macromedia Flash MX 2004
H•O•T CD-ROM

In past versions of Flash MX 2004, creating complex forms for your users to fill out was not an easy task. The sheer thought of developing a scrollable text box could take hours and a significant time investment in learning how. **Components** in Flash MX 2004 has been a welcome relief. The purpose of components is to make your life easier. Rather than build a scrollable list box from scratch that offers the user many choices that are highlighted when the mouse rolls over them, you can drag and drop the List component onto the Stage and presto: You have a scrollable list and all you have to do is add the words you want to appear in the list. This chapter will introduce to you how to work with components to create a form. In the following exercises, you will add components to a project file, configure them to display the correct information for the user, and then modify them so that they match the interface design.

What Are Components?

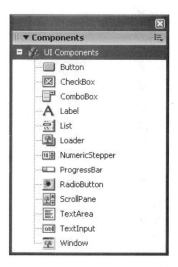

Components are like movie clip symbols on steroids—they are a special type of movie clip that has a predefined appearance and functionality. You can use components in your movie to add simple interface elements, such as check boxes and radio buttons, that have already been built for you. Flash MX 2004 ships with several user interface (UI) components, including a check box, combo box, list box, button, radio button, scroll pane, and several others. You can use the components individually or together to create user interface elements such as forms or surveys. In addition, you can modify the appearance of each component by changing such aspects as the theme color, font, font size, and font color. A chart detailing each of the 13 components that ship with Flash MX 2004 follows.

Component Types	
Type	**Description**
Button	Accepts standard mouse and keyboard interactions. This component can be programmed to carry out a specific command when the user clicks on it or presses Enter/Return.
CheckBox	Allows users to select or deselect this check box.
ComboBox	Displays a single choice with a drop-down menu revealing additional choices.
Label	Allows you to quickly create a label, similar to using a text field with an instance name assigned to it.
	continues on next page

Component Types *continued*	
Type	**Description**
List	Seems similar to the ComboBox, although this component offers a list of all choices in a scrollable menu.
Loader	A container in which you can load other movies or JPEGs.
Numeric Stepper	Allows users to step through an ordered set of numbers.
ProgressBar	Displays the loading progress while a user waits for content to load.
RadioButton	Allows you to add several instances of the radio button to your project file and prevents more than one choice in a group of radio buttons from ever being selected at one time.
ScrollPane	Allows the user to view movie clips, JPEGs, and SWF files through a scrollable window.
TextArea	Can be used to display text or allow users to type text in themselves.
TextInput	Allows users to insert text (for a username or password, for example).
Window	A draggable window for displaying content that includes a title bar and Close button.

Working with Components

There are four general phases when working with components:

- Adding the components to your project file

- Configuring the components with the correct information for the user to see and select from

- Modifying the component themes to change their appearances

- Writing ActionScript to gather and submit the data for the form

This chapter concentrates on the first three phases because phase four involves training you in more complicated ActionScripting and custom server configurations—both subjects which fall outside the scope of this book.

I. ————————Creating a Form

The first step in working with components is to add them to your Flash MX 2004 project file. This exercise will show you how to do just that.

1. Copy the **chap_14** folder, located on the **H•O•T CD-ROM**, to your hard drive. You need to have this folder on your hard drive in order to save files inside it.

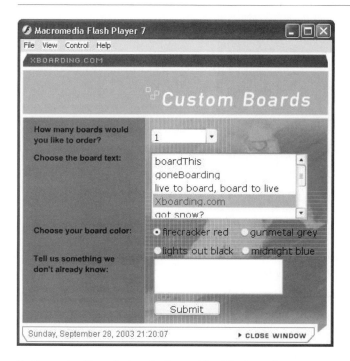

2. Open the file called **orderForm_Final.fla** from the **chap_14** folder. Choose **Control > Test Movie** to preview the file. This is the finished version of the form you'll be creating throughout the exercises of this chapter. Test out the different form elements to see how they work. When you are finished, close the **Preview** window.

*Note: If you click the **Submit** button, nothing happens because this form is not set up to submit the data to a server.*

3. Close the **orderForm_Final.fla** file and open the **orderForm.fla** from the **chap_14** folder. This file was created to get you started.

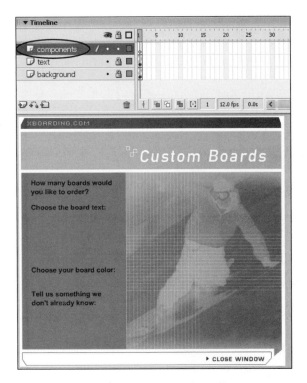

4. In the **Main Timeline**, click the **Insert Layer** button to add a new layer. Rename the new layer **components**. Make sure the **components** layer is on top, above the other two layers.

Tip: You can choose *View > Magnification > Show All* to see all of the *Stage* at one time.

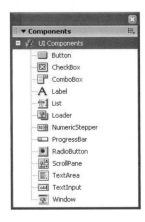

5. If the **Components** panel isn't already open, choose **Window > Development Panels > Components** to open it. This is where all the components are stored.

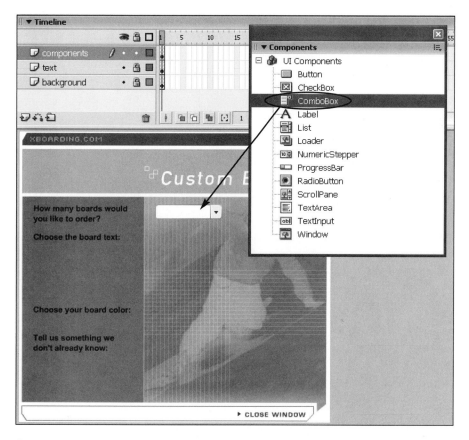

6. In the **Components** panel, click the **ComboBox** to select it and drag an instance of it onto the **Stage**, to the right of the "How many boards would you like to order?" text, as shown here.

The ComboBox is a component that will display a single choice with a drop-down menu revealing additional choices. You will configure the ComboBox choices in the next exercise. You have just added the first component to your movie!

Tip: *You can also double-click a component in the Components panel to add it to your project file. However, doing so adds the component to the center of the Stage; you then have to drag it to the desired position.*

7. Open the Library (**Ctrl+L** [Windows] or **Cmd+L** [Mac]). Notice that it now contains the **ComboBox** component and a folder called **background**, which was created ahead of time; it contains all the files that make up the interface of this project file. The **ComboBox** component was automatically added to the **Library** as soon as you dragged the **ComboBox** onto the **Stage**. For each additional component you add to your project, Flash MX 2004 will add the component to the **Library**.

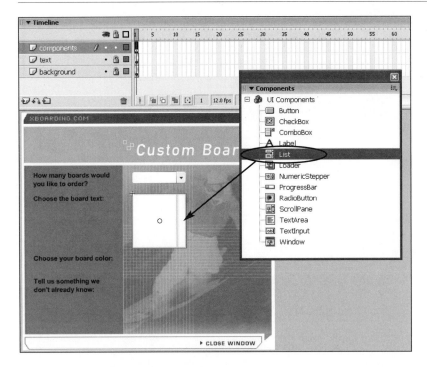

8. From the **Components** panel, click the **List** component and drag an instance of it onto the **Stage**, to the right of the "Choose the board text" text, as shown in the picture here. The **List** component offers a list of all choices in a scrollable menu.

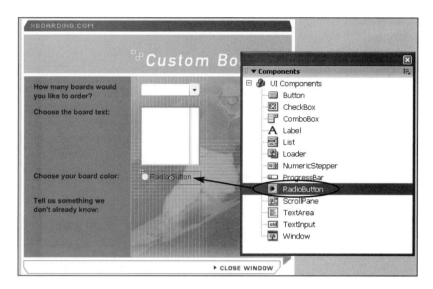

9. From the **Components** panel, click the **RadioButton** to select it and drag an instance of it onto the **Stage**, to the right of the "Choose your board color" text. The **RadioButton** component allows you to add several instances of the radio button to your project file (which you will do in the next step) and prevents users from selecting more than one choice in a group of radio buttons.

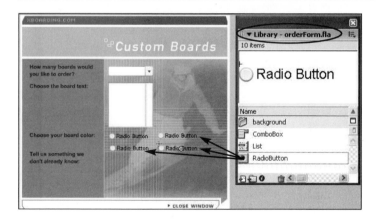

10. Using the Library (**Ctrl+L** [Windows] or **Cmd+L** [Mac]), drag three more instances of the **RadioButton** onto the **Stage** and position them as shown in the picture here. You don't have to worry about aligning them precisely because you will align all the components a few steps from now.

Note: *Why do you have to use the Library? Once you add a component to your project file, the component is added to the Library. Each time you add additional instances of the same component (just like using additional instances of any other symbol), you use the Library to add them to the Stage.*

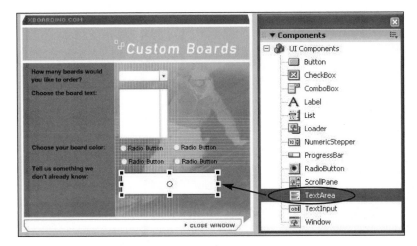

11. From the **Components** panel, click the **TextArea** component and drag it onto the **Stage**, to the right of the "Tell us something we don't already know" text. The **TextArea** component will allow users to add comments along with the form submission, and it automatically displays a scroll bar if the message becomes longer than the box. Very cool! While you're here, use the **Free Transform** tool to resize the **TextArea** component according to the image shown here.

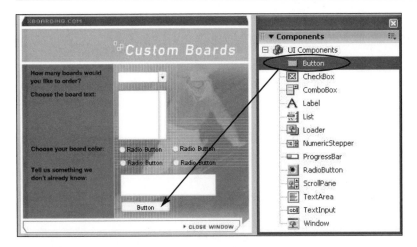

12. From the **Components** panel, click the **Button** component to select it and drag an instance of it onto the **Stage**, just below the **TextArea** component, as shown in the picture here. The **Button** component accepts standard mouse and keyboard interactions, and it can be programmed to carry out a specific command when the user clicks on it or presses **Enter/Return**.

After you add the Button in the last step, take another look at the Library. Notice that each of the components you have placed on the Stage is also located in the Library. You can add additional instances of each of these components by dragging them from the Library onto the Stage.

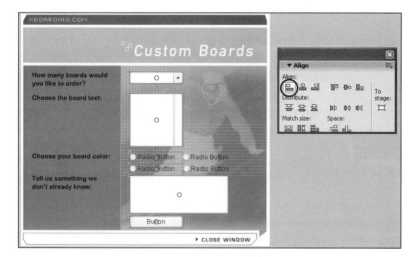

13. Choose **Window > Design Panels > Align** to open the **Align** panel. Select all the components that are nearest the white vertical interface line, as shown in the picture here. To select multiple components at once, **Shift+click** each of the components. In the **Align** panel, click the **Align left edge** button so that all of the selected components will be aligned vertically.

Note: *Because of the **Snap Align** functionality now built into Flash MX 2004, the components may already be aligned. The Align panel, though, can help in many situations to align several elements at once or distribute them across the Stage.*

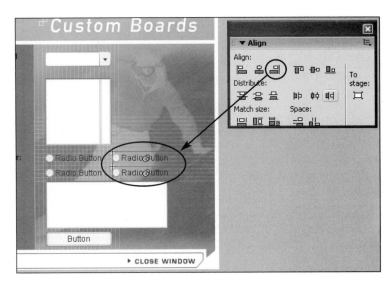

14. Click off the **Stage** to deselect everything and then **Shift+click** the two right-most **RadioButtons**, as shown in the picture here. In the **Align** panel, choose **Align right edge** to align the two components.

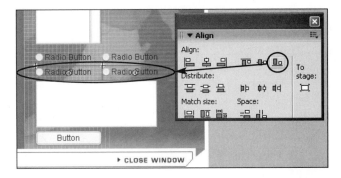

15. Click off the **Stage** to deselect everything. **Shift+click** the top two **RadioButton** components and select **Align top edge** in the **Align** panel. This will align the top of the two **RadioButtons** to each other. Click off the **Stage** to deselect everything again. **Shift+click** the bottom two **RadioButton** components to select both of them and choose **Align bottom edge** in the **Align** panel. This will align the bottom of the **RadioButton** components to each other.

16. When you are finished, save this file and keep it open for the next exercise.

2. ——————Configuring Components

Now that you have the components in place in the project file, you need to make adjustments to each component so that they display the correct information to the user. This exercise shows you how to do this by setting the parameters for each component.

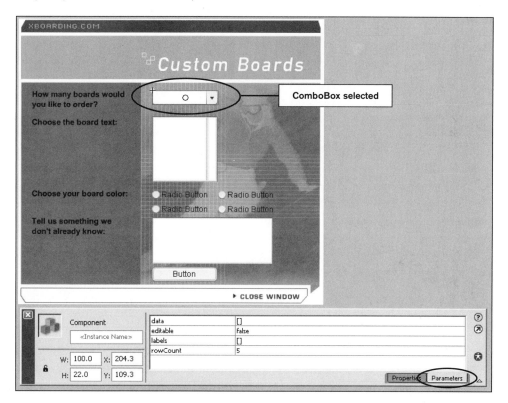

1. You should still have the **orderForm.fla** file open from the last exercise. On the **Stage**, click the **ComboBox** to select it. Open the **Properties inspector (Window > Properties)**— if it is not already open—and make sure the **Parameters** tab is selected on the right corner. Notice that the **Properties inspector** looks a little different than normal, this is part of the built-in functionality of the component.

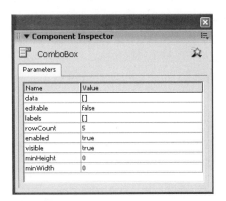

*Note: In addition to using the Properties inspector, you can also view the parameters for a component by using the Component Inspector panel. To do this, choose **Window > Development Panels > Component Inspector** to open the panel. Select a component instance on the Stage to view the parameters associated with that component. Using the Component Parameters panel will give you the same information as choosing the Parameters tab in the Properties inspector, so whichever work-flow works better for you is fine to use. In this exercise, you will be using the Properties inspector to modify the component parameters.*

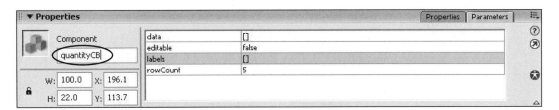

2. In the **Properties inspector**, click inside the **Instance Name** text box and type **quantityCB**. This will give the **ComboBox** on the **Stage** an instance name of **quantityCB** so that it can be referred to via ActionScript.

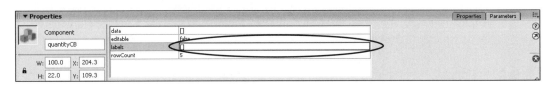

3. Double-click the **labels** parameter to open up the **Values** dialog box, where you can enter the values that will appear for the user to select from in a scrollable drop-down menu.

 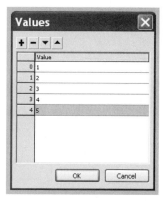

4. In the **Values** dialog box, click the plus (+) button to enter a new value. Click in the default field and type **1**. This will set the first value as 1. Click the plus (+) button again to enter the next value. Click in the default field and type **2**. This will set the second value as 2. Repeat this step to add **3**, **4**, and **5** to the list, as shown in the second picture. When you are finished, click **OK**.

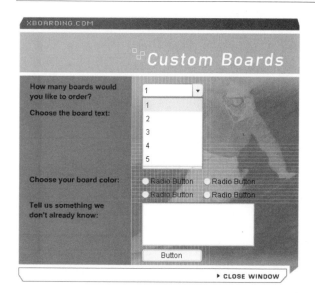

5. Choose **Control > Test Movie** to test out your **ComboBox** component. The numbers you entered will appear in a drop-down list, making the configuration for this component complete. When you are finished, close the **Preview** window.

Note: You may have noticed the highlight color when you roll over an option in the ComboBox is light green. This is the result of the "Halo" theme built into Flash MX 2004 components. You're going to change the color in an upcoming exercise to match the green in this interface design.

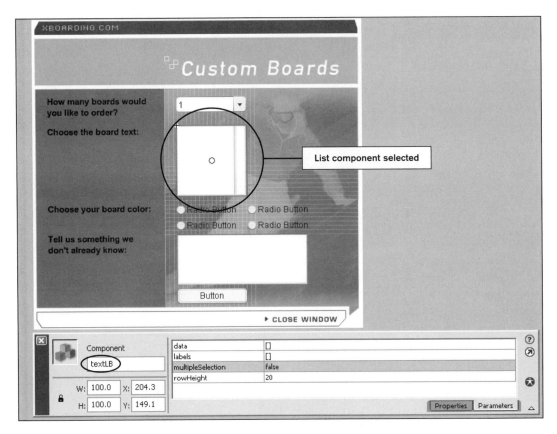

6. Back in the project file, click the **List** component to select it. In the **Properties inspector**, click inside the **Instance Name** text box and type **textLB**. This assigns an instance name of **textLB** to the **List** component on the **Stage** so that it can be referred to via ActionScript.

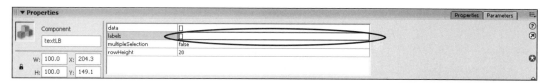

7. Still in the **Properties inspector**, double-click the **labels** parameter to open up the **Values** dialog box, where you can enter the values that will appear for the user to select from in a scrollable drop-down menu.

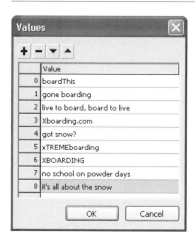

8. In the **Values** dialog box, click the plus (**+**) button to enter a new value. Click in the default field and type **boardThis**. This will set the first value for the user to select from inside the **List** component as **boardThis**. Click the plus (**+**) button again to enter the next value. Click in the default field and type **gone boarding** to set the second value. Repeat this step six more times to add text for the user to choose from that will appear on the snowboard, as shown in the picture here. You can either use the board text options I used here, or you can be creative and create your own board text. Just make sure that you add a total of eight labels. When you are finished, click **OK**.

Tip: If you want to move any of your entries higher or lower in the list, you can select the value and use the up or down arrows at the top of the Value dialog box to move them where you want them.

9. Choose **Control > Test Movie** to test out the **List** component. Use the scroll bar inside the List to see all the options you created for the user. Notice, however, that the longer text is cut off. You will change this next. When you are finished, close the **Preview** window.

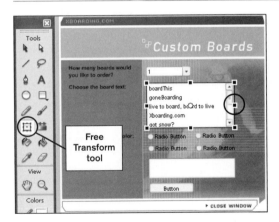

10. Back in the project file, select the **Free Transform** tool in the **Toolbar** and click the **List** component on the **Stage** to select it. Click the **right-middle handle** on the **Free Transform** bounding box and drag to the right to resize the **List** component, making all text entries visible.

Note: You can modify the width and height of List components in your project file by using the Free Transform tool. However, you can modify only the width of ComboBox components with the Free Transform tool. This is because the height of the ComboBox component is set by the font size that displays the menu choices and the Row Count parameter that determines the number of choices visible in the drop-down menu at one time.

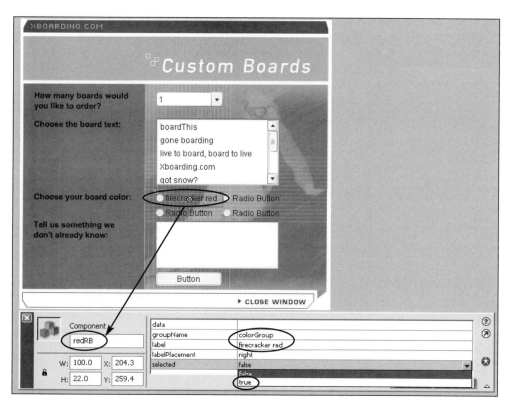

11. With the **Selection** tool, select the top-left **RadioButton** on the **Stage**. In the **Properties inspector**, type **redRB** for the **Instance Name**. Select the **groupName** parameter and type **colorGroup**. This will make this **RadioButton** part of a group of **RadioButtons** called **colorGroup**. Select the **label** parameter and type **firecracker red**. This is the label that will appear to the right of the **RadioButton** in the form. Set the **selected** parameter to **true** from the drop-down menu. A value of true for the Initial state of the **RadioButton** will make it selected by default.

*Note: Only one radio button in a group can have the **selected** state as **true**. Leave the **labelPlacement** parameter set to **right** (the default value). This parameter sets the location of the RadioButton label text to either the right of or the left of the RadioButton. When you are finished, the Properties inspector should look like the picture shown here.*

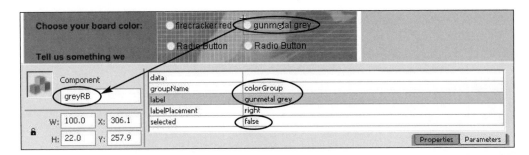

12. Select the top-right **RadioButton** on the **Stage**. In the **Properties inspector**, type **greyRB** for the **Instance Name**. Select the **groupName** parameter and type **colorGroup** to make this **RadioButton** part of the group called **colorGroup**. Select the label parameter and type **gunmetal grey** to label the **RadioButton**. Make sure the **selected** parameter is set to **false**. When you are finished, the **Properties inspector** should look like the picture shown here.

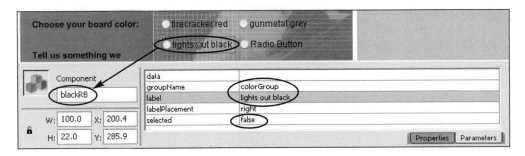

13. Select the bottom-left **RadioButton** on the **Stage**. In the **Properties inspector**, type **blackRB** for the **Instance Name**. Select the **groupName** parameter and type **colorGroup** to make this **RadioButton** part of the group called **colorGroup**. Select the **label** parameter and type **lights out black** to label the **RadioButton**. Make sure the **selected** parameter is set to **false**. When you are finished, the **Properties inspector** should look just like the picture here. You need to set the parameters for just one more button.

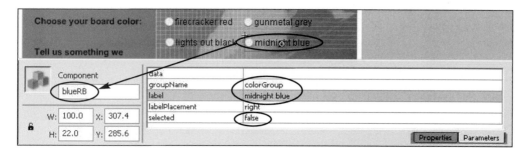

14. Select the bottom-right **RadioButton** on the **Stage**. In the **Properties inspector**, type **blueRB** for the **Instance Name**. Select the **groupName** parameter and type **colorGroup** to make this **RadioButton** part of the group called **colorGroup**. Select the **label** parameter and type **midnight blue** to label the **RadioButton**. Make sure the **selected** parameter is set to **false**. When you are finished, the **Properties inspector** should look just like the picture here.

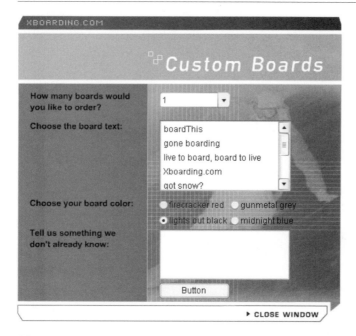

15. Choose **Control > Test Movie** to test out the **RadioButton** components. Notice that the **firecracker red RadioButton** is selected by default, although you can click to select any of the other **RadioButton** components, and only one can be selected at any time. This is an example of components in action at their finest—all of the behind-the-scenes work was done for you. By simply modifying some of the component parameters, you have a fully functional group of **RadioButton** components. Sweet! When you are finished, close the **Preview** window.

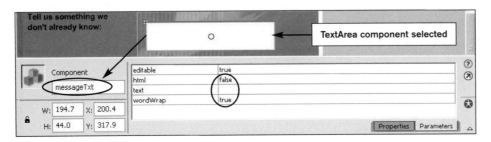

16. Back in the project file, click the **TextArea** component on the **Stage** to select it. In the **Properties inspector**, type **messageTxt** in the **Instance Name** text box. The text box needs an instance name so it can be referred to through ActionScript. Make sure the **wordWrap** parameter is set to **true**, and the **html** parameter is set to **false**. Leave the **text** parameter empty. Before you test the movie, select the **Free Transform** tool in the **Toolbar** and resize the **TextArea** component if you need to so that it matches the image here. This will make it easier for the user to see what they are typing and will help the interface look a bit better.

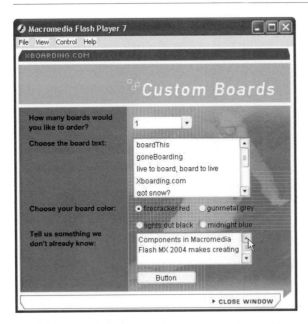

17. Choose **Control > Test Movie** to test the scrolling input text box. Try typing a large amount of text and notice that a scroll bar will automatically appear and resize as you type. Cool! When you are finished, close the **Preview** window. You have one last component to configure next.

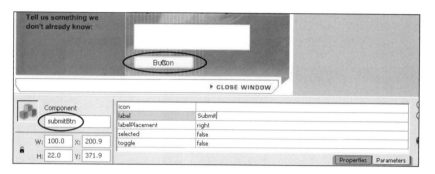

18. Back in the project file, click the **Button** component to select it. In the **Properties inspector**, type **submitBtn** in the **Instance Name** text box. For the **label** parameter, type **Submit**. This will be the label that appears on the **Button** component.

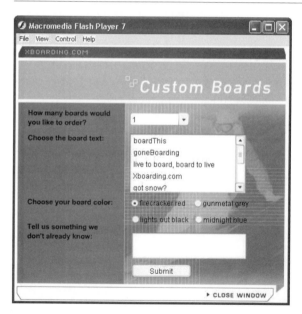

19. Choose **Control > Test Movie** to preview your **Submit Button** component. Notice that the label of the button now reads "Submit" instead of "Button."

Note: In order to test the functionality of the Submit button, including collecting all the data entered on the form and actually sending it to a server, you need to add more-complex ActionScript to the movie. Aside from the additional complex ActionScripting, you also need access to a Web server and middleware such as ColdFusion Server or Microsoft Active Server Pages (ASP), which is beyond the scope of this book. You can, however, visit the Macromedia Flash Support Center at **http://www.macromedia.com/support/flash/applications_building.html** *to find articles and resources that will teach you how to use ActionScripting to gather and submit data entered in a form.*

20. When you are finished, close the **Preview** window. Save this file and keep it open for the next exercise.

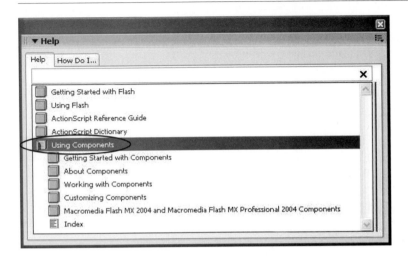

*For more information about each of the components, choose **Help > Help**. In the **Help** panel, choose **Using Components** for a listing of all the available information on components.*

3.—————————**Modifying Component Themes**

In the previous exercises, you learned how to add components to your project and create a form. You may have noticed the light green tint that appears when you roll over an item or make a selection. Fortunately, you are not stuck with the light green tint, called a Halo theme, used in the components. You can modify the Halo of the component as well as the font, font size, and font color with just a few short lines of ActionScript. This exercise will teach you how to change the appearance of the components to match the color scheme in the interface design through ActionScript.

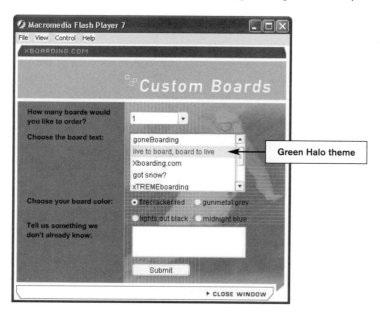

1. You should still have the **orderForm.fla** file open from the last exercise. Choose **Control > Test Movie** to preview the form you have created up to this point in the chapter. Notice that the highlight color in all the components is light green. You will change the Halo theme in the following steps. When you are finished, close the **Preview** window.

NOTE | What Is a Halo Theme?

The Halo theme is a built-in style for all of the Flash MX 2004 components that are used to set the highlight color of buttons and text when you roll over them with your mouse or make a selection. There are three colors to choose from: blue, green, and orange. To change the Halo theme, you will add a few lines of ActionScript. When you get more comfortable with ActionScript, it is possible to create new themes and graphics for components, but that is beyond the scope of this book, so for now you'll keep it simple.

2. Back in the project file, click the **Insert Layer** button to add a layer to the **Timeline**. Rename the new layer **theme** and make sure it is above all other layers. You will add ActionScript to set the color of the Halo theme next.

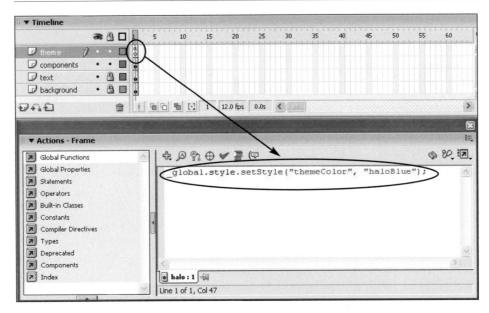

3. Select **Frame 1** of the **theme** layer and open the **Actions** panel (**F9**). Type the following line of code into the **Script** pane of the **Actions** panel as shown here:

```
_global.style.setStyle("themeColor", "haloBlue");
```

The **_global** action used here means the Halo theme used will apply to every component in the movie. The **setStyle** command is used simply to tell the components that you are setting a specific Halo theme (done with the **"themeColor"** parameter) and that the theme you want is **haloBlue**.

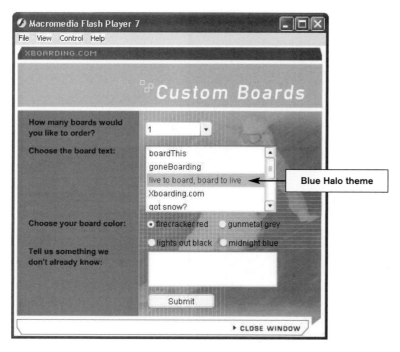

4. Choose **Control > Test Movie** to see how the theme has changed from the default color of green to blue. When you're done, close the **Preview** window.

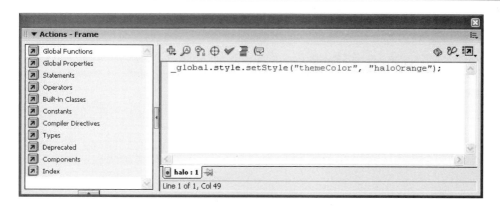

5. Back in the project file, in the **Script** pane of the **Actions** panel, change **haloBlue** to **haloOrange**, as shown here.

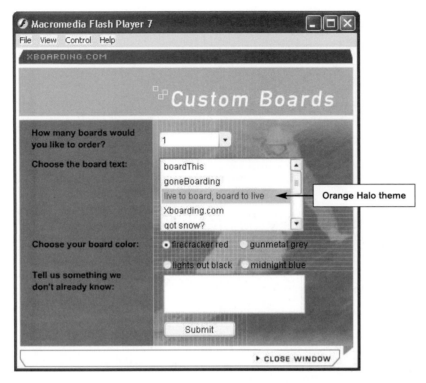

6. Choose **Control > Test Movie** to preview the Halo color theme. Notice that the highlight color is now orange instead of blue. Close the **Preview** window when you are finished.

Tip: If you don't want to use any of the prebuilt Halo themes for your components, you can simply enter the hexadecimal value for any other color in place of **haloOrange**. For example, changing **haloOrange** to **0xC1CE0F** will make the highlight color for the components match the green used in the interface very nicely. You will do this next.

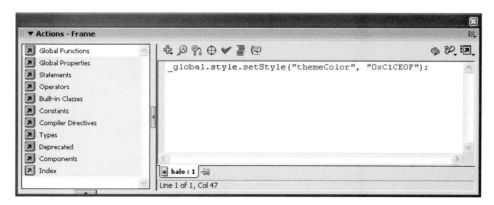

7. Back in the project file, in the **Script** pane of the **Actions** panel, change `haloOrange` to `0xC1CE0F`, as shown here.

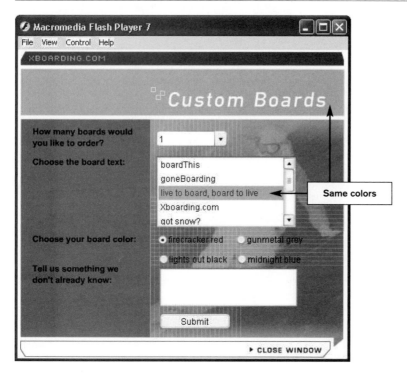

8. Choose **Control > Test Movie** to preview the Halo color theme. Notice that the highlight color now matches the green used in the interface design. Close the **Preview** window when you are finished.

Next, you're going to change the font used in the components so that it will be a little easier to read against the background, particularly for the RadioButton components.

NOTE | What Is a Hexadecimal Value?

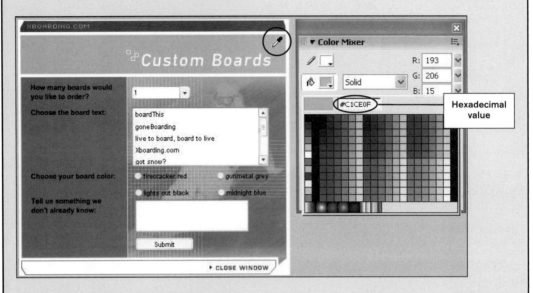

Hexadecimal
value

Hexadecimal values are six-digit number/letter combinations used to identify specific colors in ActionScript and many other programming languages. For a quick glance at which hexadecimal values belong to what colors, you can use the Eyedropper tool to sample a color used in the interface or a color swatch in the Color mixer. The hexadecimal value will generate in the Hexadecimal Value field.

If you're familiar with HTML, you may be more familiar with hexadecimal values in the format "#FFFFFF" instead of "0x000000." Why is it "0x" in front of the Hex colors rather than the standard "#" sign? Just 0 (zero), then x is short for "hexadecimal." In the old days, we also had binary, decimal, and octal to deal with. For binary and decimal, you didn't put anything before the number; for octal, you'd start numbers with 0.

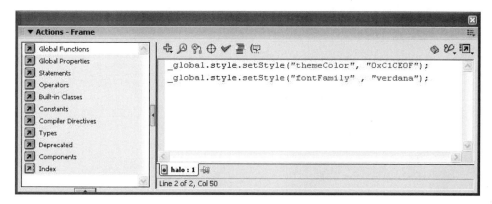

9. Back in the production file, in the **Script** pane below the first line of code, type the following ActionScript to set the font:

```
_global.style.setStyle("fontFamily", "verdana");
```

*Again, the **_global** action is used here to apply the font to all of the components. The **setStyle** command is then used to set the font family for all of the components to Verdana.*

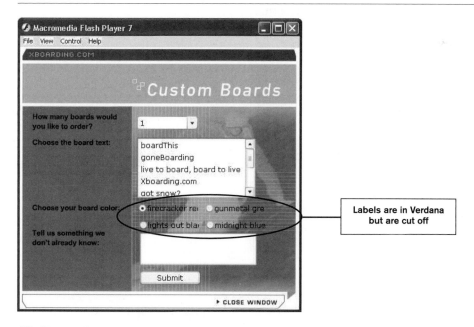

10. Choose **Control > Test Movie** to preview the font. Notice that the font is now in Verdana, but that the radio button labels are cut off. You will fix this next. When you are finished previewing, close the **Preview** window.

11. Back in the project file, **Shift+click** to select the **gunmetal grey** and **midnight blue** radio buttons. Move them to the right, as shown here.

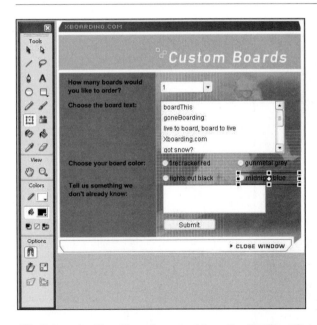

12. Select the **Free Transform** tool from the **Toolbar**. Select the **firecracker red** radio button and click the **right-middle handle** on the **Free Transform** bounding box and drag to the right to resize the **RadioButton** component so that you can read the entire label. Do this for the remaining three radio buttons: **gunmetal grey**, **lights out black**, and **midnight blue**. Resize the **List** component as well if you could not see all the text entries in Step 10.

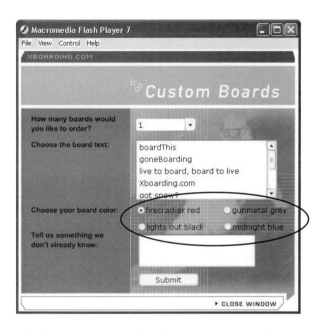

13. Choose **Control > Test Movie** again to preview the radio buttons. Notice that you can read the labels of the radio buttons now. Close the **Preview** window when you are done. You're going to change the font size next.

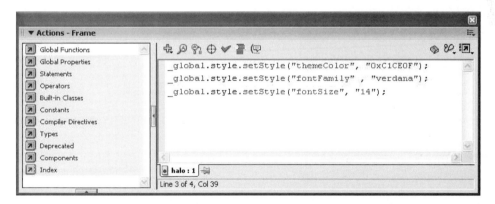

14. Below the two lines of ActionScript you now have in your **Script** pane of the **Actions** panel, add this ActionScript to set the font size:

```
_global.style.setStyle("fontSize", "14");
```

As you can probably see by now, you're applying the font size to all of the components using the _global *action, and then setting the font size to 14. You only have one more line of code to go!*

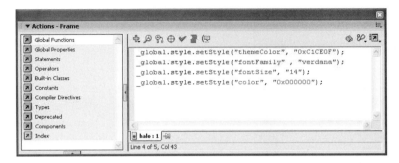

15. Once again, type the following line of ActionScript below the code you have already added. This line will set the color of the font for all of the components to solid black:

_global.style.setStyle("color", "0x000000");

Here, the **setStyle** *command is used to set the color to the hexadecimal value for black, which is #000000. If you wanted to set the color to something other than black, you would put the six-digit hexadecimal value for that specific color in place of the 000000 (six zeros) in the code.*

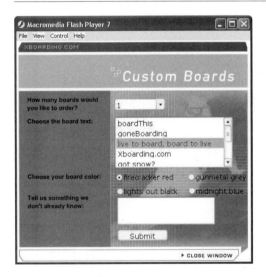

16. Choose **Control > Test Movie** to see the results of your hard work. Notice that the font is Verdana, 14 point, and black for all of the components, and the Halo theme is now the same shade of green used in the interface design, which helps to unite the color scheme used in the interface. Close the **Preview** window when you are done viewing your changes.

17. Save and close this file.

In the next exercise, you'll learn how to download extensions from the Macromedia Flash Exchange.

The Macromedia Flash Exchange

http://www.macromedia.com/exchange/flash

Now that you're more familiar with components and how beneficial it can be to use them in your movies, take a look at the Macromedia Exchange. This is a special section of the Macromedia Web site that allows users to post components and other extensions to a searchable forum, many of which have been made by Macromedia or third-party developers. You can browse through the Exchange any time and download hundreds of reusable components that do everything from provide tooltips in interfaces to generate text effects on-the-fly.

To download these extensions, simply go to **http://www.macromedia.com/exchange/flash** and search through the various categories to find a few extensions you find useful or interesting. Then use the Macromedia Extension Manager, which comes preinstalled with Flash MX 2004, to manage all of your extensions.

4. ─────────────**Downloading from Macromedia Exchange**

Macromedia Exchange for Flash MX 2004 is a special section of the Macromedia Web site that allows you to download Macromedia Flash extensions, many of which have been made by Macromedia or third-party developers. You can browse through the Exchange and download additional components to build projects, templates for designing Flash content, reusable ActionScript code snippets, additional symbol libraries, and more. In this exercise, you will learn how to download an extension from the Exchange and install it using the Extension Manager.

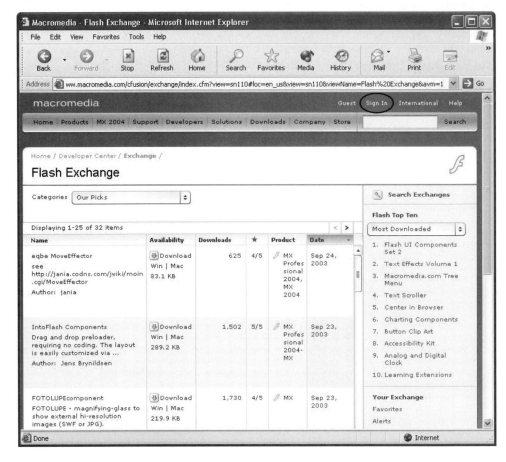

1. Open a Web browser and go to **http://www.macromedia.com/exchange/flash**. This takes you to the Macromedia Flash Exchange. If you have not created an account yet (it's free), go ahead and sign up now. You will need an account before downloading any of the extensions. If this is the case, click the **Sign In** button and follow the instructions to set up an account before continuing with the exercise.

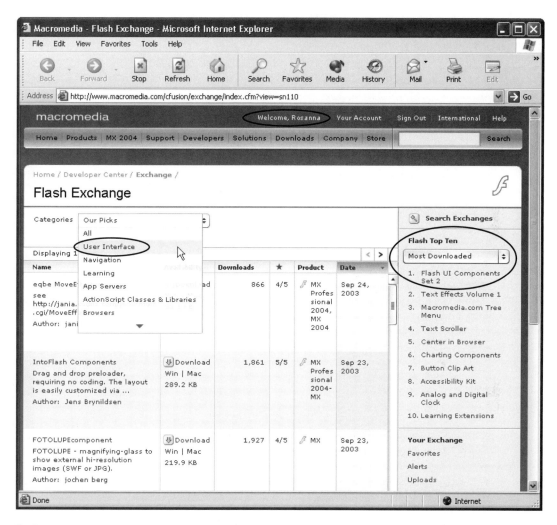

2. Once you have your own account, go to **http://www.macromedia.com/exchange/flash** and click the **Categories** pop-up menu at the top of the screen. Notice that the extensions are organized into a variety of topics for easy access. You can also check out the **Flash Top Ten** pop-up menu for the **Highest Rated**, **Newest**, and **Most Downloaded** extensions. From the **Categories** pop-up menu, choose **User Interface** from the list. This takes you to a page with extensions that relate directly to user interface topics.

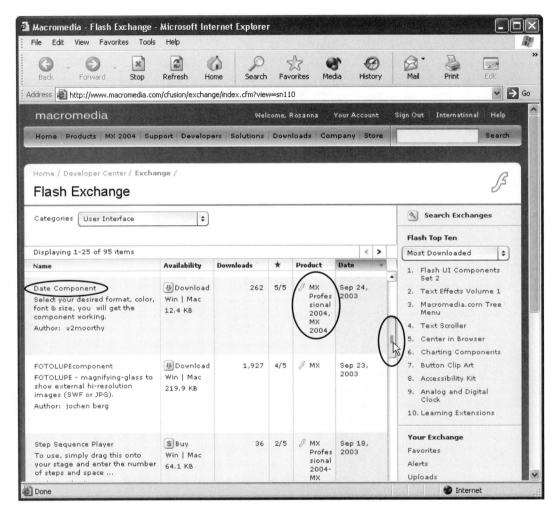

3. Notice that this page gives you useful information about each extension, such as the author, availability, number of downloads, rating, product compatibility, and date created. Scroll down to **Date Component** and notice that this extension is compatible with Flash MX 2004 as well as Flash MX Professional 2004. Click the **Date Component** link to find out more about this extension.

If the **Date Component** does not appear in the list, click the **Search Exchanges** button at the top right of the interface. In the **Search** field, type **Date Component**. In the **All Exchanges** drop-down menu, select **Flash Exchange** and click the **Search** button.

Note: At the time of this writing, few extensions were available for Flash MX 2004. Be sure to check out *http://www.macromedia.com/exchange/flash* for an update of extensions available.

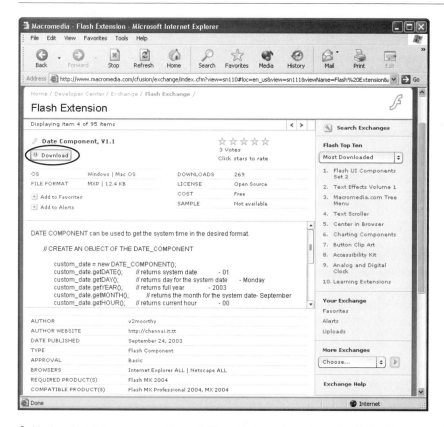

4. Notice that this page provides additional information about the **Date Component** extension, which allows you to display the operating system date and time in your Flash movies, in your desired format. To begin the download process, click the **Download** link.

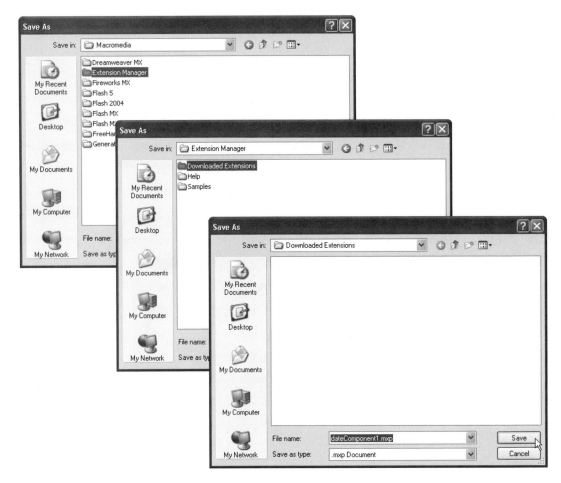

5. When you are prompted to save the extension, choose a location on your hard drive and click **Save**. Remember where you saved this file, because you'll need to access it later. The best place to store it is in the **Downloaded Extensions** folder within the **Macromedia** folder; this way you'll know where it is in the future.

Note: *Under OS X on the Macintosh, the Extension Manager will automatically launch once the extension has been downloaded. If you are on a Macintosh operating OS X, jump ahead to Step 9.*

6. You're done with the Macromedia Exchange for Flash. Return to Flash MX 2004. Choose **Help > Manage Extensions** to open the **Macromedia Extension Manager** window, which you will use to install the extension you just downloaded.

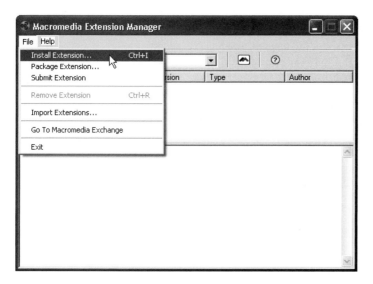

7. In the **Extension Manager**, select **File > Install Extension**. This opens a dialog box so that you can browse to the extension file you just downloaded.

Note: All extension files will have the extension of .mxp

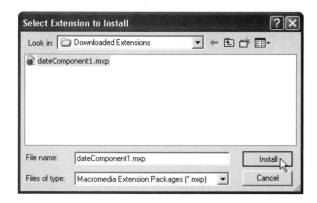

8. Locate the extension file on your hard drive and click **Install**.

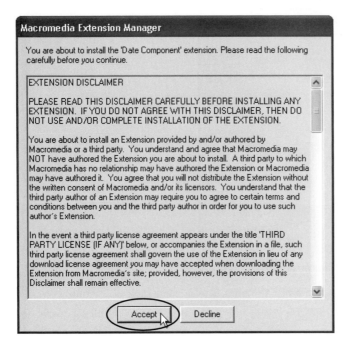

9. In the disclaimer window that appears, click **Accept** and the installation process will continue.

10. When the installation process is finished, this dialog box is displayed. Click **OK**.

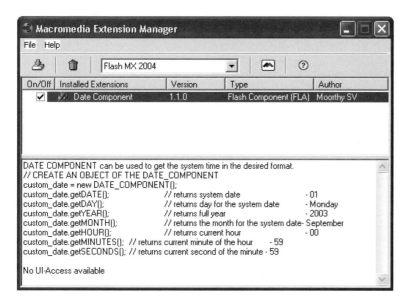

*Once the installation is complete, your new extension appears in the Macromedia Extension Manager window. To access this window at any time, choose **Help > Manage Extensions**. You can also get to the Flash Exchange from the Extension Manager by choosing **File > Go To Macromedia Exchange** within the Macromedia Extension Manger window.*

One great advantage to using the Extension Manager is that it will organize all of your extensions for any Studio MX 2004 application, and there are tons more available for Macromedia Dreamweaver and Macromedia Fireworks as well!

11. Select **File > Exit** (Windows) or **File > Quit** (Mac) to exit the **Extension Manager**.

12. Quit Flash MX 2004. You will relaunch the application so that the extension will be available for you to try out next.

13. Relaunch Flash MX 2004 and open **orderForm.fla** from the **chap_14** folder.

14. If the **Components** panel is not open, choose **Window > Development Panels > Components** to open it. Notice that the **Date Component** you downloaded has been added to the **Components** panel. You will add this component to your project file in the following steps.

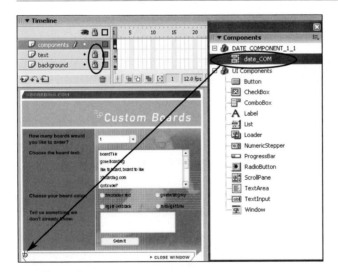

15. In the **Timeline**, make sure the **text** and **background** layers are locked and the **components** layer is unlocked. In the **Components** panel, click and drag the **date_COM** component to the bottom-left corner of the interface, as shown here. You will configure the parameters of this component in the **Properties inspector** in the following steps.

Note: When you drag the Date component onto the Stage, it will be represented by a circle. The circle is where the date and time will be displayed in your movie.

16. In the **Properties inspector** (**Window > Properties**), make sure the **Parameters** tab is selected. In the **Date Format** field, click the drop-down menu and select the fifth item from the list to display the day, month, date, year, and time in your movie.

Note: *The Date component pulls the date and time from the operating system that the movie is being viewed from.*

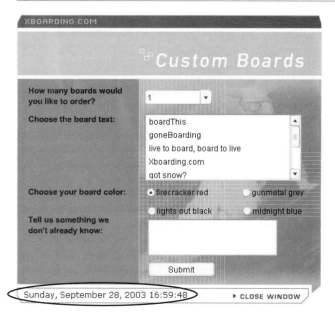

17. Choose **Control > Test Movie** to preview the **Date** component. Notice that the current day, date, and time are displayed at the bottom of the interface. Nice! You will change the font and font color next. Close the Preview window when you are finished previewing your movie.

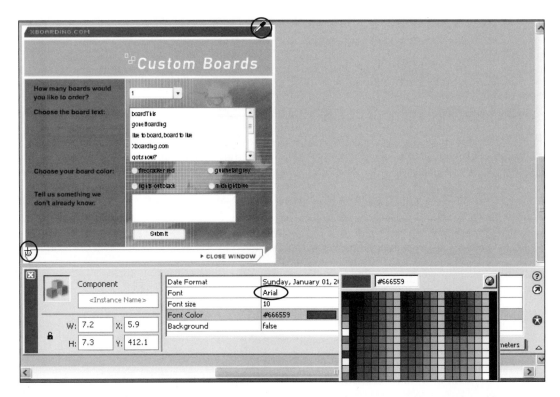

18. Make sure the **Date** component is still selected on the **Stage** and in the **Properties inspector**. In the **Font** field, click the drop-down menu and select **Arial** from the list. In the **Font Color** field, double-click the hexadecimal value or the **ink well**, and the cursor will turn into the **Eyedropper** tool. With the **Eyedropper** tool, click the **dark grey bar** at the top of the interface to sample that color so that the date and time will be displayed in that color.

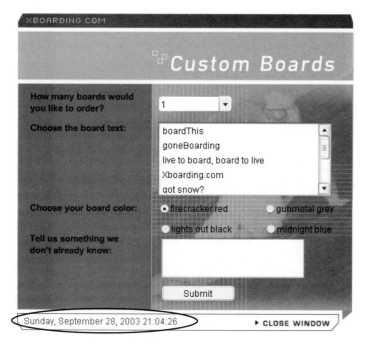

19. Choose **Control > Test Movie** to preview the **Date** component again. Notice that the date and time are now displayed in the font Arial and in the grey color that you sampled in the previous step. When you are done previewing your movie, close the **Preview** window.

This is just one example of many extensions you can download from the Macromedia Exchange. Be sure to check back often because new extensions are constantly being added.

Note: You may have noticed the "Close Window" text at the bottom-right corner of the Stage. In Chapter 17, "Putting It All Together," you will learn how to make this button work because this form will be a pop-up window in the xboarding.com Web site.

---

20. Save and close this file.

Great work! Now that you are more familiar with working with components to create forms and how to extend Flash MX 2004 by downloading extensions from the Macromedia Flash Exchange, take a quick break and get ready for the next action-packed (pun intended) chapter: "Video."

15.
Video

| Acceptable Video Import Formats | Importing Video |
| Controlling Video with stop and go Actions |
| Controlling Video by Targeting Frame Labels |
| Linking to QuickTime Video | Editing Video |

chap_15

Macromedia Flash MX 2004
H•O•T CD-ROM

The ability to include video inside a SWF file was introduced with the release of Flash MX. This opened up many opportunities for Macromedia Flash developers. Once you import video into Flash MX 2004, you can control it using behaviors and very basic ActionScript, target different points in the video to allow users to jump from point to point, transform video clips on the Stage, apply effects such as tinting and skewing, or publish a QuickTime file from Flash MX 2004. In this latest version of Flash, Flash MX 2004, Macromedia has added more video compression options and the capability to cut apart a video and organize the clips, apply color correction, and modify how the video is imported into your Flash project. The exercises in this chapter will teach you these techniques and will lay the groundwork for working with video inside Flash MX 2004.

Importing Video into Flash MX 2004

Flash MX 2004 can import a variety of different file formats. This largely depends on what software you have installed on your machine: QuickTime 4 or higher or DirectX 7 or higher. A chart follows detailing each of the acceptable video file formats.

Acceptable Video Import Formats				
File Type	**Extension**	**Windows**	**Macintosh**	**Software**
Audio Video Interleaved	.avi	x	x	QuickTime 4 or higher or DirectX 7 or higher installed
Digital Video	.dv	x	x	QuickTime 4 or higher installed
Motion Picture Experts Group	.mpg, .mpeg	x	x	QuickTime 4 or higher or DirectX 7 or higher installed
QuickTime Movie	.mov	x	x	QuickTime 4 or higher installed
Windows Media File	.wmv, .asf	x		DirectX 7 or higher installed
Flash Video File	.flv	x	x	Neither needed

Sorenson Spark Video Compression

Imported video is compressed into a format that Flash can understand using the **Sorenson Spark codec**, which is built into Flash MX 2004. A codec is an algorithm that controls the way video files are compressed and decompressed during import and export. Sorenson Spark is a video encoder and decoder that controls how video files are compressed when they are imported into Flash MX 2004 and decompressed so that they can be viewed in the Macromedia Flash Player.

There are two different methods that are used to compress video: spatial and temporal. **Spatial compression** compresses the data in each frame of video, similar to the way a JPEG image is compressed. The frames that are compressed using spatial compression are called intraframes. **Temporal compression** compares data between each frame and stores only the frame differences between them. The frames that are compressed using temporal compression are called interframes.

Sorenson Spark uses a combination of both spatial and temporal methods. It primarily uses temporal compression, which allows it to use a low data rate but produce good quality video. Sorenson Spark also uses spatial compression so that the intraframes (spatial compression) can be used as a reference for the interframes (temporal compression). Therefore with Sorenson Spark, you have the best of all worlds because many other codecs use only intraframe compression.

Flash MX Professional 2004 Video Features

Flash MX Professional 2004 offers additional video features that are not included in Flash MX 2004. The following chart outlines the video features found only in the Flash MX Professional 2004 solution. These are features that are outside the scope of this book, and will not be covered because they are not included in the Flash MX 2004 solution.

Flash MX Professional 2004 Video Features	
Feature	**Description**
Media components	Allow you to quickly integrate video into your project with streaming media components such as a seek bar, control buttons, volume settings bar, and so on that you can easily click and drag onto the Stage.
Enhanced Video Quality	Using the QuickTime FLV (Flash video) exporter, a new encoder is available with greater control and superior image quality for encoding video at larger frame sizes and higher frame rates.
Professional Video Application Integration	Streamline workflow by exporting to FLV format from leading professional video editing and encoding tools such as Avid Xpress/Media Composer, Apple Final Cut Pro, Discreet Cleaner, and Anystream Agility.

I. ————————Importing Video

The first step in working with video is importing it into Flash MX 2004. This exercise will teach you how to import a video clip into Flash MX 2004 as an embedded video.

1. Copy the **chap_15** folder, located on the **H•O•T CD-ROM**, to your hard drive. You will need to have this folder on your hard drive in order to save changes to the files inside it.

2. Open the file called **importVideo_Final.fla** file from the **chap_15** folder. This is the finished version of the project you'll be building in the next two exercises.

3. Choose **Control > Test Movie** to preview the movie. Notice the movie begins in a stopped position. Click the **Play** button to start the video clip, and click the **Stop** button to stop the video clip from playing. You will add the functionality to the buttons, but first you will learn how to import and embed the video clip into Flash MX 2004.

4. When you are finished previewing this movie, close the **Preview** window and this file.

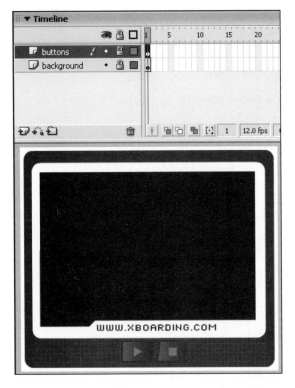

5. Open the **importVideo.fla** file from the **chap_15** folder. This file was created to get you started.

6. Click the **Insert Layer** button to add a new layer to the **Timeline**. Rename the layer **video** and make sure it is above all the other layers.

7. Choose **File > Import > Import to Stage** and select the **jumps.mov** file from the **chap_15** folder. Click **Open** (Windows) or **Import** (Mac).

Note: *This is a QuickTime video clip.*

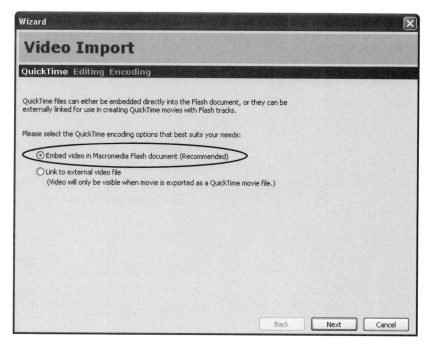

8. The **Video Import Wizard** window will appear. Make sure the **Embed video in Macromedia Flash document** option is selected. Click **Next**.

Note: You will only be given this option to either embed or link to a video file if you choose to import a QuickTime (MOV) file into Flash MX 2004. By default, all other video file types are automatically embedded.

To Embed or Not to Embed?

When you import a QuickTime video clip, you can choose to embed it or link it. If you choose to embed a video clip, the video becomes part of the movie, just as a bitmap does when you import it into Flash MX 2004. The embedded video clip will then play in the SWF file inside Macromedia Flash Player. This is wonderful because users do not need any special player to view the video—all they need is the Flash 6 (or higher) Player installed on their browsers. When you import video, you can also choose to link to an external video file. In this case, the video will not be stored inside the Flash MX 2004 document, and when you export the file from Flash MX 2004, you can not export it as a SWF file—instead, you have to export it as a QuickTime file (MOV). This means that the resulting file will not play in the Flash player, but will in the QuickTime player. You will learn about linked video in Exercise 4, but for now, the next few exercises concentrate on embedded video.

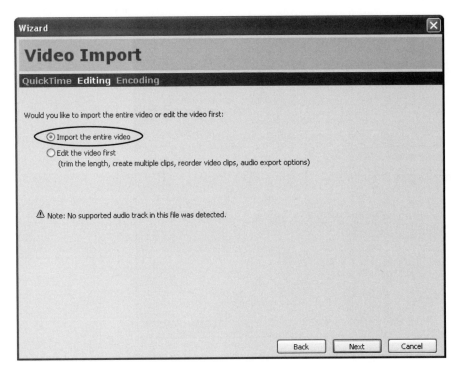

9. The next **Video Import Wizard** screen will show **Editing** options. From here you can choose whether to **Import the entire video**, or to **Edit the video first**. You will be learning, later in this chapter, how to use the editing capabilities of the new **Video Import Wizard**. For now, however, make sure that **Import the entire video** is selected. Click **Next**.

Note: You may have noticed the audio note at the bottom of the Video Import Wizard window. This note will appear if either the audio codec used in the audio track is not supported on your system or if there is no audio attached to the video file, which is the case in this exercise.

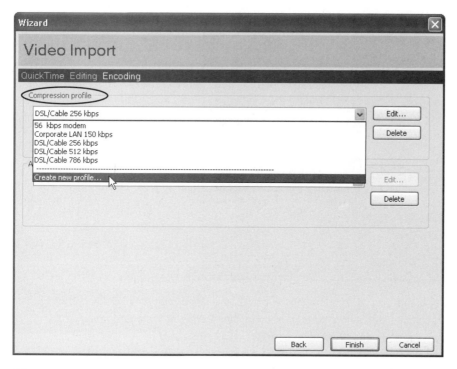

10. The next **Video Import Wizard** screen will show more **Encoding** options. From the **Compression profile** pull-down menu, choose **Create new profile**.

*From the **Compression profile** pull-down menu, you can specify a bandwidth to target. Selecting **56 kbps modem**, for instance, will compress your video in such a way that a visitor to your Web site, on a 56 kbps modem, should be able to watch the video—uninterrupted—while it is being downloaded (streamed) to his or her computer. The lower the bandwidth you are targeting, the more the video will be compressed in an attempt to reduce the file size enough to allow it to safely stream over the bandwidth target you've chosen. If you're not satisfied with any of the preset compression profiles, or you want more feedback and options about how the video is going to be compressed, you can also choose to create your own profile.*

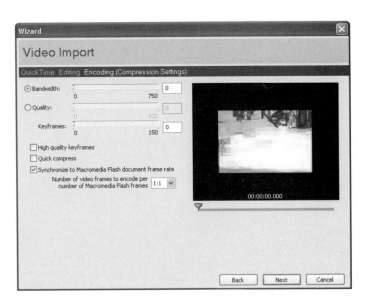

When you choose to create your own compression profile, the Video Import Wizard window will update to show you compression settings for your video clip. A chart at the end of the exercise breaks down the compression options you can specify.

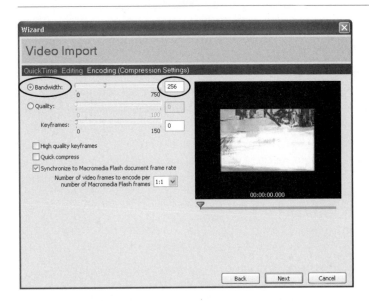

11. With the **Bandwidth** radio button selected, drag the **Bandwidth** slider to **256 kbps**, or enter **256** in the **Bandwidth** field. The **Bandwidth** slider allows you to set the download speed you are attempting to target.

12. For the **Keyframes** setting, drag the keyframe slider to **24**, or enter **24** in the **Keyframes** field. This will create video keyframes inside the video every 24 frames. For further information on video keyframes, see the "Video Keyframes" sidebar at the end of this exercise

13. Make sure the **High quality keyframes** check box is checked. This will ensure that your keyframes have consistent quality throughout the video. Make sure the **Synchronize to Macromedia Flash document frame rate** check box is also checked. This will match the playback rate of the imported video to the Macromedia Flash project file frame rate. For the **number of video frames to Flash frames** ratio, make sure it is set to **1:1**. When you are finished applying these settings, click **Next**.

14. The next screen will ask you to give a name and description to your new compression profile. In the **Name** and **Description** fields type what is shown in the picture here. The next time you want to use these compression settings, this profile will be available under the **Compression profile** pull-down menu you saw earlier in Step 10. After you name the new profile, click **Next**.

15. Back in the **Encoding** pane in the **Video Import Wizard**, click the **Advanced settings** pull-down menu, and choose **Create new profile**.

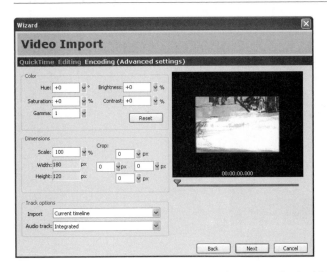

*As you can see under the Advanced settings pane in the Video Import Wizard, there are quite a few settings you can modify. Under **Color**, you can adjust everything from the color (Hue) of your video footage to the **Brightness** and **Contrast**. Under **Dimensions**, you can scale down the video footage (great for when you're importing full-scale 640 x 480 video files but only want them to display at 320 x 240), and even crop off an area of the video. Under **Track options**, you can specify where to import the video file into (the current Timeline, a movie clip, or a graphic symbol) and even if you want the accompanying audio track (if any) to be integrated into the video clip or to be its own, stand-alone sound file (so you can compress it independent of other sound clips, for instance).*

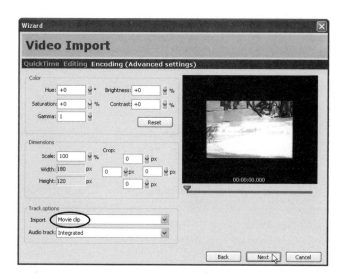

16. Leave the **Color** and **Dimensions** options set at their default settings. Under **Track options**, from the **Import** pull-down menu, choose **Movie clip** (this will keep your Timeline less cluttered because all the frames necessary to play this video will be nicely self-contained with its own movie clip symbol). Leave the **Audio track** option set to its default setting since this video clip doesn't have an audio track. Click **Next**.

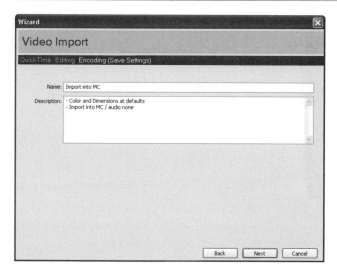

17. The next **Video Import Wizard** screen will prompt you to name your new advanced setting. In the **Name** and **Description** fields, type what is shown in the picture here. This is a description that gives a little more detail about what this advanced setting does. Click **Next**.

18. Back in the **Encoding** pane in the **Video Import Wizard**, click **Finish**.

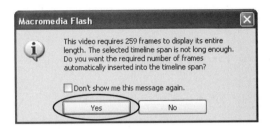

19. As soon as you click **Finish** in the last step, you will see the **Import** progress bar. Then you will be presented with one last dialog box. This dialog box allows you to decide if you want Flash MX 2004 to automatically expand the **Timeline** to accommodate the length of the video file. Click **Yes**.

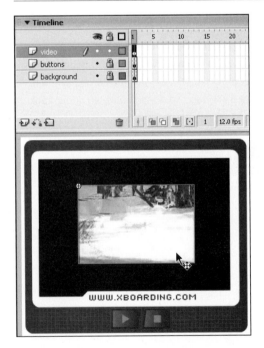

20. You'll notice that the video clip will now appear on the **Stage**. Click the video clip to select it and move it slightly higher so that it is centered inside the background window, as shown here.

When you imported the video clip into your Flash project, the video was placed in the Library, a movie clip was created, the video (and all of the frames needed to display that video) were placed in the movie clip (because in Step 16 you instructed the Video Import Wizard to import your video into a movie clip instance), and an instance of that movie clip was placed in the center of the Stage.

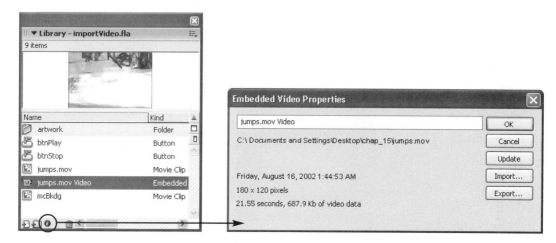

21. Press **Ctrl+L** (Windows) or **Cmd+L** (Mac) to open the **Library**. Notice the **jumps.mov** file. This is the video clip that you imported. Flash MX 2004 has automatically placed it in the **Library**. Select the **jumps.mov Video** file in the **Library** and click the **Properties** button. This will open the **Embedded Video Properties** window, where you can see the dimensions, duration in seconds, and size in kilobytes of video data. Click **OK** when you are finished.

22. Choose **Control > Test Movie** to see your movie in action in the SWF file!

Note: The buttons will not work yet—you will add ActionScript to them in the next exercise.

23. When you are finished, close the **Preview** window and save this file but keep it open for the next exercise.

Compression Settings

The following chart breaks down the compression options that you can specify in the **Compression Settings** window of the **Video Import Wizard**:

Compression Settings	
Option	**Description**
Bandwidth	This slider allows you to approximate (between 0 and 750 kbps) the download speed that you are attempting to target. When compressing your video, Flash will adjust the quality of each frame of your video clip in order to safely stream it over the bandwidth you've specified.
Quality	This slider allows you to specify the quality of all the frames in the video. A lower quality value will lower the quality of the video, but in return you get a video clip with a smaller file size. The opposite is true for a higher quality value.
Keyframes	The Keyframes slider allows you to specify the keyframe intervals (how many keyframes there are per frames of your movie). The more keyframes you have in a video clip (the lower the Keyframe slider), the faster the viewer can fast forward or rewind through a clip (if you give them that capability). But before you start thinking that's a good thing and adding a bunch of keyframes to your video clip, keep in mind that the more keyframes you add to your movie, the larger the file size. For more information about keyframes, see the sidebar following this table.

continues on next page

Compression Settings *continued*	
Option	Description
High quality keyframes	Check this check box if you are choosing to compress your video based on bandwidth instead of quality. This will ensure that your keyframes have a good, consistent quality throughout the video.
Quick compress	Checking this check box sacrifices video quality in favor of a faster compression time. If you want the best quality video, and don't mind waiting longer, leave this check box unchecked.
Synchronize to Macromedia Flash document frame rate	Synchronizes the movie frame rate to be the same as the Flash movie frame rate.
Number of video frames to encode per number of Macromedia Flash frames	Sets the ratio of imported video frames to Flash movie frames.
Playhead	Drag the playhead back and forth to preview how your compression settings will look as they're applied to a frame of your video clip.

NOTE | Video Keyframes

Video keyframes are different than the kind of keyframes you've learned about in the Flash MX 2004 Timeline. When you set video keyframes, you are determining how often a full, high-quality frame will be displayed. For example, a keyframe setting of 24 instructs the video playback to play every 24th frame. In the event that the computer cannot play all the frames due to slow processing speed, the computer playback will skip frames if it has to until it reaches a keyframe. If it can keep up with all the frames, it will play them all.

The lower the video keyframe, the more keyframes there will be in the compressed movie. The frames that are between keyframes (called interframes) will only update based on what has changed in the previous keyframe, thereby reducing file size.

You will not see the video keyframes in the Main Timeline inside Flash MX 2004. Instead, the video keyframes are part of the compression settings that compress the actual video file itself. Video keyframes are invisible to you in the project file; they simply affect the playback quality of the embedded video.

2.————————**Controlling Video with stop and go Actions**

Now that you know how to import video and work with the compression settings, you need to learn how to control the video playback. This exercise will teach you how to control video on the Main Timeline by adding ActionScript to buttons to control the video clip.

1. You should still have the **importVideo.fla** file open from the last exercise.

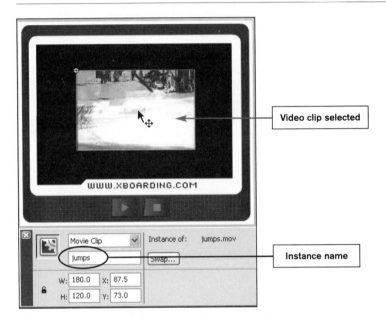

2. Click the video clip on the **Stage** to select it. In the **Properties inspector**, in the **Instance Name** field, type **jumps**. Later in this exercise, you will use the instance name to pass ActionScript to the movie clip.

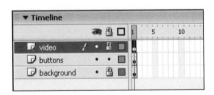

3. In the **Timeline**, lock the **video** layer and unlock the **buttons** layer.

4. On the **Stage**, click the **Play** button to select it. Open the **Actions** panel (**F9**).

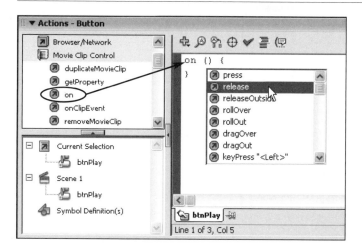

5. In the **Actions** pane, choose **Global Functions > Movie Clip Control** and double-click the **on** action to add it to the **Script** pane. From the **Code Hint** menu that appears, double-click **release** for the mouse event.

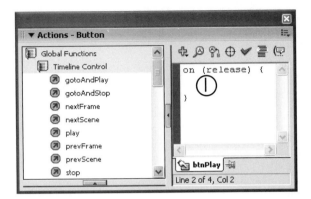

6. In the **Script** pane, place your cursor after the open curly brace and press **Enter/Return** to bring the cursor down to the second line, as shown here.

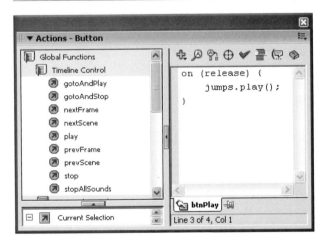

7. Type **jumps.play();**, as shown here. This tells the movie clip instance named **jumps** to play when the user clicks the **Play** button.

8. On the **Stage**, select the **Stop** button.

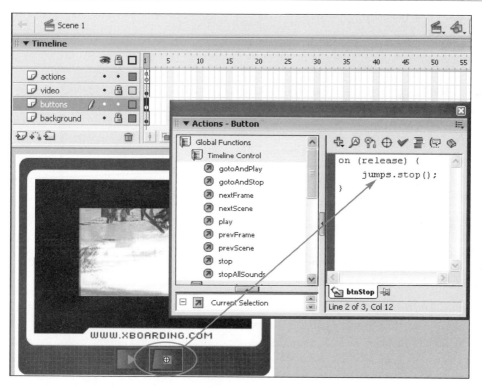

9. Repeat Steps 5, 6, and 7, but instead of **jumps.play();**, you want it to read **jumps.stop();**. Type **stop** in place of **play**, as shown here.

10. Choose **Control > Test Movie** to preview the video. Click the **Stop** button to stop the video and click the **Play** button to play the video again. Cool! When you are finished, close the **Preview** window.

You may have noticed that as soon as you test the movie, it begins to play. Next, you will add one more action so that the movie starts in a stopped position.

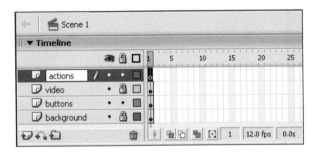

11. Click the **Add Layer** button to create a new layer. Name it **actions**, and make sure it is above all the other layers in the **Timeline**.

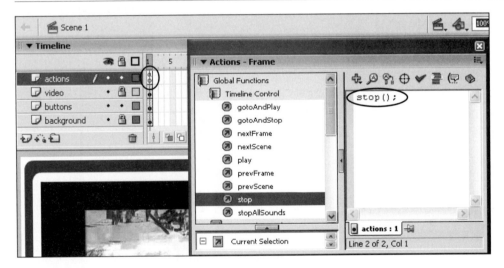

12. Select **Frame 1** on the **actions** layer. In the **Actions** pane, choose **Global Functions > Timeline Control** and double-click **stop** to add it to the **Script** pane. This will not work yet, because you are telling the **Main Timeline** to stop, and you want the movie clip instance named **jumps** to stop instead. You will add the instance name of the movie clip to the **stop** action next.

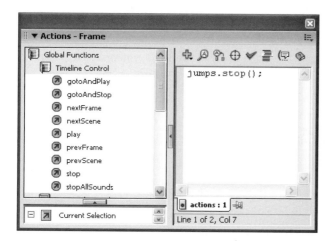

13. In the **Script** pane before **stop( );**, type **jumps.**, as shown here.

14. Choose **Control > Test Movie** to preview the video again. Notice that the video is stopped. Click the **Play** button to set the video in motion and click the **Stop** button to stop the video again. By adding a few basic actions, you can allow the user to have complete control over your video. When you are finished, close the **Preview** window.

15. Save and close this file.

3. —————————Controlling Video by Targeting Frame Labels

Not only do you have the ability to start and stop the video using ActionScript, you can also target specific points in the video using behaviors. This exercise will teach you how to use the **Goto and Play at frame or label** behavior to target different frames within the video sequence. Additionally, you will learn how to use named anchors to navigate through the video.

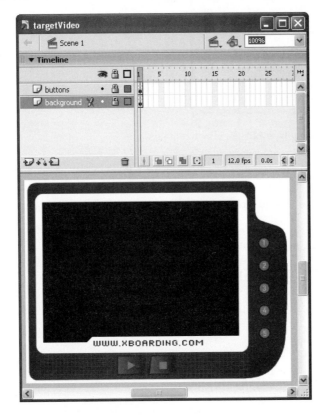

1. Open the **targetVideo.fla** file from the **chap_15** folder. This file was created to get you started.

2. Click the **Insert Layer** button to add a new layer to the **Timeline**. Rename the layer **video** and make sure it is above all the other layers.

3. Choose **File > Import > Import to Stage** and select the **catchingAir.mov** file from the **chap_15** folder. Click **Open** (Windows) or **Import** (Mac). You will then be presented with the **Video Import Wizard**.

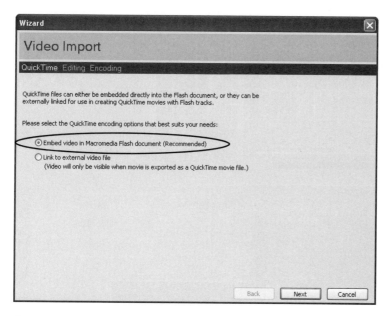

4. In the **Video Import Wizard,** make sure the **Embed video in Macromedia Flash document** option is selected. Click **Next**. You will be presented with the **Editing** window of the **Video Import Wizard** next.

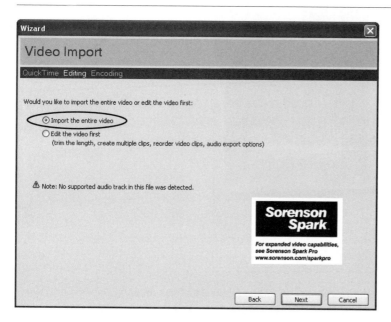

5. In the **Editing** screen of the **Video Import Wizard,** make sure **Import the entire video** is selected. Click **Next**.

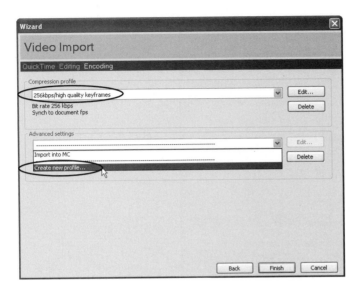

6. In the **Encoding** screen of the **Video Import Wizard**, choose the compression profile that you created in Exercise 1, **256kbps/high quality keyframes**. From the **Advanced settings** pull-down menu, choose **Create new profile**.

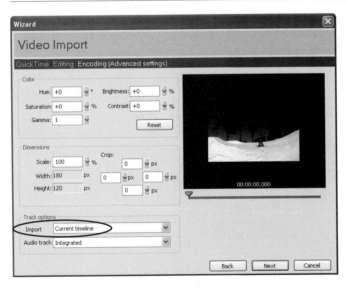

7. In the **Advanced Encoding settings** window, leave the **Color** and **Dimensions** options set to their default settings. For the **Track options**, make sure that **Current timeline** is selected under the **Import** pull-down menu. Leave the **Audio track** set to its default settings since there is no audio track for this video clip. Click **Next**. You will be prompted to name your new profile in the next screen.

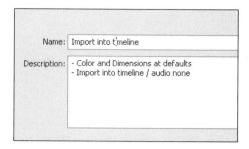

8. In the **Name** and **Description** fields type what is shown in the picture here. After you name your custom setting, click **Next**.

9. In the **Encoding** pane, click **Finish**.

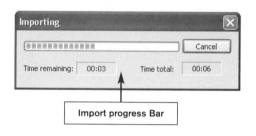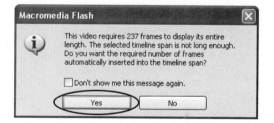

Import progress Bar

10. The **Import** progress bar will appear, and then you will be presented with the last dialog box asking if you want Flash MX 2004 to automatically expand the **Timeline** to accommodate the length of the video file (237 frames). Click **Yes**.

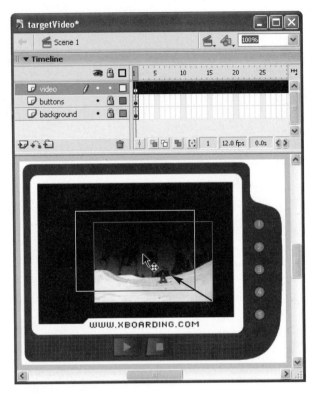

11. The video clip will be placed on the **Stage**. Click the video clip to select it and move it so that it is centered inside the background window, as shown here.

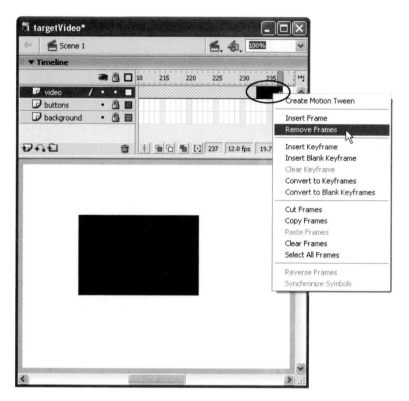

12. In the **Timeline,** move the **playhead** to **Frame 225** and scrub the **playhead** between **Frame 225** and where the video frames stop at **Frame 237.** Notice how the video fades out at about **Frame 233.** The rest of the frames from 233 to 237 are not necessary because the video has faded to black. Highlight **Frames 233** through **237** and **right-click** (Windows) or **Ctrl+click** (Mac) to access the contextual menu and choose **Remove frames** to remove the unnecessary frames from the **Timeline.**

Why remove the frames? In Flash MX 2004, video in the Timeline is treated just like Stream sound is treated in the Timeline. Only the frames that exist in the Timeline will be exported with the Macromedia Flash movie (SWF file). To reduce file size of the SWF file, you can remove frames from the Timeline to trim the video and save file size. In this example, the SWF file will be reduced from 1421 KB to 1415 KB by removing those five frames in the Timeline.

Note: *Although you deleted frames from the video clip on the Main Timeline, the original full video clip is still in the Library.*

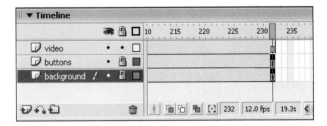

13. In the **Timeline**, click and drag down on the **buttons** and **background** layers to select **Frame 232** in both layers. Press **F5** to add frames up to **Frame 232** so that you can see the background and the buttons throughout the video.

14. Move the **playhead** back to **Frame 1** and click the **Insert Layer** button to add a new layer to the **Timeline**. Name this layer **labels**. Make sure it is above all the other layers.

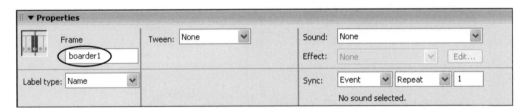

15. Select **Frame 1** on the **labels** layer in the **Timeline**. In the **Properties inspector (Window > Properties)**, type **boarder1** in the **Frame** label field. This will mark the place where the first snowboarder is shown.

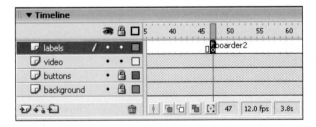

16. Scrub the **playhead** to see where a transition occurs and a new snowboarder appears in the video. Notice that a new snowboarder appears at **Frame 47**. Click **Frame 47** on the **labels** layer and press **F7** to add a blank keyframe to **Frame 47**. In the **Properties inspector**, type **boarder2** in the **Frame Label** field. This will mark the place where the second snowboarder is shown.

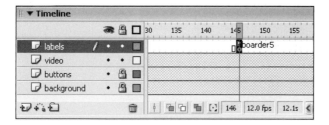

17. Repeat Step 13 to add blank keyframe and frame labels for three more snowboarders. **Hint: boarder3 = Frame 96, boarder4 = Frame 118,** and **boarder5 = Frame 146**.

In the following steps, you will add Behaviors to the buttons to target these frame labels.

18. Choose **Window > Development Panels > Behaviors** to open the **Behaviors** panel.

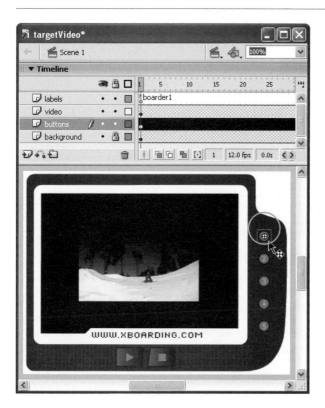

19. Move the **playhead** back to **Frame 1** in the **Timeline**. Unlock the **buttons** layer and click **button 1** on the right side of the **Stage** to select it, as shown here. You will add behaviors to the buttons in the following steps.

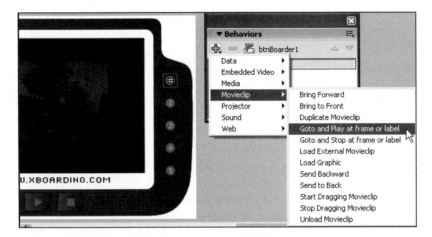

20. Click the **Add Behavior** button and choose **Movieclip > Goto and Play at frame or label**. This will open the **Goto and Play at frame or label** dialog box.

21. In the **Goto and Play at frame or label** dialog box, make sure **_root** is selected. In the **Frame Number/Frame Label** field, type **boarder1**. Click **OK**. This will tell the **playhead** to go to the frame label named **boarder1** on the **Main Timeline (_root)** when the user clicks **button 1**.

What is _root? It signifies that you are targeting the Main Timeline.

22. Repeat steps 19, 20, and 21 for the remaining four buttons. In the **Frame Number/Label** field, for **button 2**, type **boarder2**; for **button 3**, type **boarder3**; for **button 4**, type **boarder4**; and for **button 5**, type **boarder5**.

23. Choose **Control > Test Movie** and click each of the buttons to the right of the video clip to test the buttons. Each button will play a different snowboarder segment of the video. When you are finished, close the **Preview** window. You will learn to add anchors to your movie next.

Note: You may have noticed that the Stop and Play buttons worked as well. These were programmed for you using the exact same ActionScript you applied in Exercise 2.

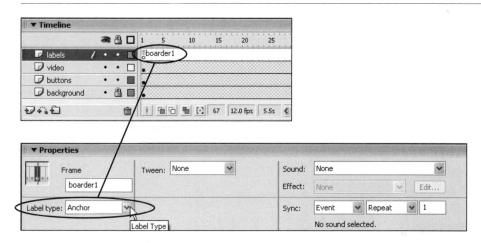

24. Back in the project file, in the **labels** layer, click the **boarder1** frame label in the **Timeline** to select that frame (**Frame 1**). In the **Properties inspector**, notice that under the **Frame Label** text box is a **Label type** pull-down menu. From this pull-down menu, choose **Anchor**. As soon as you select **Anchor**, notice that the icon next to the frame label in the **Timeline** changes. This is an indication that a named anchor is attached to that frame.

> ## NOTE | What Is a Named Anchor?
>
> In Flash MX 2004, you can create movies that work with the Forward and Back buttons in a browser. This feature is called a **named anchor**. A named anchor is a special frame label that resides on the Main Timeline and has a unique anchor icon. Once the named anchor is played in a browser window, it is registered in a browser's history. Then, when a user clicks on the Back button in the browser window, the browser will play the previous named anchor position on the Timeline.
>
> The Named Anchor feature will work in the Macromedia Flash 6 Player (or higher) on browsers that support the FSCommand with JavaScript, including Internet Explorer (Windows) or Netscape 3.x to 4.x (Windows). Named anchors do not work on browsers running on the Macintosh operating system. You will learn about FSCommands in Chapter 16, "*Publishing and Exporting*."

25. Repeat Step 24 by selecting each of the remaining four frame labels (**boarder2**, **boarder3**, **boarder4**, and **boarder5**) and then selecting **Anchor** from the **Label type** pull-down menu in the **Properties inspector**.

26. Add a new layer by clicking the **Insert Layer** button and rename it **actions**. Make sure that the **actions** layer is above the rest of your layers.

27. Select **Frame 232** on the **actions** layer and press **F7** to add a blank keyframe. You will add a stop frame action to this frame next.

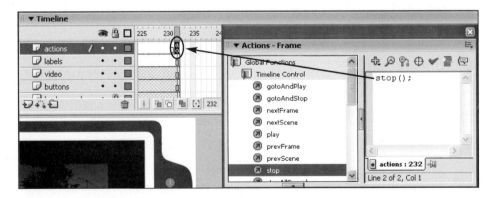

28. In the **Actions** panel (F9), choose **Global Functions > Timeline Control** and double-click the **stop** action to add it to the **Script** pane. This will stop the **playhead** at **Frame 232**, which is the end of the snowboard movie.

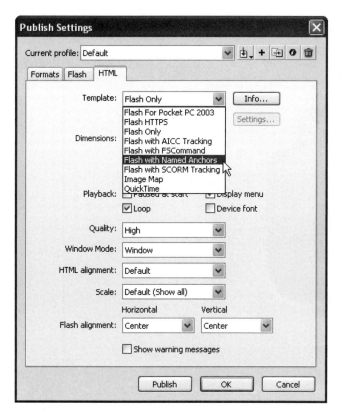

29. Choose **File > Publish Settings** to open the **Publish Settings** window. Click the **HTML** tab at the top, and in the **Template** drop-down list, choose **Flash with Named Anchors**. Leave the rest of the settings at their defaults and click **OK**. This will add JavaScript into the HTML document that will catch the named anchors as they play in the browser.

Note: *You will learn all about the Publish settings in detail in Chapter 16, "Publishing and Exporting."*

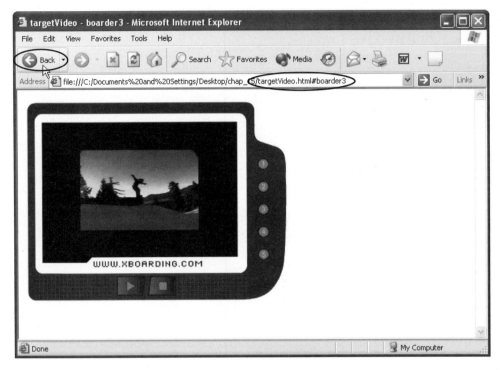

30. Publish your Flash MX 2004 movie and preview it in your browser by pressing the keyboard short-cut **F12**. This will allow you to preview the Flash MX 2004 movie in an HTML document so that you can test the named anchors. As the video plays, notice the URL in the browser window: The end will change to reflect the named anchor that is currently playing. When the movie reaches the end and stops, test the **Back** button in the browser—it will jump back one anchor to **boarder4**. Click it again and it will jump back to **boarder3**. Now click the **Forward** button in the browser and the movie will advance forward to the next named anchor. Neat! When you are finished, close the browser window.

*Note: The **Named Anchor** feature does not work on browsers running on the Macintosh operating system.*

*Tip: You can use named anchors with video or with any content on the Main Timeline. Because many users will not be accustomed to using the Forward and Back buttons with Macromedia Flash movies, you may have to add some text to your movie, instructing the users that they can navigate using the browser Forward and Back buttons. **Note:** You will learn all about the Publish Preview options in Chapter 16, "Publishing and Exporting."*

NOTE | Other Uses for Named Anchors

In the past, Macromedia Flash movies could never utilize the Back button of a browser. Because many people built entire Web sites using the Macromedia SWF file format, this created a usability problem. Using the named anchors technique, you could build back browser functionality into any Macromedia Flash MX 2004 Web site. You learned from this exercise how easy it is to add this feature, so consider this technique for any complete Web site that you build in the future. Just make sure that the named anchors exist on the Main Timeline or in the Main Timeline of other scenes because they have to be placed there in order to work correctly.

31. When you are finished, save and close this file.

4. ———————Linking to QuickTime Video

Many people and/or companies, like CNN, build QuickTime movies that have Macromedia Flash controllers. If you need to author QuickTime content, you can link to a QuickTime video clip from the Flash 2004 movie. In the following steps, you will learn about the integration between Apple QuickTime and Flash MX 2003. This exercise will show you how to use a linked QuickTime movie with a custom Flash MX 2004 interface. You need to have a current version of QuickTime to complete this exercise. A full version of Apple QuickTime 6 is included on the **H•O•T CD-ROM**. It is located inside the **software** folder.

1. Open the **linkingtoQT.fla** file inside the **chap_15** folder. This file was created to get you started.

2. Click the **Insert Layer** button in the **Timeline** to insert a new layer. Rename the layer **video** and make sure it is above the existing layers.

3. With the **video** layer selected, choose **File > Import > Import to Stage**. Select the **linking.mov** file from the **chap_15** folder and click **Open** (Windows) or **Import** (Mac). You will be presented with the **Video Import Wizard**.

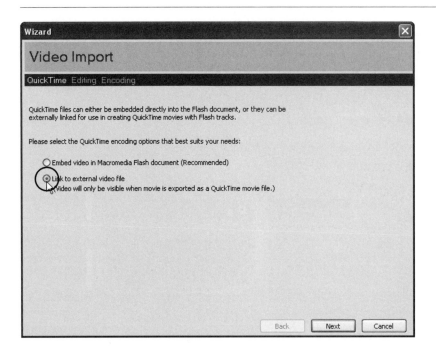

4. Select the **Link to external video file** radio button. Click **Next**.

5. You will be presented with a dialog box asking if you want Flash MX 2004 to automatically expand the **Timeline** to accommodate the length of the video file (108 frames). Click **Yes** to expand the number of frames in the **Timeline** to match the number of frames in the video.

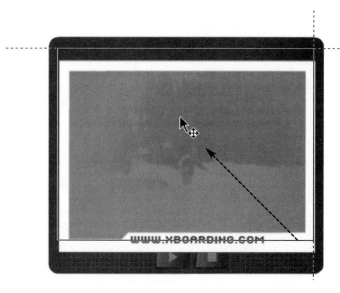

6. The video clip will be placed on the **Stage**. Click the linked video clip to select it and move it so that it is positioned inside the background window, near the top, as shown here.

7. Press **Ctrl+L** (Windows) or **Cmd+L** (Mac) to open the **Library**. Notice the **linking.mov** file. This is the video clip that you imported. Flash MX 2004 has automatically placed it in the **Library**, as well as an instance of it on the **Stage**.

8. In the **Timeline**, notice that the **video** layer is **108** frames. This is because you chose to allow Flash MX 2004 to automatically expand the **Timeline** to accommodate the length of the video file in Step 5. Move the **playhead** to **Frame 108** in the **Timeline**. Click and drag down on the **buttons** and **background** layers to select **Frame 108** in both layers. Press **F5** to add frames up to **Frame 108** so that you can see the background and the buttons throughout the video.

9. Scrub through the movie with your **playhead** to view the QuickTime content. Move your **playhead** back to **Frame 1** and press **Return/Enter** to preview the movie inside the project file.

Note: You can not preview linked QuickTime video files using the Test Movie command because you cannot export a linked QuickTime movie as a SWF. Instead, you need to export it as a QuickTime movie (MOV). You will do this later in this exercise.

10. Move the **playhead** to **Frame 1** and lock the **video** layer and unlock the **buttons** layer. In the following steps, you will add ActionScript to the **Stop** and **Play** buttons.

11. On the **Stage**, select the **Play** button on the left side of the **Stage**. Open the **Actions** panel (**F9**).

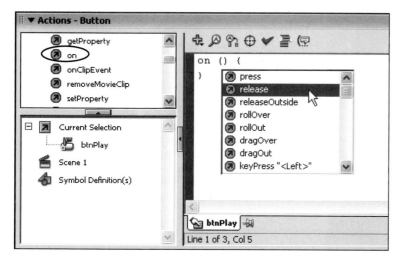

12. In the **Actions** pane, choose **Global Functions > Movie Clip Control** and double-click the **on** action to add it to the **Script** pane. From the **Code Hint** menu that appears, double-click **release** for the mouse event.

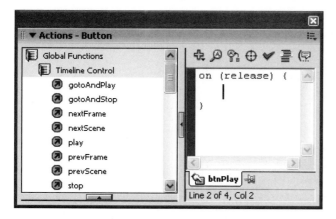

13. In the **Script** pane, place your cursor after the open curly brace and press **Enter/Return** to bring the cursor down to the second line, as shown here.

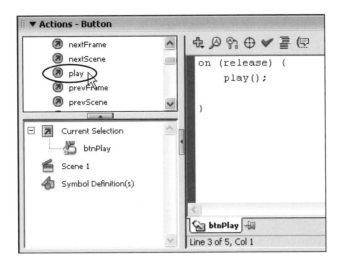

14. In the **Actions** pane, select **Global Functions > Timeline Control** and double-click the **play** action to add it to the **Script** pane. This ActionScript will tell the **playhead** to play through the frames in the **Timeline** when the user clicks the **Play** button. In the following steps, you will add the **stop** action to the **Stop** button by copying and pasting the code from the **Play** button.

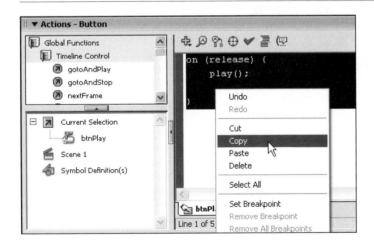

15. In the **Script** pane, select all the code that you just added to the **Play** button and then **right-click** (Windows) or **Ctrl+click** (Mac) on the selected code, and from the contextual menu that appears, choose **Copy**.

Rather than re-enter all the ActionScript onto the Stop button, you're simply going to copy the ActionScript from the Play button, paste it onto the Stop button, and change the **play();** *code to* **stop();**. *This is a huge timesaver!*

16. On the **Stage**, select the **Stop** button.

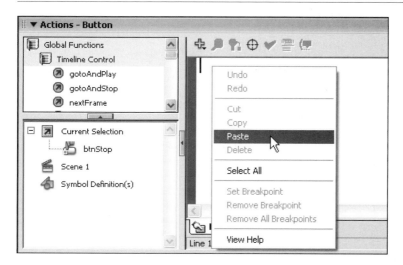

17. In the **Script** pane, **right-click** (Windows) or **Ctrl+click** (Mac), and from the contextual menu that appears, choose **Paste**. This will paste the ActionScript code that you copied from the **Play** button, onto the **Stop** button!

```
on (release) {
     stop();

}
```

18. Select the word **play**, and type **stop**. This ActionScript will tell the **playhead** to stop when the user clicks the **Stop** button.

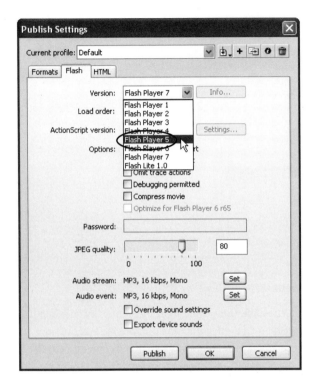

19. Choose **File > Publish Settings** to open the **Publish Settings** window. In the **Flash** tab, from the **Version** drop-down list, choose **Flash Player 5**. Leave the rest of the settings at their defaults and click **OK**. Because the current version of the QuickTime Player will play only Flash 5 content, you have to change the version of the Macromedia Flash file to Flash 5 before publishing the file as a QuickTime movie, as you will do next.

Note: You will learn all about the Publish settings in detail in Chapter 16, "Publishing and Exporting."

20. Choose **File > Export > Export Movie**.

21. From the **Export Movie** dialog box, name the movie **flashQT.mov** and select **QuickTime** as the file format and click **Save** to save it to the **chap_15** folder on your hard drive. Although you will notice many file format options here, the only way to view the QuickTime content is to save the file in the QuickTime format.

Note: You can't import a linked QuickTime file and export out the SWF file because a linked QuickTime movie simply will not play as a SWF.

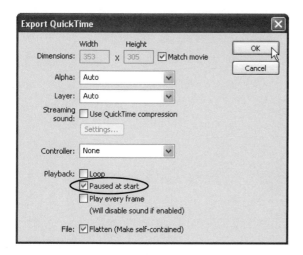

22. In the **Export QuickTime** dialog box, select the **Playback** option **Paused at start** and leave the rest of the settings at their defaults. Click **OK** and Flash MX 2004 will export this file as a QuickTime movie. The **Paused at start** option will force the movie to start in a stopped position and wait for instructions to begin playing the movie (such as a user clicking the **Play** button).

Note: QuickTime uses "tracks" to separate and store different forms of multimedia. In version 4 of QuickTime, the Flash track was added. A Flash track allows you to include content that you built in Macromedia Flash. However, QuickTime will only support ActionScript that is one version less than the version of QuickTime that the viewer has installed. (In other words, QuickTime 6 supports Flash 5 ActionScript. QuickTime 5 supports Flash 4 ActionScript, and so on and so forth.) Many people build QuickTime movies that have Flash controllers. (CNN has a lot of content on its site that is created this way). The disadvantage to this kind of movie is that it requires the QuickTime player to view the content, but it has the advantage of being able to employ cool-looking Macromedia Flash–created navigation buttons. A chart follows at the end of this exercise detailing the different QuickTime export options.

23. To check the results, go to the **chap_15** folder and double-click the file titled **flashQT.mov** file to open your file inside the QuickTime movie player. Notice that the movie is stopped. Click the **Play** button to start it; click the **Stop** button to stop it again.

24. When you're done, close the **flashQT.mov** file. Save and close the **linkingToQT.fla** file.

Note: *To recap: You can not export a linked QuickTime movie as a SWF. Instead, you need to export it as a QuickTime movie (MOV). If you want to export a SWF file that has a QuickTime movie inside, choose to have the QuickTime movie embedded (rather than linked) when you import the video.*

The QuickTime Dialog Box

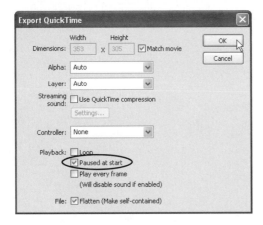

The chart on the next page explains all of the QuickTime features.

QuickTime Dialog Box	
Setting	**Description**
Dimensions	This option controls the size of the movie. If the **Match movie** box is checked, a QuickTime movie will be created that will have the same dimensions as those you set in the Document Properties dialog box.
Alpha	This option controls transparency of the Flash MX 2004 background on top of QuickTime. The **Auto** option sets the Flash MX 2004 track to transparent if it appears over the other tracks, and opaque if it is at the bottom or is the only track in the movie. **Alpha Transparent** makes the Flash MX 2004 track transparent so that you can see content under it. **Copy** sets the Flash MX 2004 track to opaque.
Layer	This option controls where Flash MX 2004 plays in the stacking order of QuickTime tracks. **Top** places the Flash MX 2004 track on top of all other tracks. **Bottom** places the Flash MX 2004 track below other tracks in the QuickTime movie. **Auto** detects where the Flash MX 2004 content is located and places the Flash MX 2004 track on top if it has been positioned in front of an imported QuickTime movie.
Streaming sound	If this box is checked, Flash MX 2004 will export streaming sound to a QuickTime sound track.
Controller	This option allows you to choose which QuickTime controller will be used to play back your exported QuickTime movie.
Playback	This option allows you to choose how your movie is played. **Loop** will play your movie from start to finish and will keep playing over and over. **Paused at start** will not play your movie until a button is pressed within your movie to initiate it, or until the Play button is pressed on the QuickTime control panel. **Play every frame** will allow every frame to be viewed, no matter the effect on playback, and all sound will be disabled in the exported QuickTime movie if this option is selected.
File	If this box is checked, Flash MX content will be combined with the imported video content into a single QuickTime file.

5. _____**Editing Video**

One of the features within the new Video Import Wizard, is the ability for you to select a video clip and choose which portions of the video that you actually want to import into your Flash MX 2004 movie. This is an incredibly useful tool if you don't have the budget to purchase a video editing program such as Apple's Final Cut Pro or Adobe's Premiere with which to edit video. Instead of opening a separate, powerful video editing program to simply extract a few clips from a larger video clip, you can now streamline your workflow by performing that process right inside of Flash MX 2004. In this exercise, you will learn how to select a video file, extract a few clips from that video, and then import *only* those clips into your Flash movie.

1. Open the **importClips.fla** file from the **chap_15** folder. This file was created to get you started.

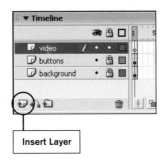

Insert Layer

2. Click the **Insert Layer** button to create a new layer. Rename the new layer "**video**" and make sure it is above all other layers.

3. Choose **File > Import > Import to Stage** and select the **jumps.mov** file from the **chap_15** folder. Click **Open** (Windows) or **Import** (Mac). The **Video Import Wizard** will appear next.

> **NOTE | Importing Video**
>
> There are two ways to import video into Flash MX 2004. The first way is to choose **File > Import > Import to Stage**, as you have done up to this point in the chapter. This will import the video clip into the Library and add an instance of it to the Stage. The second way is to choose **File > Import > Import to Library**. This command will import the video clip directly into the Library without placing an instance on the Stage.

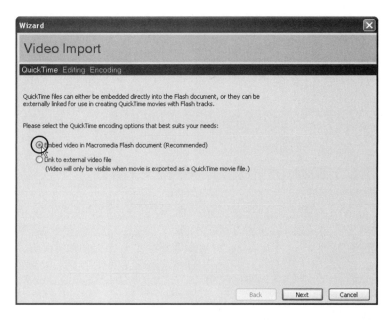

4. In the **Video Import Wizard**, make sure the **Embed video in Macromedia Flash document** option is selected. Click **Next**.

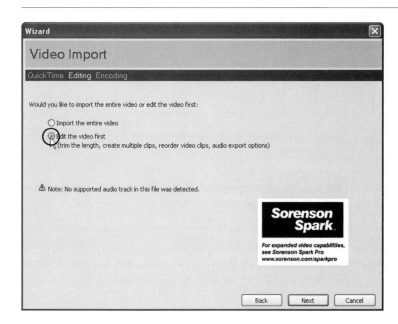

5. In the **Editing** pane of the **Video Import Wizard**, select the option **Edit the video first**, and click **Next** to go to the **Customize Editing** screen.

The Customize Editing Screen in the Video Import Wizard

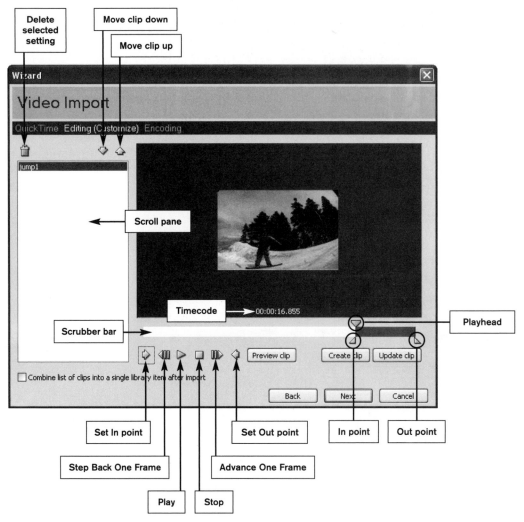

The **Customize Editing** pane of the new **Video Import Wizard** can now streamline your workflow by simplifying video editing processes right inside of Flash MX 2004. You can trim the length of your video clips, create multiple clips, and reorder video clips. You can also choose which parts of the video to pull clips from, and you can rearrange the playback order of those clips. You will do this in the following steps next.

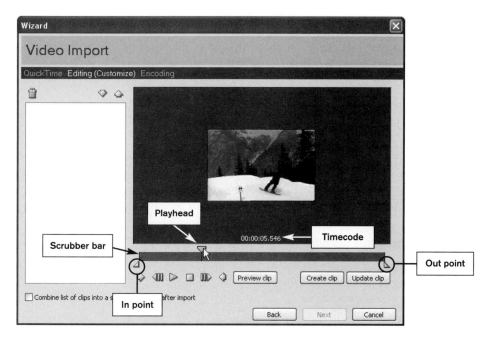

6. In the **Customize Editing** screen of the **Video Import Wizard**, drag the **playhead** until the timecode (below the video clip preview) reads **00:00:05.546**. This is the first frame of one of the jumps in this video. You will mark this as the first frame of your soon-to-be clip next.

7. Click the **Set In Point** button to move the **In** point (the beginning marker of your new clip) to where the **playhead** currently is.

8. Drag the **playhead** to timecode **00:00:07.820** (the last frame of this jump clip) and click the **Set Out Point** button. This will set the **Out** point to where the **playhead** is currently positioned.

9. Click the **Create clip** button to define your selected time (between the In and Out points) as a new clip.

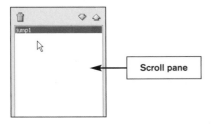

Scroll pane

10. When you click the **Create clip** button, a highlighted name will be added to the scroll pane. Rename the clip to **jump1**. You've now defined a clip!

Next, you're going to define one more clip, and then import them both into your Flash project as one video.

Out Point slider

11. Drag the **Out Point** slider all the way to the end of the video.

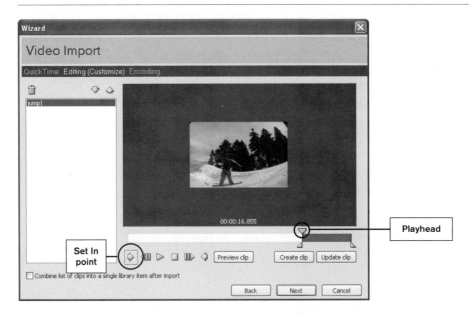

12. Drag the **playhead** to timecode **00:00:16.855** (the first frame of this last jump clip) and click the **Set In Point** button to define the beginning point of this clip. The Out point of this clip is the very last frame of the video, which you already set in Step 11.

13. Click the **Create clip** button to define a new clip. In the **Scroll** pane, rename your new clip to **jump2**.

Congratulations! You've selected a video clip on your hard drive and selected two small clips from the larger video. Next, you're going to import those into your Flash MX 2004 project. First, however, you are going to change the order the of these clips so that clip jump2 will play before clip jump1.

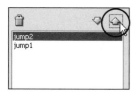

14. With the **jump2** clip selected in the **Scroll** pane, click the **Move Clip Up** button to move the **jump2** clip so that it comes before the **jump1** clip. Now, when these clips are played back, **jump2** will play before **jump1**.

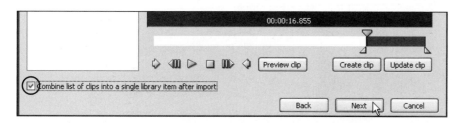

15. Click the check box titled **Combine list of clips into a single library item after import**. When this option is checked, it will consolidate the clips you've picked into one video clip within the **Library**. On the other hand, if you wanted to keep these clips as separate clips, you would simply leave this check box unchecked. After you've placed a check in the check box, click **Next**.

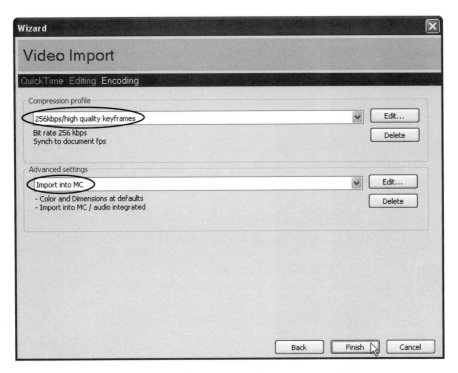

16. In the **Encoding** pane of the **Video Import Wizard**, click the **Compression profile** pull-down menu and choose the compression profile that you created back in the first exercise, **256kbps/high quality keyframes**. From the **Advanced settings** pull-down menu, choose the settings profile that you also defined in Exercise 1, **Import into MC**. Click **Finish**.

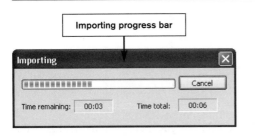

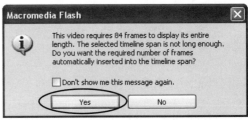

17. As soon as you click **Finish** in the last step, you will see the **Importing** progress bar. Then you will be presented with one last dialog box. This dialog box allows you to decide if you want Flash MX 2004 to automatically expand the **Timeline** to accommodate the length of the video file (84 frames). Click **Yes**.

18. The video clip will be placed on the **Stage**. Drag the video clip so that it is centered inside the background window, as shown here.

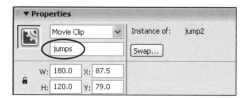

19. Make sure the video clip is still selected. In the **Properties inspector** (**Window > Properties**), in the **Instance Name** field, type **jumps**. This is now the instance name of this video clip. This name is also incorporated into the ActionScript that has already been added to the **Stop** and **Play** buttons at the bottom of the **Stage**.

20. Choose **Control > Test Movie** to preview you new video clip. As you can see, now instead of the video playing the whole way through, it is only playing the two clips that you selected in the **Video Import Wizard**!

This is a great and easy way to trim off any parts that you don't want/need of video. By trimming down your video to only the necessary parts, you are also decreasing the file size of the final SWF file.

21. When you are finished, save and close this file.

What Is Sorenson Squeeze?

In addition to using Flash MX 2004's built-in compression codec (Sorenson Spark) to compress video files as you have done in this chapter, you can also use more sophisticated technology to compress your videos outside Flash MX 2004 for higher quality video compression. **Sorenson Squeeze** is a separate product available for purchase at **http://www.sorenson.com**. Sorenson Squeeze allows you to compress video files using Sorenson Spark Pro, which is a more advanced compression codec than the standard Sorenson Spark codec that comes built into Flash MX 2004.

| Compressed inside Flash MX 2004;
SWF file size = 2,048 KB | Compressed using Sorenson Squeeze;
SWF file size = 292 KB |

The same file was compressed using Sorenson Spark inside Flash MX and Sorenson Squeeze outside Flash MX. The squeezed SWF file is seven times smaller than the file compressed inside Flash MX! It also looks quite a bit better.

Sorenson squeeze is surprisingly easy to use; Macromedia has a great tutorial, which you can find at **http://www.macromedia.com/desdev/tip/017.html**. You can also see a demo of the Sorenson Squeeze product at **http://www.sorenson.com/sparkpro.html**.

Nice job! You have made it through another chapter. Get ready for the next chapter—it is filled with useful information on how to publish your movies using Flash MX 2004's Publish and Export settings.

16.

Publishing and Exporting

Publishing Choices	HTML Files
Projector Files	Modifying Projectors with FSCommands
Exporting Image Files	Publish Settings
Optimizing Movies

chap_16

Macromedia Flash MX 2004
H•O•T CD-ROM

Prior to this chapter, you tested your movies in Flash MX 2004 by choosing Control > Test Movie, in order to see your work and generate a SWF file. This chapter will show you how to publish movies using the Publish settings instead. Testing and publishing are two different methods of producing the SWF file. You'll learn that publishing your movie instead of testing it offers many more options and greater control over the final output. As well, you'll learn how to generate an HTML file and a projector file from Flash MX 2004. This chapter will also teach you how to export an image from a project file.

A reference guide that explains the Publish settings is provided at the end of the chapter that exposes you to additional settings that are more advanced than those covered by the exercises in this chapter. In addition, a chart is provided listing the file types you can export. The chapter concludes with a look at some tips and tricks for optimizing your movies.

What Types of Content Can Flash MX 2004 Publish?

In addition to the SWF file, Flash MX 2004 is able to publish several different file formats. Here's a short chart that describes many of the available publishing options.

Flash MX 2004 Publishing Choices	
Web delivery	If you plan to publish Web content, you will need to create, at minimum, an HTML file to embed the Flash MX 2004 movie into. You'll learn how to generate this HTML code and establish how the movie will appear in the exercises provided in this chapter.
CD-ROM delivery	If you want to use Flash MX 2004 on a CD-ROM, you can create a projector file. You'll learn to do this in the exercises provided in this chapter.
Email attachment	If you want to create a Flash MX 2004 movie that you can easily attach to an email, you would create a projector file. You'll learn to make a projector file in this chapter.
QuickTime	You can generate a Flash track for QuickTime. This offers the opportunity to create Flash MX 2004 controllers or buttons for QuickTime content. You learned how to do this in Chapter 15, *"Video"*.
Image file	If you want to publish an image file, such as a JPEG, PNG, or GIF, from your project file, you can use the Publish settings to export an image. You will learn how to do this and what the limitations are in this chapter.

I. _____Flash MX 2004 and HTML

This exercise will walk you through the Publish settings interface to learn how to create the necessary HTML files for Web delivery of Flash MX 2004 content. The following steps will show you how changes that you make in the Publish settings affect the way your movie is viewed in a Web browser.

1. Copy the **chap_16** folder, located on the **H•O•T CD-ROM**, to your hard drive. You need to have this folder on your hard drive in order to save files inside it.

2. Open the **publish.fla** file from the **publishTesting** folder inside the **chap_16** folder. Notice that this is the only file inside the **publishTesting** folder.

3. Choose **Control > Test Movie** to preview the movie. This is the finished version of the effects movie you created in Chapter 8, "*Bitmaps*." Notice the title **publish.swf** at the top of the window. When you are finished viewing your movie, close the **Preview** window.

4. Leave Flash MX 2004 for a moment and open the **chap_16** folder on your hard drive. Open the **publishTesting** folder. Inside you will now see two files: one FLA file and one SWF file. When you chose **Control > Test Movie**, Flash MX 2004 created the SWF file in the folder as well.

5. Back in the project file, choose **File > Publish Preview > Default - (HTML)**, or use the shortcut key **F12**. This will trigger the **Publish Preview** command, which launches the default browser on your machine and displays an HTML page with the SWF file embedded inside it.

When you use the Publish Preview command, the Publish settings determine how Flash MX 2004 decides to publish the documents. You will work with the Publish settings in just a few steps.

> ### WARNING | Publish Preview Versus Test Movie
>
> The Publish Preview command, compared to using Control > Test Movie, gives you the most accurate indication of how your movie will look on the Internet. The preview you see when using Control > Test Movie will not always be exactly the same as the published movie appears on a Web server. For example, sound in your movie may vary slightly, and complex animations may animate slightly slower using the Test Movie command. To be safe, use the Publish Preview or Publish command to view the movie before you upload it live to the Internet.

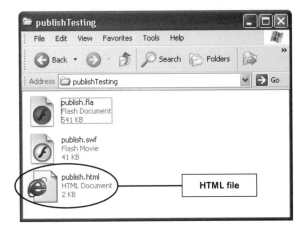

6. Open the **chap_16** folder on your hard drive. Browse again to the folder titled **publishTesting** and open it. Inside you will now see three files: the FLA file, the SWF file, and the HTML file. When you preview your movie in a browser by choosing **File > Publish Preview > Default - (HTML)**, Flash MX 2004 creates an HTML file in the same folder where you saved your FLA file.

Notice that all three files have the same name. By default, Flash MX 2004 names the additional files with the same name as the FLA file. You will learn how to change these names in the next few steps.

7. Back in the project file, choose **File > Publish Settings** to open the **Publish Settings** dialog box and make sure the **Formats** tab is selected.

The Formats tab is used to specify which file formats will be created when you publish the movie. Other tabs will appear or disappear according to which boxes you check.

TIP | Publish Settings Button in the Properties Inspector

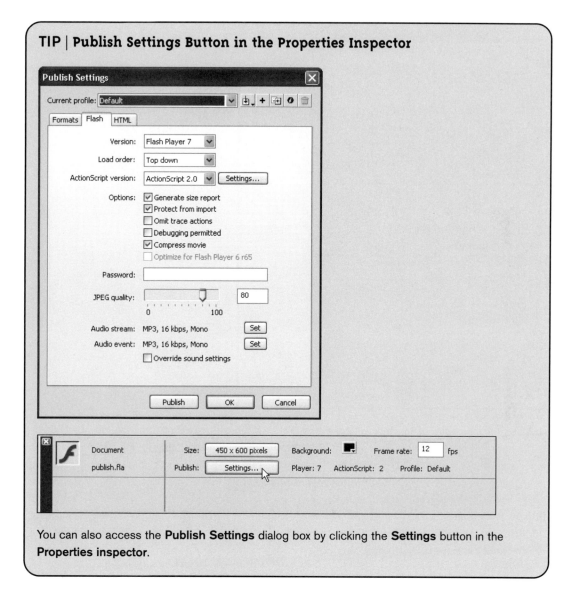

You can also access the **Publish Settings** dialog box by clicking the **Settings** button in the **Properties inspector**.

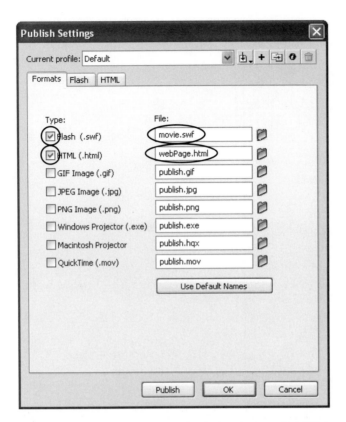

8. Make sure there are checkmarks in the **Flash** and **HTML** boxes. Notice that all the **File** names are set to have the prefix **publish**. This is because, by default, Flash uses the name of the FLA as a basis for naming the other file types. Change the name of the published SWF file by typing **movie.swf** inside the **Flash File** field. Then type **webPage.html** inside the **HTML File** field.

---

9. Click the **Publish** button to publish these two files with the names you just gave them. Flash MX 2004 will create these new files and save them in the same folder as the original FLA file. Click **OK** to exit out of the **Publish Settings** dialog box.

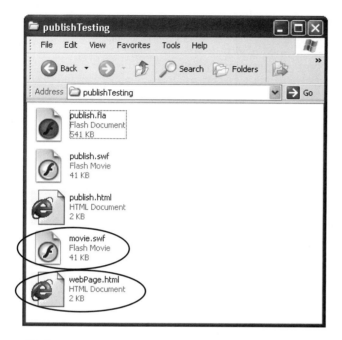

10. To make sure the new files have been published, open the **publishTesting** folder again. Inside you will now see *five* files: the three files that were already there, each with the **publish** name, and two new files named **movie.swf** and **webPage.html**.

*Each time you click the **Publish** button in the **Publish Settings** dialog box (or you use **File > Publish**), Flash MX 2004 writes and creates all of the files you have selected on the **Formats** tab in the **Publish Settings** dialog box (in this case, **SWF** and **HTML**). If you publish two or more times with the same settings, Flash MX 2004 will overwrite the existing files each time.*

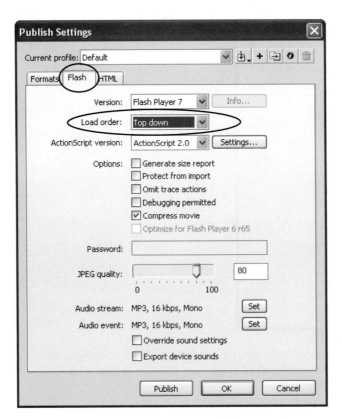

11. Back in the project file, choose **File > Publish Settings**. In the **Publish Settings** dialog box, click the **Flash** tab. For **Load Order**, select **Top down**. This will load each layer in the movie from the top layer first and continue downward. Selecting this option is a good habit to get into since, as you learned in Chapter 11, "*ActionScript Basics and Behaviors*," you should always place your actions on the top layer. When you select **Top down**, your **actions** layer will always load first in the Macromedia Flash Player.

Don't click **OK** *or* **Publish** *just yet; you will change another setting in the next step.*

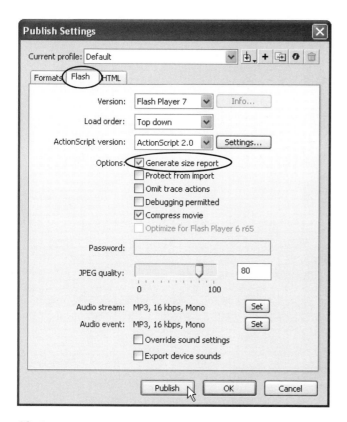

12. Place a check in the box next to **Generate size report**. Click the **Publish** button. This will cause the **Output panel** to automatically open and display the size report. Because you will be looking at the size report in a different manner, close the **Output panel** for now. Click **OK** to close the **Publish Settings** dialog box.

13. Open the **publishTesting** folder. Notice the new file **movie Report**.

*Why is it named **movie Report**? When you generate a size report, Flash creates a detailed report about the current SWF file. In this case, you renamed the SWF file **movie**, so the size report is named **movie Report**.*

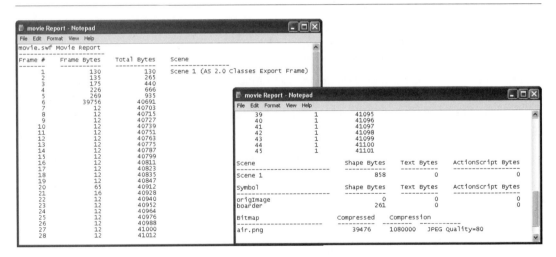

14. Double-click the **movie Report** file to open the size report file. Whenever you select **Generate size report**, Flash MX 2004 will create a special text file that gives a breakdown of the file size contributions of all of the symbols, fonts, and other elements in the movie. This is a handy tool to use when you want to know, frame by frame, how big the movie is and how many different elements are present in the movie, and even which font faces you used and which font characters were embedded in the SWF file! When you are done reviewing the file, you can close it.

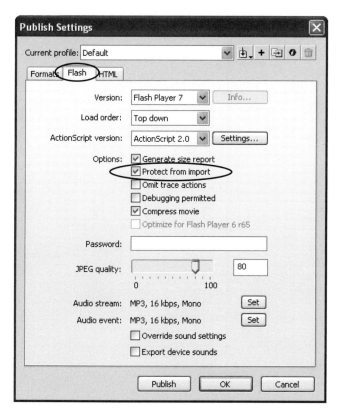

15. Go back to the **Publish Settings (File > Publish Settings)**. In the **Publish Settings** dialog box, under the **Flash** tab, place a checkmark in the box next to **Protect from import**. Checking this box prevents someone from importing your SWF movie file into Flash and converting it back to a project file.

*Be aware that checking **Protect from import** is not 100 percent secure. You can still import a protected movie into a Macromedia Director movie, and people "in-the-know" can also use third-party utilities to break into a Macromedia Flash movie. To be safe, don't put highly sensitive information into Flash MX 2004 movies, but do check the **Protect from import** box to safeguard against at least the average person opening the SWF file.*

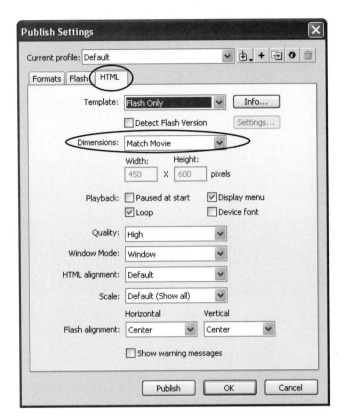

16. Click the **HTML** tab. Notice that the **Dimensions** setting default is **Match Movie**. This setting determines the dimensions at which the Flash MX 2004 movie will be set in the HTML tags. This value can be in pixels or can be a percentage of window size. As you will see in the next step, the Match Movie option will publish the movie at the same dimensions as the Stage, and will not allow the SWF file to scale. Click **Publish** to publish these changes, close the Output panel, and then click **OK** to close the **Publish Settings** window for now.

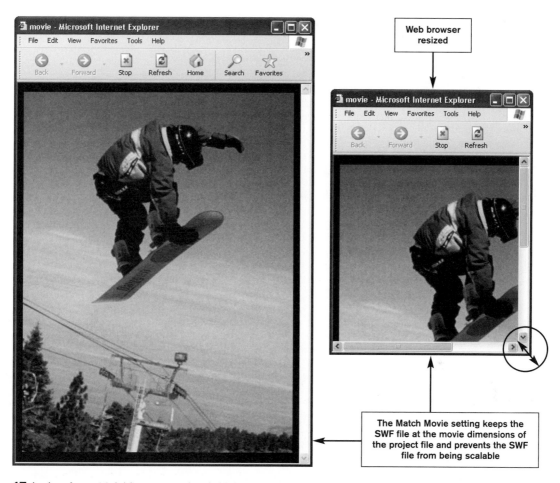

Web browser
resized

The Match Movie setting keeps the
SWF file at the movie dimensions of
the project file and prevents the SWF
file from being scalable

17. In the **chap_16** folder on your hard drive, open the **publishTesting** folder. Double-click the **webPage.html** file to open it. Resize the browser window by clicking and dragging the bottom-right corner of the window. Notice that the SWF file doesn't scale with the browser window and that, as you make the window smaller, the image becomes cut off. You will change the scalability restrictions by changing the **Dimensions** setting next.

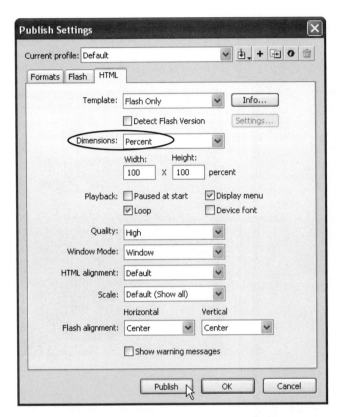

18. Go back to the **Publish Settings** (**File > Publish Settings**) and in the dialog box, under the **HTML** tab, choose **Dimensions: Percent**. Click **Publish**. This will replace the previous version of the **webPage.html** page. Close the **Output** panel and then click **OK** to close the **Publish Settings** window for now.

*It is important that you remember to click the **Publish** button if you wish to preview the new settings you have created. Flash MX 2004 will update the HTML document with the new setting applied to it only if you click the **Publish** button or choose **File > Publish**.*

Web browser resized

The Percent setting sets the SWF file to be the percentage amount relative to the Web browser, therefore allowing the SWF file to be scalable

19. To see the difference this setting makes, open the **webPage.html** file again from the **publishTesting** folder inside the **chap_16 folder**. Try resizing the browser window by clicking and dragging the bottom-right corner of the window. Notice that the SWF file scales this time! This is because the **Percent** setting allows the movie to fill the browser window 100 percent by 100 percent, so that no matter how you resize it, the movie will scale to fit the entire browser window and will not be cut off.

NOTE | Important Uploading Advice!

Flash MX 2004 publishes the HTML file with the assumption that the SWF file will be located in the same folder as the HTML file, so when you upload the HTML file to a Web server, make sure you put both files in the same directory.

This exercise has taken you through many of the common Publish settings on the Flash and HTML tabs. For a more in-depth look at what each of the settings on these tabs can do, refer to the tables at the end of this chapter. Also, in Chapter 18, "Integration," you will learn how to control the SWF file inside an HTML document by using Macromedia Dreamweaver.

20. Save and close this file.

NOTE | Scalable Bitmaps and Vector Art

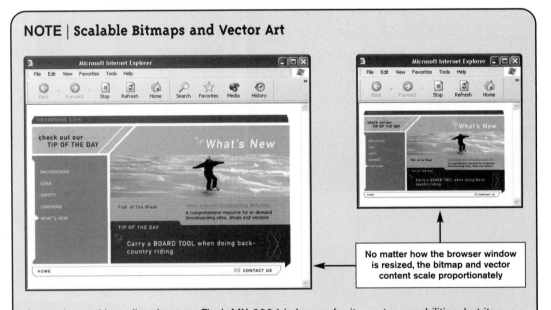

No matter how the browser window is resized, the bitmap and vector content scale proportionately

As you learned in earlier chapters, Flash MX 2004 is known for its vector capabilities, but its support of bitmap images is superb and far exceeds the support offered by HTML. Flash MX 2004 allows bitmaps to scale, animate, and transform (skew, distort, and so on) without much image degradation. This means that you can, and often will, combine bitmap and vector images in your movies. One thing to keep in mind when you are choosing to create scalable content that includes bitmaps is to import the bitmap at the largest size you plan to display it in your movie to ensure the best image quality without degradation. This is especially true if you plan to use the same bitmap at differing sizes throughout your movie.

2. ————————Creating Projectors

Have you ever received an email attachment that had the extension .exe or .hqx and found when you opened it that it was a Macromedia Flash movie that played right in its own window without a browser? If you have, you may be more familiar with projector files than you think. Projector files can be sent via email because they are stand-alone files that can play with or without the Macromedia Flash Player on most computers. Projector files can also be distributed via floppy disks or CD-ROMs or shown from your hard drive without a browser (as a great PowerPoint substitute). This exercise will teach you how to create a projector file using the Publish Settings dialog box.

1. Open the **projector.fla** file from the **chap_16** folder. In this exercise, you'll be turning this Flash movie into a stand-alone projector file in the steps that follow.

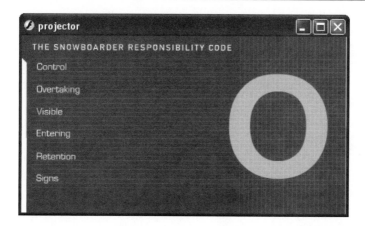

2. Choose **Control > Test Movie** to preview the movie. When you do this, Flash MX 2004 will create the SWF file and save it in the same folder as the FLA file, as you learned in the last exercise.

3. Close the **Preview** window. Back in the project file, choose **File > Publish Settings**. This will open the **Publish Settings** dialog box.

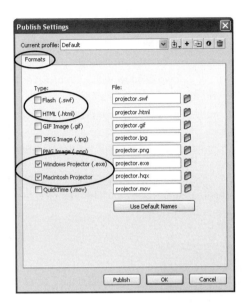

4. In the **Formats** tab, uncheck the boxes next to **Flash** and **HTML**, because you will be working with projector files in this exercise. Check the boxes next to **Windows Projector** and **Macintosh Projector**.

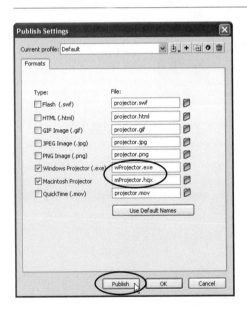

5. In the **File** field after **Windows Projector**, type **wProjector.exe**. After **Macintosh Projector**, type **mProjector.hqx**. (If you ever need to revert back to the default file names, simply click the **Use Default Names** button.) This will give each of your projector files its own unique name. Click **Publish** when you are finished.

When you click Publish, Flash MX 2004 automatically saves the projector files to the same folder as your FLA file.

NOTE | Missing Tabs in the Projector Publish Settings?

When you select the projector file types from the Formats tab in the Publish Settings dialog box, no additional tabs become available for you to alter the settings. However, you can control the way your projectors behave by using ActionScript and FSCommands. You will do this in the next exercise.

6. Click **OK** to close the **Publish Settings** dialog box. Open the **chap_16** folder on your hard drive. Inside you will see some files and a folder. Notice the two files that you just generated, **mProjector.hqx** and **wProjector.exe**.

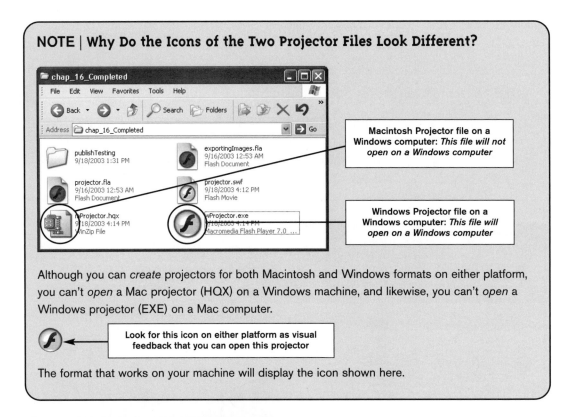

NOTE | Why Do the Icons of the Two Projector Files Look Different?

Macintosh Projector file on a Windows computer: *This file will not open on a Windows computer*

Windows Projector file on a Windows computer: *This file will open on a Windows computer*

Although you can *create* projectors for both Macintosh and Windows formats on either platform, you can't *open* a Mac projector (HQX) on a Windows machine, and likewise, you can't *open* a Windows projector (EXE) on a Mac computer.

Look for this icon on either platform as visual feedback that you can open this projector

The format that works on your machine will display the icon shown here.

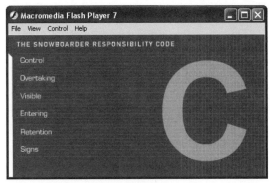

7. If you're using Windows, double-click the file named **wProjector** to open it. If you're on a Mac, double-click the file named **mProjector** to open it. You have just created your first projector file. Notice that the sound and animation play. This is because the projector file takes the entire movie, sound and all, and displays it in its own player.

8. Save this file (**projector.fla**) and keep it open for the next exercise.

3. _____Modifying Projectors with FSCommands

In the last exercise, you learned how to create a projector file. This exercise will show you how to modify the original project file by adding ActionScript to control the stand-alone projector file. The following steps will teach you how to use **FSCommands** to force the movie to take up the full screen of the computer and to disable the menu so that users cannot right-click or Ctrl+click the movie and see a list of menu items.

1. You should have the same file open from the last exercise, **projector.fla**. Save this file under a new name, **fsProjector.fla**.

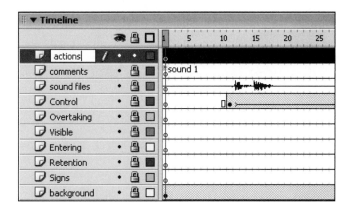

2. Click the **Insert Layer** button to add a new layer to the movie. Rename the new layer **actions**. Make sure this layer is on top of all the other layers.

3. Select **Frame 1** of the **actions** layer, and press **F9** to open the **Actions** panel. You will add the ActionScript to control the stand-alone projector file in this frame next.

NOTE | FSCommands as Frame Actions

It is usually most effective to add the FSCommands that control the window behavior to one of the first keyframes in the movie. This enables your commands to take effect immediately, as soon as the player opens.

What Are FSCommands?

FSCommands are actions that invoke JavaScript functions from Flash MX 2004. They include a command that is similar to an instruction, and an argument that checks to see if the command should be allowed (true) or not (false). A chart at the end of this exercise describes the FSCommands for the stand-alone projector.

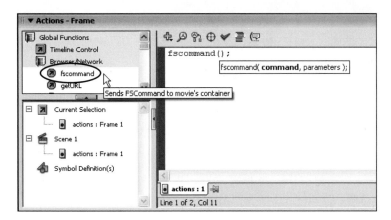

4. In the **Actions** pane, choose **Global Functions > Browser/Network** and double-click **fscommand** to add it to the **Script** pane.

```
fscommand("fullscreen", "true");
        fscommand( command, parameters );
```

5. Between the parentheses after **fscommand**, type **"fullscreen", "true"** (be sure to include the quotes). When this **fscommand** action is triggered (because it is on the first frame of the movie, it will be triggered when the movie is first launched), it will make the projector launch and completely fill the user's screen.

The fullscreen command makes the player take up the whole screen and prevents screen resizing when the parameter is set to **true***.*

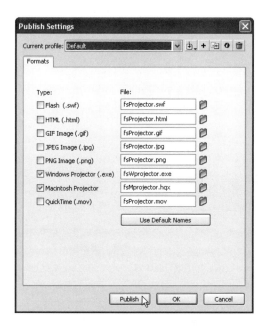

6. Choose **File > Publish Settings**. In the **Publish Settings** dialog box, rename the projector files **fsWprojector.exe** and **fsMprojector.hqx**. This will allow Flash MX 2004 to publish two new files without replacing the old projector files you made in the last exercise. When you are finished, click **Publish** to publish the projectors with the FSCommands added. Click **OK** to close the **Publish Settings** dialog box.

7. Open the **chap_16** folder on your hard drive. Inside you will see all the files you have created this far. If you are using Windows, double-click the file named **fsWprojector.exe**. If you are on a Mac, double-click the file named **fsMprojector.hqx** to open it. Now the projector will launch full screen! To exit the full-screen mode, simply press **Esc** on the keyboard.

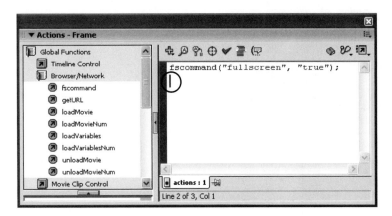

8. Back in the project file, make sure that **Frame 1** is still selected in the **actions** layer. In the **Actions** panel, click after the semicolon (**;**) at the end of the first fscommand, and press **Enter/Return** to create a line break and bring the cursor down to the next line, as shown here. This will give you a new line to add another action.

9. In the **Actions** pane, add another **FScommand** by choosing **Global Functions > Browser/Network** and double-clicking **fscommand**.

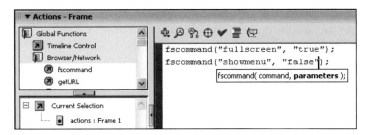

10. Between the parentheses after your newly added FScommand, type **"showmenu", "false"** (double-check your spelling and be sure to include the quotes). When the `showmenu` parameter is set to `false`, this command prevents the user from being able to **right-click** (Windows) or **Ctrl+click** (Mac) to access the full list of shortcut menu items.

*While a projector is playing, the user can either **right-click** (Windows) or **Ctrl+click** (Mac) to view a list of menu items. If the projector is set to full screen, you may not want to allow your users to zoom in or out or manipulate the way the movie is presented to them. By disabling the menu (setting* **showmenu** *to* **false***), you can limit the control that users have.*

---

11. Choose **File > Publish**. This will publish the changes you made (adding the new FSCommand) to the file formats that you specified in the **Publish Settings** dialog box.

---

12. Open the **chap_16** folder on your hard drive. If you are using Windows, double-click the file named **fsWprojector.exe**. If you are using a Macintosh, double-click the projector file named **fsMprojector.hqx**. Try to **right-click** (Windows) or **Ctrl+click** (Mac) to access the shortcut menu and see the full list of menu items. You should not be able to do it! You should see only the **About Macromedia Flash Player 7** and **Settings** menu items. This is because you set **showmenu** to **false**, thereby preventing the user from seeing the full menu and using any of the options within it.

---

13. When you are finished testing the projector, save the FLA and close this file.

	FSCommands for the Stand-Alone Projector File Defined	
Command	**Arguments**	**Function**
fullscreen	true/false	Sets the movie to fill the full screen when set to **true**, and returns the movie to a normal window when set to **false**. Setting the movie to **fullscreen** without also setting **allowscale** to **false** can result in the movie changing scale in some cases.
allowscale	true/false	Enables or disables the user's ability to scale the movie. If the argument is set to **false**, the movie will always be presented at the original size and can never be scaled. It also prevents the scaling that occurs when the movie is set to **fullscreen**. It is important to note that this option refers to the Macromedia Flash movie itself and not the stand-alone projector window, since the user can still scale the player window bigger or smaller by clicking and dragging on an edge of it. However, the movie will remain at the original size if **allowscale** is set to **false**. Note also that if **showmenu** is not set to **false**, the user can still scale the movie by right-clicking (Windows) or Ctrl+clicking (Mac) to access the drop-down Options menu, which includes Zoom In and Zoom Out options.
showmenu	true/false	When set to **true**, enables a user to right-click or Ctrl+click the projector and have access to the full set of context menu items. When this command is set to **false**, it disables the user's ability to access any of the menu items except for the About Flash Player item.
trapallkeys	true/false	When set to **true**, enables the movie to capture keystrokes that the user enters on the keyboard.
exec	path to application	Allows you to launch another application file on the local system. For this to work properly, you must know the correct path and name of the application. You must type the correct path and name of the application in the Parameters field. If you are calling a file in the same directory, all you need is the file name.
quit	none	Quits the projector.

To Publish or to Export?

In Flash MX 2004, in addition to the publishing features that you have learned in the last three exercises, you can also use the Export features, which will allow you to export content that can be edited in other formats such as an Adobe Illustrator document or a bitmap image. Why would you want to do this? Sometimes you might want to use a frame of something that you created in Flash MX 2004 in another application, such as Adobe Photoshop, Adobe Illustrator, or QuarkXPress. Many of the Export settings are very similar to the Publish settings, but the workflow involved in exporting an image is different from that of publishing an image, for example. In the following exercise, you will learn how to export an Adobe Illustrator file from a Flash MX 2004 file. A chart follows with the file formats you can export from Flash MX 2004.

Export File Types Supported by Flash MX 2004			
File Format	**Extension**	**Windows**	**Mac**
Adobe Illustrator 6.0 or earlier and Adobe Illustrator Sequence	.ai	x	x
Animated GIF, GIF Image, and GIF Sequence	.gif	x	x
Bitmap and Bitmap Sequence	.bmp	x	
AutoCAD DXF Image or DXF Sequence	.dxf	x	x
Enhanced Metafile and Enhanced Metafile Sequence	.emf	x	
EPS 3.0 and EPS 3.0 Sequence	.eps	x	x
Flash Movie	.swf	x	x
JPEG Image and JPEG Sequence	.jpg	x	x
PICT and PICT sequence	.pct		x
PNG Image and PNG Sequence	.png	x	x
QuickTime Video	.mov	x	x
WAV Audio	.wav	x	
Windows AVI	.avi	x	
Windows Metafile and Windows Metafile Sequence	.wmf	x	

Exporting Image Files

In the last three exercises, you worked with the Publish settings in Flash MX, and you learned how to publish different types of files. This exercise will show you another option for producing different file types from your project file: the Export options. If you know that you want to export only an image from your project file so that you can work with it in another application, using the Export settings can be a great solution. You will learn how to export content from Flash MX 2004 to create an Adobe Illustrator file in the steps that follow.

1. Open the **exportingImages.fla** file from the **chap_16** folder.

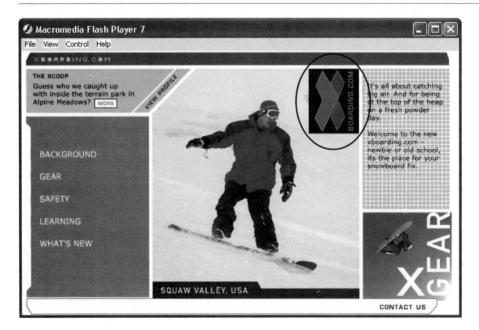

2. Choose **Control > Test Movie** to preview the movie. Notice the animating logo. This is a movie clip symbol instance that you will work with next. When you are finished, close the **Preview** window.

Suppose that you love the animated boarding.com logo, but you also want to use the logo as a static image for various identity pieces such as a business card, letterhead, and envelope. In the following steps, you will learn how to export only the logo in the previous picture from the project file as an Adobe Illustrator file.

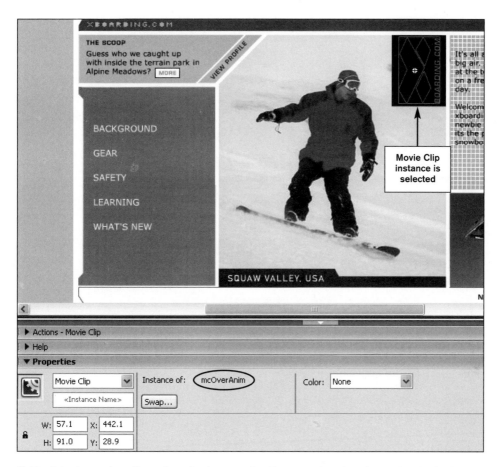

3. Back in the project file, select the logo on the **Stage** and notice the setting in the **Properties** inspector—this is an instance of the movie clip named **mcOverAnim**.

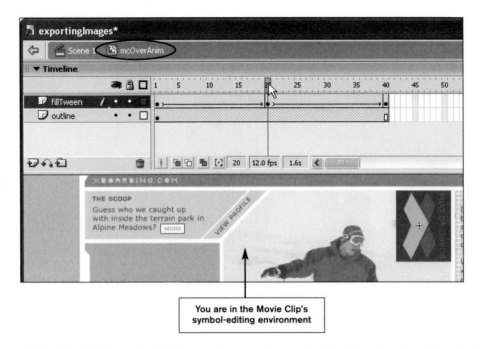

You are in the Movie Clip's symbol-editing environment

4. Double-click the movie clip instance to open the movie clip's **Timeline**. Scrub the **playhead** to find out where in the tween animation the logo is in full color.

You want to export the logo in full color, not the logo outline, so you need to find the frame that has the full-color logo. This happens to be Frame 20.

*At this point, you might be wondering, Don't I need to select the image or the frame? When you choose Export Image, you have several ways to decide what is being exported. Flash MX 2004 will either export the **frame the playhead is over** (and all layers under that frame), export a **selected frame** (and all layers under and over that frame), or export a **selected image** (including the frame the image is on and all layers under and over that frame). Therefore, based on what is selected or where the playhead is, Flash MX 2004 will export the appropriate artwork.*

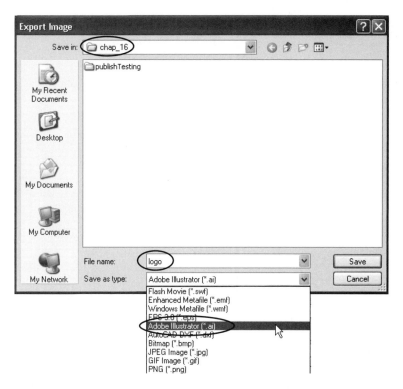

5. Make sure the **playhead** is over **Frame 20** and choose **File > Export > Export Image**. In the **Export Image** dialog box that pops up, name the file **logo** and choose **Adobe Illustrator** from the **Save as type** drop-down list. Make sure you save the image in the **chap_16** folder. Click **Save**.

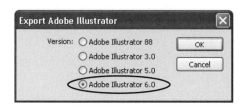

6. In the **Export Adobe Illustrator** dialog box, select the **Adobe Illustrator 6.0** radio button and click **OK**.

Adobe Illustrator 6.0 is the latest version Flash MX 2004 can export to as an Illustrator file. However, you can still open the exported file in Adobe Illustrator 6.0 and later.

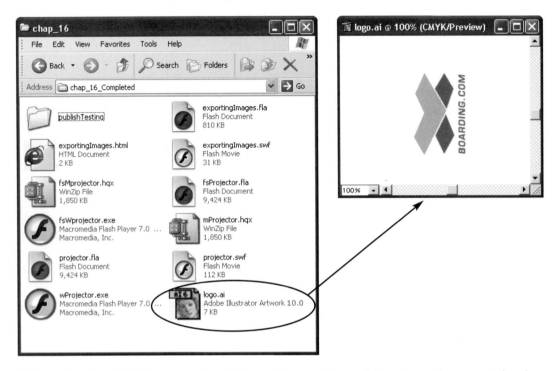

7. Open the **chap_16** folder on your hard drive. Inside you will see all the files you have created so far. Notice the **logo.ai** file. Double-click the **logo.ai** file to open it in Adobe Illustrator. You will see the logo all by itself, without any other images from the project file. Neat!

8. When you are finished, save and close this file.

More About the Publish Settings

The first three exercises in this chapter taught you firsthand how to use some of the Publish settings. I'm sure you noticed many settings that weren't covered in the exercises. This section covers how to export other kinds of media from Flash MX 2004 using the Publish settings. I will begin with the settings on the Flash tab and then move on to HTML, GIF, JPEG, PNG, and QuickTime, ending with a description of the settings for projector files.

The Publish settings are all located in the Publish Settings dialog box, displayed by choosing **File >** **Publish Settings**. You can change these settings at any point while developing or editing your project file (FLA). The Publish Settings dialog box is divided into a number of tabs.

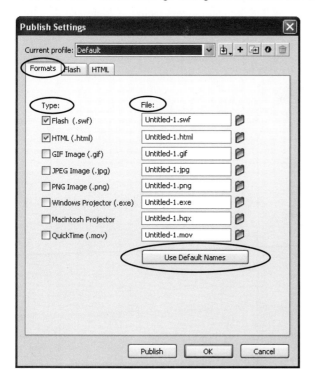

Formats Tab

The first tab is the Formats tab. It allows you to select the file formats that Flash MX 2004 will publish. As each format is selected, additional tabs will appear to the right of the Formats tab, with the exception of the Windows Projector and Macintosh Projector types. Each tab holds settings specific to the selected format that can be modified. The Formats tab also allows you to modify the file name of each selected format that Flash MX 2004 will publish.

Type

In the Type section under the Formats tab, you can select the type of files you wish to publish. Each of the types will be covered in the pages that follow.

File

As you saw in Exercise 1, the default behavior is that all file formats you choose to create will have the same name as the original project file. You can easily modify what a file will be titled when it is published by simply changing the file name to the right of the corresponding file type. To revert back to the default name(s), simply click the **Use Default Names** button. You can also publish to another directory by targeting it in the name field, like this: **swfs/movie.swf**. This way you can save and separate the project files (FLAs) from the movie files (SWFs) into their own folder and prevent clutter in your main directory.

Flash Settings

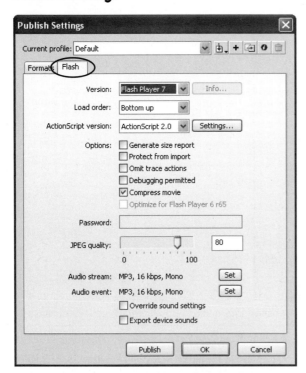

The **Flash** tab contains all of the settings that will be used for the SWF file, which is the file you have been viewing when you choose **Control > Test Movie**. The SWF file is embedded in the HTML document so that the movie can be seen properly in a Web browser. A detailed description of each option under the Flash tab appears in the following table.

Flash Publish Settings

Name	Description
Version	Allows you to export earlier formats of Macromedia Flash SWF files. The real value of this feature is that it provides you the means to import work you did in Flash MX 2004 into earlier versions of Macromedia Flash, such as Flash MX.
Load order	Sets whether the layers will be loaded from the top down or the bottom up. For example, **Bottom up** means that the lowest layer will be shown first, the second lowest next, etc. The reverse is true of **Top down.** This load setting takes place only when you have multiple elements loading in different layers in the same frame slot, and on a fast connection you may never see this happen. However, as you learned in Chapter 11, "*ActionScript Basics and Behaviors*," you should always place your actions on the top layer. For this reason, you should select **Top down** so that your actions layer will load first. The frames (not layers) will always load in numeric order.
ActionScript version	From this pull-down menu, choose whether you used ActionScript 1.0 or ActionScript 2.0 in your movie. **Tip:** If you're unsure whether or not you used ActionScript 1 or 2 in your Flash movie, just leave the version pull-down menu set to ActionScript 2.0.
Generate size report	Checking this box will cause Flash MX 2004 to create a text file that contains detailed information about the size of all the elements in your movie. It will be published to the same directory as the rest of the files.
Protect from import	Prevents anyone from importing your SWF movie file into Macromedia Flash and converting it back to a project file (FLA). This allows you to protect your work. However, there are third-party applications that can break into any Macromedia Flash movie, so to be on the safe side, don't put sensitive information into Macromedia Flash movies.
Omit trace actions	Blocks the Trace action from being exported with your movie. (The Trace action is a debugging tool.) You should select this option if you are using Trace actions and are producing a final cut of your movie.

continues on next page

Flash Publish Settings *continued*

Name	Description
Debugging permitted	Activates the debugger and will allow the Flash MX 2004 movie to be debugged remotely.
Compress movie	Compresses the Flash MX 2004 movie to reduce file size and download time. This option is selected by default and works best when a movie has a lot of text or ActionScript. This option is available only for Flash MX or MX 2004.
Optimize for Flash Player 6 r65	If you're publishing a version 6 Flash movie, you can check this check box to increase the playback performance of your movie. This performance increase will only be realized by those viewers who have Flash Player 6 r65 or later.
Password	Allows you to set a password that others have to enter before they debug your movie. This can prevent unauthorized users from debugging a movie.
JPEG quality	Allows you to set the default image quality Export setting for all of the bitmap graphics in your movie. To retain greater control over your image fidelity and file size, I recommend that you ignore this setting and set the individual settings for each file in the Library instead.
Audio stream	Allows you to set separate audio compression types and settings for all sounds in the movie that have a **Stream Sync** type and that have a compression type of **Default.**
Audio event	Allows you to separately set the audio compression type and settings for all sounds in the movie that have a **Start** or **Event Sync** type and whose compression type is set to **Default.**
Override sound settings	Checking this box allows you to force all sounds in the movie to use the settings here, instead of using their own compression settings.

HTML Settings

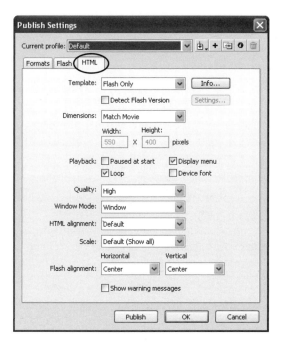

The HTML tab allows you to set values that determine how the HTML file is created for your movie. The HTML file is needed as a container to embed the SWF file if you plan to publish to the Web. By changing the settings under the HTML tab, you can change the appearance of your SWF file when viewed from a browser. The chart that follows describes the available options.

HTML Publish Settings	
Name	**Description**
Template	Allows you to choose from a list of HTML templates. Each of these templates was constructed to provide different types of support for the movie. If you don't choose a template, the default template will be used.
Detect Flash Version	Checking this check box will embed a Flash plug-in version detector into the HTML page. Clicking the **Settings** button to the right of the Detect Flash Version check box will allow you to specify which HTML pages the visitor is automatically redirected to, depending on whether he or she has the minimum version (specified by which version of a SWF file you are choosing to publish from the Flash tab) of the Flash plug-in installed or not.

continues on next page

HTML Publish Settings *continued*

Name	Description
Dimensions	Allows you to set the dimensions that the Macromedia Flash movie will be set to in the HTML tags. This value can be in pixels, or it can be a percentage of window size. A setting of **Match Movie** will not allow the SWF file to scale in the browser. A percentage setting will allow the SWF content to scale if the user resizes the browser window.
Playback	Allows you to define how the movie will act in the browser. You can check **Paused at start** to force the movie to start in a stopped position, without using a Stop action in the first keyframe. You can deselect the **Loop** check box to make the movie play only once. If you deselect the **Display menu** option, the Control menu will be disabled in the browser window. The **Device font** option applies to a Macromedia Flash movie playing on a Windows Macromedia Flash Player. If this option is selected, it allows the movie to use the local anti-aliased system font on the user's system instead of the font(s) embedded in the movie.
Quality	Sets whether the movie will be played back with emphasis on graphics quality or playback speed. **High** emphasizes graphics quality over speed, whereas **Low** emphasizes playback speed over appearance.
Window Mode	Determines how the movie interacts in a DHTML environment. This setting has an effect only on browsers that are using absolute positioning and layering.
HTML alignment	Sets the horizontal alignment of the Macromedia Flash movie within the HTML page in a browser window.
Scale	Determines how the Macromedia Flash movie resizes within the movie window on the HTML page.
Flash alignment	Determines how the movie is aligned within the Macromedia Flash movie window. This determines how the movie will look if it is zoomed or cropped.
Show warning messages	Toggles whether or not the browser will display error messages that occur within the Object or Embed tags.

GIF Settings

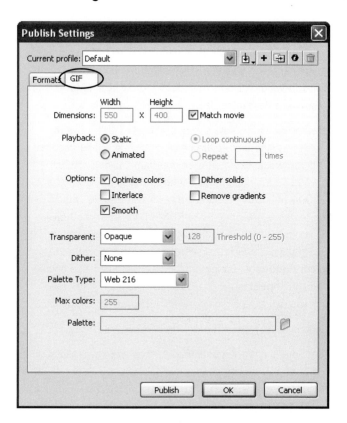

The GIF file format can be used to produce animated graphics and static graphics. For example, if you create an icon in Flash MX 2004 that you want to save to use in other applications, you can select the GIF file type under the Formats tab. By default, Flash will output the first frame of the movie as a GIF unless you specify a particular keyframe by entering the frame label **#Static** on the keyframe you select. Use caution, because Flash MX 2004 will publish all the frames in the current movie as an animated GIF unless you designate a range of frames by entering the frame labels **#First** and **#Last** in the corresponding keyframes. The GIF settings are explained in detail in the chart that follows.

GIF Publish Settings	
Name	**Description**
Dimensions	Allows you to set the size of the GIF by entering the width and height into the corresponding fields. Checking the **Match movie** box will generate a GIF that has the same dimensions that were set in the Movie Properties dialog box in the project file.
Playback	Determines whether the GIF will be static or animated. If the **Static** radio button is selected, the first keyframe of the movie will be used as the GIF image. If you would like a different keyframe to be used as the GIF image, you can add the label **#Static** to the selected keyframe, and Flash MX 2004 will export the labeled keyframe instead. If the **Animated** radio button is selected, Flash MX 2004 will export the whole project file as an animated GIF. If you want to export only a selection of frames, add these labels to the first and last keyframes: **#First** and **#Last**. If **Loop continuously** is selected, the GIF will repeat the animation over and over. If **Repeat** is selected, you can manually enter the number of times you want the animated GIF to loop before it stops.
Options	**Optimize colors:** Removes unused colors to decrease file size.
	Interlace: Causes the image to appear in stages as it is downloaded.
	Smooth: Causes the GIF to become anti-aliased, which can increase file size.
	Dither solids: Matches colors that are not part of the 256-color palette as closely as possible by mixing similar colors.
	Remove gradients: Changes all gradients to solid colors, thereby reducing file size.
Transparent	**Opaque:** Causes the background of the image to appear solid.
	Transparent: Causes the background of the image to appear invisible.
	Alpha: Controls the background and all shapes that have an alpha setting applied to them. Allows you to set the threshold so that all colors above the specified amount will be solid, and all colors that have an alpha setting below the specified amount will be transparent.

continues on next page

	GIF Publish Settings *continued*
Name	**Description**
Dither	**None:** Matches any color that is not within the 256-color palette with the closest color from within the 256 colors, rather than using dithering.
	Ordered: Matches any color that is not within the 256-color palette, using dithering from a pattern of colors.
	Diffusion: Matches any color that is not within the 256-color palette, using dithering from a random pattern of colors. This creates the closest match of colors but has the greatest increase in file size of these three options.
Palette Type	**Web 216:** Creates a GIF file using the 216 Web-safe colors.
	Adaptive: Creates a custom color palette for this specific image. This palette type yields an image that is closest in appearance to the original thousands-, or millions-of-colors image, but it also has a larger file size than the other palette types.
	Web Snap Adaptive: Similar to adaptive, except when possible, Flash will substitute colors for Web-safe colors.
	Custom: Allows you to use a custom palette for the GIF file. When you select this option, the **Palette** option becomes active as well.
Max colors	Determines the maximum number of colors created within the palette when either the **Adaptive** or **Web Snap Adaptive** option is selected. The smaller the number, the smaller the file size, but this can degrade the image quality by reducing the colors.
Palette	Allows you to select your own custom color palette from your hard drive.

JPEG Settings

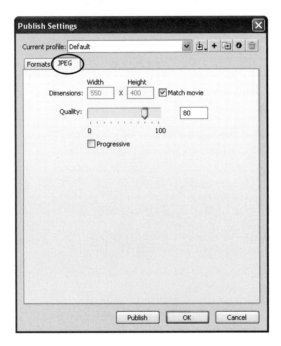

The JPEG file format can be used for images that have more detail than GIF images generally do, such as photographs. Although JPEG images cannot be animated (like an animated GIF), they can have an unlimited number of colors, rather than being limited to 256 colors. By default, Flash will output the first frame of the movie as a JPEG unless you specify a particular keyframe by entering the frame label **#Static** on the keyframe you select. The following chart describes the available options for publishing a JPEG image.

JPEG Publish Settings	
Name	**Description**
Dimensions	Allows you to set the size of the JPEG by entering the width and height into the corresponding fields. If the **Match movie** box is checked, the JPEG will have the same dimensions as the project file's Movie Properties settings.
Quality	Sets the amount of compression, from **0** (lowest quality and smallest file size) to **100** (highest quality and largest file size).
Progressive	Allows the image to appear in stages as it is downloaded.

PNG Settings

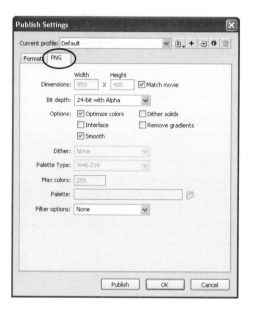

The PNG file format can be used to produce static graphics. Similar to the GIF format, the PNG format supports transparency. By default, Flash will output the first frame of the movie as a PNG unless you specify a particular keyframe by entering the frame label #Static on the keyframe you select. The PNG settings, which are similar to the GIF settings, are explained in detail in the chart below.

PNG Publish Settings	
Name	**Description**
Dimensions	Allows you to set the size of the PNG image by entering the width and height into the corresponding fields. Checking the **Match movie** box will generate a PNG that has the same dimensions as those set in the Movie Properties dialog box in the project file.
Bit depth	Sets the number of colors (bits per pixel) that will be used in the published file. As the bit depth increases, the file size increases as well.
	8-bit: Creates a 256-color image.
	24-bit: Creates an image using millions (16.7 million) of colors.
	24-bit with Alpha: Creates an image with millions of colors and allows transparency. (The higher the bit depth, the larger the file.)

continues on next page

PNG Publish Settings *continued*	
Name	**Description**
Options	**Optimize colors:** Removes unused colors to decrease file size.
	Interlace: Causes the image to appear in stages as it is downloaded.
	Smooth: Causes the PNG to become anti-aliased, which can increase file size.
	Dither solids: Matches colors that are not part of the 256-color palette as closely as possible by mixing similar colors.
	Remove gradients: Changes all gradients to solid colors, thereby reducing file size.
Dither	This option is available if the **Bit depth** is set to 8-bit.
	None: Matches any color that is not within the 256-color palette with the closest color from within the 256 colors, rather than using dithering.
	Ordered: Matches any color that is not within the 256-color palette, using dithering from a regular pattern of colors.
	Diffusion: Matches any color that is not within the 256-color palette by dithering from a random pattern of colors, creating the closest match of colors, but with the greatest increase in file size of these three options.
Palette Type	**Web 216:** Creates a PNG file using the 216 Web-safe colors.
	Adaptive: Creates the PNG using a custom color palette for this specific image. This palette type yields an image that is closest in appearance to the original thousands-, or millions-of-colors image, but it also has a larger file size than the other palette types.
	Web Snap Adaptive: Similar to adaptive, except when possible, Flash will substitute colors for Web-safe colors when saving this PNG file.
	Custom: Allows you to use a custom palette for the PNG file. When you select this option, the **Palette** option becomes active as well.
Max colors	Determines the maximum number of colors created within the palette when either the **Adaptive** or **Web Snap Adaptive** option is selected.
Palette	Allows you to select your own custom color palette (in the ACT format) from your hard drive.
Filter options	Allows you to choose a filtering method that produces an image at the best quality and smallest file size.

Projector File Settings

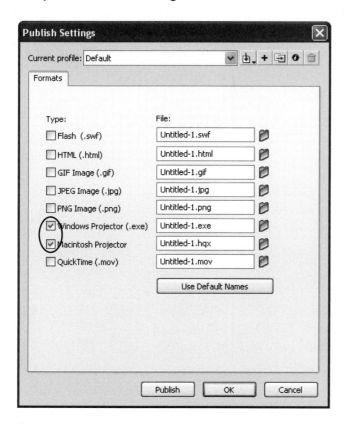

Flash MX 2004 can also be used to produce stand-alone applications for Windows or Mac machines.

Although there are no additional tabs to choose from in the Publish Settings dialog box, you can select **Windows Projector** and **Macintosh Projector** in the Type options under the Formats tab. These projectors are self-contained files that can run on any computer, regardless of whether the user has the Macromedia Flash MX 2004 Player installed or not. You learned about projector files in depth in Exercise 3, earlier in this chapter.

QuickTime Settings

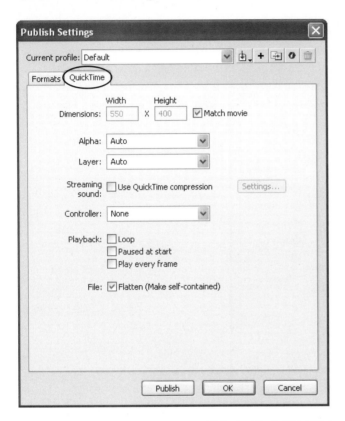

The QuickTime settings allow you publish the Flash MX 2004 project file as a QuickTime 5 movie (MOV). The layers of the Flash MX 2004 file will be converted to what is called the "Flash track" within the QuickTime movie. Chapter 15, "*Video*," covered working with QuickTime in a step-by-step exercise. The chart that follows explains the QuickTime tab options in detail.

QuickTime Publish Settings	
Name	**Description**
Dimensions	Allows you to set the size of the QuickTime movie by entering the width and height into the corresponding fields. Checking the **Match movie** box will generate a QuickTime movie that has the same dimensions as those set in the Movie Properties dialog box in the project file.
Alpha	Controls the transparency (alpha) of the Flash track in the QuickTime movie.
	Auto: Makes the Flash track opaque if it is the only track in the QuickTime movie or if it is located on the bottom of the other tracks. Makes the Flash track transparent if it is located on the top of other tracks.
	Alpha Transparent: Makes the transparent areas within the Flash track transparent. Other tracks below the Flash track will show through the transparent areas of the Flash track.
	Copy: Makes the Flash track opaque. Tracks below the Flash track will be masked.
Layer	Determines where the Flash track will reside relative to other tracks inside the QuickTime movie.
	Top: Positions the Flash track on top of all other tracks.
	Bottom: Positions the Flash track below all the other tracks.
	Auto: Positions the Flash track in front of the other tracks if Flash MX 2004 content is placed in front of QuickTime content in the Flash MX 2004 movie. Positions the Flash track behind the other tracks if Flash MX 2004 content is placed in back of QuickTime content in the Flash MX 2004 movie.

continues on next page

QuickTime Publish Settings *continued*	
Name	**Description**
Streaming Sound	Allows you to convert all streaming audio in the Flash MX 2004 project file into a QuickTime soundtrack.
Controller	Specifies the type of QuickTime controller that will be used to play the QuickTime movie.
Playback	**Loop:** The movie starts over at the beginning once the end is reached when this box is selected. **Paused at start:** The movie will start paused if this box is checked. When the user clicks a play button, the movie will play. **Play every frame:** All sound is disabled and each frame plays without skipping when this box is checked.
File	**Flatten (Make self-contained):** Combines Flash MX 2004 content and video content in one QuickTime movie. The Flash MX 2004 file and video file will be referenced externally if the box is not selected.

Saving Publishing Profiles

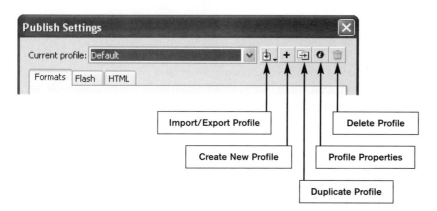

A new addition to Flash MX 2004 is the ability to take the Publish settings that you just learned about, set them up the way you want, and then save those as a **Publish Profile**. The benefits of saving your publishing settings is that you can easily use them later, or even pass them on to coworkers so that everyone has the same publishing settings as you do.

Current profile: Drop-down menu that allows you to choose from a list of profiles you have created or imported.

Import/Export Profile: Allows you to import a Publish Profile. You can also Export (save) your current profile as an XML file you can store for later use, or pass on to coworkers.

Create New Profile: Allows you to save your current Publish settings as a new Publish Profile.

Duplicate Profile: Duplicates your currently selected profile. Duplicating a profile allows you to use the profile settings as a starting point to make changes, while leaving the original profile unaltered.

Profile Properties: Allows you to change the name of the currently selected Publish Profile.

Delete Profile: Deletes the currently selected profile.

Top Tips for Optimizing Movies

All movies in Flash MX 2004 are not created equal. You can, however, use a few tricks and follow some simple guidelines to reduce the file size and increase the playback performance of your movie. The following list provides helpful tips to generate the best performance in your Flash MX 2004 files.

Use symbols. Convert your artwork into a symbol. This makes it easier on a computer's processor since there is no raw data on the Stage. Also, if you use artwork multiple times in your project file, the symbol will only have to be downloaded once and can be used over and over without having any significant impact on file size.

Use solid lines wherever possible. Try to avoid using the dashed, dotted, or jagged line styles. Each dot, dash, or squiggle in these lines will be tracked as an independent object when the file is published. The jagged line style is the worst of the three. Lines using the jagged style contribute more than 100 times more bytes to the file size of your movie than do plain lines.

Use alpha sparingly. The more alpha, or transparency, that you have in the movie, the slower the playback performance will be. Using alpha will not increase file size, but it can have a dramatic impact on playback performance. If you do use alpha, try not to have too many transparent elements stacked on top of one another.

Use gradients sparingly. Although their impact is not as serious as alpha, gradients can also slow down playback performance. Additionally, gradients that use alpha settings and are animated will significantly slow down playback performance even more, this combination of techniques is demanding on the users computer processor.

Use the Optimize command on your vector artwork. By selecting a vector object and using the **Modify > Shape > Optimize** command, you can reduce the file size of your movie.

Use vector graphics rather than bitmaps wherever possible. Vector graphics are usually significantly smaller than bitmaps, which can keep the file size down.

Be aware of complex objects in animation. The more complex your object is, the slower the playback performance will be.

Use device fonts where appropriate. When you use device fonts, Flash MX 2004 will not embed the outlines for your movie's fonts, as it otherwise does by default. Instead, Flash MX 2004 will display the text using a font on the user's machine that is closest to the specified font, saving file size.

Be cautious of looping streaming sound. When a sound's Sync option is set to Stream, it will play the sound at the same rate the animation is played. If you loop the streaming sound, Flash MX 2004 will multiply the file size by the number of times you loop the sound. This is because when the Sync is set to Stream and you specify a number of loops, Flash MX 2004 actually adds frames to the Timeline—so be careful of adding looping to streaming sound.

Turn layers into guide layers. To prevent unwanted content from being exported, convert unwanted layers into guide layers. For example, if you have artwork that you are using only for inspiration on a particular layer, and you don't want to delete it but don't want that layer to end up in the movie, turn the layer containing the content into a guide layer. Guide layers are not exported with the final movie, and this may save file size also.

Use the individual compression settings. Use individual compression settings to compress imported bitmap graphics and sound files. By compressing each file individually, you can control the file size and image/sound quality, and often you can drastically reduce the image/sound file size from the original while keeping the image/sound quality relatively high.

Use the Load Movie command. Use the Load Movie command to break one large movie up into smaller pieces and to display content only on demand. With this command, rather than having one huge movie, you can create several smaller SWF files and load them into the main movie when the user requests the content by clicking a button, for example.

Use the Generate Size Report and the Bandwidth Profiler features. Use these features to look at the breakdown of the SWF file, frame by frame. This report helps you identify places where you may be able to reduce the file size by compressing an image further, for example, or lets you spot a frame that is significantly larger than other frames.

Be aware of platform performance. Flash MX 2004 plays slightly faster (frames per second) on a Windows machine than it does on a Macintosh. Ideally, before you distribute Flash MX 2004 files or upload them to a live Web site, test the files on both a Mac and a Windows-based machine to make sure the movie performs to your expectations on both platforms.

You have completed another chapter and should be ready to distribute your Flash MX 2004 movies all over the world! Before you do, you may want to hang on and finish the last two chapters—Chapter 17, "Putting It All Together," and Chapter 18, "Integration,"—because they contain some valuable information.

I7.
Putting It All Together

The Big Picture	Examining the Scenes and Layers
Managing Layers	Organizing the Library
Using the Movie Explorer	Building a Preloader	The Bandwidth Profiler
Printing from the Project File and the Macromedia Flash Player
Exporting the Scenes	Creating Draggable Movies

chap_I7

Macromedia Flash MX 2004
H•O•T CD-ROM

You may not realize it, but after working through the exercises in the previous chapters, you have actually created all the parts that make up a full, working Web site. This chapter will take you through the completed xboarding.com Web site and will point out many elements in the site that you've created within the exercises of this book. You will then have a chance to rebuild sections of the site to enhance it even further, such as adding a Preloader and creating draggable movies. Additionally, you will be introduced to several features within Flash MX 2004 that allow you to maximize your production efficiency, including the Movie Explorer. Finally, you'll learn about the program's print capabilities.

I. ————————**The Big Picture**

This exercise introduces you to the completed xboarding.com Web site, which includes many of the exercise files you have created in previous chapters in this book. As you look through the site, you'll see references to previous chapters in which you covered the associated technique. You might find that you know more than you think you do!

1. Copy the **chap_17** folder, located on the **H•O•T CD-ROM**, to your hard drive. You need to have this folder on your hard drive in order to save files inside it.

2. Open the **xboardingSiteFinal.fla** file from the **siteFinal** folder inside the **chap_17** folder. This fully functional project file was created ahead of time for you, using many of the techniques that you learned in this book. You will learn how this was done in the following steps.

 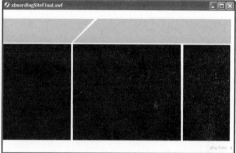

3. Choose **Control > Test Movie** to preview the movie. Notice the animation of the outline being drawn and the snowboarder fading up. This is similar to the animation you created in Chapter 8, "*Bitmaps*." Notice the next animation of the shapes turning into the interface. You created a piece similar to this in Chapter 5, "*Shape Tweening*."

> ## NOTE | Missing Fonts
>
> When you choose **Control > Test Movie**, you may see a dialog box that says, "One or more of the fonts used by this movie are unavailable. Substitute fonts will be used for display and export. They will not be saved to the Macromedia authoring document." This simply means that your computer does not have some of the fonts that were used to create the artwork in this file. Go ahead and choose Use Default so that your computer will pick a default font to replace the unrecognizable fonts in the movie.
>
> When creating your own projects, you can avoid this missing font issue altogether by working with your designer to select fonts that are common across multiple platforms, such as Arial, Verdana, or Helvetica. If you choose fonts that are likely to be included on all platforms, you will not see the "Missing Font" warning message. Also, please note that the end user will not encounter this problem, since the font outlines are embedded in the movie to be viewed with the Macromedia Flash Player. The only time this error message will occur is when you try to view a project file containing a font that is not installed on your computer.

4. On the **Welcome** screen, enter your name and click **Enter**. On the next screen, notice that your name is dynamically generated in the Welcome screen. Click the **Click to Enter the Site** button to enter the Web site. (You built a similar welcome screen in Chapter 12, "*Working with Text.*")

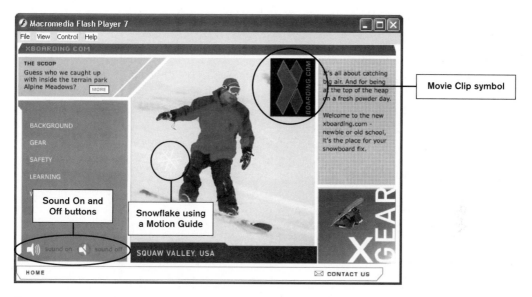

5. Notice the snowflake slowly falling down the screen. Does it look familiar? It is the same motion guide you created in Chapter 7, "*Motion Tweening and Timeline Effects*." Notice the logo animating near the top of the screen. You created this in Chapter 10, "*Movie Clips*." Click the **Sound Off** and **Sound On** buttons to stop and start the sound. You created similar buttons to control sound in Chapter 13, "*Sound*."

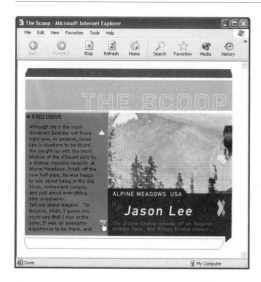

6. In the upper-left corner of the interface, click the **More** button. This opens a browser window with the **thescoop.html** file embedded inside it. You created this file in Chapter 11, "*ActionScript Basics and Behaviors*." Close the browser window when you are finished previewing the file.

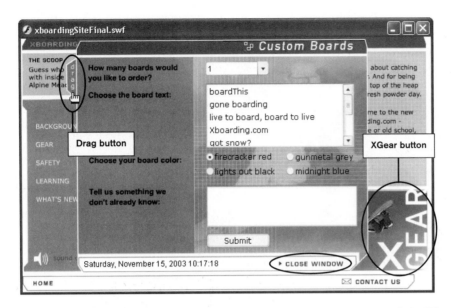

7. Back in the **Preview** window, in the lower-right corner of the interface, click the **XGear** button. This will load an order form into a level in the Macromedia Flash Player. This form is similar to the file you created in Chapter 14, "*Components and Forms.*" Go ahead and test the components and click the **Drag** button to drag the form around the window. When you are finished, click the **Close Window** button in the lower-right corner of the form to unload the form from the Macromedia Flash Player. You will learn how to make the form draggable and make the **Close Window** button work in a later exercise in this chapter.

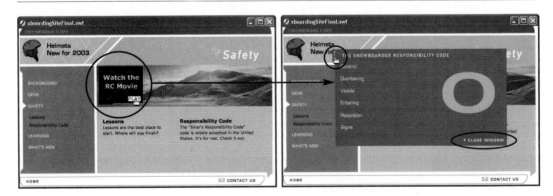

8. Click the **Safety** button in the navigation menu. You'll see the same drop-down menu you built in Chapter 11, "*ActionScript Basics and Behaviors.*" On the **Safety** page of the Web site, click **Play** on the **Watch the RC Movie** button. This will load the **Responsibility Code** movie you made in Chapter 13, "*Sound,*" into a level above the **Main Timeline**. Click the **Drag** button to drag the movie around the screen, and click the **Close Window** button to unload the movie from the Macromedia Flash Player.

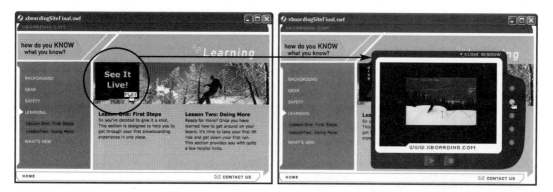

9. Click the **Learning** button in the navigation menu. On the **Learning** page of the Web site, click **Play** on the **See It Live** button. This will load a movie similar to the one you made in Chapter 15, "*Video*," into a level above the **Main Timeline**. Click the **Drag** button to drag the movie around the screen, click the buttons inside the movie to see the different snowboarders, and click the **Close Window** button to unload the movie from the Macromedia Flash Player.

10. Click the **What's New** button in the navigation menu. On the **What's New** page of the Web site, click the **Check Out Our Clip of the Day** button. This will load a movie that has features similar to the file you made in Chapter 15, "*Video*," into a level above the **Main Timeline**. Click the **Drag** button to drag the movie around the screen, click the **Start** and **Stop** buttons to play and stop the movie, and click the **Close Window** button to unload the movie from the Macromedia Flash Player.

Go ahead and explore this Web site to see how many of the pieces you recognize from lessons found in this book. In later exercises of this chapter, you'll re-create parts of this project file to learn how to add some of the sections that are new, such as the draggable movies and Close Window buttons. When you are finished, keep the Preview window open—you have one more area to look at next.

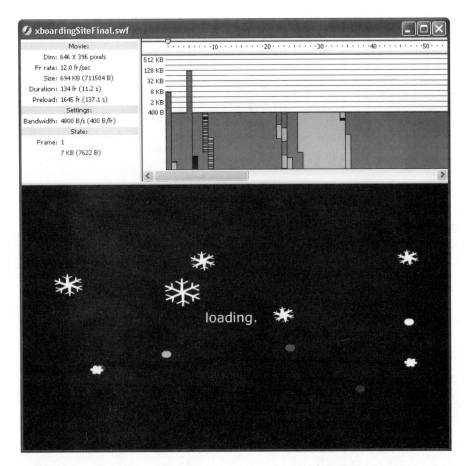

11. With the **Preview** window still open, choose **View > Bandwidth Profiler**. Next choose **View > Simulate Download**. This will allow you to see the Preloader for the xboarding.com site.

A Preloader is a short animation that plays while ActionScript checks to see how many frames from the main movie have downloaded to the user's computer. This technique is often used as a "loading" screen while a large Flash movie downloads to your end user's computer. You will build this Preloader in Exercise 6 in this chapter. The Bandwidth Profiler is a feature in the Test Movie environment. It allows you to see how the movie streams based on different connection speeds.

12. When you are finished previewing the Preloader, choose **View > Bandwidth Profiler** to deselect this option and then close the **Preview** window, but keep the project file open for the next exercise.

After investigating the complete movie in the previous exercise, it is now time to take a closer look at the FLA file to see how the Web site was put together. The next several exercises will show you how the xboarding.com site was created, will highlight certain workflow techniques, and will introduce you to a few tools, including the Movie Explorer.

2. _____Examining the Scenes

Scenes can be used to organize sections of content within the project file. You can use scenes to break up large projects into smaller, more manageable pieces. By default, Flash MX will play all the scenes continuously in order unless you use ActionScript to tell it to do otherwise. If no ActionScript is present in the Main Timeline to stop the movie, the playhead will continue on to the next scene and will play the frames in each scene, one after another, until the end is reached or a **stop** action is encountered. You'll see when the **stop** action was added in this exercise. This exercise will also point out how scenes were used in the **xboardingSiteFinal** project file.

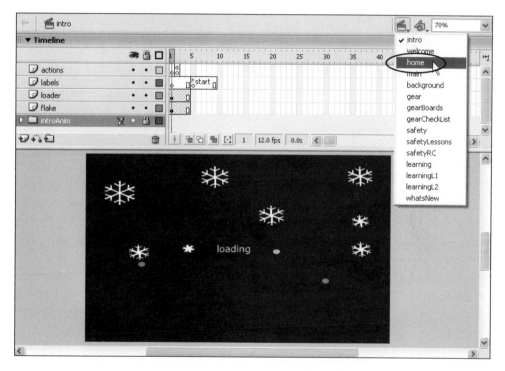

1. Inside the **xboardingSiteFinal** project file, click the **Edit Scenes** button in the **edit bar** to reveal a menu listing the scenes within this project. Select the **home** scene to open that scene's **Timeline**.

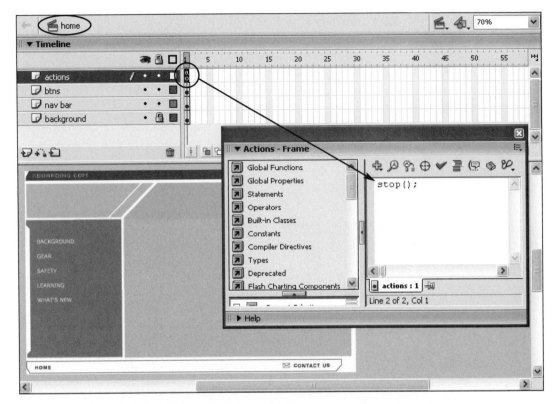

2. In the **home** scene, select **Frame 1** in the **actions** layer and open the **Actions** panel (**F9**). Notice that there is a **stop** action in the **Script** pane. This action will prevent Flash MX 2004 from playing one scene right after another—since as soon as the **playhead** hits the **stop** action in **Frame 1** of the scene, it will stop.

3. Using the **Edit Scenes** button, select the **gear** scene to open that scene's **Timeline**.

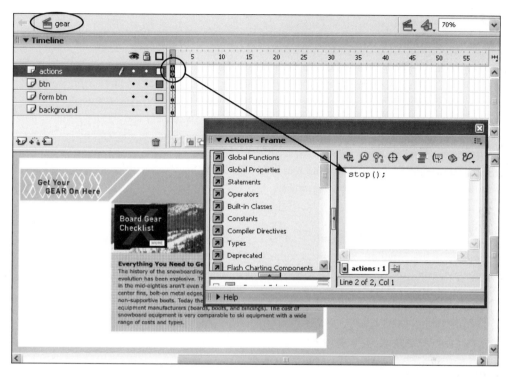

4. Click **Frame 1** of the **actions** layer to see another **stop** action. The purpose of this action is to cause Flash MX 2004 to stop as soon as the **playhead** reaches this frame and wait until the user interacts with the buttons before it continues.

5. Go ahead and use the **Edit Scenes** button to investigate each of the different scenes inside the **xboardingSiteFinal** project file.

The artwork in these scenes may look familiar to you. You used the SWF file for each of these scenes when you worked through the "Loading Movies" exercise in Chapter 11, "ActionScript Basics and Behaviors." What you never saw in Chapter 11 was the FLA file that created them. Did you suspect that there was a different FLA file for each of the SWF files? Although the xboarding Web site could have been created that way, it would have been a hassle to open each of the 15 different FLA files to change something. Instead, I used a different scene for each different "page" of the xboarding Web site, exported each scene individually using the Test Scene command, and then used the `loadMovieNum` *ActionScript, just as you did in Chapter 11, to load the correct page on demand when the user clicks a button. You will have a chance to export each of the scenes to re-create this same workflow in Exercise 9 of this chapter.*

6. When you are finished, leave the file open for the next exercise.

Layer Management

Layers in Flash are similar to transparent sheets stacked one on top of another. Layers help you organize the content of the frames in the project file. For example, in Chapter 11, "*ActionScript Basics and Behaviors*," you learned to get in the habit of adding an action layer on top of all other layers so that frame actions can always be found in the same place. In Chapter 13, "*Sound*," you learned to add a sound layer to the Timeline to keep the sounds consistently on the same layer and separate from others. Layers also play an important role in animation in Flash MX 2004. For instance, you learned in Chapter 5, "*Shape Tweening*," that if you want to tween multiple elements, each element that is tweened must be on its own separate layer. By default, all movies in Flash MX 2004 have at least one layer, although you can add as many layers as you want to your movie.

Adding and Removing Layers

You can add a new layer by choosing **Insert > Layer** or by clicking on the **Insert Layer** button in the bottom-left corner of the **Timeline**. You can click the **Add Motion Guide** button to add a guide layer. You can click the **Insert Layer Folder** button to add a layer folder. You can remove a layer by clicking on the **Delete Layer** button (the **Trash** icon).

Types of Layers

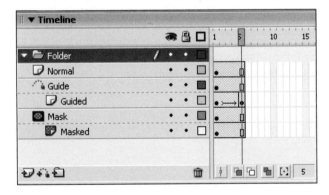

Throughout this book, you have worked with several kinds of layers in addition to a standard layer. There are three special types of layers: guide layers, mask layers, and layer folders.

Guide Layers

Guide layers come in two flavors: motion guide layers (guide layers) and guided layers. The difference between the two is that motion guide layers serve as a path for an object to follow and guided layers contain the objects that follow the path.

Motion guide layers are special layer types that are not exported when the movie is published or tested, and therefore, they do not add to the size of the SWF file. These layers are visible only in the development environment. Use caution: Although artwork on a guide layer is not exported, actions on the layer are exported.

Mask Layers

Mask layers come in two flavors also: mask layers and masked layers. A mask layer is a special layer that defines what is visible on the layer (or layers) below it. The layers that are attached or indented under the mask layer are called masked layers. Only layers that are beneath the shapes in the mask layer will be visible.

Layer Folders

A layer folder is a special kind of layer that can hold other layers inside it. It is important to note that you cannot have artwork in a layer folder—the layer folder's sole purpose is to hold multiple layers so that you can keep your Timeline compact and organized.

In the next exercise, you will see an example of both a motion guide layer and a layer folder in the **xboardingSiteFinal.fla** project file.

3. ——————Examining the Layers

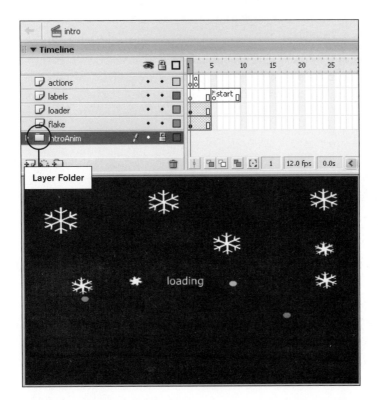

1. Click the **Edit Scenes** button in the **edit bar** and select the **intro** scene to open that scene's **Timeline**. Notice the layer folder, named **introAnim**, in the **Timeline**.

Note: The layers above the layer folder (**actions**, **labels**, **loader**, and **flake**) make up the Preloader. You will re-create the Preloader in Exercise 6 of this chapter. The section preceding Exercise 6 describes how to create layer folders and discusses how they can benefit your workflow.

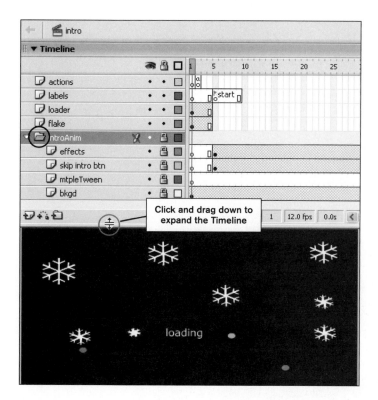

2. Click the arrow to the left of the layer folder to expand all the layers inside the layer folder.

Tip: You may have to resize the Timeline in order to view all of the layers. These layers make up the introductory animation that you saw when you previewed the movie in Exercise 1 of this chapter.

Tip: You can choose **View > Magnification > Show All** to resize the **Stage** so you can see everything.

3. Click the **Edit Scenes** button in the **edit bar** and select the **main** scene to open that scene's **Timeline**.

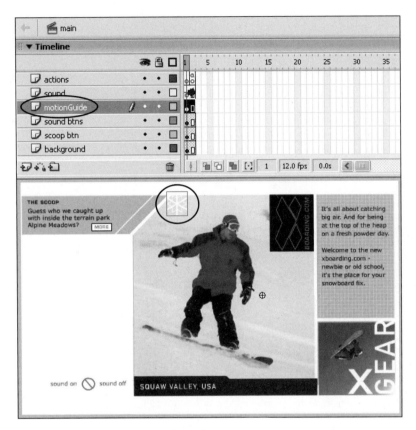

4. Click the **snowflake** to select it. Notice that the **motionGuide** layer is highlighted in the **Timeline**. This snowflake travels down the motion guide that you created in the Chapter 7, "*Motion Tweening and Timeline Effects*."

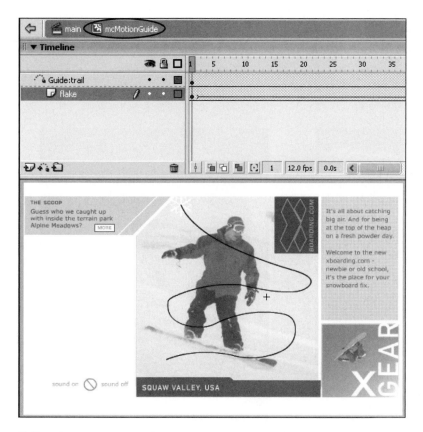

5. Double-click the **snowflake** instance to enter the movie clip's **Timeline**. Once inside, you will see the guide layer, **Guide:trail** (which contains the path the snowflake will follow) and the guided layer, **flake** (which contains the snowflake tween). This is similar to the file you create in Chapter 7, "*Motion Tweening and Timeline Effects*."

6. When you are finished, leave this file open for the next exercise.

Library Organization

Through your production work on Flash MX 2004 projects, you will frequently use the Library for a variety of purposes, including opening files, dragging sounds or movie clips out to add them to the Timeline, renaming elements, or finding elements within a project, to name a few. Since you will often use the Library, it is important to keep it organized and consistent in its naming schemes.

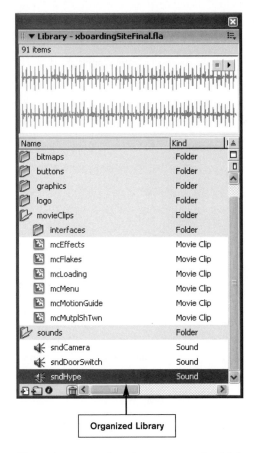

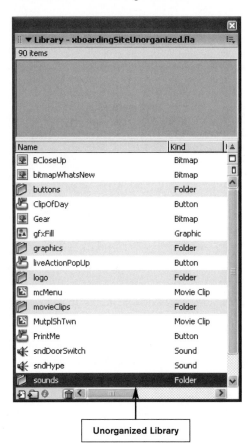

These two examples show an organized Library on the left and an unorganized Library on the right. Would you rather search for a movie clip symbol in the Library on the left, which has consistently named elements, or in the Library on the right, which is disorganized and uses many different naming schemes, as well as inconsistently placed items in the folders?

In addition to helping improve your efficiency, organizing your Library can also help other individuals who may be working on the project with you. Here are several basic "Library etiquette" guidelines to keep in mind:

• Be consistent in your naming conventions. There is no "right way" to name the items within your project file, but once you decide on a structure to follow, stick to it. Since the Library sorts elements alphabetically, I recommend using prefixes at the beginning of the item name. For example, use the prefix "btn" for buttons (as in btnHome) and use "mc" for movie clips (as in mcMenu). Again, there is no perfect way to name your elements. Instead, consistency is what matters.

• Choose brief, descriptive names, such as mcEffects, rather than meaningless letters, such as ef. This way, when you look for the movie clip at a later point, you can find it a lot easier, knowing that you have given it an accurate, descriptive name.

New Folder

• Use folders to organize the Library elements, and stay consistent with the folder names. You can create a folder by clicking the New Folder button. Short, descriptive names will help you navigate through the Library faster, and you will know what to expect inside each folder before you open it.

4. _____Investigating the Library

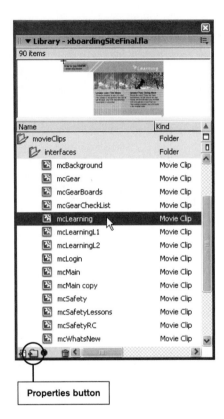

Properties button

1. Open the **Library** (**Ctrl+L** [Windows] or **Cmd+L**[Mac]) and double-click the folders to view the elements inside them. Notice that all of the elements are named consistently and are located in the corresponding folders. Double-click any **Library** item that intrigues you to open the symbol's **Timeline,** or select an item and click the **Properties** button to open the **Properties** dialog box to learn more about the element.

2. Continue to click around, expand and collapse the folders, and examine other elements inside the **Library.**

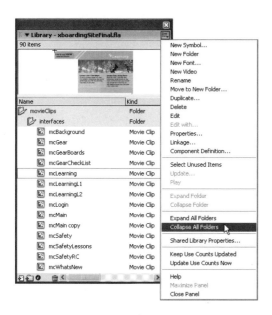

3. Click the **Options** menu in the upper-right corner of the **Library** window to view the drop-down list. Choose **Collapse All Folders**. This will collapse all the folders inside the **Library**.

4. Notice that there is one file named **bitmapLearning** that is not inside a folder. Click once on the **bitmaps** folder to expand it and reveal the files inside. Try to drag the **bitmapLearning** file that is outside the bitmaps folder into the **bitmaps** folder.

5. You will be presented with the **Resolve Library Conflict** dialog box. Choose **Don't replace existing items**, and click **OK**.

NOTE | What Is Library Conflict Resolution?

The Library Conflict Resolution feature will detect when you try to put two items with the same name into the same Library folder. If you choose to replace the existing item, it will be replaced with the new one. If you choose not to replace the existing item, the new item will be given a slightly different name, keeping the original name and adding the word "copy" at the end.

6. After you click **OK**, notice that Flash MX 2004 automatically added the word "copy" after the bitmap name. This feature is a great safeguard against accidentally writing over files!

---

7. When you are finished, save this file and leave it open for the next exercise.

---

5. —————————Using the Movie Explorer

The **Movie Explorer** is a handy tool that provides you with a visual representation of every aspect of the project file, organized into a hierarchical structure. You can use the Movie Explorer to view and locate just about every type of element within the project, including graphic symbols, button symbols, movie clip symbols, text, ActionScripts, frames, and scenes. This exercise will introduce you to the basic features of the Movie Explorer while looking at the **xboardingSiteFinal.fla** project file.

1. Choose **Window > Other Panels > Movie Explorer** to open the **Movie Explorer**.

> ## TIP | Why Use the Movie Explorer?
>
> The Movie Explorer can be used for many different purposes. It acts as a detective that displays a map that is customized to show what you want to see. For example, the Movie Explorer can be used to search and display all the text within a movie that uses the Verdana font. It can also be used to list all the graphic symbols or even all the sounds within a scene. Additionally, it can locate a particular element when you know its name but not its location. The following steps take you through some of these examples.

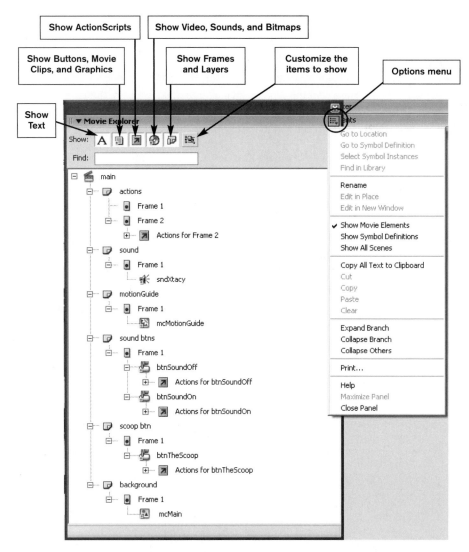

2. Click the buttons next to **Show** to select the elements to be displayed. Once you have selected the categories you want to see, you can expand and collapse the folders within the display list window to reveal or hide the contents inside.

The Movie Explorer also allows you to search for an item by name, including font names, symbols, ActionScript, and frame numbers. You'll search for a specific item next.

3. From the **Options** menu, choose **Show All Scenes** to reveal the categories for all of the scenes.

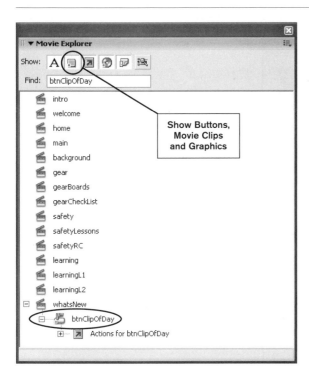

4. In the **Find** text box, type the item name **btnClipOfDay** to search for this element within the project file. When Flash MX 2004 finds the item, it will display it in the window.

Tip: Make sure that the Show Buttons, Movie Clips, and Graphics filter button are depressed.

WARNING | Finding Files in the Movie Explorer

When you use the Find feature in the Movie Explorer, Flash MX 2004 will search all the categories that are currently selected, not all the categories in the project file. If, for example, you are searching for a button, make sure you have the second button (Show Buttons, Movie Clips, and Graphics) selected. Otherwise, the Movie Explorer will not find the item you are searching for. When you open the Movie Explorer for the first time, by default, the first three buttons (including the Show Buttons, Movie Clips, and Graphics category) are selected for you.

The Movie Explorer will also reveal ActionScript applied to frames and objects within the project file. You will see this next.

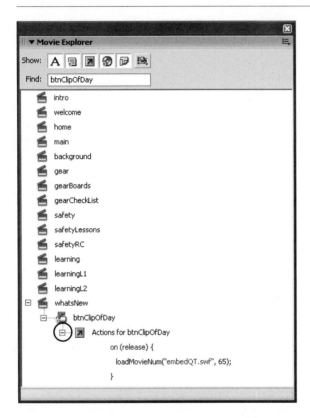

5. If it is not already expanded, click the **plus** (+) sign next to the **Actions for btnClipOfDay** text to reveal more elements related to that object. In this case, the Movie Explorer will reveal the actual ActionScript that is attached to the button instance. Using the Movie Explorer is a great way to learn how projects were built, since you can drill down to the actual ActionScripting on any object in the movie.

TIP | Viewing the Full Path

You can view the full path to the object selected at the bottom of the Movie Explorer window. Also, if the layer is not locked in the project file, Flash MX 2004 will select the element on the Stage when you select it in the Movie Explorer.

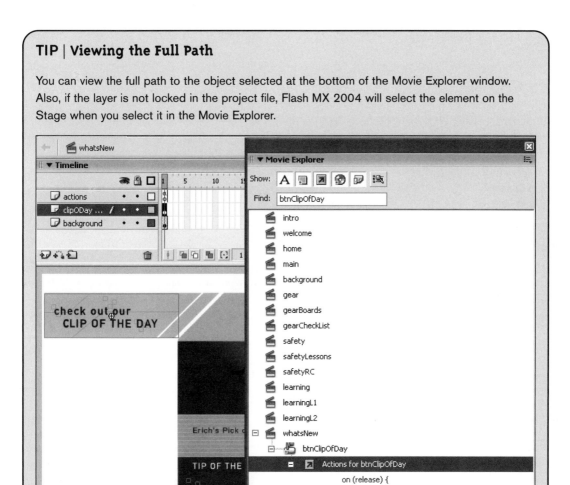

6. When you are finished investigating the **Movie Explorer**, close the **xboardingSiteFinal** project file. You will be re-creating the **Preloader** in the xboarding.com Web site in the next exercise.

What Is a Preloader?

The SWF format is a streaming format, which means that the movie can begin playing before it is completely downloaded. In many cases, this is good because the user doesn't have to wait until the whole movie finishes loading in order to see the beginning of the movie. On the other hand, there are times when you may not want the movie to be seen until all the frames have been downloaded—to assure smooth playback or synchronization with sound and the animation, for example. Additionally, there is no way of knowing the bandwidth available to the person who is going to be viewing your movie—dial-up, broadband, T1, or T3. Therefore, you may want to give users on a slower connection some type of visual feedback that the movie is being downloaded while they wait. One method of achieving both proper playback and giving visual feedback is to use a **Preloader**.

A Preloader can exist in the very first frames of the movie, in the first scene of the movie, or even at different points within the movie. It uses ActionScript that detects whether the SWF file has finished downloading or not. Once the whole movie (or an amount you specify) has downloaded onto the user's machine, the movie will play. You can put different artwork or animation into your movie to be displayed while the Preloader is doing its detection work. The animation or artwork can keep users interested while they wait for the movie to download.

The following exercise will teach you how to create a simple Preloader.

6. —————————Building a Preloader

As you build more complex projects in Flash MX 2004, you may find that the users will see the movie differently depending on their connection speed. Rather than allowing users to view a choppy animation or to click a button that doesn't work yet because the movie is not completely downloaded, you can add a Preloader to the movie that permits the movie to play once all the necessary frames have downloaded. This exercise will teach you how to create a basic Preloader so that you can control what your users see.

1. Open the **xboardingSite.fla** file from inside the **siteInProgress** folder in the **chap_17** folder. This file was created to get you started.

*The **siteInProgress** folder contains all the files you need to re-create the xboarding.com Web site. Some files are already complete, and others have been partially created to get you started. You will complete these in the next few exercises.*

2. In the project file, click the **Edit Scenes** button in the **edit bar** to access the drop-down list. Choose **intro** to open that scene's **Timeline**. You will create the **Preloader** in this scene.

The order of the scenes listed in the Edit Scenes drop-down list is the order in which they will play in the movie unless you tell the Timeline otherwise. When you have a Preloader in the movie that will control the number of frames downloaded for the entire movie, the Preloader needs to occur in the first scene.

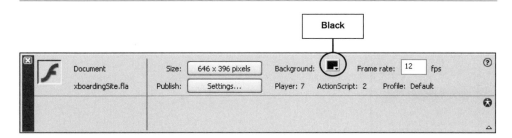

3. In the **Properties inspector**, choose black for the **Background** color.

Although the Stage looks black at first glance, it is actually white with a black graphic symbol over the top of it. Changing the Background color in the Properties inspector will temporarily change the background color of the movie to black so that you can see the artwork in the new few steps.

In the next steps, you will be previewing movie clips in the Library that have white artwork and text. When the movie also has a white background, you cannot see the animation. Changing the background color of the movie temporarily will allow you to preview the animations.

4. Open the **Library**. Inside the **movieClips** folder, click the movie clip named **mcLoading** to select it. In the **Library Preview** window, click the **Play** button to preview the movie clip. This will serve as the part of the looping animation that will play over and over until all the frames you specify are loaded.

5. Inside the **movieClips** folder, click the movie clip named **mcFlakes** to select it. In the **Library Preview** window, click the **Play** button to preview the movie clip. Notice the falling snowflakes. This will serve as the background of the looping animation that will play until all the frames you specify are loaded.

6. Click the **Insert Layer** button to add a new layer to the **Timeline**, and name it **flake**.

NOTE | Whoa! Where Did All Those Frames Come From?

When you insert a new layer in the Timeline, Macromedia Flash automatically adds frames up to the current last frame in the Timeline. In this case, there are frames up to 100 inside the **introAnim** folder, so Macromedia Flash adds frames up to 100 each time you insert a new layer. Since you don't need all those extra frames, you can highlight **Frames 2** through **100** and **right-click** (Windows) or **Ctrl+click** (Mac) to access the contextual menu and choose **Remove Frames**. This will delete all the extra frames from 2 to 100.

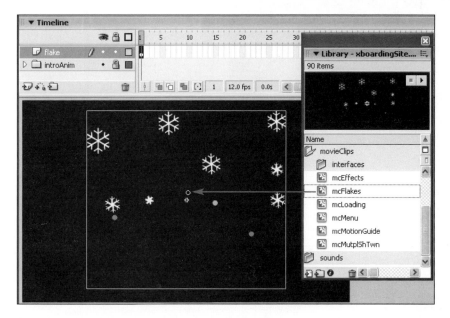

7. From the **Library**, drag an instance of the **mcFlakes** movie clip onto the center of the **Stage**.

*Tip: You can use the **Align** panel (**Window > Align**) to center the **mcFlakes** movie clip instance on the **Stage**. You can also use the **Free Transform** tool to stretch the **mcFlakes** movie clip instance so that it covers more of the **Stage**, as shown here. When you are finished, lock the **flake** layer.*

8. Click the **Insert Layer** button to add a new layer to the **Timeline**, and name it **loader**. Make sure the **loader** layer appears above the **flake** layer.

9. Highlight **Frames 2** through **100** on the **loader** layer and **right-click** (Windows) or **Ctrl+click** (Mac) to access the contextual menu. Choose **Remove Frames**. This will delete all the extra frames from 2 to 100.

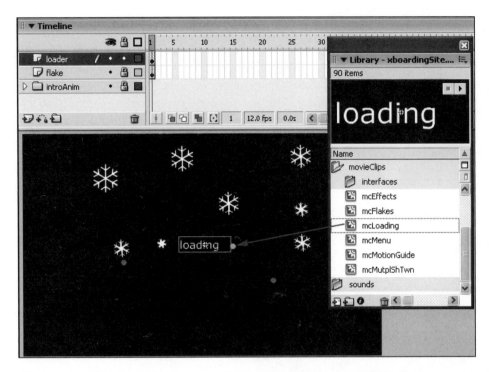

10. From the **Library**, drag an instance of the **mcLoading** movie clip onto the center of the **Stage**.

*Tip: You can use the **Align** panel to center the **mcLoading** movie clip instance on the **Stage**. When you are finished, lock the **loader** layer.*

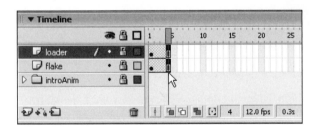

11. Click and drag down on **Frame 4** of the **loader** and **flake** layers to select **Frame 4** on both layers. Press **F5** to add frames up to **Frame 4** on both layers.

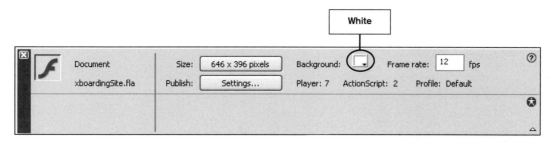

White

12. Click away from the **Stage** to deselect everything, and in the **Properties inspector**, choose **white** for the **Background** color. This will change the background color of the movie back to white.

13. Click the **Insert Layer** button to add a new layer to the **Timeline**. Name the new layer **labels** and move it above the **loader** layer. Highlight **Frames 2** through **100** on the **labels** layer and **right-click** (Windows) or **Ctrl+click** (Mac) to access the contextual menu. Choose **Remove Frames**. This will delete all the extra frames from 2 to 100.

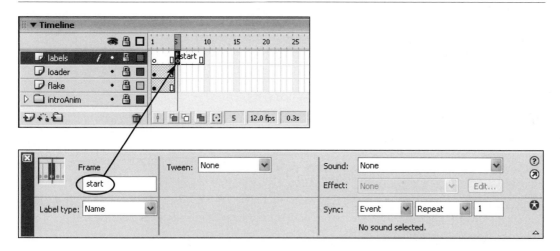

14. Select **Frame 5** and press **F7** to add a blank keyframe to the frame. In the **Properties inspector**, type **start** for the **Frame Label**. Select **Frame 9** and press **F5** to add frames so that you can see the **start** label.

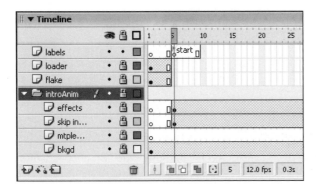

Why did you have to put the start label on Frame 5? The reason for this is that the intro animation begins at Frame 5, and in the next few steps you will be adding ActionScript for the Preloader that will check to see whether all the frames are loaded in the movie. If they are, the playhead will be sent to the start frame, and the intro animation (which begins at Frame 5) can play.

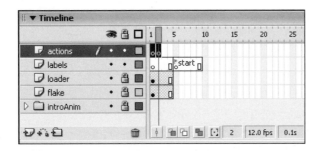

15. Click the **Insert Layer** button to add a new layer to the **Timeline**. Rename it **actions** and make sure it is above all the other layers in the **Timeline**. Select **Frame 2** and press **F7** to add a blank keyframe to the **actions** layer. Highlight **Frames 3** through **100** on the **actions** layer and **right-click** (Windows) or **Ctrl+click** (Mac) to access the contextual menu. Choose **Remove Frames**. This will delete all the extra frames from 3 to 100.

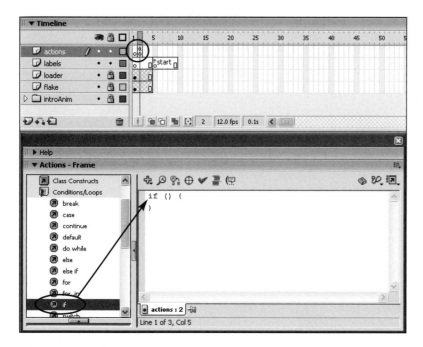

16. Select **Frame 2** in the **actions** layer and open the **Actions** panel (**F9**). In the **Actions** pane, choose **Statements > Conditions/Loops** and double-click the **if** action to add it to the **Script** pane.

*The **if** action allows you to set up a condition that tests whether or not something is true.*

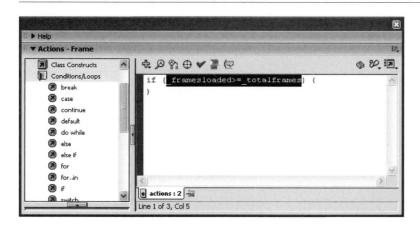

17. In the **Script** pane of the **Actions** panel, click between the parentheses and type **_framesloaded>= _totalframes**, as shown here. This tells Flash MX 2004 that if the frames that are loaded in the movie are greater than (>) or equal to (=) something, then something else will happen. You will be adding those "somethings" in the next few steps.

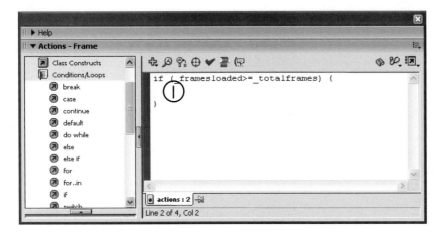

18. In the **Script** pane, place your cursor after the open curly brace and press **Enter/Return** to bring the cursor down to the second line, as shown here.

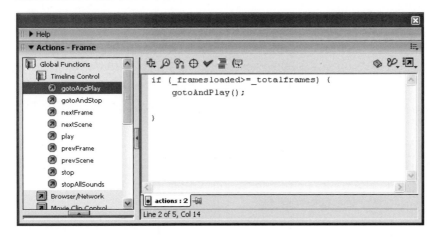

19. In the **Actions** pane, choose **Global Functions > Timeline Control** and double-click **gotoAndPlay** to add it to the **Script** pane.

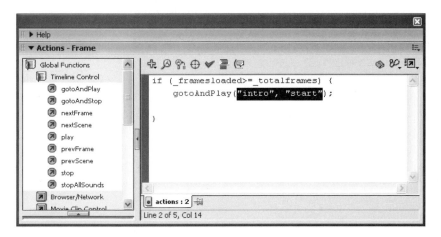

20. In the **Script pane** of the **Actions** panel, click between the parentheses after the **gotoAndPlay** action and type **"intro", "start"**, as shown here.

This ActionScript tells Flash MX 2004 to check to see whether the frames that have been loaded in the movie are greater than or equal to the total frames in the movie. If they are, it should go ahead and play the intro scene, beginning at the start label.

You have just added ActionScript to have Flash MX 2004 determine whether all the frames in the movie have been downloaded to the user's system. But what if the frames have not downloaded yet? You need to add one more condition to the ActionScript, which will cause this command to loop. You will do this next.

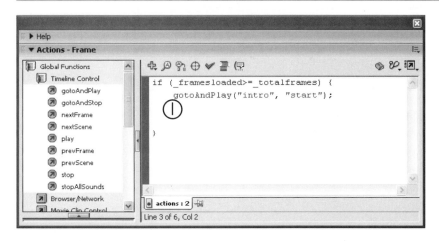

21. In the **Script** pane, place your cursor after the open curly brace and press **Enter/Return** to bring the cursor down to the second line, as shown here.

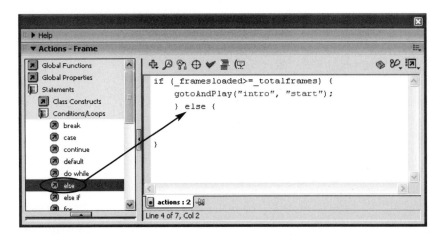

22. In the **Actions** pane, choose **Statements > Conditions/Loops** and double-click the **else** action to add it to the **Script** pane.

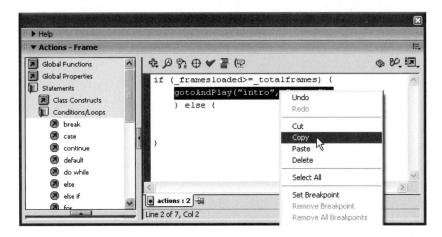

23. In the **Script** pane, highlight the second line of code and **right-click** (Windows) or **Ctrl+click** (Mac) to access the contextual menu. Choose **Copy**.

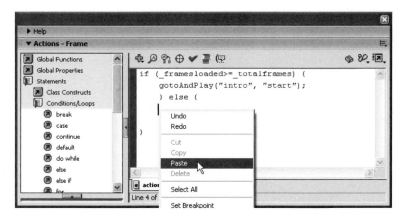

24. In the **Script** pane, place your cursor below the **} else {** statement and **right-click** (Windows) or **Ctrl+click** (Mac) to access the contextual menu. Choose **Paste**.

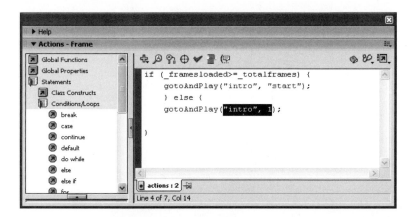

25. In the ActionScript you just pasted, change **"intro", "start"** to **"intro", 1**.

This ActionScript tells Flash MX 2004 that if the frames loaded are not greater than or equal to the total number of frames, it should go back to Frame 1. This creates a loop that checks repeatedly to see whether all the frames are loaded. If they are not, the playhead will go back to Frame 1, but if they are, the playhead will go to the start label and play the intro animation.

```
if (_framesloaded>=_totalframes) {
    gotoAndPlay("intro", "start");
} else {
    gotoAndPlay("intro", 1);
}
```

When you are finished, your ActionScripting should look like this script.

26. Choose **Control > Test Scene** to preview the movie. Make sure you select **Test Scene** and not **Test Movie**, since you need to test only the intro scene in this exercise. You may not see the Preloader!

Why? Because all the frames may load so fast that you can't even see the Preloader in action. The next step will show you how use the Bandwidth Profiler to simulate the way the movie will appear on the Internet, so that you can view the Preloader hard at work.

Note: *When you choose **Control > Test Scene**, you may see a dialog box that says, "One or more of the fonts used by this movie are unavailable. Substitute fonts will be used for display and export. They will not be saved to the Macromedia authoring document." This simply means that your computer does not have some of the fonts that were used to create the artwork in this file. Go ahead and choose **Use Default** so that your computer will pick a default font to replace the unrecognizable fonts in the movie.*

NOTE | What Is the Bandwidth Profiler?

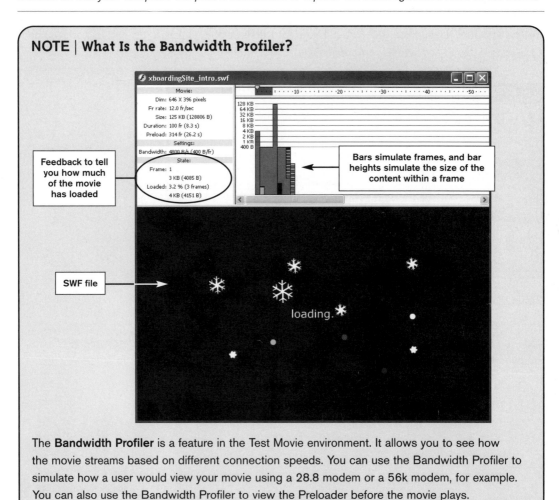

The **Bandwidth Profiler** is a feature in the Test Movie environment. It allows you to see how the movie streams based on different connection speeds. You can use the Bandwidth Profiler to simulate how a user would view your movie using a 28.8 modem or a 56k modem, for example. You can also use the Bandwidth Profiler to view the Preloader before the movie plays.

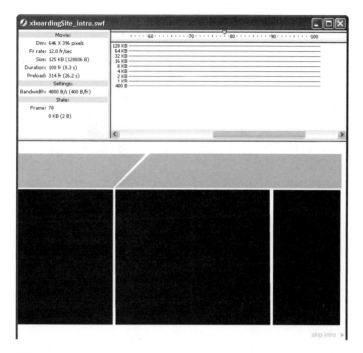

27. With the **Preview** window open, choose **View > Bandwidth Profiler**, and then select **View > Download Settings > 56K (4.7 Kb/s)** to set the test to a bandwidth connection similar to a 56K modem connection. Choose **View > Simulate Download** to see your **Preloader** work!

*This allows you to see the movie as it will appear when streamed on a live 56K connection. Notice that the loading animation loops until all the frames are loaded (you will see **Loaded: 100%** in the **State** section of the Bandwidth Profiler), and then the intro animation begins.*

---

28. When you are finished previewing the **Preloader**, choose **View > Bandwidth Profiler** to deselect it so that the **Preview** window will show only the movie and not the **Bandwidth Profiler**.

Note: What if you don't want all the frames in the movie to load before the intro animation begins? For example, what if you want only 50 frames to load before the animation will play? If this is the case, your ActionScripting on Frame 2 would instead look like this:

```
if (_framesloaded>=50) {
    gotoAndPlay("intro", "start");
} else {
    gotoAndPlay("intro", 1);
}
```

---

29. Nice work; you have made your first Preloader! Save this file and keep it open for the next exercise.

(7.) ————————Printing from the Project File

Many Flash MX 2004 users are unaware of the capability to print from inside the project file (the FLA file). You can use this feature to show a client the page layouts for a Web site or even your progress on a project. In the project file, you can choose to print all frames in the movie or just the first frame of each scene. This exercise will show you how to set up the parameters and print a section of the movie from inside the project file. Then, the following exercise will show you how to allow your users to print from the Macromedia Flash Player.

1. The **xboardingSite.fla** project file should still be open. Select **File > Page Setup** (Windows) or **File > Print Margins** (Mac) to open the **Page Setup** dialog box.

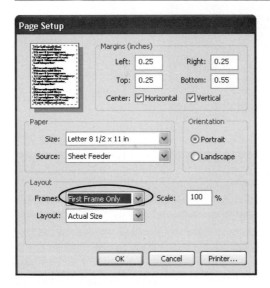

2. From the **Frames** option in the **Layout** section, choose **First Frame Only** to print the first frame in each scene.

Tip: The other option, *All Frames*, will print all the frames in the movie.

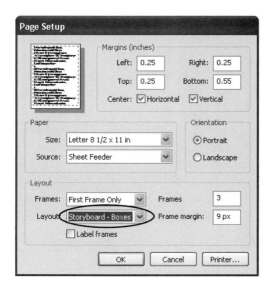

3. From the **Layout** drop-down menu, choose **Storyboard – Boxes**. This will determine how the frames will appear on the printed page.

4. After you are finished setting up the options, click **OK**.

Layout Settings

The Layout settings allow you to select from five layout options. These options are described in the following table.

Printing Layout Options	
Option	**Description**
Actual Size	Prints the frame at full size
Fit On One Page	Increases or decreases the size of each frame so that it fills the print area of the page
Storyboard - Boxes	Prints multiple thumbnails on one page and creates a rectangle around each thumbnail
Storyboard - Grid	Prints multiple thumbnails inside a grid on each page
Storyboard - Blank	Prints multiple thumbnails on one page and prints only the artwork inside each thumbnail

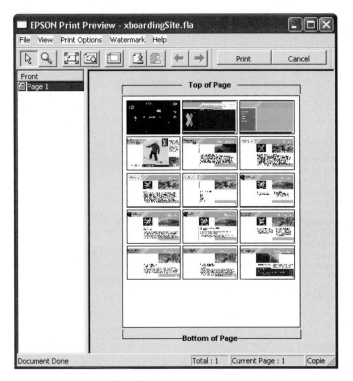

5. In Windows, choose **File > Print** to preview how the printed page will look based on the settings you selected in the previous steps. On a Mac, choose **File > Print** and then click the **Preview** button. This generates a PDF of the preview page.

---

6. Choose **Print** from the **Print Preview** window to print the first frames of each scene from the project file.

This is a great way to quickly show a client the page layouts for a Web site or even your progress on a project without having to show your client the entire project file.

---

7. You have just printed your first document from inside Flash MX 2004! Save the file and leave it open for the next exercise.

NOTE | Printing Flash MX 2004 Content from a Browser

When an end user is viewing a Web site created using Flash MX 2004, different results occur when the user attempts to print the Web site, depending on the method used:

- If the user clicks the Print button in the browser window, the page of the Web site that he or she is currently viewing will be printed. Since you cannot control the user's browser, there is no way to completely control or disable printing inside the user's browser using Flash MX 2004.

- If the user right-clicks (Windows) or Ctrl+clicks (Mac) and chooses the Print option in the contextual menu, every frame in the movie will print. However, you can change this by labeling certain keyframes as printable in the project file and thus restricting users to print only the frames you specify. You will learn to do this in the next exercise.

- If the user clicks a Print button that you created inside the Macromedia Flash movie, all the frames to which you have added a **#p** in the Timeline will print. (You will learn how to add this in the next exercise.)

Tip: You can also disable printing entirely in the Macromedia Flash Player by adding the label **!#p** to a keyframe. This will make the entire movie nonprintable from the contextual menu in the Macromedia Flash Player.

NOTE | Printing Platforms Supported by the Macromedia Flash Player

In Flash 5, Mac users experienced problems printing to PostScript printers. These issues have been resolved with the release of Flash MX 2004. Using the Macromedia Flash Player 6, you can now print to PostScript and non-PostScript printers. This includes most common printers, such as black-and-white and color, laser and inkjet, and PostScript and PCL printers. You can view a list of all the printing platforms supported by the Macromedia Flash Player at **http://www.macromedia.com/software/flash/open/webprinting/faq.html**.

8. _____Printing from the Macromedia Flash Player

In addition to printing files from within the project file, you can allow users viewing the movie in the Flash Player to print Flash content. You would add this feature if you wanted to allow visitors to your Web site to be able to print certain pages within your site. By default, all the frames in the Timeline will print unless you specify certain frames as printable or disable printing altogether. This exercise will show you how to control printing by adding a special label to the chosen printable frames, add ActionScript to a button, and set up the printing parameters for your users.

1. In the project file, click the **Edit Scenes** button in the **Edit Bar** to access the drop-down list. Choose **learningL1** to open that scene's **Timeline**.

*Note: If you receive the "missing font" message, go ahead and choose **Use Default** so that your computer will pick a default font to replace the unrecognizable fonts in the movie.*

2. Add a new layer to the **Timeline** and name this layer **labels**. Make sure it is below the **actions** layer.

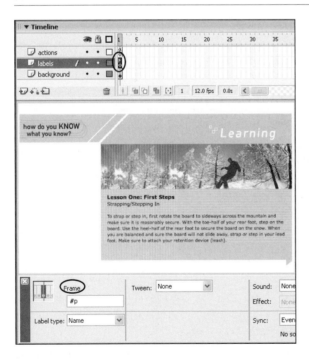

3. With the first frame selected in the **labels** layer, open the **Properties inspector (Window > Properties)**. Type **#p** in the **Frame Label** field of the **Properties inspector** to define that keyframe as printable.

NOTE | Printing from the Contextual Menu

You can permit your users to access the Print command from the contextual menu. The contextual menu will appear in the Macromedia Flash Player when a Windows user right-clicks or a Mac user Ctrl+clicks on the movie.

By default, the Print option in the contextual menu will print every frame in the movie. However, you can change this by labeling certain keyframes as printable in the project file (as you did in Step 3 by adding the **#p** label to the keyframe) and thus, restricting the users to printing only the frames you specify.

Further, you can also disable printing entirely in the Macromedia Flash Player by adding the label **!#p** to a keyframe. This will make the entire movie nonprintable from the Macromedia Flash Player. It is important to note that although you disable printing from the Macromedia Flash Player, the user can still choose the Print command from the browser. Since you cannot control the user's browser commands, there is no way to disable printing inside the user's browser using Flash MX 2004.

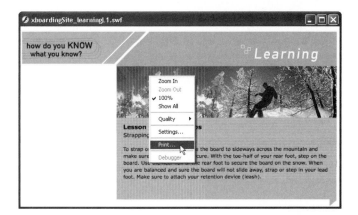

4. Choose **Control > Test Scene**. Make sure you choose **Test Scene** and not **Test Movie**, since you need to preview only the scene at this point. **Right-click** (Windows) or **Ctrl+click** (Mac) on the movie to access the contextual menu. Choose **Print** to print the frame you labeled in Step 3.

Note: After you have defined a keyframe as printable, when a user accesses the drop-down menu and chooses Print, Flash MX 2004 will print only the frames labeled as #p. When you add the #p label to a frame, you must attach the label to a keyframe, not a frame.

In addition to allowing access to the drop-down menu, you can allow the user to print frames within the movie by attaching ActionScript to a button that will print the frames you specify. To do this, you must first create the printable frame labels, as you did in the previous steps, and then you can create the button, which you will do in the steps that follow.

---

5. Back in the project file, lock the three existing layers in the Timeline and click the **Insert Layer** button to add a layer and rename it **print btn**. Make sure the **print btn** layer is below the **labels** layer.

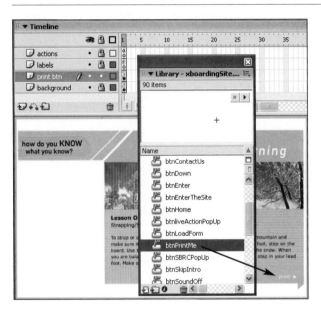

6. Open the **Library** (**Window > Library**). From inside the **buttons** folder, drag an instance of the **btnPrintMe** button onto the lower-right corner of the **Stage**, as shown here.

7. Make sure the **Print** button is selected, and open the **Actions** panel (**F9**).

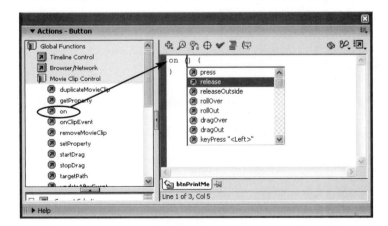

8. In the **Actions** pane, choose **Global Functions > Movie Clip Control** and double-click the **on** action to add it to the **Script** pane. From the **Code Hint** menu that appears, choose **release** for the mouse event.

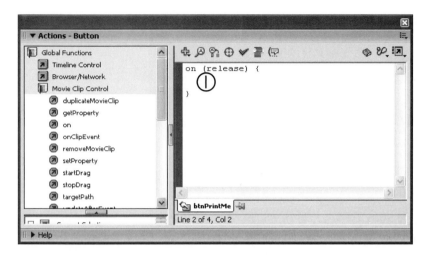

9. In the **Script** pane, place your cursor after the open curly brace and press **Enter/Return** to bring the cursor down to the second line.

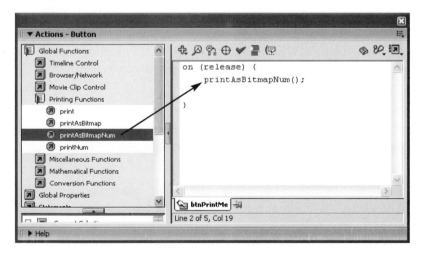

10. In the **Actions** pane, choose **Global Functions > Printing Functions** and double-click the **printAsBitmapNum** action to add it to the **Script** pane.

*The **printAsBitmapNum** action will print all the content in the frame as a bitmap, honoring any transparency and color effects in the frame.*

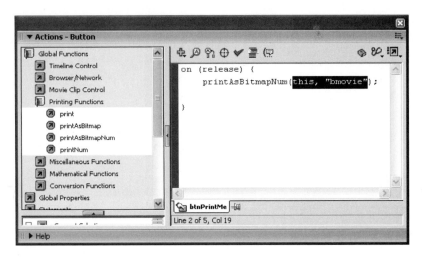

11. Between the parentheses, type **this, "bmovie"**, as shown here.

When the ActionScript is attached to a button, this refers to the Timeline that contains the button. The **bmovie** *sets the print area for all printable frames in the movie to the bounding box of the frame. In this case, Frame 1 will be printable since that Timeline is where you added the frame label* **#p***.*

Note: *The print area is determined by the Stage size of the movie, by default. Any movies loaded into levels will use their own Stage sizes as the print areas unless you specify otherwise. Also, if any object is located off of the Stage, it will be cut off and will not print.*

The chart at the end of this exercise details all the available **print** *action parameters.*

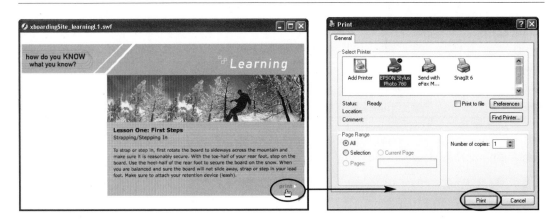

12. Choose **Control > Test Scene** and click the **Print** button to test it. Your printer will display a **Print** dialog box. Click **Print** and your printer will print the frame you labeled with **#p**.

Tip: You can use the **print** action to print frames in either the Main Timeline or the Timeline of any movie clip or movie that is loaded into a level.

Note: For a movie clip to be printable, it must be on the Stage and it must have an instance name.

13. When you are finished, save this file and keep it open for the next exercise.

Print Action Parameters		
Option	**Setting**	**Description**
Print	As Vectors	Prints frames that do not use transparency (alpha) or color effects.
	As Bitmap	Prints frames that contain bitmap images, transparency, or color effects.
Location	Level	Specifies the level in the Macromedia Flash Player to print. By default, all of the frames in the level will print unless you specify otherwise. You can assign a **#p** frame label to print only specific frames in the level, rather than all the frames.
	Target	Identifies the instance name of the movie clip or Timeline to print. By default, all of the frames in the movie are printed. However, you can designate frames for printing by attaching a **#p** frame label to specific frames.
Bounding	Movie	Sets the print area for all printable frames in the movie to the bounding box of a specific frame in a movie. You can assign a **#b** label to the frame whose bounding box you want to use as the print area.
	Frame	Sets the print area of each printable frame to the bounding box of that frame. This can change the print area for each frame and scales the objects to fit the print area.
	Max	Merges all of the bounding boxes of all the printable frames and assigns the resulting bounding box as the print area.

9. _____Exporting the Scenes

Now that you have created the Preloader and identified the printable frames, you need to export the SWF file for each scene so that the site will work correctly. This exercise will show you how to do this by testing each scene in order to export its SWF file. You will then rename the scenes to shorten their existing names so that they can be loaded into the Main Timeline on demand.

1. Click the **Edit Scenes** button in the **Edit Bar** to access the drop-down list. Choose **home** to open that scene's **Timeline**.

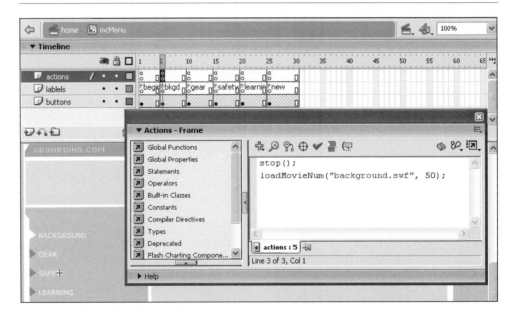

2. On the **Stage**, double-click the **menu** movie clip to open the **Timeline** for the movie clip. Notice that it looks familiar. This is the same drop-down menu you created in Chapter 11, "*ActionScript Basics and Behaviors*." Click **Frame 5** of the **actions** layer and press **F9** to open the **Actions** panel. The ActionScript should also look familiar: It is the same ActionScript that you programmed in Chapter 11. This ActionScript stops the **playhead** when it reaches this frame (**Frame 5**), and it loads a movie named **background.swf** into **Level 50**.

*In the following steps, you are going to create the **background.swf** file by exporting the background scene from this project file and renaming it to match this ActionScript. You will also create all the other interface SWF files that are loaded into levels.*

3. Click the **Edit Scenes** button in the **Edit Bar** to access the drop-down list. Choose **intro** to open that scene's **Timeline**. Choose **Control > Test Scene**. As soon as you see the **Preview** window, you can close it, since you do not need to spend time previewing the scene. Instead, the goal here is to export the SWF file for the scene.

NOTE | Why Am I Choosing Control > Test Scene?

As you learned in Chapter 16, "*Publishing and Exporting*," each time you choose **Control > Test Movie**, the SWF file of the entire movie is created inside the same folder that the project file (FLA) is saved in. Choosing **Control > Test Scene** also creates a SWF file, although instead of containing the whole movie, the SWF file will contain only the contents of the scene.

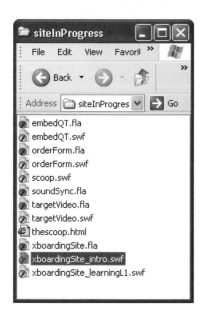

4. Leave the project file open and open the **siteInProgress** folder inside the **chap_17** folder. Notice the **xboardingSite_intro.swf** file. This is the file that was just created when you chose **Control > Test Scene**. When you choose the **Control > Test Scene** command, Flash MX 2004 automatically names the exported file, using the name of the FLA file (**xboardingSite**) followed by an underscore and the name of the scene. Notice also the file named **xboardingSite_learningL1.swf**. This is the file that was created in the last exercise when you chose the **Control > Test Scene** command to test the printing functionality. When you are finished, close the **siteInProgress** folder.

---

5. Back in the project file, click the **Edit Scenes** button in the **Edit Bar** to access the drop-down list. Choose **welcome** to open that scene's **Timeline**. Choose **Control > Test Scene**. As soon as you see the **Preview** window, you can close it, since the goal here is to export the SWF file for the scene.

6. Repeat Step 5 to export a SWF file for each of the remaining scenes: **home**, **main**, **background**, **gear**, **gearBoards**, **gearCheckList**, **safety**, **safetyLessons**, **safetyRC**, **learning**, **learningL1**, **learningL2**, and **whatsNew**.

*Note: You may get a message in the Output panel letting you know that there is an error in finding the movie **main.swf**. Click the **Close** button to bypass the message in the **Output** panel. This error will be fixed in Step 8, after you have created all the necessary .SWF files.*

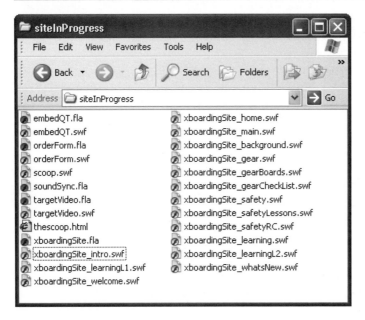

7. Open the **siteInProgress** folder again. You should now see 15 SWF files—one from each scene in the project file, as in the picture shown here.

The last task to complete in order for the site to function properly is to rename the SWF files you just exported so that they match the ActionScripting in the drop-down menu that you originally created in Chapter 11, "ActionScript Basics and Behaviors."

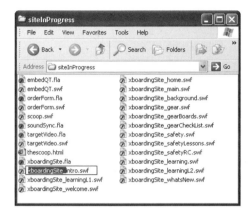

8. Inside the **siteInProgress** folder, rename each SWF file, deleting the **xboardingSite** name and the underscore so that it contains only the name of the scene. When you are finished, the 15 SWF files should be named just like those in the pictures here.

*You are deleting the **xboardingSite** name and the underscore because the ActionScript that loads the SWF files do not include the **xboardingSite** name and the underscore. In order for the movie to work, the SWF names and the ActionScript need to match.*

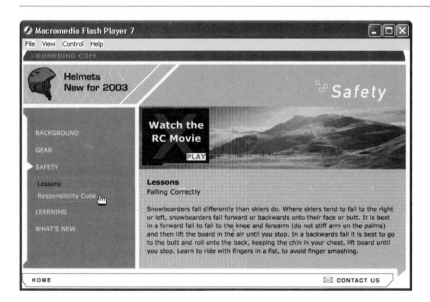

9. Back in the project file, choose **Control > Test Movie** (yes, **Test Movie** and not **Test Scene** this time) to preview the Web site. Enter your name and click to enter the site. Test all the menu buttons to make sure they work!

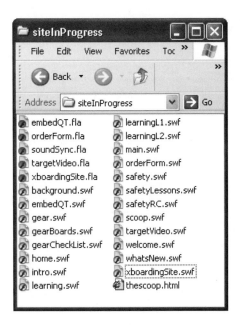

Tip: If you click one of the menu buttons and nothing happens, chances are that you have somehow named the SWF file incorrectly. If this is the case, go back to the **siteInProgress** folder and check the name of the SWF file in question to make sure that it matches this picture.

10. When you are finished, save this file and keep it open for the last exercise.

Note: Even though you can change the name of the SWF file by using the Publish settings, doing so changes the name of the SWF file for the whole movie, not just the scene. For example, if you choose the **Control > Test Scene** command after you have changed the name of the SWF file in the Publish settings to *xSite*, Flash MX 2004 will use the new name of the movie (*xSite*) followed by an under-score and the name of the scene.

Creating Draggable Movies

When you load movies into levels, you can add functionality so that they not only will load but can also be dragged around the interface by the user. This exercise will teach you how to do that. In addition, this exercise will teach you how to add the ActionScript and behaviors to allow the user to close the window when he or she is finished with it.

1. Click the **Edit Scenes** button in the **edit bar** to access the drop-down list. Choose **safety** to open that scene's **Timeline**.

2. On the **Stage**, click the **Watch the RC Movie** button to select it. Press **F9** to open the **Actions** panel. This ActionScript will tell Flash MX 2004 that when a user clicks on the selected button, it should load the movie named **soundSync.swf** into **Level 85**.

Why load soundSync.swf into level 85? As you learned in Chapter 11, "ActionScript Basics and Behaviors," the current movies are loaded into level 50, so in order to have soundSync.swf be visible it needs to be loaded into a level higher than 50. Loading soundSync.swf into level 85 gives you room to load other movies in between levels 50 and 85 if you need to.

3. Save and close the **xboardingSite.fla** file. You will not need it anymore.

*In order to make the **soundSync.swf** file draggable, you need to modify the **soundSync.fla** file. You will do this next.*

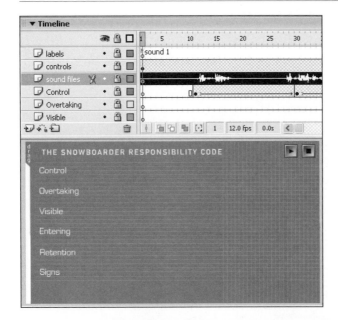

4. Open the **soundSync.fla** file from the **siteInProgress** folder. This file has been created to get you started. It is similar to the one you created in Chapter 13, "*Sound.*"

5. Choose **Control > Test Movie** to preview the file. Notice that if you try to drag the movie, you can't. This is because no button or behaviors have been added to make the movie draggable. You will add the button and the behaviors in the following steps. Close the **Preview** window.

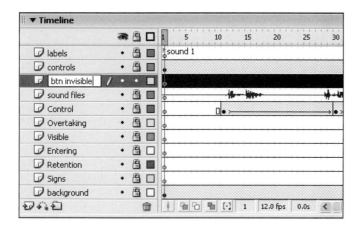

6. Back in the project file, click the **Insert Layer** button to add a new layer to the **Timeline**. Rename the new layer **btn invisible** and make sure it is just below the **labels** and **controls** layers.

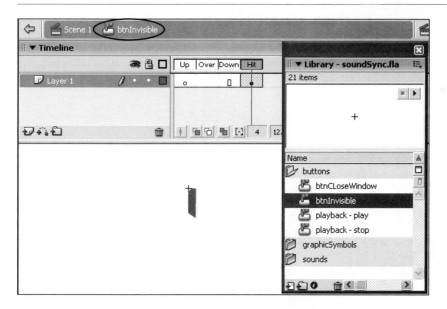

7. Open the **Library** (**Ctrl+L** [Windows] or **Cmd+L**[Mac]) and click the **buttons** folder to expand it. Double-click the **btnInvisible** symbol to open the button symbol's **Timeline**. Notice that this button has only a Hit frame; therefore, it will serve as an invisible button in the movie.

8. Click **Scene 1** to return to the **Main Timeline**.

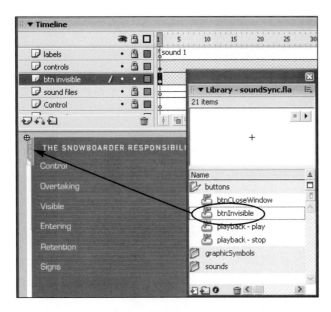

9. Back in **Scene 1**, drag an instance of the **btnInvisible** symbol onto the **Stage**. Position it so that it is on top of the tab on the upper-left side of the **Stage**, as shown here. You will add a behavior to make the button draggable next.

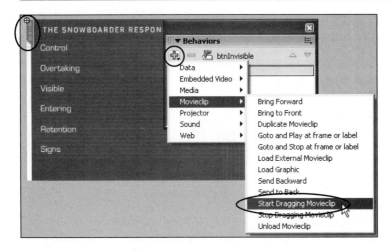

10. Choose **Window > Development Panels > Behaviors** to open the **Behaviors** panel. Click the **invisible button** on **Stage** to select it. In the **Behaviors** panel, click the **plus** sign to add a behavior and choose **Movieclip > Start Dragging Movieclip**.

11. In the **Start Dragging Movieclip** dialog box, click **OK** to accept the default settings.

12. In the **Behaviors** panel, under the **Event** column, double-click **On Release** and scroll down to **On Press**. This behavior will allow the user to drag the movie while the mouse is pressed down. You will add the **Stop Dragging Movieclip** behavior next.

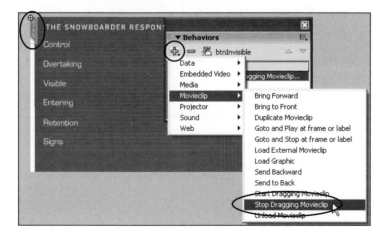

13. With the invisible button still selected, click the **plus** sign to add a behavior and choose **Movieclip > Stop Dragging Movieclip**.

14. In the **Stop Dragging Movieclip** dialog box, click **OK**.

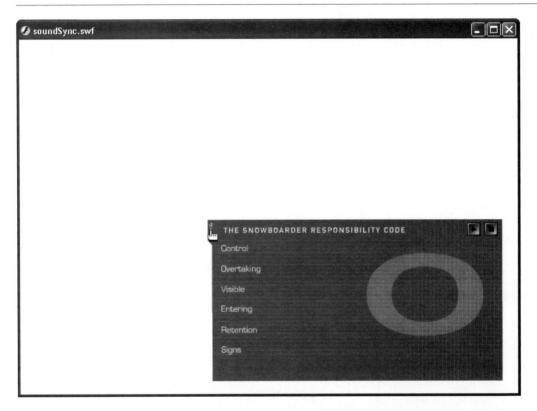

15. Choose **Control > Test Movie** to test the draggable button. Go ahead and click the **Drag** button to drag the movie around the screen. When you are finished, close the **Preview** window.

You will add the Close Window button next.

16. Back in the project file, click the **Insert Layer** button to add a new layer to the **Timeline**. Rename the layer **close btn**, and move it below the **btn invisible** layer.

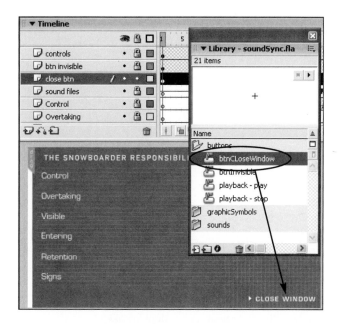

17. From the **Library**, drag an instance of the **btnCloseWindow** symbol onto the lower-right corner of the **Stage**, as shown here. You will add a behavior to this button next.

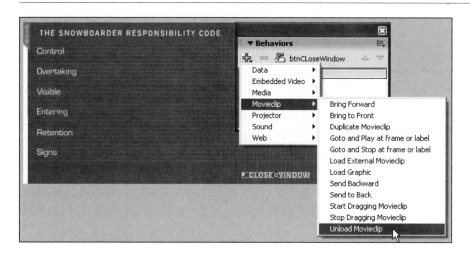

18. Choose **Window > Development Panels > Behaviors** to open the **Behaviors** panel. Click the **Close Window** button on **Stage** to select it. In the **Behaviors** panel, click the **plus** sign to add a behavior and choose **Movieclip > Unload Movieclip**.

19. In the **Unload Movieclip** dialog box, click **OK** to accept the default settings.

20. Choose **Control > Test Movie** to test the **Close Window** button and to export the SWF file. Notice that when you click **Close Window**, it does just that–the window closes! Close the **Preview** window. You will test this movie out in the actual project file next.

21. Save and close the **soundSync** file. From the **siteInProgress** folder, double-click the **xboardingSite.swf** file to preview the site movie again.

22. Once you are inside the site, click the **Safety** button in the menu.

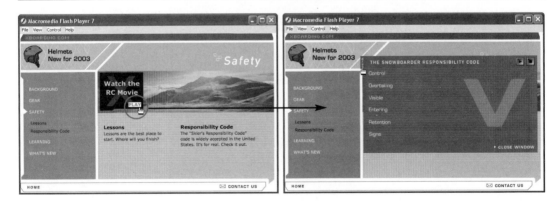

23. Click the **Watch the RC Movie** button and drag the **Snowboarder Responsibility Code** movie around the screen!

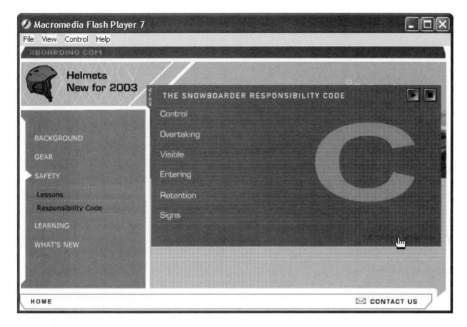

24. Click the **Close Window** button to unload the movie!

25. When you are finished, close the **Preview** window.

You have conquered another chapter! You should now have a more solid understanding of how the different pieces within this book come together to make a whole. Now there is only one more important chapter left: Chapter 18, "Integration."

18.

Integration

| Fireworks Editable Content |

| Fireworks Flattened Content | FreeHand Content |

| Macromedia Dreamweaver MX 2004 and Flash MX 2004 |

| Illustrator Content | Accessible Content |

chap_18

Macromedia Flash MX 2004
H•O•T CD-ROM

Although many designers work exclusively in Flash MX 2004, the program doesn't have to be an island unto itself. There are many opportunities to combine it with other tools. The following hands-on exercises show how to use Fireworks, FreeHand, and Illustrator content with Flash MX 2004. It also shows you how to incorporate Flash MX 2004 content into a Macromedia Dreamweaver MX 2004 Web site. Keep in mind that in order to try these exercises, you must have these programs installed on your system. The **H•O•T CD-ROM** contains trial versions of Fireworks MX 2004 and Dreamweaver MX 2004. If you don't own the other software, save the exercises for another time. You never know when you'll be adding new programs to your system, or working for someone else who has them.

Importing Vector Files

When you want to import vector files that were created in another program into Flash MX 2004, you can choose from many file types that the program supports. The following chart lists the supported file types.

Vector File Types Supported by Flash MX 2004			
File Type	**Extension**	**Windows**	**Mac**
Adobe Illustrator 10 or earlier	.eps, .ai	X	X
AutoCAD DXF	.dxf	X	X
Enhanced Windows Metafile	.emf	X	
Macromedia FreeHand	.fh7, .ft7, fh8, .ft8, .fh9, .ft9, .fh10, .fh11	X	X
FutureSplash Player	.spl	X	X
Macromedia Flash movie	.swf	X	X
Windows Metafile	.wmf	X	
PNG	.png	X	X

For a list of the bitmap file types supported by Flash MX 2004, see Chapter 8, "*Bitmaps*."

I. _____**Bringing Editable Fireworks Content into Flash**

As you continue to develop your skills, you may find from time to time that you want to use content that was created outside of Flash MX 2004. Although there are many applications to choose from for creating artwork (such as Photoshop or PaintShop Pro), the advantage to using Macromedia Fireworks is that colors and text can remain editable when you import the Fireworks MX 2004 file into Flash MX 2004. The following exercise will take you through some basic techniques for importing and working with Fireworks PNG files with editable objects and text.

Note: *You must have Fireworks MX 2004 installed in order to complete this exercise. A trial version of Fireworks MX 2004 is located inside the software folder on the **H•O•T CD-ROM**.*

1. Copy the **chap_18** folder, located on the **H•O•T CD-ROM**, to your hard drive. You need to have this folder on your hard drive in order to save files inside it.

2. Open the **fireworksFlash.fla** file inside the **chap_18** folder.

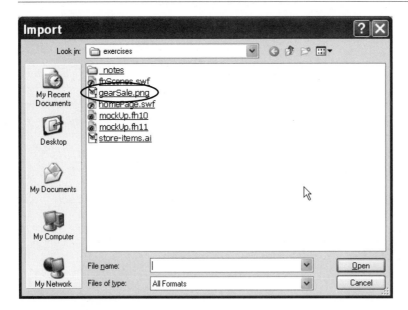

3. Choose **File > Import > Import to Stage**. Select the **gearSale.png** file in the **chap_18** folder and click **Open**.

4. Flash MX 2004 will automatically detect that you are trying to import a Fireworks PNG file. The **Fireworks PNG Import Settings** dialog box will open.

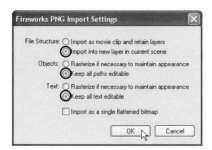

5. Choose the following settings in the **Fireworks PNG Import Settings** dialog box: **File Structure: Import into new layer in current scene**, **Objects: Keep all paths editable**, and **Text: Keep all text editable**. Click **OK**. This will import the PNG image in a new layer and allow all the text and paths to be editable. See the chart that follows for a description of each of the options in this dialog box.

Note: Importing a PNG file with editable paths and editable text allows all the vector information to remain as vector information and allows text to be editable. However, you will lose bitmap effects, such as bevels and glows. Also, if you are using an older version of Fireworks, you may notice some of the artwork aligns incorrectly upon importing.

Fireworks PNG Import Settings		
Option	**Settings**	**Description**
File Structure	Import as movie clip and retain layers	Allows you to import the PNG file as a movie clip with the layers and frames intact.
	Import into new layer in current scene	Allows you to import the PNG file into a single new layer at the top of the stacking order. When you use this setting, the Fireworks layers are compressed into one single layer. The Fireworks frames are contained within the new layer.
Objects	Rasterize if necessary to maintain appearance	Maintains the appearance to preserve Fireworks fills, strokes, and effects.
	Keep all paths editable	Keeps all objects as editable vector paths, but fills, strokes, and effects may be lost on import.
Text	Rasterize if necessary to maintain appearance	Maintains the appearance to preserve Fireworks fills, strokes, and effects applied to text.
	Keep all text editable	Keeps all text editable, but fills, strokes, and effects may be lost on import.
Import as a single flattened bitmap		Turns the PNG file into a single flattened image.

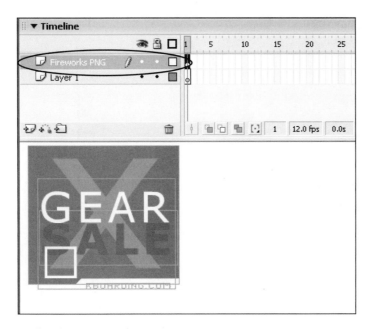

6. After you click **OK**, notice that Flash MX 2004 places the Fireworks PNG file on its own layer and even names it for you. This is because you chose the **File Structure: Import into new layer in current scene** option in the **Fireworks PNG Import Settings** dialog box.

7. Double-click the **GEAR** text on the **Stage** with the **Selection** tool. This will allow you to edit the text. Type the word **BOOT**. See how easy it is to make changes? Select your **Selection** tool again and reposition the **BOOT** text so it is centered above the **SALE** text.

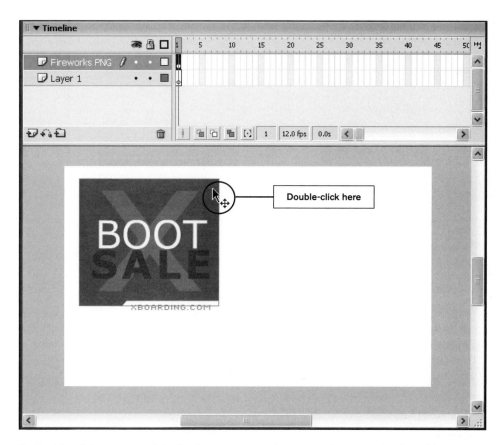

8. Double-click a corner of the background artwork to enter the group for that object.

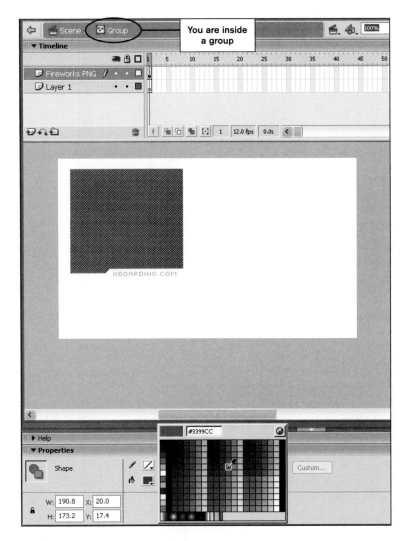

9. Using the **Properties inspector**, change the **fill** by selecting a new color from the **Fill Color** pop-up window.

When you double-click the background of the artwork in the Main Timeline, the group for the object will open, and the background will be automatically selected. If you click somewhere else to deselect it, just remember to make sure the shape is selected before you choose a new color.

10. When you are finished, click **Scene 1** in the **Edit Bar** to return to the **Main Timeline** and see your changes!

11. Save this file and keep it open for the next exercise.

You just learned how to import a Fireworks PNG file as a new layer using editable paths and editable text, which allows you to modify object attributes such as the type and object color. In the next exercise, you will learn how to import the same Fireworks document as a flattened bitmap. However, with that method, you lose the ability to edit the object as a vector because it is imported as a bitmap graphic.

2. ——————Bringing Fireworks Flattened Content into Flash

There will be times when you find you just can't create the artwork that you want in Flash MX 2004, such as artwork that contains bevels or glows. In addition to importing editable Fireworks MX content, as you did in the last exercise, you can also import a rasterized or flattened image, which is necessary if you want to preserve any bevels and/or glows contained in the original Fireworks artwork. Additionally, you can modify the flattened image in Fireworks MX without ever leaving Flash MX 2004! In this exercise, you will learn how to do just this.

1. You should still have the **fireworksFlash.fla** file open from the last exercise.

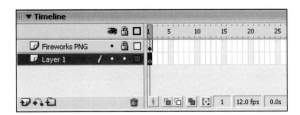

2. In the **Main Timeline**, lock the **Fireworks PNG** layer and select **Frame 1** of **Layer 1**.

3. Choose **File > Import > Import to Stage** to open the **Import File** dialog box. In the **chap_18** folder, select the same **gearSale.png** file that you imported in the last exercise. Click **Open** (Win) or **Import** (Mac).

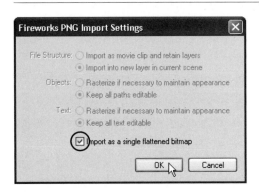

4. Flash MX 2004 will automatically detect that you are trying to import a Fireworks PNG file, and the **Fireworks PNG Import Settings** dialog box will appear again. This time, check the **Import as a single flattened bitmap** check box. Click **OK**. This will import the PNG image into **Layer 1** as a bitmap graphic.

5. Click and drag the new bitmap graphic to the right of the **Stage** so you can see it better.

Tip: By default, Flash MX 2004 automatically places imported artwork in the top-left corner of the Stage. Since Layer 1 is below the Fireworks PNG layer, it will appear behind it in the stacking order.

6. Select the bitmap you just imported and notice that in the **Properties inspector** it is a **Bitmap**. This is visual feedback that the artwork has been imported as a bitmap. Notice also the glow around the artwork. You imported the same file in Exercise 1, but there was no glow. Why? When you import a Fireworks PNG file using editable paths and editable text, some fills, strokes, and effects may be lost. However, when you import a Fireworks PNG file as a flattened bitmap, you lose the ability to edit the text and paths, but glows and bevels are preserved.

You will learn how to edit the bitmap using Macromedia Fireworks MX 2004 next.

7. Open the **Library** (**Ctrl+L** [Windows] or **Cmd+L** [Mac]) and highlight the **gearSale.png** bitmap in the **Library**.

8. From the **Options** menu in the upper-right corner of the **Library**, choose **Edit with Fireworks**. This will automatically open **gearSale.png** in Macromedia Fireworks MX 2004.

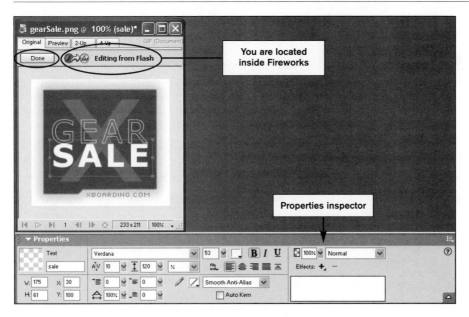

9. In Macromedia Fireworks MX 2004, select the **SALE** text. In the **Properties inspector**, choose **white** for the text color to change the color of the **SALE** text to white. When you are finished, click the **Done** button in the upper-left corner of the document window. This will return you to Flash MX 2004.

10. Back in Flash MX 2004, notice that your file has been instantly updated!

11. Save and close the file, you won't be needing it again.

TIP | **Learning More About Macromedia Fireworks**

If you are interested in learning more about Fireworks, here are a couple of learning resources and support sites:

http://www.macromedia.com/support/fireworks/

http://www.macromedia.com/support/fireworks/programs/fw_to_flash/

3. ———————Importing FreeHand Content as Keyframes

With the release of Flash MX 2004, Macromedia has strengthened the compatibility between Macromedia Flash and FreeHand. Flash MX 2004 allows you to import FreeHand 7, 8, 9, 10, or MX files and turn them into a Flash MX 2004 Web site in a few easy steps. This exercise will show you how.

1. In Flash MX 2004, open the **fhKeyFrames.fla** file from the **chap_18** folder.

2. Choose **File > Import > Import to Stage**. Inside the **chap_18** folder, select the **mockUp.FH11** file. Click **Open** (Windows) or **Import** (Mac).

Tip: If you import a FreeHand MX file that contains symbols into Flash MX 2004, it will automatically add those symbols to the Library.

3. Flash MX 2004 will automatically detect that you are trying to import a FreeHand file and will open the **FreeHand Import** dialog box. In the **Mapping** section of the dialog box, choose **Pages: Keyframes** and **Layers: Flatten**. In the **Options** section, make sure **Include Invisible Layers** and **Include Background Layer** are **not** selected. Click **OK**.

NOTE | Pages in FreeHand

When working in FreeHand, it's best to set up your document as pages, as opposed to layers (though pages can contain layers). If you set up your file using pages, you will have the maximum flexibility when importing the file into Flash MX 2004. A file created as pages can be imported into Flash MX 2004 as scenes or keyframes, whereas a file created in layers can be imported only as keyframes.

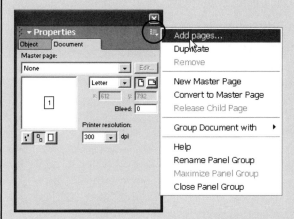

To access the pages feature of Macromedia FreeHand 10, click the **Document** panel tab. Using the **Options** arrow in the upper-right corner of the tab, choose **Add pages**.

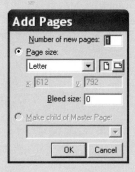

This will open the **Add Pages** dialog box.

> **NOTE | The FreeHand Import Dialog Box**
>
> The FreeHand Import dialog box appears whenever you import FreeHand files into Flash MX 2004. The settings allow you to control specific aspects of your file. See the following chart for an explanation of its features.

FreeHand Import Settings

Option Group	Setting	Description
Mapping	Pages	Controls how the Macromedia FreeHand document pages are imported into Flash MX 2004. If you select **Scenes**, each page will be transformed into a scene in Flash MX 2004. If you select **Keyframes**, each page in your FreeHand file will be transformed into a keyframe.
	Layers	Controls how individual layers are imported into Flash MX 2004 from your FreeHand file. Selecting **Layers** allows the layers in your FreeHand file to remain as layers when imported into Flash MX 2004. Selecting **Keyframes** allows Flash MX 2004 to convert the layers into keyframes. Selecting **Flatten** will convert multiple layers in FreeHand into one layer in Flash MX 2004.
Pages		Allows you to either import all pages from your FreeHand file or specify a range of pages to import into Flash MX 2004.
Options	Include Invisible Layers	If this box is checked, Flash MX 2004 will include all hidden layers from your FreeHand document.
	Include Background Layer	If this box is checked, the background layer in your FreeHand file will be included during import.
	Maintain Text Blocks	If this box is checked, Flash MX 2004 will preserve the text blocks in your FreeHand file so that they remain editable in Flash MX 2004.

4. On the **Timeline**, click Frames **1**, **2**, **3**, and **4** (or scrub the **playhead**) to see the content that Flash MX 2004 imported as separate keyframes.

Can you imagine how easy it would be to mock up an entire Web site inside FreeHand and simply import it into Flash MX 2004? This is truly powerful integration!

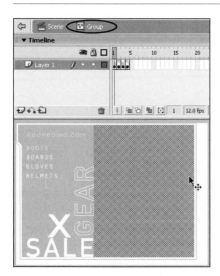

5. When you import FreeHand pages as keyframes, all your objects will still be editable, even if you select the **Layers: Flatten** option in the dialog box. (They will just all be on one layer.) Click **Frame 1** and double-click the **green background** on the right side of the artwork. This opens the group for this object. Notice that it is editable!

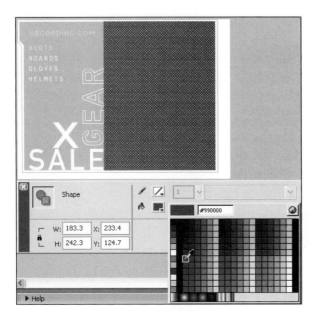

6. With the green shape still selected, choose a different **Fill Color** in the **Properties inspector**.

7. In the **Edit Bar**, click **Scene 1** to return to the **Main Timeline** and check out your changes.

8. Choose **File > Save** and then close this file.

4. ———————Importing FreeHand Content as Scenes

In Chapter 11, "*ActionScript Basics and Behaviors*," you learned to work with scenes. In this exercise, you'll get a chance to bring FreeHand content in as scenes instead of as keyframes. There is an ongoing debate within the Flash MX 2004 developer community as to whether it is better project management to use scenes or keyframes to organize sections of a Flash MX 2004 project. As you become more and more proficient in Flash MX 2004 development, you will ultimately choose the style that works best for you. In the meantime, since there is not one "correct" way to import content from FreeHand into Flash MX 2004, I want to show you both methods.

1. In Flash MX 2004, open the **fhScenes.fla** file from the **chap_18** folder.

2. Choose **File > Import > Import to Stage**. Inside the **chap_18** folder, select **mockUp.FH11**, which is the same FreeHand file you imported in the last exercise. Click **Open** (Windows) or **Import** (Mac).

3. In the **FreeHand Import** dialog box that appears, choose to have all the pages brought in as scenes by clicking on the **Pages: Scenes** radio button in the **Mapping** section. Make sure **All** is selected in the **Pages** section and **Maintain Text Blocks** is selected in the **Options** section. Click **OK**.

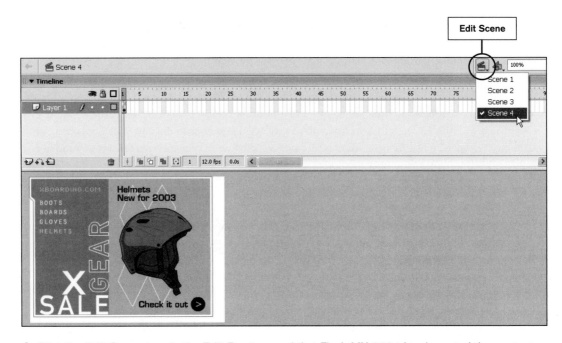

4. Click the **Edit Scene** icon in the **Edit Bar** to reveal that Flash MX 2004 has imported the content from the FreeHand file as four separate scenes! Now click a different scene to see the content within that scene. It's really easy to import a FreeHand file into Flash MX 2004 and transform each page into a separate scene.

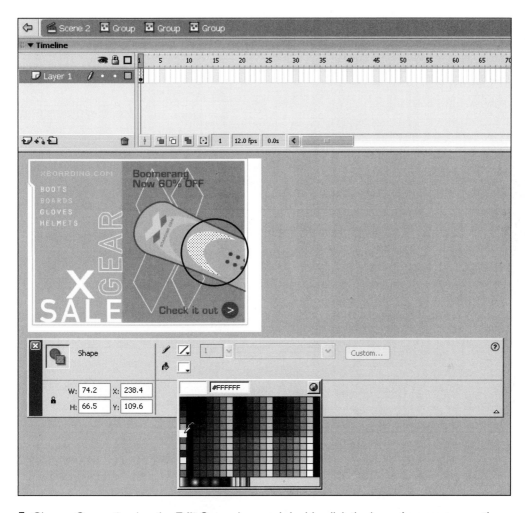

5. Choose **Scene 2** using the **Edit Scene** icon and double-click the lower **boomerang** on the **snowboard**. Keep double-clicking until you see a dotted selection mesh over the boomerang. This is an indication that you can change the color of the shape. Using the **Properties inspector**, choose **white** for the **Fill Color**.

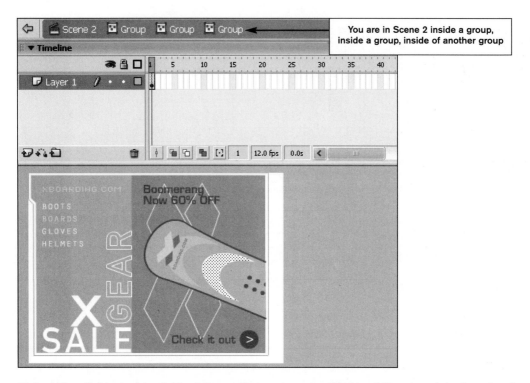

Note: Why all this double-clicking? Depending on how the FreeHand file was originally created, Flash MX 2004 will automatically group certain objects when you import the file. Grouping objects will not change the design, so just keep in mind that although you may need to click a few times, you will be able to edit any object you want, eventually! Also note that this file contains fonts that were created as outlines (because it's likely that you don't own the fonts used). If you want to keep type editable between FreeHand and Flash MX 2004, don't convert your type to outlines in FreeHand. If you want to use Flash MX 2004 to edit the text of a FreeHand file that was created without using type outlines, you will also need to have the necessary fonts installed on the computer on which you plan to edit the content.

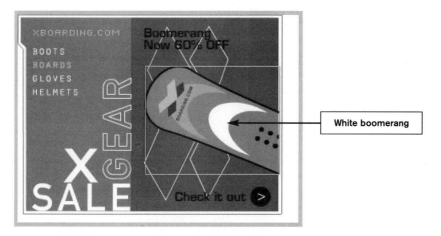

White boomerang

6. In the **Edit Bar,** click **Scene 2** to return to the **Main Timeline** and view your changes.

Just as with importing FreeHand pages as keyframes, when you import FreeHand pages as scenes, your shapes will still be editable inside Flash MX 2004.

7. Save and close this file.

TIP | Learning More About FreeHand

If you are interested in learning more about FreeHand, here are a couple of learning resources and support sites:

http://www.macromedia.com/support/freehand/

http://www.freehandsource.com/

5. _____ Dreamweaver and Flash MX 2004

Many designers create SWF files using Flash MX 2004 and then use Macromedia Dreamweaver MX 2004 to integrate the SWF file with the required HTML documents. Macromedia Dreamweaver MX 2004 is also a great tool for managing large numbers of Web site files, and it provides a way to FTP the files to a Web server. This next exercise shows how to combine HTML and Flash MX 2004 using Macromedia Dreamweaver MX 2004. Why not just use the publishing features of Flash MX 2004 for your HTML? That's fine for simple pages with only Flash content, but Macromedia Dreamweaver MX 2004 offers more control if you plan to integrate Flash MX 2004 with a lot of different HTML pages, as you would want to do in a complicated Web site. After you import the SWF file into Macromedia Dreamweaver MX 2004, you can alter many attributes of your Flash MX 2004 file, such as size and positioning. You can even insert Flash MX 2004 content inside frames, tables, or layers within a Macromedia Dreamweaver MX 2004 HTML document. Fortunately, the process is quite simple, and the following exercise will show you how.

**Note:** You must have Macromedia Dreamweaver MX 2004 installed in order to complete this exercise. A trial version of Macromedia Dreamweaver MX 2004 is included inside the software folder on the **H•O•T CD-ROM**.

1. Open the **homePage.fla** file from the **chap_18** folder.

2. Choose **Control > Test Movie** to produce the SWF file you will need in later steps for this exercise. Notice the animated logo.

3. Close the file when you are finished previewing it.

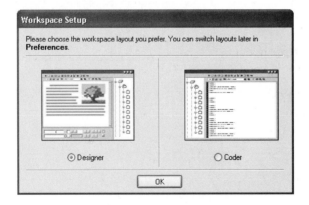

4. Open Macromedia Dreamweaver MX 2004. The Workspace Setup dialog box may appear, if so choose Designer. In Dreamweaver MX 2004 choose **File > Open**, and select the **index.htm** file from the **chap_18** folder.

5. You will see a document that has a black background. In the **Insert Bar**, choose **Common** from the pull-down menu. In the **Common** panel, click the **Media** button on the right, and then choose **Flash** from the menu.

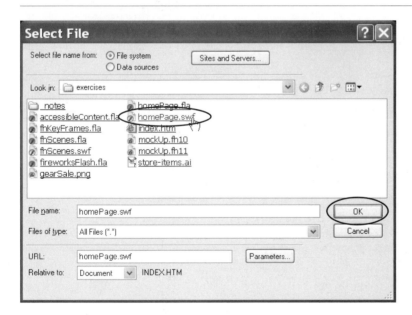

6. In the **Select File** dialog box, locate the **chap_18** folder, select **homePage.swf** and click **OK** (Windows) or **Choose** (Mac). Make sure you choose the **SWF** file and not the **FLA** file!

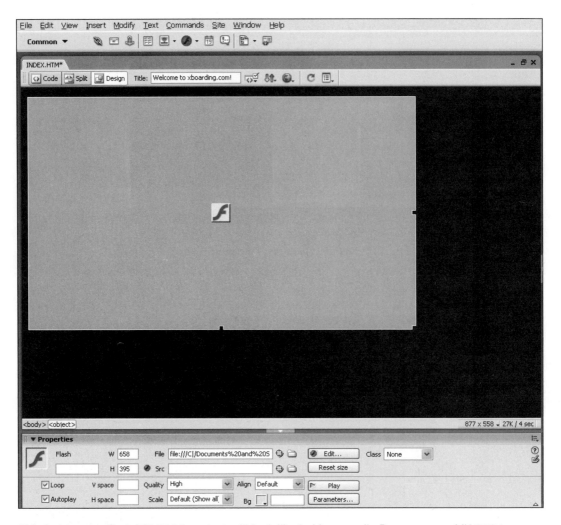

This is what the Flash MX 2004 content will look like in Macromedia Dreamweaver MX 2004.

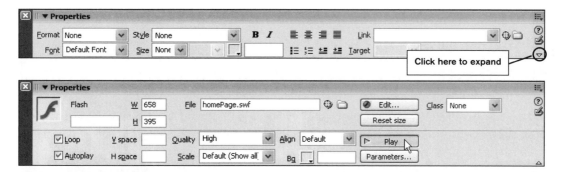

7. In the **Properties inspector**, click the small arrow in the lower-right corner to expand the **Properties inspector**. Notice the green **Play** button. Click the **Play** button to preview the Flash MX 2004 file right on the screen inside Macromedia Dreamweaver MX 2004.

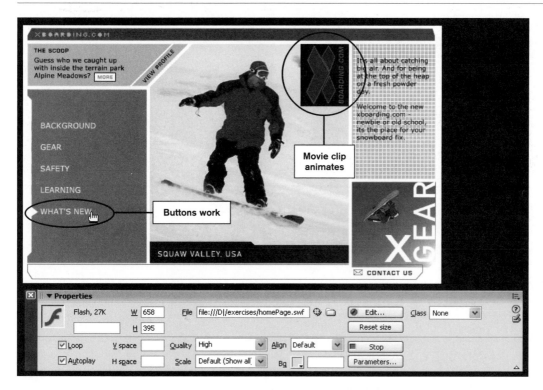

8. Check the rollover functionality of the buttons to make sure they turn white when you roll your mouse over them. Notice that the logo is animating also.

Using the Play button, you can have Macromedia Dreamweaver MX 2004 preview graphic, button, and movie clip symbols inside your Flash MX 2004 movie.

9. As you preview the file, notice that the green **Play** button in the **Properties inspector** changes to a red **Stop** button. Once you've previewed the file, click the **Stop** button to return to your work environment.

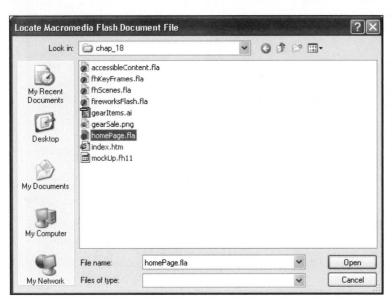

10. In the **Properties inspector**, make sure the SWF file is selected, and click the **Edit** button. The **Locate Macromedia Flash Document File** (Windows) or **Open File** (Mac) dialog box will appear. Navigate to the **chap_18** folder and select **homePage.fla**. Click **Open**. You will make changes to the source file, which will be updated in the SWF file in Macromedia Dreamweaver MX 2004.

*Tip: You can also **right-click** (Windows) or **Ctrl+click** (Mac) to access a shortcut menu and then select **Edit with Flash** to open the file inside Flash MX 2004.*

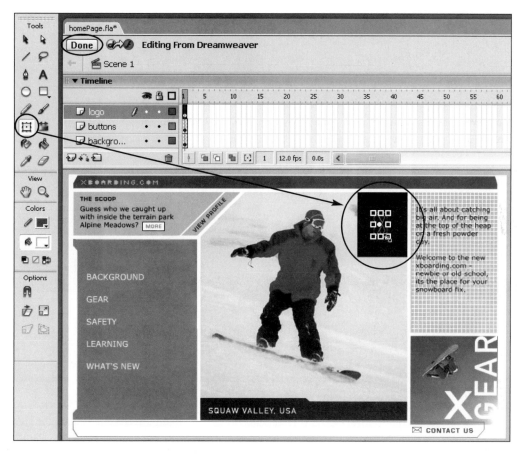

11. Once inside the Flash MX 2004 source file, select the **Free Transform** tool and scale the logo down smaller. When you are finished, click the **Done** button above the **Timeline**.

Once you click the Done button, you will be returned to Macromedia Dreamweaver MX 2004.

12. Back in Macromedia Dreamweaver MX 2004, click the **Play** button in the **Properties inspector**. Notice that Macromedia Dreamweaver MX 2004 has automatically updated the SWF file inside the document to reflect the change you made to the logo. Cool!

Note: Using the Properties inspector in Macromedia Dreamweaver MX 2004 is an easy way to edit the FLA file, assign attribute tags, change the background color, change how the content will be aligned or how the movie will scale, and plenty of other useful properties. Dreamweaver MX 2004 offers a lot of control over how the content is displayed.

---

13. When you are finished, save and close the file.

6. ——————Importing Illustrator Content as Keyframes

Many digital artists are familiar with Adobe Illustrator and prefer to use its drawing capabilities over other vector tools. The good news is that Flash MX 2004 now supports direct import of Adobe Illustrator 10 files. This exercise will walk you through the process of importing an Adobe Illustrator file as keyframes into Flash MX 2004.

1. Open the **aiKeyframes.fla** file from the **chap_18** folder.

2. Choose **File > Import > Import to Stage** and locate the file **gearItems.ai** from the **chap_18** folder. Click **Open** (Win) or **Import** (Mac).

3. Flash will open the **Import Options** dialog box. In the **Convert pages to** section, select **Keyframes**. In the **Convert layers to** section, select **Keyframes**. In the **Options** section, deselect **Include invisible layers**. Click **OK**.

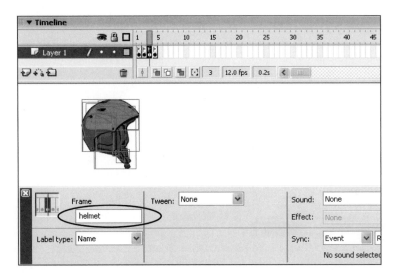

4. In the **Timeline**, scrub the **playhead** to see the content that Flash MX 2004 imported as separate keyframes. Select a keyframe in the **Timeline** and notice the frame label reflects the name of the layer in Illustrator. The ability to import Illustrator files directly into Flash MX 2004 makes creating Flash content even easier!

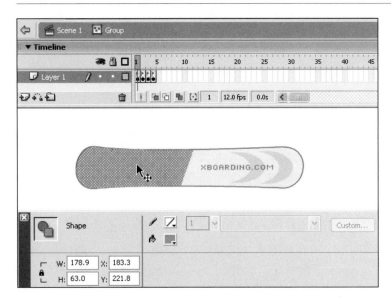

5. When you import Illustrator content as keyframes, all your objects will still be editable. Move the playhead back to **Frame 1** and double-click the left side of the **snowboard**. This opens the group for this object. Notice that it is editable.

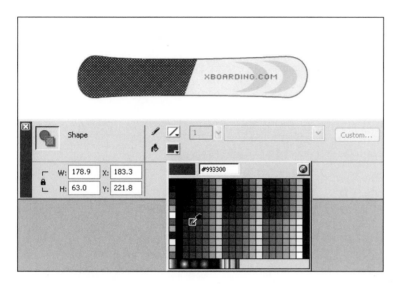

6. With the left side of the board selected, go ahead and choose a different **Fill Color** in the **Properties inspector**.

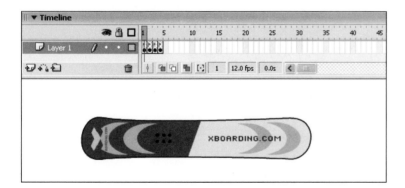

7. Click **Scene 1** to return to the **Main Timeline** and check out your changes.

8. Choose **File > Save** and then close this file.

NOTE | Import Dialog Box for Illustrator, EPS, or PDF files

Flash can import Adobe Illustrator files in version 6 or later, EPS files in any version, and PDF files in version 1.4 or earlier. You can choose from the following options when importing Adobe Illustrator, EPS, or PDF files:

- Convert pages to scenes or keyframes.

- Convert layers to Flash layers or keyframes or flatten all layers.

- Select which pages to import.

- Include invisible layers.

- Maintain text blocks.

- Rasterize everything. Choosing this option flattens layers and rasterizes text, and disables options for converting layers or maintaining text blocks.

Note: The PDF version number is different from the Adobe Acrobat number. Adobe Acrobat is a product used to author PDF files. PDF is the file format.

Illustrator, EPS, or PDF Import Dialog Box		
Option Group	**Setting**	**Description**
Convert pages to	Scenes Keyframes	Controls how the PDF document pages are imported into Flash MX 2004. If you select **Scenes**, each page will be transformed into a scene in Flash MX 2004. If you select **Keyframes**, each page in your file will be transformed into a keyframe.
Convert layers to	Layers Keyframes Flatten	Controls how individual layers are imported into Flash MX 2004 from your Illustrator or EPS file. Selecting **Layers** allows the layers in your file to remain as layers when imported into Flash MX 2004. Selecting **Keyframes** allows Flash MX 2004 to convert the layers into keyframes. Selecting **Flatten** will convert multiple layers into one layer in Flash MX 2004.
Which pages to import	All From: To:	Allows you to either import all pages from your PDF file or specify a range of pages to import into Flash MX 2004.
Options	Include invisible layers	If this box is checked, Flash MX 2004 will include all hidden layers from your Illustrator or EPS file.
	Maintain text blocks	If this box is checked, Flash MX 2004 will preserve the text blocks in your Illustrator or EPS file so that they remain editable in Flash MX 2004.
	Rasterize everything	Choosing this option flattens layers and rasterizes text, and disables options for converting layers or maintaining text blocks.
	Rasterization resolution	Allows you to set the resolution for the rasterized file being imported.

7.────────────**Importing Illustrator Content as Layers**

With the release of Flash MX 2004, integrating content from Adobe Illustrator greatly improves workflow, saving you time. In this exercise, you will learn how easy it is to import Illustrator content as separate layers inside of Flash.

1. Open the **aiLayers.fla** file from the **chap_18** folder.

2. Choose **File > Import > Import to Stage** and locate the file **gearItems.ai** from the **chap_18** folder. This is the same file you imported in the previous exercise. Click **Open** (Win) or **Import** (Mac).

3. Flash will open the **Import Options** dialog box. In the **Convert pages to** section, select **Scenes**. In the **Convert layers to** section, select **Layers**. In the **Options** section, deselect **Include invisible layers**. Click **OK**.

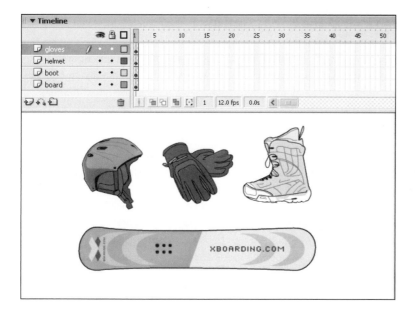

4. In the **Timeline**, notice the content that Flash MX 2004 imported as separate layers, and that the names of the layers in the Illustrator file transferred over as well. You have successfully imported artwork from Illustrator into Flash MX 2004 and isolated each Illustrator layer on its own layer and frame in the **Timeline**. From here, you can do just about anything! The ability to import Illustrator files directly into Flash MX 2004 makes creating Flash MX 2004 content even easier!

5. Save and close this file.

TIP | Learning More About Adobe Illustrator

If you are interested in learning more about Adobe Illustrator, here are a couple of learning resources and support sites:

http://www.adobe.com/support/products/illustrator.html

http://www.adobe.com/products/illustrator/main.html

Note: Adobe Illustrator 10 and later, as well as Adobe Photoshop CS, can now write files to the SWF file format, allowing you to import Illustrator and Photoshop content as SWF files. These versions provide you another possible workflow when integrating content from Adobe Illustrator and Adobe Photoshop.

8. ————————Creating Accessible Content

An increasing number of Web sites require accessible content. This means that the content must be accessible and navigable by people who have disabilities. In Flash MX 2004, you can make the content in your movie accessible to people with visual impairments who have access to screen reader software. Screen reader software uses audio to describe what is seen on the screen. In order for the screen reader to be able to read your content properly, you must set up the content in a certain way. This exercise will teach you how to make content in your Flash MX 2004 project files accessible.

System Requirements: The Macromedia Flash 7 Player uses MSAA (Microsoft Active Accessibility) technology, which is technology that communicates with screen readers. This technology is available only on Windows operating systems. It is also important to note that the Windows Internet Explorer plug-in (ActiveX) version of the Macromedia Flash 6 Player (and higher) does support MSAA, although the Windows Netscape and Windows stand-alone players do not. Also, screen reader users will need to access Flash MX 2004 content by using the Microsoft Internet Explorer browser. This is the only browser with support for MSAA.

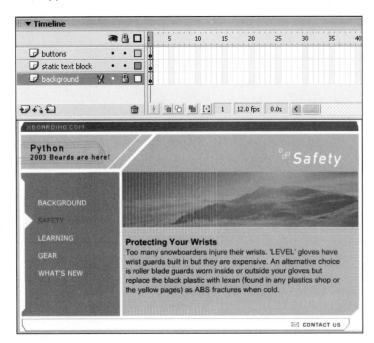

1. Open the **accessibleContent.fla** file from the **chap_18** folder. This file contains a background image, buttons, and text.

2. In the **Properties inspector**, make sure nothing is selected in the project file and click the **Edit Accessibility Settings** button.

3. In the **Accessibility** panel that opens, select the **Make Movie Accessible** box. In the **Name** field type **Safety Page**, and for **Description** type **This page offers information about snowboarding safety**. This will allow the whole movie (which resides on one frame in the **Main Timeline**) accessible to screen readers. The chart that follows describes the options in this panel.

4. When you are finished, close the **Accessibility** panel.

Accessibility Panel Options	
Option	**Description**
Make Movie Accessible	Allows the movie to be readable by screen readers; this includes all text, input text fields, buttons, and movie clips. If this option is deselected, it will hide the movie from screen readers.
Make child objects accessible	Allows the accessible objects (text, input text fields, buttons, and movie clips) located inside movie clips to be readable by screen readers. If this option is deselected, it prevents accessible objects within movie clips from being accessed by screen readers.
Auto label	Uses text objects, such as buttons or input text fields contained in the movie, as automatic labels for accessible content. If this option is deselected, screen readers will read text objects as text objects, not labels. (You will learn how to label individual items later in this exercise.)
Name	Allows you to enter a title (name) for the movie, since the screen reader will read the name of the movie even if there is no other accessible content in the movie. This option is available only if you select the **Make Movie Accessible** option.
Description	Allows you to enter a description of the movie that will be read by the screen reader software. This option is also available only if you select the **Make Movie Accessible** option.

NOTE | Accessible Objects

The Macromedia Flash 7 Player will include text, input text fields, buttons, movie clips, and entire movies as accessible objects that can be read by screen readers. However, individual graphic objects are not included as accessible objects, since graphics can't be easily turned into spoken words. On the other hand, movie clips are included as accessible objects, as are the objects inside movie clips, as long as they are text, input text fields, buttons, or other movie clips.

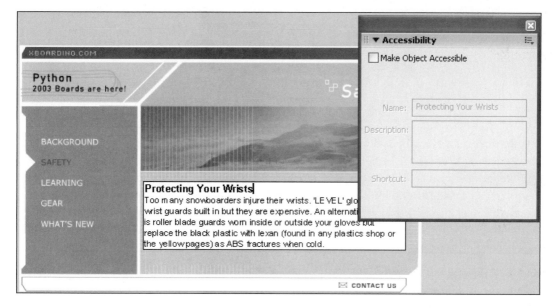

5. Double-click the **Static text** field on the **Stage** and choose **Window > Other Panels > Accessibility** to open the **Accessibility** panel again. Even though you made your movie accessible in step 3, you can have more control over what the screen reader will read, by filling out the fields in the **Accessibility** panel for this Static text field, which you will do next.

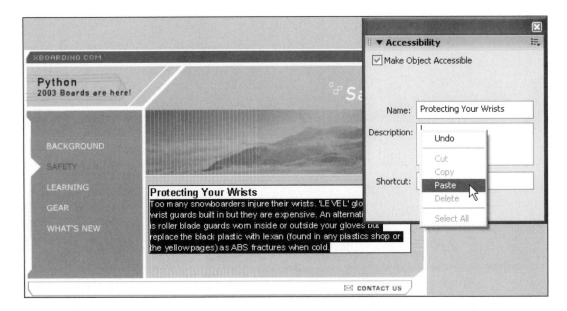

6. In the **Accessibility** panel, select the check box for **Make Object Accessible** and in the **Name** field, type **Protecting Your Wrists**. In the **Static text** field on the **Stage**, select all the text below **Protecting Your Wrists**, as shown here, and **right-click** (Windows) or **Ctrl+click** (Mac) and choose **Copy** from the shortcut menu. In the **Description** field, **right-click** (Windows) or **Ctrl+click** (Mac) and choose **Paste** from the shortcut menu to paste in the content. This will give the text field a name (**Protecting Your Wrists**) that will be read first by the screen readers, and the description that you just pasted in the **Accessibility** panel will be read after the name.

It is very important that each accessible object in your movie have a name. The screen readers will identify an object by reading the object's name first and then the description of the object. Rather than allowing Flash MX 2004 to name objects generically (by selecting the Auto label option in Step 3), it is better to take control over the names of your objects and name them yourself. By default, the Macromedia Flash Player automatically provides the names for Static and Dynamic Text objects because the names of these text objects are the actual text. Although you don't have to provide the names for Static and Dynamic Text objects, it will make more sense to the screen reader user if you do.

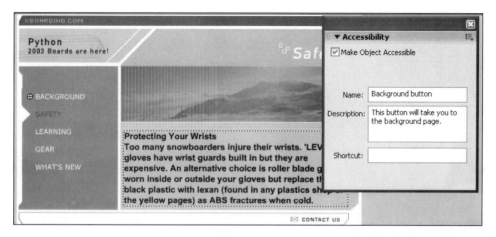

7. With the **Selection** tool, select the **Background** button on the **Stage**. With the **Accessibility** panel still open, type **Background button** for the **Name** and **This button will take you to the background page** for the **Description**. Again, rather than leaving it up to Flash MX 2004 to name your button (it may name it something like "button 17"), it is much better to name your buttons individually. When you are finished, close the **Accessibility** panel.

8. Even if you test your movie, unfortunately, it is not possible to test your movie's accessibility content using Flash MX 2004's test movie features. If you have access to a screen reader, however, you can test the movie's accessibility by playing it in a screen reader. Additionally, demonstration versions of screen reader software are available, so you can download one and test your movie that way.

TIP | Learning More About Accessibility

If you are interested in learning more about Macromedia MX 2004 and accessibility, there is a section on Macromedia's Web site all about it, and it can be found here:

http://www.macromedia.com/macromedia/accessibility/

---

9. Save and close this file. You are finished with the book!

Congratulations! You did it! I really hope this book helped you learn Flash MX 2004 quickly, and that you are now armed and ready to create your own animated and interactive projects. I wish you the best of luck with all of your future Flashing!

A.

Troubleshooting FAQ and Technical Support

| Troubleshooting | Frequently Asked Questions |
| Technical Support |

H·O·T
_____

Macromedia Flash MX 2004

Troubleshooting

If you run into any problems while following the exercises in this book, you might find the answer in this troubleshooting guide. This section will be maintained and updated at this book's companion Web site: **http://www.lynda.com/ products/books/fl04hot**.

If you don't find what you're looking for here or at the Web site, please send an email to **fl04hot@lynda.com**.

If you have a question related to Flash MX 2004 but unrelated to a specific step in an exercise in this book, visit the Macromedia Flash site at **http://www.macromedia.com/ support/flash/**, or you can contact them by email at **http://www.macromedia.com/ support/email/complimentary/main.cgi**.

Frequently Asked Questions

Q: On the Macintosh, why can't I see any FLA files when I choose File > Open?

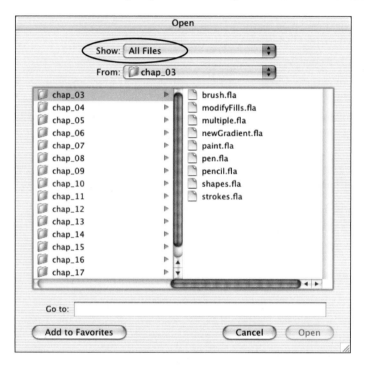

A: If the FLA file was created on a PC, you might experience a problem seeing those files when you choose **File > Open** from within Flash MX 2004 on a Macintosh. You can correct this by changing the **Show** option to **All Files**.

Q: On the Macintosh, when I try to double-click the FLA file to open it, it will not open. Why?

A: If the FLA file was created on a PC, you might not be able to double-click it to open the file. If this is the case, open Flash MX 2004 and choose **File > Open** to open the FLA file. If you don't see the FLA file listed when you choose **File > Open**, see the previous question. Once you save the FLA file (originally created on a PC) on your Mac, you will be able to double-click the FLA to open it.

Q: My Toolbar has disappeared. What should I do?

A: If your Toolbar has vanished, you can easily make it reappear again. Choose **Window > Tools** to show/hide the Toolbar. Chapter 2, "*Interface*," explains the Toolbar in detail.

Q: All of my panels have disappeared. What should I do?

A: If you lose your panels, you can press **F4** (Windows) or the **Tab** key (Mac) to show them and even hide them again. If you don't like their arrangement, you can restore them to their default positions by choosing **Window > Panel Sets > Default Layout.** This will cause all of the panels to reappear in their default positions on the screen. This command is especially helpful when someone else has undocked and changed the combination of your panels. Chapter 2, "*Interface*," describes each of the panels in detail.

Q: I undocked one of the panels, but I can't redock it again. Why?

A: To redock a panel, make sure that you drag it over the location where you want dock it. A black outline will appear, symbolizing the area that panel will be docked in when you release the mouse. Chapter 2, "*Interface*," explains docking and undocking in detail.

Q: Why does Flash MX 2004 create extra files when I press F12 (Windows) or Cmd+F12 (Mac)?

A: Pressing **F12** (Windows) or **Cmd+F12** (Mac) is a shortcut for the **Publish Preview** command. This means that Flash MX 2004 will publish the SWF file and an HTML file when you press this key. These files will be created in the same directory as the FLA file. If you want to preview your movie without publishing any other files, choose **Control > Test Movie** or **File > Publish Preview > Flash,** and only the SWF file will be created. Chapter 16, "*Publishing and Exporting*," explains the publish features in detail.

Q: I tried to create my own shape tween but it won't work, and the Timeline has a broken line. What does this mean?

A: You cannot create a shape tween using symbols, groups, or text blocks (text that hasn't been broken apart). A solid line with an arrow indicates that the tween is working properly. This is a good tween. A dashed line in the **Timeline** indicates there is a problem with the tween. This is a bad tween. Make sure you are using only objects that work with shape tweens. In Chapter 5, "*Shape Tweening*," you will find a detailed list of the objects you can use to create shape tweens.

Q: Why do all of the objects on my Stage appear faded?

You are inside the instance of the gfxFill Graphic symbol

A: This occurs when you double-click an instance or **right-click** (Windows) or **Ctrl+click** (Mac) on one and choose **Edit in Place.** This is a quick way to make changes to a symbol without having to access the **Library**; however, it can be confusing if that's not what you intended to do. Click **Scene 1** in the **Edit Bar** to exit this editing mode and to return to the **Main Timeline.** In the picture shown here, **Scene 1** was renamed **main.** So in this example, you would click the word **main** in the **Edit Bar** to return to the **Main Timeline.**

Q: I tried to create my own motion tween, but it won't work. And the Timeline has a broken line. What does this mean?

A: You cannot create a motion tween using shapes or broken-apart text. A solid line with an arrow indicates that the tween is working properly. This is a good tween. A dashed line in the **Timeline** indicates that there is a problem with the tween. This is a bad tween. Make sure you are using only objects that work with motion tweens. In Chapter 7, "*Motion Tweening and Timeline Effects*," you will find a detailed list of the objects you can use to create motion tweens.

Q: I tried to motion tween multiple objects, but it's not working. What could be wrong?

A: Motion tweening multiple objects requires that each different object exist on a separate layer. If you have all the objects on a single layer, the tween will not behave as expected. You can use the **Modify > Timeline > Distribute to Layers** command to quickly distribute each object to its own layer. Also, make sure you are trying to tween objects that are capable of being motion tweened. Objects such as shapes and broken-apart text cannot be motion tweened. In Chapter 7, "*Motion Tweening and Timeline Effects*," you learned how to motion tween multiple objects; refer to this chapter for a review.

Q: I tried to change the Alpha transparency of a shape using the Properties inspector, but it doesn't allow me to. What could be wrong?

A: To change the Alpha transparency of a shape (dotted mesh), you need to use the **Color Mixer** panel. To change the Alpha transparency of an instance, you need to use the **Properties inspector**. You learned how to do this in Chapter 6, "*Symbols and Instances*." Refer to this chapter for a review.

Q: Why won't my movie clips play when I click the Play button on the Controller?

A: You preview your movie clips on the **Main Timeline** within the Flash MX 2004 authoring environment. Movie clips can be previewed only within their own **Timeline**, in the **Library**, or by selecting **Control > Test Movie** to preview the movie clip in the Flash Player.

Q: I made an Input Text field, but when I test it using Control > Test Movie and I type inside it, nothing happens. Why?

A: Most likely, you are having this problem because when you created the text box, the text color was set to the same color as the background of the movie. Try changing the text color and testing the movie again. Also make sure that you have **Input Text** set for the **Text Type**.

Q: I see many actions in the Actions panel that I want to learn more about. How can I quickly do this?

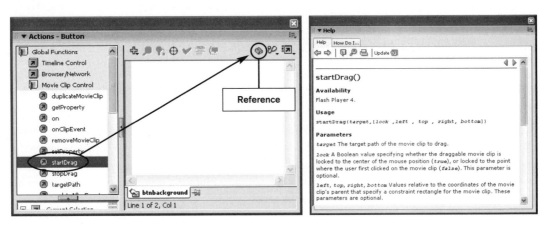

A: In the **Actions** pane, click an action that you want to learn about. On the right side of the **Actions** panel, click the **Reference** button. This will open the Reference Guide within the **Help** panel with a complete description of the action you selected.

Technical Support

Macromedia Technical Support

http://www.macromedia.com/support/flash/ or
http://www.macromedia.com/support/email/complimentary/main.cgi

If you're having problems with Flash MX 2004, please visit the first link to access the Macromedia Flash Support Center. To contact Macromedia Technical Support, use the email form in the second link. They can help you with typical problems, such as the trial version has expired on your computer, or your computer crashes when you try to launch the application. Please note that lynda.com cannot help troubleshoot technical problems with Flash MX 2004.

Peachpit Press

customer_service@peachpit.com

If your book has a defective CD-ROM, please contact the customer service department at this email address. We do not have extra CDs at lynda.com, so they must be requested directly from the publisher.

lynda.com

We have created a companion Web site for this book, which can be found at **http://www.lynda.com/ products/books/**.

Any errors in the book will be posted to this Web site, and it's always a good idea to check there for up-to-date information. We encourage and welcome your comments and error reports to **fl04hot@lynda.com**. Rosanna will receive these emails. Please allow a 72-hour turnaround and longer on weekends or holidays.

Flash MX 2004 Resources

| Online Forums | Web Sites
| CD-ROMs | Movie Library | Books |

H•O•T
_____

Macromedia Flash MX 2004

There are many great resources for Flash MX 2004 users. You have ample choices among a variety of newsgroups, conferences, and third-party Web sites that can really help you get the most out of Flash MX 2004. This appendix lists some of the best resources for developing your Flash MX 2004 skills.

Macromedia Flash MX 2004 Application Development Center

http://www.macromedia.com/desdev/mx/flash/

Macromedia has created a section of its Web site called the Macromedia Flash MX 2004 Application Development Center. This is a one-stop shop for everything Flash. For example, you can read tutorials and articles on Flash MX 2004, download sample applications, access links to other Flash MX 2004 resources, and even read the White Papers written on topics related to Flash MX 2004. This is the perfect link to use if you want to learn more about components or even video in Flash MX 2004.

Macromedia Online Forums

http://webforums.macromedia.com/flash/

Macromedia has set up several Web-based online forums for Macromedia Flash. This is a great place to ask questions and get help from thousands of Flash MX 2004 users. These online forums are used by beginning to advanced Flash MX 2004 users, so you should have no problem finding the type of help you need, regardless of your experience with the program. A list follows describing several of Macromedia's online forums.

Flash General Discussion

Online forum for general issues related to using Macromedia Flash.

Flash Handhelds

Online forum for technical issues related to creating Macromedia Flash content for handheld devices, such as the PocketPC.

Flash Site Design

Online forum for design feedback on your Flash MX 2004 animations. This forum is dedicated to the discussion of Macromedia Flash design and animation principles and practices. Other issues not specific to the Macromedia Flash tools yet important to Macromedia Flash designers can also be discussed here.

Flash Remoting

Online forum that discusses issues involved with Flash Remoting. Flash Remoting supplies the infrastructure that allows users to connect to remote services exposed by application server developers and Web services. Examples of these are message boards, shopping carts, and even up-to-the-minute stock quote graphs.

Flash Exchange Extensions

Online forum for issues relating to Flash MX 2004 extensions, including how to use them and how to troubleshoot any problems with them. (See also the "Macromedia Exchange for Flash" section next.)

Macromedia Exchange for Flash

http://www.macromedia.com/exchange/flash/

Macromedia has set up another section of its Web site called the Macromedia Flash Exchange. There you'll find hundreds of free extensions written by third-party users and developers that can help you build new features into your Web site. These features are not part of the Flash MX 2004 product, but they can be downloaded when you need them. Many of these extensions have features that normally would require an advanced level of ActionScripting. For example, some of these behaviors can give you the ability to password-protect areas of your site and to create pop-up menus, scroll bars, complex text effects, and so on.

The Macromedia site is not just for developers but for any Flash MX 2004 user who wants to take Flash MX 2004 to the next level. If you are a developer, this is a great place to learn how to write your own behaviors to share with the rest of the Macromedia Flash community.

You can also visit **http://webforums.macromedia.com/flash/** and click on the **Flash Exchange Extensions** link to access the online forum for Flash extensions.

Macromedia TechNotes

http://www.macromedia.com/support/flash/technotes.html

Macromedia has another section of its Web site listing all the issues that have been reported and answered by Macromedia Flash staff. This can be a valuable learning resource as well.

Third-Party Web Sites

http://www.flashkit.com/	http://www.actionscripts.org/	http://flazoom.com/
http://www.ultrashock.com/	http://www.flzone.net/	http://www.were-here.com/
http://virtual-fx.net/	http://flashmove.com/	http://www.popedeflash.com/

http://www.macromedia.com/support/flash/ts/documents/flash_websites.htm

Flashforward

Flashforward is an international educational Macromedia Flash conference created by Lynda Weinman of lynda.com and Stewart McBride of United Digital Artists, and sponsored by Macromedia. It's a great conference to attend once you know Flash MX 2004 and want to take your skills to a new level. The best Macromedia Flash developers and designers in the world present their technical and artistic work in an educational setting. You can learn more about Flashforward and its offerings by visiting **http://www.flashforward2004.com**.

CD-ROMs from Lynda.com

http://www.lynda.com/products/videos/index.html

Learning Flash MX 2004

Learning Flash MX 2004 ActionScripting

Intermediate Flash MX 2004

Online Training Movie Library from Lynda.com

http://movielibrary.lynda.com/html/index.asp

Lynda.com now offers a subscription service that allows you to see over 1,600 movies on a variety of subjects, including Flash MX 2004.

Books for Further Learning about Flash MX 2004

Macromedia Flash MX 2004 Bible
by Robert Reinhardt and Snow Dowd
John Wiley & Sons, 2003
ISBN: 0764543032

Macromedia Flash MX ActionScript Bible
by Robert Reinhardt and Joey Lott
John Wiley & Sons, 2004
ISBN: 0764536141

ActionScript: The Definitive Guide
by Colin Moock and Gary Grossman
O'Reilly & Associates, 2001
ISBN: 1565928520

Flash MX 2004 Games Most Wanted
by Kristian Besley, Brian Monnone,
and Anthony Eden
APress L.P., 2003
ISBN: 1590592360

Flash Web Design: The V5 Remix
by Hillman Curtis
New Riders Publishing, 2001
ISBN: 0735710988

Macromedia Flash MX 2004
Beyond the Basics Hands-on Training
by Shane Rebenschied
lynda.com, February 2004
ISBN: 0321228537

MTIV: Process, Inspiration and Practice for the
New Media Designer
by Hillman Curtis
New Riders Publishing, 2002
ISBN: 0735711658

Macromedia Flash MX Video
by Kristian Besley, Hoss Gifford, Todd Marks,
and Brian Monnone
Friends of Ed, 2002
ISBN: 1903450853

Macromedia Flash MX 2004 Magic
by Michelangelo Capraro and
Duncan McAlester
New Riders, 2003
ISBN: 0735713774

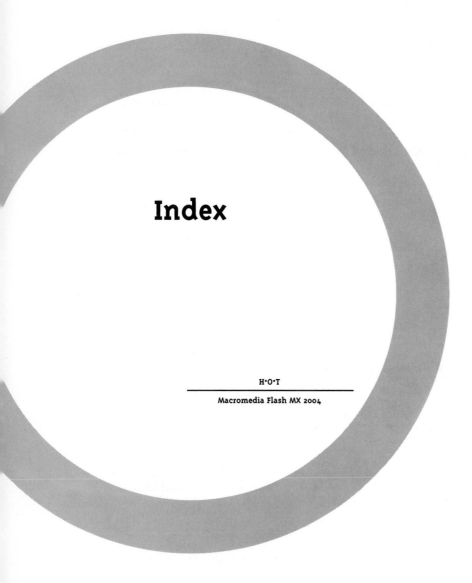

Index

H•O•T

Macromedia Flash MX 2004

A

J

JavaScript, 15
JPEG tab, Publish Settings, 814
.jpg, 315

K

kerning, 527, 530-531
keyboard events, 438
keyboard shortcuts. *See* shortcuts
keyframes, 109-110, 147
  adding
    actions to, 432-435, 503
    to Over state of buttons, 364
    sound to, 610
    stop actions to, 596
  blank keyframes, creating, 592
  copying, 130-132
  creating
    guidelines for, 179
    shape tweens between, 185
  deleting to speed up tempos,
    127-129
  frame-by-frame animation,
    112-118
  importing
    FreeHand content as,
      900-904
    Illustrator content as,
      917-919
  inserting, 117, 134
    to slow tempos, 123-127
  removing, 111
    from Hit state, 366
  reversing, 130, 132
  Timelines, 226
  video, 731
keys, shortcut keys. *See* shortcuts

L

labels, frame labels, 483
  creating drop-down menus,
    484-499
  versus scenes, 483
layer controls, 19, 21-22
layer folders, 173, 835
layer name, layer controls, 21
Layer Properties, 174-175
  accessing, 332
layers, 834
  adding, 583, 834
    for frame actions, 433
    to Timeline, 395
  deleting, 834
  extending, 231
  in final Web site, 836-839

guide layers, 266, 835
  importing Illustrator content as,
    922-923
  layer folders, 835
  locking, 22
  mask layers, 835
layers folders, placing multiple
    shape tweens in, 173-174
layout settings for printing from
    project file, 865
levels (ActionScript), 500, 504
  file cabinet analogy, 506
  loading into occupied levels, 510
libraries
  closing, 380-381
  Common Libraries, 645
  opening, 372
Library, 193
  conflict resolution, 844
  in final Web site, 842-844
  organizing, 840-841
Library Conflict Resolution
    feature, 844
Library panel, 32
limitations of motion tweening, 283
line segments, 88
Line Type, 529
  Input text, 586
linear gradients, creating, 86
lines
  adding
    to brush shapes, 67
    with Ink Bottle tool, 57-59
  creating custom line styles, 54
  hiding selections, 53
  modifying, 51
    with Property Inspector,
      52-55
  selecting, 56
linking
  to external Web sites, 462-467
  to QuickTime video, 752-760
links, email links, 465-467
List component, 672, 676
  changing, 686
  configuring, 684-686
  sizing, 700-702
lists, moving entries within, 685
Loader, components, 672
loading
  movies, 501-505, 507-521
    into occupied levels, 510
    placement of, 517
  text into dynamic text fields,
    544-553
loadMovieNum action, 500
  loading movies, 501-505,
    507-521

loadSound, 650
location of MP3 files, 657
Lock/Unlock All Layers, layer
    controls, 22
locked file destinations,
    troubleshooting, 502
locking layers, 22
looping, 233
  animation, 130
    copying and reversing
      keyframes,
      130-132
    stopping, 130
  movies, 142
  sound, music selectors,
    663-669
loops, Stream, 632
Lossless setting, 319

M

Mac projector, HQX, 792
Macintosh, docking toolbox, 24
Macintosh project, 105
Macromedia Exchange, downloading
    from, 704-715
Macromedia Flash authoring tool, 11
Macromedia Flash Exchange, 703
Macromedia Flash MX 2004. *See*
    Flash MX 2004
Macromedia Flash MX Professional
    2004. *See* Flash MX
    Professional 2004
Macromedia Flash Player. *See* Flash
    Player
Macromedia Players, 13
magnification, changing, 396
Main panel, 30
Main Timeline, 393
mask layers, 835
masking and bitmaps, 329-333
masks, 329
  and color, 330
  animated masks, creating,
    334-335
Maximum characters, Input text, 586
menus
  drop-down menus, creating,
    484-499
  Panels Options menu, 28
  Ruler units drop down
    menu, 108
  Tween drop-down menu, 226
Meta tags, 531
methods (ActionScript), 444
Microsoft Active Accessibility
    (MSAA) technology, 924
missing fonts, 468, 826

www.informit.com

YOUR GUIDE TO IT REFERENCE

New Riders has partnered with **InformIT.com** to bring technical information to your desktop. Drawing from New Riders authors and reviewers to provide additional information on topics of interest to you, **InformIT.com** provides free, in-depth information you won't find anywhere else.

Articles

Keep your edge with thousands of free articles, in-depth features, interviews, and IT reference recommendations— all written by experts you know and trust.

Online Books

Answers in an instant from **InformIT Online Books'** 600+ fully searchable online books.

POWERED BY

Catalog

Review online sample chapters, author biographies, and customer rankings and choose exactly the right book from a selection of more than 5,000 titles.

www.newriders.com

Go Beyond the Book

with lynda.com Training CD-ROMs:

**Learning Adobe
Acrobat 6**

**Learning Macromedia
Flash MX 2004**

**Learning Macromedia
Dreamweaver MX 2004**

**QuickTime Compression
Principles**

- Watch industry experts lead you step-by-step.
- Learn by viewing, and then by doing.
- Maximize your learning with high-quality
  tutorial source files.
- Over 33 active titles in our collection.

Visit http://www.lynda.com/videos/

lynda.com

Hands-on Training Books, CDs, & Online Movie Library.

Keep Learning

with More Hands-On Training Books:

Dreamweaver MX 2004
Hands-On Training

Adobe Photoshop CS/
ImageReady CS Hands-On Training

Adobe Acrobat 6
Hands-On Training

Adobe After Effects 6
Hands-On Training

- Learn by doing.
- Follow real-world examples.
- Benefit from exercise files and QuickTime movies included on CD-ROM.
- Many other titles to choose from.

Visit http://www.lynda.com/books/

lynda.com™

Hands-on Training Books, CDs, & Online Movie Library.